BY MAX LERNER

MAX LERNER

AMERICA
as a
CIVILIZATION

Volume Two

CULTURE AND
PERSONALITY

A Clarion Book
Published by Simon and Schuster

A CLARION BOOK

PUBLISHED BY SIMON AND SCHUSTER

ROCKEFELLER CENTER, 630 FIFTH AVENUE

NEW YORK, NEW YORK 10020

EIGHTH PAPERBACK PRINTING, 1967

"On an Invitation to the United States," by Thomas Hardy, from *Collected Poems of Thomas Hardy,* © 1926 by The Macmillan Company; used with the publisher's permission.

Translation of poem by Goethe, from *The American Spirit* by Charles and Mary Beard, © by The Macmillan Company; used with the publisher's permission.

"Frescoes for Mr. Rockefeller's City," by Archibald MacLeish, published by Houghton Mifflin Company.

"America Remembers," from *American Song* by Paul Engle, © 1933 by Doubleday & Company, Inc.

LIBRARY OF CONGRESS CATALOG CARD NUMBER: 57-10979

MANUFACTURED IN THE UNITED STATES OF AMERICA

PRINTED BY MURRAY PRINTING CO., FORGE VILLAGE, MASS.

BOUND BY ELECTRONIC PERFECT BINDERS, INC., BROOKLYN, N.Y.

FOR

MICHAEL

AND HIS GENERATION

CONTENTS

Foreword

AMERICANS *are beginning to turn a searchlight on themselves and their civilization, and interpret both to the world. The present study is intended as a trial essay in this direction.*

I start with what the book is not—neither a history of American civilization nor a description of life today in the American regions, states, and cities. Both have been done well by a number of scholars and journalists. Nor have I written here an indictment or apologia, either a celebration of "the American way" or a lament about it. Finally, this is not a "whither, whither" book embodying the prophecy of disaster. In short, those who are looking for the historical, the descriptive, the polemic, or the apocalyptic must look elsewhere.

What I have tried, rather, is to grasp—however awkwardly—the pattern and inner meaning of contemporary American civilization and its relation to the world of today.

A personal word may not be out of place. You write a book not for the elaborate reasons you spell out but mainly because you can't help it. Whatever I have written, thought, felt in the past has converged on the grand theme of the nature and meaning of the American experience. Whenever I have tried to chip off a fragment—on American government, on liberalism, on foreign policy, on morals—I found that it lost some of its meaning when torn from the rest. Yet to attempt the subject as a whole seemed a formidable, even arrogant, task. In 1945 I finally overrode my hesitation and started the book on its present scale. It has been more than a decade in the writing.

No American, perhaps no one alive today, can pretend to view American civilization with an anthropological detachment. The "anthropological attitude" (Kroeber) and the "sense of cultural shock" (Benedict) come from seeing values in a culture almost wholly disparate from your own. No American can achieve detachment in studying America, and I doubt whether even a European or Asian can. Paraphrasing Lord Acton, one might say that the only detached student of American civilization would be a dead one, since he would no longer care. The best you can do to achieve perspective is to keep a certain emotional distance from your subject. When the subject is your own people and civilization it is hard to keep the distance. Your hopes and fears for America manage to break through and color the analysis.

Obviously any book about America published at a time of international discord and seething world revolution is bound to be interpreted within this frame of planetary turmoil, and the question will inevitably be asked whether this book is "for" or "against" America, whether it is a rosy and euphoric picture seen in a haze of promise or an unsparing indictment.

I have tried to avoid both these sins—for an American the sin of complacency and the sin of self-hatred. I love my country and my culture, but it is no service to them, nor to the creed of democracy, to gloss over the rough facts of American life. Similarly, much have I traveled in the realms of Europe and Asia—and even in the realms of Marx and Veblen —and if there is a single count in the anti-American indictment I have not at some point confronted, it has not been through lack of diligence or realism. But it would be no service to the most committed critics of America to give them a distorted picture of American civilization only in order to nourish their distaste. Let the great world debate about America go on as it will and must: the task I set for myself is intended to have no strategic relation to it.

America is by any standard a towering technology and culture, with economic, military, and political power, the only rival power-mass being Russia. Wherever you find so much vitality packed tightly in a segment of human society, it is evidence of a striking convergence of history, environment, biological stock, psychological traits, institutional patterns, collective will and drive. When such a combination catches fire in the world's imagination and polarizes the emotional energies of men— whether for love or hate—you have a memorable civilization.

In dealing with something so provocative it is easy to be waylaid by the transient and miss the enduring. I have tried to remember that political struggles and economic programs wither and grow stale, the controversies which fill the pages of today's press become jangled images tomorrow, and party leaders end up as dimly remembered steel-plate engravings in the history books. America is not only changes and chances. It is also permanence.

That is why the questions I ask about Americans are those one would have to ask about the people of any great civilization. What are their traditions, biological stock, environments? How do they make a living,

govern themselves, handle the inevitable problems of power and freedom? How are they divided into ethnic and class groupings? What are
they like in their deep and enduring strains? What is their life history
like, in its characteristic phases from birth to death? How do they court,
marry, bring up and educate children? How do they work, play, and express their creativeness in art and literature? What are the connective
and organizing principles that hold their civilization together? What
gods do they worship, what beliefs hold them in thrall or give them
strength, what attitudes do they own up to, what convictions animate
them, what culture patterns do they move in, what dreams are they
moved by, what myths run through their being, what incentives propel
them, what fears restrain them, what forms of power invest their striving, what tensions and divisions tear them apart, what sense of society
cements them?

What, in short, is it that makes America not "a congeries of possessors
and pursuers," of individual wills and greeds and collective power, but
a civilization?

M. L.

CHAPTER VII

Class and Status in America

IN WHICH we look at the American system of class and status, asking what the modes and structures of power are in America and the modes of access to that power; also how Americans rank each other and themselves, in what kind of hierarchies, how much it means to them, how mobile and how rigid the classes are, and how they conform or conflict with the prevailing beliefs in the American mind.

After an initial over-all view, trying to sift fact from fiction about the American class system (Sec. 1, "The Open-Class Society"), we study more closely the three main strata of power and status in American life—the ruling groups, old and new (Sec. 2, "The Seats of the Mighty"), the complex emerging forms of the middle classes (Sec. 3, "The New Middle Classes"), and the workers (Sec. 4, "Class Profile of the Worker"). For each of the three we ask how cohesive or loose are the ties of the members with each other, and their bonds of common feeling and action, what are the current shaping forces that determine their power and standing, how they feel about their own position, and about the other classes. And always we ask what the struggle to achieve and maintain their desired status does to the mind and personality of the Americans in each class.

We ask somewhat the same questions about the out-groups in American life— the ethnic minority groups (Sec. 5, "The Minority Situation") and especially the situation of the Negro (Sec. 6, "The Negro in America"). We examine the extent and direction of racist feeling and discriminatory practices in America, and strike a trial balance of what has been happening in the past quarter century to the Negro and his struggle to free himself from the humiliations of Jim Crow and achieve an equal and common life with other Americans. In these sections on American stratification we are dealing less with class than with status—that is, systems of prestige and standing, and with the evidences of the breaking up of the only phase of American life that might be termed a system of caste.

We end by approaching the problem of class and status in a democracy from two angles of vision. First we inquire into the nature of the badges of belonging in America—the outward insignia of status and the inner satisfactions and scars of being accepted or being excluded (Sec. 7, "The Badges of Belonging"). Second, we test the idea that a genuine class struggle is in process in American life (Sec. 8, "The Democratic Class Struggle"), but that it has few of the features that Marxism ascribes to the class struggle, since it is focused on individual attainment of income and rank and power through individual effort rather than on the image and consciousness of collective struggle, and also because it takes place within an open-class system by methods characteristic of such a system.

Class and Status in America

1. The Open-Class Society

AMERICA was in conception a classless society. Behind its settlement and growth was a heritage partly borrowed from revolutionary Europe, partly shaped by the American experiment. It included four related elements: hatred of privilege, the religion of equality, open channels of opportunity, and rewards based on achievement and not on birth or rank.

This was the image of a classless American society. No man was to get a better or worse start than another; each was to have the same chance to show the stuff he was made of—to begin and end as a man; none was to bare his head or bend his knee to another by reason of birth, rank, or vested power; each was to be judged by what he was and could do. In the phrase that Jefferson picked up and adapted from an English rebel, "the mass of mankind has not been born with saddles on their backs, nor a favored few booted and spurred, ready to ride them legitimately by the grace of God." This is what he had meant in the Declaration of Independence, by his assertion that "all men are created equal": not that there were no individual differences between men, but that no man-made differences of class, caste, and subjection were to be added to those that nature had made.

One gets here a picture of a society with no depressed and subject classes and without aristocracies of blood, race, or position. The only elites recognized were those of ability and achievement. In the hierarchies of European society it was blood that talked; in America it was to be achievement and success that talked. The difference between the two meant a difference in the *élan* of the society. For blood and rank are given facts which a man has himself done nothing to achieve and cannot undo. Thus a society of blood leads among the privileged to an indifference about effort and among the pariahs to a hopelessness about reward. But a society where achievement talks, and where the marks of worth can be acquired as they can also be dissipated and lost, is by its nature a society shot through with effort and suffused with hope. Even when it is a plutocracy its top members are *novi homines,* and where all the members of an elite are *novi homines* none of them are. The fact of being "self-made" men is their signature of honor. The place of the

Great Estates is taken in America by the Great Fortunes. But unlike an estate, which is the result of status, a fortune is held by Americans to be the result of will and skill. Some can lose it, others acquire it. "From shirt sleeves to shirt sleeves in three generations" is part of the American myth.

Thus the American image of a classless society is one with a minimum of resentments, with few class tensions to rip it apart, without menace for the future, and with unlimited hope because of almost unlimited social mobility. There is an idyllic quality in this image, as in Eden before the Fall. It is not, however, the ideal of a stagnant society but of a freewheeling, perhaps even a freebooting, society.

As such it is part of the Great Folklore of America. This does not mean that it is all moonshine. It has a strong basis in American social reality. But it also has accumulated a distinct folklore, which is uncritically accepted by a large body of American opinion and often used as propaganda. In fact, the great reliance of the corporate propaganda in America is on the symbols of the free economy and the classless society. "I have heard thirty sets of lectures in defense of the Christian religion," a Scottish professor once said, "and, thank God, I'm a Christian still." After reading all the corporate defenses of the American "classless" society, it is only the saving remnant of sanity that allows one to hold on to the belief in the American open-class system.

The trouble with the class image of American folklore is that it rests on doctrines which tend to close the class system rather than to keep it open. The theory of "natural selection" assumes that a man who gets rewarded must therefore have deserved the reward. Yet it does not follow that the animal who survives in the jungle has proved anything more than his power for survival. To say that an able man ought to be rewarded is not the same as to say that those who are rewarded are therefore the ablest, and those excluded from the prizes must be dolts and weaklings. This distortion has led to a crass apologia for the existing distribution of income and economic power.

Similarly, even in a society with rapid social mobility not everyone can move upward. Beyond the expansion and dynamism of any society, it is inevitable that if some move upward others must be replaced and move downward. This process of downward mobility, or of declassing, mars the perfection of the legend of American classlessness.

One consequence of the Great Folklore is what may be called the Great Hunger. In any society in which the people have a great deal of freedom, they want more. Where privilege is minimized, it is belligerently hated. "This never dying, ever kindling hatred," De Tocqueville called it, "which sets a democratic people against the smallest privilege." Americans have, by the very fact of a high degree of equal opportunity, formed the habit of making ever-greater individual claims on their culture. It is a hunger, as De Tocqueville saw, that "grows by what it feeds on"—the material out of which a psychic dynamism has developed to match the economic dynamism. The American has been encouraged by this psychic dynamism to expect that it will fulfill his legitimate life demands. More than by anything else he is moved by a hatred of privilege and a passion for equal opportunity which is the true "permanent American Revolution."

The Great Hunger sets its face against privilege and against hierarchy of any kind. It is the stuff on which much of the infinite hopefulness of American life feeds—the hope for a chance to get at the goods in American life and at the good life in America. Yet bitterness also feeds on it. The struggle for civil rights, for example, would not be possible without the Great Hunger. Every advance in the legal status and social opportunities of Negroes is seen as a steppingstone to another advance, and if it is blocked the bitterness is intense. There can be no end to the dynamism which seeks a continually better job, income, and social position in the community.

The meaning of "classless" in American usage is different from the European. It does not, in the American ideal, mean an absence of rank, class power, or prestige. More exactly it means a class system that is casteless and therefore characterized by great mobility and interpenetration between classes. American thinkers since Madison and John Taylor have been preoccupied with the economic basis not only of politics but of social prestige and position as well. Ward, Sumner, Small, Giddings, Veblen, Cooley, Ross—all the first-rate sociologists—had to grapple with the problem of class and based much of their thinking on it. When therefore the Americans speak of their "classless society" they do not mean it in the Marxist sense but are rather answering the Marxist challenge. What they mean is better expressed by the phrase "open-class society."

How classless is this society? Only in the sense that the class formations in it are fluid, that mobility is the rule rather than the exception, and that class change is impressively obtainable. The most striking trait of the American class system is what the theorists call "vertical social mobility," the rate of movement up and down the ladder of income and social prestige, which has probably been greater in America than in any historical civilization. Partly this came about because of the break with the relatively closed class system of Europe, partly because there was a continent waiting to be opened and exploited. The idea of rigid and untraversable class lines is not a plant that grows well on wind-swept plains spanning long distances. It is more likely to flourish where the horizons are cramped and the margin of life is meager. Even in the big American cities the same dynamism which expressed itself on the plains was transmitted into a restless, unremitting movement of men and ideas that accompanies the movement from one income and prestige rung to another.

There are evidences that the class reality of America is moving steadily away from the image of the classless ideal. Compared with this image and with the intensely fluid character of the class system on the frontier, some scholars say, there has been a creeping closure of mobility. If this were true it would be disquieting to those who believe that the heart of the American social system lies in continuing mobility and in the access of all to opportunity. One would not argue this position from the spread in the distribution of income, wealth, and power, drastic as that spread is. The ladder of mobility, along which are stretched the rungs of income and position, has always been long enough to reach from the extremes of luxury down to the extremes of privation. The rich have grown richer in the last generation of Americans, but the poor have not grown poorer: in fact, many of them have become tolerably comfortable.

A study by Anderson and Davidson in California of the groups at the bottom of the ladder during the Great Depression showed a considerable shift of job and occupation as between father and son, but overwhelmingly inside the same larger class; and it showed also, as might be expected, a shift away from the number of small businessmen toward the professional, white-collar, and semiskilled occupations. Finally a recent study by Form showed that seven out of ten manual workers had started as such and remained where they had started, and that the same applied to eight out of ten white-collar workers. Mills reports that nine out of ten wage workers were wage workers at the time of their marriage and had never moved beyond, that none of the well-to-do professional men or big businessmen in the community he studied had come from wage-earner's or lower white-collar worker's backgrounds. On the other hand, the Mills study also showed that two out of three foremen had started as wage workers, and four out of five small businessmen had also risen from the lower ranks. Nor is the income spread in itself conclusive, since it has in the past existed alongside very extensive mobility. Actually the rise of living standards at the bottom and the impact of heavy taxation at the top are tending to diminish the spread, although for many Americans the steep disparities will remain as the never forgotten denial of the genuineness of the open-class system.

A similar debate has raged on the question of whether mobility has slowed down and rigidity has increased in the class layers at the top and at the bottom. A number of recent studies show pretty well the nature of this trend. In the 1920s a classic study of the class origins of business leaders by Taussig and Joslyn showed that half of them were sons of business leaders, although in the previous generations the big business-men had come from the farms and small towns, from clerks and sales-men and small business families. The adherents of the view that Ameri-can class is growing more rigid hold that in each succeeding genera-tion there has been a tighter closure of the top control positions in big enterprise as the capital required to start or sustain them has grown ever larger, keeping many of the sons of the rich in the charmed circle by the fact of their wealth and inheritance and shutting most of the others out.

One criticism of this viewpoint is that it assumes a classless or wholly open-class society in earlier America to start with, from which present-day America is moving with ever-greater class rigidity. It is a case of Eden and the Fall. Yet the original picture needs revision. America did not start with a relatively classless society, nor is it moving rapidly to a class society. In the America of the Puritans and the Cavaliers there were classes which were marked off as distinct styles of life, even though the aspect of power may not have been as important as it is in America today. Perry Miller has shown that even the Puritans, after their first years of settlement in the New World, made their peace with class dis-tinctions and even gave them a blessing, although they supported the principle of open access to all positions for the believers. In Southern society, as well as that of Philadelphia and New York in early times, the idea of the gentleman had considerable strength, although again it had more to do with a mode of life than a structure of power. The famous essay by James Madison, which appeared as Number Ten of *The Federalist* papers, showed a consciousness on the part of intellectuals of the existence of economic power and interest groupings on which class distinctions as well as political "fractions" could be based. The often crotchety and radical, but nevertheless meaningful, pamphleteers of the Age of Jackson, as Arthur Schlesinger, Jr., has depicted them, could not have written and spoken as they did in a society without class distinctions.

It would be truer to say that the movement in America has not been from classlessness to class or from an open to a more rigid class system but from relatively clear divisions and modes of life to a situation where the divisions have become more blurred, the stratification has become more subtle with shadings that are imprecise and elusive, and the modes of life have tended to converge in a large category of middle-class living.

The changes in the American class system have involved increases in mobility and in rigidity in different areas and at different times, but it would be a mistake to view those changes outside the larger framework which gives them meaning. The greatest mobility is from the lower strata, particularly the industrial wage earners, up into the ranks of the salespeople, clerical workers, foremen, small businessmen, and the lower corporate managerial group. The mobility of American life in this middle area is probably greater than in any comparable society, and there is a steady stream of movement up into the middle class and within it from one stratum to another. But it is still hard to rise from the very lowest ranks of the unskilled and depressed class at the bottom of the income pyramid, although the diffusion of education has begun to reach even to that stratum and promises in time to make it relatively mobile. While the great mobility has been the movement into the middle classes, the rigidity should not be overestimated. It is still true that some of the bottom dogs are able to break away, although it requires will and ability.

The most difficult question has to do with mobility at the top of the pyramid. What has been happening to the channels of access to top income, wealth, power, and prestige? Here we must distinguish between two trends. One is the continuity of class, by which a son inherits the enormous advantage of his father's position. The other is the constant creation of new managerial elites who occupy the strategic operative positions in big business, and who often come from below.

Actually there was more upward and downward mobility in the top class positions in the America of the mid-1950s than appears from studies like Taussig's which were done a generation earlier. A study in 1955 by Warner and Abegglen, focused upon the top ranks of the new managerial elite, gave a different picture and showed that the trend noted by Taussig was being reversed. It was still possible for young men starting in technical or sales positions in the corporate bureaucracy to move into executive positions. And the Warner study shows that a considerable number of them came from families that had not been in big business—either farmers or workers, professional people or small business.

Another study, however, a *Fortune* study of "The Executive Life," which drew its material from the 900 top management executives, shows that in one respect the Taussig picture still continues to be true. The fathers of 43 per cent of these men came from business occupations, while 15 per cent came from the professions. In the case of almost 26 per cent of the top executives studied, their fathers had been either the founders or the executives of corporations. In very few of the cases did the fathers come from nonbusiness and lower-income ranks: less than 13 per cent of them were farmers, and less than 8 per cent were workers. What is even more striking is the fact that the figures for the fathers of executives who were under fifty years of age showed an even lower percentage: only 11 per cent were farmers and 2½ per cent were workers. In short, conclude the editors of *Fortune,* new members of the nine hundred are tending to come increasingly from economically comfortable families. And they go on to comment that the struggle of impoverished forebears to fight their way to better living standards is no longer the heritage of the manager of the big corporation. He is more likely to come from a "tranquil family"—that is, while he may still have bettered himself compared with his father, the struggle has not been a sharp one, nor has the mobility been as marked as in earlier generations.

The transfer of education, skills, and relative economic comfort enables the new generations to live in ease and inherit also the jobs of their fathers or jobs comparable to them; but unless they show a good portion of the ability of the parents they are less likely to remain in the strategic posts. New men keep coming up, and while they do not become the owners or build great fortunes, they are recognized as part of the top class stratum. Thus, what occurs at the top is more a rigidification of income than one of business operation or power. This may explain why American society has not had to pay a heavy price thus far for its recent rigidity. It has escaped paying the price either of stagnation at the top or of revolutionary class conflict at the bottom.

To draw the profile of the American social strata is more elusive than almost anything else in American life. American society is still in the continual process of being formed and re-formed, and there are still few signs that it is settling down long enough for the observer to delineate the structure of the social hierarchy and the lines of division within it. It may well be many years before one can formulate a coherent theory of power and class in America.

In analyzing the nature of the American class system we must separate the question of the modes of power that define a man's strategic place in relation to his fellows from the modes of access to higher positions that are open to those below; and we must distinguish both of them in turn from the modes of status or prestige which define how a man looks in the eyes of his fellows and, by reflection, in the mirror of his self-image.

In terms of power, there has been a broad shift in the past three generations from industrial ownership to stock income and managerial position in the corporations, the trade-unions, and to some extent in the government; in the middle classes there has been a corresponding shift from small middle-class property to the new middle-class skilled occupations and professions, many of them in the tertiary service areas of the economy. In terms of access and mobility, American society seems to have countered every tendency toward closure by opening up new channels in other areas of effort. Thus it would be difficult to say, despite the growth of monopoly tendencies in the economy, that the actual or potential degree of mobility has declined in America since the nineteenth century. In some areas it is even possible that it has increased. The chances of moving into a commanding position in the economy as a businessman in control of his own business have become, of course, considerably less. But the independent entrepreneur has, as I have emphasized, become far less the type-figure he was in an earlier economy; and the chances of rising to top managerial positions, through apprenticeships in every phase of the company's activities, are still open to young men of the middle classes as well as the ruling class, although they are slimmer for the sons of workers and farmers. As for movement from those groups into the intermediate ones of power and income, the channels are still open except for the poet at the very base of the pyramid, which the impulses of ferment and change through the whole society take longer to reach.

What I have said about the increasing closure of the top power and income positions to the sons of workers and farmers may offer a clue to the character of the newly emerging class system. Men make their way up to the top less because of inherited wealth (although that is still an appreciable factor) and less because of technical and specialized skills: more and more the qualities called for are the generalized skills of making men work together in a "team," of "keeping everybody happy," of riding out crises, of "making contacts" and "being in on deals," of being alert to new developments in technology, marketing, advertising, and public relations, and being hospitable enough to the new ideas so that the company doesn't "get into a rut." This is another way of saying that education and brains are not enough in themselves to insure movement to the top; they are more important in the more technical aspects, such as science, engineering, market analysis, and corporate law. The more generalized skills are related to a style of personality, and this "personality market" is open only to those who have been conditioned to it by the mode of their education and the range of their "contacts." This may suggest why the boys from the lower classes and the lower middle class, and particularly from the minority ethnic groups, are less apt to rise to these positions than their fellows from the strata above.

As for the modes of status and prestige, some considerable degree of income and power is necessary for them, but there is no one-for-one correspondence between the two categories. There are top income groups in American life who elicit prestige within their own area of action—in their own industrial or professional or political circles—but have not achieved the same community standing as families of lesser income who have had the badges of status over a number of generations. At a lower stratum the white-collar occupations may carry a better status in the community than higher incomes which derive from skilled labor or from the petty trades.

I speak here of the levels of prestige and status, but not of their security. One of the striking facts about the whole American status system is exactly its high degree of *insecurity*. This is understandable in a society of such rapid change and movement, where the social image of a man and his own image of himself are interlocked, and where both of them derive not only from the objective facts of his income and strategic position in life but from a whole array of intangibles as well. This is one of the points at which the American picture of mobility differs most sharply from, let us say, that of the Russians. Some studies done at the Research Center for Russian Studies, at Harvard University, estimate that the likelihood of vertical mobility is about the same in the two societies—a striking fact when you consider how recent the Russian Revolution is and how profound were the changes that it sought to achieve in the society. But in the Russian case the insecurity of prestige and status changes mainly with political factors inside the regime; in the American case the political factors are of slight importance, and the array of intangibles is crucial.

2. *The Seats of the Mighty*

THE CREATION OF new elites, as Pareto saw, is the product of the circulation of talents. In that sense the American ruling groups are part of the picture of class mobility, rather than of the rigidification of caste at the top. America has had a series of aristocracies, although it has overwhelmingly rejected the aristocratic ideal. The men of religion who governed some of the original New England colonies formed elites in the quite literal sense, for they considered themselves the "elect" of God, and they shut out the unbelievers and the nonbelongers not only by class taboo but by the flaming sword of everlasting damnation. They represented status-by-religious-belief; accordingly they did not last in American life, since they performed no function linked with personal success or national survival.

The American Revolution, which was to a degree also a social revolution, swept away the beginnings of the second aristocracy of America— the landed aristocracy—along with all the cluttering accompaniments of British land law. To some of the conservative thinkers this removed the basis for government, as John Adams put it, by "the rich, the well-born, and the able." But their thinking ran against the American grain. Only in the South, with its prewar plantation economy and its linking of prestige with hereditary land and gentlemanly leisure, was there an economic base for an aristocracy of land and blood. It was demolished in the Civil War, and its pitiful residues in the frayed gentility of the postwar South turned inward into the bitterness of a frustrated elite. It is the memory of this aristocratic tradition and the nostalgia for it that have produced some of America's best writing.

There have been some other aristocracies in American life, as in the effort to build an aristocracy of prior immigration among the F.F.V.s ("First Families of Virginia") or the descendants of the Dutch patroon families in New York. And in New England there lingered deep into the nineteenth century the only vital aristocracy of culture and education, linked to some extent with family, that America has had—that of Concord, Brook Farm, Cambridge, and Beacon Street in Boston. While all these aristocracies had an effect on the taste and intellectual life of America they were only marginal to the structure of class as power.

In this sense of power the place of the aristocracies was taken in America by a plutocracy unparalleled in any prior culture, including the Roman Empire at its height, or the Italian merchant princes and the Dutch capitalists, or even England at the peak of its nineteenth-century commercial and industrial power. But because it had not been attached to land, blood, and dynasty, it was more fluid than the feudal and even commercial aristocracies, and gave access to some of the most resourceful talents. Its hallmark has been not nobility but mobility, not family dynasty but individual dynamism. De Tocqueville was struck by the fact "that amongst the Americans all honest callings are honorable," and that the contempt which the European aristocracies felt for "labor with a view to profit" had no place in American life. The fact that the field was left clear for the business ruling group enabled America to avoid the conflict which every western European country had experienced between capitalism and the authoritarian tradition. America did not have on one side the eagerness of the parvenu, nor on the other the condescension of the nobility. Nor was there the steady infiltration by the commercial class into the landed aristocracy—the conquest of blood and honor by money—which colored the thinking and politics of both Germany and England.

The American business class became the pivotal elite of the country because in an acquisitive society there was no other to challenge it. It had no time or taste to govern politically, as the European aristocracies did. It had not yet learned how to use its leisure. It pursued business not only for the profit in it but also, as De Tocqueville saw, "for the love of the constant excitement occasioned by that pursuit." It was attracted by magnitudes and got a sense of confidence in itself by its constant relation to those magnitudes. It did not care much about the people it employed: "the object is not to govern that population but to use it." And at the end of his classic chapters discussing the new business group, De Tocqueville wrote: "The manufacturing aristocracy which is growing up under our eyes is one of the harshest which ever existed in the world; but at the same time it is one of the most confined and least dangerous. Nevertheless the friends of democracy should keep their eyes anxiously fixed in this direction; for if ever a permanent inequality of conditions and aristocracy again penetrate into the world, it may be predicted that this is the channel by which they will enter."

De Tocqueville's brilliant insight has been confirmed by a century of history. Yet the "permanent aristocracy" which he foresaw does not accurately describe the American rich, since they too are somewhat subject to downward mobility and very much to the upthrust from below. And if De Tocqueville overestimated the rigidity this class would assume he underestimated its cohesion as a class. "To say the truth," he wrote, "though there are rich men, the class of rich men does not exist; for these rich individuals have no feelings or purposes in common, no mutual traditions or mutual hopes; there are therefore members, but no body." Not more than a quarter century after he wrote this, his generalization was contradicted by the bitterness with which the "rich men" resisted the new union organizing drives. In their labor relations, as in their pressures on government, the ruling business groups acted more consistently as a self-conscious class than any other groups, even including labor; the Marxist thesis of class-consciousness applied more aptly to them than to any American proletariat. In recent generations also the business elite has learned how to shift some of its energies to the arts of government, how to use its wealth and leisure as patrons of the arts, and how to live with a degree of imagination which the earlier business pirates did not share.

Much has been written about how the steep taxes and the diffusion of wealth have diminished with "great American fortunes," about which Gustavus Myers once wrote; yet the facts are against this view. In a careful study of the admittedly incomplete and shaky data on the "very rich" —whom he defines as men with fortunes of thirty million dollars and over—C. Wright Mills examined the top ninety in the generations of 1900, 1925 (the top ninety-five), and 1950. In each group there was one in the billionaire class (Rockefeller in 1900, Ford in 1925, and Hunt, and perhaps Cullen, in 1950); there were three in the first two generations with $300 million and over, and six in 1950; in each generation a

fifth of the group were in the $100-million-and-over group. The geo-
graphical shift of the sources of wealth away from the East is shown by
the fact that of the richest ten in the 1950 group, five were Texans, and
of the richest ninety there were nine Texans. Despite the inheritance
and income taxes and the loud outcries against governmental interference with the accumulation of wealth, the acquisitors in the mid-1950s
in America were still active in acquiring wealth and still able to hold on
to it.

To this group of the top rich, and cutting across it, there should be
added another—the big-income group. The profile one gets of American
wealth from this angle of vision—not the accumulated fortunes but the
continuing annual income—is a striking one. There were in all, in the
mid-1950s, fewer than 14,000 persons with declared incomes of $100,000 a
year and over. Of these, roughly 11,500 had incomes of between $100,000
and a quarter of a million dollars a year; 1,383 had incomes of between
a quarter and a half million; 379 had incomes of from a half million to
a million; and 120 a million or more. The notable fact here was that
this group of 14,000 (Mills calls them the "corporate rich") got roughly
two thirds of their income from corporate dividends and capital gains,
and from estates and trusts, while the remaining third came from corporate salaries, direct business profits, and professional services. The
"unearned" income was thus double the "earned." There were, moreover, known methods in corporate and income-tax law for excluding or
concealing income for taxable purposes, or for declaring income at a
minimum taxable rate—including "capital gains," "depletion allow-
ances" in oil and mineral incomes, and tax-free municipal bonds. Given
these methods and also the tax-free family foundations, the amount that
the top-rich Americans were able to keep for expenditure and accumulation was considerable and ranked with any high-income, big-fortune
ruling group in the world.*

The question of access to the seats of the mighty—to these positions of
the top rich and the corporate rich—sheds light on the American class
structure. Studying his 275 "top-rich" multimillionaires, Mills found
that access to the accumulation of these big fortunes was being restricted
to an ever-smaller group. In the 1900 generation 39 per cent came from
lower-class families; in the 1925 group it had sunk to 12 per cent; and in
the 1950 to 9 per cent. The proportion coming from the middle classes
remained relatively stable—between 20 and 30 per cent. The proportion
coming from the upper class was 39 per cent in the 1900 group, 56 per
cent in 1925, and 68 per cent in 1950. Almost nine out of ten of those

---

* On the business leaders of America, see Ch. V, Sec. 2, "The Rise and Decline of
the Titan." On the inequalities of wealth and income, see Ch. V, Sec. 9, "Poverty and
Wealth."

who came from upper-class families inherited fortunes of at least a half million dollars, and there can be little question that they found their path toward wealth, power, and status eased by the fact of the wealth, power, and status that were transmitted to them. Of Mills's whole group, roughly one out of three had to make his way to his position of wealth and power: the other two either rose in firms which were owned or controlled by their families or else got their wealth by the fabulous increase in the value of stocks during the past generation.

W. Lloyd Warner, studying the corporate decision-makers rather than the top rich, found that the problem of access to their positions of power and income yielded quite different results. He took the 8,000 business leaders who held "the highest positions in the largest companies in all types of American enterprise." He made a basic division between the "birth elite" and the "mobile elite" and found that the numbers in each were roughly even: 52 per cent of his 8,000 business leaders were "born to business," while 48 per cent "moved into business"; actually, the degree of mobility of access was greater than these figures show, since of those "born to business" only 23 per cent came from families that belonged to the birth elite, while the others came from families that had had to achieve their position. Mills found that the typical road of advance among the top rich was, in one way or another, to come into command of some strategic position, to have a sufficient sum to take advantage of it, to make the "big jump"—and then to pile up an "accumulation of advantages," partly by skill and partly by exploiting the position achieved through the big jump. Warner, on the other hand, found that the "royal road" to business leadership (and the income wealth and power going with it) was higher education, which is available in America to middle-class as well as upper-class groups.

Looking at the whole problem of rigidity as against mobility in the elites of top wealth and top corporate jobs, several generalizations are possible. So far as the very big fortunes are concerned, the process of rigidification has set in, and it is difficult for men to move all the way from the very bottom of the pyramid to the very top; yet they can still move from a little below the middle of it to the top. Looking at the top income group, it is also hard for a member of the submerged group, or even of the working class or the independent farmer group, to get to them; yet mobility still takes place from the middle classes to the top income. Looking at the small number of top executive posts in business, the rigidity is considerably less and mobility greater: men can move into them along the road of education, energy, and resourcefulness; although it is still true that those who come from families that have possessed such power over one or more generations find the going much easier. But if we broaden the range of our vision to take in the whole group of

8,000 business executives who held the high posts throughout the industrial structure, Warner's conclusion jibes well with the empirical experience of most Americans: the possibility of moving into these posts from the middle and lower ranks is still decidedly open. Warner's results were the more striking because he compared them with a similar study of access to posts of business leadership made a quarter century earlier by Taussig and Joslyn, which I have discussed above. He found that mobility has increased rather than lessened.

This leads to some general reflections on the nature of access to the elites in an open-class society. The important fact about those who have a differential advantage is that what is transmitted to them is not just wealth or income but a chance to show their ability which they might not have got otherwise; but unless some measure of ability is there, they will in time be pushed out of decision-making posts and become *rentiers* living on dividends and interest. What is transmitted then is not just money but the chance to make more; not just power but the chance to increase it; but both depend upon maintaining a level of ability. For those without the differential advantage of birth and opportunity, the meaningful channels of access are not those that lead to the big fortunes and income but to comfortable wealth and income. While the top berths may be pre-empted, those just below are still fairly open. Those that are most open have to do less with piling up big wealth and income than with the decision-making power in the managerial posts. Here the American business elite is still fluid—perhaps more so than ever in its history after the earliest beginning.

One difficulty with much of the research that studies the biographies of the members of the American ruling group and tries to treat them statistically or by questionnaires—and this applies both to Mills and Warner—is that such a method must omit the factors of personality, will, and even genius. By its inherent nature an elite is made up of selected men; it does not therefore lend itself easily to statistical uniformity. It is true that there are "insiders" and "outsiders" among those trying to make their way upward into the positions of power. This is underscored by the fact that the channels of success are growing less specialized, and that they have more to do with "personality" in a broad sense, and with the blurred contours of personal relations. This is where the "insider" has the "inside track." Yet here again, unless he has the qualities to exploit his advantage and maintain it, he can be passed (especially on a rough track) by someone coming from far behind with zeal and resourcefulness, and sweeping around and beyond him.

It must be added, however, that the new people, who come up from the lower middle classes, usually do not have final control over corporate decisions even though they are in the managerial posts. That decisive and final control often remains in the hands of those who, by the fact of being a birth elite and having money and power over generations, have the prestige that adds weight to their functional qualities and equities within the corporation. To that extent one can still regard this group as *the* ruling group. Yet those who rule from week to week, from day to day, and from year to year, ruling interstitially (as it were), between crisis decisions of others, are largely a new elite, and they bring a new point of view.

Somewhere in between an aristocracy of blood and land and a power elite of acquired wealth there is the domain that the American newspapers call "Society." Wealth alone does not open the portals of this domain, as a number of rich men and their wives have ruefully learned in studying the "Social Register." Birth and family are the key to entrance, although a number have declassed themselves by marrying below their station, and there is a question of how long the birth and family continue to exercise their spell without the added witchery of wealth. In communities such as the old New England cities, only the "old families" hold the top social positions. The "new families," while they may belong to the plutocracy and command much greater wealth, do not carry the same charismatic quality.

There was a period in American life when "Society" meant, however, a good deal more than it does today—the period of the great Fifth Avenue mansions, the estates at Newport, and the consciously modest houses of Louisburg Square. Henry James's *The American Scene,* written after a tour of the watering places and Society centers, is a brilliant evocation of these evidences of a way of life which even then was beginning to crack and which today—in the remains of the Vanderbilt mansion at Newport or the great hotels at Saratoga Springs—are studied as monuments of a past era. What has happened is not that there is less money to spend—actually the very rich families have far more—but that it is no longer fashionable for the elite of wealth to swagger in the old way of "conspicuous consumption." The more established it has become as the top social stratum, the more sophisticated does it become in expressing its dominance. It is the radiant moon toward which all the other tides of American life are drawn. There are still particular focal points at which it gathers, from Nob Hill in San Francisco to Aiken and its "horsy set," and from the east shore of Maryland and the Hamptons on Long Island to Sun Valley in the Rockies. Yet these are playgrounds which one finds ever harder to differentiate in their outer trappings from the playgrounds of the upper middle class or of the "New Families," and the consciousness of the social elite exists more in the valuation placed on them by the rest of the community than in any differential social display.

The rise of an upper class of newly rich families has transformed the upper American social status, both in small and large cities, and has introduced a ferment of new moral standards. The earlier America had a number of cities, each of which boasted its "old families" and its inner circles of blood and standing. The emphasis was upon kinship, intermarriage, landownership (especially in the South), and wealth over time. These local "social sets" not only dominated the more intimate social life of the city, making decisions about who belonged or did not belong: they were also the people who made decisions about economic and political power. But increasingly this local "society" has been subordinated to the power groups and social sets of the big metropolitan centers, where celebrities cluster and the Social Register operates, and men make decisions affecting the whole nation. In most cases the "country club" groups of the small city link their aspirations and dreams with the society of the big urban centers and especially of the night-club and "café society" groups.

The fact is that there is no longer a single "400" as there used to be but a whole constellation of "social sets" which interlock and overlap, some of them more exacting than others about their membership and their moral standards. As class lines became more fluid there was an epidemic of "Cinderella marriages," with an invasion of pretty and ambitious girls from across the tracks into the once jealously guarded inner circles, and a dilution of the birth elite of the old families with this new blood. The aristocracy of taste and manners got blurred around the edges. Moreover, with the spread of wealth in the days of the Big Money, and with the incursions of the income tax, it became more difficult to distinguish between the real social set and the phony one on the basis of money and spending power alone. Where so many were rich it became harder for the rich-over-time to hold their distinction or their sense of assurance. The breakdown of status lines accompanied a breakdown of standards. Whenever the newspapers featured some sensational murder or other scandal in the "social set" the nation had a chance to look behind the façade and to see the rather pathetic lives and loves inside. Any authority that the wealthy and well born might have exercised in the past over the standards of the lower-status groups was thus corroded.

The Big City social sets have themselves been transformed. The older upper class still furnishes the great names, but a new upper class has forced its way in, with a surer sense of what it wants and with the power to get it. Hungry for recognition and status, it has opened the gates to "celebrities" whose social origins would have shocked the dowagers and patriarchs of the earlier inner circles. As a result, "society" in the Henry James and Edith Wharton sense no longer dominates American rank and taste, except residually in those lingering social centers that Cleveland Amory called the "last resorts." It has been replaced by the arbiters of "café society" and Hollywood—a group of talented and attractive young men and women who are the celebrities of the Big Media and have proved the revolutionary element in the new situation. In many cases their members are parvenus whose love life is carried on in public, whose morals are fluid, whose education is dubious, and whose financial position is momentarily thriving but insecure. What they have that is decisive is their public éclat. Their pictures appear in every newspaper in order to give it the febrile vitality that Americans call "glamour." Their exploits are dutifully chronicled, their frailties are exposed, their marriages and divorces become headline news, and a whole new set of scandal magazines has cashed in on the business of laying bare their infractions of the moral code.

It would seem strange that, in the face of this kind of image, the linkage would persist between society and the celebrities. Yet each gets from the other something it seems to need: the society groups get the infusion of new vigor, and the gods and goddesses of the Big Media get the feeling of being linked with wealth and power. A list of those who are given priority at the Cub Room of the Stork Club or at Twenty-One has taken the place of Burke's Peerage and the Social Register. The list of the "ten best-dressed women" may have been thought up originally as a public-relations stunt for American tailors, but it became part of the folklore not only of fashion but of glamour and social standing. Inevitably the newspaper and picture layouts of the magazines have replaced the records of birth and lineage as the focus of social attention. The avoidance of publicity by the great families is a thing of the past. Where once no reporters or photographers were allowed at the great balls and parties, a "Society function" scarcely counts as such now unless it has been reported and photographed and the gradations of social rank have been recorded under klieg lights. What counts in American status is thus not money alone—not even primarily—but closeness to the sources of power, publicity, and popular success.*

The Big Media constitutes a different kind of elite as well—the power elite of opinion-molders and taste-shapers whose symbol has become "Madison Avenue," where the offices of the broadcasting chains, the advertising agencies, and the public-relations firms cluster. This is a differ-

* For a further discussion of American "Society," see Ch. IX, Sec. 3, "Manners, Taste, and Fashion."

ent kind of power from that of the top executives of the corporate managerial group, and different also from the elite of Great Fortunes and Big Income. The power they represent does not flow from their control over strategic decisions but from their capacity to shape the stereotypes and mold the tastes of the opinion public and buying public who are reached by the Big Media. Americans set a good deal of store by "public opinion" and are conscious of its transient quality and its fickleness. The elite of Madison Avenue are the high priests who are considered to have a magic way with the changing moods of the public. It is they who advise the politicians about how to sway voters in elections, they who guide the big corporate executives in their "public relations," they who have to worry about the private lives of celebrities, they who do the "motivational research" on which sales policies and advertising campaigns are based. They are the new symbol manipulators of the American power structure, the new "invisible government," the "hidden persuaders"—and therefore themselves a symbolic target of a good deal of popular resentment. Some of them reach the top posts in their organizations because of their verbal facility and their capacity to manipulate symbols. Others have the same generalized ability to co-ordinate these skills and the same impact of personality which marks the successful top executive in the corporate managerial group.*

There is, finally, the new elite of the officers of the Armed Services. I shall have occasion to deal later† with the role of the military in relation to American government, foreign policy, and freedom: what concerns me here is its relation to the class system. It is the only one of the strata of American society which does not depend on the operation of the market for its valuation but has developed a sense of dedication and an *esprit de corps* linked with patriotism, discipline, and the arts of killing. It comes thus closer to forming a caste, despite its rotation of rank and its very high recruitment of new abilities, than any other elite.

Even more important, the vast increase in the Armed Services means that the experience of caste is transmitted for at least several years to every young American male and many of the women. Since it is a totalitarian society, with an iron hierarchy of rank, obedience, and deference, this experience may habituate future generations to a new kind of subservience hitherto unknown in American life, and to a concern with what their "station" in life is rather than their inner worth. Yet in several respects this long-range trend has been qualified in more

* For the opinion-molders as a force in the economy, see Ch. V, Sec. 5, "Business and Its Satellites"; for their role in elections and in party politics, see Ch. VI, Sec. 4, "The Party System and the Voter."

† For the role of the military, see Ch. XII, Sec. 4, "Landscape with Soldiers," where the power of the generals and admirals over decisions is further discussed.

immediate terms. Many young Americans, after their Army caste experience, suffer a violent revulsion against it, as witness James Jones's *From Here to Eternity* and other recent novels of the seamy side of Army life.

But the totalitarian rigor of the Army makes it also a great leveler. The Negroes especially have recently found in its ranks a break in the Southern tradition of segregation, a tapping of new experience, and the chance to learn new mechanized skills which enable them to move out of the depressed class of sharecroppers, field hands, and mill workers into the skilled trades. Finally, the "G.I. Bill" has opened for millions of young Americans who have survived the battles a chance for vocational training and higher education under government subsidy, which comes at just the right time when they have measured their capacity and are mature enough to know where they want to go. In this sense the Army experience has brought new stir and mobility into the American class system, even while it promises to exercise in the long run a deadening effect upon a sense of initiative and the resistance to authority.

If we ask then who are the Americans who sit in the seats of the mighty, the answer must be that there is no single "ruling class" in America—well defined, articulated, conscious of its role and power. There is, to be sure, an upper class, in the sense of a top-rich and big-income stratum for whom leisure is at once habit and burden, which is the recipient of privilege and (to a limited extent) the shaper of ideal living patterns and an imitated life style. But such an upper class is different from a ruling class, whose essence is power over the behavior and destiny of others that flows from its strategic control of production and its decision-making in industry. The conditions of American society, which is geared by its history and mood to accept innovation, where the base of economic power is constantly shifting under the force of social mobility, and where pluralism and ferment pervade the whole, are not such as to favor either the emergence or the encrustation of a unitary ruling class.

Robert Lynd has argued, in an incisive criticism of the work of Mills and others, that the concept of "elites" (or even of some "power elite") as a substitute for the class concept is an illusory one, and that even in America there is a dominant class which is the center and source of the meaningful community power, and of which the various elites are only branches or tributaries. There is force in this view, in two senses. First, it is in the nature of power that it feeds on itself; economic power, whether or not it "determines" other forms of power, casts its shadow on them, so that there is at least a *prima facie* assumption that the holders of economic power will also have a strong hold on political elections, on decisions that affect war and peace, on education and religion, on the world of opinion, ideas, and the arts, and on social standing and values. Second, there is a common attraction that the holders of power have for one another, and a community of viewpoint ("class conscious-ness" is one way of putting it) which they inherit and perpetuate: this is especially true at a time of common danger, when they feel the *novi homines* or the trade-unions hard at their heels.

But my own tendency throughout this book is to approach America in terms of its nature as a richly pluralistic society. The pluralisms I find in American stock and regions, in American loyalties, in the American character structure, in religion and the sects, in political and economic life, I find also in the class system and even in the ruling groups.

Within the frame of this pluralism there are what may be called *power and prestige clusters,* which include the social elite ("Society"), the intellectual elite, the big-wealth and big-income elite, the top church leaders, the opinion-industry elite (press, radio, TV, movies, advertising agencies, public-relations men), the government managerial elite, the corporate managerial elite, the labor managerial elite, the military elite. Merely to list them thus conveys a sense of what I have said in my discussion of power in American life—that the whole of American so-ciety is power-saturated.*

But to say that there are many such clusters of power, prestige, and privilege does not mean that all are equally powerful, or that their powers balance each other out of existence. Quite clearly there are some power clusters which are more pervasive and dominant than the rest. The four fairly obvious ones are the corporate executives ("Big Business," "Wall Street," to use the popular symbols), the political decision-makers (again, in popular usage, "the Administration," "the Hill," "the White House"), the military leaders ("the brass hats," "the Pentagon"), and the opinion-shapers ("Madison Avenue"). I mention the popular designa-tions of these groups because on the question of power the instinct of the "man on the street" is likely to be closer to the truth than that of polemicists, students, and apologists. The interesting thing about the American popular consciousness is that it does not fix on a single and central power symbol but on a number of them.

Mills, in speaking of his "power elite," combines the first three of the four elites I have mentioned, in a kind of coalition of elites to form a cen-tral one. But, as Lynd points out, he does not assign primacy to any one of them. I should myself say that there have been shifting constellations of these power clusters in American history, and that at each period one of them has had primacy over the others. At the present time, at the height of the role of a business economy in a business culture, it is natural for the corporate executives to be the dominant elite. But this

* See Ch. VI, Sec. 5, "Power and Equilibrium."

does not exclude or minimize the importance of the others, especially (in an age of nuclear science) the military elite.

This is very far from the key image, in Marxist theory, of the ruling capitalist class as engaged in a naked warfare, including the force and violence that war uses, the hostilities on which it feeds, the bitterness it engenders, the survivors who emerge from its ordeal as victor or victim. In the view of Max Weber, there is a different key image of the elites, taken from that of the German governmental bureaucracy and the German army of the Weimar period, which were highly organized around the principle of professional competence and distinction and of a certain life style. Neither of these applies in the American case, where the image of naked warfare holds only for the underworld and among the racketeers on its margin, as it holds also *inside* the corporate world and in the top positions of the Big Media. As for the bureaucratic image, it is true that each of the four elites I have mentioned is a bureaucracy of a kind; but it would be truer to say that the power group uses the bureaucracy yet stands above it and apart from it, unfettered by its orderliness and its routineering.

Mills makes a good deal of the interchangeability of leaders in the three elites that form his "Power Elite." It is certainly clear that the same kind of person and the same kinds of talents will make good in each of his elites, and that there is even a kind of understanding by which the members of each "co-opt" men of their own kind to work with them and succeed them. But one need not conclude from this that there is a rigidity or even a cohesiveness within the elites that unifies them. In fact, the more important conclusion would stress the element of mobility rather than of rigidity. The striking thing about the elites in American society is their continuing mobility. This applies to the high government posts (despite the exclusions on ideological grounds at the time of the McCarthy hunt for dangerous ideas), to the military posts (as witness Eisenhower, Marshall, Ridgway, Bradley, Gruenther, and others), to the Madison Avenue opinion-makers, to the corporate executives who form the most important of the elites.

This still leaves open the question of whether there is a unifying element—other than mobility—that holds the elites together in the shifting constellations I have mentioned. They are not just Dantean circles in an upper-class Hell, but neither are they tied together by some historic determinism. If there is some common substance I should look for it in the ethos of the society and the tension between the power of the elites and the prevailing social values—to which the elites, however amoral they may seem, are not wholly immune. The curious fact about the elites in American life is not that they corrupt democracy or destroy it but that they are part of the continuing dialectic of what may be called the democratic class struggle.

3. The New Middle Classes

THE EMERGENCE OF a strong, broadly inclusive middle class is the characteristic class achievement of America. Where the pivot class of other civilizations has been some aristocracy, merchant class, or peasantry, the culture carriers of America are the middle classes. Earlier in American history they comprised the independent farmers, the small businessmen and shopkeepers, the professions, and the middlemen. But in the last two generations there has been a revolutionary occupational shift away from agriculture and even manufacturing—away, that is, from the extractive and industrial jobs—to the distributive phases of the economy, the white-collar jobs, the bureaucracies in government, industry, the trade-unions, and the public services like schools and hospitals. This has broken up the old class structure and thrust a new one into being: a new one in which, while the power elites still have the power and the working class has remained relatively stable, the growing points of American life have become a variety of middle-class occupations.

I have already discussed the result of this shift in the creation of a powerful group of technicians, managers, and business and governmental bureaucrats.* Even more important is the emergence of the new white-collar groups, including salesmen and sales girls, office workers, advertisers, middlemen, and the talent professions. The older middle classes, including the farmers, shopkeepers, and small businessmen, have diminished in their relative importance in the middle-class constellation; the newer ones have given the whole constellation less a productive and commercial than a technical and white-collar character. They form a loose collection of occupational strata, probably more anxiety-ridden than the rest of the culture, dominated by the drive to distinguish themselves from the working class, uncohesive, held together by no common bond except the fact that they are caught in a kind of Purgatory between the Hell of the poor and weak and the Heaven of the rich and powerful. Yet they have thus far managed to give stability to American society and to form a massive chain of social experience which links the changes in America's technological revolutions with the changes in the consumer's revolution, and which gives American society its characteristic stamp. When an American speaks of the "common man," it is these classes that he refers to along with the industrial workers.

A somewhat similar shift took place in English society in the eighteenth and nineteenth centuries, when England ceased to be a nation of

* See Ch. IV, Sec. 3, "Big Technology and Neutral Technicians," Ch. V, Sec. 3, "The Corporate Empires," Ch. VI, Sec. 6, "The Governmental Managers."

yeomen and became "a nation of shopkeepers," even more than one of factory and mill workers. Engels complained in his letters to Marx that in mid-nineteenth-century English society even the workers had become bourgeois. And it is clear enough to the sharp observer today that even British Socialism, under the Labor party, is largely a middle-class Socialism. Yet the American middle classes are not a duplication or imitation of British experience. The "shopkeepers" have in America diminished in importance as the big chains have crowded them out. The solid British citizen who rose every morning in a London suburb and went to the "City" in frayed frock coat and bowler hat, with rolled-up umbrella, and returned every evening to his newspaper and garden, was only in externals the forerunner and prototype of the American white-collar employee. He was the residue of the diminished middle-class strength of an England which had once been a great middle-class society and not—as in America—the cutting point of new class formations and transformations.

The new white-collar middle classes of America have emerged as a result of new modes of mass production and specialization, new routines of organizing, new techniques of salesmanship and advertising, and Big Distribution. They are therefore the product of American dynamism fully as much as the elites of big-business ownership or the corporate managers, whose *élan* and confidence take them out of the scope of the white-collar classes, although technically they belong with them. Grim as is the class profile of the white-collar people in such an analysis as Wright Mills's *White Collar*, it must not be forgotten that they are the outgrowths of an expanding economy and a society of rapid movement.

So rapid—in fact, for some time so unnoticed—that the new middle classes emerged on the American scene almost unobtrusively, with no cataclysmic revolutionary clangor and no fanfare of messianic change. Yet the transformation they have brought goes beyond anything else in the American class system. The middle classes as a whole made up 6 per cent of the labor force in 1870 and 25 per cent in 1940; roughly two thirds of them are office and sales people. In the early 1800s, Mills points out, four fifths of the Americans were self-employed or in some way "entrepreneurs"; in 1870 there were only one third; in the 1940s only one fifth were self-employed. Since 1870 the number of the self-employed in America has increased by only 135 per cent; the wage workers by 255 per cent; but the salaried employees have increased 1600 per cent, until they now form more than half of all the gainfully employed and four fifths of the wage receivers in the economy. America has become a salaried rather than a profit-making or wage-earning society. For a time the greatest increases were among the corporate and governmental civil-service people, the professions, and the sales people, but recently the office workers and clerical staffs have outstripped them.

What holds this loose collection of new social strata together? Objectively it is the fact that none of them owns the enterprises for which they work: that is to say, they are as propertyless as the industrial workers, except for those who may be speculating or investing in the stock market as part of their effort to become secure or rich, which is irrelevant to their jobs as such. The other fact is that they all receive salaries rather than wages, have no heavy manual labor to perform, don't get their hands dirty, and wear their street clothes to work. Like the industrial workers, they are employed by business units over which they have no control and in which they have no property shares or stakes. Unlike the industrial workers, however, they do not think of themselves as belonging to the working class but are oriented toward the values of their employers; they are only marginally unionized (only 16 per cent of them were in unions at mid-century, compared with 44 per cent of the industrial workers, and many of their unions have renounced the ultimate weapon of the strike) and they get most of their psychic satisfaction through the consumer's and Big Media culture to which their income and status give them access.

To deepen the shadows in the picture, especially as Mills draws it with bold and dramatic strokes, even this differential prestige is being stripped from them. In the 1890s the average white-collar pay was double that of the wage workers; today the margin between the two is very slight, and in many cases the skilled industrial jobs are higher paid than the white-collar jobs; tomorrow the margin may swing in the direction of the worker's average pay. The biggest factor in the fluidity of American classes—namely, the spread of access to college education and technical training—may be digging the grave of white-collar distinction, for as the market for college graduates gets saturated the differential salary a college education can get grows ever slimmer. The day may be approaching when the prestige of wearing a white collar may disappear because everyone does.

This then is a possible portrait of the new middle classes, from the managerial employees and the "idea men" in the talent professions at the top to the file clerks and sales girls at the bottom: a formless cluster of groups, torn from the land and from productive property, with nothing to sell except their skills, their personality, their eagerness to be secure, their subservience and silence. Since they must act as the personal eyes, ears, hands, and brains of impersonal corporations they are no longer the "masterless" men of an earlier America: they must always wear the public mask of their occupation; to be marketable they must shape themselves to a personality pattern of efficiency, smoothness, sales vigor or charm or deference—which is what is expected and what will be paid for. They end by not knowing themselves, all the more fearful because they have no core of self-knowledge and no collective consciousness that leads them to act with their fellows, caught in a "status panic." The only fact that gives them cohesiveness is that together they hold the middle position in the occupational hierarchy and the prestige scale of American society.

One can paint this kind of picture which dooms them forever beyond redemption to their peculiar Purgatory. Yet, as with many oversharp analytic schemes, this one misses some of the realities of a changing America. You can look at the picture as a deterioration story when compared with a Jeffersonian or Jacksonian society of independent farmers, self-employed artisans, and self-reliant small businessmen. But you can also look at it from another angle, in terms of the upward movement of depressed and minority groups, of Negroes and Catholics and Jews, of the sons and daughters of industrial workers, thrusting their way into occupations that give them the badges of belonging to a middle-class society and therefore the standing for which they have hungered.

The same Irish Catholic worker's family that watches one son go into the priesthood may see another move up the corporate ladder from the sales force to the lower managerial group, and get an equal sense of prestige from both. The Italian or Jew whose son becomes a college teacher, a writer, a lawyer, or surgeon may have the feeling that America has been good to him and has put the stamp of success upon his migration from Europe. Their striving may be riddled with social illusion, their values may be borrowed, but if these are illusions they belong to a social position that is fought for with eagerness: its psychic satisfactions belong to them and not to others, and both the illusions and the satisfactions furnish the social cement that helps hold them and the society together. Many of the men and women who work in the bureaucratic posts of government or corporation or trade-union, who become teachers or script writers or TV performers, who play in the jazz bands, who turn out advertising copy, who stand trimly at the counters of the big department stores or travel about as buyers for them, who work as inspectors and sales engineers for the public utilities, who preach the sermons or write the books and magazine articles, who staff the news papers or run the political parties of America—many of these men are far less aware of the tragedy of their plight, the emptiness of their values, or the slipping security of their prestige than the stern observer who measures them by the standards of a simpler technology and of a society as it was before the property atom was split and before the Big Media emerged.

There are three tests we may apply to a class system: how well it fills the psychic hungers as well as the objective needs of the people; how much stability it gives to the social structure; and how much fluidity it gives to it. Judged by these tests, the new middle classes are imperfect on each but don't come off too badly on any. To most of their members they offer to some degree the "career open to talent" and the sense of upward movement on the income and prestige scale, or at least the sense of not being outsiders. As for stability, I do not deny the possibility that the new middle classes may in a time of stress turn against the industrial and union workers from whom they distinguish themselves and become the dupes of a totalitarian leadership, much as happened when the middle classes of the Weimar Republic turned in panic to the Nazis: but I doubt that it is inevitable or even likely. The German middle classes were mainly the bureaucracies of a stratified society, in which the career open to talent had never strongly taken root, and in which deference was traditional and authority habitually accepted. They were also part of a defeated society which had, at least for a time, lost its power of expansion and was caught in political paralysis and inflation disaster.

As for the test of fluidity, the perception of Max Weber laid bare the outlines of the "three hierarchies" of the social structure, and he saw that the middle class was caught in an "iron cage" between the two others. The difference between the situation of the German and American middle classes is found exactly in this symbolism of the iron cage. German middle-class society was at once too rigid and too amorphous. When economic disaster came there was no underpinning that could save the middle classes from being wiped out by inflation and thrown into the arms of the Nazi adventurers by political hysteria. The new American middle classes are so diverse that while some of them suffer the scars of the chances and changes of economic life, they have never all been affected at once. They are far less rigid and more fluid than the German classes which Weber described, possessing a flexible capacity to adjust themselves to economic transformations which—more than anything else—gives the American class structure the resilience it has.

The fact is that no class structure ever offers a solution to social problems except in the Marxist canon, and it ought not to be judged by the test of whether or not it does. Toynbee has said that the two big rocks on which every civilization has foundered have been war and class. In each civilization there has been the choice between a frozen class system, managed and manipulated from above, and a mobile one; among the mobile ones there have been those which have moved from crisis to crisis through the mechanism of class struggle, always sharpening class distinctions and aligning the people in one camp or another without any intermediate middle ground; and there have been, on the other hand, the class systems which have always sought a moving equilibrium to give the society some stability. The American class system belongs with the latter. It does not—as no class system by its very nature can—make people happy or creative, rooted or alienated, powerful or weak, active or apathetic. All that it can hope to do is to organize the differentials of life choices and life chances with a maximum of access to opportunity and social experience and a minimum of the riving social tensions.

Seen in this frame, the American middle-class society is an operative effort to distribute power and prestige, opportunity and social experience, among the major sectors of the American population which comprise neither the owners of industrial power nor their challengers, neither the powerful nor the embittered, neither elites nor proletarians. By the very nature of the social function they perform, the middle classes cannot be the great militant or assertive force of American life. They are mediators and twilight people, and the most that can be asked is that they should occupy their middle positions with a tolerable measure of social energy and personal fulfillment. Unless a society is dominated by a single class, or is caught in the lethal struggle of two armed class camps until one or the other becomes the dominant one, only a middle-class society can furnish the pattern of a class equilibrium. Obviously the economic and technical changes of the society will be most strongly transmitted to these middle classes, which have received the shock of the changes, cushioned them, transformed them into new forms of social energy.

A middle class which is frozen or is caught in an iron cage has, by this token, ceased to perform its broadly mediating function, and it is doomed along with the society to which it belongs. But in recent American generations the dynamic movement that so swiftly and silently brought the new middle classes onto the stage of American history may also usher them out and bring new forms of class power, prestige, and experience in their place. Where change is so constant and active the strength of the class system is to be measured not in terms of the stability of any particular class formations, nor the happiness or security of the individuals who form it, but by the fact of the change itself. The dynamism that has produced the present middle-class formations in America can produce others as well. This is the growing point of American social experience, and these are the shock absorbers of American social change.

Thus America has become a great historical experiment in a shifting middle-class society. The middle classes do not hold the power of government or rule the economy; they do rule the culture, set the tone of consumption, serve as the crucial audience for the Big Media. They are in this sense the pivot class of America. It is they who read the books and the "slick" magazines, and see the plays and movies with just enough of a cultural veneer to make them palatable and give them gloss. They do not have either the burdens or satisfactions of manual labor, nor the daring that comes from large-scale enterprise. They are middling folk with middling goals, caring for comfort, a competence, and security. Although they still pride themselves on their individualism, they have lost much of the old individualistic stress on hard work and self-denial. They are not out for the old virtues but for some new, relatively safe gamble, whatever it may be. The feel for the safe gamble is the key to their conformism, politically and culturally. They look up to the high places of big business that they hope to reach and down at the lowly places of the workers that they wish to avoid.

Yet I am stretching this too far if I imply that these are barren leaves on a barren tree. Much as it may pain some of the intellectual elite to say so, it is often the middle-class people who dream the dreams, see the visions, and push forward the new formulations that make a people great. The paradox is that out of the middle classes have come some of the most creative talents of America, including the movement for governmental reform and for collective international action. Even the New Deal was as much a movement of the middle class as it was of labor: it first had to shape itself as a movement of middle-class reform and then it went out to find a labor movement which would furnish it a base of mass action.

Like Toynbee, De Tocqueville felt that no civilization could survive unless it resolved the problem of class; his own conviction was that only a middle-class society could sustain political and social democracy. Since then the analysis of thinkers like Veblen, and more recently Laski, Lynd, and Mills, has argued the opposite: that in the key struggle between capitalism and democracy, the middle classes more or less consciously serve the cause of capitalism and are therefore dangerous to democracy. The trouble with this argument is that noncapitalist societies, with very little of a middle class, notably those of eastern Europe and of Asia, have been drawn more strongly than the middle-class societies to totalitarianism and have become managed societies, linked not with democracy but with its antithesis.

De Tocqueville's argument also needs rethinking. The middle classes he knew in the America of his travels were very different from those of today. They were the middle classes of masterless men—farmers always seeking new land, self-employed artisans and mechanics, shopkeepers, small-town editors and lawyers, small businessmen. The independent middle class with which he linked the fortunes of democracy has grown less independent, less secure, more complex. There is no certain demo-cratic health in it as there is no certain democratic destruction.

An effort must be made to distinguish between types of middle-class experience—between the corporate bureaucracies, for example, and such professions as teachers, writers, scientists; between the middle classes with crucial skills which keep them in social demand and those whose living standards become indistinguishable from the average workers; between those who have risen from the ranks and those who, starting at the top, have become declassed; between those, like the technicians and some of the sales and advertising and distributive people, who are the product of economic expansion and those who are caught in a back eddy of history. The fact that they are neither proprietors nor workers defines their outer boundaries but sheds no light on the social functions or the creative force of the groups which are the growing point of American society.

The more functional middle-class groups, especially when they have moved up the class scale, have an *élan* too, which flows from the feel-ing of not being frozen in a permanent lower class, and therefore of seeing the possibilities of life ahead. Thus the middle classes are not automatons, nor merely the hollow men. When politicians and parties have sought to use them by manipulating them politically, they have sometimes succeeded, but just as often they have been disappointed in finding that their material was not as pliable as they had thought. The middle class has done much to mute the jangling sharpness of American competitive tensions and blur the class divisions. It has had to pay the psychic cost of such a role. It is the most vulnerable, perhaps, of the American social strata, and as permeable by fears, hates, and frustra-tions as the depressed classes or the rat-race executives and the top rich. Nevertheless it exerts a mediating force, at once flexible and massive, fluid and resistant, which has helped keep American society from the class agonies that others have experienced.

4. Class Profile of the Worker

UNLIKE THE MIDDLE classes, the American working class is neither the pivot of the culture nor its mediating force, nor is it so vulnerable to the shifting tides of change and opinion.* Yet here too there have been far-reaching changes since the days of Jefferson and Jackson, especially in the last half century.

The American working class disappointed both its champions and its enemies by proving less revolutionary than the former had expected and less docile than the latter had hoped. Unlike the working classes in more clearly stratified societies, it has never shown any of the marks of a permanent proletariat. Nor has it, on the other hand, wholly submitted to the process of *enbourgeoisement* which defeated the hopes of European trade-union organizers who had counted on the continued militancy of their working class. The American workers have been militant enough, but only in trade-union terms, and not in the ideology or politics of revolution. They have shown little proletarian potential and have persisted in refusing to isolate themselves from the main currents of American life. But they have also refused to be absorbed by the other classes and have maintained a sturdiness of viewpoint which makes them neither subservient nor class-embittered. This is part of the anomaly of the American working class.

As with other classes in American society, the dominant historical drive among the workers has been that of fluidity. From the start they saw in America vistas of possibility that were denied to the permanent proletariats of Europe, caught in the iron mesh of a system of status. As early as the Jacksonian period, however, the shadows began to fall on the American workers. Part of the radicalism of the "Workingmen's Associations" and of the Knights of Labor came from the effort to keep the sluices of opportunity open—by fighting off centralized banking and corporate power and by demanding full educational facilities for their sons which would enable them to compete for the prizes of an opening continent. At mid-century the workers, to keep from getting caught as a class, had to rely upon cheap government land; but the process of getting to the frontier with a family required in itself a considerable capital outlay, which in turn became an inhibiting factor. By the 1870s it had become clear to some of the farsighted leaders of the workers that unless they could keep the class system fluid by fighting the new power groups, it would imprison them. Hence the militancy of the Knights of

* See Ch. V, Sec. 7 and Sec. 8, for the history and role of trade-unions and the position of the working force as a whole in the social structure, and Ch. IV, Sec. 4, for the transformations within the factory culture itself and within the concepts of work and the job.

Labor, which reached for weapons of political organization as well as economic and sought alliance with farmer and middle-class groups outside the labor movement. When that effort failed, and the job-conscious unionism of the A.F. of L. took the stage, it spelled the end of one phase in the class development of the American workers. They did not become a proletariat in the sense of becoming hopeless or embittered. But they emerged with a definite consciousness of their common interests, geared to the job rather than to social transformation, yet nonetheless aware of their need for cohesiveness as a class in the struggle with the massed power of the employers.

This phase of class conflict in America has sometimes been slurred over in the eagerness to prove that America is a classless society. There were debt struggles in America as there were in Rome, but in the American case they were between the farmers and the mortgage companies. There were struggles over access to markets, sometimes between farm shippers and the railroads discriminating against them, more often between small businessmen and big monopolies. Yet the class militancy of the farmers and small businessmen largely ebbed away, with the one becoming wards of the government and the other feudatories of the big corporations. The militancy that continued has been in the conflicts over wages and work and life conditions for the workers. Their antagonists have been not only the big corporate managers but even more the small entrepreneurs who have encountered the workers in the face-to-face struggles of collective bargaining, strikes, and lockouts. Since they have been the most direct antagonists the class bitterness between them has been the greatest. This has tended, as I have suggested earlier, to isolate the working class from the middle classes and has imposed upon it the burden of taking on another antagonist along with corporate power.

The class militancy of American workers has not been, therefore, the product of a taste for violence or of the dogma of social change. The magnetic attraction of middle-class and elite values has operated strongly on the workers; often their leaders have been drawn off and lost to them because of that attraction; and the rank and file would have preferred to be absorbed in the rest of American society. The continuance of the workers' militancy has been largely due to the businessmen and the corporate managers who have shown themselves most tenacious of their power, as they have been most resourceful in their use of every means of resistance to union organization and demands. They have used their control of press and propaganda, their vast economic power, and—when pushed hard—even violence itself. How far this had gone beyond sporadic instances was shown in a *Harvard Law Review* article commenting on the National Labor Relations Act (1936) by Professor (now Judge) Calvert Magruder. "Away with yellow dogs,

company unions, black lists, deputy sheriffs in the pay of employers, barricades, tear gas, machine guns, vigilante outrages, espionage, and all
that miserable brood of union-smashing detective agencies." It was an
epitaph on a phase of the labor-management class struggle that was
never to return in full force.

For the American worker to be a worker—that is to say, to belong to
the working class—is an act of involuntary association, but one sealed
in the fire of historic struggle. The antagonism and coercions are not
what he would have wished, since his whole pull is toward acceptance
in the community, away from proletarian consciousness. Yet, given
his refusal to be placed below the salt and given also the tenacity of
the Big Business owners in resisting his claims, the antagonisms have
been inescapable. The worker has suffered scars and met defeats, and
he has also tasted of victory. He has learned a little about the "prowess
order" in American society, and what goes with the status of the bottom
dogs as of the top dogs.

In the process he has caught a glimpse of the power he can exercise in
common action with his fellows. He has refrained from exercising that
full power—at once economic, political, and social—despite the fervent
prayers and upbraidings of side-line coaches who want him to act for
the salvation of society. He acts, however, according to the laws of his
own being within the American frame—peaceful when he can be, violent
when he must, an economic man most of the time, a political man in the
great crises, an individualist when he can indulge himself in that
luxury, but acting with class solidarity when he can do no other. As a
result of the struggle, some traits in him have become desensitized, others
sharpened; on the whole a democratic dynamism has come out of it,
since the worker's fulfillment of at least a good portion of his life
claims upon the culture is a condition of vitality in a people's society.

To a desolating degree these life claims remain unfulfilled. The
worker often leaves school as a child, to keep the family vessel from
foundering, and he never gets back to equip himself with the needed
skills for advancing out of his job. Often a worker who has started
with eager hopes for thrusting his way up has wound up with the job
he had at the start. The hope for advancement becomes a youthful
memory, and he accedes to the quenching of his hopes and the drab
limits of his uneventful historyless life career. Thus forces which in
other cultures expressed themselves in a permanently depressed proletarian class have in America been transmuted into defeated life
claims and "deadened choices" for a segment of the unskilled and
semiskilled workers—and perhaps even some of the skilled workers and
lower white-collar groups.

Why then has not the American worker asserted his resentments more strongly? The German scholar, Werner Sombart, put this question at the turn of the century in a book called *Why Is There No Socialism in the U.S.?* The two Lynd studies of "Middletown," which are powerful attempts to trace the logic of class relations in America, suggest that he has been bemused by the mass media which the business class controls and the legendry it has fashioned, and has forgotten his own interests, allowing his militancy to be absorbed in "the Middletown spirit."

Yet at least three additional factors should be mentioned. One is the democratizing influence of public education, which is free and universal for all social classes through the public high schools and which can be had at a minimal cost in the city and state universities. Even the private universities have increasingly been opening their doors, through scholarships and subsidies, to the sons and daughters of workers. What I have said above, about the working-class child having to leave school to help support the family, is happily true only of an ever-decreasing segment of the workers. Second, there is the democratizing effect of mass consumption, which has meant that the worker and his family now have access to many of the things from which they were formerly cut off. Third, there is the persistent hope that the worker's children will "do better" than the parents did, with respect to a job and education and the class into which they will marry. I must add that in terms of both mass education and mass consumption the real problem for the worker has been not that of being able to cut across class lines but of finding in the new norms to which he has penetrated some content with richness enough to nourish his personality. Generally these norms have been filled with the values of the middle classes, for which the worker has hungered because they have been alien to his experience, yet which have often left him with the frustrated sense of achieving less than he had hoped for.

There has been considerable evidence since the Lynds that subjectively the workers think of themselves in middle-class terms and yearn for a middle-class status. In 1940 a *Fortune* poll found that 79 per cent of the American people called themselves "middle class" rather than "lower class," and a Gallup poll found the percentage to be 87 per cent. But a Princeton study by Richard Centers, which put the question differently, got very different results. Centers asked a sampling of Americans whether they belonged to the "upper," "middle," "working," or "lower" class. This time 51 per cent put themselves in the "working class," and 43 per cent in the "middle class."

While there are serious doubts about what any of the attitude studies really show, the shift in percentages between these studies is striking.

The American worker does not think of himself as part of a permanent underlying proletariat. He refuses therefore to put himself in the "lower class." He will bow subserviently to no man. But he is not ashamed of his role as worker, and when confronted with "middle class" and "working class" as a designation, he chooses the latter. Although in income terms he belongs below the middle of the hierarchy, he does not feel an outsider in his culture. His whole striving has been to shun proletarianism and seek equality of status with other common men, whether they be in the middle or working class, yet not to give up his militancy as a worker and not to hesitate about calling himself one.

The three crucial indices of class are power, income, and status. In terms of power the American worker as an individual does not have the formal economic and social power that the corporate owners and managers have, in the sense that he cannot strategically shape the behavior and destiny of others. Yet acting collectively in the trade-union the workers do have a vast power over the destinies of the economy as a whole, and, whether they choose to exercise it or not, it gives them a feeling of assurance. In terms of income, the worker's purchasing power and living standards have risen steadily, although not as rapidly as the wealth of the owners, and in many cases are higher than those of the lower white-collar groups. In terms of his social standing in the community, however, the worker does not have the badges of social rank that the middle class has. In this area of status and prestige he tends to imitate not, as Veblen thought, the prowess and ostentation of the businessmen in the "leisure class," but the comforts and living standards of the middle class: he hopes to have his daughters marry into it and his sons move up into the professional, technical, managerial, or small-business ranks, while his wife moves into its churches and clubs. This is a slow process, but it is taking place in America, especially for the upper income ranks of the working class. The middle classes have become, in status terms, a compassable goal for the working class while it retains its own identity and solidarity on the job.

Thus, when Europeans ask why there has been so little "proletarian potential" among the American workers, the answer is the multiple one I have suggested. It runs in terms of education, mass consumption, the Big Media, the fact of high living standards and income, the constant movement into the middle-class status, the sense of hope for the future of the next generation. The greater democratic atmosphere of social intercourse in America has shorn membership in the working class of much of the social stigma that it has carried elsewhere. The outlets offered for democratic political activity, where the worker has the same vote as the employer and is protected by the same legal right, have a similar effect. But above all, there has been a steady increase in the productivity of American workers, unequaled in world history. The role that was formerly played by continued access to free land, in cutting down a sense of class inferiority and class bitterness in the worker, was later played by the continuing rise of the productivity curve due to technological advance. It is notable that there is no exactly parallel word in the European languages for the sense in which Americans use "productivity."

In fact, technology had at least as much to do as the much mooted frontier with shaping the profile of the class system in America. The task has been to transmute a substantial part of the productivity gains into higher real wages and lower hours for the workers, which has been the task of a job-conscious, astutely led, tenacious trade-unionism. The result of all these influences together has been to drain off the "proletarian potential," which is to say, the revolutionary energy of the American worker.

While he has functioned on the economic level with class solidarity, the worker has been drawn on the social level toward the values of the middle class which he often rivals in his income. His reading, sports, amusements, hobbies, heroes, are the same as those of the white-collar classes, the small merchants, the professional people, the businessmen. He is caught in the contradiction that while his political and economic attitudes recognize his class identity and are an expression of it, he persistently refuses to give up his belief in a fluid class system. Thus is created the great class anomaly of American society—that of the worker who acts militantly as one, but whose leanings and dreams are toward the values of the middle class.

5. The Minority Situation*

EVERY NATION, seen realistically, is several nations, and in every historic civilization, stock and race—as well as class—have been the traditional lines of cleavage. In America, where the class lines have been blurred by social mobility and where most of the society is middle class, the more stubborn cleavage lines have proved to be race, color, religion, and the social hierarchy of ethnic and national stocks. Visitors to America, especially from Europe and Latin America, have for generations been puzzled by the ordeal by contempt to which the American

* I have already touched on this theme in Ch. III, Sec. 1, "Is There an American Stock?" and Sec. 2, "The Immigrant Experience," both of which deal with the composition of the American people. I deal here with the social situation of the ethnic minorities in relation to the majority.

ethnic minorities have been subjected. The Negro, Chinese, Japanese, Mexican, Filipino, Italian, Jew, Catholic, the foreign born (and to some extent the second generation) of almost any stock have found to varying degrees that their standing and acceptance depend less upon themselves as persons than upon the labels attached to them.

It is difficult to get at accurate figures on the size of minority groups, partly because of definition and partly because the census figures are lacking. But G. E. Simpson and J. M. Yinger have made some calculations that are worth setting down. They indicate that as of 1950 there were fifteen million Negroes in America, one half million other non-whites, two million Mexican Americans, ten million foreign-born whites, and five million Jews. Allowing for overlappings, they estimate that thirty million Americans, or a little less than one fifth of the total population in 1950, belonged to one or another of these minority groups. This was a smaller percentage than forty years earlier, in 1910, when the Negroes and the foreign born formed more than a quarter of the total number of people.

Thus the trend has been toward a more homogeneous population. This is especially true of the foreign born, whose proportion to the total has been decreasing since 1910 and whose actual numbers have also been falling since 1930. If we move beyond the foreign born to the second generation, there were in 1950 somewhere around twenty million "of foreign or mixed parentage." When added to the thirty million figure above, we get over fifty million Americans—roughly one third of the nation—who could be said to belong to the minority groups or to feel the impact of the current attitudes toward minorities. In their sum they form a system of not very disguised lower status. They have again in varying degrees become the targets of socially sanctioned hatred, contempt, and fear upon the part of the majority. They occupy the lower positions in what has become a hierarchy of belonging and alienation which can scarcely be squared with the clangor of American ideals, the professions of churchmen, or the pronouncements of political spokesmen.

This hierarchical pattern is not, except for some state laws and ordinances in the South, embodied in statute or legal decision, but more dangerously in the practices of everyday living and the emotions of everyday thinking. To assign it to the crude energies of a lusty, growing nation—a kind of sowing of cultural wild oats by an otherwise generous and equalitarian people—contains a core of truth, however bitter the rind may be. One of the paradoxes of American life has been the simultaneous passion for equality among "insiders" and the almost equally passionate rejection of the "outsider." This is, in effect, a kind of American tribalism expressing itself through a system of upper caste and pariahs—grudgingly recognized, accompanied by a sense of agonized guilt, inveighed against by some of the "best people," yet nonetheless practiced.

Amidst the varieties of racist experience represented here, one may trace the main lines of the historical graph by which the "outsiders" were isolated from the culture. As long as America's greatest need was for more manpower to clear and settle the land and build the industrial plant, men of all nations and creeds were accepted, if not welcomed, by the earliest arrivals. From the beginning there were stereotypes imposed upon the more marginal immigrants. As was perhaps natural, the members of each new wave of immigration were assigned the lowliest tasks, the longest hours of work, the poorest and dirtiest living quarters. The basic pattern was, however, for the immigrants of each new influx to be in time absorbed by the rest, yielding the role of strangeness in turn to the still later comers. Most of them moved up the hierarchical ladder, while those who followed grasped eagerly the lowly places that had been relinquished. But during this period the discriminations were (so to speak) objective: it was taken as a fact of life in the New World that the earlier arrivals got the favored positions; what prejudice existed was more against immigrants as such than against any particular groups, although even in the 1840s the Irish immigrant was a favorite target of abuse.

The entering wedge of a new order of prejudice came with the racism developed by the struggle between North and South. The first Negroes, even when they came as indentured servants, were not regarded by the other Americans as a separate order of mankind. The whites who had come as indentured servants, and even those who had come as convicts, were later absorbed, and their descendants are today merged with the rest. But the cotton gin, and with it the development of large-scale methods of cotton growing on the Southern plantation system, made necessary the importing of a whole population of cheap black slave labor, recruited from the easy sources of African supply. Since the Southern spokesmen could not square this with their democratic or Christian ideals of the brotherhood of man, they developed a doctrine to justify the ways of the master race to the subject race—a doctrine of the biological superiority of one and inferiority of the other. This effort to create a permanent legal and social caste system clashed not only with the American ideals of equality but also with the efforts of the other sections to keep the society open for free labor and investment. The North won, with its belief in free labor and an open-class system; yet in the South the bitterness of defeat and the postwar urge to keep freed slaves in subjection served to harden the mold of racist doctrine.

Its consequences to the American mentality were not restricted to the South. In the free West, which had joined with the antislavery cause, movements developed after the Civil War for the exclusion of Chinese immigration, again on grounds of a biological racism. The peopling of the continent grew less pressing, and the scarcity of man power was less felt. New currents of thought came in from Europe—those of Gobineau and Alfred Schultz, and later of Wagner and Houston Chamberlain; in America there was a response in the racist writings of Lothrop Stoddard and Madison Grant. As Oscar Handlin has noted, the liberal thinkers were not guiltless on racism and immigration: the Populist campaign (sometimes with anti-Jewish overtones) against "Wall Street," the campaign of Gompers and the A.F. of L. against Chinese immigration, and the writings of Edward A. Ross and John R. Commons (and later of H. P. Fairchild) were all the more influential because they were known liberals on other scores. Immigration policy grew tighter, and with the passage of the quota laws racism came of age in America.* Not only did caste thinking develop on color lines, but America in effect declared officially that the stocks of eastern Europe, the Mediterranean countries, and Asia were less welcome as permanent residents than the supposedly "Aryan" stock of northern Europe and the British Isles. The revival of the Ku Klux Klan in the twenties and the spread of anti-Semitic forgeries like the "Protocols" gave a new dimension of hatred and violence to the prejudices of previous generations. With the Great Depression, the anxieties of survival and status were deepened for millions of Americans who were ready to turn their frustrations on the vulnerable groups. The rise of Nazi power in Europe, and the spread of Rosenberg-Goebbels propaganda by the Bund and other organizations, completed the graph.

The sources on which racism had fed and grown strong were deeply related: some of the same domestic tensions which led to the closing of the immigration gates led also to inner economic and political struggles, as in the Depression and the New Deal, which in turn served as arenas for deepened racial and religious hatreds. The impact of world struggles was also felt, as witness the internment of the Japanese in California in World War II and the efforts both of anti-Semites and of Communists to turn some of the atom-spy episodes involving persons who happened to be Jews to the purposes of their own propaganda.

One could tell the story of minority-group Americans in a very different fashion, turning the seamier side inside and displaying some of the less gloomy aspects: that the whole minority experience in America has been a successful one; that, except in the South, no local

* For a fuller discussion, see Ch. III, Sec. 2, "The Immigrant Experience."

prejudices have been translated directly into law; that, again excepting the South, no political candidate or party since the Know-Nothings has run successfully on a platform of racism; that these irrational prejudices, which form the chief outlet for social tensions and frustrations, have resulted in remarkably little violence; that mingling of majority and minority groups in the Armed Services during World War II resulted in considerable erosion of racism; that statutes like the Ives-Quinn Law in New York helped whittle away discrimination in employment, without coercion and with little publicity; that recent Supreme Court decisions, especially in housing, transportation, and education, show the secular trend of constitutional law; that the political party on which the racist Southerners depend for their power is the same party that won five successive Presidential elections in the span of a quarter century by a coalition which included labor, anti-racist liberals, and the minority groups; that the prejudice against Negroes, Orientals, Catholics, Jews, and the various national minorities has been steadily decreasing; that when Hitler relied on American racist discords to pave the way for victory, he calculated badly; that the similar reliance of the Communists, using very different techniques of propaganda, is also based on a miscalculation.

While each item in this defense is valid, their sum still leaves standing the massive fact of a "divided America." To a degree the class inequities and the ethnic discriminations in American life are both subject to erosion by mobility, which, however slow it may be, makes the open-class system one of hope. But I doubt that it makes a status system open enough to stand alongside the open-class system. If there were still the kind of open-caste system there was for a time, when only the most recent immigrants were made the targets of stereotyped ridicule and discrimination, that too would be tolerable. But in the case of Negroes and Jews, and to some degree Catholics, Orientals, and Mexicans, the lines of division are drawn tightly. The danger, of course, lies in the idea of two Americas—one a presumably authentic America of traditional blood and ways, the other an inferior and supplementary America of second-class citizens, made up of those who do not belong to the exclusive club and who have to fight for equal access to opportunity.

It would not be hard to make out a rational defense for the philosophy which wants to keep a society from becoming too "mongrelized" or "cosmopolitan." There are social values in the tightly knit, relatively cohesive communities—Sparta and Puritan New England and Renaissance Italy come to mind—for which one can at least make out a case: values of like-mindedness about manners and morals, common assumptions, a common pace of living. Even the best of these societies have foundered on the problem of growth: to expand means to take in variant ways of life and thought. But if the choice ever existed for America —which I doubt, since from the beginning it was founded on the idea of inclusiveness, not tribalism—it exists no longer. America has moved far beyond the limits of a simple tribalism. It has so successfully absorbed diverse stocks and strains that the warnings about being overwhelmed by "mongrel" groups sound a little like the forebodings of a future in which the insect kingdom will overwhelm the human race. Even those who plead that the spirit of the immigration restriction laws is not racist argue at most for a "breathing spell" in which to consolidate the population gains, but not for discrimination against those who have become Americans.

Actually the logic of the "breathing-spell" position should lead more powerfully toward the idea of an inclusive America, in which the "foreign" parts are brought into a synthesis with the whole instead of remaining as excrescences. A civilization does change in its ways of life and thought as it absorbs elements from diverse biological stocks and cultural traditions. One can even understand the fear of the more prolific birth rate of the minorities, but since they are largely the product of lower living standards the strategy of keeping the living standards low by enclosing the minorities in walls of caste would seem self-defeating. However, this fear of being "swamped" by alien stocks and ways of thought is in itself a curious contradiction, since from earliest times the Americans welcomed accessions of individual vigor and cultural strength, from whatever ethnic source.

The rituals of expulsion and purification, which can only rest on the premise of a core stock which is alone pure and the assumption that everything else is polluting, are themselves grotesquely alien to the traditional American spirit. The individual has the right to be wrong in choosing his social associates and intimates on the basis of attraction, taste, snobbery, or conviction. Nor is there anything unhealthy about the existence of ethnic communities within the larger American community, each of them trying to hold on to elements of its group identity and in the process enriching the total culture pattern. What is unhealthy is the freezing of ethnic lines into caste lines, especially when they purport to be also dividing lines of "Americanism" and "loyalty." When these lines are congealed, so as to separate top dogs from bottom dogs, and are made tests of belonging regardless of an individual's own worth, the explanation cannot be found in the intellectual rationalizations that pass as "arguments," or even in the traits of the minority groups themselves. They must be sought in forces within the society which the racist impulses somehow mirror or express.

If we try to understand these forces and tensions, anti-Semitism in America offers a case study a little sharper than the other minority groups, although less sharp than the case of the Negroes. Until the turn of the century the problem of anti-Jewish feeling was little different from that of anti-immigrant feeling in general. In fact, one could not have found anti-Jewish movements similar to the Know-Nothings or the American Protective Association, nor were Jews anywhere in America treated as the Irish immigrants were treated by the Boston Brahmin community in the 1850s and 1860s. In common with the others, the anti-Jewish stereotypes could be expected to yield to the mellowing effects of time and mutual acquaintance. In a Bible-conscious America the Jews had one advantage over the other minorities—the affinity between Protestant militancy and the tradition of Hebraic prophecy.

If one holds, with Carey McWilliams, that anti-Semitism is "the mask of privilege" and therefore crucially related to the class struggles in a capitalist economy, then the refusal of a famous Saratoga hotel in 1871 to admit the wealthy Jewish banker J. W. Seligman becomes a symbolic turning point in the treatment of the Jews. But I should be inclined to see the incident more narrowly as part of the elite thinking of New York "Society" and its pettiness in seeking to close its gates to the parvenu Jew. To see anti-Semitism as a deliberate "diversionary issue," created by a ruling class in order to turn away the gathering anticapitalist wrath, seems somewhat too pat. In more complex terms, one can see a triple separation—at once stock (ethnic origin), recency of immigration, and religion—which made the Jew seem more of an outsider than other minorities, and a heavily Jewish city like New York more exotic and sinister to Americans from the South and the Midwest.

Thus anti-Semitism gained a cumulative force, fed even among the other immigrants themselves by the centuries-old hatreds of Europe, by echoes of Chaucer and Shakespeare and Dickens, of Oberammergau and Wagner, of the traditions of the Slavic peasant and the German bourgeois. The economic struggle contributed its competitive rivalries-turned-to-hatreds. McWilliams notes rightly that there was little outcry against the Jews from eastern Europe as long as they stayed as proletarians in the needle trades, but when they moved into the middle classes and made a bid for higher living standards and better schools, residences, and resorts, the anti-Jewish tensions mounted. Yet it was not until the era of Depression and Nazism that anti-Semitism took its place, after anti-Negro racism, as the most serious movement of ethnic hatreds in America. This was not due so much to capitalism or economic exploitation, nor to any logic in the racial doctrines themselves, but to the aggressions and frustrations of life in a rapidly changing, highly charged society. The Jews became in a sense the residuary legatees of other stored-up and unexpended hatreds.

What this has meant scarcely requires review. The planes and dimensions on which it is expressed are complex: exclusion from residential areas, resorts, and clubs; exclusion from many colleges of standing except on a rough quota basis, and dwindling admission into many professional schools, especially medical and engineering; as well as economic discrimination, in getting employment and advancement; a depressing number of anti-Semitic episodes. Obviously these forms of discrimination run from the genteel and perhaps largely unconscious, through the instances where they are used as a kind of group style in conforming to dominant habits of thought, all the way to the open incitements of fanatical professional anti-Semites. In the large they comprise an effort to isolate and segregate the Jews, and to squeeze them by pressures, gentle or otherwise, into a system of status for which they have not proved tractable material.

On any rational level there is a wild paradoxical quality in the charges made against the Jew in America. His position in business and finance makes him a target for nativist "Populist" movements, while his position in liberal and labor circles makes him the target of the Radical Right. By using the Jew as the symbol both of Bolshevism and of international finance, his enemies have managed to link him at once with the two movements that have invoked widespread hostility. They also get him coming and going on the score of his ways of living. If he seeks to embrace the ways of the larger community—in work or play, in marriage, in social intercourse—he is either repulsed as an intruder or condemned (not the least by his own people) as a fawning "assimilationist." If, either as a response to the rebuffs or out of pride in the Jewish tradition, he lives and marries and brings up children largely within his group, he is condemned as clannish and unassimilable.

A similar paradox invests the passions of the small rabble of violent anti-Semites. Although they regard themselves as part of the American majority, they speak and act more as if they were a victim minority themselves and as if the Jew somehow represented the dominant cultural profile. They see him as the center of a successful conspiracy to dominate the whole of American life—its banks and trade-unions, its government, its colleges and school system, its Big Media, its book publishing and reviewing, its judiciary and even the Supreme Court. Making a bid for the role of pursuer, they retain the mentality of the victim. They manage to bridge both roles, as Theodor Adorno has noted, by saying vaguely that "blood will flow," thus implying that it might be theirs at the hands of the Jews, and rationalizing their own role as that of counterviolence. Much of their literature and their speeches contains a sense of discovery, as if they had found "the key" which so many of the bemused and bewildered are seeking—the key not only to American salvation but to the solution of the world crisis.

Some of these racists come from the working class and some from the wealthy strata, but most from the lower middle classes. As a result of the new phases of American life that have cut many away from internalized codes of thought and behavior, they have developed a malaise. Whatever the established patterns of hatred, they move to them because they find them socially sanctioned hatreds. But in addition to a sense of status, they also get a sense of being rebels fighting to overthrow the reigning idols. They join the racist "crackpot" organizations, are proselytized and in turn become fervent proselytizers. They become obsessive, as much the victims of their hate as the hated ones.

In a massive collaborative study, *The Authoritarian Personality*, a number of American social scientists, mainly with a European background (Adorno, Frenkel-Brunswik, Levinson, and others), sought light on the personality pattern of those who succumb to racist prejudices and become their carriers. Using various schematic scales for attitude measurement, interviews, and projective techniques, they found racism most pronounced in two types: in a California study of college girls they found an insecurity that came from their need to maintain status in their genteel, well-groomed, upper-middle-class groups. They were overtrained for the status struggle and full of social anxieties. Another group was made up of war veterans in Chicago, largely from the working class. In them the violent and rebellious strains were more apparent. As Nathan Glazer has pointed out, there is no contradiction between the strain of nonconformism at one stratum and of conformism at another, both entering as ingredients into the racist syndrome. Both are manifestations of a malaise that may take either a chip-on-the-shoulder form or that of status anxiety. In both cases the family context and the processes of child-rearing, rather than experience with minority groups, seem decisive in the formation of the personality pattern. In both also there is a haunting sense of failure in the life goals. The traits that each individual most feared or disliked in himself were found to be projected onto the symbol of the target victim.

Finally, the investigators found an interconnected pattern of attitudes: anti-Semitism almost always was linked with hatred of Negroes and of other ethnic minorities. (This was proved accurate in the agitation against school integration in the South in the controversy of the mid-1950s.) These in turn were linked with a hatred of labor, the New Deal, and liberalism, and a tendency to use highly charged nationalist and religious symbols in condemning them together. Thus the racist hatreds are not to be seen as isolated prejudices but as an interconnected web of hatred whose scope, like its sources, embraces the tensions and problems of the whole of American society.

I have used the status of the Jews as an extreme example of ethnic hostility toward a minority whose members, unlike all except a few Negroes, could "pass" if they wished—that is, could renounce their minority membership and join the majority. Strikingly very few American Jews have availed themselves of this chance. Instead there has been an alternation, almost cyclical in nature, between the urge toward assimilation with the larger culture and the urge toward a militant assertion of the identity of the subculture. These cycles of changing emphasis have probably been true of immigrant groups in general—of the Scandinavians, the Slavs, the Irish, the Italians, the Greeks, the Arabs, the Chinese and Japanese; but the conflict has been sharper in the case of the Jews, partly because they have been more articulate about it and have thrashed it out in novels, Community Center meetings, and in their newspapers and magazines. In the quarter century after the rise of Hitler to power, during which the profile of Jewish life abroad included the experience of martyrdom, the needs of the refugees, and the crises of the new Jewish state, the emphasis within the American Jewish group shifted away from assimilationism toward a sometimes overmilitant assertion of their uniqueness and separateness as a historical community.

As with other minority groups in America, this was partly a carryover of earlier ethnic patterns, partly a response to the hostility, partly a tenacity of group survival under the great assimilative force of American life. One result has been a continuing tendency toward ethnic endogamy, not only among Negroes upon whom it is forced but also among Catholics and Jews where it is also a willed community act. It is especially true in the towns and cities where there is a heavy concentration of minority population and where they have built up a community life of their own. It is a striking fact that even in cities like New York, Chicago, Detroit, Cleveland, Philadelphia, and Buffalo, where the ethnic minorities are substantial and often together form a majority, they still retain minority attitudes. The isolating ghetto pressures, both from without and from within, build up little ethnic pockets which make for cultural diversity but which also perpetuate needless frictions and divisions, and contribute to a sense of minority isolation and (especially among Jews and Negroes) even a victim psychology. There is among Negroes a surprising amount of "passing," where pigment and conscience allow it. Like the other white ethnic groups, the Jew, to "pass," has only to become "assimilated," which is a matter of cultural conformity and absorption. Yet even the Jew who strives hardest for such absorption finds that it is not enough for him to wear his religion lightly or even discard it and break his ties of identification with his ethnic group. In many instances his offer of assimilation is not acknowledged: it is only his children and in turn their children who are finally accorded a substantial measure of acceptance. Even where the pride of Jacob has been discarded, the fear of Ahasuerus lingers.

It is a hard thing for a member of such a minority group to hold the balance even between his sensitivities about status, his temptation to overreact toward hostility and either belittle himself or hate himself or flaunt in the face of the majority the very minority traits that have been called in question, his pride in his ethnic heritage, his ties with the victims and martyrs of his tradition, his hunger amidst it all to prove himself and fuse his own experience into the larger cultural pattern. It is these crosscurrents of impulse and emotion that made the Negro or Jewish youth a stock figure in the problem novels of the 1940s and the 1950s. His quest for identity was a voyage that had to survive dangerous shoals and rapids. He had two cultures rather than only one with which somehow he had to make his peace—identifying himself with segments of both as he grew up, sifting both of them through his fears and insecurities, his hopes and strengths, accepting and rejecting, and out of it having to discover who he was. The young Negro or the young Jew who managed to come through this experience was perhaps the sturdier personality for having been through it, and he carried with him a richer freightage of family and cultural memories. But in too many cases the experience warped or broke him.

Concentrating on such problems, there is a danger of slighting the very substantial progress that American minorities have made in finding their place in the larger culture without surrendering a saving remnant of identity. The Jews themselves, for all the restrictions on them, have advanced more rapidly on the social scale than the other minorities. But the Negroes have also won an increasing measure of socially recognized as well as legal equality. To many foreign observers what is remarkable about America is not that there should be the conflicts I have recounted but that in the midst of so many tensions there should be so striking a measure of success in living together. On the score of religious freedom the Catholic and other churches have been given by the Federal courts the right to run their own parochial school systems as alternatives to the public schools; the Jehovah's Witnesses have been protected against local ordinances restraining their activities; the sects of conscientious objectors to war have been recognized as such by the draft boards. Negroes and whites, Protestants and Catholics and Jews, ethnic groups from every part of the world, live together in the big cities without violence. Even the racist syndrome itself is in one sense a response to the democratic creed: confronted with equalitarian ideals which he dare not openly reject, the embittered and frustrated person who seeks a purge for his frustrations may find refuge either in the fantasy of an elaborate Jewish or Catholic conspiracy or else in a theory of the biological inferiority and superiority of the subject and master races.

Yet America remains a house divided against itself so long as the minority groups are kept from normal access to a wide range of life choices and from the normal processes of absorption. With perhaps a fifth of the population and considerable strength as a voting force, the Catholics have in recent years effectively protected themselves against Know-Nothings of contemporary America and have achieved a degree of power in the government, especially in Congress and in some of the administrative services. The anti-Catholic crackpots who are bemused by a world "Catholic conspiracy" are still to be found, and there are also serious students who fear objectively that Protestant America will not show the strength to resist the organized pressures to make the Catholic viewpoint prevail in a number of areas in American life. Yet on the whole it can be said with some assurance that the dangerous phase of anti-Catholicism in America is a thing of the past. Lower in the scale than either Jews or Catholics are the three million Mexican Americans, who are either migratory workers or live ghetto-wise in the "colonia" of the cities of the Southwest, where they rank just above the Indians and the Negroes: provided with poorer schools, discriminated against in hiring and firing, kept out of unions, given a shabby justice by local police and court officials, largely ignored in the choices for public office.

There is a curious paradox to be found in the American attitude toward minority groups, as disclosed by a recent Roper public-opinion poll. When asked whether various minorities should be given "a better break," one third of those questioned said that Negroes ought to get it, yet 79 per cent expressed a distaste for the idea of intermarriage with Negroes. The figures on the Jews were reversed: only 8 per cent thought they deserved a better break, while 50 per cent were against intermarriage. It is worth noting that the latter figure comes closer to the 40 per cent who thought the Jews had too much economic power. The response on the Catholics was 7 per cent for their deserving a better break, and 21 per cent against intermarriage. It is clear that intermarriage carries a decisive emotional freightage, since on the question of working side by side in factory or office or store and on the question of entertaining them in one's home, Jews and Catholics had evidently been pretty much accepted. The groups against whom prejudice persisted here were the Chinese, Filipinos, and Mexicans, and especially the Negroes. Two out of five Americans prefer not to work with Negroes, and more than half do not want them in their homes. Thus there is a hierarchy of sensitivity in the attitudes toward minority groups, ranging from the casual contacts of everyday life, through work and social intercourse, to the intimacies of family relation.

Whatever may be the current state of ethnic prejudices, it is never the "majority" that holds them. Except in the attitudes toward the Negroes, the majority of Americans hold—at least on a conscious level —enlightened views. In the wake of the Nazi excesses, a relativist concept of race has become widespread, and increasingly in the scholarly literature the older idea of a correlation between biological stocks and such traits as intelligence, disease, and criminality has been discarded. The kind of "cultural pluralism" which Horace Kallen and Randolph Bourne championed has become a staple of American writing and teaching. The carriers of racism are intense individuals who represent only the minority forces in American life.

Yet by their intensity, and by appealing to traits and tendencies on the level of the often unconscious and irrational elements in the majority, they have been able to exercise a disproportionate influence on American behavior. No Negro, for example, has ever gone beyond the House of Representatives in an elective office; none since Reconstruction days has ever been chosen in state-wide elections either as governor or Senator. Negroes have recently been appointed to the Federal courts, but none has reached the Supreme Court. Jews and Catholics have been governors and Senators, held Cabinet posts, and have even sat on the Supreme Court, where among the Catholics (Taney, White, Butler, Murphy, and Brennan) and the Jews (Brandeis, Cardozo, and Frankfurter) there have been some who have made judicial history. No Jew has ever been nominated for the Presidency, and in the one instance where a Catholic ran he was greeted by a revealing campaign of bigotry. Nevertheless, Senator Kennedy came close to getting the Democratic Vice-Presidential nomination in 1956, in a setting that made the Southern delegates paradoxically his most ardent supporters—which must be taken as a revolutionary turning point in the American attitudes toward Catholics. For a Jew, even a converted one, to head up the American imperial power as Disraeli headed up the British or Blum and Mendès-France the French, would still seem to most Americans politically unthinkable. To choose either a Jew or Catholic for the highest symbolic post in the nation would seem like choosing an outsider, and a political party which ventured such a candidacy would be challenging an encrusted tradition.

This is one of the things that sticks in the craw of the ethnic minorities. It has been suggested that ethnic pluralism breaks up some of the rigidities of the class system, and there is truth in it, but what counts for the minorities is that they have one additional hurdle—and often a steep one—in the competition for life's goods. What they resent is not just the prejudice but the closure of the otherwise open-class system in their case, just as what the Negroes especially resent, even more than racial hostility, is the lingering rigidity of caste in a society whose every fiber otherwise cries out against it. More than anything else, this accounts for the persistence of fairly cohesive voting of minority groups in political elections. It would be exaggerated to say that they vote as "blocs," yet in practice the politicians go on the assumption that the blocs do exist, and make their appeals accordingly in the campaigns. Usually the minority groups vote not so much their interests as their fears, their insecurities, their resentments, and the eagerness of their hopes.

These hopes must not be left out of the total picture. The central fact remains the vast assimilative force of American life. In a sense the xenophobic and racist hatreds are a response to it—a form of protest by the more backward and primitive elements against the onrushing pace of this force, an effort by embittered men and women to stay the strength of the current which is bearing them out to a chartless sea. In a sense also the elements of hope and affirmation in the lives even of the victims of hostility are also a response to it, for they sense that even the victories of their enemies are victories in a rear-guard action. The assimilative force of American life is more powerful than the logic of the liberal arguments, more powerful than the specialized sense in which "assimilation" is used, more powerful even than the economic and voting strengths exerted by the minorities. For it is intrinsic to American growth and experience, and as such it is itself a nonrational dimension which can match and overshadow the irrationalism of the racist impulse.

6. The Negro in America

I WANT TO deal separately with the case of the Negro in America because there is nothing in the experience of the other minority groups quite like it. The Negroes are the real outsiders of American life, and their situation is not one of disguised caste but almost nakedly of a pariah caste, kept in subjection by law, social custom, terrorism, and fear, at its worst in the South but even in the North anything but a thing of beauty. The "Negro problem" is a "white problem" as well: it is at once the ugliest scar on the American conscience and its gadfly. In terms of America's class system it presents the hierarchies of class in heightened and more rigid form, with (until recent years) relatively little of its mobility and sense of hope.

The case of the Negro can be spelled out in the relation between race, class, and caste. On race one can only say that it is a reality whose precise definition has defied generations of study. The Negroes form a more sharply defined ethnic group than most in American life. Coming as they did from the isolated and primitive life of African tribalism, their cultural heritage differed drastically from the culture to which they were brought. But even with the strongest differences in pigmentation and in cultural heritage, one misses from the factual picture of race any clear-cut evidences of superiority and inferiority.

In the jungle of American physical diversity, as I have said earlier, any notions of ethnic "purity" or prescriptive ethnic superiority become incongruous. Among the more recent theorists, Cox has defined race as any population with a large "penetrance" of a particular genetic trait, and the UNESCO statement defines it in closely similar terms. In this sense the Negroes form a race. But even when you single out pigmentation from all the other genetic traits, there are still a bewilderingly large number of color gradations and combinations in America that would defy a corps of skilled ethnologists: the varieties of black, white, yellow, red, mulatto, quadroon, octaroon, almost white, "passing," Creole, Indian-white, Indian-Negro, Caribbean-Latin, Hawaiian-Filipino-Chinese mixtures. Where the culture is, like the American, made up of human material from many ethnic groups that were crossbred to start with, and where it has carried the biological and cultural crossbreeding so far, the stalking of ethnic purity has an ironic irrelevance, and to base social caste on it becomes a cruel fantasy. The richness of ethnic composition that makes America a microcosm of the larger world transforms racism into a bad joke. It was the American school of anthropologists, headed by Franz Boas, that did most to lay bare the absurdities of racist thinking, even before the Nazi theorists had raised the absurdity to a political dogma.

The roots of American racism are to be found partly in the tragic history of both blacks and whites in the South.* Slavery itself, the "peculiar institution" of the South, was a way of life for both peoples. But once the Negroes got their freedom, their progress toward equality—however slow—could not be stopped. Partly this has been due to their own quality of tenacity—the asset side of that necessary obsessiveness with their plight which has been (as Kardiner puts it) the "mark of oppression." Less noted, but no less striking, is the role played by certain phases of the same American society which for many of the em-

* For an earlier discussion of the Negro strain and influence in America, see Ch. I, Sec. 2, "The Sources of the Heritage." For the problem of Negro and white in the Southern regional mind, see Ch. III, Sec. 11, "Regions: the Fusion of People and Place."

bittered Negroes seemed the chief actor in the whole diabolic drama.

To see this clearly one must start with the situation of the "New Negro"—new, that is, since World War I. The beginning of this phase came with the great migrations, north and west from the South. The Negro migrated for the best of possible reasons: because life in the South became intolerable, because he glimpsed the horizons of freedom elsewhere, but mainly because America was a society of restless, mobile striving. The two world wars gave them the chance they wanted, jobs in the North, money flowing so richly that some of it trickled into Negro pay envelopes in St. Louis, Detroit, Chicago, Pittsburgh, New York. From 1915 to 1920, 50,000 Negroes moved into Chicago; by 1938 there were 150,000 Negroes in the slums of Detroit, along with the lower-class whites and the mountain people who also migrated to the new auto center—all of them, white and black alike, drawn by unparalleled wages like the highly publicized five dollars a day that Henry Ford was paying. "It was kind of crowded on McComb Street," Joe Louis recalls. "It was kind of crowded there, but the house had toilets indoors and electric lights. Down in Alabama we had outhouses and kerosene lamps." In the two years from 1940 to 1942, 60,000 Negroes came to work in Detroit.

The combination of the New Deal and the Second World War gave the Negro struggle another fillip. The Northern Negro, who suffered terribly in the Depression (the first to be fired, the last to be hired), found jobs again. In the Armed Services he finally won a measure of equality: Jim Crow in the business of death was too grim a jest to be tolerable. But mostly what the Negro found in the era of the New Deal and Fair Deal was a new confidence in his collective power. For the first time, along with the other ethnic groups and the unions, he found himself part of a coalition forming the base of a victorious political party. For the first time he had the bargaining strength that went along with a decisive balance-of-power vote in crucial states.

His settlement in the big Northern cities had a double consequence. In immediate terms it meant the creation of new ghettos. In New York's Harlem the crowding of Negroes is worse than in Atlanta, and the spatial separation of blacks and whites is perhaps greater. In Chicago's South Side, which holds 250,000 of Chicago's 400,000 Negroes, in Detroit's East Side (called bitterly "Paradise Valley"), in St. Louis and Kansas City and Pittsburgh, in Philadelphia's "inner city" crowded with 300,000 Negroes, in the hideous clustering Negro shacks that scar Washington, the Negro ghettos are the worst slums in America—dingy, crowded, dive-dotted, whore-patrolled, disease-ridden. The Negro migrations were a bonanza for the owners of the tenements and cold-water flats in the areas where they settled and within which they were circum-scribed: it was a landlord's market, and they could extort higher rents for the sleazy ghetto quarters than had to be paid for a clean, well-lighted space outside the ghetto.

When the Negroes tried to break out of their cage the real-estate boards—in a panic lest a leak in the segregation dike might mean an inundating Negro mass movement into white residential areas and sub-urbs—"covenanted" the houses. Behind the real-estate boards with their profit fears were the status fears of the white middle classes. Even under Federal housing aid the FHA accepted the "local real-estate reaction" as a standard for decision and refused to insure most mixed housing projects. After the Supreme Court had held the covenants unconsti-tutional, some of the white-collar Negro families sought to move into "white" areas, but too often they were met by terror. When the Clarks, for example, moved from the Chicago slums to an apartment in near-by Cicero, ironically it was another minority ethnic group, the Czechs, who loomed large in the group that stoned and burned them out.

Recent studies, challenging the idea that there can be no interracial housing because of the encrusted attitudes of hostility, have stood the idea on its head. For example, a 1950 study by Deutsch and Collins, comparing integrated public-housing projects in New York with segre-gated projects in Newark, showed that the fact of living more closely together leads to greater friendliness and tolerance between the Negro and white groups, and that it even has a healthy impact on relations inside the white groups themselves and produces a more closely knit community as a whole. As a result the Newark policy was changed, and the segregation elements were eliminated—again with healthy results. There have been similar experiences on the job in factories and work-shops, in department-store selling, and most strikingly in the defense forces, where every step toward eliminating segregation made the next step possible by breaking down hostile attitudes on both sides.

The same concentration of the Negroes in the large Northern cities which spread panic fears of mass inundation, also helped them as a political and economic force. Since they bunched themselves in their jobs and living quarters, they bunched their votes as well. As Henry Lee Moon has pointed out, this has meant a decisive Negro vote which gives them not only the balance of power in the state elections of New York, Illinois, Michigan, Ohio, and Pennsylvania, but also may at times give them the same kind of marginal power in swinging Presidential elec-tions. It is this power which revived the movement for Federal civil-rights legislation, and in turn caused the urban Negro to be wooed by both major parties. In terms of economic force, it meant that much of the fifteen billion dollars the Negroes spent annually in the American market was also concentrated, giving them a considerable economic pressure force against discrimination.

An even more powerful weapon the Negroes have had has been that of the law. In the South more than in the North, but in both areas, the machinery of police and law enforcement has operated unequally, protecting the Negroes least, bearing down on them most heavily. Yet their greatest advance has been achieved through the instrument of the law. They have waged an unrelenting fight for legal equality, knowing that the law on the statute books or in the court decisions may not settle things in practice but does set a frame. On the issue of voting without burdensome poll taxes, on getting free of housing covenants, on breaking out of Jim Crow schools for their children, on access to law and medical schools, on travel across state lines, on hotel accommodations and restaurant service, on parks and swimming pools and hospitals, and on equality of job opportunities, they have fought with a tenacity which has enraged their enemies all the more because they have known that this force, once set in motion, was irresistible.

Recent Federal Court decisions in the Sweatt, Henderson, McLaren, Seipuel, and Clarendon cases must be seen as forerunners of the final victories to come. The great decision in the school segregation cases in 1954 represented a climactic point in a long series of earlier constitutional battles. They were hard-gained and dearly paid victories, and sometimes the pace seemed heartbreakingly slow both to the Negroes and their allies, South and North. Yet the debate has been about the wisdom, validity, and workability of legal action. Particular Court decisions have been attacked, but even the most extreme of the Negro's opponents have not dared deny them in principle the right to make use of the legal weapon.

I have spoken of political, economic, and legal action. More powerful than any of them, and what gives them their momentum, is the American conscience. It has had a sorry enough state of facts to operate on. I cite a few dramatic figures from the report of the President's Commission on Civil Rights, which had a striking impact on later events. The average annual income for Negro families in 1947 was a little over $1,000 compared with three times as much for whites. Forty per cent of the whites had incomes of over $2,000, but only 11 per cent of the Negroes. Twenty-two per cent of the whites were below $1,000, and 75 per cent of the Negroes. In the segregated Southern states, where nine of the fifteen million Negroes lived, the value of the school plant used for the Negro children was $52 per child compared with $224 for a white child, and the amount spent every year for a Negro child's schooling was $57 compared with $104 for a white child. In 1900, before the Jim Crow laws became hardened, a Negro in Washington, D.C., could enter any hospital; by 1950 there were only two that admitted them. Throughout the South there was not a "white" hospital which would admit a sick Negro or a "white" church that would allow him to pray to the God of all races. Until 1950 the only chance for a Negro in the Navy was as a mess attendant, and in the Army as part of the segregated transport units; since that time the color walls have been broken down with increasing success. No Negro in the South could break the laws and traditions of segregation when he went to work on a bus, or wanted to eat lunch or dinner in a restaurant, when he tried to travel on a train, when he wanted to see a movie or a play. In most Southern cities no Negro would dare park his car in front of the post office without running the risk of being considered "an uppity nigger," nor would he dare walk late at night in the white section of the town. The life expectancy of a Negro child in the South was eight years less than that of one born white. And from birth to death the Negro lived in constant tension and insecurity, walking always in the shadow of uncertainty and fear.

It is this image which spurred the American conscience, and that conscience in turn goaded Americans of all kinds into action. While there are still poll-tax states in the South, the Negro votes in growing numbers in every Southern state, and while there have been efforts at intimidation there has been a reluctant acceptance of the fact of the Negro as voter. His children have forced their way into a number of Southern colleges, with several thousand Negro students squeezing their way through the college gates, and the siege of the professional schools now is in full swing. The 1955 case of Autherine Lucy, in Alabama, represented a temporary setback in this steady advance, but no one believed it would long hold back the tide. Even the "separate but equal" doctrine, fatefully enshrined in *Plessy v. Ferguson* in the 1890s, finally crumbled sixty years later, and a unanimous Supreme Court under Chief Justice Warren held that "separate" (segregated) schooling could not by its nature be equal because it stunts the whole growth process of the child. Southern legal resourcefulness, of course, was able to invent new strategies of state action ("interposition") to evade and nullify the Supreme Court decision. The movement of Southern resistance, especially in the smaller towns where the White Citizens' Councils made effective use of the weapon of economic boycott, was bitter and protracted. Yet all along the line white supremacy was waging a losing battle.

Thus it has been the context of American society and the "American creed" that has reduced the walls of the caste system. The American economy, with its impersonal relations in the market of buying and selling, gave the Negroes a new bargaining power. So also has the American political system, with its formal principle of counting each head once no matter what the pigment of the face, and its reliance on an equilibrium of pressure groups. The American legal system, with its tradition of growth to meet the changing demands of a changing society, gave the Negro a slow and belated but irresistible measure of justice. Even American social science, especially sociology and psychology, were drawn into the constitutional struggle and played the great role in the reversal of *Plessy v. Ferguson.* The dynamic quality of American life allowed the Negro to shift from section to section, from sharecropper farm to auto and airplane factory and steel mill. It raised his income and living standards, in the South as in the North, gave him entrance into the trade-unions in spite of the persisting hostility of many of the union leaders. The emergence of new big-audience media enabled him to break through the walls of his ghetto, and radio and TV sets brought even into the dingy living rooms the spaciousness of a world hitherto denied to them.

Even in the South the economic, political, and educational levees are being broken by the rising waters. Until the Great Resistance after the schools decision the white students in Southern colleges were increasingly demanding the entrance of Negro students. In Northern colleges there were sporadic revolts against the system of segregated fraternities. The Negro can no longer be treated as the child, savage, or beast—which were the stereotypes applied to him ever since he came out of the holds of the slave ships. The classic statement of Lincoln about a "house divided" has proved true, in a sense which he may himself never have foreseen: not that the moral principle makes it impossible for such a house to stand, but that the laws of action in the society as a whole are bound to break down the enclaves inside it which defy the principle by which the society lives. Just as the American class system rejects a permanent proletariat, so it rejects a permanent pariah class buttressed by a caste system.

It has been argued that the erosion wearing away the soil of Negro segregation came not from the society of a liberal capitalist democracy itself, and from its economy, its law, and its conscience, but primarily from the changes wrought by two world wars, and from the needs of a permanent "readiness economy" during the cold war. Those who hold this view call this a process of "negative democratization," which comes because the ruling groups in the society need the Negro for their own purposes and must yield him his rights out of self-interest rather than out of conscience. This is an ungenerous view which would deny that any reform is ever achieved except by force or any privilege ever relinquished except through selfishness. It denies any sort of creativeness within American society except one flowing negatively from the power struggle. It is true that the progress in civil rights for Negroes came partly through their own bargaining strength and partly through the self-interest of the whites, but that progress could never have been achieved except through the operation of law and public opinion and the impulsion of the idea of equality. Without these even the needs of war and cold war would have been powerless to achieve the same ends. Strikingly, the South, which has met the advance of Negro civil rights with the greatest resistance, has also been the region most committed to military pursuits and the idea of total war.*

There remains, even among those prodded by conscience, the unyielding issue of "social equality." As noted in the preceding section, many of the majority group, who when polled felt that the Negroes ought to get a "better break," recoiled from the image of Negro-White intermarriage. Actually, there has been very little of it even in those Northern states where the law allows it: only five out of every 10,000 marriages—or one twentieth of 1 per cent—represent a crossing of the color lines. Yet in twenty-nine states there were drastic laws against miscegenation, carrying in some cases the penalty of imprisonment. Even more oppressive are the sexual taboos in the Southern states. Although the promiscuity of whites with Negro women has long been recognized as the perquisite of a master race, the Negro boy who dared court a white girl in the South would expiate his effrontery only by death.

Under the slave system the most terrible punishments were reserved for cases of "rape," and the intensity of feeling on this issue has scarcely subsided since then. White supremacy in the South has always used lynching as the ultimate sanction against the defilement of white blood. While these lynchings have steadily decreased (the Tuskegee figures show that the five-year period from 1900 to 1905 averaged 105 lynchings a year, while the 1945 to 1950 period averaged three, and then practically ceased), the Southern courts have operated on a double standard of justice in applying the laws against rape: most of the prosecutions are against Negroes, and even where whites are brought to trial they are not given the death penalty that is visited upon the Negroes.

Modern psychiatry, especially in the trail-blazing study by John Dollard, *Caste and Class in a Southern Town,* takes the view that the

* For a discussion of civil liberties, as distinguished from Negro civil rights, see Ch. VI, Sec. 10, "The Struggle for Civil Liberties."

deepest roots of Southern hostility on the Negro problem are sexual:
that the male Southerner brought up by a Negro "mammy" finds the
Negro woman his abiding sexual symbol, and that the Southern woman
is at once attracted and repelled by the sexual vitality of the Negro.
Certainly there is a complexity to race relations in the South which is
better expressed in the nuances of a novel like E. M. Forster's *A Passage
to India* than in the thunderous simplicities of the denunciations on
both sides. Lillian Smith, writing about her own Southern upbringing
in *Killers of the Dream,* underscores the terrible blight which the treatment of the Negro has left on the white family, with the wife set on an
impossible pedestal of "purity" and cut off from her own children, and
the husband ridden by guilt about breaking the taboos he himself has
set up. Yet the whole question of "social equality," aside from these
psychoanalytic probings, is largely a straw issue. The bounds of class and
status have proved strong enough to prevent intermarriage not only between Negroes and whites but even between the class extremes within
the social system of the whites themselves. The Negro does not ask (because no one could ask) any kind of Force Bill to compel intimate social
relationships which the whites are unwilling to engage in—or at least
acknowledge. All that he asks, as Robert Carr has put it, is "freedom
to enter the main stream of American life."

The most tragic fact about the long effort to maintain the Negro
caste system is that it has left its scars upon whites and blacks alike. The
effect on Southern whites, at once in economic and psychic terms, can
scarcely be calculated. To keep nine million people in poverty—and
in ignorance, so that they will not get ideas that will make them unruly
—impoverishes the economy itself and forms a drag both on the market
and on technical development. It means a social system riddled with
formal taboos and with furtive violations of them. It means a constant
sense of living, as a white garrison, in the midst of a hostile surrounding
Negro population, with alternating moods of anxiety and aggression. It
means, finally, an obsessive concentration on a single theme of racist
exclusiveness which has for many Southerners become more deeply their
religion than religion itself. This obsession, bred into the children from
infancy through adolescence and maintained in the adults by the constant agitation of politicians and press, keeps many Southerners of good
will from seeing that fair treatment of Negroes would improve the lot
of the whites as well. The fears of the elite groups, who resist the organization of Negro labor and want to keep their cotton profits high
and their domestic labor cheap, do not express the interests of the South
as a whole. Yet the obsessiveness continues, making the efforts of the
militant Southern liberals and even of the Southern moderates one of

the most difficult in the American experience. It takes courage to be a liberal in the South.

The greatest psychic cost for the Southern white is the constant sense of guilt, accompanying the constant feeling of being misunderstood. There are, of course, psychic consolations. The greatest of them is the sense of power in the elite itself, and among the poor whites the feeling that no matter how low you sink on the status scale there is always a Negro whose status is below yours. Yet this is a shabby compensation for the frustrations and aggressions that life offers the Southern whites. For them the "Negro question" is a twisted folk bias that permeates every phase of their consciousness—religion, sex, family life, the economy, education, the legal system, and literature. The only gainer has been literature itself, which, in the agonies of the Southern novelist and playwright, has found an inverted tragic strain which gives their work an emotional dimension not found in other regions.

If the psychic burden on the Southern white is heavy, the burden on the Negro is intolerable. The stereotype which describes the Negro as a carefree child singing and dancing his way through life, unmindful of his scars, is a pitifully partial one. The American Negro inherits most of the tensions of the white culture, and to its heavy load he adds his own. So much of his everyday energy has to be expended in a constant struggle against discrimination and taboos, a constant anxiety, a constant need for making choices and uncertainty as to what to expect from people and situations. "There is no time in the life of the Negro," say Kardiner and Ovesey, "that he is not actively in contact with the caste situation." These two men had a series of long interviews with a cross section sampling of Northern Negroes. Their psychological profile of the Negro is one of self-hatred, depression, emotional instability, frustration, because the goals of the whites which he has accepted are for him unattainable.

This portrait is obviously overdrawn, and to get a more balanced view one must set it against the equally overdrawn folk picture of the Negro as a happy and carefree savage. Yet of the two the psychiatric profile is the more relevant to the tensions of the Negro's life. The cruel paradox of that life is that even the success of the Negroes—I should say especially the success—in wresting gains in living standards and freedom from the white society makes life more difficult psychically for him. For it is the Negroes moving up on the social scale who encounter the sharpest doubts as to their status. At one end is the inverted psychic security of being wholly a subject caste and knowing therefore where you stand; at the other end is the security of complete equality with the whites; it is the area between the two which exacts the heaviest psychic toll.

The Negroes have developed social and economic class lines of their own within their own hierarchies. A new Negro elite has arisen—"black millionaires" (as the Negro magazine *Ebony* puts it with a curious pride) who "travel by Cadillac," send their daughters to debutante parties, and despise their own caste inferiors almost as much as the whites do. There is also a new Negro middle class, the "black *bourgeoisie*," as Frazier has called them, that is riddled with the same status fears as the white middle class: "No self-respecting Negro [again I quote *Ebony*] would smoke a cheap cigarette." Frazier's theme is that the Negro middle class, caught between a status it rejects and one it has not achieved, has been reduced to a *nothingness* of values and identity. The Negroes have also developed their own remedial measures: the racist Garveyism of the 1920s and the messianic Communism of the 1930s have lost ground, but an intense nationalism persists whose excesses are the product of the racism and fanaticism of the whites. They find themselves caught, as every struggling caste is caught, within a compulsive frame which shrinks the horizons of the world at large until it encompasses only the world of their own grievances, sufferings, strivings.

Yet the striking fact is not that a Negro population, striving to free itself and enter fully into the stream of majority life, finds its effort a terrible ordeal but the fact that the effort is made and that it is succeeding. The striking fact again is not that 12,000 light-skinned Negroes disappear every year from their ethnic ranks—"pass" into the white world—but rather the fact that so many who could pass choose to remain Negroes. It is an affirmation of the worth of being an American without surrendering your ethnic heritage. And on the side of the whites the remarkable fact is not continued hostility but the irresistible force of acceptance.

Under the impact of this acceptance, the Negroes themselves grow more relaxed. Roi Ottley offers as evidence a recent trip of his through Europe and the Middle East, as described in *No Green Pastures*. Among the Negroes in Europe he found that the American Negroes were considered an aristocracy with the highest living standards and the great symbolic leaders of the race. Since 1900 a half million Negro immigrants have come to America, despite its caste system, and today there would be few Negroes elsewhere who would not welcome the chance—despite the realistic understanding of what the ordeal of life would be. Here again one confronts the overmastering fact about American society—its mobility and stir. They count for more than the fears and anxieties that carry over from the breaking of the chains of caste, and they alone are making it possible for the chains to be broken.

7. The Badges of Belonging

THIS THEN IS the picture of the over-all stratification of American society—the open-class system, with its mobile and rigid elements; the ruling groups of the wealthy and powerful; the new middle classes, vulnerable and uprooted, yet with a sense of well-being that defies all predicted dooms; the working class, tenacious of its gains, job-conscious, with none of the marks of a permanent proletariat; the minority ethnic groups whose peculiar status cuts across the class strata; the Negroes, whose history marks them for the role of a depressed caste but who have enlisted all the force of American dynamism to break through their constrictions.

Any assessment of the American class system must ask two sets of final questions: how are the class distinctions mirrored in the minds of Americans, and transmitted and transmuted into their daily lives? And what is the nature of the competitive struggle for status in the American open-class system? To these questions this and the following section are addressed.

The writers who shy away from the harsher phases of the class system lag behind the ordinary American whom they study. He recognizes pretty well the objective facts of class: that "money talks" more frequently than merit or grace; that income and what it can buy give a man access to power and privilege, from which the moneyless are cut off; that class power is not only command over commodities but command over obedience—the ability to decide what shall happen to those who depend on you for livelihood; that for the classes toward the bottom of the hierarchy, and for their children, the chances for scope and expressiveness of living are less than for those toward the top.

It is remarkable that he has cherished few rankling resentments. Class consciousness, in the sense of hostility at the service of the conscious understanding of the class role in history, is almost absent from the American scene. It does exist in the secondary sense of divergent class attitudes on the issues of the day. But the characteristic form it takes is that of a subjective rating system. "How does he rate?" may apply to any aspect of a man's personality, or to his technical credit rating, but mostly it refers—not necessarily with any snobbish overtones—to the community's valuation of his income, wealth, power, standing, repute.

This process of rating oneself and others is, consciously or not, a constant part of daily life. It has often been noted and satirized by the critics of American life as "keeping up with the Joneses." Veblen, using

his most barbed phrases, called it "invidious distinction" and "pecuniary emulation." A nonmoralizing view would see, however, how
closely it meshes into a society possessing high mobility. When people
in a class system are in constant movement they are likely to reassess
constantly one another's position and their own. How healthy this process is depends on the kind of qualities chosen for rating, and whether it
is a single factor (like income or the size of one's house) abstracted from
the whole. Even at its best there is a vicious-circle quality about the
rating system: those who have prestige receive even greater deference
because of it; those who have power assume even greater authority;
those who lack them are further shorn of what little they have. This is
a rigidifying process, and often a cruel one. Yet it is at once the price
of mobility and the product of effort. When it becomes a form of closure
of the channels of opportunity it is most destructive. Taken as a whole,
it is part of the valuing process which is integral to life in society—a way
by which every individual puts out antennae to feel where he is in relation to others.

It should be clear then why the characteristic school among contemporary American class studies should be that of Lloyd Warner, which
tends to slight a man's objective power over others as it also minimizes
the actual conflicts of class interest, and which makes his class position
depend so strongly on the community's valuation of him. Similarly, the
dominant school in the study of human relations in industry is that of
Mayo and Roethlisberger, which minimizes the inherent relation of
mastery and dependence where men work for other men and holds that
frictions can be lessened and production increased by fortifying esteem
and self-esteem in the factory-as-society.

The impetus to the Warner community studies, as earlier in the
Lynd studies of "Middletown," came from anthropology and is linked
with the American passion for the inductive method. The Warner class
concept is almost wholly statistical: it finds and charts the position of
a man on the graph of social standing according to a number of indices
of community rating. Instead of starting with the European theories of
class structure and class conflict, the students of American society prefer
to start, as businessmen do, with a factual survey. Obviously they do
bring to it an intellectual scheme which perhaps unconsciously shapes
what they find. Obviously also a good deal depends on how much of a
cross section of America their sample community is, whether it be
Muncie, Ind. (the "Middletown" of the Lynds), or Newburyport, Mass.,
and Grundy County, Ill. (the "Yankee City" and "Jonesville" of Warner), or Burlington, Vt. (which Elin Anderson studied in *We Americans*),
or the Illinois town studied by Hollingshead in *Elmtown's Youth*, or
the Southern communities that John Dollard, Allison Davis, and Hor-

tense Powdermaker wrote about. These are all small towns or cities, chosen as such to be compassable for study, but they do not tell us much about the class experience of big cities, which is likely to be at once more mobile in some phases and more extreme in class contrasts. Nor do they make allowance for regional characteristics: the Midwestern town is likely to look eastward for its patterns of living, while the Eastern towns are more self-sufficient; in the Deep South and New England the class lines are more set and the elite groups more firmly established than elsewhere; and very few of the surveys deal with the Far West. Yet with all these caveats the community surveys have heaped up considerable evidence on the nature of American society, which is particularly valuable on the class system because most of them made class cleavages and strata the focus of their analysis.

The survey team (it has been waspishly described in Marquand's novel, *Point of No Return*, set in his home town of Newburyport) moves into a community with letters of introduction, gets acquainted, settles into the community life, and observes how people talk of one another. Class is a local reality in every community, with local designations for each of the classes. Warner found the "old families" at the top of the pyramid, with wealth inherited over time, living in the old mansions "on the Hill," the arbiters of manners, taste, and social distinction. Just below them in the upper class he found the "new families," with more recently acquired wealth, the heads of the corporations and Chambers of Commerce, the "country club set" who often associated with the "old families" and were *in* but not *of* their class. In the middle classes he found toward the top the "comfortably situated" and "highly respected" men, substantial, self-made, either small-business or professional men or members of the corporate managerial group, living in the suburbs, belonging to social clubs and the good churches. Below them in turn are the salaried people of the lower middle class—the store managers, white-collar workers, little shopkeepers, salesmen, who make up the most fluid and rapidly growing phase of the American "common man." Then there was the upper layer of the lower class—the skilled industrial workers, "poor but honest," who work for wages, belong to unions, are unlikely to belong to clubs but are members of the poorer churches, drive small cars, and have clean-looking small houses or "flats" on the "other side of the tracks." Finally there was the bottom layer of the lower class—the unskilled workers, the Negroes, the Puerto Ricans or Portuguese or Mexicans, who live in run-down houses or in the slums or in trailer camps on the outskirts of the town, the "ne'er-do-wells" who "don't belong" and are often unemployed and on relief.

In developing this six-class system (upper-upper, lower-upper, upper-middle, lower-middle, upper-lower, lower-lower) Warner and his associates relied mainly on criteria that correlate roughly with the economic indices of occupation and income but rest principally on prestige (who is above, who below), associations, clubs and cliques (who goes with whom, who belongs to what), family standing, taste in spending, and the veneer and trappings of life. In Newburyport he found 3 per cent in the top two classes, 39 per cent in the middle two, and 58 per cent in the bottom ones. He recognized the fact of continual movement between the classes, but what he observed and described were the divergent privileges, prestige, and standing of a stratified system of status whose individual members may change but which does not itself change as a system. With the American talent for reducing abstractions to a statistical rating scheme, he worked out an Index of Status Characteristics (I.S.C.) to guide his staff interviewers, with a point scale assigned to four objective facts about a person: his type of home, his neighborhood, his occupation, and his income source (more important than income size). To this he added the results of the Evaluated Participation (E.P.) scale, or the ranking assigned to a person by the community, especially those toward the top who run a community and preside over it and therefore ought to know it.

One may ridicule the pseudo-precision of ranking the sons of Mary and the sons of Martha, but it is hard to laugh off its reality. One gets a similar picture, more sweepingly drawn, in Hollingshead's Elmtown study, which found a five-class system: the top class, with money and family; the upper middle class, still based on money, family, and marriage into both; the lower middle class, with good steady jobs, who form the America of the "common man"; the factory workers and clerks who "live right but never get anywhere"; and the bottom class of the unskilled and unrooted who "aren't worth a damn and don't give a damn."

The image that people have of a man's class standing and his image of himself are important facts about him. An influential element of the class system is what is in people's minds, in rating their fellows and judging between those who belong and those who don't. Even wealth and income are not in America the ultimate badges of belonging: they are currency to be converted in time into the "right kind" of associations and thus into the "right kind" of manners, clothes, behavior, in which each person shapes himself to the model of the class to which he aspires. Although this has phases of snobbism and conformity, it cannot be dismissed thus. It is the point of all the straining and striving, the ambition, agony, and ruthlessness of competitive living from the bottom rungs of the class ladder right up to the top ones. And, to round out the circle, Americans also know that social standing is in turn a key to further income and job advancement: that by getting into the "right crowd" they get access to those who have power, and thus get a trial for their talents or a hearing for their plans. Thus there is a continuous circuit by which money is converted into prestige and power, which in turn are converted into money, and so on.

Most Americans recognize these facts of their class life. While there has been a drastic shift of people from one set of occupations to another in the past generation, the rule-of-thumb ratings of the occupation have not changed appreciably. It depends on how much skill each occupation requires, what income it affords, how much authority and power over others it carries, the standing and respectability it affords in the community. Thus the American combines a realistic sense of the objective facts of class power and income along with the subjective factors of prestige and position.

There are elements of American life which still cut across the class divisions and give it the rough kind of social equality that De Tocqueville noted. People work together in the factories and on the farms, shop together in the markets, worship together in the churches, compete in and attend the same games and sports events, read the same papers and magazines, vote in the same booths. Except for the Southern Negroes, they ride in the same trains and busses, go to the same movies and theaters, send their children to the same schools; and even the Southern Negroes have increasingly been winning equal access to these areas. Americans of all classes buy and drive the same cars, watch the same TV programs, eat the same packaged foods. In a standardized economy there is a leveling effect produced by the wide diffusion of standardized goods. Add the fact that gas stations, recreation and amusement centers, transport systems, automatic vendors, and professional services are available pretty much to all on an impersonal market. Add also the free public services—parks, swimming pools, band concerts, public dances, libraries —where at least technically no distinctions of class or caste are allowed.

Yet every American knows the breaches in the observance of these ideals, as he knows also the extent to which social equality has been eroded by the crystallized system of class ranking. The divisive effects of this system and the social expression of class differences are manifested in everyday life.

They bear hardest on the children. There is no double-class system in the American schools, as there is in the British, although the emergence of a network of private schools augurs the start of one. The real double-class system is to be found in the lingering residues of segregated schools in white-supremacy areas. Yet even in the school systems that admit children of all classes and races, there are gerrymandering devices by which children of similar class or ethnic origin are assigned to the same schools. And where a class cross section exists inside the school, children from families who "belong" tend to segregate those who do not by a tacit understanding which they derive from their elders and from the social atmosphere. Children from the higher income levels develop ways of acting, thinking, feeling, that keep them apart from their fellows. Recent studies of the youth in Midwestern public elementary and high schools (Warner and Havighurst, *Who Shall Be Educated?* and Hollingshead, *Elmtown's Youth*) found evidence of "cliques" and "sets" that form in the school system on class levels, with the insiders feeling a snobbish satisfaction and the outsiders experiencing heartbreak. They suggest that popularity depends partly on the insignia of class membership, and that whoever strives for it pays a heavy psychic price. There are few places where the pathos of social imitation is more striking than in the American school system.

The schools are at once agencies of class equality (for many children there are no other means for breaking across class lines) and agencies of class conditioning. When schoolchildren are asked to name those who are "clean," "good looking," and "always having a good time," they usually choose the children from the upper social levels and ascribe the negative qualities to children from the lower ones. While there is little sense of class or ethnic differences at the start of schooling, by the time a child has reached ten (fifth grade), he has become "socialized" and his preferences are marked. Thus the roots of class superiority and ethnic hatreds lie less in propaganda than in social training through one's peer groups. This is, of course, especially marked in the South, where the Federal courts found that the training in segregation demonstrably hurt the personality growth of the children of both groups. But even in a nonsegregated high school in the North, Hollingshead found that school disciplines involving both rewards and punishments (high grades, failures, and disciplinary measures) bear more heavily on the children of the lower strata and are skewed in favor of the upper; and Allison Davis found that the values which the teachers underscore and which run through their teaching as unquestioned assumptions are middle-class values. Thus the lower-level children learn early the gap between their actual status and the desirable ideal.

This insulation of the classes is carried beyond school through life: in food habits, etiquette, reading tastes, health opportunities, courtship and sex habits, marriage, divorce, taste exchange, clubs, lodges, even churches. In every phase of social expression the badges of belonging separate one class from another and pervade subtly the whole expression of personality. There are, of course, wheels within wheels—the big wheel run by the fate of class, and the little wheels run by the grace or talent of a particular person. But the picture of social distinction, seen in terms of differential life chances and life conditioning, is nonetheless roughly true.

Much of the stream of energy is turned into the channels of social acceptance. Life in every community is lived with a yearning eye cast toward the class above. Middle-class families scrimp to send their children to private schools and good colleges, at least long enough for them to make the right kind of "contacts" and be out of reach of the wrong kind. Some are steered toward careers that will bring money and success, while the vigil of protecting daughters from giving their hearts too cheaply to an unrewarding love gives the American middle-class parent that air of watchful anxiety and dissatisfaction that the novelists have noted. In the lower classes there is the steady hope that education will turn out to be a means for improving the social position of the children, and the wild hope for the occasional Cinderella marriage of the daughter of a Slav steelworker to the heir of an oil fortune, or of the rise of a girl sprung from a seedy music-hall troupe to become the Love goddess of the Hollywood screen and a familiar of the "International Set." But there is also the constant anxiety among the "moral poor" of the lower middle class that the son or daughter will slip down into the ranks of delinquency and crime.

This burden of class watchfulness is not a light one, no matter what the class is. To go to the right schools, to attend the right dances and parties, to belong to the right churches, to be accepted in the right social and country clubs, to be a "potentate" in a lodge, to drive the right make and model of car, to wear the right clothes and have the right manners, to have your daughter (at certain social levels) "introduced" to "society" and presented at the cotillion, to have your son spend his military service in the officer corps and not as a lowly private: these become for their appropriate class members matters not of choice or opportunity but a social necessity. The burden of these obligations, and the psychic tension of keeping intact the margin that distinguishes you from your inferiors or of overcoming the margin that separates you from your superiors, can become not only exacting but destructive. It is an all the greater burden in an open-class system because the chances of advance upward and the dangers of incursion from below are real. In a society of more or less permanent and crystallized classes, grown too rigid for redress, the anxieties of the psychic class vigil are likely to be less. In the pursuit of American status the pursuers are also pursued.

I have mentioned several areas of life in which one finds important differences among the classes in behavior and attitude. The cleavage can be extended into almost every area. We have seen that you can make rough predictions of voting behavior in politics, depending on whether the voter belongs to the trade-union or managerial groups, whether he is an urban Catholic or a rural Protestant, whether he is of Midwestern German or Scandinavian descent or a Southern cotton farmer or a Jew in one of the new talent professions. The children of these various groups will usually take over the political attitudes of the parents, which reflect their social stratification: the child of a Detroit auto worker's family or of a TV writer in Hollywood is likely to vote and think differently from the child of a General Motors executive.

There will be differences also in the stability of a Negro or Irish slum family when compared with that of a middle-class Protestant family. There are recognized class differences in fertility, depending on the differential choices made between more children and, let us say, better education and life chances for fewer: although I have pointed out in an earlier chapter that some of these differences have been badly blurred in the recent population trends. There is a different life expectation at birth between Negroes and whites, and lower and upper classes. There are, as the Kinsey studies have shown, differences in sexual behavior—especially in the case of American males—as between the lower and upper educational groups: the street-corner adolescents in the city slums have a different profile of sexual activity and a different set of sexual attitudes from the adolescents in an Ivy League college. In courtship and in marriage the prestige of a middle-class or upper-class girl of "native" stock is far higher than that of a working-class girl or one from a minority ethnic group. There are important class differences in the class composition of the various religious sects—between, let us say, the Catholics and the Episcopalians, the Baptists and the Jews, although in recent years the differences have become more blurred, and all the major sects are reaching a higher percentage of people in the lower classes than they did and spreading out into the whole class range. Even in the case of mental illness, there are likely to be differences in neurotic and psychotic behavior among the various income and occupational groups, with a higher rate of mental disturbance and breakdown, as well as of hospital commitment, in the low-income groups as compared with the upper ones.

These again are some of the badges of belonging and they serve not only to differentiate one income and prestige group from another but also to explain why the upper groups try to insulate themselves from too much encroachment and the lower ones strive to push their way up. But the class insulation does not always have its impetus from above. Sometimes it comes from below. I have noted the prides and resentments that cause some of the minority ethnic groups to impose a taboo on intermarriage. Observers of the social structure in New England point out how little the new immigrant groups intermarry with the earlier stocks, but also how little they intermarry even with each other. The crossing of national origin lines is not frequent, and when religious barriers are added, the crossing of both becomes for many families an inconsolable infraction of the code. The class lines are not the only ones that count. For an impoverished Catholic to marry a rich Jew, or for a Jewish middle-class boy to marry the daughter of the Protestant banking family in the town, might in both cases be considered a catastrophe, despite the class advance. The latter situation is treated movingly in Norman Katkov's novel, *Eagle at My Eyes,* which has a Midwest setting but might happen anywhere.

The force of class-bound marriage, added to the force of race-bound and religion-bound marriage, makes the system of social distinction a gridiron instead of a set of stratified layers. Whatever the freedom of social relations—including sexual relations—before marriage, the act of marriage itself becomes the testing ground of group cohesion. For it is through the exclusions and inclusions of marriage that the class-ethnic system becomes the transmitter of stored experience, and through it also that the cohesion or exclusiveness of the group is broken down and its experience changed and enriched.

It is in this area of conflict between the insulation of the old class experience and the vitality of the new that the American novelists of manners have found their best themes. Since the elite of the "old families" is strongest in the old established regions of the South and New England, the anxieties of status are most searchingly explored in the fiction of these areas. Hardly a Southern novel or play is written in America which does not deal with the theme of a family of high standing that has lost its money but holds on fiercely to its sense of distinction. Faulkner, who has carried this theme to its highest pitch, deals therefore (as Irving Howe points out) not so much with *class* as with *clan.* The setting of these Southern families in the larger frame of rapid American class mobility, and therefore of rapid disintegration, is what gives Southern writing its added dimension of the "nerve of failure" in the sense of courage in the face of doom. In the case of New England, Marquand has almost pre-empted the theme of a young aristocrat pulled by the attraction of sexual vitality and the exotic toward the plebeian strength of some "outsider," but choosing in the end the ties of class and tradition: but on this level Marquand is only Edith Wharton and William Dean Howells rewritten, diluted, and given modern instances. Yet so crucial is the understanding eye and ear of the novelist that Marquand's insights into the nuances of the social hierarchy of New-buryport, in his *Point of No Return,* form a necessary supplement to the factual picture that Warner gives of the class structure of the same town.

It is more difficult, both for novelist and sociologist, to chart the gradations and resistances of class mobility in the big cities. Class differences
in the cities are more impersonal in their daily expression. The occupational shift has been greater there, and most relationships are the
more casual ones of the market, business, and the professions rather
than of intimacy over time. This diminishes some of the subtle cruelty
and anxiety of class gradations in small-town America; and while it has
all the faults of a depersonalized life, this depersonalizing—in the flow
of city living—may make the cleavages of class more tolerable for those
below, just as the glamour of city living makes wealth itself more re-
splendent and the miseries of city living make the distance from extreme
wealth to extreme poverty more desolating.

Yet this holds out hope for those who do not relish the prospect of
a class-encased American society. The important class differences are
not so much the rural-urban ones as those between communities of
economic growth and those of economic decline. The sway of cliques
and respectability, the tyranny of the "old families," and the rigidities
of caste are more likely to be found in static areas from which the
younger and more vigorous are moving out, while the less class-bound
situations are in areas of the greatest economic stir and therefore social
mobility. A rapidly expanding economy is thus, in spite of the power
it piles up at the top and the groups it uproots from their old skills,
the best insurance against the meannesses of class distinction, which
fester most wherever energy is turned inward toward social introspec-
tion rather than outward toward social growth.

I have used marriage as an example mainly of class insulation in
American society, but this is only a partial view. Compared with other
class societies, marriage in America crosses class and caste lines so frequently as to create the continuing mixture of stocks I have described
earlier (the estimate in the mid-1950s was of 300,000 marriages a year
crossing religious lines alone) and also so frequently as to raise the
problems of divergent class conditionings between the generations in
child-rearing. The ethnic and class differences that apply to marriage
apply also to divorce. It has often been remarked that there are three
class levels in American divorce methods: the rich can afford to go to
Reno or Florida; the middle classes stay in their home states and resort
to courts where they must often commit perjury to fulfill the requirements of the state law; and the lower class falls back on desertion, which
has been called the "poor man's divorce."

These distinctive badges of class membership help explain also some
of the phases of the changing American personality. Instead of the

static injunction to "learn your station in life" and stay within it, there is the constantly haunting question "Do I belong?" The decisive answer rarely is forthcoming, since every move upward on the class scale is an invitation to another, so that the sense of satisfying your status hungers and of feeling secure in your standing is rarely achieved. This may be expressed in terms of a class-personality cycle: a man's income and power go to determine his social standing, which in turn determines how others value his personality and even how he values it himself; these valuations help mold the personality, pushing it to orient itself toward income and power, and the cycle starts again. The end result is at once a drive toward success, a recoil from failure, and a hunger for security. Many who celebrate a mobile class system deplore these qualities of the American personality, forgetting that they are qualities that are bound to accompany the mobility. You cannot have at the same time the freedom and fluidity of an open society and the values of security that go with a closed one.

The serious aspect of the dilemma is how the personality can grapple with the terrible sense of failure, and of being left behind in the race. Most observers of American society are aware of the pathos of social distance and the neuroses of frustration that come in the wake of failure. Some of them have stressed the individual's need to adjust himself to his place in the system, and they have defended the TV "soap opera" and "daytime radio serial" as a mode of consoling working-class and lower-middle-class women for their sense of failure. It is not so much that these people console themselves with the Big Media: rather they derive from them a set of fresh impressions and enjoyments, however trite to the sophisticated, which serve as substitutes for continued class advance.

The real warpings must be sought in the constant tendency to see every phase of life through the lenses of advancement. Thus education is viewed almost solely as a step toward a new social ranking, which it often is, and rarely for its effect on the personality. This applies often to clothes and fashions, to marriage, to clubs; in fact, much of the American's life is focused on the fulfillment of status hopes.

Thus far the emphasis in the American system of class and social distinction has been on mobility. The question that follows logically is: mobility for what life purposes? I shall deal with this question of American life purposes in the next chapter. There remains, however, to put the second question posed at the beginning of this section: To what extent does the American open society offer the individual access to social opportunity, and therefore a base for the American folk belief in his society?

8. *The Democratic Class Struggle*

"No WESTERN SOCIETY," writes A. J. P. Taylor, "will ever again tolerate great extremes of rewards." The American extremes have in recent years been somewhat lessened by the steeply graduated tax structure at one end and the shrinking of the poverty group at the other. A big spread remains both in wealth and income between the top and bottom dogs, yet it is not the crucial inequality, either in America or in any other democratic class society. It would be truer to say that no society will ever again tolerate the large-scale damming of aspiration and hope on the part of the plain people. This danger the American class system has thus far averted.

This is why it has been for Americans, in Popper's phrase, an "open society." But how open is this open society? I have reviewed the mobilities and rigidities of American class, the changes in the alignment of classes, the nature of the caste strata, the way in which class distinctions are expressed in the differentials of thinking and action. It remains to point out that the crux of the openness of an open society is the degree of access it affords to the opportunities of life.

This is the "religion of equality" of America—not equality of reward or of social standing but of access. It is roof, center, and underpinning of whatever "classlessness" there is in American society. Nor is this, like other religious feelings, a mystical or dedicated one. The Puritan conscience, which once kept watch over the growing inequalities to keep them in bound, no longer operates to the same degree. In its place has come a hard empirical feeling that sharp inequalities make very little sense. The margin of tolerance has narrowed for whatever shuts the door against the life chances for any boy or girl. To be sure, this is qualified by the new status vigil that gives many Americans a sense of satisfaction at the status discomfiture of those below them, as well as anxiety about their own status. But this satisfaction has little to feed on if the position of the depressed classes is due to their never having had a chance. Just as the American's demand for class advancement for himself is unsparingly concrete, growing by what it feeds on, so he will refuse to tolerate a caste setup which puts unpassable obstructions in the way of a reasonable chance at making a living and a life.

This suggests a functional definition of class for Americans—a stratum with similar economic opportunities, similar access to education, health, courtship, and the other major elements that fit a man for the voyage of life. Thus, to dam up equal opportunity for travel or recreation, for holidays and leisure, for the acquirements of taste and the refinements of manner, is only secondary to damming up the equal opportunity for schooling, nourishing food, housing, medical attention, and job chances. The principle of equal access embraces not only physical fitness and vocational skills but preparation for all the major social experiences that mean the growth and health of the personality. Seen in this frame, the idea of class is neither narrowly economic in the Marxist sense of income and power nor narrowly subjective in the Warner sense of prestige and status, but is broadened to include the total strategic situation of the personality in the culture—the sum of the chances he gets at life and the preconditionings to life which flow not from his heredity or personality but from his location in the society. If the deadened life chances of the worker who gets stuck in his groove or the caste exclusions of the Negro from the main stream are seen in these terms, then the doctrine of equal opportunity becomes a decisive fact about the society rather than what Justice Holmes once called "a fiction intended to beautify what is disagreeable to the sufferers." Given such access, the class system then becomes itself a means toward continued class mobility within it and uncovers the truth of Woodrow Wilson's "I believe in democracy because it releases the energies of every human being."

This may also suggest a fresh way of seeing the meaning of the class conflicts in American history—as phases of a democratic class struggle whose purpose was never (as in other contexts) the extermination of the other classes, nor even always class domination, but the effort of the majority to achieve access to the means of a good life from which the shifts of technology and of economic power were cutting it off. It is clear enough that this was true of the Jeffersonian revolution of small farmers and planters and artisans against the landed and funded wealth and the shipping interests; it was equally true of the new farmer class of the West and the new artisan class of the cities when they swept Jackson into power. How characteristic it was, then, for the Jeffersonians to emphasize, as a set of means for their class struggle, the freeing of land tenure from feudal restrictions, and guarantees of religious freedom, and the establishment of colleges where a democratic elite could be trained. How characteristic also that the Jacksonians should have fought so hard to broaden the base of the franchise, to outlaw imprisonment for debt, to establish a free school system for all, to keep the financial power of the new banking group from blocking a fluid currency and credit, and to keep the new business groups from achieving monopoly through their corporate charters. Each of these measures was aimed at destroying the obstructions to what Joseph Blau has called "the enterprise of freedom . . . and freedom of enterprise." A class of journalists, lawyers, skilled artisans, and small farmers was struggling with a class of merchants, *rentiers*, businessmen, and clergy to keep class closure from setting in.

This analysis could be extended through the major class conflicts of American history that were to follow, from the struggle between the landowning and slave-working class and that of free workers and businessmen in the pre-Civil War period to the struggle of the New Deal coalition of small shopkeepers, trade-union workers, ethnic minorities, small farmers, and professional classes to build a welfare economy. In every phase of the New Deal program the struggle ran in terms of class interests, but always with a view to blasting away the obstructions that corporate power and a rigidified class system had placed in the path of class mobility. Throughout their history, in this kind of democratic class struggle, Americans have used not only the methods of trade-union and economic action but also of pressure politics, bloc voting, and other forms of interest-group political action. This kind of political action has been at once a form of the democratic class struggle and a solvent of class frictions that might otherwise have resulted in violence.

Why such a result has not occurred is one of those miracles of the class system which, like all secular miracles, may be subject to explanation. It has not been due to the lack of class resentment or the absence of sharply divergent class attitudes. The richest prizes and most desirable strategic positions in the economy have been pre-empted by the big corporations and all but frozen by the legal maintenance of privilege. The insecurities of the market, where a whole family's destiny depends on the earner's capacity to sell his skills or products and buy his materials and means of living within what he gets, have further sharpened class attitudes. America is a class society in the sense that its people fall into more or less well-defined income groups, living-standard groups, and status groups, although the lines between them are blurred. Those within each group are affected much the same way by the same ups-and-downs of prosperity and depression, employment boom or recession, inflation or deflation, or by tax laws and social legislation. Although they do not always think together, they do tend to act, lobby, and vote together for their common ends, especially when an emerging leadership makes them conscious of the identity of their interests.

Recent attitude studies—those by Arthur Kornhauser and by Richard Centers are most striking—have documented the differentials of political and economic opinion as between the occupation groups in the class system. This cracks the veneer of hypocrisy about class attitudes, but it could scarcely have been a surprise. There is as great a social distance between a South Side Negro and the head of the Chicago *Tribune*, between a Southern white sharecropper and the top managers of the absentee-owned new industries of the South, and between a fitfully employed unskilled worker in Wilmington or Newark and the directors of great chemical corporations, as there was in Rome between a landless soldier and a Crassus, or in feudal England between a noble and his lowest retainer. The great difference between these earlier societies and the American is that the Americans in the lower classes—and certainly in the middle ones—have (in Max Weber's phrase) a "culturally induced discontent" which flows from the aspirations of the culture and is based on the actual experience of actual class mobility. It is this disaffection-linked-with-hope which sets the tone of American class life. The classes have a roughly common plight, common vulnerabilities, common prospects, but they have also common levels of what Werner Sombart called "ascent aspiration." The democratic class struggle is sparked as much by the aspiration as by the disaffection. Together they explain why the lower classes think liberally in many of their political attitudes and vote New Deal, yet cling to a belief in the open society and retain the hope that their children will do better than they did.

This sheds light on the Great Paradox of the American class system. It has two phases: first, although political and economic attitudes differ sharply between the upper and lower classes, those below reject the notion that they are there permanently; second, despite the often big gap between the encouraged claims of each class, especially the lower ones, and the limited fulfillment possible in any one generation, there is neither great class tension nor loss of cultural hope. It sheds light also on the relaxed quality—along with the militancy—of the American class situation: the sense of "taking it easy" which has been the despair of the class-obsessed radicals. I do not account for this, as Russell Davenport does, as "a social partnership that only the craziest optimist would have dared foretell." The term "social partnership" elides the elements of class difference and class struggle, but it is true that the struggle is carried on within a framework of mobility and hope.

Much of this may be a form of folk belief, and writers like Robert Lynd have bitingly asked students of American society to shape their class doctrines to social reality rather than to this folk belief. There is value in such prodding, but it ignores the fact that folk belief is in itself an important phase of social reality, especially when the belief finds considerable support in past experience. There is a distinction between folk belief and folk fable, as there is between a social myth concocted and sustained by propaganda techniques and one rooted in a people's history and in the genius of their institutions. You cannot dismiss the American folk belief about class as untrue on the ground that its truth is mainly a psychological one. It does distill the American experience with class as sifted through the popular mind over the generations. Obviously there is a deep surge of feeling coming up from below, merging with and strengthening the inherent cultural optimism of America. There is in it an inextinguishable hopefulness that keeps corporate power and the hierarchy of social distinction from breeding that despair which is the matrix of class revolution. What is bred in the American situation is quite a different thing—not the resentment of the rebellious but the pathos of the excluded, and the unremitting anxiety under which life in any status system is lived.

Yet even taking account of the pathos and anxiety, the dominant tone is hope. It is based on a number of trends: on the expanding college attendance, especially for the children of the working class and the lower middle class; on the movement to the suburbs, which has added to the buoyancy of the class system by giving a people largely torn from the land and from home-owning a new sense of roots and a new stake in community living; the growth and social acceptance of the trade-unions, which have brought the bargaining power of the working class to its height; the new Mass Media, especially TV, which have reduced the sense of class isolation and opened vistas of experience for all to feed on; the fact that 70 per cent of the American population is in the areas where upward mobility still operates, so that in almost three out of four American families the sense of social possibility and the upward pressure on the levels of aspiration are still operative; finally, on the history of the New Deal and its successor administrations which have proved that government action can help remove the obstructions that stand in the way of the immediate upward goals attainable for many. In other words, at the base of the folk belief is the fact that the recent experience of most of the strata of the class system has kept their members from feeling caught in the trap of a closed class.

Big gaps still remain. If they did not, what I have described as the Great Paradox of the class system would be no paradox. But neither is it a blind alley. In a frame of hopefulness even the class gaps perform the function of spurring individuals to greater effort and providing strength to the failing individual incentives of the economy. As long as the immediate goals continue to seem and be compassable they spur whole classes to span the distance that lies between. If in delineating American life we are to borrow anything from the Marxist armory of class concepts, let it not be that of a classless society, which is as false in the American as in the Russian context, but the concept of class struggle, which goes back before Marx to the early American political writers and takes on a special meaning when it is placed in a frame of democracy.

CHAPTER VIII

Life Cycle of the American

WE MOVE away here from American technology, economy, government and class structure, and shift our attention to the growth of the American personality. We trace what happens to the American in the course of his life cycle from birth to death, focusing on the interactions between the developing personality and the pervasive culture at each of the turning points of the individual's life (Sec. 1, "The Personality in the Culture"). It is here that we take stock of the American family, noting its flux and transformations and seeing it as the primary laboratory for the forming of personality and the basic attitudes on authority, freedom, and individual expressiveness (Sec. 2, "The Family As Going Concern"). We look into the cultural anxieties involved in the cult of the child, and the recent reassertions of the parental role (Sec. 3, "Children and Parents"). We trace the process of growing up and coming of age in America as one of finding models to identify with and roles to play, of earning one's spurs, and finally finding one's identity (Sec. 4, "Growing Up in America"). We go on to the courtship years, with their "dating" and "pairing" patterns, and look into the American attitudes toward love, and the failures and successes of marriage in America (Sec. 5, "Courtship, Love, and Marriage"). We then turn to the situation of the American woman, at once the most vaunted and least fulfilled of the American cultural products. We analyze the roles the culture assigns to her, the rebelliousness she has engaged in, the social revolutions that have transformed her situation, the multiple lives she leads and the deaths she dies, the dilemmas she still has to face, and how she is confronting them (Sec. 6, "The Ordeal of the American Woman"). We carry the American on into the middle years of his life, noting the changes taking place in reorienting toward middle age in the light of the lengthened age span and the changing conditions of leisure, but not omitting the desolate spaces on the landscape. And we end with the new American in a new conception of old age and its possibilities, and with American attitudes to the eternal but un-American fact of death (Sec. 7, "The Middle and End of the Journey").

Life Cycle of the American

1. The Personality in the Culture

ONE way to get at the quality of a culture is to ask how the human personality fares in it through the life cycle. In the more primitive folk societies, where there was a close collective concern with magical and religious rituals, and where a member's relation to his tribe and the tribe's relation to the supernatural world were almost blended into one, the society intervened ceremonially in the life cycle of the individual. The Belgian anthropologist Van Gennep has used the term "rites of passage" for the ritual transition points at which the individual is inducted into the succession of crucial life experiences.

Like other modern cultures, Americans have almost lost the impulse to magical ceremonial. What survives of that impulse is found in a few desultory religious services at birth, puberty, marriage, and death, when the occasion is restricted to family and friends rather than celebrated by the community as a whole. Yet from cradle to grave the community does come in with its norms and codes, if not with its ceremonies, to shape the stages of the life cycle. In one sense the true American ceremonials are not the rites of passage but the rituals of the scientists and doctors. As James Klee has said, the Salk polio vaccine may be a more important ceremony to them than Confirmation.

In every civilization the life cycle is culture-bound. One may say that the life history of the American is the unfolding of the person-in-the-culture, and equally the condensation of the culture-in-the-person. There are some truisms here that tend to be forgotten: that people make their culture, as their culture makes them; that no culture can rise in its quality above the kind of human material developed in it; but equally that the final test of a culture lies in the quality of the setting it provides for the individual personality to form itself.

There is a risk of overstating the importance of the particular culture, and how unique a stamp it can place on its human material. The phases of the life history are much the same in every culture: birth, the forming of infant habits of eating, talking, walking; child growth to adolescence; the onset of puberty; adornment and courtship that come with sexual awakening; the induction into the community and its adult patterns; betrothal, marriage and procreation, starting another life cycle; child-rearing; the assumption of the economic burdens of family and the civic and religious duties of the community in the maturity of one's powers; the middle years and the sexual climacterics; sickness and the decline of physical powers; old age, with its dependency; death.

But if the invariables of human life make the life cycle itself pretty much a constant in its skeletal structure, they have to be filled in by the history of the culture and the biography of the individual, leaving room for the interplay of "culture" and "personality." John Dollard emphasized how powerful the culture is in shaping ahead of time what will happen to the individual: "All the facts we can predict about the organism . . . will define the culture into which it comes. Such facts can include the kind of clothes it will wear, the language it will speak, its theological ideas, its characteristic occupation, in some cases who its husband or wife is bound to be, how it can be insulted, what it will regard as wealth, what its theory of personality growth will be. . . . These and hundreds of other items are or may be standardized before the birth of the individual and be transmitted to the organism with mechanical certainty."

These cultural shaping forces, although lying below the surface of the individual life, are powerful in their effects. Even in America, with its stress on the uniqueness of the individual, the strong common elements that place diverse personalities in similar cultural molds are undeniably present. Sometimes it is the role in a subculture that is more important than the culture: the life of a Mississippi Negro sharecropper will in most respects differ from that of a Du Pont, but it will parallel the life of other Negro sharecroppers, just as Du Pont's will parallel the lives of other families who have enjoyed wealth and power over a long time.

In some respects the culture or subculture will act through some short cut that eases the individual's growth, as for example through formalities of language, manners, or moral codes. In other ways it will act through controls that circumscribe the individual's expression, as through rigid standards he must live up to and taboos he dare not violate. Anatole France had such cultural burdens in mind when he said that every child born into civilization is born with a beard. Changing the figure, the journey of the personality in any culture is like walking under water, or struggling past heavy obstacles in an enveloping dream.

How much control does American society, compared with others, exercise over the individual? It is usually said that American society is "restrictive" rather than "permissive," but this applies mainly to the control of sexual relations. On premarital intercourse, especially for girls, and on homosexual relations, Americans are severely restrictive in their formal codes, but a good deal less so in their operative ones. On the other hand, on the child's behavior in the household, on discipline in the school, on the freedom of the individual to move about physically and to cross social lines, on freedom to change and exchange opinions, and especially on its refusal to demand deference to any priestly, magical, parental, or governmental authority, American society is among the most permissive in history.

Since these two extremes are found in the same society, it is useless to apply either term to it. One finds here again an instance of the polar nature of American life. But this fact is in itself important in assessing the impact of the culture on the personality, for it means that the American goes through life meeting not one but a number of varying degrees of pressure or permissiveness. He is like a diver changing quickly from one sea level to another: if it doesn't make him bleed profusely or kill him, he emerges more able than most people to adapt himself to contrasting changes. But most of all, the contrast of tight pressures and permissive freedoms must seem confusing to the young American and produce in him a sense both of being boxed in and of being left bewilderingly alone.

The same problem may be put in terms of how purposive American life is. The formal codes are mainly negative, in the shape of taboos. The positive goals for individual striving are never imposed or enforced as such by the community. The individual is seemingly allowed the utmost latitude in making his own choices—choosing his interests as he grows up, his companions and friends, his job and career, his mate, the size of his family, the color of his opinions, his recreations and hobbies, his books, his tastes, his residence. This degree of freedom of choice leads some observers to count America as the most permissive of societies. Yet there is some constriction under this deceptive aspect of extreme freedom. From birth to death there are pressures molding the individual in the direction of "what is expected." The major and minor goals for individual striving—to succeed, to have a job, not to waste time, to do and not to dream—are pounded into him. The fact of his freedom of choice makes it more imperative for him to choose rightly, not aimlessly or heretically. Thus again he is torn between seeming freedom and the persistent process of social molding.

Such a society has little patience with the "marginal man." I have been discussing here the person-in-the-culture, but every society develops also the man-out-of-the-culture. There are some, for example, which make a place for the homosexual even while they recognize his divergence: they give him a social function to perform for which he is temperamentally fitted. There are probably few societies in which as much divergence for the man-out-of-the-culture is allowed as in the American, yet few also in which there is so much anxiety to hide that fact. The poet, the exotic, the dilettante, the political and social rebel, the Thoreau-like idler, the aesthete, the saint, the devotee of one crotchety "cause" after another: all of them are allowed to live without molestation, and even the sexual deviants are harried less by the penalties of law than by the censure of their shocked neighbors. All that Americans ask of their people on the margin of the culture is for them to pursue their eccentricities privately. They provide them with a reluctant neglect, but only rarely do they relax the obvious and continuous disapproval of what clashes so deeply with the main currents of community energy.

In discussing cultural patterns, Ruth Benedict has noted the problem of continuities and discontinuities in the cycle of the generations. In folk societies where occupations are stable, and even in most of the European societies from which the Americans came, a boy or a girl grew up in the calling, the crafts, the ways of life and thought, of ancestral generations. These continuities have been broken by the drastic geographical movement, the occupational shift, and the social mobility of Americans. It is rarer than in the past for children to grow up and raise their families in the homes, or even in the towns or neighborhoods, where they were born—or on a similar level of living standards. As a result the crucial process of social education, of inducting the growing child into the ways it is expected to follow, is carried on mainly not in the primary group of the family but in the larger society-as-a-whole.

This is especially true of sexual education. In some primitive groups, as Margaret Mead has noted, the child is brought early into contact with the later sexual role it will have. The girl, for example, is encouraged to think of herself sensuously as a coming mother, and by observing and imitating she prepares herself for her role. In the American case the taboos upon premarital sex make such imitation and preparation more difficult, so that the continuity of the cycle of generations is broken. Each generation makes its start afresh, learning through trial and error, in a new city and a new setting with new attitudes toward parental and child relationships. For most the effort of self-reliance is too great, and they try to learn from the current tastes, fashions, and taboos of the larger community, so that the result is almost as constricted as in the traditional societies.

The image thus received from the legislators of emotional development and the arbiters of character is never wholly stereotyped or clear. But there are assumptions in the culture by which the growing person learns to judge his effectiveness. These are the more powerful because they are never codified but are taught by the indirection of what is taken for granted. It is assumed that the child will "do well"—that he will be part of the main currents of play in the nursery or early primary grades, and not stay on the margin; that he will be "popular" in high school and a "leader" in college; that he will be a "success" at his job or career and in gathering his portion of the world's goods; that when he gets into emotional difficulty he must become "adjusted"; and, most of all, that he will strive to be "happy."

Although happiness is an elusive intangible, the individual is assumed to be more or less indifferent to the whole cluster of other intangibles—the sense of wonder and mystery, the sense of honor not because it is the "best policy" but as its own end, the awareness of beauty, the dedication to what will not pay off. He is not expected to tap successive layers of his personality, except in a competitive situation—at sports, or in some heroically demanding piece of work which is regarded as a "character builder" ("the Army will make a man of you"), and where he is praised for drawing upon his reserves of strength and will. He finds little value placed upon growth through suffering, nor (despite the Christian base and overtones of the culture) is he likely to learn that it is by a series of deaths that men have reached fulfillment in life. It is assumed that personality growth pretty much takes care of itself as a by-product of the pursuit of the immediate goals.*

Such a scheme of assumptions leaves the American without much sense of wonder at the successive phases of the individual's life history. Primitive groups, by contrast, are so close to the life-cycle experiences that they celebrate it in ritual drama and build their great folk myths around its stages. In the case of the generic mythical hero, one finds him achieving his effects by some exaggeration or inversion of the usual human role. Thus, as Joseph Campbell has developed the theme in *The Hero with a Thousand Faces,* the hero is likely to be born of a goddess or at least of royalty and not a human being; abandoned on some mountaintop or left floating among the bulrushes in the river; suckled by a wild animal, perhaps a wolf; discovered as a foundling and brought up in isolation in the extremes either of poverty or of nobility; courting and winning the beloved one through the ordeal of danger; mating, by the fateful inversion of incest, with mother or sister; slaying his father; wrestling with demons and living out a life of penitence on the desert or in the mountains; in the end founding a new religion or nation.

The American folk myths are of a different type. Their exaggerations and distortions are more likely to be applied to feats of work prowess, or rollicking boasts of superhuman effectiveness, or life in a mythical

* For more on American cultural goals, see especially Ch. IX, Sec. 8, "Life Goals and the Pursuit of Happiness."

paradise of splendor, or the Superman feats of magical science.* Thus the popular imagination is torn away from the great transitions of the life cycle, which are conceived as burdens somehow to be borne, and it is fixed upon the more abstract goals of the society.

In the process the sense of wonder is replaced by anxieties and tensions. Malinowski, in his studies of the Trobriand Island culture, held that the rituals of primitive life fulfill the deep psychic needs of the person. He cited the anxiety felt by the husband and relatives of a woman in childbirth and later by the parents of the newly born child, and saw the community birth rites as a response to these anxieties. But A. R. Radcliffe-Brown, who had studied the Andaman Islanders with equal care, shrewdly pointed out that in some instances the rite is not a response to the anxiety but itself creates it. The best way of putting it is probably the way that G. C. Homans uses: that in the group life of every society there is a circular process of creating and satisfying needs, so that the same primitive rituals which are a response to the tensions and anxieties of the life cycle also help to bring them into being. The whole elaborate hierarchy of customs and codes in America is partly a response to the tensions of a new industrial culture and the anxieties it begets, but also the existence of the customs and codes helps create the tensions and anxieties.

In the life history the individual American may, however, take part in a great drama of cultural transformation, especially if he is a second- or third-generation member of an immigrant family. His life expectations and aspirations change, his notion of means and ends changes, his whole personality style changes. Anyone reading Handlin's *The Uprooted* cannot help feeling that he has witnessed the broad sweep of a ritual drama in which millions of new Americans and their children and grandchildren have had a role. Much of it, to be sure, is adaptive and imitative rather than creative, but the creativeness is not lacking. This is one of the great typical interactions between culture and personality in America. And if, in the case of many of the immigrant cultures, the rites of passage have tended to wilt in the new social climate of America, it is because the intensity of the cultural transformations has overshadowed the sense of regular life transitions brought over from another cultural world.

One of the striking facts about the American scene, however, is the absence of a ritual drama except in the sense I have described, and even the unofficial extrusion from the culture of the artist-dramatist. He is marginal to the culture and moves on the periphery of it. Among the primitives the ritual drama was a means toward the defining of tribal

* For a discussion of American folk myths, see Ch. XI, Sec. 3, "Heroes, Legends, and Speech." For children's literature, see Ch. VIII, Sec. 3, "Children and Parents."

tradition and the discovery of individual identity: since it has diminished in America, the task of the discovery of identity becomes correspondingly harder.

Yet the process of discovery does go on and is perhaps the crucial phase of the interaction of culture and personality. As he grows up the young American finds himself and develops his sense of identity partly, at least, by identifying with aspects of his culture—with the heroes of its competitive sports, with its figures of glamour in the Big Media, with the image of swift movement in a convertible or a plane, or equally swift success in the rise to the top of one's field, with the discoveries of scientists, the building feats of engineers, the swagger of the newspaperman, or the solid achievements of the executive life.

American social scientists have recently talked a good deal of "role-taking" in this process of the discovery of identity, and it is true* that the growing-up process runs largely in terms of experimental probing of the roles of wooer and wooed, pupil and teacher, son and daughter, husband and wife, soldier, adventurer, man of substance. Yet surely this fragmentizes the whole process far too much, breaking the total personality up into separable phases which are never in actual fact separated from each other. The process of self-discovery is one that keeps taking place of, by, and for the total person. The dynamics of this process lie hidden in the recesses of personality itself, which the Freudians think of at least partly in terms of a dark battlefield swept by confused alarms of struggle and flight, but which some of the more recent American psychologists have interpreted also in terms of a more expansive feeling of creativeness.

The difficulties arise, of course, with the question of whether the individual absorbs and identifies with all the phases of his culture, meretricious as well as healthy, repressive as well as releasing, in the process of his growth toward maturity. Much of the confusion of the inner life of the American derives exactly from the terrible burden of making a selection of what one will identify with, and thus having to sit in a kind of judgment on the culture—which one cannot do without having already arrived at a sense of one's identity. This is the vicious spiral that the individual runs into in any culture: that he is infected with its confusions and contradictions unless he can detach himself from them, yet by the fact that in most cases he cannot, he is pervaded by them and adds to them. It is usually the innovator and the marginal man of the culture who achieves enough of a detachment from it to help it to clarify itself and grow more creative. One is likely to forget, in the stress on the identity and growth of the individual, that the culture too has an

* See Sec. 4, "Growing Up in America."

identity, that it has continuities, that it is faced with the chances and the problems of growth, and that the kind of culture which serves as a frame for the individual's life may make all the difference in deciding whether that life is to be stunted or expressive.

In his cultural frame the American has shown a resilience of mood and a variety of temperament. The end product of the life process is not the cultural type but the individual himself in all his multiple forms. American society does not encourage individual diversity where it conflicts with the standards of an often ruthless peer group or community. Yet individualist tradition has managed to break through even these layers of conformity. American society is both overorganized in some areas and underorganized in others, but it allows ample room at the joints for individual development. The real question is not whether particular divergences are allowed, but whether the whole social climate is one in which the impulses to know yourself and to be yourself can grow strongly.*

Let us now see how this climate operates and how these impulses fare through the stages of the American life history.

2. *The Family As Going Concern*

THE AMERICAN FAMILY has been caricatured both by American and foreign observers, and in one sense it is a caricature of itself, since it always seems to be parading its excesses. In the more dramatic and distorted version the American family is an anarchic collection of delinquent adolescents, spoiled cacophonous brats, a domineering wife, and a harassed, two-timing husband, their discords frequently aired in divorce courts and tabloids, the whole of it watched by Dr. Spock for baby care, Dr. Gesell for child growth, and Dr. Kinsey for the record of erotic successes and failures.

On a less caricatured level the picture is still somber enough. Americans tend to marry young and run into divorce problems often, have small families whose size they seek to control, give their children unparalleled freedom; they marry romantically for love and are often disillusioned, experiment a good deal sexually, and then in most cases they remarry for love or money, pleasure or companionship; the husband tends to be absent, the wife unhappy, and both to be sexually unfulfilled. There are many broken families, insecure children, possessive mothers; the family seems uprooted and unstable, scarcely performing

* On the problem of conformity, see Ch. IX, Sec. 4, "Varieties of American Character." On codes, see generally Ch. IX, especially Secs. 5, 6, and 7, and Ch. X, Sec. 1, "God and the Churches."

its traditional functions; and the instability of the family seems both to express and intensify the general sense of cultural disintegration.

I have put the indictment as strongly as I can, yet anyone except the special pleaders and Juvenals will see that it is overdrawn. With all its weaknesses and excesses the American family is a going concern reflecting less the disintegration of the culture than its mobility and genius for innovation. For that reason it is a pain to moralists, traditionalists, religious absolutists, bourgeois-baiting Marxists, and professional cultural pessimists. If the American family system is sick, then the class system must also be sick, and the whole economy, the democratic idea, the passion for equality, the striving for happiness, and the belief that there can be free choice and a future of hope. For it is on these that the American family is founded. You may feel varying degrees of approval or disapproval of the American institutions and ideas I have listed, but the point is that the American family is part of the totality and reflects its virtues as well as weaknesses.

The elements of the traditional family that took root in the American soil have largely been stripped of their function. In the Europe from which the American stocks came, the father was the unquestioned head of the family, since he was the ruler of his farm or had a clear status in society; in America he is unlikely to have an economic domain of his own to rule or a sharply defined social position. His sons leave him to carve out careers of their own, just as he left his own parents; his daughters follow their husbands and set up families of their own. He no longer tills the soil as he did: the large New England or Midwest farm family, which was the product both of overflowing pioneer energies and the need for family labor, is no longer the rule. Thus the traditional family —large, three-generation, patriarchal, attached to the land, closely integrated in performing the collective economic functions of farm homestead or small shop or family business—has almost gone out of the picture. It is more likely to be small, two generation, mobile, whole-family-centered, equalitarian. The family no longer performs to the same degree the old functions of economic production, religious cohesion, kinship continuity, educational and cultural transmission.

But this does not mean that the American family has found nothing to replace what it has given up of these functions. No longer a production unit, it has become a more demanding consumption unit, based on the earning power of both husband and wife and the spending power and tastes especially of the wife and daughters. It is still a residence unit, even when it is highly mobile. No longer an educational and religious entity, it is becoming a more broadly cultural one. It seeks to supplement the traditional bondage to father or husband by free decisions

among its members. It tries to make companionship and common interests rather than social duties its psychological basis. It is cemented, if at
all, by the pursuit of happiness rather than the exercise of authority.*

I have no alack and alas for this. The oldest function of any family,
that of producing and caring for children, it still performs. The relation between husband and wife, between parents and children, between
brothers and sisters, is less traditionally regulated than it was. But who
will say that bonds of kinship maintained in a spirit of free commitment, with a continuous inquiry about their meaning, are any less
strong for that fact? Given the necessary elements of obligation and tradition, the American has fashioned anew the features of his family institutions, as he does everything else about him—his clothes, income,
technology, production, government, class system, laws, occupations,
ideas, and opinions. The result may seem chaotic, but only because it is
also revolutionary.

The American family is "nuclear," by which is meant that it is not
the old "organic" or "extended" family and has come further from the
clan than is true in any other culture. Certainly it is sharply different
from the Moslem family with its man-centered polygamy and its depressed caste for women; or the Indian "joint family," run by the elder
women; or the Chinese father-son family axis, run for and by the old
men; or the continental family based on the marriage of convenience
and still father-oriented; or the various concubinage systems; or the
Soviet family, in which the parental or filial roles, whether of power,
obedience, or affection, have been largely diluted by a state which has
tried to distill away for itself the essence of all these roles. Along the
path of its development the American family shed in-laws, grandparents, cousins, aunts, and retainers; it handed over production to the factory and office, religion to the churches, the administration of justice to
the courts, formal education to the schools, medical attention to the
hospitals, and it has even begun to hand over some of the basic life decisions to the psychotherapist. It has been stripped down to the spare
frame of being marriage-centered and child-fulfilled.

Actually there are at least five definable family types in the American
culture. Four are still largely traditional. First, the rural family (in the
Midwest or New England), which still is large, where the children still
do field and household chores and do not usually disperse when they
come of age and get married. The second is the "old family" unit, especially in the elites where there has been wealth over time, considerable
pride of standing, and little geographical mobility, so that the old ideal

---

* I am, of course, giving a generalized portrait. The precise picture presents a good
many overlappings.

of the "Great House" of the Southern plantation or the "family on the hill" in New England still holds. The third is the family of second- and third-generation immigrants, especially Slavic, Mediterranean, Irish, and Jewish, with residual traditional elements: it shows instances at once of great cohesiveness (largely because of the carry-over of the old ways and the old urgency for holding together in a strange and changing social environment) and of a persisting break between the generations. The fourth is the Negro family, shaped by the plantation heritage caste conditions in the South, great geographical and social mobility in the North, and a high desertion rate: the father is often absentee, the mother has a factory job or lives out in domestic service, and the children are often raised by grandparents in a truncated three-generation family.

The fifth type is the middle-class, big-city, small-town, or suburban family, which is the dominant American form. The father is a somewhat transient figure and the mother a pervasive one. This new archetypal family may best be described in terms of the social changes that brought it into being. One was geographical dispersal, the constant physical and occupational mobility of Americans that flings them around over the face of the land in constantly shifting internal migrations in search of jobs and opportunity. Another was the technical revolution that turned America from a farming society into an urban and suburban one and made it possible for women to become machine tenders or to take their place in a vast clerical and office hierarchy. Aided by a "sexual revolution" and a "kitchen revolution," the American woman of the upper and middle classes (not the lower ones) achieved the kind of freedom from household chores which the slave system gave the wives and daughters of the plantation owners of the Old South. Operating on all these changes has been a ceaseless equalitarian impulse, whittling away the subordination of wives to husbands and of children to parents, and making romantic love and free marriage choice the center of the family relationship.

There are several levels on which the dominant American family type can be analyzed: its structure of authority; its inner emotional climate, and how it mediates between its members and the world of outer social experience; how stable and viable it is; how it brings up children. To the first three of these I now turn. The fourth will be discussed in the next section.

One of the things that has struck European travelers and observers sharply has been the comparative difference in the authority of the fathers. Busy at job or office, the American father cannot exercise the continuous direction required in the patriarchal family. His authority is still recognized in theory, and usually he is the court of last resort on questions of discipline. But he is no longer backed up by a religious sanction of his paramount authority, nor does he have the will to assert it. On daily matters his wife is his deputy, and under the absentee sovereignty of the husband the deputy becomes king—only to give up her authority on week ends to the husband or at times to the children themselves. Thus the libertarian tradition is reinforced by the changes in the inner authority structure of the family. The children think in terms of claims and rights, more than of duties and obedience. Their world is not that of deference to authority but of "talking back" to parents and bargaining to exact a set of rewards for their surrender to family rules on food habits, manners, and behavior.

This portrait of the child-centered anarchy of the family is again overdrawn. In effective families there is little of that tyranny of the weaker which has caused the family to be described as the "dictatorship of the sickest member." The rules are made together, to be followed together. Money saved up is not something to be scrambled for by competing children, but it is used for trips and treats for the family as a whole. Family rituals which meet with strong objection from any of the members are likely to wither away, nor can the authority of the parents alone sustain them if they lose their meaning for the children. There are, to be sure, constant opportunities for neurotic distortions of the emotional structure of the family. For reasons inherent in their own personalities the unconscious bias of one or both parents may be toward one child or against another, and a child may grow up as a "golden boy" or as a family scapegoat. The rivalry of the children for affection and concessions makes the shaping of family decisions difficult in the extreme.* More difficulty is introduced by the fact that comparisons are continually being made with rules and decisions in other families. Yet, however faltering the process is, the decisions are part of what may roughly be called a democratic family process.

The resulting democracy is vulnerable, as all democratic structures are. The attacks on the American family on the ground of its dissolution of authoritarianism are a good deal like similar attacks on American political democracy. The family is more vulnerable, of course, because it must bear the heavy burden of making its democracy function. This burden is placed on a large number of small family units, many of them broken and disorganized, with ignorant, confused, neurotic, or dissolute parents. They often make a mess of bringing up children in a framework of affection and responsibility. In the society as a whole the failure of some persons to live up to the democratic burdens, through ignorance

---

* For more on the emotional structure of the family, as expressed in the parent-child relation, see Sec. 3, "Children and Parents."

or frustration, may be balanced by the greater maturity of others. But exactly because the family is the primary group, no other family can do much to rescue it. Thus it sinks or swims depending on whether its members can make a go of the co-operative venture. If they fail, the authority structure becomes tyrannical, possessive, or anarchic.

It is often said that because of the individualist authority structure of the American family a political dictatorship is impossible in America. If this is true it is not because of any carrying over of the rebellion principle from the family into the political sphere. Actually it is the over-possessive, domineering parents, in insecure family situations, who are more likely to create in their children the drive to search for a father or to displace him with another. What links the family structure with democratic political habits is a two-way relation: only in a democratic political milieu could the family have thrown off the burdens of arbitrary authority and sought equality for its members; and—even more crucial—the process of coping with the problems of government-by-consent in the primary social group, through joint rule-making and rule-observing, makes the family an unparalleled laboratory for government-by-consent in the larger political sphere. Children and parents trained in such a joint effort are unlikely to become cogs in an authoritarian machine or find their fulfillment in following a leader blindly—although the evidences of conformism in recent American political attitudes show how much the family is itself caught in the cultural pressures.

The nostalgic amusement and archaic flavor, as if from a museum piece, which American readers and theatergoers got from Clarence Day's *Life with Father*—a patriarchal father who claimed a religious sanction for his authority—attested the span that the American family has traveled in the intervening generations. The current folklore which shows Father at the other end of the authority scale—having to squeeze his way into a family bathroom pre-empted in the rising hours by an aggressive group of children, or manipulated by children and wife in the "Bringing Up Father" comics—is a genial recognition of the loss of his power. Yet the satire is gentle, for the American father has accepted his diminished authority partly because his work takes so much of his time and energy, partly because his role fits into the spirit of his society as a whole.

In comparing the American family with that in authoritarian societies, the difference between them is striking. The authority structure of the pre-Nazi German family spilled over into the rest of German society. Under the Nazis the influence ran the other way, and the *Führer-prinzip* in society reinforced the position of the father. But there was a degree to which the German family remained, as Max Horkheimer put it, a "shelter against the mass-society" of the Nazis, which was why the Hitler regime had to "reconstruct" it, for even with its authority principle it did not go far enough in the discipline of the Nazi virtues. It may be noted that recent studies of the German family indicate that the father is losing his authority and coming closer to the American image. In the Soviet system the Communist party has tried to reinforce the authority structure within the family after the model of the same structure within the state. The Latin-American family has recently been throwing off both the dominance of the church and the tyranny of the father; and the anticlerical movements in Latin-American countries have developed alongside the steady penetration of the society by the image of the free-choosing American family structure. In fact, there is every evidence that Western nations are quite generally following the American lead in family development, just as America carried further the tendencies already present in European society.

The concern of the American family is with raising and socializing the child. At the heart of the recent family changes in America is a hedonic revolution which asserts that life can be pleasurable, that the size of the family can be planned and the sequence of children spaced, that bearing them need not be a curse, nor raising them a burden, that happiness can be found for both partners in a freely willed marriage and freely willed children, that family decisions should be made largely with a view to preparing the children for a good life. I stress the children as the focus of the nuclear family, and their rearing and socializing as its chief function. Yet part of the hedonic revolution is the growing belief that there can be a life for husband and wife alike even after the children are raised. With the average age at marriage for the woman somewhere at twenty, the childbearing cycle may be completed for her before thirty, and the last child has outgrown dependency before she has passed her mid-forties. This gives her a chance, at the prime of middle age, to turn back to her earlier interests and assume new ones, as it also gives the husband a chance to ease up on his work and tensions—if he knows how.

In the early years of family building, however, the whole focus is on children and home, at least for the woman. His job and career strivings allow the husband little scope for continuous attention to his family. He becomes a residual father, and his wife what Geoffrey Gorer has called the "encapsulated mother."

The American mother is not only the organizer of consumption and spending but also the one who reads books and magazines and studies the mysteries of child psychology: she thus becomes the child's rearer, cajoler, censor. Her ways are less authoritarian than manipulative. She is a matriarch not in exercising firm power but in managing the family.

Since she is the chief socializing agent—along with the usually female schoolteacher—the American boy comes to identify moral codes with women, and thus either to think of them as "sissy stuff" or else to associate the sexual life with an impossible goal of purity. If she proves too possessive the result is shown in the psychiatric records of battle-shock cases in World War II, when the boys from mother-sheltered families found the transition to the realities of an all-male world too sharp. In the cases where she is the dominant adult the boy may find it hard to establish his own later role, having no effective masculine model. The daughter may seek a strong father symbol in her future husband, or come to think of him as an object for the exercise of her own power. What Philip Wylie has termed "Momism" in America may be, as he suggests, an overcompensation for the boy's rebellion against a mother-dominated home life. Or it may be a nostalgic harking back to the idyllic days of mother and home from which the grown man regrets having moved so far.

An idyl the "home" is, at least in later memory. It is the most lyrical of American symbols. It may mean a sharecropper's hut, a tumbledown shack near the railroad tracks, an estate at Newport or on Long Island or the east coast of Maryland, a company house in a mining or steel town in West Virginia, a government housing project in Detroit, a Lake Shore Drive mansion near Chicago, a movie star's estate-cum-swimming-pool at Beverly Hills. But generally the image is that of the middle-class suburban or small-town home, with memories of pies eaten in the kitchen, and a radio or TV set in the living room, a tool shed, a bicycle to ride to school, perhaps (in the earlier days) a swimming hole and sand-lot baseball games.

The fact that America has been so mobile makes this home idyl the more evocative. Until the suburban revolution most Americans grew up in crowded city quarters, which meant that the home idyl, with its small-town and semirural associations, became for the culture all the more a figure of the Golden Age. It is not nostalgia alone that moves Americans but the longing for a social unit to stand firm in the wrack of a dissolving world.

The young people, as they sit courting, spin their dreams around the "dream home," and they turn the pages of the apartment and house-for-sale ads and the magazines embodying the latest architectural plans and interiors. They want the home for the comforts it gives them but also because it sets a seal on the marriage, provides a frame within which children can grow up, gives the family a clear standing in the community, and certifies in a tangible way the ideals of security and permanence for which Americans hunger. This attachment to the home underlies the vast housing boom that developed after World War II, and which has been discussed in an earlier chapter. It also inclines Americans to associate a number of social ills, especially juvenile delinquency, with bad housing—a mode of interpretation that has a core of truth but also carries with it a favorite American thesis in linking the nature of the home neighborhood with character formation.*

I am thus more than a bit skeptical of the predictions of decay and doom freely made for the American family. It is true that its kinship ties are not as strong as, for example, the father-son ties in China, nor does it perform so well as the extended family the function of transmitting the social heritage from one generation to the next. The strength of such ties varies in every society with the rate of social mobility. Those who care about an America in which the channels of social movement are not closed can scarcely quarrel with its consequences for the family.

As for the rising divorce rate, it may show not so much a disbelief in marriage as an intent to take seriously the American premise that a marriage is held together by love and common interests. The steadily rising rate of remarriage after divorce shows that Americans still believe in marriage even after a disastrous experience with it. The stability of these post-divorce marriages does not differ markedly from that of first marriages. As for the children, many of them learn to get along even after the family ties have been broken, and after the remarriage of one of their parents they again become parts of a whole family. The worst consequences of broken families are in the cases where they lead to neglect of the children or brutality toward them, but family life even without divorce has its seamier side in the same social strata. The evidence of psychotherapy is that it may be even worse for children to grow up in families where the bonds are held together despite the unremitting hatred, unhappiness, and sadism of the parents.

One image that we shall have to discard after studying the recent divorce figures is the romantic image of the lower-class family as stable, integrated, and happy, while the middle-class family is divorce-ridden and neurotic. This is simply not borne out by the facts. Actually, as William J. Goode has shown, there is an inverse relation between class and divorce, the lower-class families having higher divorce rates and the middle- and upper-class families lower ones. The factors behind this are complex. It is probably true that there is more effective sexual understanding between husband and wife at the lower income strata than at the upper ones. But it is equally true that the economic strains at the

* For an earlier discussion of house and home in America, see Ch. III, Sec. 6, "The Sinews of Welfare."

lower strata express themselves in family conflict which often disguises their origin and becomes a nagging relationship making marriage intolerable. The easier economic means at the higher-class levels will often enable a marriage to survive that could not have outlived privation. Similarly, there is a broader network of social involvement at the upper levels, in leisure, recreation, and "going out," which can make life tolerable for both husband and wife even with an unsatisfactory marriage. It is possible that divorce was originally an upper-class institution which has been taken over into the lower strata and carried further, but it is more probable that family instability has changed its form among the lower strata: where once it found an outlet in desertion and protracted separation, it now finds divorce a simpler solution. I do not deny here the reality of the objective facts on the increase of divorce, but I suggest that they do not tell the whole story.

In any event, the middle-class family cannot be caricatured any longer as an unstable and neurotic chaos. It carries the burden of family changes in the culture as a whole, being usually in the vanguard. This was true of the growth of sexual experimenting, especially by the American woman, and the practice of contraceptives. The widespread acceptance of such "birth control" led to considerable anxiety about population decline and childlessness, as in the case of the Roman Empire. But again the evidence points the other way. Certainly the first effect of "family planning" is to cut down the birth rate, with the family income going into higher living standards and better education for fewer children. But the next phase is quite different—the raising of the birth rate when young parents, especially among the better-educated classes, find that the psychic satisfaction of having children is greater than extra house furnishings or clothes without them.*

The greatest strengths of the family system must be sought among those parents who have made a willed choice to stay together because they find their deepest expressiveness in family life. This expressiveness is again part of the much ridiculed American search for happiness. It is a search which goes beyond the sexual partnership itself and even beyond the marriage relation, finding its fulfillment in the pattern of children, home, community status, and warmth of human relationship which together form the family.†

* For more on divorce, see Sec. 5, "Courtship, Love, and Marriage." For the larger aspects of the birth rate and family planning, see Ch. III, Sec. 5, "Human Resources: Population Profile."

† For a fuller discussion of some of the material of this section, see Sec. 5, "Courtship, Love, and Marriage," Sec. 6, "The Ordeal of the American Woman," and also Ch. IX, Sec. 7, "Society and Sexual Expression," and Sec. 8, "Life Goals and the Pursuit of Happiness."

3. Children and Parents

THE CHILD BORN into an American home has a better chance of survival and health (as does also its mother) than in the comparable social classes of most other societies: the American record ranks roughly with the best on these scores, including New Zealand, Australia, and Holland. The death rate in infant births was cut in a single generation from 64.6 per 1,000 births in 1930 to 29.2 per 1,000 births in 1950. Katharine Lenroot noted that in the sixteen-year span of her tenure as head of the Federal Children's Bureau the maternity death rate dropped from almost sixty per 10,000 live births in 1934 to seven per 10,000 in 1950.* In the mid-1950s a large corps of psychiatrists, welfare workers, graduate students, and volunteers was scattered around the nation, hidden behind screens in child clinics, hovering over the children in nursery or playground, stalking them from one activity to another, all busily studying child behavior, taking action photos and movies, making countless records, running the results through electronic sorting machines, and presenting conclusions on conflict, co-operation, competition, aggression, and frustration among children with an alluring if illusory mathematical precision. If research funds and statistical surveys could purchase understanding of the great mystery under the heavens—the way of a child with an adult, of an adult with a child, and of a child with itself inside its own universe—Americans would today be certain of having penetrated that mystery.

But they are not. While the American child's chances of survival, health, and economic competence are good, his chances are not equally good for growing into an emotionally mature adult, with a stable personality, a sense of identity, and the capacity for living a productive life.

The defect does not lie in science or social rationality. The problems of underdeveloped countries, where the birth rate outruns current living standards, do not apply to America. Birth control and birth spacing as part of a family life plan, although still not officially accepted among Catholics (many American Catholics probably accept it in practice in some form), have become the rule for most American families. To a considerable extent the blighted areas of child life still exist in America: malnutrition, slum living, squalid housing, substandard schooling, family neglect, teen-age prostitution, and narcotics addiction. Some cities use their budget for less relevant items and leave the schools overcrowded and the diagnostic clinics and child-health centers under-

* See also Ch. III, Sec. 5, "Human Resources: Population Profile."

staffed. As for child labor, there are still two or three million children under seventeen employed during the year, many of them during school hours. But the factory children and the "climbing boys" of eighteenth- and nineteenth-century England, or even the child-labor situation in America at the turn of the century, find no parallel in America today. The problem of the American child is less that of the poor and exploited than of the comfortable and even the pampered. The blight is not one of economic privation but of emotional deprivation.

Americans today sometimes idealize the life of the child in colonial and early agrarian America. Actually there was a struggle of parents and children with the hobgoblins of Original Sin, a continuing war with the Devil, and an adamant effort by parents and clergy to repair the child's ignorance and willfulness by catechisms and prepare him early for the trials and duties of life and the deliverance of death. It is easy to note in the history books the recorded successes of this method of child-rearing and to forget the obscure failures, the "lives of quiet desperation" that Thoreau saw around him, the wild outbursts of family rebellion. The early ills of excessive piety and family authority have been conveniently overlaid by the later ills of excessive materialism and family confusion. Several generations of Americans received their impression of childhood in agrarian America from Louisa May Alcott's *Little Women,* with its picture of happy domesticity and of cheerfulness in meeting the shocks of genteel poverty. But it must be remembered that the author was the daughter of Bronson Alcott, himself the child of the Enlightenment, a devotee of the ideas of Rousseau's *Émile* transplanted to the new world.

It was roughly at this time, in the 1840s, that De Tocqueville saw and described the democratic structure of the American family, the ease and equality of manners within it, and the new paths opened up in the education of girls. The one disharmonious note he reported was the assertion of independence of the sons from the father as they moved away from the family to hew out their own careers. A solvent was already at work which, through American mobility, prevented the incipient rebellion against the father's authority from becoming chronic and violent, as in Europe. The revealing documents of the American family structure are less concerned with the tyranny of the father than with the domination of the mother or the absence of any family core.

Bringing up children in America is not the product of impulse followed by neglect. If anything, the approach is too rational. Most American children (especially in the middle class, much less in the lower classes) are born only after a careful calculation of whether their parents can afford them, both in "initial investment" and "upkeep." There is heart-searching about whether the child will get a good education, will live in a "good neighborhood," will meet the "right people." Under highly skilled medical attention the children are put through a process of "factory childbirth" in a hospital, with a speed and detachment that make American birth the most sanitary in the world but also the most impersonal. During the early months every energy is focused on a rational schedule of bathing and feeding the child, and on the other rituals of a highly sterilized regime. Studies of a number of cases of autism (or extreme withdrawal) among children found that the parents usually were members of the educated middle and professional classes who had shown the children no emotional abandon and had given them no feeling of sensual contact. In these extreme instances the children, as a psychiatric study put it, were "kept neatly in a refrigerator that didn't defrost."

The entire family plan, especially on the middle-class level, centers around the child. It is dressed up, coddled, socialized early. In an effort to set the stage for what Margaret Mead calls the "expected childhood experience," the parents sometimes squeeze themselves dry of spontaneous emotion. They watch the stages of the child's growth against the statistical norms of Gesell or (on a lower-class level) the traditional folklore of expected growth. They brood over the moot questions of child-rearing: the child's thumb-sucking, the choice of feeding and the time for weaning, its toilet training, its bed-wetting, its temper tantrums; and later its speech and reading difficulties, lying, stealing. An agonized parental debate is always in process: is the child too timid or too brash, is he a "sissy" or a bully, does he withdraw or does he "show off," does he eat like a little pig or is he too finicky? Does he suffer as an only child or is he the victim of "sibling rivalry"? Is discipline too stern or too permissive? Does he need most (as an earlier generation put it) "the Bible and the birch rod," or a psychotherapist or psychiatric social worker with some "play therapy"?

It is evident that in no other culture has there been so pervasive a cultural anxiety about the rearing of children. Here is another instance, as noted above, where in meeting anxieties a culture manages to create and intensify them. In a culture with rising living standards, smaller families, a "kitchen revolution," greater leisure for women, uprooting from the land, physical and social mobility, and universal schooling, there came also the stirrings of self-criticism in the rearing of children. As Stendler has put it, along with the excitement about railroad reform and antitrust reform in the first decade of the century, there was bound to be excitement about baby reform too. We might add that in the 1920s, along with the sexual revolution and the kitchen revolution, one had to expect the baby revolution. G. Stanley Hall had already in the 1880s started lecturing about "child development," emphasizing the changing physical structures and attitudes of the child. He was followed by reverberations from Europe of the work of Freud and his followers. But in America the impact of John B. Watson's behaviorism preceded the full force of Freudianism. Watson taught that except for the primary impulses of fear, rage, and hunger the child came into the world a *tabula rasa* on which the parents and culture could write what they wished. This put a heavy burden of anxiety on the parents, made all the more onerous by the Behaviorist injunction to the parents to decide on routines for the child, treating it like any other object of conditioning, but otherwise to restrain themselves and leave it alone, not encumbering it with the irrelevancy of pampering love.

The Freudian period proved even more fertile of anxieties. The parents were taught that childhood is the fateful molder of the later personality, with the Oedipus romance as its decisive crisis. This was followed by the revelation that the first five years, those discussed in Freud's *Three Essays on Infantile Sexuality,* were the crucial ones, and that afterward everything was closed; then the determining period was narrowed to the first two years, before the formation of language; then the first year, before weaning; and finally, the first six months, with some schools pushing back even further into the intra-uterine period and the trauma of birth. Americans had moved all the way from the Puritan view of the life history as a battlefield on which the virtues were pitted against the Devil to the post-Freudian view of the formation of "destiny in the nursery."

If the fate of the personality was sealed in the earliest phase of childhood, it became crucial to learn what the experts advised on child-rearing. The debate raged around issues like "schedule" as against "demand" feeding, permissiveness as against limit-setting, *laissez faire* as against early socializing, ego-strengthening protection as against the rude preparation of the child for the realities of adult life, "pouring love" into the child as against the exercise of discipline and control. In these debates material was drawn from troubled, delinquent, and even psychotic children, including extreme cases of withdrawal and regression, and from the life histories of schizophrenics, and was applied with admonitory overtones to something like forty million normal children under the age of fifteen. Easy guides for infant care and child-rearing flooded the book market; parents flocked to meetings where psychiatrists discussed "penis envy" and "sibling rivalry"; a whole new vocabulary containing the gobbledygook of child care was added to the American language, and a new technology came into being, to be ranged alongside the other technologies of the machine age.

As with all technologies, it had its roster of "authorities" on whom the conscientious parent leaned. Like every group of experts dealing with life, death, and salvation, this one too became a priesthood, whose oracles were studied for their cryptic meanings. Even when the liberation movement got under way at the turn of the 1940s, the Declarations of Independence from the experts invariably appealed to other experts: "the authorities agree," Americans were told, that little definite and scientific data is known on which to base the sway of the authorities in the nursery and home. Thus the priesthood was invoked to place its stamp of approval upon the secular revolt against the priesthood.

But it was a healthy skepticism that came to change the cultural climate in which parents lived. They had oscillated between fads, alternately repressing and expressing their parental longings and rages, until their natural confidence reasserted itself and the recoil swung them back to the attitudes of the 1890s, when parents had worried less and mixed their permissiveness with a measure of discipline. The snake was coiled full circle, tail in mouth. A residual reliance on the authorities still continued, except that the parents now listened to the experts who tried to repair their basic confidence in themselves. Studies were now made of groups of "normal" and "healthy" children, emerging with the discovery that they had been reared and disciplined with a variety of techniques, but whichever technique it was, had been applied with consistency. Parents began to relax their anxieties and trust their instincts. So sensitive a barometer of the new moods as Lewis Mumford, in his *Conduct of Life,* stated the problem of the growth of personality as one of the "increase of effective love," with the real problem being "how to make ourselves capable of love and ready to receive love." Not only had the cycle come full swing but a new one had started, its anxieties centered not on the fateful early events inside the child's psyche but on the dehumanizing of all personality—adult and child alike.

This is not, of course, wholly new. Much of the anxiety directed toward the child had always sprung from the insecurity of the parents about themselves and their society. Some child experts speak of the "good child in the bad culture," as if what happens to a child is always the result of bad cultural situations and pressures, and never of its own predispositions. One finds the same premise, in more ironic form, in Brock Chisholm's foreboding that despite all the care lavished on children they "may turn out to be the same kind of people we are." This conception of the child as a Noble Little Savage possessed of an artless innocence which is corrupted and distorted by civilization, and also the attitude that the child is always the victim, the adult always the guilty fumbler, bumbler, meddler, and destroyer, are part of the cult of the American child. The other strands in the cult are that the child must be "understood" instead of being allowed to become a functioning part of a functioning family and community; that he must be continually "adjusted," (which seems curious if it is true that his fate is sealed early); that the culture and the future are founded on him; that he will have it better in a better future and will himself *make* the future better. Thus the American overvaluation of the child is compounded of equal parts of guilt, anxious concern, and cultural hope.

There is evidence that this portrait is heavily weighted toward the middle-class family and is less true of the working-class one. Certainly there are differences of family and childhood experience that measure differences in income strata, class, residence, prestige, and ethnic derivation. What is true of a child brought up in a Back Bay house in Boston, or a Park Avenue apartment in New York, or a suburb outside of Chicago or Los Angeles will not be true of one brought up in a Kansas City slum or a California migrant camp or a Negro quarter in Detroit. In *The Father of the Man,* Allison Davis and Robert Havighurst studied child-rearing in different income strata in the Chicago area and found a greater freedom and less tension in the attitude of slum mothers to their children than of middle-class mothers.

Throughout the nation the class posture is a distinctly different one: where middle-class parents are restrictive—on sex, cleanliness, toilet training—the working-class parents tend to be permissive; where middle-class parents are permissive—on talking back, on discipline—the working-class parents tend to be restrictive. The working-class mother never quite caught up with the reliance on experts, nor could she afford the psychotherapists and play therapy. There were enough troubled and sick-minded children coming out of the lower classes, especially from the economically deprived strata and from the Negro and Puerto Rican ghettos, to cause a delinquency problem; but the roots of the delinquency—the alcoholism of parents, family disintegration, the resentment at a lower social status for the ethnic group, the eagerness to overcome the economic and ethnic gap by short cuts—were different from the roots of the middle-class cases of delinquency, which were more likely to be overpossessiveness and overprotection. The feeling of the working-class mother about her children was less one of anxiety, guilt, and overconcentration than the sense that they were something of a burden and that housework had become a bore, and the wish to get away for a while to the movies or a TV audience-participation show. Living on a thin economic margin, moreover, the working-class children had a necessary role in the family as helpers in a common struggle, and in the large families the older children had the added function of caring for the younger ones. In the case of middle-class children there was little of this functional sense: instead of finding their useful place in the family, the children tended to feel that the family existed for them, and too often the parents failed to disabuse them.

It is possible to see the general American overconcentration on the child as marking a phase in American social and class history. Many writers seem to put the blame for what we may call the child panic on the psychologists and psychiatrists. But the deeper source lay in the rapid social mobility and the consequent emotional insecurity of the families that were pushing up into the middle and upper classes. Of the millions of American families which moved into these classes in the years between 1915 and 1955, many had come from farms and small towns, many others were of immigrant stock—most of them second generation, some third. Having achieved income and position, and seeing limitless vistas ahead, they hoped their children would keep moving upward and fulfill the dreams they had themselves fallen short of. In many cases they had broken their ties with their own parents or felt that the old experience would not apply to the new situation, and so they had no traditional rules for bringing up their children. It was into this vacuum that the "experts" and "authorities" had moved.

Seen thus, the focusing on the child was a stage in America's total development, but in a period of constant movement into the middle class it took its character largely from the emotional problems of that class. Yet when compared with corresponding classes in other cultures, even the rural and working classes shared it, since all of them shared the culture's emphasis on success and happiness and the belief that if you took the right path you could achieve both. In a more traditional culture the stress on raising children might have been on the mastery of the tradition in a mold of civic discipline. In a more materialist culture (i.e., one in which material achievement was harder and therefore counted more deeply) the amassing of money at any psychic cost would have been stressed. But the dreams that American parents dreamed for their children were those of mobility (success, partly in money terms, mainly in terms of education and prestige) and happiness. In the past two or three generations the emphasis in the perspectives of parents for their children shifted from material well-being to psychic well-being. The main concern was to give the child a good start in life and to protect him against the social jungle outside the family until he could "adjust" to the demands it would make on him. If he was "badly adjusted" he would prove a failure in "popularity" and happiness. The ultimate disaster might strike him—a "nervous breakdown."

The trouble here was that the parents became cultural surrogates for the child, building for him a substitute world not always relevant to the problems of emotional maturity, offering him an emotional diet that fell short of what he was capable of absorbing. An example was the children's stories and the difference between the kind that parent and school fed them and the kind for which they themselves reached out. The orthodox children's literature in America presented a pastel, two-dimensional world in which only cute or trivial things happened, with surface experiences and unreal emotions. Even the great children's myths that have carried over from other cultures—like the Grimm and Andersen fables—became suspect to modern parents, perhaps because they reached too far to the deeply emotional folk experiences of the human family. There was a quality of primitive terror in these experiences, and American parents avoided them as the Medusa head that might turn the fragile child to stone. Even the Bible stories came out prettified. As for native American children's literature, except for the Br'er Rabbit versions of the widely dispersed "coal-tar baby" myth and the Paul Bunyan "tall stories," America produced little to compare with the continental cultures, where the peasant families made the child part of their own imaginative world. The world of Mark Twain's boyhood America, with its cave and hidden treasure, its tramps and drunken fathers, its raft on the Mississippi, has not been paralleled by any contemporary creations of the same imaginative power. The American child sought a substitute for these in the culture heroes of the popular arts—of baseball, the prize-fight ring, the TV screen. He also reached out, with a perversity that was the despair of his parents, to the heroes of the comic strip and the comic books, to the masks of evil and terror and Superman derring-do which might heighten the anxieties in him, but which managed to take the place in the child's imagination that nothing else had filled.*

If the parent tries to be the culture surrogate for the child, the child is often the emotion surrogate for the parent. American living, for all its outward gusto, is emotionally unexpressive. To the American the emotional richness of Latins, for example, seems wayward and explosive. It is not that he maintains an emotional passivity, like the Orientals or the native Indians of his own continent. It is rather that the combination of success hunting and sexual repression often starves the emotions. All the frustrated hopes of men and women who have come to adulthood without fulfilling their dreams and drives are poured into the child's upbringing, which becomes a means of vicarious living or reliving for the parents. They seek to fashion the child into their own cherished image, using him eagerly to fill the emotional void in their own lives.

* For folk tales and legends in American life, see Ch. XI, Sec. 3, "Heroes, Legends, and Speech"; also Ch. VIII, Sec. 1, "The Personality in the Culture."

It may be said in paradox that the American parents, and especially the mother, do not begin to live emotionally until the child's rearing gives them function. So deeply felt is this need that a black market for the adoption of illegitimate children usually operates, children often being "placed" in families before they are born, at prices reaching into thousands of dollars. Since Americans start with an intensely romantic ideal of love and courtship, and then find they must live realistically in their marriages, they transfer their romantic fixation to the child, thus preserving their belief in the miracle of love-into-happiness. The child, on his part, instead of developing affectionate relationships with a variety and succession of adults, finds himself often fixing on a particular one. In a small "nuclear" family, often isolated from the outside world, having to narrow his whole emotional life in his earlier years to the compass of his family and depend on it for emotional security, his alternatives are few. This means, as Arnold Green has noted, a "capture" or "personality absorption" of the child by the family, often by one parent. Depending on whether parent or child is dominant, it may be regarded on the parent's side as a love imperialism, and on the child's as a form of juvenile blackmail.

In either event the tyrannies of love are substituted for the less exacting relations of affection, friendliness, and respect. When the parents believe they must mute their own personalities in their anxiety about the ego of the child, the result is a deference vacuum. It is underscored in the case of second-generation immigrant children, where there is a cultural break between the generations, while little in the new culture teaches respect for Old World values. It is also true in situations of rapid social mobility, where parents of humble class origin seek to rear their children on upper-class living standards, or where college sons and daughters recoil from the trade sources of family wealth. Finally it is underlined by the influence of the Big Media, which displace the father-hero with the TV, sports, and other popular culture heroes. The more deference the parents pay the child, the less deference they get from him.

In the already child-centered American family this deference vacuum often brings the family close to a child-centered anarchy. This is not because of indifference or lack of love: the attachments are often intensely demanding. In the American variant of the Oedipal "family romance," with a crisscrossing of the mother's concentration on the son and the father's on the daughter, the emphasis is not on the child's moving toward maturity but on the "staying young" of the parent to remain attractive to the child. This is one reason for the extreme American emphasis on youth. As Jean Cocteau put it petulantly on one of his New York visits, "Everyone in America seems so youthful. They all drink milk, as though they were still near their mothers."

If I have stressed here the cultural anxiety about children, I have not meant to imply that American family life is merely ridden with burdens and drenched in anxieties. In the traditional paternalistic families of Europe, Asia, and Latin America, children were almost without rights except what the head of the family granted them. In the recoil the American family has replaced children-without-rights by children-with-too-many-claims, and the transition to a freer structure of family authority has been attended by pains and near chaos. Yet the effort to replace the bonds of one-sided authority by those of mutual consent has meant a social gain. The crucial experimental element has given a new meaning to the child's role in the culture. In no other culture has the rearing of children been so earnestly approached as a problem to be solved, not in terms of conscious purpose or choice but because it grows out of the whole configuration of American life.

Fortunately, in the mid-1950s there were signs that the child panic, as one might call it, was relaxing, and that the cult of the child was giving way to a new perspective which sees both parents and children as worth attention from each other. The popular child experts, like Benjamin Spock, were those who counseled parents to go back to their instincts and rely on common sense. There was a trend toward firmer discipline and a reassertion of the personality of the parents.

But the problem reached deeper than merely that of freedom of discipline, *laissez faire* or authority. At its core is the question of how young children can best be given an effective start on the road toward growing up, without too many crippling limitations. There were things about this process that Americans had not yet learned, but which they were equipped by many of their traits to understand.

One was the idea that parents educate their children less by what they say than by what they are in their totality—by their body stance, their muscle tensions, their rhythm of life, their anxieties or repose, their fears or courage. If this is true, then it follows that effective love —so necessary for healthy emotional growth—cannot be transmitted to a child by a parent who sets no limits on him and who clearly does not value himself. A child must learn how to deal with freedom as a reality principle, which means that he must learn the nature of the limits staked out for him in the primary group of the family, and the reason for them. He will thus more confidently discover the area within which he can make his own choices, more effectively than if he were confronted by either tyrannical or too indulgent parents. As he finds both his limits and his freedom, he will feel that the parents have helped him find them and will take it as a mark of their concern and love for him.

This is linked with another idea—that of the effective model and the sense of identity. During the early years when the child forms his crucial image of himself and of his future role, he may miss the firm model of a self-respecting adult and encounter instead the anxiously wooing parent who pours love into him, exacts it in return by a love imperialism, demands always that the child prove himself worthy of love, and makes the granting or withholding of love the guerdon or punishment of the child's behavior. With this blurred model, the child is bound to fumble in his efforts to discover his identity. Parents who have lost their own identity in their anxiety about their child cannot expect thus to help him find his. Similarly those who live in the shadow of their children—who sacrifice so that their children can spend, or stunt their own lives in order to live in the right neighborhood for their children, or hold a loveless marriage together "for the sake of the children"—cannot complain if their children get a distorted view of personality.

Finally there is the idea of the child's having a functional place in the family. One of the losses in the passing of the large, rural, traditional family was the loss of function for the children. But there are utilities to be rendered, functions to be performed, and crises to be met in the family type of every era, and this applies as much to the new American family as it did to the old. When the child helps to perform these utilities, fulfill these functions, and meet these crises he learns to fuse responsibility with freedom. At the same time he will be measuring himself against brothers and sisters, and other children of his age outside the family; and he should encounter as many adults as possible so that he may have a choice of models broad enough to give him the freedom to find his own identity and individuality.*

4. Growing Up in America

THE GROWING UP years are not easy in America because the choices to be made are so many and the securely prescribed areas of conduct relatively few. I shall deal in this section not so much with the biological

---

* See also, on the family and mental health, Ch. IX, Sec. 8, "Life Goals and the Pursuit of Happiness"; on the problems of TV and "comic books" for children, Ch. XI, Sec. 2b, "The Reading Revolution," and Sec. 6, "Radio and TV: the World in the Home." On the folk heroes of the American child, see Ch. XI, Sec. 3, "Heroes, Legends, and Speech," and Sec. 4, "Spectator and Amateur Sports."

universals involved in growing up as with the interplay of the biological, the emotional, and the cultural in the American frame.

In his early years the child is mainly concerned with the discovery of his body and its functions, and with his emotional relations to his parents and family. He "catches on" to social experience as well, but it is largely filtered and mediated, as if by osmosis, through the envelope of the family. As the child grows into adolescent, and the adolescent in turn into the young adult, the agencies by which his personality and character are shaped broaden out from family to community, from immediate kin to the whole social milieu. These are the years of the "latency period" in the Freudian description, when little is really latent, followed by the period of puberty and its immediate consequences. They are the years when the young American, bursting with discoveries and searching always for new experience, reaches outward from the family to the peer groups of school and "camp," to street gangs, cliques and clubs, sand-lot and water-front sports, dating and dressing, odd jobs, summer adventures, college, and military service.

The American family does not let go of him early but tries to hold on as long as possible, recognizing his need for self-reliance but anxious to protect him and eager to enjoy him. Unlike the British, it does not push the boy abruptly into the "public school," where he is away from home and wholly on his own, subjected to the cruel rules and taboos of his fellows. It allows the boy or girl to make the break away from home by easier stages—at first in the "summer camp," whose use is growing among middle-class parents, then perhaps in a private boarding school (still confined to the upper income groups), finally (for the boys) in the Army. This blending of home and away-from-home experience is one of the things Americans are learning to do best, although one must remember the large number of still overprotective parents who cling to the child, and the equally large number of working-class parents who let him drift off into a job of his own as soon as he has passed school age or been in a trade school. There are also the middle-class parents who send him off very early to a military academy or school on the convenient theory that he will learn independence and discipline but actually to shift to someone else the burden of the decisions about his rearing.

On the formal level the qualities he is taught, both in the family and the peer groups, are those that will fit him best into the competitive race: to be resourceful, industrious, persuasive, friendly, popular, an easy mixer, strong of purpose, inventive, self-reliant. The emphasis in a mobile society built on immigration is on outdoing your parents—getting a better education, marrying into a better social stratum, making more money, living in a better neighborhood and with higher living standards. The traits stressed are those of packaging your abilities in the best salesman's fashion, and of a constant quality of *push.* These traits, inculcated and renewed in each generation, take on a cumulative strength in the culture. They leave little room for the withdrawn and reflective personality, who may be detached from the competitive struggle. In fact, when American parents or teachers find these traits in a boy, they may regard them as signs that he is "badly adjusted" and in need of therapy.

Some American scientists, like W. H. Sheldon, see the physical constitution as shaping temperament and even character, and a number of biologists stress the "built-in" mechanisms which set the frame for all growth. Yet there is little of determinist thinking in the attitude of most Americans toward the growing-up years. The pluralism of stocks, the high living standards, and the strides in medicine, all tend to disarrange any preconceived frames of physical growth for Americans and put the stress on will. Similarly, the stress in popular thinking about personality and career is not on the limits but on the potentials of development. "Be a king in your dreams," said Andrew Carnegie to the young American. "Say to yourself, 'My place is on the top.'"

Thus the young American grows up to see life as a cornucopia spilling its plenty into the lap of those who are there to take it. Within the limits of his family's income, and sometimes beyond it, there are few things denied to the growing son and daughter. Their attention is focused on what they can *get,* first out of their parents, then out of life. The growing girl learns to get clothes and gifts from her father and later from her husband. The boy fixes his attention on a succession of artifacts, from a toy gun and an electric train to a car, preferably a convertible. Their levels of aspiration stretch to infinity. Often the parents are blamed for this pliancy and indulgence, yet it is also true that the culture, with its sense of plenty, contains the same principle of infinite possibility. It tells the boy that if only he wants something hard enough, even the Presidency of the nation, he can achieve it. This spurs his striving but it also sets unrealizable goals, since his capacities may not equal the tasks he sets himself, or his class and status handicaps may be too crippling. Thus he misses the sense of security which one gets from the compassable. No limits are set to his goals, and often he reaches for incompatible sets of goals. Rarely does he learn the tolerance of deprivation or the recognition of limits which are a matter of course in less dynamic cultures and which exact a lesser psychic toll than the sense of infinite possibility.

Such an oceanic sense of possibility has its elements of strength for the boy or girl in growth. The feeling of impasse that so many of the youth of Europe have, in cul-de-sac economies where the job chances are narrow and they feel they must break through doors shut against them, does not crop up often in America. It is hope and not hopelessness that runs like a repeated chord through the growing-up years. They are the years in which heroisms are dreamed, tight-lipped resolutions made, values first crudely formulated. The emotional life awakens in all its tumbling confusion, the imagination ranges far, the lights and shadows of the moral life are accented, the shapes of good and evil take on their most intense forms. Anything is possible, and everything is fraught with far-reaching meanings. There is a sense of limitless potentials, of obstacles to be overcome by a surpassing display of energy and talent. At home, as in school, the archetypal prizes held up are the big ones and the stories told are the success stories. There is a constant demand for vitality, in season and out, regardless of whether it is charged with meaning. The emotional dangers that the young American runs are not those of apathy 'or despair but of anxiety about success or failure. He finds it hard to keep from wondering whether he is swift and strong enough to win in so exacting a race. Even within the minority ethnic groups, with their residual sense of status restrictions, the young American feels the pressure to succeed within the standards of the minority mold, or even to break out of it—especially to break out of it. And if he fails he cannot assign the failure to his goals or society but only to himself.

Growing up with the assumption that he will "make his mark" and "knock them dead," he is rarely allowed to forget that he lives in an expanding civilization in which he must accomplish "bigger and better" things. Just as he is enveloped by the sounds of cars, trains, planes, so the symbols investing his life are those of speed and movement, violence and power—the symbols of competitive drive. They don't have to be preached to him: they come through the culture-in-action. He picks them out of the air—from how his family behaves, from what his teachers and schoolmates say and what he reads and hears, from the men and careers held up to him for emulation.

Asked for more than he feels he can fulfill, he comes in turn to ask more of his family and milieu than they can fulfill, with a resulting insecurity and bleakness of mood. He turns to his age peers to find with them the expressiveness and sense of kinship not to be found among their elders. Their families may be too distraught to pay much attention, or too protectively concerned with providing for their children's outward wants to be able to gauge their inner nature with wisdom. An adult society, with churches that seem distant and "preachy" and with spinster-staffed schools that seem only an extension of the nursery, offers little that exacts loyalty or heroism from young people who are hungry for both. Their hunger arises from the fact that when they are torn away from the primary ties to their parents there is no corresponding growth in their confidence of their own strength. They yearn for the sense of belonging which will restore those primary ties, and they attach them now to agencies of their own peers.

Into this vacuum come the teen-age activities, some of which amuse the elders, while others worry them. Among the first are the hero worship of the gods of popular culture, the love affair with the TV screen, the calf-love obsessions that turn the teen-agers "girl crazy" or "boy crazy," the jazz or jive madness that "sends" them. Less amusing are the "hot-rod" frenzies in which they court mechanized suicide, the escapades of bored baby-sitters that break into the headlines, or the sexual antics of the high-school "non-virgin" clubs which shock parents and teachers without jolting them into an understanding of their emotional sources.

There is a passage in Thomas Wolfe's *You Can't Go Home Again* describing "the desolate emptiness of city youth—those straggling bands of boys of sixteen or eighteen that one can always see at night or on a holiday, going along a street, filling the air with raucous jargon and senseless cries, each trying to outdo the others with joyless catcalls and mirthless quips and jokes which are so feeble, so stupidly inane, that one hears them with strong mixed feelings of pity and shame." Wolfe asks "what has happened to the spontaneous gaiety of youth," and answers that these youngsters "are without innocence, born old and stale and dull and empty . . . suckled on darkness, and weaned on violence and noise." In his *Studs Lonigan* novel sequence James Farrell shows similarly the social violence and cultural emptiness which condition the emotional bleakness of a boy's life on the city streets.

Yet in his formative years the city boy, especially from the working class, learns more—bad and good—from the gang than from any other group except the family. The gang is a group on the margin between rebellion and crime, forming a clannish community in play and war against parents, elders, teachers, police, and rival gangs. Sometimes it is a harmless effort of normal youngsters in a disturbed and impressionable life phase to huddle together for human warmth, sometimes it is a desperate attempt to channel floating aggressions. The gang brings into the emotional vacuum of the boy's life a structure of authority which makes demands on loyalty, on spartanism in the face of adversity, even on honor and heroism of a sort; above all, on a sense of acting together. That is where the boy learns crudely and even brutally the mystery of sex, the warmth of friendship, and the heady sense of prestige gained not through class position but through strength and natural leadership. It is ironic that the lack of effective codes in the larger society should leave the gang codes as the only substitutes: or perhaps these are only negative parallels of the middle-class codes from which the boys (most of them coming from the lower classes) feel themselves shut out as from an Eden; and so they turn the Eden upside down into a Hell. But even the gang codes prove tawdry and worse as the gangs move over the margin into the pathology of violence and rape and crime.

Not many young Americans follow them that far. But most of them look back to the adventures of their all-male peer groups as their time of expressiveness. It may be that the gang gatherings on city street corners, the loitering counter at small-town drugstores, and the crossroads taverns in the rural areas where you smoke and buy cokes and play the juke boxes are for American boys the playing fields of Eton.*

What is true of the gang for the urban working class is also true of college for the educated classes. It is remembered as the Golden Age of their lives. It has relatively few economic pressures and is the last phase of growing up, just before the boy breaks wholly from the tutelage of family and local community and goes off on his own. It makes its demands in terms of prowess, popularity, and prestige: intellectual content in most American colleges is secondary to friendships, fraternities, "contacts," "bull sessions," sports, and the furious crossfire of campus politics and extracurricular activities. The boy can wreak some of his strongest drives on college life, including heroisms and hero cults, fierce intellectual loyalty, combativeness, the sense of honor, the straining of nerve and will for a cause which at the time seems real enough to evoke an effort beyond the human. In most college novels, as in Scott Fitzgerald's *This Side of Paradise,* there is always an Amory Blaine—a grown man who goes back nostalgically to the time at college when he caught a forward pass and wooed a beautiful girl. They may be mock battles and mock victories, a preparation for something that in the end fails to come off. But here too, as with the gangs, the later remembrance of these rivalries and loyalties reveals them as an outlet for youthful energies that the growing boy does not otherwise express.†

What happens in the process of growing up in America is an emphasis on the individual that results in a feeling of separateness with-

* For more on the teen-age gangs, see Ch. III, Sec. 9, "City Lights and Shadows," and Ch. IX, Sec. 5, "The Disorders of a Society."

† For the college as a sub-culture, see Ch. X, Sec. 3, "The Higher and Lower Learning."

out the quality of distinctiveness. The growing boy (or girl) is taught by the whole cultural environment to assert his individual self, and the way he is expected to find himself is by breaking his ties with his family and rebelling against parents, teachers, neighborhood. In the process he wrenches himself free of bonds and codes, only to find himself isolated from what had given him security. He comes to miss most the sense of belonging, or relatedness, to the "primary ties." Much of the feeling of loneliness in the growing-up years comes from this sense of loss and isolation, and the yearning to recapture the primary ties from which he has been too sharply separated.

In the families where there is close contact between parents and children, in a freewheeling, affectionate atmosphere, these ties can be recaptured adequately enough to tide the child over until he has made ends meet in his personality struggle and is on the threshold of adulthood. It is true that the old cohesive relations, which families had when they did their work together and had to stick together, have largely been lost. But with the new leisure there is a chance for families to spend vacations together, go on automobile trips together, watch and discuss the media programs together, talk and play together. This does something, if not enough, to alleviate the sense of isolation. It is in the families where this closeness of relationship does not exist that the yearning to belong is left unsatisfied. They may be families where both parents are at work, or where the father is hardly ever at home, or where alcoholism or grinding poverty or lovelessness creates a destructive vacuum. At the other extreme they may be families which, even with a high living standard and an outward show of affection, are emotionally empty. It is from the families at both these extremes that most of the cases of failure in the growing-up process come.

I must add the factor of discrepancy between class perspectives. Most commentators on American life have moved away from discussion of class experience and class conditioning. Yet much of the human material that comes to grief in American society will be found in the working class, in the case of youngsters brought up in working-class families and working-class neighborhoods but surrounded everywhere by middle-class and leisure values. That is to say, their subculture is a working-class subculture, while the larger culture is a middle-class culture. Their whole sensate world of striving and their glory dreams are middle-class strivings and middle-class dreams. Yet they find themselves shut out of the world they long for, much as Adam and Eve (as I have suggested above) were shut out of Eden after the Fall by a flaming sword.*

* For an elaboration of this theme, with respect to the "mutiny of the young," see Ch. IX, Sec. 5, "The Disorders of a Society."

Thus the "opportunity line" which exists for young people in America, given its rapid class mobility, is accompanied by an insecurity line—or better, by an isolation line. There is scarcely a culture in the world where the longing to belong in the growing-up years is as intense, and where the failure to satisfy it is as destructive of the potentials of personality.

When a culture trains young people there is much that it tries to train out of them. Growing up thus becomes not only a process of *inculcation* of the socially approved virtues, but—shall we say—of *exculcation* of the socially disapproved ones as well. Thus there is a need of exculcating the primitive sense of equality with which children start. In the early years before the social norms begin to harden, as I have noted above, the children of every stock and religion play together: only later does the society teach them what is expected of them. Lillian Smith, in her novel *Strange Fruit*, pictures a beating a young Negro mother gives her small son when he has dared dispute something with a white boy: she must show him that his mortal life is in peril if he does not observe the man-made fence between him and those who hold supremacy. And from the side of the whites, Miss Smith has told how "the mother who taught me what I know of tenderness and love and compassion taught me also the bleak rituals of keeping Negroes in their places—which could be applied to other minority groups as well." The mingling of status groups becomes less frequent as the child moves through the grades into high school and college, and goes dating and dancing and week-ending. The growing-up process in America involves the loss of the social innocence with which children start.

Similarly, the growing boy is taught to develop mainly his vendible talents. "I couldn't stand Asheville now," Thomas Wolfe wrote in one of his remarkable letters to his family from college. "I couldn't stand the silly little grins on the silly little drugstore faces. I couldn't stand the silly little questions of 'What're you doing now?'—and the silly little 'oh' and the silly little silence that follows when you say you are writing."

For all except the strongest-willed youngster (and Wolfe was one) the cult of the vendible means the exculcation of other talents and impulses. Neither family nor school can protect him against these tyrannies of the culture: for are they not themselves caught up in the same tyrannies? So they discourage "woolgathering" and "daydreaming," which lead nowhere, get you into mischief, don't pay off as action and business do. Rarely is a protective sheath thrown around the contemplative impulses that are as crucial in the growth of personality as the impulses to action. Rarely is there support for the brooding exploration of the whole enriching range of emotional life in a culture as complex and paradoxical as the American. In the end the children become themselves the taboo-enforcing censors, and anyone violating their canons of orthodoxy is an outsider, a "square," a "goon."

This is reinforced on the side of the parents by the pressure to "mix well" and be "popular"—but within socially acceptable groups. The impulse toward popularity flows at once from the cult of success and the shaky self-image of its devotee. It narrows the complex realm of personal relations to the art of manipulation. Tragically, it cuts the child from his fellows just at the phase where such a severance is most destructive to him. For the tissue of human connections cannot be reduced to the manuals of popularity. Which may explain why, in the most glittering of cultures, so many Americans are scarred—as Fitzgerald's Jay Gatsby was all through his years—with the sense of having lost what they have so insistently been taught to capture.

To strive for popularity, yet to feel alone and unwanted; to hunger for use, yet to go unused; to carry the sense of comradeship like a burning city in your heart, yet to have to extinguish it in order to keep your position in the hierarchy; to replace the idle impulse and the brooding intensity by the attitudes of Faustian power, of violence, of speed and aggrandizement: for all too many youngsters this is what growing up comes to mean.

Aside from what the society tries to inculcate into him or exculcate from him the growing child has a double task of preparation: for making a living and for making a life—one, the problem of finding a career; the other, that of finding himself. In the case of the girl—except in the instances where she is in earnest about a career—the two preparations are merged into the preparation for marriage, which is viewed as both a living and a life. With the boy the pressures are to give primacy to making a living, so that he finds himself thrust into choosing the job or career for which he must train before he has gone far enough in his emotional unfolding to have much basis for choice. The result is often a gnawing conflict between what is expected of him and what he finds welling up within himself, rebelling against the plans for him.

Both processes—of finding himself and finding his vocation—involve the boy's spur-winning. He measures himself against the strength of his age peers, of his older brothers, even his father. A time comes when his father notes proudly that the son has caught up with him in stature and strength, and even towers over him. He has a "paper route," mows lawns, shovels the snow off sidewalks, does odd jobs after school; in the summer he perhaps overestimates his age to pick up some quick money in a factory or at the shipyard. He saves his money carefully to buy some prized possession, with the calculation of a junior capitalist. He starts learning the trades, skills, tactics out of which competence and success will later come. In American society his expected growth as a person takes largely the form of the kinds of spur-winning that lead into a career and into business habits. And the way he is assessed by his elders and assesses himself is also in those terms.

The American theory is that a boy "chooses" his job or career. For many, however, the choice is narrowly restricted. Sometimes the limited choice of jobs, especially on the lower-class level, is frustrating and embittering. Sometimes, however, it may be a saving fact physically, since it does not burden the boy with the sense of inadequacy which a middle-class boy has when he finds few choices where there are supposed to be many and comes to blame himself. To avoid this self-doubt he may be more precipitous than is good for him as a person. The process John Milton described, of seeking what was to become his epical life work—"long-choosing, the beginning late"—is a luxury that most Americans deny themselves. Even at college American students (like German university students as well) are anxious to choose the courses that will lead directly into their chosen career and thus give them a start in the competitive race. Only a good deal later do some of them come to understand the cost that the personality had to pay for their career haste. But in a culture so nervously paced and so poised for the big killing, any other choice is difficult.

On some scores it is easier in the American case than in others. There is not the same need to rebel against a tyrannical father, or the same galling sense of being caught in a blind alley with no chance either to develop or show one's abilities. On other scores it is harder. The boy (or girl) comes to biological maturity a good while before either of them comes to emotional maturity. The society—permissive in so many other respects, restrictive in this—cracks down on sexual expression before marriage. In the case of the boy, the military draft has recently become an organic part of the life cycle: while the sexual taboos are relaxed for military personnel, the all-male society and the severe discipline of the Army conflict; and the need to postpone both career and marriage during the most crucial years is a chafing one.

From the parents' behavior and their responses to his own the child forms the crucial image of himself. He has a need to understand and emulate his father's job, as the girl has a need to play house, but a job at "the office" is a hard one for the boy to use as an effective model, and often the substance of the job slips out of the child's mind and all that remains with which he can identify himself is its aura of respectability or power. In an earlier society, where the struggle with nature and the conquest of animals had meaning, the boy's spur-winning might take the form of the hunt or the fishing expedition. Americans today who read Faulkner's long story, "The Bear," or Hemingway's *The Old Man and the Sea,* find it hard to attach much meaning to the hunt for the killer bear or the apprenticeship of a boy to an old fisherman, since it has no parallel in their own experience; yet they are drawn to such stories because of this vacuum in their growing up.

Their own spur-winning experiences are likely to follow more closely the pattern of the American boyhood in *Tom Sawyer* and *Huckleberry Finn,* with the swimming hole, the fence-painting, the treasure hunt, the bloodcurdling oaths of gang secrecy, the cult of male separateness from females. One of the striking facts of this Mark Twain tradition of boyhood is its emphasis on both the "badness" and the maleness of boys. Every American boy is expected, as he grows toward his teens, to be intractable about soap and water, to look (whatever his family's means) like a ragged and tattered waif, to resist the blandishments of school and teachers, to be awkward with little girls and flee their advances, and to regard any dancing class or other frippery as a conspiracy of the Devil. This tradition of the good-bad boy is one the elders cherish as part of their recognition that the American household and school are governed by a regiment of women, and its antifeminine bias (included in the anti-"sissy" complex) is the price they pay for continuing that government. From the boy's side, however, it is part of the necessity for breaking away from this domination and of finding who he is.

In the process his reading helps him, and it is notable that he seeks out the reading about bad men (the old frontier and bandits have given way to whodunits) and science fiction. In the city life that has replaced the farm and frontier, spur-winning gives new forms to the old activities—learning how to smoke and swear, hearing about sexual exploits, showing athletic prowess, taking part in school pranks and escapades. One can view this as the impact of crowded city life on the boy, but it is better to view it as part of the quest for identity. "Who am I?" the boys asks, and his answer is first given in terms of being part of a male peer group.

Then in the teens comes the further process of awakening identity, in which he splits himself from even his earlier boys' groups. He is breaking away from the ways of a child but has not yet learned the ways of an adult. He goes to parties and dances, he needs spending money, he works and saves in order to learn his own nature: for it is his own job, his own car, his own girl, that he now wants. Even in his courtship he is perhaps less concerned with erotic aims than either Freudians or Americans generally suppose and more concerned with that ceaseless problem of probing and parrying by which adolescents of both sexes come to discover their identity. They want their own sense of rightness, grope for their own codes. This is where they come to feel most split away from their elders, and that struggle between the generations which the parents find so intolerable an ordeal emerges most sharply. In fact, the two generations become almost subcultures, the younger one finding both its goal and its modes of expression within the new social situations more readily than the older one.

It is in the teens, unhappy as they are because of this struggle and the difficult quest for identity, that all the new wealth and excitement of social experience in America impinge on the young people. They experiment with adult modes of consumption, learn the terrifying ways of speed and travel, enter into the kingdom of the Big Media. They are able to move about the country, trying themselves in a variety of occupations. The typical American first novel, for example, is likely to be a novel of these apprentice years, and every first novelist puts on his dust jacket the calendar of his job and migratory experiences, just as he is likely to focus his story around his boyhood, with its trials and triumphs. The critics may continue to call for a novel of manners or of mission, but the kind the American first writes is either a novel of adolescent unhappiness or one of the tribulations of early life and loves, and at the end of it the hero has finally discovered who he is.

I have not meant to say earlier that America crushes every diversity and irons out the nonconformers. The adolescent finds ways of evading many of the cultural pressures and often grows adept in the process of finding his own growth pattern in spite of them. Success and power and competitiveness are not the only American growth goals, even though they are the principal ones. For they are only one aspect of the individualist ideal. The other is self-fulfillment, and the young Americans (sometimes a minority) who learn how to know themselves are on the way to learning how to become themselves.

They develop, in the process, a life style which they partly shape and which partly is shaped for them, inside the frame of their work, their class, their locale, their culture. They have first to find some models on which to mold the personality through imitation: they find them in their parents, older brothers and sisters, teachers, age peers. Out of these and out of the personality images presented to them in the culture as a whole they form an ideal image of self toward which they probe experimentally as they play one role after another, fitting each of them on for size and looks in the mirror of others as well as of themselves.

But in this copying and playing of roles a dangerous clash takes place

—the clash between what I want to call the *cultural image* of self and the *identity image* of self. The cultural image is the one borrowed and imposed from without, and inevitably it tends toward conformity. The identity image is one that emerges from the quest for a distinctive self-hood and is the product of a continual interplay between the individual's need and whatever measure of cultural elements he is able to absorb in growing up. The clash is always there because there has been no culture in history in which the individual has been able to ignore the cultural demands and pressures. But where it is too great the result is alienation on the one hand, or else an overreceptiveness to the cultural pressures in order to resolve it, or else some form of breakdown. Yet there are unmistakable evidences that the child growing up in America is learning to make the resolution tolerably well. When he does, there is a richness of the final personality style which is itself both the index and product of the difficulties encountered in the process of growing up.

5. *Courtship, Love, and Marriage*

LOVE COMES IN the American's life cycle as the harbinger of life's ful-fillment, with a violence of expectation characteristic of a culture built on promise. "Love is sweeping the country" ran a tune in *Of Thee I Sing*—the Kaufman-Gershwin musical which was a satirical take-off on star-spangled politics and on the national pastime of being in love with love. More than any other people, Americans believe in love and make a cult of it, lose themselves in it and feel lost in it. Every French school-boy, it has been said, dreams of becoming a *flaneur*, happy in his numerous erotic affairs. The young American schoolboy is more likely in his daydreams to see himself the sole and successful wooer of a creature who combines Hollywood contours with the steadfastness of Penelope; and the young American girl is eager for a handsome young man who will be coveted by her rivals but will cherish only her forever. They expect obstacles in their quest: how could there be victory in the scheme of romantic love if there were no obstacles to be overcome? But they expect also to triumph over them, as witness the moot Hollywood formula: boy-meets-girl, boy-loves-girl, boy-wins-girl. If the girl whom the American middle-class or working-class boy is likely to meet has not always the long-limbed, busty perfection of the "pin-up" girls or the prize winners in the annual "Miss America" contest, the courtship is nonetheless carried on within a frame of idealization and is suffused with a springtime eagerness.

The roots of this need for love go back to the emotional structure of the American family. The child, asked constantly whether he loves and assured he is loved, learns that love can be a weapon in the emotional power struggle of the family, to be granted as reward or withheld as punishment. Thus he comes to test the success of his relations with the outside world by whether he is accepted and loved, and is more swayed by a panicky fear of deprivation than by the expectation of love and bounty. By becoming an early life goal, love is made part of the calculus of failure and success.

The emphasis on parent-child love yields, in the life history, to the later romantic love, and perhaps some of the psychic mechanisms are carried over from one to the other but with a strongly different emphasis. The romantic ideal came into the Western tradition from the Middle Ages, when it emerged as passionate love. Denis de Rougemont, its most learned and astringent historian, traces it intricately back to the Cathar heresy, which held that the Devil had intervened to complete God's work. The current of passionate love came into the main stream of Western sensibility through the "medieval courts of love," the love lyrics of the Troubadours and Minnesingers, and the Tristram-Iseult story.

It is pretty clear that this ideal of passionate love came as a reaction against the anti-erotic strain in Christianity and the cult of virginity, and that it was a convenient literary way of providing a cover for the new erotic energies of European society. It started as an aristocratic and feudal idea, but it flourished best in the middle-class societies of Europe, giving rise to the European novel and drama. It reached its most intense form, however, in American culture, with its novels about romantic love, its slick-paper magazine stories, its Hollywood formula movies, its radio "daytime serials." Neither the heritage of guilt left by the Puritan tradition nor the mechanization of American life—the two great enemies of romantic love—has succeeded in destroying it. The Puritan heritage, with its *Scarlet Letter* pattern of shame and secrecy and its furtive pleasures stolen in the face of harsh community punishment, led to a recoil which actually strengthened the hold of the romantic cult. As for mechanization, love in the American machine age is still, in its ardor and intensity, closer to the old romantic tradition than it is, let us say, to the new Puritanism of another machine culture—that of Soviet Russia.

The crux of romantic love, in this larger Western and American frame, lies in two elements: the conviction of uniqueness and the submission to fatality. Behind the quest for the love partner is the premise that there can be for each person only the exactly right "one person." Love in America is thus an intensely individualist emotion in an intensely individualist society. The fatality idea, on the other hand ("falling in love"), is a deposit left from earlier societies where star-crossed lovers drank love potions and thereby committed themselves to the destiny of their love. It is true, of course, that the romantic ideal of the ordinary American is borrowed not from the Tristram-Iseult theme and the Arthurian cycle but from Hollywood; yet the Hollywood image, in turn, is taken from the fiction writers whose obsessive theme reaches far back. What the Tristram-Iseult legend has shed in its sea change is its death sequel and its tragic overtones. Instead of committing himself to death, the American lover surrenders to the irrationals of his passion, but the target is life and happiness.

Thus the American has taken over a medieval theme and has shaped it to the temper of his society, combining the strain of fatality out of an earlier era with the strain of uniqueness out of his own. The American stamp, however, has become so dominant that even the fatality emerges largely as uniqueness.

One reason the American is obsessed with romantic love is that it is the only socially acceptable secular escape from the iron individualistic prison of himself. It is one of the few instances in which the philosophy of free will is swept away by a sense of submission and fatality. Here is the point in the life cycle of the American when he ceases to play God in his own universe, losing himself in a passion of surprising power and in the play of forces that for once seem to be not of his own choosing but to possess an awesome inexorable quality. The surrender of the American to love has about it for the moment an appearance of completeness not frequently found in other cultures. In each great Henry James novel—*The Portrait of a Lady, The Ambassadors, The Golden Bowl*—the sophisticated detachment about love comes from the foreign partner to the match, the sense of love as compelling and absolute comes from the American. There are suggestions in James that this may be because the American brings to whatever he touches a fresh and generous energy that contrasts with the somewhat jaded feeling of the European. It is more likely, however, that the impulsion comes not from surplus energy but from the loneliness of the American and his impulse to escape from it into a secure harbor where he can find the absolute of love with his loved one.

This overvaluing of love is reflected in contemporary American fiction. The creative novels dealing with love take it seriously as the great business of youth—in many cases as the only lasting life value. But one must add that it is also a literature compounded of violence, disillusionment, and frustration. In Dos Passos's documentary trilogy of American society, *USA*, the characters (mainly on the make) use love as a commodity of exchange, and are incapable of anything but its hollowest forms. Ring Lardner's short stories (as in "The Love Nest") lay bare the heartlessness behind the show of heart. In Faulkner the symbols of love are often associated with the violence of incest and rape. In Farrell the *Studs Lonigan* worthies gang up on a girl in a drunken brawl and use her in succession. O'Hara portrays with compassion, in *Appointment in Samarra* and *10 North Frederick,* and with more violence and disillusionment in *Butterfield 8* and *A Rage to Live,* the defeat and dissipation of the generous impulses of love. Even in Hemingway, whom two generations have found deeply moving, the symbol in *The Sun Also Rises* is that of a mutilated incapacity for love, in *A Farewell to Arms* it is the cup dashed from thirsty lips, in *Across the River and into the Trees* it is that of a mingled ritual of war and eroticism. I cite these almost at random, not as an accurate transcription of the operative force of love in American society but because the reflections of American attitudes in the minds of sensitive and creative writers, however transmuted, are an index of what people believe about themselves.

In an acquisitive society, moreover, love somehow is charged with the power and violence of the acquisitive drive. It is as if the two circuits had become crossed, and the way Americans feel about money and success had got tangled up with the way they feel about love. There can scarcely help being some continuity between economic success and erotic success in a culture where both are viewed as forms of prowess. Consciously or not, the American carries over into his erotic life the drives of his economic life. This is especially true since the days of courtship are also those in which the adolescent is preparing to make a start in his career or in the Armed Services. On the threshold of manhood, he is concerned about proving his strength to himself and to the world. With a sketchy sex education, casually acquired through the family or distorted in transmission by the "gang," he is often a prey to feelings of inadequacy and guilt. In such instances he cultivates love not as a creative relationship between like-minded people but as a testing ground for his virility. Courtship becomes a matter of personal success in a quest whose goal is that of proving oneself. In marriage also the man who is a hardheaded competitive businessman or corporate executive outside comes home to play the role of tender husband and father. Money talks during the day, but love is expected to dominate the evening and night. These shifts from one mode of personality to another make it hard for many Americans to discover their sense of themselves on which the art of love depends. The sense of loneliness, the hunger for fulfillment, and the search for identity become tangled with the compulsion to power.

For Americans, courtship is localized in the later adolescent years. By the age of seventeen, when the American boy is likely to be a high-school senior, he is (at least quantitatively) somewhere near the threshold of his sexual powers; and at eighteen the pattern of his later sexual behavior has been pretty well foreshadowed.* Thus the five or six years after seventeen, when the boy and girl seek a mate, are also (at least for the boy) the years of fully awakened sexual interest and activity when both partners are looking for the new personal experiences and sexual adventures. This double purpose and the crisscrossing pattern of biological drives, social pressures, moral intuitions, and inner anxieties make these years at once troubled and eager. These are the years of "dating," of dancing and driving together, of "necking" and "petting," of "going steady" or "playing the field." However constricting they may seem to the young people themselves, they are years of great freedom, if one compares the American culture with most others. Since an American strives to marry for love this involves a far greater variety of courtship experiences than where marriage is arranged or moves in highly traditional grooves or is severely held within class lines. The American conception of love-as-encounter is possible only in a society of relative physical and class mobility and the free mingling of the sexes.

There are considerable class differences in courtship practices, ranging from encounters on campuses, at proms, house parties, and "deb" parties and night clubs at the top levels, through movies, "church socials," and bathing beaches or resorts at the middle levels, to amusement parks and taverns at the low-income levels. "Pickups" are likely to be somewhat casual on the lower level, sophisticated on the top ones, most frowned upon in the middle classes.

Yet what all the classes have in common is the institution of "dating," which foreign observers regard as strikingly American while the Americans themselves take it for granted. To "have a date" is the raw material of courtship; to date the same partner a number of times is a sign of being smitten; to change dates frequently is, on the other hand, a token of being heart-free; for a girl to be "dated up" is proof of being "popular," and (as on any market) the high rate of demand enhances the value of the commodity. Thus, in what Willard Waller has called the "rating-dating system," there is a reciprocal valuation process by which dates are made on the basis of popularity and sexual attraction, but both sexual attraction and popularity increase with the number of desirable dates each partner has.

What has interested students of American society even more than the rating system is the ritual of granting and withholding favors. The boy is expected to make advances, to boast of his prowess and conquests, to exult over each step of kissing, "necking," "petting," and to aim at the

---

* For a further discussion of sexual behavior during courtship and marriage, see Ch. IX, Sec. 7, "Society and Sexual Expression."

ultimate sexual surrender. The girl is expected to yield just enough to keep her partner interested, yet to withhold the final sexual boon. Put in this way American courtship seems loveless and joyless, a calculated exercise in prestige and self-satisfaction. It has been ironically described as such, particularly by observers with an anthropological training, who view it as they might the rituals of a primitive tribe. Geoffrey Gorer has called it a "competitive game of chess," and Margaret Mead has defined a successful date as one "on which there is no petting at all, but merely a battle of wits, of verbal parrying, while the boy convinces the girl that he is so popular that he has the courage to ask for anything, and the girl convinces the boy that she is so popular that she has to give nothing." Compare with this the more common view, shared chiefly by anxious parents and teachers, that young Americans even of the high-school age are teen-age Casanovas and Liliths, experts at seducing and being seduced, members of "non-virgin clubs," practitioners of the wildest promiscuity, little monsters who are wise in the ways of contraceptives and old before they have grown mature.

Each of these divergent pictures has enough core of truth to make it believable. The violence of some of the adolescent sex behavior is the result of rebellion against home and school repressions, and embodies an effort to use sex as a weapon of power or as a way of buying personality acceptance. The mechanical elements of much of the dating complex—at once loveless and sexless—go along with any ritualized behavior.

But it would be a mistake to consider this a meaningless ritual. Much of dating involves the effort of each partner to find his identity—to discover the limits of acceptance and rejection, to exchange experience with an age peer who shares his problems and perplexities, to explore the corners of another's personality, and therefore of one's own. Both the boy and girl know the human and social costs of too easy a conquest. Their "necking" seeks to avoid the emotional entanglements of a liaison, without complete abstention. It is their way of setting limits for themselves and mediating between the conflicting pulls of the biological impulse and the social code. Dating is thus a way of welding in courtship the need for marriage choice with the impulse to experiment. Obviously this requires at best a high degree of skill, and what some have viewed as heartless calculation in a mechanized society may be seen better as the diplomacy and statecraft of courtship, including power politics, strategic maneuver, cold war, and the peace that passeth understanding.

The attacks on dating and the defenses of it have both lagged behind the actual institutional change. The dating pattern, without being replaced, is being supplemented by a petting-and-pairing pattern which is really a form of early, steady, and sustained dating. Those acquainted with American college life have observed the growing tendency of sexual inhibitions to break down at the last moment, especially for girls seeking emotional security and the knowledge that they are desired. "Necking" has been to some extent replaced by what Kinsey called "petting to climax." In fact, this is the most marked of the very few changes in the pattern of overt sexual behavior in American life since the "sexual revolution" of the 1920s. Kinsey's figures show that by the age of twenty almost half the college-level boys have taken part in such petting, while this applies to less than a fourth of the grade-school-level boys at that age, and that the frequency on the college level is three times as great. The same study shows also less frequent intercourse as part of dating than on the grade-school level. Assuming that the college-level partners set standards of courtship which are followed by the others at a time removed, one may hazard that young Americans are seeking a way of expressing their sexual drive while maintaining technically the community forms and the sense of limits.

There seems also to be a growing tendency of daters to "pair off" very early and for extended periods. Dating in the strict sense of rapidly shifting fencing matches is being replaced by the "steady dating" where a boy and girl stress continuity rather than experiment. The "pairs" may last during a whole college year, or even during most of the four years; more and more frequently they are found even in the early high-school years and may stretch on after college, during the years when the boy is in a professional school or trying himself at a job. Usually, though not always, they lead to formal "engagements." What they represent is something distinctly this side of the experimental "companionate marriage" which was so moot an issue in Judge Ben Lindsey's time; it is a semi-companionate of two young people who have no living quarters together and who may restrict themselves (often they do not) to "deep petting" with both its satisfactions and frustrations, but who nevertheless are together almost constantly and are recognized as a "couple" by their friends. Especially in the early high-school years the result may be precocious sexual involvement (which is the basis for the stand that the Catholic Church has taken against it in parochial schools), or it may often become an *égoïsme à deux* which narrows social experience long before the marriage itself. Yet often also it is a working compromise between the necessity of postponing marriage and the wish for a constant compatible partner. It must be seen as another expression of the craving for psychological security among the younger Americans.*

I have spoken above of the debt of American romantic love to the medieval ideal. The great difference is, of course, that in medieval cul-

---

* For more on moral codes and the succession of the generations, see Ch. IX, Sec. 6, "Morals in Revolution."

ture romantic love was a frill to embroider the institution of chivalry and a make-believe ritual under whose cover the women of the knightly order could get release from the bleakness of medieval marriage. It had its being outside the marriage vows and was in fact hostile to the marriage institution, which was a product of caste and church and which excluded romantic love. But in the American case romantic love looks to marriage as its fulfillment. Pouring so much into courtship and expecting so much of marriage, Americans find themselves frequently disillusioned, as witness not only the divorce figures but the disgruntlement and smoldering conflict in many of the ménages that hold together. The slick-paper love stories generally end with orange blossoms and wedding bells: beyond that, all is silence; but American novels about marriage are usually problem novels. It is not that the path of love is smooth in the courtship novels: by its nature it cannot be, for romantic love feeds on obstacles; but in marriage, the love obstacle turns into conflict, frustration, and often a sense of desolation. In courtship the obstacles arise from an outside source—family interference, religious or class differences, economic difficulties—and the lovers face them together; but in marriage the obstacles become conflicts *between* the former lovers inside the marriage relation, and the feeling of facing them together is dissipated.

This may explain why Americans associate the idea of romantic love only with the premarriage years: afterward they are likely to speak of love ironically as of a deflated ideal or of a pleasant but foolish dream. The young wife has perhaps had in her mind an idyl of marital suburbia acquired from magazine fiction and the movies. The husband finds perhaps that his earlier image of his wife as June Allyson in an apron is jarred by the reality of crying babies, economic worries and tensions that make sexual understanding difficult. The result is the well-known marital "letdown." Yet it is characteristic of Americans that neither husband nor wife wholly discards the romantic ideal. The wife continues as its principal carrier, reading the novels and poems, seeing the movies, continuing the daydreams of a not-impossible-he. The husband, with more preoccupations outside the home, may plunge into his job, haunt his club or lodge, or find on "back streets" the concealed liaison which suggests that he has not abandoned the love ideal. More often perhaps than the critics are willing to admit, the partners resolve their conflicts and find a depth of epic quality in love-as-marriage that they did not find in the lyrical love-as-encounter. In other cases a merely tolerable working solution is reached, with a grudging working arrangement inside the marriage tie and sexual adventure outside, or else with frustration and neuroticism as the steep cost of the maintenance of the tie. More and more frequently divorce is the outcome. But the rate of remarriage among the divorced is so high as to suggest that Americans get divorced not because of disillusionment with marriage itself but because they believe in it deeply enough to want to be part of a successful going concern rather than a bankrupt failure.

It is idle to urge Americans, as recent moralists and "marriage counselors" have done, to abandon the ideal of romantic love and base marriage upon more rational and stable concerns. In a much discussed polemic novel, *Marjorie Morningstar,* Herman Wouk has his heroine turn away from her illusions about romantic love to a safer, more secure and more rational marriage that fits better with the traditions and way of life of her Jewish ethnic group. Certainly the novel expressed a current counter-trend to the great Western myth of fatality and uniqueness in love. But it is something of a misnomer to speak of the "cult" of romantic love in America. It would be better to call it part of the folk belief, which hangs on tenaciously in the American mind even when there is so much to shake the faith in it, very much as the belief in a wholly open-class system hangs on. In fact, there is some relationship between them. The American believes in romantic love not only because of the mystique of fatality but also because of the sense of choice and possibility it carries. What both partners hope to get from a love marriage is happiness; and while at any time it seems that only one person can bestow it, the finding of that one person is an act of free will appropriate in an open-class society, to be tried again if it fails.

Obviously the freedom of marriage choice is also largely myth, at least for many. There are class limits, income limits, race limits, the accidents of geographic and ethnic closeness. You may dream of a rich, handsome, and gallant corporate executive who will swoop down to woo you, but you actually marry the boy down the street, whose mother knows your mother and who gives you his high-school fraternity pin to wear. Only the very attractive and successful have anything like a large range of choice. Many young men, in their awkwardness and fear and their income limits, settle for something less than Helen of Troy. For many middle-class and lower-class women, who don't want work or a career of their own, or are fearful they will lose their value on the marriage market, marriage becomes a way of finding a means of support and getting status in the group. Sometimes money becomes important enough to cut across the field of choice, as with Lily Bart in Edith Wharton's *House of Mirth.* Lily Bart will not marry merely for money if it will demean her socially, but she has been brought up to the view that a marriage of love *without* money is an intolerable fate: thus her values are conventional values, not money values as such, but under the conventions there is a money base.

There is also another and deeper sense in which marriage choice is not free: even in the most romantic matches the American is likely to seek out the partner who is selected not by his conscious choice but by stronger unconscious currents which flow from his character structure and his early life history. What applies to courtship applies also to the years after marriage, as attested by a symposium published in the mid-1950s on *Neurotic Interaction in Marriage,* in which a number of psychiatric writers point out that two neurotic partners may out of their unconscious drives make life intolerable for each other or—by some Freudian destiny—may luckily find that their neuroses intermesh.

Since Edith Wharton's day Americans have increasingly made happiness the test as well as the goal of marriage. Were I to say that this has been a movement from the romantic to the hedonic ideal, I should be distorting both of them somewhat, since the romantic ideal in the American setting always had an element of pleasure in it, and the quest for happiness does not end with the libidinal pleasure principle. Yet it would be at least a half truth. The American wants happiness out of marriage, and he believes in a love marriage not because he makes a cult of love but because he thinks there can be no happiness when love is wholly lacking. This leaves Americans vulnerable to the charge sometimes made, that marriage is but a joining of two *egotisms*—a mutual orgasm pact between two self-centered individuals, maintained not until death do they part but only as long as desire remains fresh.

But this is unfair. Marriage in America is no more to be summed up as a transient pleasure pact than as a permanent maintenance pact. In part, it has elements of both. But mainly it is an earnest partnership quest: on the part of the man, for someone with whom he can achieve self-expression and build an effective going concern; on the part of the woman, for self-expression through children, a home and the status it brings, and the figure she can cut in her group. These are human goals but not ignoble. And in their restlessness they express the dynamism and mobility of American society.

A study by Geoffrey Gorer (*Exploring English Character*) concludes that an English husband wants his wife to be a good housekeeper, an understanding and faithful person, and a good cook—in that order. The English wife wants her husband to show understanding, a sense of humor, moral qualities, fidelity and generosity. There is little stress on beauty and attractiveness, on financial ability, on sexual qualities: only in the prosperous classes does the question of sexual compatibility in marriage assume any importance. By contrast a successful American marriage is closely linked with love, with financial competence, with continuing elements of attractiveness, and with sexual compatibility and fulfillment. Thus the British marriage criteria have to do more with personality factors and with making everyday life smoother, while the American criteria (as I have suggested above) are at once more romantic and hedonic.

The American situation has its drawbacks. American husbands and wives develop anxiety about whether they fulfill each other's expectations. Young married people read the popular sex and marriage manuals, both to prepare themselves and to overcome whatever difficulties they may encounter. Often the manuals are helpful in dispelling ignorance and fear, sometimes they produce more anxiety than they allay. American husbands and wives tend to worry overmuch about their sexual adequacy and performance, just as they worry overmuch about bringing up their children. But these mark the growing pains in a rapidly shifting cultural pattern—a sign that Americans have not yet found themselves in their happiness society and wonder whether they are getting out of marriage everything they should be getting.

Nor do they complain about sexual incompatibility just because they make sexual gratification an end in itself. If they did they would seek for gratification outside, as husbands did in European cultures for centuries, when prostitution served to bolster the institution of "respectable marriage." The reason this is less true in America (professional prostitution has grown less important in America) is because they feel that sexual response is crucial for love and for personal expressiveness, and that both are integral to marriage as a going concern. The American husband does not pose as the family boss, as his grandfather did; and he wants much more out of marriage than the sense of power and authority. Similarly, the American wife is coming to feel that marriage is a joining of partners, each of whom is a person in his own right. Both of them see a chance to enjoy life and find personal expressiveness, and they don't want to be left out.

This unwillingness to be left behind and cheated out of important life experiences is assuming importance in the minds of Americans whether in or out of marriage. It may be the negative phase of the happiness quest, but it is not negligible. It is too easy to see American life wholly in terms of power and glamour and the sexual experimenting of *avant-garde* intellectuals. One thinks of Sherwood Anderson's novels and of the stories in his *Winesburg, Ohio,* and the record they offer of the hunger of obscure people for a sense of connection. America is, at least in part, millions of such obscure lives, seeking at least one event that will transform the humdrum into the meaningful. That is why Nathanael West, in his novel *Miss Lonelyhearts,* chose as the central symbol for his novel a newspaper hack who runs an "Advice to the Lovelorn" column and—still possessing a capacity for empathy—suffers every day the crucifixions of the agonized letters he gets. More often these columns, which are an established part of the American press, are saccharine in content, and sometimes cynical in their conventional values, advising the questioner not only to forgive her *fiancé* or understand her husband, but sometimes to resort to callous strategies in holding him. For all the vaunted camaraderie at the service of American life, the individual has a sense of isolation. It is the fear of loneliness which also helps account for the high rate of remarriage after divorce, and for the forlorn men and women who join "Lonely Hearts Clubs" because they recoil from evenings spent alone and want someone to talk to.

Despite the fears of marriage decline commonly expressed by commentators and moralists, the marriage rate in America has not shown signs of falling away, as in the often invoked case of the Roman Empire. While population increased 14½ per cent in the decade of the 1940s, the number of married couples increased almost 24 per cent. With all the cultural forces (the rise in living-standard imperatives, the longer span of professional and technical training for careers, the required period of military service) pushing in the direction of marriage postponement, the "propensity to marry young" seems if anything to have more than held its ground. The median age at which American girls marry has dropped to 20.4 years; the husband is likely to be only two or three years older. Some moralists have attacked this as a sign that the American girl doesn't want to work and is eager to be taken care of as early as possible; others interpret it to reveal an eager sexuality on the part of both that cannot wait to be fulfilled. But, as I have noted, the Kinsey figures and the growth of the "pairing-off" pattern show that the sexual impulse is not wholly unfulfilled even before marriage, and the increase of married mothers holding jobs to supplement the family income shows that they are not entirely lazy.

The propulsive force leading to early marriages must be sought elsewhere. In both cases the clue is the pursuit of happiness. For the woman it is likely to lie in a home, children, and social status, for in the woman's case—far more than in the man's—marriage is the determiner of status. For the male the impulse to marriage is not—as Freud suggested, with his eye on the European social structure—to emulate the image of the father's family authority. For the American male it is rather the desire to be part of a family which is a going social unit, with a wife who is a good homemaker, a good mother, a good hostess, and wears clothes well; and on her part, with a husband who has a good job, is respected in the community, is a good father, and has a circle

of friends with whom the couple can "spend the evening." Both partners
are told often enough that the marriage may fail, but they take the risk
because for them the stakes are crucial.

The hazards of marriage in America are real enough. The boy and
girl about to be married are constantly advised to make sure of their
ground. A pamphlet intended for high-school and college students lists
—among the "test of love"—the test of the "electric spark," of "time,"
of "separation," of "companionship," of "crisis situations." But, with
all the warnings, mate selection (as I have suggested above) is more
likely to reflect hidden and unconscious drives. It is part of the new
folklore of American marriage counseling that the best marriages are
those based upon what has been called the "myth of common interests," and that husband and wife ought to concern themselves with the
same range of interests and friends. Yet this is to stress the rational
approach in an area in which the demands of the irrational cannot be
overlooked. In marriage, as in love, it is the covert drives rather than
the overt rationalizations that are commanding. The sense of the uniqueness of the loved one is likely to be a recognition of the striking extent
to which he (or she) meets one's psychic hungers, which in turn are the
unconscious product of the whole buried life experience. When these
psychic needs and values dovetail and supplement each other there is a
"meeting of true minds"; when they clash or are irrelevant to each
other the result is conflict or vacuum. A successful marriage must thus
manage to meet not only the conscious purposes and life goals of the
two partners tolerably well but also their unconscious drives.

The probing of marriage failure in America has been intensive. The
principal causes usually listed are incompatible temperaments, loss of
attraction of the partners for each other, infidelity, money worries, and
quarrels. The statisticians have even charted the most dangerous years
of a marriage, when divorces are most likely to come. But it is a mistake to think that these tensions arise wholly from the marriage relation itself. They reach further back to the life cycle of the partners,
each of whom is likely to reproduce in his marriage role the characteristics he developed during childhood and adolescence in the emotional
structure of his family. They reach back also to the society itself—its
economic demands, its tense rhythms, its stress on glamour and security,
on sensuality and power and success. One thinks here of John O'Hara's
best fictional portrait—that of Julian English in *Appointment in
Samarra*, beset by economic difficulties which help turn his sexual life
into barren and violent gesturing, until the fear of losing both his
business and his wife's love breaks up his marriage and drives him
toward a tragic suicide. Thus the marriage relation has to bear the
total burdens of the personality and the society.

There are no people in the world who make greater demands upon marriage than Americans do, since they lay greater exactions upon it and also expect greater psychic satisfactions from it. They do not make the necessarily right demands, but whether right or wrong, they don't settle easily for a small fraction. Again the comparison with the Gorer study of the English may shed some light. The English husband and wife don't ask for the stars plus sexual fulfillment; they don't restlessly demand happiness, nor do they worry so much about extramarital errancy. The difference between the two situations may be the difference between a more established society which has resigned itself to a limited economy and a diminished place in the frame of world power and a more swaggering society with an expanding economy and a feeling of unlimited life chances.

Yet alongside this earnest quest for happiness one may find in American culture a bitter folklore on the tribulations of marriage. There is a mythology of comic-strip quality dealing with the bored husband and the bridge-playing wife, the hardened husband who pays the bills for the many hats his wife buys, the tired husband who comes home from the office and doesn't take his wife's conversational gambit seriously, the husband with a roving eye and wife with a prim policewoman's vigilance, the husband who talks ironically of his wife as "my better half" and "my ball and chain," the husband and wife who are engaged in a cold war of extinction and survival. This cruel public banter reveals a good deal more than it intends. The ritualistic buffoonery of a people is likely to convey in its overtones more than a hint of the accumulated frustrations and aggressions that are to be found along with the swagger and the power.

The more serious concern is with the problem of marriage fidelity and infidelity. I shall deal later* with some recent findings on extramarital sexual behavior in America. What is of interest here is the paradox of a culture in which sexual infidelity has become extensive but is not taken lightly, and is a matter of great anxiety and concern. This again is part of the experimental pattern of American marriage, in which the evasion of moral standards is not a matter of moral disintegration but of a quest for personal fulfillment within a shifting frame of morality. As with most other problems, Americans tend to view infidelity as a question of mental health, usually as part of the crisis of the middle-aged male in his search for sexual reassurance. The psychiatrist is likely to say that it is only the compulsive types of infidelity that present a serious problem, since their compulsiveness makes them self-destructive—and therefore destructive of others as well, and of the whole family pattern. In other words, instead of thinking of infidelity

* See Ch. IX, Sec. 7, "Society and Sexual Expression."

as a rigid moral category Americans tend to think of it in terms of what it does to the personality and to the web of relationships. Yet this does not mean, again, that Americans take it lightly. When it is dealt with in an American novel, unlike a French novel, it is treated as a crisis matter, where the failure to resolve it leads to the destruction of the personality. This is also the way American novelists treat the problem of incompatibility within marriage, with an emphasis on the emptiness it leaves inside the personalities of both partners.

Judged in terms of viability, a large number of American marriages are failures. The high and steadily increasing divorce rates* have given great concern to commentators who regard it as the sign and proof of the disintegration of American culture which will make it topple as the Roman Empire did. Some writers have compared divorce with bereavement and the divorce trauma with the trauma of the mourning period. As William Goode puts it (*After Divorce*), they think thus because they tend to feel that divorced people ought to suffer for breaking up the romantic American image of marriage. Studies like Goode's, based on field interviews in Detroit in 1948, should lead to some revaluations of long-standing American myths about divorce.

Foremost among these is the tendency to attribute divorce to the willfulness that comes from wealth and materialism, seeing it as a special middle-class disease which is rampant among the spoiled and neurotic who can afford it, while the simple lives of the working-class folk are presumed to be less riddled by it. No doubt there is some relation between the laxity of divorce standards and the laxity induced by American creature comforts and material values. But divorce in America is not the prerogative of the rich. The available studies show that there has been an inverse relation between class membership and the divorce rate: that the service and white-collar groups and the unskilled labor groups show a higher divorce rate than the skilled labor, professional, and managerial groups. Thus the divorce rate is higher among the lower-income classes and is lower as the income rises.

The reasons are complex. Partly they are economic: when it is hard to make ends meet in family maintenance, the irritations pile up and the clashes of personality are heightened; similarly, a comfortable economic margin may make many irritations tolerable. Moreover, a wife in the upper-income groups may find that there is a wide gap between her living standards within marriage and her living standards as a divorced woman (this does not take account of the mounting alimony figures), while a working-class wife may find that she can do almost as

* I have already touched on the subject of divorce in my discussion of the family: see Sec. 2, "The Family As Going Concern."

well with a job of her own as with a ne'er-do-well husband. The evidence shows, at any rate, that divorce is not due merely to the self-indulgence of the rich or of the Hollywood elite whose marital difficulties enliven the press headlines and the weekly picture magazines. It is true that studies of families during the Depression years show a shifting of divorce figures with the changes in the business cycle, with a lower rate in the "hard times": the grimness of economic reality presumably pulls the marriage together and dispels fancied hurts and secondary grievances. But a closer study, by Mirra Komarovsky, shows that the Depression strengthened certain types of families but weakened others. Thus, economic pressures, whether in good or bad times, are rarely to be seen as final causes of the breakup of marriage or of its strengthening: they are important mainly as they express themselves in the psychological postures of the two partners toward each other. It may be true that marriage is largely a maintenance contract, but it has a psychological as well as economic structure. It is the shift in American attitudes, rather than the materialism or prosperity of the economy, that accounts for the changes in the marriage institution.

The question of the divorce trauma is an elusive one, and certainly no one will underrate the impact of anxiety, sleeplessness, and heartache. But the evidence fails to back up the belief that divorce in America is shattering to the personality. Goode found that once the final separation was achieved, even before formal court action, the psychic shock tended to lessen, and when dating began again the post-divorce adjustment was on the way. While the statistics are not wholly clear, most divorced persons (as I have said earlier) pay marriage the homage of trying again, and in many cases they make a success of it where it had been a failure before. This is not to say that the divorce experience improves the stability of marriage. The figures show that a marriage is more likely to break up if one or both of the partners have been married before than if they have not. Yet it remains true that for the divorced woman her second marriage is likely to prove more stable than her first.

The greatest anxiety that Americans show about divorce is about the children of divorced parents. There is no question that they suffer in divorce—not necessarily from the divorce itself but from the conflict it involves and from the separation from one of the parents, generally the father, since American courts, by a curious quirk of gallantry and a tenacious belief in mother love, almost invariably award the children to the mother. Yet the mothers who remarry report their belief that the lives of the children are better than they were before the divorce, when they were the victims of an atmosphere of lovelessness and conflict.

The important shift in American attitudes about marriage has been the tendency to believe more deeply in the possibilities of finding marital fulfillment. This carries with it an experimental feeling toward marriage, with divorce seen no longer as a final disaster but as a temporary setback in a continuing quest. What is relied upon to hold the marriage together is not the religious and social prohibition of divorce, or even the extreme legal difficulties placed in its path in some American states (notably New York), but the feeling of inner unity that expresses itself in the sense of a going concern. In its deepest currents of feeling the American consciousness is now more apt to condemn a marriage entered into or continued without love, than even a love relationship outside of marriage. A Soviet professor recently charged that "bourgeois marriages are mere business matches in which love gets dirty and trampled." This was even wider of the mark than most Communist utterances on Western societies. The burden of concern that Americans feel about marriage has been shifting away from the economic toward the psychological, from the maintenance contract toward the pursuit of happiness. The whole question of sexual activity, which was once considered a phase of moral codes alone and only incidental to the marriage relation, is now viewed as an integral part of it, and sexual fulfillment has become one of the prime tests of marital happiness.

In fact, it is here that American marriage has developed a new area of vulnerability. With the quest for happiness, as with the fight for social equality, great expectations feed on themselves, and every new gain means a more critical view of the gap that remains between reality and promise. The high divorce rate does not necessarily mean that there is more unhappiness than there was in American marriages, but only that there is less propensity to accept unhappiness as part of the eternal frame of things which cannot be mended. Americans have become more watchful of unhappiness and more clamant in their demand for an expressive life. This means a far greater emphasis than ever upon sexual fulfillment, whether in or out of marriage; it means a sharper conflict than ever between moral codes and operative behavior; and it means, for that reason, a resort to the marriage counselor, the psychotherapist, and the pastor as well as to the divorce courts.

The changing patterns of attitude and behavior on marriage have thrown the courts into confusion, as the "crazy quilt" of divorce decisions testifies. They have also thrown the older moral standards into confusion. Premarital intercourse and adultery tend to be regarded as only venial sins: the mortal sin is coming to be considered the lack of a productive life. Someone has remarked that, given the different pace at which the partners may develop, marriage is a "mutual mobility wager." What has happened to the American attitude toward marriage, as it has happened to the family and society as a whole, is a growing earnestness about making the whole pattern work without sacrificing the values of individual independence and fulfillment. The emphasis here is not just on the self-indulgent individual but on an effective partnership. A viable marriage has come to depend on whether the two partners keep pace with each other in their sexual rhythms, their attitudes toward children, their awareness of the world, their structure of values, and whether they "work at" the marriage in the sense of putting their creativeness into it.

6. The Ordeal of the American Woman

RARELY IN HISTORIC civilizations have women been as free, expressive, and powerful as in America: yet rarely also has the burden of being a woman, and trying to be a fulfilled one, been as heavy to carry. That is one of the many paradoxes which characterize the social role of the American woman. Everything in American life seems to conspire to make her a glittering, bedecked, and almost pampered creature, yet also one bedeviled by a dilemma that reflects the split both within herself and her culture. She is torn between trying to vie with men in jobs, careers, business, and government, and at the same time find her identity as wife, mother, and woman. The tussle between them accounts in great measure for the ambiguous place she holds in American society and for the frustrations and neuroses commonly associated with her.

The growing-up years of the girl differ from those of the boy. She is welcomed less enthusiastically: to the low-income families she brings consuming rather than earning power, to the middle-class families she presents the problem of being married off. She is shunted away from the "gang" in which her brothers are accepted and must exchange giggly and self-conscious confidences with "girl friends." She feels left out. Yet she is carefully tended and decorated, taught how to wear clothes by her mother, pampered and worshiped by her father, and given by both a greater degree of independence than in most contemporary cultures. It is, however, less independence than her brother gets: one of the consequences of her training is that her sheltering as a girl by her own family makes her more dependent on her husband after marriage.

She is more closely watched than her brother, by the family of which she is part, by the community outside, and by the censor inside her. Since she is considered the frailer vessel, she must be shielded; since she is to marry well, she must be marriageable; she must be careful not to cheapen herself, not be "talked about," to encase herself in the triple armor of inaccessibility. A small town or suburb, where everyone knows everyone and where the Puritan heritage in morals still lingers, is especially stifling for her. As a result, many a small-town girl seeks the blessed anonymity of the big city. Yet even there she is plagued by her dilemma: with one side of her she wants an adventurous and exciting life, but another voice tells her that she lives in a culture where few women can make a go of it on their own, and where therefore she must find the marriageable male who will invest her with security and status. As for the city girl, especially in the minority ethnic groups, she too is encased in a protective armor of what is "expected" of her.

This means the narrowing of her range of absorptions until they focus mainly on what makes her feminine and desirable. The American male, who specialized in the lamp of power, has left the lamp of beauty to the female. In fact, America's greatest work of art may well turn out to be the American woman, from sixteen to fifty, whether stenographer or society belle, shopgirl or movie queen. She is known the world over for her pertness, her spirit, and her looks, for the contours of her figure, the smartness of her clothes, and the vitality of her person. Some of this derives from the image left by the spread of American movies, but mostly it is the deposit left by her place in her culture. Simone de Beauvoir has said, "One is not born a woman. One becomes it . . . by the ensemble of civilization."

The American woman, who must accept the assumptions of romantic love and also those of the merchandising economy in which the sale depends on the packaging, channels her pent-up energies largely into dress and decoration. She finds here an expressiveness and feeling of power that are not balked as they are in other channels. She finds available in the economy around her an array of fabrics, colors, furs, jewels, cosmetics, and even in the middle and lower income groups she finds copies of expensive items scaled down (almost) to her ability to pay. In decorating and beautifying herself she discovers a talismanic admiration, "dates," popularity, and the right kind of husband, all of which are counted as signs of female success. As she grows older, some of her hopes fade, her jauntiness wilts, and she must work harder to contrive lesser effects, but the task itself she dares never relax.

Out of this arises what the advertising copywriters call the "American look," on the premise that the American woman does have a *different* total look from that of the Roman woman, Chinese, British, Latin, or Russian. It is hard to distinguish the reality from the *imago*, which the movie magazines, TV, the advertisements, and the "pin-ups" have projected, representing the American male's dream symbol. In some ways the image is almost a Petty or Varga caricature, with shapely silk-clad legs longer than the torso, with small waist, narrow hips, long neck, swollen breasts, pert features, dilated and inviting eyes, blond or red hair, sinuous body, and an expression at once vacuous and sophisticated, helpless and predatory. In actual statistical measurement and look the average American woman falls short of this dream, as the range of motley sizes and shapes in women's clothing testifies. Yet the cultural ideal is often approximated in height and slenderness, ankles and legs and contours, and even where it is not its hold is tyrannous.

The effort to approximate it has absorbed generations of skill and concentration, the suiting of techniques to taste and to the prevailing modes and moods. I shall discuss later* the shifting codes of fashion that have governed the cycles of American taste in women's dress and profile from the crinoline-and-stays period, to the Gibson girl, to the interwars flapper, to the current norm I have tried to describe. Within these larger and baffling cycles there are the whims and tyranny of the short-run changes in fashion on which whole industries may be built and by which they may be ruined. For the Goddess of the Right Thing is an exacting one. She demands specialized clothes for city and week end, for work and play, school and church, for beach, ski resort, mountain resort, for the seasons and sub-seasons, for evening and afternoon, for the shopping trips themselves—so that by an endless circuit one must dress correctly in sallying out to buy the things which will dress one correctly. She demands also the matching of the elements of the ensemble and the accessories, including hats, hair-do, shoes, stockings, handbags, gloves, jewelry, and furs. On the level of the Big Money this Byzantine profusion is, of course, achieved without much difficulty. Where it hurts is in the middle and low income groups, but even there —by smart buying of low-priced "copies"—one manages to respond to the unrelenting demands.

Being "smart" means, for the American woman, staying within the frame of fashion but adding her own individual touches. Her skirt length must be neither too long nor too short, her suit cut must be in style, her hairdo must not depart too far from the fashion magazines. All this involves an array of handbooks of fashion, from the expensive fashion arbiters like *Vogue* and *Harper's Bazaar,* through *Charm* and *Seventeen,* down to the picture weeklies and even the cheap movie magazines: in fact, the movies themselves serve many women as tips for clothes. The editors of the fashion magazines have become female Napoleons ruling their domains. Yet even they can rule only by giving their subjects room for individual creativeness. The lipstick, compact,

* See Ch. IX, Sec. 3, "Manners, Taste, and Fashion."

hatbox, shopping list, become part of a freemasonry which give scope to the most impassioned rivalries, out of which come the artistries of a minor art, perhaps, but one carried on at a fever pitch.

The arts of advertising and salesmanship lose no chance for encouraging this rivalry. If the American woman were in danger of forgetting a moment about clothes and cosmetics, lingerie and nylons and "foundation garments," deodorants and perfumes, the advertisers make sure the lapse is brief. "It is our job," said the head of a trade association of women's retail stores, "to make women unhappy with what they have in the way of apparel and to make them think it is obsolete." From every side there are focused on her the cozenings and admonishments of advertising, using every technique from open seduction to concealed terror. The models are languorous, the images sensuous, the language tactile and erotic.

Yet for all the tyrannies and blandishments with which she is surrounded, the American woman remains the center of the constellation. Are we wrong in sensing some of the qualities she thus expresses: *triumph* ("see the richness of my setting"), *boredom* ("what's new? what's different? what's a bit shocking?"), *craftsmanship* ("I'm an artist, and I am my own work of art"), and *seductiveness* ("take me—I'm trim and smart and the slightest bit expensive, but that's all the more reason for taking me").

The miracle is that with all this world of make-believe she has not succumbed wholly to its tyrannies. She has kept a measure of independence, wrecking many a big investment built on the premise that she would follow the command decrees of the great designers and clothes manufacturers. Even in the elite arts of dress and decoration, steeped in the vocabulary of exclusiveness, the democratic note has been sounded ever more insistently. The language of the fashion magazines and the advertising copy has increasingly become that of a democratic snobbery —an exclusiveness that includes shopgirl and stenographer along with debutante and young Park Avenue matron. Mail-order fashions, patterns for those who do their own clothes, mass-production models that are a triumph of cheapness and taste, "home permanents" that have cut into the role of the beauty shops—these are part of the great paradox of the American woman as artist and artifact.

I have already discussed* the strategic role of the American woman as organizer of consumption. But her economic function is only part of her larger social one, shaped by a series of changes so drastic that

* See Ch. IV, Sec. 5, "The Wilderness of Commodities."

they are usually spoken of as "revolutions." The most continuous American revolutionary is the American woman.

First there was the *suffrage revolution,* as part of the long, hard-fought movement for equal rights in which a succession of strong-minded women, in the face of jeers and humiliation, broke into previously barred professions and won the right to an equal education with men, to speak in public, to vote for and hold office. Second, there was the *sexual revolution,* directed against the double standard of morality and aimed to gain for women some of the same privileges of sexual expressiveness as the men had. Coming in the wake of the equal-rights movement, it was a phase at once of the revolt against Puritanism and of the dislocations caused by the first World War. Related to the revolution of morals was, third, the *revolution of manners,* with women shedding their cumbersome garments and adopting form-fitting clothes and revealing swim suits and shorts, taking part in sports, driving cars and even piloting planes, serving in wartime as WACS and WAVES, smoking cigarettes and drinking in public. Fourth, there was the *kitchen revolution,* with mechanized kitchens and canned and prepared foods giving some women greater leisure and enabling others to get industrial and clerical jobs. Finally there was the *job revolution,* which transformed the American working force as it also transformed women's role in the economy. In 1920 there were eight million women holding jobs; in 1955 there were more than twenty-seven million, comprising over 30 per cent of the labor force. For the first time in American history, married women outnumber single women in paying jobs, although most of the women in clerical and professional jobs are single.

One can see these "revolutions" as a succession of liberating movements. They have come in semicyclical form, each of them with a recoil at the end which overlaps with the start of another cycle of liberation. They have come as part of a double thrust of aspiration, with the American women trying to be equal to the men and therefore like them, yet also to be themselves and find their own identities.

On one score the American woman has not had to struggle for her economic position. While there are no hard figures, the usual estimates are that women control up to 70 per cent of America's wealth, that they have 60 per cent of the savings accounts and are the beneficiaries of 70 per cent of the insurance policies, that they represent more than half the stockholders in the big gilt-edge corporations, that they own close to half of the nation's homes, and that at least three quarters of the nation's purchasing power is funneled through them. The catch is that women hold their purchasing power largely as wives and have acquired their wealth mainly as widows: economically they are disbursing agents, not principals. Or as one unmarried woman has put it with some acerbity: women have trust funds, stocks, and real estate, mainly "because their husbands die early, of overwork for these economic parasites." Not only do American women live longer than men, but many rich Americans who marry for a second time marry younger women who outlive them by a number of years.

But it does not follow, as some would have it, that this has turned America into a matriarchate, or that the American women are idlers who spend their husbands' salaries or clip interest coupons. The real control even of the wealth of wealthy women is in the hands of male trustees, lawyers, and bankers. Few women are directors of big corporations, just as there are few who form government policies. As for the women in industry, most of them work for a living or to supplement a family income too low for decency. Thus American women, like men, are divided between an elite arrayed in glory and a majority who must work for what they get; and even the minority of women who are powerful in their ownership of wealth are functionless with respect to their wealth, because they lack the strategic control of it.

During the first quarter of the present century the American woman strove for equal rights with men: having achieved them, she has spent the second quarter wondering about the result. The struggle for the vote, for the right to hold and transfer property in her own name and to have legal control of her income, to go to the same colleges and professional schools as men, engaged the stubborn and persistent energies of a succession of woman leaders, from Emma Willard, Mary Lyon, Fanny Wright, Margaret Fuller, Elizabeth Stanton, Catherine Beecher, Lydia Child, Jane Swisshelm, to Jane Addams, Carrie Chapman Catt, and Eleanor Roosevelt. There were career women all through the nineteenth century, but the gap was great; in the twentieth it was narrowed. The boos and cheers that greeted the suffrage parades in the early twenties seem quaint now, when there have been women mayors and Senators, UN delegates, and even Cabinet officers, along with judges, doctors, scientists, commentators, novelists, playwrights, war correspondents. To be sure, a few of the "equal-rights" militants still resent the protective social legislation for women, on the ground that to single them out for protection is to doom them to a subordinate role.

But there can be no question of the glowing victories won in the successive cycles of emancipation. In theory, in law, and to a great extent in fact, the American woman has the freedom to compete with men on equal terms: but psychically and socially she is caught in a society still dominated by masculine power and standards. That is her dilemma.

What disturbs her most is a doubt that what she wants most is her rights. However important the legal and economic struggle, it has brought no ease to her unquiet spirit and her turmoil of mind, and so her heart is not in it.

I do not mean to underplay her effect in humanizing the rigors of a society bent on power and acquisitiveness. The great achievements in the history of American reform movements—in civil service, prison reform, labor and social-security legislation, temperance, social case work, settlement houses, slum clearance and housing, public health and movements for international organization—have owed their patience, passion, and compassion to women. These women may often have acted the Lady Bountiful, and sometimes laid themselves open to derision as caricatures in the Helen Hokinson style. But they have been moved—as Helen Keller and Julia Lathrop were moved, Jane Addams and Lillian Wald—by the defeated and embittered lives of obscure people, and they often showed a capacity to see the world through their eyes. Partly this was because their energies, dammed up by the denial to them of careers normally open to men, overflowed into social protest and swept the men along as well. It was Maria Lowell who inflamed and sustained the antislavery radicalism of James Russell Lowell in the *Biglow Papers*. And no small part of the great role Eleanor Roosevelt played in history was to help keep the power aspects of the New Deal in perspective within the human aspects.

Kept out of the full stream of American power expression, the women often had a capacity few men develop to insulate themselves against the ruthlessness of an expanding young nation. Although Hawthorne was contemptuous of the "damned mob of scribbling women," Henry Adams later said grudgingly, "I suspect that women are the only readers—five to one—and that one's audience must be created among them." It is the view of most American college teachers that the girl students keep alive the flame of the liberal-arts education. American music and literature depend largely upon women for an audience.

In a society tending to grow more militarized, American women blunt the sharpness of the obsession with arms and power. Discussing the history of the Spartan state, Arnold Toynbee points out that the men were caught in the rigidity of overspecialization to arms, and only the women in the end could adapt themselves to changing conditions, winning thus the moral superiority over the men and even the political and economic control. This was not the last time in history that men's concentration on power stripped them of their flexibility and gave the women a moral edge on them. But it may also be true, as Stanley Diamond suggests, that in every culture the woman's concentration on child-rearing and the family provides her with a kind of built-in insulation against cultural shocks which hit men when they are deprived of their traditional social roles. Among the Jews of East European origin, for example, torn from the shelter of the "shtetel" (small town) and its culture, the women emerged as sources of family strength and as the practical tacticians in the new competitive struggle of the big American city.

One aspect of the history of ideas is worth noting here. The cycles of women's emancipation came relatively late in American history. Thus American woman's intellectual and social coming of age, and her alertness to the vanguard ideas of her time, came recently enough so that she was able to equip herself with a less obsolete set of ideas than her husband or brother. This does not mean that American women have been consistently more "liberal" than the men; actually women have tended in party terms to divide pretty much as the men have. Often their desire for the security of the family has ranged them against radical political programs; but by the same token they have been more vulnerable to human values, and in each of the major parties have tended to gravitate toward the liberal wing. Unlike the women of continental Europe and Latin America, they have not been swayed politically by the church authority which in those cultures has made the political role of women a conservative one.

However important the humanizing role of the American woman, her creative achievements at the top level have not matched those of the men. There have been good novelists (Edith Wharton, Ellen Glasgow, Willa Cather), poets (Emily Dickinson, Edna Millay, Elinor Wylie), short-story writers (Katherine Anne Porter, Eudora Welty), dramatists (Lillian Hellman), dancers (Martha Graham). But except perhaps for Emily Dickinson none has seemed to break through to the furthest reaches of achievement. They have been good craftsmen, as Jane Austen and George Eliot were in England, and have shown sensitivity, taste, and insight. But the woman who gets a good start in a career or in writing and the arts seems to falter before the goal is reached. The writers I have mentioned have not shown the sustained strength of, let us say, Hawthorne, Melville, Mark Twain, Henry James, Faulkner, Dreiser. One quality that women seem to lack, in a masculine culture like the American, is staying power. They would have to possess greater self-confidence than they do and be free from the psychic constrictions that come from trying to lead their lives on several levels at once.

But this merely shifts the analysis and poses the question of whether there may not be certain modes of creating that are closer to the feminine temperament and for which the dominant cultural drives in

America offer little scope. One could, for example, conceive of an American woman novelist who might be another Henry James, but not of one who would be another Melville, Dreiser, Hemingway, or Faulkner. We would have to conclude that the main drives in American culture are creatively less assessable and congenial to women than to men, and that the "creative component" in women finds less hospitality within the American cultural frame. For the dominant energies of American culture are power-saturated, violence-ridden, filled with pursuits and triumphs, so that the creative woman finds herself cut off from them and less expressive within them. Hence she turns to the novel of manners, to the short story, to the dance, in all of which she can either operate as a marginal commentator on the American scene or express her own form of protest against it.

This does not mean that the American woman belongs, as several writers have put it, to the "lost sex." She is no more "lost" than her husband or her brother, except that she finds it harder to perform her variety of social roles without feeling the full weight of the cultural contradictions that bear down on her. Like men, she has suffered a loss of function in losing the productive place she once had in the frontier and farm home; nor has she been able to replace it with a sense of new power over the environment, as the men have largely done. But it is a distortion to think of her as suffering badly from a lack of function.

If anything, she is bedeviled by too many functions. She leads simultaneously a multiplicity of lives, playing at once the role of sexual partner, mother, home manager, hostess, nurse, shopper, figure of glamour, supervisor of the children's schooling and play and trips, culture audience and culture carrier, clubwoman, and often worker or careerist. Of the two sexes, it is the man who is specialized to making a living or money, or working at whatever productive job he is doing; the woman, remaining unspecialized, becomes the converging point for all the pressures of the culture. The usual portrait in the foreign commentaries, picturing the American woman as idle, wasteful, and pampered, is not one she will herself recognize. If she has lost some of the stamina of her slightly mythical pioneer grandmother, she has had to take on jobs and problems that her ancestors never dreamed of. She is prized and bedecked as never before, is freer of a tyrannical husband than ever, is equal to him before the law, and has had opened to her a range of opportunities and activities that no civilization before has ever offered to a woman. Margaret Mead's studies have made clear the range and malleability of women's interests and capacities in a variety of cultures: she has added the significant comment that even in the cultures where women do the things we regard in ours as men's prerogative, prestige continues to attach to whatever it is the men do. Thus the relation between prestige and sex status cannot be ignored. Yet what the American woman has already accomplished in a masculine culture and the multiple tasks she assumes and performs show that there is no biologically fated block against her achievement or her happiness.

The crux of it lies neither in the biological nor economic disabilities of women but in their sense of being caught between a man's world which they have no real will to achieve and a world of their own in which they find it hard to be fulfilled. Thus Thurber's famous drawings of the "war between the sexes" (where but in America could so savage a conception, so furiously executed, strike so deep a response?) do not reach that most tragic theme, which is the war within women's own hearts. When Walt Whitman exhorted women "to give up toys and fictions and launch forth, as men do, amid real, independent, stormy life," he was thinking—as were many of his contemporaries—of the wrong kind of equalitarianism. The American woman did it, thinking she was doing it to show she was as good as the man. In the sense that she achieved a new kind of freedom of action for herself and the whole family structure, the movement for equal rights and jobs was a fruitful one. Yet the bobbed hair, the latchkey of her own, the cigarette, the cocktail, the ballot, the pay envelope, proved to be symbols of a quest not so much for equality as for identity. Much of her energy may have been motivated, as the more waspish critics have suggested, by envy of the man, and some of it by a hard-driving emulative rivalry which displaced much of her frustration. But she has primarily aimed at discovering who she is, as a woman and as a person.

She has been kept from finding herself mainly because all her cultural conditioning—in the setting of American equalitarianism and the American economy—has been at once to compete with the man and to manipulate him. As she grows up, her preparation is to find the right man for marriage and marry him before her attractiveness and bargaining power have been diminished. What resources she will bring to the marriage are left to the chance of the individual instance. The whole duty of parents is held to be that of teaching their daughters the code of what girls do and don't do, dressing them to the extent of the family means (and sometimes beyond), giving them accomplishments and schooling, and marrying them off well. As to what will happen after marriage, it is assumed that the sum of her wisdom will be to have children (not too many) and look after them, furnish a house or apartment, keep her looks and figure, build a circle of friends, and prevent her husband's attention from wandering too much. The question "Are you happy?" is more often addressed to the woman than to the man and has come to have almost a technical meaning in the American cultural context, as if to say, "Are you content with your domestic arrangements, and are you getting along pretty well with your husband and children?"

What women become is thus largely what they are expected to become by the standards of a culture in which the male is held to be the prized quarry and the female the lucky or luckless hunter. The ultimate disaster for women is to miss out on getting a husband. In college courses on "Marriage and the Family," readings are included on how and when to make the best use of the opportunities for meeting men; and the newspaper "Woman's Page" often runs a series of tips to unmarried women which take much of their predatory quality from the culture; it is the method of salesmanship and business aggressiveness transposed to the area of personal relations. "You're going a bit far, Miss Blanchard" is the heading of a Thurber cartoon showing a weakly protesting male as the woman carries his helpless body to the waiting couch. But the unhappiness of the unmarried woman is less the cultural problem of America than the unhappiness of the married one. To have caught up with the prized quarry, and then to find that the excitement of the chase is over and there is only a sense of emptiness left, is too common an experience to be set down as a matter of individual unhappiness.

This applies, of course, not only to the woman but to her husband as well. There are mutual antagonisms, rivalries, fears, recriminations. Sometimes the only important thing the two of them have in common is the sense of emptiness. The husband may feel that the wife does not give herself sexually to him in a satisfying surrender. The wife in her turn may feel that after marriage the husband forgets how to woo with either ardor or imaginativeness. The psychic casualties are drastic—not only in the heavy incidence of frigidity among American women and (to a lesser extent) of impotence among the men, but on both sides the feeling that life and happiness are passing them by.

The unhappy wife has become a characteristic American culture type. She may feel that what her husband expects of her is trivial and trivializing. In the low-income groups she spends her best energies as the heroic family economist, but not always with a sense that the heroism leads anywhere. In the upper income groups she is often forced back into the erotic dream world of plays, movies, and novels, into psychoanalysis, even into astrology and spiritualism and all the thousand ways by which a discontented woman expresses the autumn of her discontent. Where psychoanalysts are too expensive, there is no less need for help: a recent American study of "where people take their troubles" has revealed the quackeries and charlatanisms that shoot up like weeds out of this psychic need. The classic studies by G. V. Hamilton and Katherine Davis show to what extent women of all income groups feel themselves sexually unsatisfied, and a number of recent studies—including the insights offered by the Kinsey volume on women—evidence the fact that a substantial percentage of American women find fitful sexual adventures in extramarital relations.* This sense of being emotionally unfulfilled, along with the sense of being socially unused and functionless, combine to create what Pearl Buck has called the "tinderbox woman" in America.

Nor has it helped the unhappy woman to know that she has become the focus of the system of consumption and adornment, the moon that radiates the shimmering surface of American life. What she wants is not to be treated like a well-dressed toy or called "Baby" but to be a person in her own right, with an emotional and intellectual life that makes her a person. As a brainless charmer, who needs to be protected and who learns to manipulate her protector and provider, or—in recoil from that —as the determined careerist who demands the chance to show she equals the male on every level, the American woman finds herself in a blind alley.

One key to her plight is the freezing of models and roles for the behavior of the sexes in the culture. There is an idealized model for both male and female at which each has been culturally conditioned to aim, as an image of oneself and also as an image of one's desired partner. These cultural models may have little relation to the real life goals of the person. As Margaret Mead has suggested, a woman may have a low level of sexual vitality and a slow life rhythm, and a man may in his own terms be of the same type, yet instead of finding happiness in each other, each is bludgeoned by the demands of the culture into aiming at a model of sexual vitality and aggressiveness which may represent the exactly wrong mate.

A similar freezing of roles applies to the whole life cycle of the woman. In girlhood she is brought up to measure her effectiveness by the standards of popularity and success. In her late teens, on the eve of marriage, she becomes the overvalued darling of the culture on whom concentrated attention is lavished, but what she is valued for is her youth and good looks and not any talent she may have or any function she will fill as wife and mother. Once married and started on her childbearing, she is transferred from one frozen role to another, this time as presiding spirit over the home, where she may feel isolated or crowded; the spotlight is shifted from her, but she takes on a series of tasks for which her education has scarcely prepared her. Where the social role of her hus-

* For a discussion of the sexual patterns of American women, see Ch. IX, Sec. 7, "Society and Sexual Expression."

band is that of a man growing to the height of his powers, the ideal of a mature woman is strangely absent in American thinking; from the time she passes the peak of the socially fixed ideal of youthful beauty she feels herself on the downward slope, and much of her psychic energy goes into fighting off her anxieties on this score. When her children have grown up and left the home, she tries again to pick up the old threads of her life, but she no longer has the self-assurance of her youth, nor is she likely to have built up a real competence in any field: she marks time until she is frozen again in the role of an elderly lady whose life is filled by grandchildren and good works.

There are signs, however, that these rigid social roles are being relaxed and more fluid ones are taking their place. There are as yet no signs of a clear direction in which the American woman is moving. But if she is to discover her identity, she must start by basing her belief in herself on her womanliness rather than on the movement for feminism. Margaret Mead has pointed out that the biological life cycle of the woman has certain well-marked phases from menarche through the birth of her children to her menopause; that in these stages of her life cycle, as in her basic bodily rhythms, she can feel secure in her womanhood and does not have to assert her potency as the male does. Similarly, while the multiple roles that she must play in life are bewildering, she can fulfill them without distraction if she knows that her central role is that of a woman.

America has realized better than any other society the vision of Mary Wollstonecraft's *Vindication of the Rights of Women:* yet equal rights do not mean an interchangeable identity with men but scope to lead a diversified life while remaining a woman. In this spirit the American woman is groping for a synthesis of her functions in her home, her community, and her job. Her central function, however, remains that of creating a life style for herself and for the home in which she is life creator and life sustainer. She is learning that she need not lose functions simply because she has talents and because she aims at a productive life which will develop her interests and her inner resources. In using these talents she will not follow what the man does simply because of his prestige in a masculine society, but will seek through them to fulfill her own life style.

7. *The Middle and End of the Journey*

THE MOST DIFFICULT years in American life are the middle years, when the first bleak intimation comes to a man that he has fallen short of the standards of the culture and his own life goals. He may find that the success he strove for either has not been achieved or has offered little satisfaction, that the tensions of living have left him depleted, and that the pot of gold at the end of the rainbow looks tarnished and insubstantial. The middle years ought to be the pay-off years in the American scheme—the reward for the work and saving and competitive striving. There is a good deal in the recent Kansas City study, covering people in the age span from forty to seventy, which indicates that they are indeed the pay-off years. But there is also evidence that they are years filled with intimations of mortality and with anxiety about the future.

I have spoken of how the American woman, with her children grown up and away, is faced with the problem of picking up again the severed threads of life and finding new interests to fill the emptiness. Something of the same is true of her husband, except that he continues to be absorbed by his job or business. But the mounting crises of life come for both of them in these years: of declining sexual powers for men and the menopause for women, of anxieties about health, of the prospects of loneliness, and of economic and psychological insecurity, of having to face the inner self and finding there perhaps poverty of spirit and failure to grow. These are parts of the life cycle, in any culture, but in the American their impact is greater because the original promise is greater.

Americans live in a rapidly changing culture but, since all their changes tend to be equated with changes for the bigger and better, they are reluctant to face the fact of change in their own bodies and personalities—at least, changes that might be for the worse. Middle age is the time when the individual must recognize that while he lives in an expanding society he is being passed by others in terms of promise and career, and perhaps being by-passed by life itself. His problem is to find a universe of possibility that is not restricted to the shrinking compass of his own skin. In the case of a man he may make a final attempt to break out of that compass, sexually and emotionally, in what Edmund Bergler called "the revolt of the middle-aged man." A woman's restlessness and revolt are likely to take less concrete form, and—especially when her children are grown—are directed into channels of club and community work. In recent years the extension of the life span and the spread of leisure time have intensified the problem of middle age by presenting Americans with the question of what they will do with their leisure during the middle years; but the new leisure has itself also offered a potential solution to the problem in the form of tours and vacations, part-time jobs, voluntary jobs, and the various new life interests that may result.

All this applies even more strongly to the group that Americans call the "aging." I have spoken of the American cult of youth, especially of the growing boy and of the girl on the threshold of marriage, and later of the successful young executive. There is, as I have noted, no pride in the mature woman, and little even in the mature man except to the extent that he may have reached success and power. If Americans in the middle years of the journey, passing over into the later ones, do not accept and value themselves it is partly because they sense that the culture does not value them.

This is linked with the American time conception. The American is usually held up as Exhibit I of the time sense of Western man. Note, however, that he thinks of time mainly in precision terms—the regular reiterations that are like equally spaced pegs on which the net can be hung which meshes together the parts of his world. He has little sense, such as one gets, for example, in Thomas Mann's *Magic Mountain,* of the relativity of time and its changing pace and emotional density. Time, to the American, means make-haste-and-get-to-your-appointment; one minute slips into another and all are part of a democracy of equal quality. There is no cumulation in the succession, no leaving of residues. The movement of time is on a flat plane, so that the passage of time may mean "progress" or growth in magnitudes, but it does mean a three-dimensional qualitative development and growth.

Given this time conception, it is natural for the culture to treat the old like the fag end of what was once good material. It requires a different sort of time conception to see that a man who has ceased to be a hustler may have deepened thereby, and that the urgencies may have given way to something of greater value. The most flattering thing you can say to an older American is that he "doesn't look his age" and "doesn't act his age"—as if it were the most damning thing in the world to look old. There is little of calm self-acceptance among the old, of the building of the resources which give inner serenity and compel an outer acceptance.

There is correspondingly little cultural valuing of old people. One finds nothing like the Japanese reverence for ancestors or the valuation the Chinese set on the qualities of the old. Since the American has been taught that success belongs to push and youth, it is hard to revere those who no longer possess either. One can be fond of them, tolerate them, take reluctant care of them, speak whimsically of their crotchetyness and frailties; but these are far from the genuine homage of heart and mind. To build a code of conduct toward the old requires not only personal kindliness but generations of the practice of values from which the old are not excluded—of which indeed they are the summation. The cement of the filial relation crumbles. Where there are few codes of honor, it is difficult to build a code that will pay honor to the old.

Every culture has what may be called a style of aging, as it has a style of growing up and a style of maturity. The style of aging in America is not a graceful one. It is filled with constant efforts to fight off anxieties, until one encounters what Martin Gumpert has called the "shock of aging"—the sharp recognition (usually associated with disease) that one is "done for," and the final loss of confidence that comes with it. There come then, as Albrecht and Havighurst have put it, the "insults" that assail the aging person—the loss of physical attractiveness, the loss of life partners and friends through death, the loss of status, the loss of useful and respected roles in the family and culture, and the final insult of being imprisoned in a body which is the shell of its earlier self.

The two-generation nuclear American family, usually constricted in living space, has little room for the old people, nor does it allow them any participating role. In a society of rapid change the gap in outlook between the generations is too great to leave the older people any sense of their function in transmitting the mores of the culture. They retire from business or are arbitrarily retired from their jobs. Absorbed as they have been with making money, making a living, or running a household, they are unprepared for the burden of leisure, and helpless when the family web has been broken. They are left almost functionless, with no status and no sense of being useful. What remains for them? To become spectators, in a culture that values only participants and puts a premium on action; to crowd into the lodges and fraternal orders, the bridge clubs, the women's clubs; to go to church regularly, watch censoriously over what others are doing, dwell increasingly on the compensations in a future life for the shortcomings of this one; to tinker with doctors, drugs, and patent medicines, to worry about failing health and alien ideas and subversive influences; to be anxious, to nurse fears, to find scapegoats.

These are the most conservative years of the life cycle. Instead of bringing political revaluation and opening the mind to new influences, the years of disillusion make even more tenacious the hold on what seems so precarious. Property, possessions, status and superiority, prejudices and stereotypes never seem so important as when all else seems to be slipping away. A culture is made up of people living by different clocks, each age group with bundles of habituations formed in a different period, each with different sets of conditionings and different outlooks on the future. The American population trends make it increasingly a nation of aging people, with corresponding attitudes.

In increasing the life span* the new medical techniques and the declining death rate have increased the proportion of the population in the later age groups. By the 1955 figures there were twenty-nine million Americans over the age of fifty-five, an increase of 45 per cent over the

* For an earlier discussion, see Ch. III, Sec. 5, "Human Resources: Population Profile."

1950 figures. In 1900 there were three million Americans who were sixty-five and over, forming 4 per cent of the population; in 1955 they had grown to fourteen million, forming 8½ per cent; the Census Bureau estimates for 1975 were almost twenty-one million, forming more than 10 per cent of the population. Thus the old people constitute the most rapidly growing portion of the American population. During the half century since 1900, when the total population doubled, the number of people sixty-five years and over nearly quadrupled. Much of this increase is due not only to the new techniques for prolonging life in the old years but to the drastic cutting down of mortality at birth and in infancy. The current American emphasis on medical and psychological advances in "gerontology" promises to prolong the life span further, thus intensifying the trends and problems of an aging population.

There has been a growing recognition of these problems, and, characteristically, Americans have bestirred themselves to cope with them. Although there was a lag in introducing social-security legislation, compared with what had been done earlier in Britain and Germany, the pace of advance has recently been swift, and Republican administrations have confirmed what the New Deal began. The Social Security Act was passed in 1935, and twenty years later, by 1955, the benefits paid out under it totaled thirty-four billion dollars, of which the old-age benefits were sixteen. The demand for greater benefits continued, however, and social-security coverage was extended to new groups, while there were residues of the movements for old-age pensions—like the "Townsend Clubs"—which had flourished in the 1930s.* But the greatest advance was made as the result of trade-union action, especially in the steel, coal, automobile, and garment industries, where pension plans incorporating and extending the government benefits were made part of the "fringe benefits" of the collective-bargaining contracts.

The problem of "retirement" has occupied a good deal of attention in America recently. It has two aspects: for most Americans it is a problem of discriminatory barriers against the employment of the aged; for a smaller but increasing number it is a problem of finding new interests after leaving their business pursuits.

One of the facts about American industrial organization is its haphazard and ruthless waste of human resources and potentials. The industrial machine demands the young. When a worker has reached fifty—sometimes even at forty-five—it is rarely that he continues in demand. Where possible, except in wartime, he is brusquely cast aside and replaced by a younger man. Even in the corporations, in the top business posts, the older men are pushed up into do-nothing positions in order to

* For the problem of social security, see Ch. III, Sec. 6, "The Sinews of Welfare."

make room for "young blood." The result is a reserve army of productive capacity which is kept largely unused and unpaid. In 30 per cent of the cases where the head of the family was sixty-five or over, the mid-1950s figures showed the family income to be less than $1,000 a year; in more than half it was less than $2,000. There were still six million workers—almost one out of ten among the gainfully employed—who were not covered by a retirement program of any kind, while only seven million were covered by industrial pension plans. The odds against a worker of over forty-five finding a new job were something like six to one. In some of the Utopian schemes, like Bellamy's *Looking Backward,* the state was to underwrite the leisure of every citizen after the age of forty-five. In the American case one might say grimly that for many there is a similar "Inca Plan"—but one of enforced retirement, where the underwriting of leisure is absent or very skimpy. The resulting effects on the self-respect and the attitudes of the older people are disastrous.

Americans generally use the term "retirement" to apply to people in the middle and upper income range who have given up their business or work, and whose children are grown up and married off. Retirement in this sense is one of the great cultural dreams. Since it involves a sort of "means test" for distributing latter-day leisure, it works for only a small minority. They may be living on insurance or annuities or on savings invested in stocks, and in some cases on pensions. They may either have given up their business or work or may be tapering off. For them the symbolic paradise has become Florida or California, where they dream of spending their time in the sun, gossiping or visiting, listening to the radio or watching TV, pursuing their hobbies.

For a period the idea of complete retirement had great appeal for those who could afford it, and the doctors recommended it as a way of prolonging life, especially since the greatest killers among the chronic diseases in America are heart disease and hypertension. But more recently the old people discovered that to be functionless, even with comfort and leisure, is to eat out your heart. Away from your old haunts and interests you are lost; and you find yourself more miserable out of harness than in harness. "Retirement" becomes in this sense mainly a design for self-indulgent dotage ridden by loneliness. The students of geriatrics now emphasize that the problem for old people is not to drop their work but to slow its pace, rechannel their energies and fuse them with broader interests. The trouble here is the question of whether strong enough psychic resources have been stored up to make the latter years a time of harvest and not of emptiness.

I have not taken account here of the differences in the aging process by reasons of class, occupation, region, ethnic group—and sex as well. To start with the last: the American woman, who is culturally expected and conditioned to be "well preserved" at fifty-five or later, takes aging with a more calculated deliberateness (although not with less anxiety) than her husband or brother. In a sense she has to face the "shock of aging" much earlier than he, since the cultural ideal of youthfulness applies more stringently to women than to men. Even at thirty-five she is beginning to look back at her mirror with awakening doubts, and in her forties and fifties they reach a crescendo of anxiety. By sixty she has encased herself in an habitual wariness about the aspect she presents to the world, her family, and herself. Being thus gradually conditioned to adjust herself to aging, she is likely to suffer fewer scars than the American male, who rushes headlong into a seemingly indefinite future, playing the role of the alert young executive until he is brought up sharply by an abrupt awareness of bodily and psychic changes.

The differences in the aging process between classes, occupations, regions, and ethnic groups still remain to be studied. But there is enough material to suggest that aging hits the working class harder than the professionals, artists, or business executives. One might also speculate that it leaves more psychic casualties in the rural areas and small towns than in urban centers, on the theory that the older person can find more stimulation in city surroundings and is not thrown back on himself too bleakly. But we also know that there can be a terrible loneliness for the old in cities as well—a loneliness which is enhanced by the fact that there is so much vitality all around them. The whole problem still awaits study. But we do know that the lonely American is all the more lonely when he is old.

The most difficult question is the degree to which an individual's ties with the culture enable him to weather the inner storms of aging. In a suggestive typology Riesman ventures the guess that there are three types of reaction to aging—the "autonomous," the "adjusted," and the "anomic." At one end of the scale there are people who find sources of self-renewal as their physical capacities shrink, and they move beyond their accustomed limits to discover new levels at which they can function productively. At the other end there are people without a sense of identity, who crumble under the encroachments of age. In between them Riesman places the "adjusted" who are kept going in the later years by their ties with the culture, getting their resistance to the inroads of age not from their own inner strength but from the cultural roles they have learned to maintain. In the case of some ethnic groups, as with Negroes and Old World orthodox Jews, the ties are not so much with the larger American culture as with the immediate ethnic subculture, and the result is likely to be something more than merely "adjustment": it is rather an inner harmony between the personality and culture which enables the life cycle to fulfill itself without much strain and without the "transcending" quality which the "autonomous" must have.

I may have given here a picture of aging in America with too few lights and too many shadows. The response of Americans to the aging process is varied. It may run all the way from hurt vanity or resigned acceptance to the creative tapping of new resources; their feelings range from anxiety or panic to a mellow affirmation. An attitude study of people over sixty-five in a small Midwestern city showed 17 per cent of them checking the statement "My life is so enjoyable that I almost wish it could go on forever"; another 20 per cent checked "These are the best years of my life"; and another 40 per cent checked "My life is still busy and useful." This would indicate that three out of four elderly Americans have come to terms with the fact of aging. The obvious difficulty with these figures is that old people are likely to draw a veil over their sense of isolation and failure, and to show by a cheery response to such questions that they are taking their burdens with courage. Robert Havighurst, who has been close to the research and interviews in this field, believes that "the age period from sixty to seventy-five is just as happy as any other age period for Americans, and is actually a good deal happier than the period of adolescence." This does not jibe with my own impressions, nor with what we know about the strong major currents that flow through the life history of the American; yet it is good to have this counteremphasis to balance the prevailing pessimism about this period of American life.

How any particular individual will respond is likely to depend more on his whole psychic history than on any category in which he may be placed in a typology. If Americans do not grow old gracefully it is not because of any failure of awareness of the problem. They try earnestly and self-consciously to meet it, yet it is also a harder task for them. For old age is the time when, as Martin Gumpert put it, "fewer and fewer things are done for the first time, and more and more things are done for the last time"—and American culture is the kind that places its premium on firsts rather than on finalities, and on challenge rather than acceptance.

Much of the American anxiety about old age is a flight from the reality of death. One of the striking qualities of the American character is the unwillingness to face either the fact or meaning of death. In the more somber tradition of American literature, reaching from Hawthorne and Melville and Poe to Faulkner and Hemingway, one finds a tragic depth that belies the surface thinness of the ordinary American death attitudes. By an effort of the imagination the great writers faced problems which the culture in action is reluctant to face—the fact of death, its mystery, and its place in the back-and-forth shuttling of the eternal recurrence. The unblinking confrontation of death in Greek times, the elaborate theological patterns woven around it in the Middle Ages, the ritual celebration of it in the rich peasant cultures of Latin and Slavic Europe or in primitive cultures: these are difficult to find in American life, except among the Negroes or where immigration and its cultural transfers may have left some colorful residues of death customs within some of the ethnic groups.

Whether through fear of the emotional depths or because of a drying up of the sluices of religious intensity, the American avoids dwelling on death or even coming to terms with it: he finds it morbid and recoils from it, surrounding it with word avoidance (Americans never die, but "pass away") and various taboos of speech and practice. A "funeral parlor" is decorated to look like a bank; everything in a funeral ceremony is done in hushed tones, as if it were something furtive, to be concealed from the world; there is so much emphasis on being dignified that the ceremony often loses its quality of dignity. In some of the primitive cultures there is difficulty in understanding the causes of death: it seems puzzling and even unintelligible. Living in a scientific culture, Americans have a ready enough explanation of how it comes, yet they show little capacity to come to terms with the fact of death itself and with the grief that accompanies it. "We jubilate over birth and dance at weddings," writes Margaret Mead, "but more and more hustle the dead off the scene without ceremony, without an opportunity for young and old to realize that death is as much a fact of life as is birth." And (one may add) even in its hurry and brevity the last stage of an American's life—the last occasion of his relation to his society—is as standardized as the rest.

Americans repress closely the emotional drives concerned with death and sorrow—so closely that what the psychiatrists call the "grief work," in Erich Lindeman's phrase, is given little scope. It is true that the death of a husband or father leaves a great void in the American family, and that widowhood is a difficult state to bear, especially when the widow—who is generally left with adequate insurance and other economic resources—is left without the psychic resources to live her own life self-sufficiently. (The mid-century figures show nine out of every 100 families in America broken by widowhood.) But however intense the personal grief may be, there are cultural pressures to put an end to it, to keep it from interfering with the survivors' effectiveness, and to recapture one's "peace of mind." Because the great values of American culture are all associated with the power and pulsing of life, there is felt to be no point in dwelling on the values that transcend life and reach into death, nor any profit in trying to see the everyday values take on a new meaning in the withering perspective of death.

In almost every culture there is a fear of death, yet the fear may carry along a fascinated absorption. But in America there is little of this fascination. The recoil from death betrays in itself a lack of sensitivity toward its implications for the spirit. One reason why Hemingway's *The Old Man and the Sea* came from outside the culture (Hemingway wrote it in the setting of the Cuban fishing villages) was its celebration of old age and its heroisms. There had been little in American literature about the dignity of old age, as there is little also (except in the war novels) about the grace of dying. As for suicide, although it has lost some of the fierceness of the taboos that were thrown around it by medieval Christianity, it is still regarded as the act of an unhinged mind and the final insult to a culture which underscores effectiveness in life. It is not, as it has been in some other societies, a culturally recognized way out of the human dilemma; nor would it be easy to imagine an American thinker writing the kind of philosophic defense of suicide one finds among the French existentialists. Conversely there is little in American philosophical speculation that deals with the theme of immortality. American culture cuts away the sensitivity to death and grief, to suicide and immortality, emphasizing the here-and-now as it emphasizes youth and action.*

And so, from birth to death, "from the cradle to the grave," the life cycle of the American.

* For a further discussion of the American time scale and time perspective and the American attitudes toward death, see Ch. XII, Sec. 7, "The Destiny of a Civilization."

CHAPTER IX

Character and Society

WE DEAL here with a variety of themes, all of them relating in some way to the wholeness and fragmentation of American life, to the codes by which Americans live or which they break, and to the relation between the structure of American society and the lineaments of the American character. First we stand back a bit and ask what elements of cohesion there are that hold America together, and what it uses for a social cement in the absence of the traditional cementing forces of the great societies in the past. In the process we inquire into the curious fact of the lonely American amidst all the bustle and swagger and power, and the alienated American in a society that sets so much store by the quality of community (Sec. 1, "The Cement of a Society"). This brings us to the associative impulse which has made America a nation of joiners (Sec. 2, "The Joiners"). And this in turn leads to the emergence of new standards and codes in manners, taste, dress (Sec. 3, "Manners, Taste, and Fashion"). From the discussion of these nuances in American behavior we take a sweeping look at the whole gallery of emerging American character types, noting that there is no single new "American character" but rather a plurality of diverse and conflicting personality trends that take shape in a number of new character portraits (Sec. 4, "Varieties of American Character").

We turn then to face the Gorgon head of all discussions of the American social structure—the question of the forces of disorganization in American society, and we ask whether the "cracks in the cement" mean that the whole structure is disintegrating, or whether they mark the excesses of the same tensions and strivings that give America some of its qualities of strength (Sec. 5, "The Disorders of a Society"). We continue with the theme of changes in American codes, grappling with the convulsive changes in moral codes and standards, and concluding that as the older ones are transformed newer ones take their place (Sec. 6, "Morals in Revolution"). On the question of sexual morality we note the gap between the American obsession with sex and the sexually repressive codes, and examine the stratagems of "patterned evasion" of the formal standards (Sec. 7, "Society and Sexual Expression"). Finally we look at what these strivings are, in the form of basic life goals that move Americans to their actions and passions (Sec. 8, "Life Goals and the Pursuit of Happiness").

CHAPTER IX

Character and Society

1. The Cement of a Society

WHAT holds America together? A democracy, De Tocqueville wrote, cannot function without a religion and a philosophy. Which is to say that while every civilization needs some principle to hold it together, a democracy has a special problem of cohesion. Paradoxically, it may be easier to hold a people together through inequities sanctioned by tradition, religion, or monarchical authority than through the equality that is always questioning itself and being questioned. To the extent that American culture is tangled and various, diverse in ethnic tradition and geography, free of recognized social hierarchies, obsessed with the individual and his rights, averse to the claims of social duties, it is a wonder that it holds together at all. The paradox is that so atomistic a civilization should have found so effectively the stuff of cohesion.

In any tribal culture there is always the clannish differentiation of the "we" from the "they" to serve as a cohesive force. But more important are the ties of institutions and ideas. The Greeks had pride in their city-states, yet Plato suggested myths for the ruling Guardians to instill into the underlying population. The Romans had a conquering zeal and a sense of historic destiny to link them, yet they also used an imperial religion to which both Machiavelli in his *Discourses on Livy* and Gibbon in his *Decline and Fall* assigned an important role in the Empire's fortunes. The Japanese used the Emperor God. The medieval world stressed a universal church and a system of feudal statutes and personal allegiance; and the Catholic societies of Europe and Latin America have relied on the residues of these and on the close-knit rural communities tied by honor, loyalty, and social obedience. In feudal China and in India the cement used has been a caste system, again fused with religious traditions. England relied on a social aristocracy, an established Church, the Monarchy, and the rule of law. The French since 1789 have used their revolutionary tradition and their attachment to the native soil. Russia has a myth of hostile encirclement, plus a messianic belief in the invincible march of Communism, plus a surviving if incongruous mystique of "Holy Russia."

The American case has been different. None of the cementing forces which have held together these other societies—feudal hierarchy, caste, aristocracy, monarchy, state Church, religious or revolutionary mystique —has counted for much in America, with the exception of an idea like Manifest Destiny. Nor has authoritarianism taken hold, whether military or clerical. When the new American society broke with that of the Old World, the break was not only with the outer ties of dependence but also (to a lesser extent) with the inner ties that held the old society together.

What many American settlers did have, to start with, was a deep religious feeling and the sense of social commitment that came with it. They had in addition the sense of a new community being hewn out on a new continent, with the world's eyes on its course, and the belief in equal opportunity. Returning to De Tocqueville's remark, that a democracy cannot survive without a religion and a philosophy, the Americans had as their stuff of cohesion the religion of free worship and the philosophy of equality.*

A philosophy and a religion cannot operate effectively, however, unless they are at harmony with current practices. We have seen the nature of the atomizing forces which came into American society. The diverse immigration and the mingling of races and religions meant group differences in ways of thought and living, and tensions pulling apart the society. The operation of competitive capitalism brought with it the coldness of a business spirit which measured men as items in a market economy. The expansion of American power meant the assumption of new political burdens in the world and exposure to new influences. To a great extent the old codes and the old consensus based on them dissolved. Americans were confronted with the most difficult task that a society ever has to face—that of finding organic continuities to keep its life from being pulverized.

One can argue, as F. S. C. Northrop has done, that the atomizing principle was present even in early American thought; that it had been taken over from John Locke's theory of ideas, which saw reality as only a collection of atomic sense data, and which saw society similarly as a loose collection of atomic individuals. Northrop points out that the British based their own polity on Thomas Hooker, who conceived of the Church of England as an organic society of individuals whose individuality was absorbed in the common mystical body. But this leaves open the question of why the thinking of Locke and Hume, rather than of Hooker, had so strong an appeal for Americans. Perhaps it was be-

* For religion in America, see Ch. X, Sec. 1, "God and the Churches." For the philosophy of equality, see Ch. VI, Sec. 2, "The Democratic Idea," and Ch. X, Sec. 2, "American Thought: the Angle of Vision."

cause their thinking was congruous with the surging strength of the new economy and the competitive spirit and with the force of business materialism. It is idyllic to believe that whatever breakdown there has been of faith and morals is a recent event in American life, part of a cataclysm sweeping away the original system of faith and morals. The fact is that these were already broken with the later advances of science, the machine, and the market economy.

Nor were they peculiar to America. Karl Polanyi, studying English economics and social history at the turn of the nineteenth century, noted that the automatic market mechanism became the principle for organizing not only the economy but also the society—although the automatic market was constantly haunted by reform movements, Chartism, and a variety of religious cults. The older controls of British society, which Edmund Burke had celebrated, were replaced by the free-market-as-control, and the mutual responsibilities between society and its members were replaced by *laissez-faire*-plus-the-poor-laws. Using Polanyi's term, this was the "Great Transformation." Something of the same transformation took place in American life in the 1840s and 1850s, when the landless industrial worker first became a permanent part of American life; and in the decades after the Civil War, when the market economy came to be accepted as the principal regulator not only of the economic but also of the social and moral order. As Mr. Featherstone put it in one of Thomas Love Peacock's novels, "Every man for himself, sir, and God for us all." Again it must be noted that in America, as in England, the automatic market was haunted by Fourierism, Transcendentalism, and reform movements. Yet the religion of freedom and the philosophy of equality were steadily transformed into the creed of the automatic market, whose religion was individualism and whose philosophy was the competitive and acquisitive spirit.

A drastic critic of American society could draw a quite terrifying picture of the dominant role of money in effecting outward ties without any inner ones. From birth to death the centrifugal pull of money values is felt. There is little equality in the surroundings of birth: in the hospital wards there is a hierarchy of solicitude for mother and child depending on income. In school there is a similar gradation in the way children are dressed and the homes they come from which shapes the child's attitude toward other children. The child learns quickly the gulf between those who have everything assured and those who have to struggle for them. In the years of growth the conditions that make for an expanding personality must be paid for—leisure from work in the early years when work can be oppressive, adequate medical care, the chance for recreation and travel, access to sun and sea, music and art and books. In adult life the principles of business operate, and even friendships are overridden by the principle that "business is not philan-thropy." In his job life the worker often comes to feel that the cor-poration is not a benevolent father, and in turn he gives his work grudgingly and without enthusiasm. Those who care about honor and love, about fighting for causes that yield no return and spending them-selves for people with whom they have only the bonds of a common humanity, are called "idealists," "do-gooders," and "eggheads." In old age those who can no longer pay their way are forgotten. And even in death they are hurried away silently into an obscure grave.

This may be overstressed. The nonpecuniary values of generosity and honor, friendship and comradeship and love, workmanship and cre-ativeness, are present to a high degree in American life. The whole force of American literature supports them. It is also true that Ameri-cans can be as sentimental as any people in the world. Yet aside from personal sentiment the pressures of the culture run the other way. A market economy means a market society, in which the great crime is to be "taken in," and the great virtue to be tough and illusionless. This means resisting the pitfalls of fellow feeling and breaking whatever it is that ties person to person in the web of a common plight. The night-mare of American life is to be left dependent and helpless—a greater nightmare than failing to help others when they need help. The result is the desensitized man whose language is the wisecrack and whose ar-mor is cynicism.

It is interesting that the characteristic American contribution to psy-chiatry should have been Harry Stack Sullivan's concept of "interper-sonal relations." It is, of course, true that in the last analysis a society is composed of persons, and in such a sense all social relations are inter-personal. Yet this misses the big fact that—without assuming any actual social organization above persons—a society is more than the sum of the individual atoms in it. There is a whole web of symbols and going concerns that weaves together the lives of people, and the greatest of these is the notion of society itself. The American emphasis, however, is individualist and atomist. It gives rise, for example, to such a char-acteristic popular myth as the feeling that the social services under-taken by government are a rape of the public treasury by incompetents who have fallen behind in the battle of life and that all collective ef-fort is a betrayal of the laws of life. This jungle attitude is coupled often with a moral neutrality which makes the "innocent bystander" keep hands off even when he sees someone victimized, lest he become too involved. The conditionings of American life are to flee needless entanglements and vulnerabilities ("Don't stick your neck out," "Don't be a sucker"). This vacuum of the passions of fellow feeling is the most desolating measure of what Nietzsche in another context called the "pathos of distance."

How to bridge that distance has been a constant problem for American humanism. Since most Americans fear the role of playing Santa Claus to countries in need, the internationalists have had to argue that every dollar lent or granted abroad is an act not of generosity but of national self-interest in fighting the nation's enemies. The same appeal to self-interest is made by those who plead for the civil liberties of minority groups: "If you let it happen to them it will in the end happen to you." In one of the movies about anti-Semitism, there is an eloquent speech by the hero-detective to a hillbilly soldier from Tennessee, saying that unless he takes to heart the brutal slaying of a Jew, the irrational madness might spread until Catholics become the victims, then Protestants, then redheaded men, and perhaps even men from Tennessee. Thus the argument is one of skin-saving rather than belonging to an organic social whole or being implicated in a common human plight: and while it is true that skin-saving is an impulse that goes back to a fundamental human selfishness, a cohesive society can never be securely founded upon it. If the depersonalized quality I have mentioned were the whole truth about America, it would be hard to explain—in the face of all the fragmentizing pulls—how American society has managed to hold together as it has.

In negative terms, the answer lies partly in the tradition of toleration which is one facet of *laissez faire*. Given the pluralism of American life and the bewildering array of group differences, the agreement to disagree is an important force in avoiding tensions and conflicts. Americans have learned a toleration of ethnic and religious differences (although not of personal nonconformism) which amounts to a kind of mutual insulation. Even the ghettos—the closely packed ethnic communities of Irish, Italians, Jews, Puerto Ricans, Germans, Czechs, Negroes, Chinese—play an important part in this insulation. They are little islands or enclaves, and as such they may seem to fragmentize American life further. But actually they are the natural response of like-minded persons who find themselves a minority in a culture still strange to them; and until the new generations can take their place in the main stream of American striving, these little back eddies serve to minimize the turbulent conflicts of group differences. For a sensitive observer like Alistair Cooke, the remarkable thing about life in New York City is not that there are tensions among the ethnic groups that make it up but that they manage to live together with an almost unparalleled absence of conflict. In time the ghettos are themselves atomized, and as they break under the disruptive force of standardized ways of living, the danger is not one of too slow but of too rapid absorption of the American subcultures. They are one form of insulation against the violence of change which would annihilate the identity of the individual within his group.*

Something of the same process may be found even in the market society. The relations of purchase and sale, of work in big corporations, of standardized consumption, and of large-scale advertising are depersonalized relations. Yet in fact there is a saving quality that many observers may miss. To take the American Negro group as an instance, despite the persistence of job and wage differentials the place where segregation begins to break down first is exactly in the market society, and the place where it holds on unyieldingly is in the intimate social relationships that are least governed by the market. It is true that in many cases the Negro's money may still fail to buy him the house he wants or an equal place in a restaurant or theater. Yet in the national market his purchasing power is eagerly sought by the makers of competing commodities, and in local retail outlets the Negro purchaser finds increasingly a freemasonry of the dollar which puts his money on an equality with the others. There is thus an impersonality about the contacts of the market place which qualifies even caste divisions and reduces the loneliness of status. Even what Riesman calls the "false personalizing" of relations between salesman and customer serves as the starting point for diminishing prejudices that had been uncritically accepted. Studies of department-store buying show that the addition of Negro or Jewish clerks helps rather than hinders the volume of sales. Thus the social changes in American life are being absorbed into American consciousness through the operation of the profit motive. Even more important is the impersonality of the job relation, which leads workers of diverse origin to work side by side in the day-to-day relations of the factory, meeting common problems and fighting against common enemies, until finally they develop the sense of fellow relation which is at the heart of any society.

The social theorists draw an important distinction, which goes back to Frederich Tonnies, between "community" or "society" (*Gemeinschaft*) and the "association" (*Gesellschaft*). It is the distinction between the close-knit unit of community living, as found mainly in traditional rural societies, and the loosely organized unit familiar to modern urban industrial living. No one would claim that the concept of "community," as it existed in a society like that of sixteenth-century Spain, based on the common traditions of land, church, and hierarchy, comes anywhere

* For an elaboration of this theme, see Ch. III, Sec. 2, "The Immigrant Experience" and Ch. VII, Sec. 5, "The Minority Situation."

near applying to American society. In its place has come a social organization created by the people of an industrial culture, fashioned (in Helen Mims's phrase) as their "master artifice." American society may stand as the characteristic expression of this master artifice. It is looser than a "community," which has a freightage of meaning that conveys inner traditional ties of long standing. But it is a good deal more than is usually conveyed in the word "association," which Americans use for specific voluntary groupings.

In fact, the "master artifice" of American society contains in it more of the affirmative element of mystique than most students have been willing to find. The avoidance of disruption and conflict and the impersonal market forces, which I have stressed above, do not in themselves hold together the fabric of a society. The real cement of society lies in the folk beliefs about it. These are not as abstract as the philosophic ideas, nor are they a religion in any formal sense. Yet they serve effectively to link people with each other and with the culture.

I have spoken above of the folk belief in the American open-class system. Just as important, in the political area, is the belief in fair play and the "rules of the game," which accounts for the difference in ideological intensity between political conflict in America and Europe. In the legal area there is the belief in law which gives the underlying groups a chance to invoke the slogan of equality before the law and prevents a society of frozen status from forming. In terms of models of living, there are the common symbols and type-figures in the realm of sports, business, movies, and television to serve as folk heroes.

This is mainly the stuff of standardization, and a valid doubt may be raised as to whether genuine social cohesion—or even (as Erich Fromm puts it) the capacity to love—is possible in a thoroughly standardized society. This doubt has been raised especially about the Big Media, on the ground that they are corrupting and disintegrating forces rather than cohesive ones. But while the media may dilute the aesthetic quality of popular culture and of the American experience, it is hard to deny their striking role in effecting communication between individuals and their society on every class and ethnic level. The fearers and doubters should reckon with the force of individualism in American life, which keeps it from becoming wholly a mass culture, valueless and normless.

The weight of this individualism, plus the impersonality of a market society, plus the insulation and later the integration of conflict groups, plus the effects of participation on the job and in the market, plus the ideal of equality before the law, plus finally the symbols and hero figures of folk belief—these have somehow added up to the cement of American society.

2. The Joiners

A STANDARD CLICHÉ about American society is that the Americans are "joiners" and "belongers." The derisive attack on the symbol of Sinclair Lewis's Babbitt, who belonged to the Elks, Boosters, and a network of other service clubs and lodges, became a stereotype of American social criticism. It is true that the associative impulse is strong in American life: no other civilization can show as many secret fraternal orders, businessmen's "service clubs," trade and occupational associations, social clubs, garden clubs, women's clubs, church clubs, theater groups, political and reform associations, veterans' groups, ethnic societies, and other clusterings of trivial or substantial importance.

When the intellectuals speak scornfully of Americans as "joiners" they usually forget to include themselves: there are more academic organizations in the United States than in the whole of Europe. They have in mind a middle-class American who may be a Shriner or an Elk, a Rotarian, a Legionnaire, a member of a country club or outing club, and at least a dozen other organizations. In the Warner studies of "Yankee City" (Newburyport) which had 17,000 people, there were over 800 associations, about 350 of them more or less permanent. Taking some random figures in the mid-1950s for illustration, the fraternal orders included in the past at least twenty million members; there were about 100,000 women's clubs; there were two million young people who belonged to the rural and small-town "4-H" clubs. At least 100 million Americans were estimated to belong to some kind of national organization.

Max Weber, the German sociologist, visited America in 1905 and spoke of these "voluntary associations" as bridging the transition between the closed hierarchical society of the Old World and the fragmented individualism of the New World, and he saw how crucial a social function these groupings perform in American life. After World War II the students of German society, looking back at the Nazi experience, thought they could trace a connection between the lesser role of such voluntary groups in Germany and the rise of totalitarianism. Their assumption was that when the associative impulse is balked, it may express itself in a more destructive way.

Certainly one of the drives behind "joining" is the integrative impulse of forming ties with like-minded people and thus finding status in the community. Americans joined associations for a number of motives: to "get ahead," to "meet people" and "make contacts," to "get something done," to learn something, to fill their lives. These drives shed some light on the human situation in America. Constantly mobile,

Americans need continuities to enable them easily to meet people, make friends, eat and drink with them, call them by their first names. The clubs and lodges help fill the need. They are at once a way of breaking up "cliques" and "sets" and at the same time forming new ones. They are a means for measuring social distance, narrowing it for those who break in and are included, lengthening it for those who are excluded. For a newcomer in a community it is hard to break the shell of the tight local social groups unless he comes with a recognized stamp from a national organization or makes his way into a local one. Once in it, he joins with the others in a critical surveillance of the next new-comer. This is a way of solving the need in any society both for clannishness and for social flexibility.

In the midst of constant change and turbulence, even in a mass society, the American feels alone. In a society of hierarchy, loneliness is more tolerable because each member knows his position in the hierarchy—lower than some, higher than others, but always known. In a mobile, nonhierarchical society like the American, social position does not have the same meaning as in a vertical scheme of deference and authority. A man's status in the community is a matter of making horizontal connections, which give him his place in what would otherwise be a void. It is this social placing of an American—in church, lodge, service or women's club, eating club, Community Fund drive, veterans' group, country club, political party—that defines his social personality. Through it he gets the sense of effectiveness he does not have as a minor part of the machine process or the corporate organization. Here he can make his way as a person, by his qualities of geniality and friendliness, his ability to talk at a meeting or run it or work in a committee, his organizing capacities, his ardor, his public spirit. Here also he stretches himself, as he rarely does on the job, by working with others for common nonprofit ends.

Thus Americans achieve a sense of collective expression which belies the outward atomism of American life. "Not to belong to a *we* makes you lonesome," says the adolescent girl in Carson McCullers' *The Member of the Wedding.* "When you say *we,* I'm not included, and it's not fair." Since there is little emphasis in America on some mystical community of religion, there is a greater hunger to belong to a "we." This was less true in the earlier history of the nation. The American rarely thought of himself as "lonely" until the twentieth century. Before that time the dominant note in his thinking was that he was a self-sufficient individual. But he is no longer sufficient unto himself. He gets a certain degree of shared experience from his job at the factory or office, and from his trade-union, but he needs a good deal more from personal relations outside his job life. Margaret Mead notes that at their first meeting Americans are distant and ill at ease, but at their second they act like old friends. It is because they have had a shared experience, no matter how slight, which removes their inhibitions and makes them feel expansive because of it. Karen Horney, coming from Germany to America, was compelled to change her whole theory about the neurotic personality when she found how different were the inner sources of conflict in America from those in Germany, and how much of a role loneliness played in American conflicts.

It is a striking fact that friendships in America, especially male friendships, are not as deep as in other cultures. The American male suspects that there is something sissified about a devoted and demonstrative friendship, except between a man and woman, and then it must pass over into love, or perhaps just into sex. In their clubs and associations, however, at first in school clubs and college fraternities and later in secret lodges or women's clubs, Americans find a level of friendship that does not lay them open to the charge of being sentimental. In his clubs a man is not ashamed to call another man "brother," although outside of the lodge, the trade-union, and the church the term "brother" is used sardonically in American speech.

It is the hunger for shared experience that makes the American fear solitude as he does. More than a century ago Emerson spoke of the polar needs of "society and solitude." The days in which Americans pushed into the wilderness to find solitude are largely over. Many of them still leave the crowded cities for "the country," but their search is not so much for solitude as for greater living space and smaller and more compassable groups. Lewis Mumford has made a plea for housing arrangements that will assure each member of the family a room of his own to which he can retreat when the need for solitude comes upon him, to rediscover the shape of his personality. But for many Americans solitude is still too frightening, whether because they dare not face the dilemma of their own personality or because they recognize themselves more easily by reference to their association with others.

There are many ways of dividing American associations into broad types, none wholly satisfactory. The best one can do is to point out some dramatic contrasts between them. There are the occupational and economic groups at one end of the spectrum, geared to self-interest, and the crusading and cultural ones at the other. There are the patriotic societies of the "old Americans" and the newer ethnic societies of minority groups. There are broadly inclusive associations (political parties, trade-unions, *ad hoc* reform groups) at one end, and at the other there are highly personal groups that run all the way from high-school cliques to the adult eating clubs and the "country-club set." There are, as Warner has put it, "secular" organizations and "sacred" ones, matter-of-fact ones and highly ritualistic ones.

Some of these are more saturated with symbolism than others, yet all of them in one way or another deal in symbols and take their appeal from them. The symbolic complexity of American life is largely expressed in these clubs, lodges, and associations, which fulfill to the hilt what Durkheim long ago laid down as the essence of religious groupings—"collective representation." The degree of ritual varies, being very high in the case of Masonic lodges and church groups and less so in the case of *ad hoc* reform groups. Yet the symbolism and the ritual are present, explicitly or implicitly, in all of them.

Behind the urge toward "joining" is the sense of the mysterious and exotic. To belong to a secret order and be initiated into its rites, to be part of a "Temple" with a fancy Oriental name, to parade in the streets of Los Angeles, Chicago, or New York dressed in an Arab fez and burnoose, to have high-sounding titles of potentates of various ranks in a hierarchy: all this has appeal in a nonhierarchical society from which much of the secrecy and mystery of life has been squeezed out. The fraternal groups flourish best in the small towns of the Middle West: the drearier the cultural wasteland of the small town, the greater the appeal of the exotic. Americans have an ambivalent attitude toward secrecy: they want everything out in the open, yet they delight in the secrecy of fraternal groups, as Tom Sawyer's gang of boys in Mark Twain's books did, and as the cellar clubs and the boys' gangs in the big-city slums still do. Much of the appeal of the Ku Klux Klan lies in this mysterious flim-flammery, at once sadistic and grimly prankish. In many ways the American male of adult years is an arrested small boy, playing with dollars and power as he did once with toys or in gangs, and matching the violence of his recreation to the intensity of his loneliness.

This is especially clear in the veterans' groups, like the American Legion or the Veterans of Foreign Wars, which banded together not only for bonuses and other lobbying purposes but through a nostalgia for the ultimate shared experience of killing and facing death. Under the form of vigilant patriotism they are an effort to recapture the adventure of youth and death in a life that seems humdrum by contrast with the memories of war and derring-do. Since they have the self-assurance of being patriots and hunters of subversives, they come to feel that they have earned a license for license. Their political views take on something of the same cast as their prankishness at conventions, and there is a peculiar irony in the spectacle of drunken and boisterous middle-aged men whose leaders deliver solemn speeches about saving the nation. Curiously, some of the men who are pursued by these Hounds of God got themselves into trouble originally by reason of the same proclivity to become joiners, sponsoring a series of liberal and Leftist letterheads through a mixed impulse of gregariousness and reformist action.

For many American women, the women's club fills the emotional void of middle age, helping in the fight against loneliness and boredom. For others it means a chance to act as culture surrogates for their husbands, who are too busy to keep up with the trends in literature, the arts, or the community services. Americans have learned to take the clubwomen with a kindly bantering acceptance, much as in the Helen Hokinson caricatures. The jokes about the ladies' club lecture circuits cannot conceal a measure of pride on the part of a new nation in having wives with leisure enough to spend on veneer, like garden clubs, reading and discussion clubs, parent-teacher associations, and child-study clubs. In every American community the lecture forums, Little Theater groups, concerts and symphonies and poetry readings are in the custody of little groups of devoted people—men as well as women—who combine the sense of community service with a feeling of membership in a cultural elite.

These cultural groups are part of the array of *ad hoc* organizations which Americans form for every conceivable purpose. Some of them are meddlers and priers, seeking to impose their will upon the society by hunting other Americans down and boycotting and censoring their activities; others are formed to combat them with equal militancy. There are vigilante groups and civil liberties groups; there are radical, conservative, liberal, reactionary, and crackpot groups. Each of the three great religious communities—Protestant, Catholic, and Jewish—has its own welfare, charity, social, recreational, social work, and reformist clubs. In fact, the Negroes as well as the newer minority ethnic groups have a more intense participation in associational life than the "old Americans": it is their way of retaining their cohesiveness and morale in the face of the pressures of the majority culture. Cutting across the religious and ethnic divisions are Community Chest drives, hospital societies, private schools, settlement house and welfare groups, and groups built around every conceivable hobby. They go back in their impulse to the idea of self-help, and many of them combine the pressure group with self-interest and "do-goodism." To some degree they embody the fanatical energy drive that has transformed the face of American life.

It is through these associations that Americans avoid the excesses both of state worship and of complete individualism. It is in them, and not in the geographical locality, that the sense of community comes closest to being achieved. Through them also the idea of neighborhood has been re-created in America: for in most American cities the neighbors next door, who may be fellow tenants or fellow houseowners, have little else in common. The real common interests are shared by people working in the same industry or profession, sending their children to the same school, belonging to the same welfare organization or club, fighting for the same causes. Sometimes this involves "sets" and "cliques" which form from the encrustation of shared experience; sometimes it involves common membership in leisure-and-recreation groups whose chief tie is an interchange of taste and experience. But through the sum of these ways the American manages to achieve a functional set of social relations with like-minded people, the core of which is not propinquity of place but community of interests, vocation, preferences, and tastes.

The propensity to join is not new in America. It goes back to the ladies' reading clubs and other cultural groups which spread on the moving frontier and softened some of its rigors, and which were the forerunners of the parent-teacher associations and the civic and forum groups of today. The jungle of voluntary associations was already dense enough for De Tocqueville to note that "in no country in the world has the principle of association been . . . more unsparingly applied to a multitude of different objects than in America." The permissiveness of the state, the openness of an open society, the newness of the surroundings, the need for interweaving people from diverse ethnic groups—or, conversely, of their huddling together inside the ethnic tent until they could be assimilated—all these shaping forces were present from the start. What came later was the breaking up of the rural and small-town life of America and the massing in impersonal cities, bringing a dislocation that strengthened the impulse to join like-minded people.

Yet here again one runs a danger in generalizing about Americans as a nation. There are phases of class and status that must be taken into account. There has been a tendency to believe that because Babbitt was a joiner all joiners and belongers must therefore be Babbitts and must come from the middle classes. But the studies show a different picture. Warner found in Newburyport a direct correlation between the height of the class level and the propensity to join associations. Using his own six class categories (two uppers, two middles, and two lowers), he found that 72 per cent of the people in the upper classes belonged to associations, 64 per cent in the upper middle, 49 per cent in the lower middle, and 39 per cent and 22 per cent in the two lowers respectively.

Moreover, each of the classes tended to join different kinds of groups, for somewhat different purposes, and each of them had a different "style" of behavior within them. The elites used the associations chiefly as instruments for the strategic manipulation of the life of the community—through their control of the country clubs, the eating and discussion clubs, the civic associations, the fund-raising drives. Even when they belonged to such middle-class groups as the women's clubs or the businessmen's service clubs, they brought with them a prestige which enabled them to run the show, and sometimes they used their social power as a form of blackmail in extracting larger civic contributions from the parvenu groups. The middle classes used the associations largely as a way of improving their social status and for training themselves in articulateness and leadership. For the lower classes the emphasis was mainly upon church activities. Actually, the figures for their participation in club life would be even lower if it were not for the fact that a large proportion were in the minority ethnic groups and belonged therefore to their ethnic societies. The lower-class "old American" has very few associational ties.

An added word as to why the "low-status" people (as a number of studies have shown) belong to relatively few associations: partly it is because the nature of their work leaves them less time, partly because they lack the needed money for membership, partly because their interests and perspectives are more limited. With more limited life chances there is a corresponding shrinkage of participation in community experience through the associations. In fact, the Lynds found in their *Middletown* studies that the low-income and low-status groups made few visits except in their immediate neighborhood, formed few ties outside it, and had few friendships: their contacts of a more intimate sort were with their "own kin." Thus the low-status groups in America tend to become isolated, and their isolation is all the greater because they are part of a culture in which everybody else "belongs." I have spoken of the differences in class style. One of the striking differences is that the club activities of the lower and middle classes tend to be more symbolic, emotional, and ritualistic: those of the upper classes are more rationalist, with greater emphasis on speeches and discussions.

There are certain common elements, however, in the whole range of associational life. Members are expected to be "active." They belong to committees, take part in campaigns, try to get publicity for their activities in the local press, lay a good deal of stress on fund-raising (especially in the case of the women's groups), and engage in a kind of gift exchange by a reciprocity of contributions which Warner compares to the potlatches of some of the American Indian tribes. A good deal of American humor has concerned itself with club life, including Robert Benchley's classic film on "The Treasurer's Report." But club and com-

mittee work has also meant a training in democratic forms and procedures and an instrument for integrating the community.

Some commentators have guessed that Americans are intense joiners
because they need some way of alleviating the tensions and anxieties that
arise in their competitive living—which would account for the large
number of philanthropic, service, and reformist organizations. Certainly
the ritual of the fraternal associations may be an answer to the humdrum character of the daily tasks, and the sense of brotherliness and of
service may be a way of allaying the accumulated hostilities and guilt
feelings. E. D. Chapple, using an anthropological approach to the theory
of associations, suggests that a person who has suffered a serious disturbance may get relocated either by some form of ritual (the *rites of passage* mentioned above) or by changes in his "tangent relations," which
he achieves by activity in clubs and associations. This is a technical and
roundabout way of saying that the American propensity to join meets
a need of the personality and mediates disturbances within that personality, and that keeping busy in association work is one way of meeting,
avoiding, or channeling tensions within oneself. Yet this seems a negative and partial approach. Like other human beings, Americans don't
do things just to avoid trouble or allay guilt. In a deeper and more affirmative sense the joining impulse is part of the expansion of personality, even while it may often help to create some of the insecurities it
seeks to allay.

This jibes with what I said above about class differences in community participation. If joining were only an answer to inner tensions, then
the low-status groups would be fully as active as the middle classes, or
even more so: yet they are much less active. Their lesser activity derives
from their lesser income, lesser education, narrower perspectives and life
chances. The urge to associate is thus linked with the expansion of perspective and personality, at least in the intermediate stage, since there is
plenty of evidence that a highly developed personality tends in the end
to seek solitude. But solitude is different from isolation. Another bit of
evidence is to be found in the trend toward suburban living. The theory
has been that the impersonality of the big city breeds associations. Yet
recent experience shows that when people move from the mass city to
the more compassable suburb, their participation in club and association life increases deeply. Again this indicates that the American is a
joiner because he feels the freedom to expand, to fill out a personality-
on-the-make, and he has an inner need to find outer symbols of the fact
that he belongs to his culture and has not been left behind by it.

The clubs and associations which he joins do not, however, simplify
his life but make it more crowded and complex. The demands on his

time and participation multiply. The "new leisure," which is in itself the product of mechanization and the shorter working week, is getting filled in with the beehive activities of common ventures. Keeping up with club work has become one of the new imperatives of middle-class life. What makes it worse for a small group is that the range of leadership is a constricted one, and the most difficult tasks fall upon a few. America has become overorganized and association-saturated. Yet it may be worth the cost since the associations serve as filaments to tie people together in a community of interests less accidental and casual than it may seem.

Such filaments reach across the continent, so that periodically Americans gather in "conventions" of every sort, which serve formally as legislative bodies but actually as ways of tightening the ties of interest by face-to-face encounters. It may be a convention of a political party or of a trade-union or trade association, sales representatives of a big national corporation, scientists or scholars, church groups, or women's clubs, Shriners or Elks or Legionnaires. In the case of a big national organization as many as 100,000 people may descend upon the convention city to stay for a week, although usually it means only a few hundred or few thousand. They outdo one another in antics and pranks; they swarm over the hotels, sustaining the hotel industry, bars, night clubs, and call girls. In the case of conventions called by big corporations or trade associations, the purpose is to build morale and give a personal touch to an otherwise impersonal organization. The dominant note is that of "greeterism," in which the managers and inside groups seek to make the "visiting firemen" feel at home.

But changes have come over American conventions, as over the whole institution of "joining." The "service clubs" such as Kiwanis and Rotarians—a combination of Big Brother, Good Neighbor, and Greeter—are regarded with some amusement even among their own circles. The world of Babbitt exists in perfect form only in the pages of Sinclair Lewis and in the "Americana" items enshrined in the faded issues of Mencken's *American Mercury*. Even the antics of veterans' groups and fraternal orders are coming to be regarded with boredom and annoyance. The emphasis is shifting from adolescent hoopla to the concerns of particular interest and taste groups. Even in the conventions, as Raoul Denney has pointed out, the "greeters" are becoming "meeters"; and the techniques of "participating" sessions, in which work experiences are exchanged, have reached the trade association and corporate meetings.

Yet with all this sobering current of change, Americans as joiners have not wholly lost the *élan* which has made their associational impulse a cross between promotion, interchange of ideas, and the exorcising of loneliness through modern saturnalia.

3. Manners, Taste, and Fashion

THE HURLY-BURLY I have been describing, of clubs, "greeters," and "meeters," would be impossible in an aristocratic society where the minutiae and *elegantiae* of conventional behavior are part of its being. Obviously they are not unimportant in the American living scheme, as witness the question-and-answer columns in the newspapers, the etiquette books by Emily Post and Amy Vanderbilt, and the anxiety with which stenographers and salesgirls, adolescents and young wives, study "the right thing" to do. The difference is that the aping of one's social superiors in America takes other and more meaningful forms than the aping of their manners. The imitation is directed rather at their business ways, their genteel ferocities and their modes of consumption. Besides, there are today no established arbiters of American manners and taste, as there were in English and French society of the seventeenth and eighteenth centuries, so that the compendia codify diffused popular usage rather than class edicts.

Despite Veblen's satire about how the underlying population apes the leisure class, what sets the emotional tone in America is not so much *imitation* as *striving:* not the aping of the behavior of superiors but the straining to catch up with their living standards. Where a society is in rapid movement, class differences are not sharp or stable, and manners become fluid. Their function becomes not so much that of setting off groups from one another as of merging them. That is why De Tocqueville spoke of the "democratic manners" of the Americans of his day. He was writing for an audience of nineteenth-century Europeans who valued *la politesse* as a mode of class expression; and he was struck by the fact that manners in America crisscrossed the class strata, expressing neither deference nor condescension but the easy give-and-take of equals.

This was truest, of course, in the frontier communities that De Tocqueville visited, as it continued to comprise a large constituent of the democratic spirit of the frontier: manners counted not as etiquette—what was "correct"—but as a valuing of the person by others. The earliest American books of etiquette (as Arthur M. Schlesinger, Sr., has shown in his little book, *Learning How to Behave*) dealt with the theme of deference to rank; and in the South these books continued to present the way of life of the English landed gentry and "the chivalry." After the Civil War the rise of the newly rich in the North brought with it a new solicitude about manners on the part of those who wished to gloss over their class origins.

The contemporary foreign travelers, who can now be read as amateur anthropologists of American behavior, were impressed with the gap in manners between the Americans and the Europeans. Mrs. Trollope especially, in her famous book on *Domestic Manners of the Americans* (1832), wrote about the American people, "I do not like their principles, I do not like their manners, I do not like their opinions." She was shocked at the male habits of tobacco chewing and spitting, at the execrable theater behavior of both sexes, at the silent bolting of food in public eating places, and at the rudeness both of women and children. Anthony Trollope, trying to heal the wounds his mother's book had caused, was able to add very little in the 1870s that could correct her picture of the 1830s. He agreed with her about the American "lower orders" who did not know their position, yet he had a grudging admiration for people who scorned subservient manners and demanded respect for what they were as persons. The comments of Charles Dickens on the materialism of American life and the grossness of manners that flowed from it are now classic. Yet despite the strictures of these travelers who came from a more rigidly stratified society, De Tocqueville's judgment that American manners were on the rough side but had the ease of an equalitarian society seems to give a better perspective.

After World War I, when leisure was spreading among the new middle classes, the problem of good manners took a new form—that of correct etiquette. Books of etiquette were marketed by artful advertisements presenting embarrassing moments, with the caption "What's Wrong with This Picture?" The 1930s were filled with "fear ads" showing the discomfiture of a well-meaning young American who didn't know the right thing to do. Peter Arno caricatured this whole literature of fear in a cartoon which showed a bride resting her wrong arm on her father's hand, the caption reading, "A Laugh Went Through the Congregation." But while the sophisticates laughed, a million copies of Lillian Eichler's *Book of Etiquette* and an equal number of Emily Post's *Etiquette* were sold in the quarter century between 1920 and 1945.

In an essay on Emily Post, Edmund Wilson has pointed out that her world of the 1920s is peopled by "characters" like those of La Bruyère: Mr. and Mrs. Worldly, the Gildings of Golden Hall, Mr. and Mrs. Kindhart, Mrs. Littlehouse, Mr. and Mrs. Oldname, and Mr. Richard Vulgar. The archetypal life that Emily Post had in mind was that of the Oldnames, who lived not lavishly or ostentatiously but in a style that was (as Wilson puts it) "costly and glossy, smart, self-conscious" and always with the perfection of taste which made every piece of furniture and every item of clothing "priceless." The America of today has moved away from this impossible norm. The new books of etiquette, like Amy Vanderbilt's, are written on the assumption that "it is no longer smart to be stuffy," that the mannerly American housewife may be running a servantless apartment, mingling with Catholics and Jews and needing to know their customs, and that she may even herself be a "new citizen." Yet the need to know the "correct thing" in every situation is still an insistent one in a mobile society in which the codes are difficult even to formulate. This is especially true since so many Americans came from cultures whose patterns of behavior were different from the American, so that they had to strip themselves of one pattern and take on a new one.

With the expanding life of the middle-class American in a consumer's civilization, new rules are necessary for dress and manners, entertaining, social letter writing, conversation, bringing up children, speaking before a club audience, travel abroad. The vogue of the cocktail party, night club, football, or World Series baseball games, "dinner and the theater," country week ends, summer vacations, has raised new conventional anxieties, from what to wear at the cocktail party to the "etiquette of the road." But the manners, fashions, and tastes of a society of widespread leisure, which govern its minutiae of social relations, are different in character and function from those of a society where leisure is sharply stratified by class.

These codes are not needed in a democracy, as they are in an aristocracy, to hold the society together, but to clarify the confusions that arise from class mobility and diverse ethnic origins. In the South, where status is more rigid, manners have always been much more formalized: visits, dances, dueling (in the earlier days), even conversation, were governed by a highly developed ritual. To a lesser degree this was true of New England society, and it is notable that the "novel of manners" flourished mainly in the regional literature of the South and New England. Both on the frontier and in the big cities the rigors of manners were dissolved: but even the frontier developed its own codes of rough-and-ready social relations, and in the early mining days of California there was a punctilio of violence. Thus "democratic manners" do not mean that codes are discarded but that the same etiquette and the same freedoms apply to all classes; as a result, the classes develop an ease of manner toward one another not found in more rigid societies. But this ease is not without its own anxieties. Especially among the white-collar classes and the parvenu rich, there is a malaise which reflects a fluidity of social movement without fixed standards of social behavior.

Each society infused its codes of etiquette with the characteristic tone and overtones set by its dominant ideals. The ideals in America are neither those of chivalry and status nor those of the aristocratic *noblesse oblige*. They are the ideals of making your way, of being popular and charming, of being a success. Etiquette books and columns are read in America largely as part of the "how to" literature. The problem in knowing the correct thing is not to fix your station but to avoid discomfiture and learn how to be popular and charming. The dominant drive is social acceptance.*

In societies with codes of good manners, there is likely to be good conversation, which at its best contains ritual elements. American conversation, while it has a ceremonial of its own based on the radio gag writer with his routinized "wisecracks," is not good conversation. On every class level it is built around much the same staples—gags about marriage and sex, banter about sports and parties, offers to bet someone on practically anything, jokes about politics and corruption, shop talk about business or office, women's talk about clothes and shopping, family persiflage, scandal about figures in the headlines, ripostes about "dates" and attractiveness. Thus conversation in America is fragmented and stereotyped, tending to copy the talk on TV and in the movies. An evening of conversation becomes a succession of stories, jokes, retorts, and discontinuous comment, where little is sustained and nothing explored. It is not so much a probing of personality or an exchange of ideas as a discharge of nervous energy.

Conversation thus holds a mirror up to popular culture and not to the life of intellectuals or artists. Even in popular culture it does not today parallel the traditional "tall stories" of the frontier or the "Southern conversation" which was a ritual prelude of every visit in Southern families of breeding, just as it marks a break from the conversation at the dinner tables of the New England Brahmins. But a society must be judged by its ideals, and the conversational ideal of the London of Samuel Johnson and Alexander Pope or the Paris of the great literary salons is not that of America. There is a racy quality in the Broadway characters of Damon Runyon, so cherished as an American image by British intellectuals, and there is a vitality in the rapid-fire dialogue of the American suspense thrillers which is admired by French intellectuals. But they have little relation either to the cultural ideals or reality of American everyday convention. Similarly, letter writing, which was one of the great arts of a stratified society in the days before the communications revolution, is practically an extinct one in America. The published letters of Henry Adams and of Justice Holmes—graceful, barbed, learned, wide-ranging—are unlikely to be duplicated among the literary men of today who don't have to write letters since they can phone or fly, or are too busy for leisurely correspondence, or have a ready financial market for whatever flows from their typewriters.

The problems of taste are more important to most Americans than those of conversation. Like etiquette, taste is a new empire brought

---

* For a discussion of "Society," see Ch. VII, Sec. 2, "The Seats of the Mighty."

within the reach of lower- and middle-class groups by the spread of leisure. The violent attacks on American mass culture should not obscure the role of leisure in breaking the old fences which used to shut millions of people from the elite standards of appreciation and taste. There are great popular audiences in America for good concert and recorded music, as well as a new mass audience of perhaps a hundred million readers for books in popular reprints—most of them trashy but some on a level which never had a mass audience before:* on questions of food and cooking, of household furnishings, of dress, of the choice of schools and colleges, of vacation places, of movies and plays, of methods of child-rearing, there is a constant "taste exchange." This has been true in other societies on the upper-class levels. But there has never been so wide a range of choice for so many people, nor so demanding a task in making the choice.

The standards of taste in America have been decried repeatedly by those who feel that Americans neither like the right things nor know what they do like and why. This is not wholly the product of recent commercialism. Even in Emerson's and Hawthorne's time the superficial and gracile "Zenobias" and "Cleopatras" that American sculptors fashioned on their trips to Europe became the rage among a public that found prestige in the appreciation of classical themes; and the flaccid Hiram Powers statue of *The Greek Slave* was admired at exhibitions and became, in miniature copies, a standard embellishment of the American home. In the new American society there was a collapse of the taste standards of the European societies from which Americans had come. The principle of social equality made impossible the European idea that the lower classes were to derive their tastes from those above who acted as arbiters. Most Americans prided themselves on having become liberated from their bondage to aristocracies, in matters of taste as well as in matters of politics. "You are in a country," wrote the novelist James Fenimore Cooper to the sculptor Horatio Greenough, "in which every man swaggers and talks, knowledge or no knowledge; brains or no brains; taste or no taste. They are all *ex nato* connoisseurs, politicians, religionists, and every man's equal and all men's betters." Inevitably the large new middle class that became dominant in America failed to show the requirements of taste found in a society clearly divided between patrician and commoner, or one in which the crucial relation was between patron and artist.

Yet it was not for want of trying. American women filled their houses in the 1850s with bric-a-brac, knickknacks, and *bibelots*. American husbands dreamed of building houses which looked like Greek temples.

* For a further discussion of this theme, see Ch. XI, Sec. 2b, "The Reading Revolution."

James Jackson Jarves, who was an art critic and collector in the 1850s and 1860s, wrote that "it has become the mode to have taste." Jarves and his family had lived in Florence, and many people since him have measured American taste by the standards of that great Italian city. Obviously American taste could not touch the height of Florentine society in the Renaissance, and there were many depths of vulgarity that it did touch. Yet the taste it fashioned was its own, set not by the arbitrary standards of a specialized group but by energies within the whole of American society. Edith Wharton believed that if the taste of the rich could be elevated, this would seep down and reform the taste of the rest of American society. Other writers and critics have fondly hoped that the taste of an intellectual elite could perform the same function. But they have all been proved wrong.

I shall return* to the problems of taste posed by a Big Media culture where the artist does his work for a mass market, and where new designs are mechanically reproduced in millions of copies. What I am concerned with here is the codes that shape American taste, and the pressure toward conformism in taste as in morals and personality.

It is true of most cultures that the popular taste is derived from the high-income upper class, and to an extent this has become true of America as well. But where America is different is in the fact that its middle classes have access to much the same goods that its top rich possess. Thus both good and bad taste are diffused through the whole society instead of being specialized to particular classes. The work of designers of some distinction is brought into millions of homes. Even when it gets there through imitation rather than through genuine taste, it may often succeed in molding taste. As a result the stuffy ornateness of much of nineteenth-century living, especially in American home interiors, is being replaced by designs and fabrics more closely related to the needs of American living.

There is an obvious leveling-out process going on in American taste. The eccentrics who gave flavor to eighteenth- and nineteenth-century American life find fewer counterparts in the mid-twentieth century. The grotesquely bad taste of the frontier society, or of the immigrant and working-class culture of big cities, had at least an element of lustiness, and the same is true of the lavish extravagance of plutocratic society from the end of the Civil War through the 1920s, which has been often caricatured by American satirists. The great danger in this area is not that Americans will accept conformism—as they tend to do in matters of opinion—but that the middle-class impulse toward "good taste" tends in itself toward the anemic. As Louis Kronenberger has

* See Ch. XI, Sec. 8, "Building, Design, and the Arts."

put it, the nerve-grating, teeth-on-edge qualities of American life come not from a people that is "overbred" (as in aristocratic societies) but from one that is "overburdened." This is another way of saying that taste is not a dominant cultural ideal in America, as it is in more stratified societies. The dominant ideals are prestige, security, and success. It is they that produce the strain and tension and cause the psychic burdens to mount. They, as well as the taste, are part of the price that a society of rapid mobility has to pay.

American taste has moved through successive layers and transformations, as through the phases of a cocoon. Russell Lynes, writing the history of the *Tastemakers,* speaks of the three broad eras of "public taste," "private taste," and "corporate taste." While one may argue whether this is not too neat a categorizing of history, there is little question that all three are present as elements shaping American taste today. The combined anarchy-plus-tyranny of democratic taste is still a reality in a mass-production society; so also is the new role of the corporations acting as Maecenases, and the tax-deductible efforts of the private collectors; so too is the autonomous taste of the individual who uses what is usable from the domains of public and machine-made taste, yet is bold in forming his own judgments and tenacious in holding to them against the current.

All of which does not mean that there are no leaders in fashioning taste, even in a democracy. The vogue of a sculptor like John Rogers, an architect like Richard M. Hunt, or an interior designer like Elsie de Wolfe in past phases of American taste has given way to the vogue of new "tastemakers" like Loewy, Dreyfuss, and Bel Geddes in the domain of industrial design. The plush-and-crystal crazes of past periods, expressed in the garish hotels, river boats, and Pullmans that were advertised as "palaces for the people," have become muted in contemporary America, where there is a fear of being too loud, and where glitter-and-gold seem too reminiscent of the parvenu decade. Ostentation has become unfashionable. Yet it would be too early to predict that the aesthetic energies of so rich a civilization will remain leashed very long.

The most striking taste development in America is the emergence of a consciousness of strata of taste which parallels to some extent the class stratification. The now classic division between "highbrows," "lowbrows," and "middlebrows" is an expression of prestige levels, not in the area of economic or social position but in the areas of dress, speech, reading, and preferences in art. Lynes has rightly pointed out that in this area there is a different kind of power politics from the one that applies in class stratification as such. There is a working alliance between highbrows and lowbrows, in the sense that the highbrows value the folk impulses of the lowbrows and take over such popular preferences as the taste for comics and jazz. Very different from both is the taste of the middlebrows, toward whom the highbrows feel a condescension, and who in turn fear to be confused with the lowbrow. When one adds the distinction currently being made between the taste of the "upper middlebrows" and that of the "lower middlebrows," and between the "old highbrows" and the "new highbrows," the whole picture takes on some of the quality of Warner's six-level scheme of class stratification.

What is involved here is that the middle class, which has come to dominate the rest of the culture, has found forceful challenges in the realm of taste and feels isolated between the snobbery of the highbrow intellectuals and the vulgar energies of popular culture. Yet this is in itself evidence that there are no class tyrannies in American taste, and that the whole process of social change is still fluid enough to allow for the upward movement of popular culture from below, and the downward movement of critical taste standards from above. The middlebrow is caught between the two currents, yet he does not long remain the middlebrow. Nothing is more rapid in American life than the changes in taste which form part of the same ferment as the changes within the social order itself.

In dress as in other living standards, the lines of distinction between the wealthy and the middle class have been almost wiped out in America. This is not due to a redistribution of income: the buying capacity at the top levels is still many times what is available at the middle and lower levels. Nor is it the product of the willed simplification of technology which shows itself in the industries of women's clothes as elsewhere. To make big profits American designers have had to break through the luxury trade, to tap new middle-class and mass markets. To do so they have reduced the number of their basic models and distributed widely "copies" of the work of the great designers of Paris and New York. The differences are still there—in quality of fabric, in detailed work of finish, in the time differential before new models are available for mass distribution. Yet a degree of smartness and taste is achieved even with cheap fabrics and in factory-made designs, and they have also speeded up changes in fashion.

Few societies in history have been as fashion conscious as the American, and there have been few in which styles and clothes have changed so often.* Students of human society know that changing fashions are

* For an earlier discussion of fashions, as they affect the social role of American women, see Ch. VIII, Sec. 6, "The Ordeal of the American Woman." For dress as living standard, see Ch. IV, Sec. 5, "The Wilderness of Commodities."

an index of the pace of social change within the society: in the great Oriental civilizations, which were closed societies for centuries, there was little change in styles of clothing, whether for women or men; the stability of dress expressed the stability of status. In the class societies of the West, notably the French and British since the Industrial Revolution, changing dress fashions expressed the changing class relations, and the Victorian middle classes dressed as differently from those of the seventeenth and eighteenth centuries as the Europeans of today when compared with the Victorians. In the American case, however, women's fashions have changed more rapidly than can be accounted for by shifting class relations. Skirts rise and fall in length with a baffling periodicity; the female figure is first constricted in corset and hobble skirts, then flattened out into a shapeless tubular frock which gives it freedom as within a flour sack, then blossoms forth in the seductive outlines of the "glamour girl." "New Look" follows "New Look," revolutions and counterrevolutions in fashions succeed each other with bewildering rapidity, especially when the dress industries are in need of rescue.

America produced in Thorstein Veblen's writings one of the seminal theories of the relation of dress to society. He saw "dress as the expression of the pecuniary culture," especially in setting off those who don't have to work from those who do. He saw the modern woman as a prime exhibit of "conspicuous waste" and "pecuniary emulation" on the part of her husband, to impress the underlings. *The Theory of the Leisure Class* was written at a time of corseted and restricted women's dress and of garish display by the captains of industry. It explained a good deal about women's clothes in America, but not enough. For Veblen's theory is far less applicable to the American case than to any other of the Western societies. The fact is that American fashions are neither set by the "leisure class" in the sense of the capitalist elite nor could they be sustained by that elite. It is the upper middle class, including the girls of the college generation and the young matrons of the professional and small-business class, who are the carriers of fashion change. They vie with the women of wealth in showing that they can be as smart and modish on a much smaller outlay; and the women in the lower middle class, pushing up the ladder of mobility, vie in turn with them. As Quentin Bell has put it, "The society which produces changing fashions must itself be changing," and the transformation of the middle class has constituted the crucial class change in America. But American women are likely to wear their clothes not so much to impress the class below, nor even to ape the class above, as to show their distinction and individuality on their own class level. Dressing becomes for them at once an expression of status and a form of creativeness.

Efforts have been made to trace the changing profile of the American woman through the shifting male attitudes toward women and the shifting responses of the women. Some of these theories have focused on the impact of a war, the premise being that in war and postwar periods the male feels heroic and wants his women to be feminine and seductive. Thus the Gibson girl of the turn of the century is seen as a response to the Spanish-American War in her elegance of dress, her emphasis on feminine hips and bust, and her ankles peeping out from yards of skirt. The profile of the American woman in the era of the suffragette and of the militant feminists was reflected in the hobble skirts and the sheath gown. After World War I, the pendular swing was once more toward the sultry femininity of the "vamp." But during the rest of the 1920s the women, with their knee-length skirts and their concealed or flattened bust and hips, again took on a boyish and sexless look. In the 1930s and 1940s Hollywood emerged as the archetype of fashions, with Jean Harlow and Rita Hayworth as the "love goddesses" toward whom the world of women's creations moved. Toward the middle 1950s there was a struggle going on between the forces tending toward a return to the "Dark Ages" of the tubular, shapeless figure and those emphasizing the natural attractions of the female.

This theory, typically formulated by Winthrop Sargent in a *Life* series, has the merit of reckoning with the currents that govern the emotional life of the woman and are therefore reflected in her dress and adornment. Since fashions, like fads, contain much of the element of recoil that springs from the boredom of the repetitive, a cyclical theory can be maintained with only a measure of distortion. Yet it leaves out of account the long secular trend in American fashions, which has steadily drawn away from the cumbersome garments to the freer ones and from the concealing to the revealing ones. Again, as part of the long secular trend, each of the "vamp" or "glamour" phases is a step further toward the cult of legs and breasts that expresses American sensuality. With its sleek and shining quality of the "siren look," it adds the elements of danger, expressiveness, and accessibility to the sensual cult. Again, each of the "Dark Ages" counterrevolutions toward the masculine and assertive in women's dress and attitudes falls ever shorter of the goal of women's revolt. In the mid-1950s there were efforts at reviving the fashions of 1900 and 1920, but they were tongue-in-cheek affairs, largely by college girls whose freshness of looks and mold of figure allowed them to "get away" with almost anything, and who underscored Quentin Bell's suggestion that the American woman adds "conspicuous outrage" to Veblen's other categories of conspicuous display.

Moving steadily, despite occasional retrogressions, toward freedom of dress, the American woman, however, fails to be a free agent. She responds to the tribal compulsions that move in waves of tendency.

Simone de Beauvoir calls the world of women an "immanent" one, and Gina Lombroso has suggested that women tend to fix their sentiments not on ideas but on objects, deifying them and using them as symbols. If this is true generally, it would be doubly true of a civilization in which women live among a wealth of objects and means of adornment. The American woman lives in the ever-recurring hope that a change in her silhouette can achieve the miracle of a change in her life cycle or life destiny. Emerson quotes a lady as saying, even in his day, that a "sense of being perfectly well dressed gives a feeling of inward tranquillity which Religion is powerless to bestow." But is it always tranquillity? Obsessive interest in fashions is more likely nowadays to be a response to boredom or frustration, or to a failure of life goals. Thus the woman is the more ready to accept the gyrations of fashion because she half hopes they will compensate for what she has missed in life.

The great designers know this: if clothes help unhappy women to forget, then the way to sell new clothes is to force them to remember. "We must accelerate obsolescence," one businessman said. Another told his trade colleagues in 1948, when the "New Look" had swept the country, "We must have a New Look every year. It is our job to make women unhappy with what they have. You might call us the merchants of unhappiness." American designers have arisen to challenge the Parisian empires of Balenciaga, Dior, and Fath. New synthetic fabrics on the market have added novelties of texture to those of design and have placed both within the reach of lower-middle-class women. The art of dressing up and photographing models to bring out their height and slimness and the sculptured grace of their characteristic skull formations has been carried to a degree of perfection never achieved elsewhere. The dress industries have only a limited power to create fashions, but they can prod them.

The creative role is in the culture and in the woman herself. If women are birds of plumage, American women have a special assurance in the knowledge that the resources of the consumer's culture are at their command. College girls at the height of their social valuation are especially resourceful in dress, since they are pretty enough to take risks. They ransack the centuries and vocations for ideas, using jockey caps and the British soldier's tam-o'-shanter, ranchman's overalls, Peruvian Indian capes, Indian moccasins, American army jackets. They use every available fabric from the finest silks to fish netting and potato sacking. From hairdo down to shoes, they seek novelty and turn everything that strikes their attention to decorative uses. Yet these individual variations are within the frame of the larger fashion cycles, which are, at bottom, tribal compulsions.

As for men's clothes, they are equally subject to tribal compulsions, but in a quite different sense. While the conventions dictate constant change of style, design, and material for women, so that last year's fashion is as archaic as some monster of the Reptilian Age, the conventions dictate much the same men's clothing year after year. There are some exceptions to this, notably the "sports" garb of Miami and Hollywood, where a certain garishness is held modish; the "sharp" styles of the man-around-Broadway, as also the Harlem dandy; and the Texas-Western style copied from the ranch boss or ranch hand, with cowboy boots and ten-gallon hat. But for the rest there is the "standard business suit" or "N.A.M." garb, in blue or brown or gray, which has varied little for a half century. The great dividing line in clothes is between the work clothes of the manual and the white-collar occupations. The difference in clothes look between a corporation executive and his salesman or advertising copywriter is very little, except for the quality of the fabric and the cut of the suit. The difference between both of them and the railway or steel worker or elevator operator is much greater.

There is little valuation in America of the dandy, except in extremely limited cosmopolitan circles: there is no one in American life who takes the place of the French dandies of the eighteenth century, partly because Americans regard one who has no visible occupation as a wastrel, partly also because there is a fear of overdecorated male finery and refinements of taste in men's clothes lest one be suspected of a homosexual bent. Only recently, especially in the suburbs and at the resorts, has the American male broken away from his traditional drabness and ventured into experimental colors and styles. But here too it is the middle class, not the elite, that has been the innovator.

The possessors of power in America feel at once fearful of fripperies of dress and contemptuous of them. Their wives, who must express the decorative impulse for the husbands as well and who must win and hold their affection, are absorbed with fashions and clothes. In both cases it is the code that governs, but in the case of the woman there is greater scope for expressiveness within the code and greater need for it, since it must help fill the haunting sense of being unused.

4. Varieties of American Character

DESPITE THE simplified versions of the "American character" that fill the commentaries on American life, it is in reality diverse and multiple.* This is a product of the geographic variety, the crisscrossing ethnic strains and cultural traditions, and the intermeshing forces and

* For a preliminary statement of the problem of the American character, see Ch. II, Sec. 5, "National Character and the Civilization Pattern." See also Ch. VIII, Sec. 1, "The Personality in the Culture."

counterforces in a changing American society. The crucial fact is that there is no single pattern that can be called the "American character," nor is there a neat set of categories into which the American personality fits. Riesman, who developed a striking set of character types for America in *The Lonely Crowd,* stressed the ambiguities within each and the fact that any individual American contains elements of all. When he brought together a series of interviews and case studies of particular contemporary Americans, in his *Faces in the Crowd,* he found that they eluded his categories. Each personality is a battleground of forces sweeping from every direction of the cultural landscape.

Whatever makes America a relatively open society makes it also more mobile in developing a potpourri of personality traits. The plasticity I have noted in American ethnic types is also present in the personality patterns. I do not mean that American personality is less rigid than personality in other cultures: it may actually in many instances be more rigid. But the mobility which gives Americans access to new forms of leisure and experience exposes them also to the new postures of personality that go with unaccustomed modes of life.

Seventeenth-century England produced a number of books on *Characters* depicting English society through the typical personality patterns of the era. Trying something of the same sort for contemporary America, the first fact one encounters is the slighter emphasis on a number of character types that stand out elsewhere in Western society: to be sure, they are to be found in America as well, but they are not characteristically American. One thinks of the scholar, the aesthete, the priest or "parson," the "aristocratic" Army officer, the revolutionary student, the civil servant, the male schoolteacher, the marriage broker, the courtesan, the mystic, the saint. Anyone familiar with European literature will recognize these characters as stock literary types and therefore as social types. Each of them represents a point of convergence for character and society. Anyone familiar with American literature will know that it contains stock portraits of its own which express social types. I want to use these traditional types as backdrops and stress some of the social roles that are new and still in process of formation.

Thus there is the *fixer,* who seems an organic product of a society in which the middleman function eats away the productive one. He may be public-relations man or influence peddler; he may get your traffic fine settled, or he may be able—whatever the commodity—to "get it for you wholesale." He is contemptuous of those who take the formal rules seriously; he knows how to cut corners—financial, political, administrative, or moral. At best there is something of the iconoclast in him, an unfooled quality far removed from the European personality types that always obey authority. At worst he becomes what the English call a "spiv" or cultural procurer.

Related to the fixer is the *inside dopester,* as Riesman has termed him. He is oriented not so much toward getting things fixed as toward being "in the know" and "wised up" about things that innocents take at face value. He is not disillusioned because he has never allowed himself the luxury of illusions. In the 1920s and 1930s he consumed the literature of "debunking"; in the current era he knows everything that takes place in the financial centers of Wall Street, the political centers of Capitol Hill, and the communications centers of Madison Avenue—yet among all the things he knows there is little he believes in. His skepticism is not the wisdom which deflates pretentiousness but that of the rejecting man who knows ahead of time that there is "nothing in it" whatever the "it" may be. In short, he is "hep."

Another link leads to the *neutral* man. He expresses the devaluing tendency in a culture that tries to avoid commitments. Fearful of being caught in the crosscurrents of conflict that may endanger his safety or status, he has a horror of what he calls "controversial figures"—and anyone becomes "controversial" if he is attacked. As the fixer and the inside dopester are the products of a middleman's society, so the neutral man is the product of a technological one. The technician's detachment from everything except effective results becomes—in the realm of character—an ethical vacuum that strips the results of much of their meaning.

From the neutral man to the *conformist* is a short step. Although he is not neutral—in fact, he may be militantly partisan—his partisanship is on the side of the big battalions. He lives in terror of being caught in a minority where his insecurity will be conspicuous. He gains a sense of stature by joining the dominant group, as he gains security by making himself indistinguishable from that group. Anxious to efface any unique traits of his own, he exacts conformity from others. He fears ideas whose newness means they are not yet accepted, but once they are firmly established he fights for them with a courage born of the knowledge that there is no danger in championing them. He hates foreigners and immigrants. When he talks of the "American way," he sees a world in which other cultures have become replicas of his own.

It is often hard to distinguish the conformist from the *routineer.* Essentially he is a man in uniform, sometimes literally, always symbolically. The big public-service corporations—railroads, air lines, public utilities—require their employees to wear uniforms that will imprint a common image of the enterprise as a whole. City employees, such as policemen and firemen, wear uniforms. Gas station attendants, hotel clerks, bellhops, must similarly keep their appearance within prescribed limits. Even the sales force in big department stores or the typists and stenographers in big corporations tend toward the same uniformity. There are very few young Americans who are likely to escape the uniform of the Armed Services. With the uniform goes an urge toward pride of status and a routineering habit of mind. There is the confidence that comes of belonging to a large organization and sharing symbolically in its bigness and power. There is a sense of security in having grooves within which to move. This is true on every level of corporate business enterprise, from the white-collar employee to "the man in the gray flannel suit," although it stops short of the top executives who create the uniforms instead of wearing them. Even outside the government and corporate bureaus there are signs of American life becoming bureaucratized, in a stress on forms and routines, on "going through channels."

Unlike the conformist or routineer, the *status seeker* may possess a resourceful energy and even originality, but he directs these qualities toward gaining status. What he wants is a secure niche in a society whose men are constantly being pulled upward or trodden down. Scott Fitzgerald has portrayed a heartbreaking case history of this character type in *The Great Gatsby,* whose charm and energy are invested fruitlessly in an effort to achieve social position. The novels of J. P. Marquand are embroideries of a similar theme, narrated through the mind of one who already has status and is confronted by the risk of losing it. At various social levels the status seeker becomes a "joiner" of associations which give him symbolic standing.

The foregoing personality types are, in one way or another, forms of what Erich Fromm has called the "marketing orientation." Their chief concern is with what is vendible, what can be quickly marshaled and exchanged for valuable commodities. I do not mean this as a stigma on the American society which is built around the market. It was inevitable that when the exchange of commodities for money—which in turn will buy more commodities—became the focus of social energies, the logical final step would be to make man himself a vendible commodity. Marx had an insight into this when he spoke of the "fetishism of commodities" in his era, pointing out that the commodity (especially money) is personalized and becomes a fetish, while human labor becomes a commodity. Were he writing today he might stress that it is not labor only which is up for sale but also love and the whole human personality. He was so preoccupied with class exploitation that he failed to see the *vendible personality* as a fixture on every class level, so that even the ruling groups themselves become its victim. What this character type seeks is not so much the money into which it can turn its talents as the assurance—which the money partly offers—that by being in demand it is an effective personality. In a society where the measures of value become increasingly external, the vendible personality strives to be in demand so that it can be sure of its identity—sure, in short, that it exists.*

The vendible personality has aspects of the hollow, but it contains little that is destructive. That quality lies rather with another facet of American life, the *authoritarian personality*. One of the historical functions of the free market and the open society was to break up the authoritarian mold of the society of status which preceded it. But the Devil cannot be driven out with a pitchfork. The authoritarian bent reasserted itself in American life as did the drive toward status and security. On every class level at mid-century one found signs of a cocksure intolerance which expresses the "true believer" who does not hesitate to impose his belief on others by an imperialism of will. A number of American psychologists, who had learned something about the classic Fascist and Communist personality patterns in Central Europe, made extensive studies of the same personality types in the American context (*The Authoritarian Personality,* by T. W. Adorno and others) and found the essential pattern present, although it took a specifically American form under American conditions.

As pioneers in the Big Media, Americans are also sensitive to the authority of the media. As a result, the *publicity seeker* became an organic part of a society in which the Big Media are crucial in achieving status. He gets a glow from seeing his "name and face" in the papers. He will often work hard in organizations mainly to become an officer, and he reaches the summit of his dreams when his picture is taken with a visiting celebrity. In the small town he may be in the church-and-club set, and in the big city in the café-society set, but always he does what he does in order to be seen doing it. He is happiest in the goldfish bowl of the public eye. The surrender of privacy which has been a marked trend in recent American life is for him no sacrifice but an assurance that he is "in the swim."

Another aspect of the whittling away of privacy is the emergence of the *informer-confessor* as a recognizable character type. In the earlier days of evangelistic religion the confessor came forward and bore witness to having been saved from the flames of Hell. In latter-day America (I am speaking of the avid confessor, not the reluctant one) he bares his political past with a virtuous sense of having achieved salvation after sin. He exposes others who worked with him in the past, either to save the nation or his skin, or to compel them to save their own souls.

The confessor impulse is not confined to former Communists or even to politics. The obverse side of the confessor-informer is the *voyeur,* who

* See also Ch. V, Sec. 6, "The Reach of the Business Spirit," and Ch. XI, Sec. 9, "Artist and Audience in a Democratic Culture."

craves a glimpse into the private lives of others, especially the noted and notorious. A by-product of the Kinsey interviews was an epidemic of fake "investigators" who got a thrill out of interviewing women on their sex lives—and in a remarkable number of instances the women were willing to tell all to men they had never before seen. Social workers have also encountered this confessional urge; and it is obvious that part of psychiatric treatment is the chance it offers for baring the soul, however painful the process. This helps account for the American vogue of the gossip columnist and the gossip magazines, several of whom have built a following and a structure of power unparalleled in other societies. By catching the great with their guard down, the ordinary man is reassured that they are of the same human condition as he.

The Age of Anxiety has also seen the emergence of the *fearer-pursuer*. He is convinced that he is encircled by enemies; at the same time he is a hunter for dangerous thoughts. He can combine these two seemingly contradictory sets of traits because each serves as psychic source and reinforcement of the other. The paranoiacs who feel themselves surrounded by conspirators are likely to become the Hounds of God in hunting them down; those in turn who spend their lives in a sustained quest for subversives are likely to feel themselves caught, like the Emperor Jones, in the jungle of their own anxieties. To breathe they require the constant euphoria of the chase, alternating with the shivers of conspiratorial fear. This personality pattern is also closely related to that of the debunker, since it thrives on the conviction that the institutions of a capitalist democracy are window dressing behind which a secret enemy—Communist, Fascist, Liberal, Wall Street, or Jewish—is carrying on his machinations.*

I have mentioned the vendible personality and the authoritarian one. Two other broad character types need to be added to them. One is the *adjusting* personality—and, as a counterweight to it, what Peter Viereck has called the "unadjusted man." The loss of clear life goals,† the fragmentizing of the mind, the feeling of being part of a going concern too vast for any one individual to resist, have all contributed to the outer and inner pressures of the American to "adjust." This is a different matter from selling oneself in a talent and personality market, as it is also different from wreaking oneself on others or surrendering to an authoritarian hero.

The adjusting man may have little of the authoritarian animus within

* For aspects of the authoritarian personality in action, see Ch. VI, Sec. 10, "The Struggle for Civil Liberties," Ch. VII, Sec. 5, "The Minority Situation," and Sec. 6, "The Negro in America."

† See Sec. 8, "Life Goals and the Pursuit of Happiness."

him and little of the aggressive drives of salesmanship. He just wants to merge into his social landscape, to offer as little exposed and vulnerable surface as possible to the storms of life, to take his place in the scheme of society with a minimum of effort and an economy of psychic hurt. This applies to his political behavior, as it applies also to his behavior on his job, in his neighborhood, in his family, among his friends, and in his social set. There is an aspect by which the American "common man," who seemed so vigorous and assertive a figure from the Age of Jackson to the New Deal Era, has become merely the "little man," who asserts only his urge not to assert himself.

If these portraits of social roles that have emerged during the past half century in America seem to have unnecessary shadows and even smudges, it is because the stormy experience of a half century of social dislocation and change, war and cold war, is bound to take its psychic toll from the personality. It would be strange if this experience had not produced far-reaching changes in the American personality pattern. But one could set up a similar gallery of portraits and roles, done in very different colors, that would express the other side of the American personality pattern and might be as faithful to the varieties of American character.

I have mentioned the *unadjusted man*. He is, of course, the *rebel* American whose life history stretches all the way from the Revolution to the present moment. He may be the highly sensitive and socially conscious American, derisively called "bleeding heart," who has not lost the antennae of fellow feeling and who suffers every ordeal or injustice and deprivation to which others are subject. He may be the *libertarian* who has broken away from the illusions of revolutionary theories born in very different cultural milieus and is all the more stubborn in defending the freedoms of his tradition. He may be the writer or artist who uses irony as well as indignation as his weapon and who stays in his own society to fight it out, unlike his predecessor who went to Rome or the Left Bank of Paris. He may, however, find a different kind of solution, not in civic battle but in retirement to the realm of the private life, where he can be an amateur of the arts and of thought and release his imagination by making his own personality into a work of art. Or he may be the *committed* American, whether the roots of his commitment be religious or aesthetic or moral, who survives the wrack of change because his primary drive is to be part of something meaningful which transcends himself, without ceasing to be himself. I might add that the very use of the phrase "unadjusted American," with its negative reference, is itself a sign that the personality types within this broad category of the marginal American have not yet found themselves within their new setting.

I have left to the end a personality type which may reach closest to the heart of the American experience. For want of a better term I call him the *operational* American. Again he falls into a number of subtypes. He may be the *engineer-businessman* of broad perspectives, whose pride is that of construction and who thinks in terms of welfare. He may be the *organizing* American, able to translate dreams from a blueprint stage into reality. He may be the *commanding* American who adds energy to whatever situation he finds himself in and carries with him always the prospects of achievement. He may be the *footloose* American who roams through the new empires carved out by his technology, with a generosity of outlook that few conquerors have had. But the generic trait of all of them is the creative impulse that takes its characteristic shape through the urge to get a job well done, so as to release rather than constrict the spirit.

No one of these portraits is more than a facet of the complex multiple personality that we call "American." What makes the new American of inexhaustible interest is that he can be interpreted by every observer so as to bear out his own bias. Much depends on the accident of the particular moment of history at which the composite portrait is drawn. I know, of course, that all these personality patterns have changed as they have responded to contemporary changes in the social situation, and that they will continue to change. It is a risky business therefore to set down these temporary frames of personality as if they were permanent. But it is a risk that must be taken. For even if the particular social roles and character types are transitory, the larger patterns that I have sought to sketch out will probably survive.

5. *The Disorders of a Society*

WHETHER OR NOT every punishment should be made to fit the crime, it is pretty clear that most crimes and disorders fit their culture. To those who take pride in the normalities of the "American way" it may come as something of a shock to consider that it is exactly the excess of that same "American way"—the norm gone beserk—which represents the disorganization and pathology of the culture.

Every society has its characteristic types and styles of disorganization, its inner nature being illumined by the breakdowns of its codes. Thus where postwar Europe had its black markets, America had its rackets; where other societies are riddled with widespread illegitimacy of birth, America has the problem of illegal abortions; where other societies have their legalized prostitution districts, America bans them but has the call-girl trade and the adolescent "amateurs"; where other societies may encourage childhood thievery and marauding adventures, America is deeply concerned about its fourteen- to sixteen-year-old delinquents; where crimes against the person prevail elsewhere, in America the characteristic crimes are against property, and particularly the white-collar crimes of business and professional groups.

Americans are likely to worry most about juvenile delinquency. This is because of the sense that the young people are the foundation of the American future, and if they are corrupted, then the future becomes blank. Boys of fourteen and over who pilfer and steal, and girls of the same age who show "ungovernable behavior" or become sexual delinquents, pour through the juvenile courts in increasing numbers. The problem is not usually in their intelligence but in the conditions under which they grow up. The spate of statistical studies and life history "documentaries" shows them to come from "delinquency areas" where several subcultures are in conflict, and from homes whose emotional and moral atmosphere is unhealthy.

There are recurrent waves of guilt about these facts that periodically sweep over American society. The denunciation of slums and poverty gets the best responses when they are depicted not as ills in themselves, ugly and debasing, but as the breeding ground of child delinquency. The studies of rejected and unloved children leave their mark on the American mind less because the lack of love mutilates the personality than because it makes vulnerable material for delinquency. There are citizens' committees, surveys, conferences on juvenile delinquency. The newspapers dutifully record the solemn, scolding speeches, the moralists moralize, and the denouncers denounce. Usually there is a cry for more "recreation facilities" (recreation has been called the "nostrum of the citizens' committees"), which sheds light on the guilt feeling Americans have about delinquency. In contrast with the original image of immigrants who saw America as a wonderful playground, they have been compelled by the condition of the children to think of it as a condemned playground.

A persisting question is whether the volume of delinquency has actually increased during the past two decades or whether there is merely greater sensitivity to the problem and a more intense fixation upon it. The official figures show an actual and dramatic increase. Focusing on the ten- to seventeen-year-old, and taking as a base the estimate of annual delinquency at the rate of 1 per cent of the young people in this age group before World War II (between 170,000 and 200,000 children), the figures for the mid-1950s were just about double, meaning an annual rate of 2 per cent (around 385,000). If we add the children who are picked up by the police without having their cases brought before the courts, the total figure becomes roughly a million; and, according to the estimate of the Federal Children's Bureau for 1953, the probable total figure for 1960 is likely to be a million and a half. If, finally, we add the figures of children involved in dependency and neglect cases, which are the breeding grounds for delinquency, the official delinquency estimates are increased by 25 per cent.

The crisis moment in the life of a child in his encounters with the law comes at the age of fifteen to sixteen, a fact that underscores the relation between delinquency and the sexual and psychic problems of adolescence. The 1952 figures showed boys outnumbering girls about five to one in delinquency cases—a not very surprising fact when you consider the different demands that the culture makes upon growing boys and girls and the different roles it assigns them. The attitude of the society is a good deal more permissive toward the growing boy ("boys will be boys") and a good deal more solicitous in the parental control of the adolescent girl, especially in lower-class families. One should add that just as the society is more permissive about the code of the growing boy, it is more lenient in punishing his infractions of the code; in the case of the girl, there is a far higher percentage of referral to social agencies and commitment to correctional institutions. While delinquency is still centered largely in cities, the rate in rural areas is rising rapidly. Yet the basic problem remains one of the rejection of the children of minority groups by the larger culture. The normlessness which underlies what has been called the "mutiny of the young" finds more intense expression in those groups which have not made the transition to a new milieu and which feel themselves excluded from it.*

The human harvest of these seeds of disorder may be found in the ominous "statistical profile" of crime in America. At mid-century there were about fifteen million arrests annually in those cities where the statistics are fairly regular—a figure which represents only a fraction of the total offenses committed. Most of the arrests are for larcenies, burglaries, auto thefts, and other offenses against property. In only one case out of twenty does the offense result in imprisonment. In the case of white-collar crimes, involving business cheating, embezzling, illegal stock-market manipulation, tax evasion, defective merchandise, the proportion of offenses discovered to the total number committed is even smaller.

Despite a long history of prison reform and the relatively high standards of administration in Federal prisons, the condition of American prisons is still backward in most states, especially in the South, where the chain gangs are used to get cheap labor for public works and where

* For an earlier discussion of the adolescent gang, see Ch. VIII, Sec. 4, "Growing Up in America."

race feeling is added to the usual inhumanity between captor and captive. In most prisons the inmates are still kept shut up in cell blocks,
given largely meaningless labor, and cut off from the responsibility
which alone can restore a man to a productive life. In a society which
stresses sex they are also cut off from normal heterosexual relations, so
that prisons fortify and even breed homosexual tendencies. A few voices
are now asserting that "prisoners are people too," and experiments are
being made in informal prison farms where the men can come closer
to normal patterns of daily living and have their confidence in humanity restored.

But the individual criminal dwindles in importance before "rackets"
and "syndicates." The racket is a pattern of extortion and tribute which
urban brigands levy on night clubs, shopkeepers, bars, manufacturers,
trade-unions, waterfront companies, and truckers, under threat of de-
spoiling their goods or premises and even death. The syndicate is a business combine with a feudal structure of authority, organized to exploit
activities beyond the law or on its margin—gambling, betting, slot machines, houses of prostitution, "call-girl" services, and narcotics.*

These activities are not as marginal to American life as they are to
American law. One trait on which the rackets and syndicates build is the
belief in luck, which is deeply ingrained in a culture that underlines the
big prizes. There is widespread betting on sports events—on horse racing, prize fighting, baseball, basketball, football. Slot machines are the
center of rural and roadside taverns as well as of urban bars and luxury
clubs. One of the purest forms of the belief in luck is the "numbers" or
"policy" game, in which bets are placed on what numbers may turn up
each day in officially published reports, such as Federal Reserve Bank
statements. The crowds gathered around New York's newsstands for
early editions of the morning tabloids are probably more interested in
getting the racing results and the "numbers" pay-off than in the international news. The annual "take" from slot machines has been estimated at two billion dollars. The income from "policy" betting in Chicago alone, largely in the Negro areas, is estimated at fifty million
dollars, most of it in nickels, dimes, and quarters. In such low-income
Negro areas, "policy" may mean destitution for thousands of families—
and wealth for the few men who organize and run it as a big business.
For the gambling industry as a whole, including bookmaking, legalized
or pari-mutuel betting, the "numbers" game, "policy," slot machines,
and lotteries, the annual business has been calculated at fifteen billion
dollars, involving an industry that ranks in gross sales with such major
American industries as chemicals.

* For the "racket" and the "fix" in the context of American politics, see Ch. VI,
Sec. 4, "The Party System and the Voter."

To protect these industries against the uneasy conscience of the community, an alliance is sometimes formed between the syndicates and rackets on the one hand, and on the other the political bosses, machine politicians, police-force officials, wire and phone services, trade-unions, and seemingly respectable business concerns that operate as "fronts." It was this alliance which was the principal target of inquiry by the Kefauver Committee in 1951 and the McClellan Committee in 1957. The importance of these inquiries, as also earlier of the writings of Lincoln Steffens and the muckrakers, was that they made the American people aware of the tie-up between lawlessness, politics and the marginal aspects of business and trade-unionism. What they saw did violence to their cherished belief not only in law and order but in the healthy organization of their society. A few men went to jail, a few local administrators and labor leaders were thrust out of office, new Federal tax laws made the "bookie" profession a good deal more dangerous—but the basic pattern of the rackets and syndicates went on.

America today, as in the past, presents the picture both of a lawless society and an overlegislated one. In some of the earlier societies the reliance was less upon detailed legal norms and penalties than upon custom and the sanctions of community opinion. But America is the type-society of the West in which little is left to loose community action, and the characteristic way of dealing with crime is to set down definite statements of legal transgressions and punishments. Nevertheless, Americans consider crime a problem they cannot master, which will continue to grow because it is an outcropping of some inner disease of their society. Recognizing this, they also recoil from it, thus displacing on the criminal their own guilt and powerlessness—which may help explain why the treatment of crime has lagged. To feel mastery over the environment, over things and money, and yet to feel baffled by so elementary a fact as crime, has become a source of frustration.*

Like the belief in luck, the habit of strong drink is something Americans worry about while many of them continue to practice it. The frontiersmen prided themselves on their drinking excesses: the isolation of life, along with its rigors, led to a plentiful consumption of homemade spirits. For the plantation leisure class of the Old South, heavy drinking was at once an antidote to boredom and the mark of hospitality for the landed gentry. Among the miners and cattle ranchers of the Far West, the frontier saloon was an outlet for the turbulence of new and lawless settlements. All these strands of social inheritance may still be found in American drinking, yet while the old reasons for heavy drinking no

* For the concept of the criminal in American law, see Ch. VI, Sec. 8, "Law and Justice."

longer apply in the urbanized indoor society, the drinking remains. The new reasons for drinking are probably more closely connected with the driving tempo of life in America and the anxieties, frustrations, and aggressions it engenders. It should be added, however, that the practice of "local option" means that a large part of the nation is legally "dry," and what drinking there is must be done in private homes or by subterfuge. The heavy drinking is to be found in the Eastern centers, on the West Coast (California leads the nation in alcoholism), and in the centers of new wealth and social change, like Texas.

Not the least of America's mores are woven around the night club, the roadhouse, the public bar—and the private bar at home. Just as betting and gambling take on emotional overtones from the ritualized competitiveness of American sports, so liquor in the night hours and night spots takes on sexual overtones from the orgiastic arts of "hot music" and sexually revealing "revues" and "floor shows." The sexual revolution of the 1920s removed the restraints against drinking by women; except in the small towns, where the older mores prevail, women will be found drinking in public restaurants and bars, or at private parties at the "cocktail hour," which is as basic a national institution as afternoon tea for the British or the Continental apéritif. So crucial did the consumption of alcohol become in America that the Prohibition episode came closer to dividing the nation into two camps than anything since the Civil War, and the cleavage between "wets" and "drys" became a struggle between Guelphs and Ghibellines. Much of the network of rackets and syndicates goes back to these Prohibition days: so strong was the feeling against "law enforcement" that the American attitude toward the Prohibition agents in the 1920s was very like that of a Resistance movement toward an army of occupation.

Distinguishing between "social drinkers" and compulsive ones, there were some forty or fifty million of the former and about two and a half million of the latter, of whom at least a half million were confirmed alcoholics. While these figures seem large, the problem of alcoholism in America is not as serious as in European countries like Sweden and Germany. In their efforts to deal with alcoholism, Americans characteristically resorted to the device of a club, "Alcoholics Anonymous," whose members supported one another in their efforts to refrain from drinking. As for narcotics addiction, the narcotics traffic increased after World War II, and the vigilance against it tightened. About a fifth of the fifty or sixty thousand drug addicts were teen-agers, mainly from the metropolitan centers and especially the Negro areas. The smoking of "reefers" (marijuana) was more widespread among teen-agers than drug addiction: its danger lay in its leading so often to heroin or morphine.

To these items of social pathology we must add organized prostitution, illegal abortion, homosexuality in its more compulsive forms, and sexual offenses—especially against children—which were often in the headlines and roused intense popular anger.*

These are all departures from the dominant norms of cultural health. Some of them, like crime, are deliberate attacks upon the norms; others, like delinquency, alcoholism, drug addiction, and prostitution, are forms of failure in living up to the norm. In some instances, as with homosexuals, or heavy drinkers who are not alcoholics, or those migrant and homeless men who are unemployed and who cluster in the flophouses, it is a question of being on the margin of the norms. In the case of mental defectives (which Americans tend to push away without much discussion except when there are drives to sterilize them by law) and in the case of sexual psychopaths, we are dealing with the clearly pathological. Some forms of disorganization fall under none of these categories, but—like many cases of suicide, for example—flow from normlessness, or the failure of any kind of values to take hold of the individual.

Americans are concerned and baffled about these phases of their society. Having found that many of their problems yield to technology and organization, they feel ordinarily that their way of life ought to move toward purpose and contain solutions. Yet in the norm-breaking and normless behavior we have discussed they find a spectacle to shake their belief in their own institutions. They see the social breakdowns as symptoms of the decadence and disintegration of American society as a whole. Things "fly apart at the center," reversing what Americans regard as the natural order: children grow up to become criminals, gangsters, gamblers, the face of innocence takes on the hideous mask of the narcotics addict, families are broken up by divorce, "nice girls" engage in promiscuous sex or even become professional prostitutes, the image of the clean-cut young businessman turns into that of the uncontrolled alcoholic or the compulsive homosexual, respectable citizens are revealed as white-collar criminals, and the basic activities of life are turned into rackets. Thus the Americans find the most cherished symbols of their society turned topsy-turvy.

Yet does disorganization always violate the essential spirit of the culture? Does it always mean the abnormal, pathological, anticultural? Actually the departure from norms may shed extraordinary light on the inner nature of the culture. In trying to explain why Americans are themselves deeply drawn to the gangster films which they know to be distortions of their urban life, one notes that a gangster is an American

* For sexual deviants, see Sec. 7, "Society and Sexual Expression."

"cultural hero" in whom Americans recognize a symbol of the energy of their culture. Or take American criminologists, who stress the paradox of the "rationality" of the habitual criminal, in the sense that given his twisted antisocial premises, his acts flow logically from them. What they often ignore is a different kind of rationality: that the criminal takes seriously the barely concealed premises of the culture itself. He sees easy money being made and predacity practiced, knows that the rules are constantly broken, knows that there is an internal violence in the act of exploiting the market and ravishing the environment.

Thus the forms of American disorganization arise from the more naked drives within the culture itself, with the workaday masks stripped away that have hidden the sadism and ugliness which are part of the human condition and are to be found in every culture.

In every society forces are generated that are harmful to its functioning and in the end destroy it. It would be strange if this were not happening in America as well. But those who fix upon crime and rackets, divorce, prostitution, and alcoholism as proofs of American decadence and degeneration may be fixing upon the wrong symptoms of the wrong disease. Most of the phases of social pathology I have listed are the extreme applications of principles which, in lesser degree, may be healthy. The delinquent and the criminal, so greatly feared by Americans, are not so dangerous to the social fabric as they seem to be. The point about the gangster, the racketeer, and the syndicate operator—even the housebreaker and the burglar—is not that they scorn property but that they value it enough to be ruthless in seeking short cuts for making it their own. The adolescent delinquent, in turn, in the act of rebelling against family or school or community, may be seeking the cherishing love upon which the family and other primary groups must be based.

The principles by which American culture lives are those of freedom and acquisition, and—where the two meet—the freedom of acquisition. There are always a number of people who feel themselves left out of the operation of these principles, or who are too much in a hurry to wait, or who feel resentful because others seem to start with an unfair set of principles, and who therefore seek some equalizer. Since they feel at a strategic disadvantage in the competition of life, they feel justified in ignoring the usual inhibitions and in tearing down the accepted cement of social relations. Because they use a distorted version of the cultural energies to destroy social bonds and rip apart the cohesiveness of the society, they in effect pit the culture against the society.

One may deplore these dislocating energies, but they would seem to be an inherent part of a society in which the pace of life is set by freedom, competitiveness, and acquisitiveness, and they are part of the price the society pays for those informing principles. A society less free and less dynamic—one of tradition and status, or one of totally state-directed power—may escape some of these dislocations but be beset by others. The whole impulsion of American culture is to raise hopes and claims in the individual and spur him on to fulfill the hopes and nail down the claims. At the same time it is too young a society to have developed the kind of inner discipline which—let us say, in England—can serve to inhibit the full sway of the impulsion.

Take, for example, the extreme case of the narcotics "pusher," who is even willing to corrupt children and develop the narcotics habit in them in order to make customers for his product. He represents the principle of creating a market, inherent in the market economy. In the mid-1950s he was thriving in America mainly because the severely repressive Federal narcotics laws, with constant "crackdowns" by enforcement officials, kept increasing the danger of narcotics distribution and therefore the price and profits—without reaching at all the terrible sense of isolation which underlies the use of narcotics. But he is also an example of the desensitized man in whom the principle has run wild, like cells in a cancerous growth. Or consider the case of the racketeer, who on principle recoils from the notion of earning his bread by the sweat of his brow, but who invests great resourcefulness in applying *force majeure* at the most vulnerable points of business enterprise.

The racketeer is likely to come up from the slums, reaching for quick affluence by breaking the windows of the mansion of American success rather than by entering at the door. There are studies showing how the prominence of Jews, Irish, and Italians in urban crime has swung from one immigrant group to another as each has flooded into the United States, sought to orient itself in American society, and become assimilated to it. At the beginning they are dislocated from their old culture but have not absorbed anything of the new culture except its cruder aspects; they have demons within them to assert themselves in a challenging new environment, they have few inhibiting fences around them, and they are in a hurry. The violence with which intense slum youngsters imitate the values of the culture, even while distorting them, may be seen as their own form of flattery. What they do is legally and morally wrong, but instead of being a sign of the decay of American life it may be taken almost as a sign of its vitality.

One of the clues is the dynamism of rapid social change. Racketeering crops up mostly in the areas of new business enterprise which have not yet been reduced to order or become subject to tradition, and where economic change moves more rapidly. The most serious outcroppings of violence and crime come also at the times of greatest social change, involving a rapid migration of population, the shifting of industries, the contact and clash of subcultures, the improvement of living standards, and the opening of new perspectives for which people are not yet prepared.

As a case in point we may take the known fact of the prevalence of reefer-and-dope addiction in Negro areas. This is usually explained in terms of poverty, slum living, and broken families, yet it would be easy to show the lack of drug addiction among other ethnic groups where the same conditions apply. One may guess that the rapid movement of Negroes from a depressed status to the improved status and partial freedoms of today, with new jobs and new living standards, has led also to the breaking down of old goals, while the new ones are still vague and seem inaccessible. I have noted in an earlier section that the passion for equality feeds on itself, setting the goals ever higher and making the distance from them more embittering. Drug addiction thus becomes one of the expressions of the isolation and normlessness that are the by-products of social advance, achieved under nerve-wracking stress, bitterly paid for. Where rigid status is being broken up and class lines shifting, and where a sense of social hope persists, social disorders are the tribute which the unbalanced individual pays to the naked premises of the culture.

Their real danger lies not in the pathology of cultural values but in their denial. The delinquencies and moral breakdowns which flow from the sense that only power counts and all American life is a racket are less dangerous than those which flow from the sense that nothing counts —not even the rackets. The breakdowns of family life or of sexual morality, and the crimes against property, by threatening the foundations of the American social structure, evoke counterforces in turn which solidify the social structure in its own defense. A frontal attack tends to be met by a defense in depth. Yet the disorganization which flows from the desensitizing of men, and from a lack of belief in any values, is a threat to the idea of social structure itself.

6. Morals in Revolution

ALMOST SINCE THE beginnings of their society, Americans have been as troubled about the everyday infractions of the moral codes as about the pathologies of social disorders. Their moralists are forever talking of the "moral breakdown" of their time. In few civilizations is there so constant a sense of moral crisis—to which one might remark that where there is so continuous a crisis there is no crisis at all, but only an unremitting malaise and anxiety. It is shown by the nostalgia for the "good old days"—the primitive simplicities of an agrarian society where right and wrong were clearly delimited. They have a Golden Age feeling of a lost Eden, and of the face of innocence covered over with latter-day Babylonianism.

Much of this anxiety focuses on the young. In the 1920s the American moralists were shocked at the "revolt of the younger generation," with new freedoms of smoking, drinking, petting, and premarital sex. Some saw it as the end of the world, others as a passing rebellious whim. Actually it was neither, but a phase of a continuing revolution in morals. The form it first took in the 1920s has been described by Lloyd Morris in terms of a semantic change: "The word 'neck' ceased to be a noun; abruptly became a verb; immediately lost all anatomical precision." Armed with bootleg liquor, the young and the old flaunted the codes of the bluenoses. The flapper-and-flask "lost generation" of the 1920s gave way to the "social significance" generation of the Depression and the New Deal in the 1930s, hot for certainties in political causes. This in turn gave way to what one of its members has described as the "beat generation" of the 1940s, canny and de-emotionalized, addicted to bebop, its boys dazed by wars and cold wars, its girls torn in the lonely debate whether "to sleep or not to sleep." As for the 1950s, the "beat generation" in turn has given way to what may be called a "sure-thing generation," anxious to find moorings early in an insecure society.

With every change in the nuances of rebellion and despair on the part of the young, the elders cluck-clucked and the moralists viewed with alarm. In the realm of morals Americans tend to regard man as fundamentally good and are shocked when they find men breaking the codes and turning out untamed and evil. This sense of shock has become chronic. While the moralist finds widespread evidence of the disintegration of controls over the personal vices (sex, alcohol, and gambling), his outcries against public corruption are as loud as against private immorality.

All moral codes are experiments in social control—instruments through which the family, church, school, Army, community, and state maintain their hold on the individual. As long as religion held a central place in belief and organized the lives of individuals, the codes were a corollary of religion but secondary to it. When faith in God began to slip, the Americans of the later nineteenth century tried to put secular morality in its place.* The weaker the religious bonds became, the more rigid the moral codes grew. Since they largely lost their religious sanctions, the effort to prop them up with the supports of community

---

* One should separate out the Catholics from these generalizations: what I say here applies less to them than to other religious groups. They have tried to maintain a religious rather than a secular control over morals.

opinion and secular hell-fire became more frantic. Inevitably the next step was taken—the use of legal measures through censorship, Prohibition, and the revival of old statutes against sexual offenses. America thus became an overlegislating and overmoralizing society.

Censorship is a case in point. There has been no central political censorship to seize upon ideological heresies, but there is a Legion of Decency under Catholic auspices, plus a handful of state censorship boards to watch over the moral level of films. In addition, there is a network of new unofficial groups that watch over the reading habits of their neighbors, imposing a private ban on the publication and sale of "obscene" books and magazines. These censors have built their moral case on the mushrooming growth of magazines and book reprints that blatantly display sexual drawings and photographs on their covers and deal with those who exceed the limits of obscenity. Most of the cases fall short of those limits, and the policing problem is too difficult for government machinery to handle. This has left the field open to the private groups, which try to impose their moral imperialism on the public and periodically force local booksellers to remove books and magazines (including some good ones) from sale under the threat of community boycott.

Professional moralists, from Anthony Comstock in the 1870s to the vigilantist local busybodies of the 1950s, have had little effect upon actual behavior. Americans remember that sensitive foreign observers were shocked by the widespread American habit of tobacco chewing and tobacco spitting, and that the moralists once included smoking, lipstick, theaters, and novels among the vices. Today smoking is accepted for women and adolescents, and is the base for major American industries. The recent medical research on the relation of smoking to lung cancer in males has probably done far more to inhibit American smoking than all the homilies of the churches and elders.

The turning point in the American attitude toward the moralists came with the "Great Experiment" of Prohibition. The efforts of the "women's crusade" and the Anti-Saloon League over a number of decades had finally pushed the nation into a large-scale suppression of drinking. The result, in Herbert Asbury's graphic language, was "a horde of bootleggers, rumrunners, highjackers, gangsters, racketeers, triggermen, venal judges, corrupt police, crooked politicians, and speakeasy operators, all bearing the twin symbols of the Eighteenth Amendment—the tommy-gun and the poisoned cup." This experience made Americans recoil from what Gerald Johnson has called "the illusion that you can establish morality by law," and they came to take a less Catonian view of human frailties. Its most revealing result was the light it shed on the organized evasion of the law. The "speak-easies" and "bootleg" liquor were a dramatic expression of the process of "patterned evasion" observable throughout the social system.

More subtle than individual code-breaking, patterned evasion is a collective circumventing of the codes, paying lip homage to them as codes while allowing the individual to tailor the code to his life and personality. One finds a parallel in Great Britain, where—if a law has been made archaic by social changes—the practice is not to repeal it but quietly to disregard it. There is a similar parallel in the French attitude toward the collection of taxes. American examples may be found in divorce practices as against the formal law of divorce, in "graft" and "influence peddling" as against the formal administrative procedures, in sexual promiscuity as against the codes of marriage and chastity, in white-collar crime and corporate "rigging" as against the theory of business morality. Some writers have spoken of the "structured corruption" in American society, through which the principle of "each for himself," "what's in it for me?" and "I might as well get mine" finds expression in practices socially recognized even while they are legally and morally ruled out. A notorious gangster, Willie Moretti, put it plaintively to the Kefauver Committee during its crime investigation: "Everything's a racket today. Everybody has a racket of his own. The stock market is a racket. Why don't they make everything legal?"

The answer to Moretti, of course, is that legal and moral codes have their function, setting norms for the conduct of life and fixing the direct and indirect penalties that serve as control instruments. But patterned evasion also has its function, which is to allow interstitial room for those who must deviate from the letter of the code while accepting its framework. In this sense, structured corruption and patterned evasion are the price society pays for the survival of the codes when too great a rigidity would break them. They furnish, in short, a way of living with codes without an intolerable psychic strain.

Thus to say that one cannot have one's moral cake and eat it is to reckon without code evasion. The evasion is not merely hypocrisy, although an element of hypocrisy does enter. It rests rather on a collection of social or cultural fictions, which James Woodward has termed "functional deviousness." In the clash between strong impulse or self-interest and the moral code, men may resolve the clash by giving it the homage of a stereotyped fiction, while following the impulse or self-interest which conflicts with it.

A characteristic instance is the practice of padding expense accounts for the purpose of tax deductions. Much of the luxury restaurant, bar, hotel, and night-club business in the larger American cities is based on a new "expense account aristocracy" which writes off many of the amenities of life against the "necessary expenses" of business entertainment and travel. Strictly, it breaks the legal code and is subject to fine or jail, but usually it is accepted even by the government as a convenient fiction by which the structure of heavy taxation remains while the individual is able to cushion its rigors. A distinction is often drawn between tax "evasion" and tax "avoidance": the latter stays inside the margin of legality while the former falls outside. But Justice Holmes, who believed that law expresses the operative rather than rhetorical moral practices of society, protested against this hair-splitting. He held that law enforcement has to draw a line at an arbitrary point, and that everything this side of the line must be considered legal and not simply "avoidance" of the law.

What is true of expense accounts is true also in the area of sexual adventure. In business it is true of the evasion of antitrust laws by the fictions of corporate organization and reorganization; it is true of many practices of the stock market, of the construction industry (where the codes are so cumbersome as to be nonsensical), of trade-unions. It seeps down into school and college, as shown by instances of collusive "throwing" of basketball games and "cribbing" in examinations.

The margin between immorality on one hand and patterned evasion and cultural fictions on the other is a narrow one, yet the basic dividing line is clear: the group accepts the evasions and fictions while it rejects the immorality. But even in the acceptance there is an ambivalent quality. For a nation with a Puritan tradition, there is a measure both of guilt and triumph in the stolen sweets acquired by eluding the outer and inner censors. What are the psychological sources of this evasion of norms? One can discern in the mixture the desire for freedom of action, the constrictions of small-town morality in an expanding society, the greed for profit, the impulse to "have fun," the reasoned willingness to take social risks within the community in the interests of the "pursuit of happiness."

I have left out of account the morality-breaking impulse itself. In an individualist America there have been many individuals who lived in deliberate defiance of morality. The history of American radicals who fought with this Nietzschean beyond-good-and-evil impulse against the encrusted codes, especially those who broke the rigid taboos on American women until the first World War, is a history of men and women who courted martyrdom in order to achieve social liberation. Some of them flaunted the codes in order to dramatize their archaic quality.

The story of Robert Dale Owen and Frances Wright, of Bronson Alcott and Orestes Brownson, of Josiah Warren, Stephen Pearl Andrews and Victoria Woodhull, of John Humphrey Noyes, Ezra Heywood, Benjamin Tucker and Moses Harman, is one of struggle for a society in which the hold of codes would be broken and the individual left free to enter into "natural" relationships. The invasion of Socialist thought brought with it another crop of moral debunkers who hoped to substitute the utopia of a "rational" collectivist society for the code shackles presumably imposed by the capitalist system. They did not see that they would destroy one set of codes only to replace them by another.

To measure the impact of these morality breakers upon the American mind, one may quote a sentence from Mark Twain, who was a sensitive barometer of the climate of American thought: "We have no real morals, but only artificial ones—morals created and preserved by the forced suppression of natural and healthy instincts." Mark Twain assumed here what Rousseau had assumed—that the "natural" instincts are "healthy," that man is born in innocence and freedom and only by society and its codes is he corrupted and enslaved. This was the credo of the moral reformers I have called "morality breakers." They must be distinguished from another type of "reformer"—the code fanatic like Anthony Comstock or Bishop Cannon or the small-town moralists whose task was to nail down the code provisions. Thus Twain's credo had its countercredo in these moralizers, who held that the natural instincts are corrupt and the human passions dirty, that human sin can be checked only by community vigilance and the individual's inner censor. They held that codes are broken only by willfulness or weakness, and that the answer is a system of legal and social penalties, since morality can be established by law and enforced by community scrutiny.

Caught between the morality breakers and the moralizers, the American has fumbled for a moral credo of his own. This credo takes the biological drives as neither wholly good nor wholly evil, but faces the need to reckon with them. It looks to the main chance. It is the credo of people in a hurry, striving for their quota of money, power, and "fun," snatching at what they can get while they run—although not without anxiety and guilt. To assuage their guilt and square conscience with impulse, they rely heavily on institutional evasions.

De Tocqueville in the 1830s was impressed by the strictness of American morals, which seemed far more chaste and severe than the European. He attributed the difference to freedom of marriage, the education of women, the cohesiveness of the family, the sway of religion, and the single-minded preoccupation with business which seemed to

him to make life more orderly. But he also thought that once immorality set in, the equalitarian impulse in America would level the
moral codes as well as the political ones, fixing them from below rather
than above; in America, he notes, "no class exists which can undertake
to keep society in order."

He was partly right in his analysis. American moral codes have been
small-town codes, fixed in a simple agrarian society by the austere
standards not of the dominant economic or social class but of the lower-
middle-class "respectable" churchgoing groups. The wealthy and powerful did not shape the codes but lived largely on their margin. The
business Titans whom I have called the "Puritans" shared the small-
town morality, paying it at least lip service; those whom I have called
the "magnificoes," like Morgan, flaunted them. Unlike the codes of
manners and fashions, the moral codes are not copied from the groups
with social status by those who yearn for it. The upper groups, with
their mobility and prestige, manage to purchase only a degree of freedom from the codes. The shaping force of the codes is the Judaeo-
Christian tradition as taken over by a Bible-reading people, who transposed the taboos from ancient Hebrew to modern American society.

The great moral revolutions in American history came with the
changes in technology that gave rise to new classes—especially the white-
collar and professional middle classes—and gave them access to new
experience. Just as it was the old middle classes that fixed the moral
standards of American life, so it was the continued flux of the new
middle classes and the new elites that forced a change in the operative
moral codes. Only a society with rapid social mobility can carry through
so drastic a series of moral revolutions without being shattered or becoming cynical and sophisticated.

One can trace several phases in the continuing recent moral revolution in America: the revolution of morals and manners of the 1920s, the
revolution in the status of women, and the continuing sexual revolution whose results are shown in the Kinsey studies. The striking fact
is that they were not accompanied by the open cynicism one may find
in Paris, Rome, or Vienna. Nor do Americans show the lack of self-
consciousness one finds in the Scandinavian countries. Being troubled
by their moral lapses, they feel neither wholly sophisticated nor wholly
pure in heart. Yet they resolve their problem by continuing to observe
formally codes which operatively they evade and sometimes even ignore.
They use their new mores to relieve the pressure of the rigid older codes.
These new mores generate a momentum of their own as they are more
widely practiced—a momentum which carries them beyond the original
goal of a convenient device for evasion and sets up a new norm in the
form of an operative code.

As the shift from the formal to the operative codes took place, the force of the mores in American life became stronger than the force of morals. Americans are apt to denounce strong drink, inveterate gambling, and loose sexual morals—yet embrace them in practice. The formal code says a man must be temperate in drink, prudent in avoiding games of chance, continent in sex, and governed by the values of religion and honor. It says similarly that a woman must be chaste and modest. But this formal code has been replaced by an operative code which says that men and women may drink heavily provided they can "carry" their liquor and not become alcoholics; that they may gamble provided they pay their gambling debts, don't cheat, or let their families starve; that a girl may have premarital sexual relations provided she is discreet enough not to get talked about or smart enough to marry her man in the end; that husband or wife may carry flirtations even into extramarital adventures, provided it is done furtively and does not jeopardize the family; or (if they are serious love affairs) provided that they end in a divorce and a remarriage.

If these operative codes are broken, life can become intolerable in the smaller communities, and even in the cities it will be conducted only on the margin of respectability. These codes are an effort at approximating the life experience of Americans. They seek to arrive at new rules of conduct which will be more than merely the mores of the community but will prescribe for the good life in a manner not too widely separated from the mores.

What Americans are suffering is not so much a moral breakdown as (to tear a phrase from Nietzsche out of its context) a moral interregnum. One king is dead and a new one has not yet been crowned, as with the moral interregnum at the time of the Roman Empire, when the pagan codes had broken down and the Christian codes had not yet been shaped. In fact, although American writing and thinking show signs of a constant search for a new formulation, it is not even clear out of what line the new kingship will come—out of what ethos the new moral code will emerge.

Whatever the new codes emerge from, they will have to reckon with the cultural life goals. It is difficult to make the ideal of honor persuasive in college sports when it is not applied to business, labor, and politics. It is hard to preach homilies to young people who have witnessed the triumph of shams in their communities and homes. There is a popular quip that a man who steals a small sum from another is sent to jail but one who extorts a huge sum from the public—by his control over legislators, his lobbying power, or his ability to hire smart lawyers in a tax deal or a corporate reorganization—is an honored citizen and can flout the code from the top of his heap of money. Government administrators who cry out against the vices of the trusts are themselves often captured by a big corporate job. Corporate executives who cry out against union racketeering and government corruption tend to forget the role of businessmen who are in complicity with both. For every bribe taker in the government, there is a bribe giver, generally in business; for every union racketeer there is a context of collusion between a cynical employer and a cynical union official. From the defective muskets of the Civil War to the embalmed beef of the Spanish-American War, from the Teapot Dome scandals in the 1920s to the lobbying corruption of the natural-gas industry in the mid-1950s, the record of American economic and political power is not one to reinforce moral preachments against individual private infractions of the code. Thus American moral standards have had to fight a difficult battle against the mounting hypocrisy of institutions.

If the knowledge of this hypocrisy spreads it may produce a feeling of hopelessness about enforcing the codes in the case of the top power elite. Where this hopelessness exists, morality is hard to inculcate. Even the traditional control agencies—including the churches, schools, courts, and home—become infected with it. In the end the strength of a code depends less on the penalties it can threaten or the taboos it invokes than on the conditionings which produce inner restraints within the individual. He is responsive to a code only as he has a sense of belonging to the society which it helps to hold together. In America the cultural life goals—success, competition, power, prestige, security, happiness —speak more loudly than the moral codes. The indices of belonging are belongings. What gives a person status is less integrity than success; what drives him is the emulation of the possessors; what is likely to fill his thoughts is not the right way of life but new access to the goods of life.

Other people's actual values may be more effective in shaping a person's morality than the codes they preach. If public opinion frowns on stealing it frowns also on poverty and gives grudging admiration to a quick dollar made quickly. A girl who is generous with her charms may find that "the whole town is talking," but if it finds that she has no talent for interesting or holding men, its silence and its indifference to her may be more scathing than talk. A successful Hollywood starlet or TV actress is expected to move toward her goal with few scruples about the moral price she has to pay. A cynic may say about American life, as Balzac and Thackeray said about nineteenth-century European society, that the effective immorality is not code-breaking but failure.

I do not mean to leave the impression that what I have said applies equally to all Americans. There is a diversity to be found in moral beliefs and practices in American society. There are still a large number of Americans, especially in the small towns and among the stricter religious sects, who adhere pretty closely to the formal moral codes. Recent studies of American soldiers indicate that about one third of them, during World War II, did not make use of their "leaves" to let off steam and contented themselves with the operative codes of Army behavior. Moreover, in the case of many parents the anxiety or dismay over the conduct of their children is not hypocrisy but the result of a real shock because of the discrepancy between the formal and operative codes. There is a constant stream of young people coming from the small towns and villages to the large cities, where they can find an escape from the censure and censorship of their neighbors: but the older people whom they leave behind often still cling to the codes.

This brings us back to the primary truth that the source of morality in a society is the culture itself and the operative (not rhetorical) valuation that it places upon the comparative goods of life. Morals arise not from a vacuum nor from lawgivers but from the common apprehension of men, and they change as that apprehension changes. If there has been a breakdown of morals in America, its clue is in the relation of the unfolding personality to the values of acquiring, possessing, competition. These are hammered in on the growing child by movies and TV, by the press and schools, by the family itself. The cyclical recurrence of prosperity, depression, and war only serves to heighten the impact. For depression brings the disintegration of old ties; prosperity brings the heady sense of the big money; war—and there has been a war in every generation—brings both. None of these can produce deep moral belief or a stable moral code. When the moral middle classes in America bemoan the "moral breakdown," they are bemoaning something which they and their life values have largely brought about, corroding the old moral code without bringing a new one into being. That is the moral interregnum in America.

Meanwhile the reigning moral deity in America is "fun." Martha Wolfenstein has noted the role of "fun morality" as a shaping force in the operative moral code. There may be little that is novel in this morality, at least for the upper classes. The latter part of the eighteenth century was a period of intemperate pleasures; the period from the end of the Civil War to the turn of the twentieth century was one of ostentation and garish display, as noted by such chroniclers of the rich as Alva Johnston and Cleveland Amory. There is a similar garishness in the contemporary New York and Chicago night clubs, displaying dancing girls in diaphanous nylon net or in panties trimmed with mink.

The big change that took place, therefore, was in the democratization of fun. The quest for it was no longer limited to the rich but became pervasive through the whole social structure. "We had fun" or "It was lots of fun" became an almost compulsive description of a successful party. The turning point came in the moral revolution of the 1920s, whose spirit Scott Fitzgerald caught as being "like a children's party taken over by the elders." In fact, much of the emphasis on fun was a recoil from the responsibilities of adulthood in an iron age, and a recasting of the American's image of himself in the image of a gay and irresponsible child. From another viewpoint "fun morality" may mark the passing of the older belief that life in this world is of little worth and only a preparation for eternity: since the present is the only life there is to live, then why not have fun?

Thus the idea of having fun is a protest against a number of the traditional sources of morality—the Puritan conception of seemly deportment, the solemn values of the elders of the community, the ideal of purposeful work, even against the business and money pursuits which make the fun possible. It is a way of standing American life on its head, reversing its solemnities with a jesting mockery. Thus Max Eastman, in his autobiography, could speak of his moral heritage from his ancestors as "my load of virtues"—which makes the Greenwich Village revolt intelligible because the fun was a recoil from the unendurable load of virtue. Most of all, fun came for many Americans to represent an abbreviated way of expressing the sexual freedom which flowed from irresponsibility. It meant dates, parties, autos and speed, drinking, dancing, late hours, necking, and petting. It came to be an elastic word whose meaning could be stretched all the way from the wholly innocent to the delightfully culpable. In the end it took on a final ironic twist, becoming itself a social compulsive, so that the necessity for having fun became as rigid as the old Puritan taboo of it. Parties, dates, or vacations that could not be described in terms of fun had a lingering sense of failure attached to them. Instead of freeing himself from the old codes, the American was caught in a new social imperative, often a curiously joyless one. One should add here the stretching of the life span, which means that even middle-aged and elderly Americans now have far more time for fun than was possible for their parents and grandparents.

Despite the spread of relativism in many areas of American thought, it did not triumph in the sphere of morality. As each of the generations came of age, it did not discard the idea of enduring moral values but was skeptical as to whether the values it inherited were those it could live by. Americans must live in three universes—a natural or biological universe with impulses they can neither ignore nor suppress, a social universe with life goals and institutional practices of which they form part, and a moral universe with values that give life much of its meaning. As each generation breaks away from the standards of the preceding one, it is moved not only by rebellion but by an experimental impulse. It is the impulse to find the warmth of fellow feeling which it needs, or a sheath within which it can insulate itself from the harshness of contemporary life and develop its own values. Thus these rebellions express as much the effort to achieve belief as they do disillusionment.

The blinkered critics of American life see only the corruption and the sensuality, the chasing for fun, the moral breakdown: they fail to see the elements of strength behind the continuing moral revolution. American morality is not summed up by its emotional frustrations and its tongue-in-cheek code evasions. The quest for new standards is itself a sign of cultural strength. The revolutions in morals come not out of weakness or resentment but out of a ferment which pervades the society and especially the groups moving up the social ladder and getting new increments of experience. Obviously this new experience is at first disintegrating in its effect, when the individual on his new level of living gropes for a freedom of action he had never had. But out of this groping there may emerge challenger codes which will distill, as all successful codes must, the ambivalent sense of social discipline and of individual striving for emotional expression.

7. Society and Sexual Expression

THE TUMULTUOUS CHANGES that overturned the codes of moral behavior and of manners, fashions, and taste could not help affecting sexual behavior in American society. It is a truism that sex is sex the world over and has been all through the ages. But unless this is meant as a joke it would scarcely imply that anything so deeply culture-rooted and socially conditioned as the relations of the sexes would remain untouched by the storms that swept across character and society in America.

Every society imposes regulations and codes upon sexual relations, but the striking fact here is that American codes, permissive in most other areas of behavior, are more restrictive about sex. The American girl, with wide leeway in choosing friends, clothes and schools, books and magazines, movies and plays, places to go and people to see, with freedom of movement, education and opinion, is nevertheless closely watched and admonished on everything affecting sexual relations. Even the American male adult, who may be ruthless in business and is expected to be inventive and adventurous about his work, comes up against a strong taboo when he is tempted to show the same qualities in his sex life. Thus sex is locked in an anomalous position within the frame of American society. The American cannot help becoming aware of the gap between what the society formally exacts of him in this area and what it allows in almost every other. From the start sex is separated from the rest of life, surrounded with stronger (and therefore more exciting) prohibitions, banned except within the traditional forms and inside the limits of marriage.

After puberty and menarche the American boy or girl must make a choice between curbing the biological impulses or breaking the codes. In the small-town society before the sexual revolutions of the twentieth century, the choice was generally toward curbing the drives. Since World War I the choice has generally been toward evading or changing the codes. But there has been little relaxation of tensions. The figures on mental health suggest that the psychic strains of American life were at least as heavy in the mid-1950s as they were before World War I. What happened is that the forms and sources of the strain changed. Sexual life in America grew freer in breaking and evading the taboos, but conscience in the face of the codes remained, and as long as it did the evasion of the taboos remained a source of anxiety and guilt. Since freedom generates its own tensions, which grow more assertive with every new gain by freedom, every gain in sexual freedom in America has generated the appetite for further gains and has widened the gap between code and conduct.

America has become in many ways a sensual and sexual society, but with a curious blend of blatancy and deviousness. The marks of the blatancy are in evidence throughout, but especially in the advertisements, the picture magazines, the movie posters, on the covers of paperback books, in musical comedies, and on TV programs. America has come to stress sex as much as any civilization since the Roman. When the buried ruins of New York and Los Angeles are uncovered by some future Winckelmann they will show erotic pictorial images not strikingly different (allowing for the difference in American conditions) from those of Herculaneum and Pompeii. The cult of female legs and breasts will be noted by future historians as characteristic of Americans: "beauty contests" turn upon the contours of both these anatomical features; newspapers and magazine picture layouts exploit both, and the "cheesecake" of a movie starlet's legs enticingly displayed for the photographers at the airport, or the half-exposed breasts of a Hollywood love goddess who is outstanding for her natural resources are recognized publicity stunts.

But the combination of this sexual emphasis with the Puritan taboos results in a sexual furtiveness. The American movie code, for example, is rigorous about how nakedly the sexual attractions may be revealed, but the publicity agents expend great ingenuity to promise seductive delights. In the actual production of a movie a minor fortune may be spent in filming a tantalizing bathtub sequence and a king's ransom in publicizing it. Thus what is most expressive about American culture is not sex in itself but the public furtiveness in the use of the sexual appeal as a way of stimulating the senses and suggesting images of secret delight—at the same time that there are outcries against it. The culture betrays itself in the conflict between the sensual pulls and the Puritan restraints.

In a study of the "folklore of sex" Albert Ellis noted the split between the overt repudiation of sexual behavior infringing the codes and the covert acceptance and even celebration of it. He found mass media authors explicitly supporting the conventional sex attitudes while introducing sexually inciting themes and hinting admiration for those who get away with the illicit pleasures. The impulse to have one's cake and eat it, in the sexual realm as elsewhere, offers an insight into American personal relations. Undogmatic, making no fetish of principle in itself, the American follows the hedonic impulse in a happiness civilization, while he refuses openly to flaunt the accepted moral standards of the community. This is not so much hypocrisy as it is part of the pattern of accommodation to reality, which treats both conventional attitudes and the hedonic side of life as realities and tries to make the best of both worlds.

The American absorption with sex has been put under a crossfire of attack—from the Left as evidence of "capitalist decadence," from the Right as proof of the horrendous results of "atheistic materialism." Pitirim Sorokin, finding it the climactic expression of the widespread disease of the "sensate culture" of the Western World, sees American sexual freedom as leading directly to the inner collapse of Western society and the conquest of the American imperium by outer barbarians, as in the case of the Roman Empire. One of the weaknesses of the argument that sexual freedom dooms America to destruction and oblivion is that it mistakes the sources of the American absorption with sex. It derives less from sexual freedom itself than from the centuries of the Puritan heritage of repression. This applies not only to the overt and covert sensuality of American life but also to the heavy incidence of sexual neuroses, which are the product of the conflict between human drives and social goals and codes, and the internalizing of that conflict within the developing personality.

The life goals of success, hedonism, and power, and the preoccupation with magnitudes and statistics, are reflected also in American sexual behavior. Thus the characteristic American contribution to the study of sex—the work of Alfred C. Kinsey and his associates—is statistical in method and emphasizes the calculation of average and modal sexual "outlets" in a statistical sample. Kinsey was anxious to break with what he called the "philosophic" tradition in the study of sex, in which he included not only the moralists, poets, and philosophers but also the psychoanalysts and psychiatrists. Trained as a zoologist, he sought to limit himself to what could be measured and classified. Yet this expression of behaviorism in a realm reserved for sentiment and moralizing is itself characteristically American. It helps account for the popular emphasis upon the sexual calculus, which is the contemporary American successor to the Benthamite calculus of happiness. One may guess that the effort to keep track of sexual frequency became merged in the American mind with the cultural ideals of success and happiness, which came to depend partly upon the test of sexual activity.

The two volumes of Kinsey studies, however—*Sexual Behavior in the Human Male* and *Sexual Behavior in the Human Female*—met with considerable criticism. The interview method was widely attacked as unreliable in studying sexual behavior, since the subjects in their unconscious mind were likely to distort the versions they gave of their sexual record, either by boasting or by covering up. In any event (it was contended) human sexual behavior cannot be measured statistically, like an animal's: to try to study it as if it were the wingspread of the gall wasp is to miss the depth and emotional content of human sexual relations. Finally (it was argued) the frequency of the sexual "outlet" sheds little light on its morality. It became a stereotype in the Kinsey criticism to say that the frequency of sexual outlets no more makes them moral than the frequency of the common cold makes it healthy—an equating of sex with disease which in turn sheds considerable light on the heritage of Puritan repression.

In answer, Kinsey and his defenders said that he had set himself the task of studying measurable sexual behavior and not sentiments and emotions; that he left morals to the moralists, love to the poets, and the unconscious to the psychoanalysts; and that he wrote only as a biologist when he put men and women in their setting in the natural universe of the mammals. The answer had force, yet it left a core of validity in the indictment. Kinsey understandably swung the balance away from past moralizing in the direction of measurement and behaviorism. The history of all human knowledge is the record of this kind of seesawing from underemphasis to overemphasis. As a biologist, Kinsey sought the source of human sexual drives in the natural universe and in man's animal behavior—which does not mean that a person's animal behavior sums him up as a human being.

If Kinsey had one foot planted in the world of nature he had the other in the social universe, emphasizing the taboos and codes that seek to hem man in. In the spirit of Rousseau's "Man is born free yet he is everywhere in chains," Kinsey put the responsibility for repression upon the social heritage. If the American could be unshackled from the traditional moral codes (he reasoned) he could be restored to his natural and healthy state. Thus, despite his dedication to his massive work in the spirit of a detached scientist, there was a reformist element in Kinsey which sought to bring legal and social attitudes closer to the nature of human sexual drives. The weakness of his premise was the assumption that the "natural" was the healthy and that the social and moral were almost necessarily repressive. This was to take a negative view of the intricate web of social arrangements (in Freudian terms, the "superego") which not only check the biological impulses but give them dimensions of emotional and aesthetic meaning scarcely to be found among the "infra-human mammals." Kinsey failed to see that it is not only the biological drives but also man's emotional needs that are part of human nature and require fulfillment.

This does not diminish the importance of the insights derived from Kinsey's work. He found a far greater spread and variety in the forms and extent of sexual activity for both sexes than had been assumed earlier. He shed light on the sexual life history curve of American men and women. The profile of male behavior shows the adolescent, at seventeen or eighteen, to be at the threshold of his full sexual powers, while in the case of women there is a much slower development, with the peak not being reached until around the age of thirty. After that, the woman's curve of capacity levels off to a plateau which remains relatively stable often well into the fifties; by contrast, the male curve, starting earlier and rising more steeply, also declines more precipitously. Kinsey also found a greater prevalence of premarital and extramarital sexual relations than had been previously established; while the percentage of such activity was higher in the male than in the female, it was the findings on female behavior that caused the greater stir. His figures on deviant forms of sexual behavior, especially homosexuality in the male, were equally striking. Just as dramatic was his contention, based on a sample of almost 15,000 subjects of both sexes, that women respond less frequently and intensely to psychological stimuli than do the men, and that the role of the imagination in sex is therefore a more important one for the male.

In the case of the American male, the sexual life pattern he is likely to follow is, in Kinsey's view, set during his adolescence. But while this life pattern is in large measure genetically determined, the forms in which the sexual drive expresses itself are shaped by class, education, and social environment. One of Kinsey's striking conclusions was that male sexual behavior in America varies greatly with the class and educational level. He found the strongest sexual activity among the lower middle classes, who get to high school but not beyond it, while he found the lowest activity among males on the college level. More important than frequency, however, are the differences in the forms and styles of sexual behavior. "Petting" starts mainly on the college level, although it has spread to the groups on the high-school level. Premarital relations are most frequent on the grade-school and least frequent on the college level. Homosexual relations are lowest on the college level. Nudity and kissing, which are held in suspicion on the elementary-school level, are most accepted among college groups. On marital fidelity the lower educational groups start in a more vagrant mood but come increasingly to confine their relations within marriage, while on the higher educational level the relative fidelity to marriage vows is corroded and there is an increasing tendency to seek sexual adventure outside of marriage.

These class differences apply far less to the case of the American woman. Instead, Kinsey found striking differences in the sexual behavior and attitudes of women depending on the decade of their birth. This was especially true of "petting" and other forms of premarital sexual experience. Kinsey's findings served to document other evidence that a sexual revolution took place in America around the time of World War I, and that since then every successive generation of women has followed the new pattern of sexual freedom and pushed it further. In fact, Kinsey's work is best seen in the context of a continuing sequence of sexual revolutions that go back for many generations. A little more than a century ago Orestes Brownson attacked Hawthorne's *Scarlet Letter* for its blatant parading of adultery. Theodore Dreiser's novel, *The Genius,* expressed the drive toward sexual reform, although it made its hero a Nietzschean man-out-of-the-culture, whereas actually the sexual revolution came to permeate the lives of ordinary Americans. In its initial phase, its aim was to liberate the American woman from her status as a chattel of her husband and a ward of community opinion. But once started, the revolution was extended from women to men, from the young people of the 1920s to the middle-aged people of today. The latter are being told in the popular magazines—what most of them have already discovered—that sexual expression need not end with the end of youth, and that the middle years can be sexually the richer because the tensions of youth have diminished.

In the midst of changing sexual behavior, the legal codes and attitudes remained relatively rigid. Kinsey made a good deal of the point that the legal and moral codes derive from the Judaeo-Christian tradition, chiefly from the Jewish tribal laws as set down in the Old Testament, which accept only reproductive sexual relations within marriage and which were carried further by Christianity. Students of religious history have seen considerable differences between the Jewish and Christian traditions on this score, and—within Christianity—between the Catholic and Protestant traditions. Yet there can be little doubt that much of the harshness of the American legal codes toward sexual offenders is due to the harshness of the religious heritage. In spite of a good deal of recent insight into the psychogenic factors in homosexuality, all homosexual relations are still subject to severe penalty under the law. The problem of sexually obsessed psychotics who prey upon the young and defenseless is being given intensive study, and in some states there has been considerable progress toward treating these cases as problems in mental disease. Yet the problem of sexual deviants—or "perverts," as most Americans tend to call them—remains a baffling one.

The political debate early in the 1950s on the presence of "sex perverts" in the State Department and in other "sensitive" government posts opened a broader debate on homosexuality. There was an uneasy sense that it was increasing in America, due mainly to widespread social disorganization and the distorted emotional patterns within the family; yet there were no comparative historical figures to indicate the secular trend. Some students took a wholly relativist view in the debate, contending that "normality" in sexual behavior had little meaning; that homosexuals ought not to be treated as a pariah caste; and that the task of mental health was to help these deviants to live at peace with themselves and their partners so long as they did not hurt the community. There were others, however, who, without either hostility or hysteria, regarded homosexuality as a form of neurosis and therefore of unhealth, and as a departure from the heterosexual cultural norm, which was deeply interwoven with the whole web of social institutions and moral codes. This view rejected the harrying and ostracism of sexual deviants but sought—wherever possible through psychiatric aid and through preventive work within the emotional structure of the family—to cut down to a minimum the growth of homosexuality and the harshness of social attitudes toward it. Its underlying premise was that of flexibility of view within a broad frame of sexual norms. It held that sexual behavior is a matter of personal growth, deeply impelled by biological drives, taking place within a social and moral frame, and in turn affecting the style and quality of social experience as well as the basic health of the civilization.

Despite crosscurrents and counter-eddies the full sweep of the broad stream of the American sexual revolution has scarcely yet been felt. As against the legal prohibition of their sale before 1920, contraceptives have been passively accepted as a functioning part of social practice and are made widely available. Their basic rationale is the need for birth planning and family spacing in marriage, and it should be noted that American scientists have recently been at work to develop cheap and effective contraceptives for the fight against overpopulation in areas like the Caribbean and the Asian countries. Yet in the setting of American sexual behavior the new knowledge has been closely related to the sexual revolution. The same is true of the development of effective treatment of venereal diseases, removing much of the sense of menace that served as a taboo against sexual experimenting in the past.

One of the results has been a sharp decline in commercialized prostitution. I do not mean that commercial sex is not still substantially present. While the streetwalkers and the segregated districts of the big European and Asian cities are less important on the American landscape, there are still teen-age "B-girls" to be picked up at dances or bars, "call girls" who are available by phone, "kept women" who are the American form of the Old World concubines, and attractive "V-girls" who may have jobs and live on the margin of the respectable but supplement their income by selling their sexual favors to out-of-town businessmen or convention visitors in the big cities.

But the great change that has occurred is outside prostitution, in the availability of men and women alike for sexual adventure. The files of marriage counselors and of psychiatrists and psychologists are crammed with material about sexual episodes hidden in the shadows of the lives of outwardly conventional people of every class and ethnic and religious group. By comparison with the Restoration period of sexual license in England and the eighteenth-century sexual revolution in France, the new American sexual orientation is far more pervasive. In the British and French instances the sense of sexual release was felt chiefly among the upper nobility and often took the form of perversions and libertinism—as witness the erotic literature of both periods, especially in the writings of the Marquis de Sade and the licentious romances of the British. In the American case there is considerable spread through all the classes, although Arthur Hirsch is probably right in calling attention to its concentration among the "upper-cultured"—that is to say, the college-trained groups. It is part of the folklore of America that the greatest release from restraints is to be found in the Hollywood colony —as witness a novel like Norman Mailer's *The Deer Park*. Yet there are other segments of American life where sexuality is more privately conducted and is incorporated into the busy lives of hard-working executives and professional groups, without the white glare of publicity that focuses on Hollywood.

The important fact here is that a shift has taken place from the commercial to the private sexual releases outside of marriage. With the failure of the religious sanction, with the new geographic and social mobility and the gospel of personal fulfillment and happiness, a new sexual orientation has taken shape. The carrier of the revolution has been the American woman rather than the man. Recent novels present her as expecting sexual fulfillment and confronting the male with the challenge of developing a "psychological potency" which will equal hers.

On a different level Americans have had to contend with disturbing developments in the sexual behavior of adolescents. It is here that the gap between the codes on the one hand and the biological impulses and social stimulants on the other has shown itself most dramatically. The adolescent boy at seventeen finds himself in high school, probably in a classroom with an unmarried middle-aged female teacher, and watched over at home by censorious parents and neighbors. He knows that he is old enough soon to be subject to the military draft—to be given a gun and sent to the far corners of the world, perhaps even not to return. The adolescent girl, having newly discovered lipstick and grown-up clothes, living in a culture where marriages come earlier in each generation, is equally impatient of the taboos and restraints that encircle her. In both cases the adolescent is surrounded by clamorous sensual stimuli—the movies and TV, juke boxes, newspapers, and magazines. The resulting conflict between the codes and the biological and social stimuli has resulted in a considerable breakdown of community moral standards among adolescents.

The fact is, as Herbert Blumer has noted, that adult practices and attitudes in the area of sex have been pushed down increasingly to early age levels. Dating, formal dances, and petting may be found at the age of twelve or thirteen, and sometimes even earlier in the pre-adolescent age. There is constant pressure on the parents for permission to act the role of precocious adults. The power of decision about sexual behavior seems to have largely shifted from adults to adolescents and preadolescents. This has meant a strikingly earlier sexual sophistication than in the past—another instance (along with advertising, consumption, and TV) of how America is basing its society on the triumph of adolescence.

The question of how to deal with this phase of "the mutiny of the young" still baffles most Americans. Exposés of "non-virgin clubs" and sexual "orgies" among high-school students have been splashed in headlines across the nation. The community has tried to deal with the problem by periodic "cleanups" which soon subside and are forgotten. The courts have tried to deal with it by reform schools and correctional institutions, and often by severe jail penalties in the case of "statutory rape," where the girl is below the age of consent. The trouble is that in the case of premarital sexual relations, the law classi-

fies as criminal the types of behavior that are practiced and tacitly accepted by a large part of the population. Given the gap between actual
behavior and formal codes, Kinsey estimates that 85 per cent of the
younger male Americans could be convicted as sex offenders. In the
gap and conflict between these two forces he finds a source of much of
the American sense of guilt and anxiety, which form the heavy psychic
toll that Americans pay.

A curious fact is that Kinsey did not follow up this insight adequately
in his work. Instead of regarding sexual deviants and sexual disturbances
among both men and women as evidence of the psychic devastation
wrought by sexual conflict, and instead of viewing the sexual precocity
of the young as a phase of the complex interaction of instinctual, social,
and moral factors, he allowed his naturalistic emphasis to triumph and
refused to regard these forms of behavior as posing difficult problems
for American society. While he did not explicitly make statistical frequency the test of the normal, his whole emphasis was on sexual expressiveness whatever the nature of the "outlet" and its surrounding
emotional tone. There was also an element of the naïve in the premise
that gave him his faith—that once the operation of the taboos is exposed
and the accumulated moral hypocrisies laid bare, the hold of archaic
laws, codes, and attitudes will be broken. He failed to understand that
despite the fluid nature of American society there is a tenacity in the
codes that is hard to break through, and their hold is all the greater
because the loose and sprawling character of the society frightens most
Americans and makes them cling all the harder to the challenged codes.
However vulnerable they may be, the Kinsey studies nevertheless
represented a monumental advance in the understanding of American
sexual behavior. The courage and candor with which they were pursued
would have been impossible if the sexual revolution starting in the
1920s had not paved the way for them, but, equally, the social challenge
that provoked the studies as response would not have been possible if
it were not for the depth of resistance to the revolution.
The American society that Kinsey studied was in its sexual aspects
half Babylonian and half Puritan. There was an explosiveness of release from the older taboos which was largely a recoil from the re-
pressiveness of the past, especially in small-town America. But the
shocked, angry reaction to the Kinsey findings, especially those in the
volume on the American female, showed that the repression had not
been torn out. Kinsey's own response to this hostility was a bristling
one, perhaps because he was so certain that future generations would
vindicate him. Even in his own day the fact that a team of responsible
scientists undertook the studies and that responsible foundations fi-

nanced them was a sign of growing maturity in American sexual attitudes. The size of the statistical sample, surpassing that of any previous
studies, and the care with which the interviewing techniques were developed, were themselves indications that—within their limits—the
studies were thorough.

It is somewhat ironic that the Kinsey studies should have been attacked as an invasion of privacy, when much of their impact was to
strengthen the right of each person to his individual decisions in the
area of his greatest privacy—his sexual life. It was in this sense that
Kinsey, like Freud, must be counted a liberator. Not that his work can
be proved in itself to have wrought much change in the actual pattern
of sexual behavior: it would be truer to say that it had its effect on
American attitudes and gave some scientific sanction to the underlying
forces that were changing the behavior patterns. Thus Kinsey's impact
was that of a kind of Guilt Killer. After all the valid criticisms have
been made, it remains true that Kinsey's work has broken the taboos
surrounding the last area of human behavior which had been left almost
wholly unexplored. In that sense Kinsey's pioneering work was characteristic of American pioneering in the large.

Sexual revolt in America has asserted three freedoms: the freedom
to break the formal codes; the freedom to diverge from the majority
sexual patterns into deviant behavior; the freedom to lead a fully expressive sexual life in the pursuit of happiness. It is the last of these
three which has become most meaningful in recent years. It is not
revolt for its own sake, nor revolt to bait the community censors, nor
to establish the rights of sexual deviation, but revolt for a healthily
expressive life.

In an important sense this liberation movement differs sharply from
the sexual revolts of the past. It has become in its own way a protest
against the lack of standards characterizing the earlier sexual revolts.
It calls for liberation from a kind of sexual anarchy which was becoming
in itself a new tyranny. It emphasizes the sustained relationship as
necessary to a healthy sexual life. Even while it is willing to treat sexual
deviants with humanity, it does not regard them as expressing a satisfactory way of life. It is not moved by status panic or fear of conventions, since most of the people who form part of this new mood are
not averse to iconoclasm in other fields and are the effective enemies
of social conformism. It is less a question of the observance of codes
than the fulfillment of life purposes.

Looking backward, one sees that the more rigid Puritan tradition
stressed the Biblical virtues which limited sex to procreation and then
led to widespread repression, hypocrisy, frustrations, and neuroses. It

was challenged by a series of sexual revolts which started as far back as the 1840s and were climaxed by the great revolution of the 1920s. The extension of these forces into the 1930s and 1940s, in a world torn by social struggle and personal insecurity, led in turn to the excesses of sexual cynicism and normlessness.

If I am right, this mood too has passed its crest, and a countercurrent has set in, replacing it by an outlook far less restrictive than the Puritan. It takes more account of sexual needs both in adolescence and adulthood, and is thus permissive of experiment, especially in premarital relations. It is also more favorable to a wider range of sexual techniques. But these freedoms are all directed toward the fulfilled relation between a man and a woman as the core of a healthy society. Put in a different way, the sexual freedoms won in the last century are unlikely to be relinquished. But there is discernible an American attitude which insists upon directing these freedoms more and more into the channels of happiness. That, in turn, is being redefined not in terms of success or material goods or power, but in terms of the broad personal expressiveness which includes sexual expressiveness.

This may, of course, be somewhat wishful on my part, discerning a stream of tendency where there is only a whirlpool of crosscurrents. Americans are probably engaged in a complicated struggle in the building up of definitions as to what is permissible and truly expressive in the area of sexual behavior. There has been nothing approaching an accurate account of this struggle, with its agonies and blindnesses and earnestness, taking place on the darkling plain of the American psyche. One possible outcome may be a reversion to a new form of the Puritan codes, with new and more indirect repressions. But the more likely outcome is the newer expressiveness which I have outlined above.

8. Life Goals and the Pursuit of Happiness

THE SEARCH for personal expressiveness and happiness leads into the question of American life goals.* To find the life goals of a culture one must look for the impulses toward value that come out of the culture and take the shape of a Grand Design for living. I do not have in mind those virtues or "value clusters" which family, school, and church seek to instill into the young. They are listed in every book on American society, including such traits as freedom, democratic equality, competitiveness, thrift, honesty, loyalty, social mobility, practicality, and the

* For earlier material on American cultural goals, see Ch. VIII throughout, especially Secs. 1, 3, 4.

belief in the individual life and its worth. Together they add up to a kind of cultural superego. Yet the question is not what Americans believe they believe, but what animates them and what their main energy drives actually are.

They grow up in a quasi-individualist society, expecting great things of life, and they are disappointed if they don't achieve them. The point is that they measure their lives against these expectations mainly in terms of what the culture accepts as life goals. Robert and Helen Lynd showed with great force in their *Middletown* studies how bitter the disillusionment can be when the expectations are not matched by the outcome.

Life goals are a complex interweaving of strands from both the culture and the personality. They are given shape as stereotypes derived from the culture, but they are constantly changed and enriched by stirrings from within the personality which cannot long be denied or belied. Whether or not "human nature" can be changed, there is no question that the life goals which have shaped American striving have changed decisively. It is difficult to trace them in their changing forms, since they are never codified and are rarely made articulate.

In an idyllic vein American social historians look back to an earlier society in which the operative life goals were related to the Puritan virtues of work, pride of craftsmanship, thrift, achievement, and the fulfillment of the vocation and tasks to which one was called. To spoil this Garden of Eden view, it must be added that these virtues were from the start contaminated by those of money, materialism, and success: or, to put it differently, these life goals were all along implicit in the earlier ones and grew out of them. By the turn of the twentieth century a new pattern of life purposes emerged. Its components were *success, prestige, money, power,* and *security.* This is loosely termed the "success system," and it is true that at its core is the cult of what William James called scornfully "the Bitch Goddess, success." But it might be better to call it simply the *five-goal system,* since each of the goals has enormous pull for the American imagination and a sovereign place in the constellation as an equal among equals.

The system as a whole stresses achievement—or, in James Plant's terms, *whatness* as against *whoness.* I have tried to trace in an earlier section* the changes in American character and society that are interwoven with the acceptance of these life goals. One might say, with Lawrence K. Frank, that people on the move, geographically and socially, are bewildered about their "whoness" and look to "whatness" for security and for a definition of their personality; also that persons

* See Sec. 4, "Varieties of American Character."

who have only a blurred sense of their "whoness" turn to "whatness" as a surrogate.

To understand the importance of *success* as a goal, one must remember that for the ordinary American the test of an idea is in the end product of action, and the proof that something is valid lies in its being effective. He cares about success because he prides himself on living in an illusionless world and cannot let himself be bothered with futilities. Hence his homage is given to the best-selling book, the candidate who is elected by a "landslide," the stock speculator who makes a "killing," the play or performer that gets "rave" reviews, the general who wins the battle, the businessman at whose touch every enterprise turns to gold, the football player who catches the decisive pass or breaks away for the winning touchdown, the song on the "Hit Parade," the movie star who gets on all the magazine covers. It adds to the American's stature to be associated with a going concern.

The only disaster is failure. But even failure is tolerated if it is used as a springboard for a "comeback" which is a success underlined by a dramatic reversal. The golf player who came back after an auto smash to win all the tournaments, the faded movie star who was found to have a revived box-office appeal, the Wall Streeter who lost several fortunes only to make a new one—these are the American equivalents of Lazarus come back from the dead. I do not say that the success drive is stronger now in America than it was in William James's time: the chances are that it is somewhat weaker, not in itself but relative to some of the other components of the American system of life goals, especially prestige and security. But it is still an integral part of the larger pattern.

Prestige is at once the subjective aspect of success and its reward. To achieve success is to receive the respect and applause of one's fellows. In a society of competitive striving a man's standing in the community is measured against others by what Veblen called the "invidious" emulative bent of his fellows—the differential advantage he has over others in income and status, and the "pecuniary emulation" that he practices or of which he is the target. The sources of prestige in the socially mobile American society are less likely to be birth and family than job, income, spending habits, clothes, car, residence, club and group memberships. In his studies of stratification, Lloyd Warner makes prestige the nucleus of the class system, getting at the social rating a person has in the community by asking neighbors and friends to rank each other in the prestige hierarchy. One must agree that the drive toward prestige has done much to release American energies. But the price has been high—the hollowness of values in a system where life is lived in the mirror of how people rate you, and whether (in Arthur Miller's phrase in *Death of a Salesman*) you are not only "liked" but "well liked." Life becomes thus a joyless and derivative affair, laden with endless anxieties in an endless prestige rat race.

In a society where the traditional goals have been undercut, the goal of *money* has an alluringly tangible and massive quality. In speaking earlier of the "cement" of American society and of the changes in the American character, I noted the role and the limits of pecuniary values in a society in which most things become marketable. It is true that the American expectation is largely measured in money terms, and that the "law of the fast buck" is a powerful force in American striving. This is not uniquely American. Older civilizations, like the French, combine the values of culture with those of greed.

There is at least some evidence, especially in recent novels (which serve as telltale documentaries in such matters), that the role of money as a decisive life goal is being questioned. Americans are aware that "money talks," but they are also aware that "you can't take it with you" and that there are things that "money can't buy." That it needs constantly to be challenged is, of course, a mark of the hold of acquisitiveness on the American mind. Yet the fact is that challenger goals are emerging. Mary McCarthy has noted, speaking of American materialism, that Americans live *among* things but not *by* them: similarly, one may add that they find money necessary but not adequate in the system of life values. They agree that other values count more but add that men without money find it difficult to achieve them.

As for *power*, I have noted earlier* how it pervades every phase of American society, which is not power-starved but power-saturated. One source that feeds the power drives is the American emphasis on the life of action: the imperialism of action demands control over the actions of others. The critics of American machine society have also built a seductive theory by which machine power is projected into the human personality and generates a similar power drive in men. I suspect that it is less the machine than the bureaucracy which feeds the power impulse. For those whose lives are geared to their status in a hierarchy, power has meaning. Government bureaucrats, corporate managers, trade-union leaders, Army officers, press and radio barons, and all the minor gods and demigods of America may find in power a psychic reward they cannot find elsewhere. But except for the mutilated personalities, most people in a dynamic society are unlikely to feed and live on power alone. The "authoritarian personality" is far less dominant in America than it was in Nazi Germany or than it is today in

* See Ch. VI, Sec. 5, "Power and Equilibrium"; also Ch. VII, Sec. 2, "The Seats of the Mighty."

Communist societies or in the feudal societies of the Arab Middle East. One must remember also that a market society is less power-ridden than a wholly bureaucratic one, and a mobile society less dependent on power than one where the personality can find little fulfillment except in the strategic control of others.

The important newcomer in the five-goal system is the stress on *security*. Anyone studying the emerging personality pattern in America must note how the propensity for risk-taking has slackened, and how risk-cutting and security-seeking have come forward with a new strength. The stress on insurance is, of course, the base on which one of the biggest private industries has been built. The newer stress on "social security," especially since the Great Depression, is the base on which much of the welfare state is built.

However, it is not economic security alone but a whole psychic security syndrome that is involved. Each new generation seems less geared to risk-taking and more bent on nailing down the future beyond chance and doubt. Elmo Roper's annual polls of college graduating classes show life goals that have moved far from those of the adventurous entrepreneur, the intellectual pioneer, the social maverick. What the graduating classes envisage as the "good life" is a home, two or three children, one or two cars, and a salary of ten thousand a year. They are wary even of the harsh competitive struggle and the driving quest for success. They look mainly toward merchandising and "personnel" work ("because I like people"). As one of them put it, he didn't want to become a "big operator with blood pressure and coronary thrombosis." Instead of setting up an independent business, they aim at joining a corporate organization ("A.T.&T. might not be exciting—but there will always be an A.T.&T."). Their goal is to become "good technicians, good managers, good neighbors," to cut risk and dig in for a sure if unexciting income. To some extent this is the result of the draft experience of the young Americans, but it goes beyond that.

I do not share the anxieties of the corporate personnel managers who deplore the lack of "enterprise" among American youth. Generally what they mean by it is the lack of a sense of "push" and "go," and a passivity which does not infuse energy into the "team." For me the real tragedy lies rather in the psychic insecurity which carries with it a yearning for a secure niche in a known and orderly structure, and which thereby strips the individual of his individuality. This is true of adults as well. Polls of adults in the working class and lower middle class show that the groups which are least secure economically—Negroes, the unskilled, white-collar workers—are also the most willing to take a job at low pay if it will assure them a steady and secure income.

How much of a clash is there between this yearning for the secure life and the belief that the future holds hope and that one's children will be better off than oneself? It may be a case of trying to have the best of both emotional worlds—that of a dynamic society with its hope, always breaking continuities and making new beginnings, and that of a security society where there are few breaks and no risks. By precept and by the example of daily living, Americans teach their children both the creed of risk and the creed of security. They are torn by polar pulls in both directions. The most corrosive element in the security syndrome is its narrowing of the margin of generosity toward others. To think of your own safety means to fear involvement in the plight of the victim, lest you be tagged with the stigma of the outsider. It is to develop the yearning for the securely normal which leads to a massive conformism.

If asked to reflect on what was their main aim in life, most Americans would probably shrug the question away, since they tend to take life goals as given; but if pressed, they would probably say, "To be happy," or "To lead a happy life." If asked what they want for their children, their answer would again be happiness. As I have several times noted, America is a happiness society even more than it is a freedom society or a power society. The underlying strivings may be toward success, acquisitiveness, or power, toward prestige or security. But what validates these strivings for the American is the idea that he has a natural right to happiness.

Howard Mumford Jones has traced the web of meaning in the concept of the "pursuit of happiness" since it was introduced into American thinking in the eighteenth century. One phase came from the aristocratic idea taken over from the classical writers, who saw happiness (as Jefferson himself saw it) as a gracious way of life led by landed gentry or farmers, with leisure for contemplation and a taste for books and for science, the arts, and Nature. The second came from the Puritan idea of obeying God's laws and having a store of worldly goods to show for it. This in turn was linked with what became in the nineteenth century the core idea of a happy life—the idea of material success.

Even in nineteenth-century America the seeds were present for a conception of happiness that was to go beyond materialism and success. Emerson defined happiness as self-realization within the spiritual laws of the universe. Later in the century William James helped give it a fateful twist of meaning as the "agreement" of a man's inner life with the realities of his outer experience. James himself, as we have seen, rejected material success as a goal. Yet his "agreement" came to be translated into "adjustment," and the idea of adjustment was taken over by vocational guidance counselors, personnel experts, and scientific managers, and interpreted as making one's life effective within a society of business and money values. The "mental health" movement also for a time made adjustment its central concept, adding its own twist of meaning. It saw adjustment as whatever fits a person into his social frame to lead a useful and normal life, so that he does not feel himself a rebel and outsider. This was soon challenged by the more perceptive people in the field of mental health. The question some psychologists raised—among them Robert Lindner in his *Prescription for Rebellion* —was whether the individual does this at the cost of trimming away his own individuality and his impulses toward uniqueness. If this is true, then what William James meant as a way out of the trap of conventional values became instead a way of leveling down the jagged ends of personality. Thus "adjustment" became, along with "security," a life purpose that modified the five-goal complex but did not seriously challenge it. Under its influence the pursuit of happiness came to be defined mainly as the pursuit of conformism and the avoidance of neuroses.*

If it is true that every civilization has its characteristic culture style and social structure, it will also have its characteristic pattern of neuroses. I do not mean to assert that neurotic behavior arises from specific social strains, rather than from the underlying and perennial human situation. But there has been enough recent exploration by psychiatrists and anthropologists to enable us to draw a rough correspondence between the culture and the neurotic pattern.† The neurotic-personality-as-American may feel caught in the conflict between the stated ideals and operative drives of his society. Because of this gap he may feel guilty, anxious, and insecure, and may seek to build himself up in the mirror of other people, or may seek the elusive inner security in the feverish effort to achieve money, power, and an outer security.

The neurotic patterns of continental European societies are likely to be those of people who feel caught in a blind alley, unable to extricate themselves from the encrusted habits of their fathers and their community, desperate to make a fresh start. The characteristic American neuroses, on the other hand, are those of people who have to pay a heavy psychic price for freedom of movement and decision, and the flux of fortunes, station, and values. In a constantly shifting social situation, with a high rate of personal mobility, few Americans have an anchorage in traditional values. This may mean an intense anxiety

* For the "adjusted man" and the "unadjusted man" as contrasting American character types, see Sec. 4, "Varieties of American Character."

† I deal here with mental health and disease. For other aspects of health and disease, see Ch. III, Sec. 6, "The Sinews of Welfare."

about the changes and chances of life, and a feeling of inner emptiness.

There is an interesting difference in the nature of the "family romance" in the European and American situations. The Freudian doctrine developed in Central Europe, in an authoritarian family frame where the son grew up resenting a tyrannical father: the Oedipus relation and the repressed libidinal energy thus came to occupy a central place in the Freudian system. In the middle-class American family, where the authoritarian father has all but disappeared, the family romance is more likely to revolve around the emotional relationship between son and mother, and an overemphasis on loving and being loved. While the repression of libidinal energy has proved important in a culture that still carries some of the scars of Puritanism, the more important problem in the American personality is that of insecurity and identity—the lack of models to follow, the absence of a sense of self, and the feeling of failure in living up to one's own expectations or those of others.

It has been suggested that while the European neuroses are those of the id and the superego, the American neuroses are those of the ego. This jibes with Erik Erikson's observation that the central problem of American personality is the "quest for American identity." It is a quest that takes place in the growing-up years in every culture. But it is especially hard to find your identity in a society where the temptation is to live in the mirror image that others have of you, where the patterns of group living are still unstable and your role in the group is not clearly outlined. Thus the American yearns for unattainable goals set by the shifting standards of his group, yet he does not exact from himself the willed effort to live within his own psychic limits and resources and to be a personality in his own right. To add to the difficulty, there is the outer image of the abundance of life opportunities in American society, so that the individual feels he is falling short of his duty to exploit them and therefore is inadequate for life. He has thus the sense of starving psychically amidst psychic plenty, and hence of being cheated in life.

When William James heard Freud's lectures on the latter's visit to Clark University, he told Freud and Ernest Jones: "The future of psychology belongs to your work." James may have spoken from his interest in motivation and in nonrational beliefs such as the varieties of religious experience: he had himself had a breakdown as a young student. Yet despite his remark the characteristic psychological interest of America, which he expressed in his own work, was with normal behavior and the area of the conscious. It is true that a number of doctors —including Benjamin Rush, the elder Oliver Wendell Holmes, and

S. Weir Mitchell (all three of them writers as well)—showed sharp insights into the irrational phases of behavior. Adolf Meyer at Johns Hopkins and William Alanson White in Washington had also moved beyond neurology into psychiatry. Nor should we ignore the insights of such literary figures as Hawthorne and Melville into the realm of the unconscious. Yet the development of American psychiatry came mainly as the result of a major borrowing from Central Europe, with the importation of Freudian ideas and techniques. When President G. Stanley Hall, who had made important studies both of adolescence and senescence, invited Freud to speak at the Clark University Centenary, the impact of his visit was startling. Freud's ideas eventually found fertile soil in an American society in which new insecurities, anxieties, and tensions had arisen to assault the psyche and produce blockages in the effective functioning of personality.

What was still lacking was a trained corps of men to apply the insights to the new American experience. This was provided as a result of a great migration of Austrian and German analysts and scholars in the 1930s from Nazi persecution, among them such figures as Karen Horney, Erich Fromm, Theodor Reik, and Bruno Bettelheim. There have been few migrations of skills with such far-reaching consequences. So complete has been the transplanting of these ideas in the American soil that most foreign observers have come to identify psychoanalysis with contemporary America.

Yet the mobile, bustling, power-drenched American society of the twentieth century was drastically different from the exhausted cosmopolitan society of Vienna in the early days of Freud's career—culture-proud, highly skeptical, conscious of the shutting off of avenues of mobility and power. Such key ideas of the Freudian school as the Oedipus complex and castration fears made their appeal to a narrow group but could not hope for a wider appeal in the common-sense atmosphere of American popular thinking. The European doctrine had to find new roots in the characteristic American family structure. The conditions of American life did as much to transform Freudianism as Freudianism did to change the intellectual atmosphere of America.

One may speculate on the forms that neurotic behavior has taken in America—or what may be called the characteristic American neurotic posture. In the late nineteenth century the typical case was that of the neurasthenic upper-class woman who had convinced her family and herself of her chronic invalidism and used it to tyrannize the household. To some degree she is still a fixture on the American psychic landscape, disillusioned after an impossible romantic courtship, using the psychoanalytic couch to give her life some importance.

But new figures have come on to the scene. There is the daughter or son who, within an overprotected milieu, has been torn away from many of the life experiences which once gave the young American a sense of identity. Some psychiatrists have called the result the "Smith-Vassar" or "Harvard-Princeton" syndrome. There is the "silver cord" relation between an obsessive mother and a weak son which has blighted the lives of many young Americans and paved the way for a considerable growth of homosexuality. Add the portrait, so often met in the contemporary American novel, of the alienated young Jew or Negro who feels himself an outsider in a culture he has tried at once to fight and woo, and who carries with him the scars of the struggle. But the scars are not restricted to minority groups. There is also what Arnold Green has called "the rural Protestant in the modern metropolis," who finds that the codes developed in a small-town agrarian society do not fit the rootless conditions of urban life and is riddled with anxieties in a society without landmarks.

I have left for the end the case of the schizophrenic, which has come to engage so much of the attention of American psychotherapists. At bottom, schizophrenia marks a breakdown in communication, so that the afflicted person is unable to cope with the world of reality but lives instead on two levels which move ever further apart. There are some who believe that American culture is itself schizophrenic, split with a deep fault line which is driven between the clamorous exactions of the culture and the confused responses of the individual. Certainly schizophrenia has proved more of a problem in America than elsewhere. It may be called a home-grown psychosis, just as the diseases of tension—the heart, the circulatory system, ulcers, and colitis—have proved home-grown psychosomatic diseases. It is notable that one of the native Americans who made a great name in psychiatry was Harry Stack Sullivan, a disciple of Meyer and White, and that at the start of his career he put in long years of work at the Enoch Pratt Hospital in Baltimore with schizophrenics, for whom he seemed to have a particular empathy.

The common thread in these characteristic American neurotic and psychotic situations is the inability of the personality to find any clearly defined and culture-sanctioned patterns of ideas, conduct, and feelings which will express its deepest drives. A number of writers have described in rich detail the defensive strategies and ruses by which the neurotic personality tries to bolster itself. There is a certain fitness in this way of putting it. For it is understandable that in a power society like the American, the neurotic situation should be focused on what Harold Lasswell has called "security, income, and deference" and that it should revolve primarily around the use of the stratagems of power to relieve

the sense of the inadequacy of the personality to the demands and possibilities of the culture.

Foreign commentators have often remarked that America seems to be
one vast mental hospital, but no one can be more conscious of the problems of mental health in America than American observers themselves.
Granted the inherent vagueness of definition that plagues statistics in
this area, the psychiatric profile they give of America is a striking one.
By mid-century the estimate was that 8,500,000 Americans—one out of
every eighteen persons—were suffering from some form of mental illness;
that in the course of his life, one out of every ten would need some kind
of psychiatric care; that there are as many patients in mental hospitals
as in all others combined, and an equal number who require hospitali-
zation are crowded out; that close to a million Americans who reported
for the military draft were found to be suffering from some kind of psychic difficulty.

Even with a training program for turning out more psychiatrists the
magnitude of the problem goes beyond the available resources of
therapy, which are geared to the intensive treatment of the few. The
answer seems to lie in two directions—that of group therapy and the
development of low-cost clinics, and that of preventive therapy. The
latter, of course, would involve a considerable change in the prevailing
life goals of the society. To avoid so drastic a change, the home-grown
American modes of thinking have brought a shift of emphasis from
Freudian "depth psychology" to the idea of "adjustment" within the existing social frame. Dating from the dramatic case of Clifford Beers, as
a "mind that found itself," the American genius for organization mustered the resources of the new psychiatry into a Mental Health movement which developed local groups in a number of communities. It addressed itself to the problem of organizing mental health in the same
deliberate way that Americans have gone about the problem of social
work, factory legislation, and juvenile delinquency. It declared that its
goal was not the diagnosis and treatment of mental ills—necessary as that
might be—but the development of healthy minds and personalities.

For all these vexing questions the key ideas of psychoanalysis have
permeated the American intellectual atmosphere. In American social
science the psychological approach is more common than the economic. In the novel, theater, and movies the unraveling of hidden
memories and the removal of psychological blocks to personality have
become dominant themes. Popularizations of Freud and Jung have become stock literary material. A mushrooming group of popular magazines is devoted to the self-knowledge and self-improvement of salesmen,
secretaries, small businessmen, corporate executives, and housewives.

The psychoanalyst and his couch have been enshrined in a legendry of popular jokes and cartoons and have become imbedded in American folklore.

Beyond the controversies and the cult, the spread of psychiatric thinking serves a long-range function in American life. Partly it measures the strength of revulsion against the repressions and denials of the instinctual life. Partly it marks a fumbling for the identity of the individual in a bewildering culture. It has served to tide America over the period between the life meanings and goals of a simpler society and the emergence of new ones. Most important, it has led to a questioning of shoddy purposes and too easily accepted conformisms within the frame of the pursuit of happiness.

CHAPTER X

Belief and Opinion

WE TURN in this chapter to the influences that shape the convictions, opinions, and attitudes of the American people and the forms they take. We start with the religious tradition, the role that religion and the churches have played in American intellectual history, and the recent varieties of religious experience (Sec. 1, "God and the Churches"). We go on to trace the history of American social thought in its main stream and its tributaries, noting how it has expressed itself politically in the three principal angles of vision—radicalism, conservatism, and liberalism (Sec. 2, "American Thought: the Angle of Vision"). We follow this by a close look at the American school system and its educational philosophy, analyzing the school as a subculture within the larger culture and as an agency for control, and moving on to a similar analysis of colleges and universities and the increasing access to them which has been made available to young Americans (Sec. 3, "The Higher and Lower Learning").

We then examine American journalism and the press, both in their inner structure of power and in their impact on the public mind (Sec. 4, "Profile of the Press"). We end with the technological changes that have produced a revolution in the opinion industries, viewing them not as "mass media" but as Big-Audience media—new forms of power in shaping opinion which cut across the classes and hold an immense potential for good and ill (Sec. 5, "Revolution in the Big Media"). This chapter restricts itself to the opinion and belief aspects of the Big Media, leaving the aesthetic and cultural aspects to the chapter that follows.

Belief and Opinion

1. God and the Churches

IS America a religious culture, shaped by men who sought freedom of worship, with God constantly present in their minds even when the Church has become formalized? Or is it a secular culture, with a "wall of separation" between Church and State, and with religion playing only a marginal role in men's daily lives? Each of these questions can be answered affirmatively, which indicates how deeply the religious ambiguity cuts into American culture. America is as secular as a culture can be where religion has played an important role in its origins and early growth and has been intertwined with the founding and meaning of the society. It is also as religious as a culture can be whose life goals are worldly and whose daily strivings revolve not around God but around man.

De Tocqueville rightly underscored the strong religious base of American life and thought, both in the older Puritan communities of New England and in the new frontier states. The Calvinist doctrine of predestination, which played a dominant role in the early colonies, was a hard and bleak doctrine fitting the mood of communities founded on the "challenge of hard ground." It called for ascetic living, but its asceticism became part of the secular world rather than the religious and led to an activism which left its mark on American history. Similarly, the earlier intolerance felt by men who had an inner sense of loneliness as they waited for a sign of God's grace was in time replaced by the doctrine of toleration.

This mixture of theocracy and secularism, of dogma and indifferentism, is one of the striking features of the American religious heritage. One finds a clue to it by noting the difference of religious climate at each important stage of American history. The colonies were settled under the stress of religious revolt, in an age of creative religious feeling; American freedom was won at the end of the eighteenth century in an age of Deism and revolutionary freethinking; the major growth of America took place during the century which followed the Jeffersonian era and which was strongly marked by scientific rationalism; in the contemporary Atomic Age there has been a revival of religious feeling under the stress of social tensions and personal insecurity. This mixture of seventeenth-century Calvinism, eighteenth-century Deism, nineteenth-century rationalism, and mid-twentieth-century anxiety may help explain some of the contradictions in the relations between God and man in America.

Religion has lost a good deal of its former hold on the American character and no longer pervades the daily content of living as it once did. Yet we must not underestimate the hold it still has. While there was an atheist strain in the writings of Tom Paine, and while atheism is still protected by Supreme Court decisions, there is less and less room for the "godless" in America, since godlessness is usually associated with Communism and depravity. America is regarded as a "Christian country," with an emphasis on "Christian" that carries it beyond the tolerant deism of the Founding Fathers who wrote of "Nature's God" with an inclusive anthropological sweep. There is no candidate for even minor political office in America today who would dare to mock religion or alienate any of the denominations. In every major speech a President is likely to include what Franklin Roosevelt used to call the "God stuff."

Yet religion plays more than a surface part in the conduct of American government. Woodrow Wilson was a Presbyterian, Franklin Roosevelt an Episcopalian, Harry Truman a Baptist, and Dwight Eisenhower grew up in Kansas among the mushrooming religious sects of the frontier, although he turned to Presbyterianism on the threshold of the White House. Examine the Presidential tenure of each and you will find features of it illumined by the particular kind of religious training he received. The religious ambiguity of American politics is further shown by the fact that every President (and Vice-President) has belonged to one of the Protestant sects, yet few pay much attention to the particular sect to which he belongs.

As the child of the Reformation, Americans took over not only its dominantly Protestant heritage but also its deep individualistic strain. Every European sect that found itself constricted or in trouble emigrated to the New World, which thus became a repository of all the distillations of Reformation thought and feeling. Since the Reformation had broken with the authority of the Church and left to the individual the meaning of the Scriptures, America became a congeries of judging individuals, each of them weighing the meaning and application of the Word. A Bible-reading people emerged, drenched in the tradition of the Old and New Testaments. This may help explain the stress on the idea of "convenant" in American thought, which Helmut Richard Niebuhr has noted. It also suggests why a people so concerned with the meaning of the Holy Writ has been the first to give a sacred character to a written Constitution but has at the same time remained a nation of amateur interpreters of the Constitution.

Two basic concepts of the Christian belief—the soul and sin—took on a new emphasis in individualist America. Each man was the judge of his own religious convictions, since his possession of an immortal soul gave each man an inner worth regardless of color, rank or station, political belief, wealth or poverty. Thus the foundation was laid in religious freedom for a political equalitarianism which no later history of privilege has been able wholly to extirpate from the American mind. But if each man had an immortal soul to save, it was because it had been steeped in sin. As a Bible-reading people, the Americans took over many of the preconceptions of the Hebraic society in which Judaism and early Christianity were rooted. Among them was the sense of individual—aside from original, or inevitable—sin, without which there could be no individual salvation.

There is a resulting ambiguity between the sin-and-salvation strain in Christian doctrine and the organic optimism of American economic and social attitudes. The Hebrew prophets, as they lamented the disintegration of Biblical society, called on each Jew to ward off God's wrath from his people by cleansing himself of his own inner guilt; the Christian allegory added to the somberness of this conception. But there have been few occasions on which Americans could believe with any conviction in an impending collapse of their social structure and their world. The sense of sin and the sense of doom were therefore importations from the Old and New Testament that somehow flowered in the American soil in spite of the worship of money and success—or perhaps exactly because of this worship, which required a compensating doctrine to ease the conscience.

The result has been an American religious tradition which is at once deeply individualist, anti-authoritarian, concerned with sin and salvation, yet secular and rationalist in its life goals, Bible-reading in its habits, with its emphasis on man's relation to his own conscience and therefore to his private religious judgment. The Americans have been salvation-minded, each believer being engrossed in his relation not to the church but to God, in Whom he was to find salvation; yet they have also formed a secular rather than a sacred or hieratic society. Since they were believing and judging individuals, they did not lean on a priesthood: even their churches were based less on the authority of a hierarchy than on lay presbyters or the congregation itself.

This conflict between secular social goals and the religious conscience has colored both the religious and the democratic experience of America. It underlay the agonized conscience of early New England, the preoccupation with God's way with man in good and evil which characterized American Fundamentalism, the fear-drenched frontier religion filled with literal-minded terrors, the Social Gospel movement; and it will be found in the latter-day movement of neo-Calvinist religious thought, with its Atomic Age setting of apocalyptic guilt and terror. For all its optimism and its cult of action and success, American culture has been overlaid with a sense of both agony and evil.

America owes much of the effectiveness of its democracy, as well as much of its dynamism, to this strain in its religious experience. I am suggesting that the fiber necessary for democracy is not the product of any particular religious doctrine but of the lonely debate within the free conscience. Democracy is the polity of individual choices and of majority consent; it can be run effectively only where there is a habituation to hard choices. Those who are certain of the simplicity of revealed truth make the initial choice of submission and do not have to make any subsequent choices; they do not furnish a fertile soil for the democratic seed. Those who expect miracles will not take the risk of dissent. Those who are sure of dogma given to them will not make the arduous effort of winning the slow and gradual victories of an always unfinished society. Finally those who suffer no conflict within the arena of their own minds will not generate the needed dynamism to transcend the conflict and resolve their conscience.

American democracy, in the sense that it is linked with private judgment and freedom of dissent, is thus also linked with the stir and turmoil of free religious choice. To be sure, the psychic toll of this conflict and dynamism is a heavy one. But the stakes have been great—nothing less than the creation and sustaining of an open society which is based on the judging and the choosing individual caught on the battleground of his own mind.

In an era when the threat to democracy is conformism of mind and stereotyping of character, one of the great counterforces is the traditional American religious nonconformism. This nonconformism had its roots, as Arthur G. Parker has put it, in "a religiously inflexible New England, with its mores forged upon the anvil of Jeremiah by the sledge of Calvin." Something of the dark intensity of this religious commitment has persisted in America until the present day. It gave American history some of its Calvinist dourness from the time of the Mathers and Jonathan Edwards to the current revivalists whose chief stock in trade is still hell-fire and brimstone. For all its optimism and its cult of action and success, American history has been overlaid with a brooding sense of agony and evil. One finds it in Hawthorne, Melville, and Poe, as also in Mark Twain and Henry James, Thomas Wolfe and Faulkner. While this strain persists, there is less danger of the flattening out of personality and of a herd-mindedness in opinion.

It is here that American religious Fundamentalism has its roots. The brand of Christianity that the earlier Americans took to their hearts was not the mildness of Jesus's teachings or the doctrine of brotherly love, but the probing of man's relation to good and evil and of God's ways to men. In the mid-eighteenth century, as Perry Miller pointed out, a deeper shadow came over American Puritanism. It remained during the century and more of frontier expansion, forming a frontier religion of the Right Way, filled with literal-minded terrors, with swift rewards and stern punishments. Its basic image was that of life as a hard pilgrimage pursued by temptations and dangers, an unrelenting quest beset with trials and testing. Much of this view has survived even into the contemporary era of diluted and sophisticated religion. Its continuing strength suggests that it fulfills a function—that of keeping alive a ferment of enthusiasm within individuals surrounded by collapsing moral standards, who face denials and frustrations in their own lives. Sometimes, as in the case of the religion of the American Negroes, there is a quality in their religious expression akin to the simplicity and creativeness of the primitive Christian church in its catacomb days. But in many other instances of enthusiastic religion the fervor lacks creativeness and represents a mechanical reassertion of faith in the face of inner fears and emptiness.

One of the striking facts about American history has been the linkage of the "religion of the fathers" with what Mencken delighted to call the "Bible Belt" mentality—a narrow view of life and morals, a belief in the literal inspiration of the Bible, and a reactionary code of political belief. The passion of the "Hot Gospel" and the archaism of the hell-fire-and-damnation religion have been put to work as a counterforce to the inherent humanism of the Christian teachings. It has enabled a number of demagogues, especially in the rural Midwest and South, to clothe their racist and reactionary appeals in Biblical references. In the big cities the tradition of Charles G. Finney and Dwight L. Moody was continued with modern publicity techniques by Billy Sunday, Aimee Mac-Pherson, and Billy Graham. They were evidences of how broad is the gulf in American religion between the loudly committed and the deeply committed. Unlike Puritanism, which with all its excesses embodied an internalized religious conviction—the product of people who wrestled with God as Jacob did—the current evangelism is a form of religiosity externalized in a public spectacle.

The question here is not one of "liberalism" and "conservativism," whether in religion or politics, but of the inner relations between religious attitudes and democracy. There is a curious example in the Populist political movements in the South and Midwest, in which the stress on saving one's soul and preserving religious orthodoxy was linked with an anticapitalist radicalism. The type-figures were William Jennings

Bryan and Tom Watson. In them a crusading Populism was fused with
a harsh Catonian moralism. The common element was the need for the
salvation of the believer from the wickedness of the Cities of the Plain
where both wealth and freethinking accumulate. The anticorporate
strand was thus intertwined with the moralistic, and Bryan's famous
Cross of Gold speech was in direct line with the crusade for Prohibition
and the Scopes anti-Evolution "monkey" trial. In its characteristic latter-
day form this amalgam has lost its anticorporate militancy, replaced by
an antilabor, anti-Negro, and anti-Jewish emphasis. Thus in these areas
religious Fundamentalism has damned minority groups along with the
urban liberal intellectuals who are vaguely felt to be undermining the
tribal traditions.

I take another example from the relation of Christian ideals to the
American business spirit. Modern Protestantism and the modern business
spirit were born out of the same historical soil. The real problem for
religion came with the harshness of the acquisitive spirit. Confronted
with this, the churches too often faltered, and instead of challenging
business enterprise they emulated its premises, investing business power
with religious sanctions. In the case of figures like Dwight Moody, Sam
Jones, and Billy Sunday, Christian exhortation either became an
apology for the acquisitive and competitive or gave religious confirmation to the caste system in race relations and to the status quo in industrial relations. This approach came to be vulgarized to the point where
one writer depicted Jesus (*The Man Nobody Knows*) as the Great
Salesman, and the campaigns for the revival of religious faith were
mapped out with salesmanship strategy. In the hands of such men religion became conventionalized, status-fulfilling, and smug.

Yet, having said this, one must add to this phase of American church
history the Social Gospel phase, given impetus by Washington Gladden
and Walter Rauschenbusch, which dedicated the churches to a militant
role in economic and social reform. Some of the best energies of the denominations, including the Methodists, Presbyterians, and Baptists—the
three sects which also made the greatest headway on the frontier—were
turned toward the new pathways of social action in the spirit of a Jesus
who had given himself to the poor and been denounced as agitator and
revolutionary. In this spirit some of the pastors of every denomination
have fought for racial equality and economic justice and have explored
settlement work, adult education, and psychiatric pastoral counseling.
Wherever this has happened, whether with Catholics, Protestants, or
Jews, it has been attacked as a secularizing of religion. It is true that it
has turned the main stress of religious energy away from the supernatural to the social, from transcending the human to the serving of human
needs. It is also true that such a humanist emphasis has in many in-

stances become theologically thin. It is easy for sophisticates to deride religious liberalism, to caricature the sermon-turned-book-review, to depict the wrestling of the spirit with God in the form of the muscular Christianity of young men in the YMCA gymnasium or in the sports activities of settlement work. Yet it has served the function of making religion a living part of the needs of the people and keeping it militantly alert to the furthermost stretches of social possibility.

A reaction has, however, set in against this humanist emphasis. Increasingly the young American intellectuals have been turning not to a social religion but to a new theological intensity which is at once radically pessimist in its premises about human nature and social possibility, and also a return to some of the old Calvinist themes. Theologians like Paul Tillich and Reinhold Niebuhr, while affirming a deep interest in contemporary social struggles, put their chief stress on the corruption of the human enterprise, the limits of human will and action, the difficulties of spiritual growth as well as of social struggle in the process of history, and the heroism called for in the "courage to be."

But the crucial division in American religion is not between fundamentalists and modernists, or between liberals and neo-Calvinists. It is between active and passive belief, between those for whom religion is commitment and those for whom it is lip service or conformist respectability. The Social Gospel and the new Calvinism have at least one trait in common—that of seeking to bring vitality once again to the religious commitment. Both feel the difficulty of the human situation and the unremitting arduousness of the struggle for belief. The enemies of both are smugness, apathy, an easy optimism, and a short-cut conformism. The introspective religion flourishes best where man feels isolated, struggling against the eidola of secular society. The early America, with its lonely frontier communities torn up from their European roots, furnished such a soil. But when American society came into the full swing of prosperity and became itself a great artifact with numberless institutional relationships, the lonely meeting of man and God became more difficult.

Much the same can be said of prophetic religion. Prophecy is the product and sign of social failure, and in the American myths there is no room for failure. Even the mid-nineteenth-century sects which used to forecast the doom of the world at an appointed time could not survive the ridicule of their contemporaries when the time of doom came and the end was not yet. The voice of ridicule was the voice of a culture built on boundless hope and optimism. Even the Fourierist and other Utopian communities of the nineteenth century were the product of millennialism rather than of social despair. Everything in America has seemed to conspire against pessimistic and other-worldly religions. It is hard to talk of the mysteries of Nature where science exploits it, or of compassion in a culture that flees failure, or of humility in an imperial culture that makes an idol out of wealth and power. It is hard to see how a religion of poverty can strike continuing root in the richest civilization of the world, or a religion of denial in one of the most Byzantine.

How then account for the strong pulsation in America today toward a religion which is imbued with a sense of the corruption and weakness of human institutions, and which is once again ridden with pessimism? I suggest that the revival of this impulse comes in an age of anxiety and alienation, when Americans are disillusioned with the idea of automatic progress, when the world struggle and the menace of atomic doom have become pressing anxieties, and when optimism, liberalism, and modernism have come under suspicion. But while this new mood has led some of the best elements in the churches toward new depths of religious feeling, it is part of the dilemma that history presents to American religion. The religion-creating capacity, as witness the great period in the Middle East at the time of the Roman Empire, depends on social failure and catastrophe, while the open society depends on prosperity and peace. To put it another way, the creative soil for religion is social anxiety, which may be the product or the harbinger of democratic failure.

I do not believe that such a sense of failure is likely to thrive long in the American cultural setting. The cultural strains that have given America its power and greatness are those of dynamism rather than despair. Perhaps a new religion will someday emerge from some impending world catastrophe as the religions of the Orient emerged from the collapse of the Greek and Roman worlds. But short of such an apocalyptic vision the American religious future is likely to grow out of the American past, whose chief features have been social optimism, dynamism, and a continuing equilibrium between the conflicting pulls and tensions of American society.

This may offer a clue to the creativeness of the American religious experience. It differs from the religion-creating genius which showed itself in Asia and the Middle East. Its striking characteristic lies in the luxuriant growth of religious denominations splitting off from each other amoeba-wise. Pluralist in so many other phases, the American culture is supremely pluralist in religion. Staying mainly within the broad frame of historic Christianity, Americans have explored new ways of life in new communities (from the Shakers to Father Divine) or proclaimed new particular insights (as with the Mormons, Christian Scientists, Jehovah's Witnesses) or fragmented a denomination into cults and sects. Nowhere else could William James's *Varieties of Religious Experience* have been so congenial to the cultural temper. Nowhere else did the tradition of religious dissent lead to such a spread of denominational forms—not only the broad religious divisions of Protestants, Catholics, and Jews, but also Episcopalians, Presbyterians, Methodists, Baptists, Congregationalists, Unitarians, Friends, Lutherans, Moravians, Christian Brethren, Christian Scientists, Jehovah's Witnesses, Seventh-Day Adventists, Disciples of Christ, Mormons, and the adherents of The Church of God with Signs Following After.

The sects have been derided because they split what might have been religious unity and cast themselves out of the "Eden of infallibility." Yet to attack them for this is to ask America to be other than it is, not only in religion but in every phase of its life. For the pluralism of the American churches is like the pluralism of America's regions, its diverse economic forms, its political localism, its ethnic and immigrant stocks. It is closely linked with religious freedom which, as Madison put it at the Virginia Convention of 1788, "rises from the multiplicity of sects which pervades America and which is the best and only security for religious liberty in any society." The competition of creeds has prevented Americans from erecting intolerance into a principle of government.

There is perhaps less meaning than meets the eye in the figures on the growth of American church membership. It is estimated that, as of 1954, there were ninety-seven million church members (of whom fifty-seven million were Protestant, thirty-two million Catholic, five million Jewish, the rest scattered) comprising over 60 per cent of the population, a larger percentage of the total population than at any time in the past century. This represents a "return to religion" of some sort, but what sort is far from clear. It could mean a new groping for faith as a compensation for the ugliness and danger of life. Or it might mean that in most American communities church membership is a badge of social status, and that membership in them represents safety in a conformist, churchgoing society. Clearly the traditional social nonconformism has been giving way to a conformism which accepts the power structures either as a positive good or as an evil which it would be futile to resist. It is not that the churches practice a conscious hypocrisy about Christian teachings but rather that religious doctrines have been turned into counters in a game men play to bring their consciences to terms with their universe. It is less a question of what the pastors say than the fact that they are no longer listened to; having lost the capacity for belief, they have lost also the power to instill belief.

On the question of the relation of the churches to the class composition of their membership there have been some recent changes of note.

On the whole the Protestants and Jews are more strongly represented in the upper and middle classes, while the Catholics draw more heavily upon the lower-income groups, especially among organized workers. Nevertheless the strength of Protestants in the lower class has been growing, especially since World War II. Of the Protestant sects the Methodists, Baptists, and Lutherans have their heaviest membership in the lower class and are lightly represented in the upper class, while the Presbyterians, Episcopalians, and Congregationalists show a higher proportion in the upper class and a considerably lighter one in the lower class. Yet these figures should not obscure the fact that Protestants and Jews, especially the latter, are largely middle-class groups and most typically come from business and the professions and from the white-collar and service strata of the population. The Protestants and Jews also draw from a higher educational level than the Catholics.

The church affiliations of the American Negro offer a special case. The available figures are at least a decade old (most of them come from the year 1946) and there are considerable differences between the figures given in the studies by Liston Pope and William W. Sweet; yet the main outlines of the profile of membership are fairly clear. Sweet estimates that 70 per cent of the fourteen million Negroes in 1946 belonged to churches—a higher percentage than whites. Of the nine and a half million Negro church members, more than eight million were Baptists or Methodists (Pope's figures are six million out of the almost seven million Negro church members). The studies agree that only a small fraction of the Negroes are Catholic (the number has been growing rapidly in the past decade) and, of the Protestants, only a small fraction belong to the predominantly white denominations. The striking fact about Negro church membership is the heavy emphasis upon the all-Negro denominations. This is partly due to the force of white discrimination and partly to the Negro's own desire to control the organization of his church, in which he has found the freest expression of his leadership and his emotional life. The latter fact does not relieve the white churches of their responsibility for religious jim-crowing. The estimate is that less than 1 per cent of the white congregations have any Negro members—usually only a handful—and less than one half of one per cent of the Negroes who belong to these congregations worship regularly with them.*

There remains the question of the nonchurchgoer and his religious outlook. If 40 per cent of the American population are not claimed as members by any of the denominations, this comes to some seventy million people: taking into account the exaggerated claims of a number of

* For a further discussion of the religion of the American Negro, see Ch. VII, Sec. 6, "The Negro in America."

the churches, the figure is probably considerably higher. It does not follow that they do not have religious beliefs. Abraham Lincoln refused to belong to any particular church, yet he was a deeply religious man. No doubt some of the number are atheists, a good many are agnostics, many are indifferent, many are puzzled, many may feel themselves too poor to afford church membership and its social obligations, and still others prefer to keep their religious beliefs to themselves instead of joining a church and worshiping in common with others. Since Americans are, as I have pointed out, a nation of "joiners," the substantial percentage which has stayed out of the life of the church is all the more striking. There is a current tendency to emphasize church membership, which is bound to put pressure upon the nonmembers and reduce their numbers. But it remains true that one of the articles of the democratic belief in America is the disbelief in any state church or any equation between membership in a church and membership in the American commonwealth. This distinction is crucial to the idea of religious freedom as Americans have practiced it.

The issue of religious freedom in America thus goes beyond discrimination and also beyond the pluralism of the sects, to the core principle of the separation of church and state, as embodied in the constitutional prohibition against any "establishment of religion." Given the experience of Europe as well as that of the early Puritan settlers, the generation of Madison's famous *Remonstrance* saw that an official recognition of a "religious establishment" would hamper religious freedom.

There are some polemicists who ask whether a democracy can remain indifferent to religion when its deepest faith is based on religious premises. One might answer that the official religious neutrality of the government does not imply the personal religious indifference of its members. An American President, Senator, or Supreme Court Justice may have his own explicit religious views, including President Lincoln as Protestant, Senator Lehman as Jew, or Justice Frank Murphy as Catholic. But each knew that unless he refrained from using his official power to propagate the strength of his creed, all the creeds would become entangled in a murderous war.

As Justice Rutledge stated clearly, there is a double price Americans pay for religious liberty: one is the self-restraint of the government in noninterference with a man's creed; the other is the ban on the use of governmental machinery by or for any church. That is why the Supreme Court has tried carefully to draw a line of distinction between valid aid to parochial and public schools and the kind that violates the principle of separation. Another problem that confronted the Court involved the sect of the Jehovah's Witnesses, against which a number of local ordinances were directed on the ground that house-to-house visits for the sale of their religious literature created a nuisance. The Court majority ruled against the ordinances, seeing more in these cases than the importunings of a minor religious sect—nothing less than a central principle of American religious freedom.

No creeds have had better occasion to profit from this principle than the Catholics and the Jews, living among a Protestant majority. Swelled by a great immigration from the 1840s to the 1920s, the Catholic population grew from fewer than two million in 1850 to thirty-two million in 1954. Despite some anti-Catholic movements of bigotry, they have grown in popular acceptance, community importance, and power. Nowhere in a non-Catholic society do they enjoy the freedom and prestige they have in America. The same is true of the roughly five million Jews, who—despite sporadic anti-Semitic outbursts—have flourished in the climate of American religious freedom and economic opportunity. It may be noted that no other Catholic community contributes as much to the Vatican world position as do the American Catholics, and that the American Jews form one of the two polar centers (the other being Israel) of the Jewish world community.*

In fact, while America is still dominantly Protestant, it can no longer be described as a primarily Protestant culture with Catholic and Jewish minorities: it is close to becoming (in Will Herberg's phrase) a three-religion culture. One might predict that in the latter half of the twentieth century these three religious groupings will harden rather than dissolve. They are becoming increasingly self-contained. There is, for example, greater mobility within the class system in America than among the three religions; to put it another way, an American (especially if he is a Catholic or a Jew) is less likely to marry outside his religion than outside his class. The Catholics are critical of intermarriage, pointing out that Catholics who marry outside their faith are likely to abandon that faith. The Jews, anxious to maintain their identity in the face of world hostility, have also strengthened their resistance to intermarriage. The Protestants, less unified in organization and in religious consciousness, have been slower to join this trend. It is in American politics that the trend toward a three-religion society is most clearly reflected: in a city like New York, for example, the political slates of candidates are likely to be carefully composed of representatives of the three major faiths, and as much care is given to the ingredients of this political-religious recipe as to any recipe of a gourmet —and deviation from it is as sensitively noted.

In the days of the great migrations from Europe, the immigrants brought with them to America their own religious denominational be-

---

* For a further discussion of the Catholics and Jews in the American class structure, see Ch. VII, Sec. 5, "The Minority Situation."

liefs, along with their language and customs. It was part of the American creed of freedom that while the immigrant was to assimilate "Americanism" in all other respects, he was expected to keep his religious separateness. The second generation often moved away from this religious heritage, and the third and later generations have returned to it—but in a different form. Again a phrase Herberg uses (taken from a study of intermarriage in New Haven by Ruby Jo Kennedy) is illuminating: that the descendants of the immigrants have fused their religious beliefs in a "triple melting pot." For the new generations it is important to be a Protestant, a Catholic, or a Jew "as the specific way, and increasingly perhaps as the only way, of being an American and locating oneself in American society."

This becomes then a new kind of secularism—not outside the churches, as with the seventy million Americans who are nonmembers of any denomination, but inside the churches. The best illustration of this trend is the recent movement to introduce religious teaching into the schools in the form of a stress on "spiritual values." While some Americans, alert to the danger of the erosion of the "wall of separation," have regarded this as a dangerous offensive by the religious vested interests, it may also be seen as a sign of the flattening out of religious belief. This flattening out takes the form of the conviction that religious faith is somehow "a good thing." Or, as President Eisenhower has put it, "our form of government has no sense unless it is founded in a deeply felt religious faith, and I don't care what it is."

It was part of the disquiet and disorder of the era of anxiety that Americans should be seeking some inner link between religion and democracy. One may cite the characteristic intellectual pilgrimage of Russell Davenport, who first sought the meaning of life in the "permanent revolution" of the American free economy, then tried to link it with a Republican political renaissance under Wendell Willkie, and finally left as his testament an unfinished manuscript asserting that the future of democracy and of the "dignity of man" lies in charting the still uncharted and nonrational elements of religious faith. It might be truer to say, however, that instead of finding their democratic faith in supernatural religion, Americans have tended to find their religious faith in various forms of belief about their own existence as a people. The deepest element of Lincoln's faith, as Edmund Wilson has pointed out, lay in a religious *mystique* of the national Union. If Americans have been turning toward the vague phrases about "spiritual values," it may be because their existence as a unified people is no longer threatened as it was in Lincoln's day.

There is little doubt that the American religious community is linked with democracy, but the linkage is less through "spiritual values" than in the fact of America as an open religious society. What is most striking about it in this sense is the fact that, with its multiplicity of faiths speaking as with a confusion of tongues, there have been no religious wars or massacres. You will find in American history few of those blood-encrusted crimes which in world history have been committed in the name of the only true God and the only true religious way. No other civilization offers a parallel in this respect. There has been marked bitterness between Catholics and Protestants in the struggle for political power, and between the Jews and both of them in economic rivalries. But the principle of the open society, with its rapid class mobility, its religious intermarriage, its respect for the right of religious dissent, has proved a dissolvent force both for bigotries and hostilities.

By the same token it has been corrosive not only of bigotry but also of religious intensity. An example may be cited in what has happened to the religion of American Negroes, whose church affiliations I have already discussed. It has been said that the real inheritors of the creative Christian tradition were not the Protestant descendants of the Calvinists or the powerful Catholic church but the humble and despised Negroes. To them fell the role of continuing the dynamism of frontier religion. Toynbee has written eloquently of the primitive Christianity of the American Negro as one of the few strong growths of spontaneous Christian faith in a "post-Christian era." But as the social lot of the Negroes has improved, their characteristic religion—with its buoyancy, tragedy, and myth-making imaginativeness—has been diluted. With prosperity and a measure of equality has come respectability. Today the middle-class Negro finds himself increasingly caught in the same churchgoing middle class as the white.

A note may be in order on the relation of religion and the economy. The historians of Protestant societies have stressed the doctrine of vocation and its carry-over from religious to secular uses. Given the history of American democracy, one should add another aspect—the inner relation between religious pluralism and a pluralist economy. What both have in common is the process of decision-making through the exercise of private judgment. The free-market economy, as Karl Polanyi has shown, was alien to the ethos and psychology of medieval Europe. It carried in its wake some devastating social irresponsibilities for the human costs of industrialism. But what we have not seen until recently is that the decentralized decisions involved in capitalism put the burden of decision-making on numberless individuals. True, the growth of monopoly has diminished the scope of this, but in great measure it still applies. I do not say that every small businessman or corporate manager or highly skilled worker carries the moral burden of the decision-making well. In many instances he does not. But I do say that a society in which

he ceases even to make the attempt is a society in which the habit of decision-making in moral and political terms becomes also constricted. It
is a striking fact that the same societies which have maintained a decentralized choice in religion have tended to maintain it also in the economy and in politics.

To those who believe, finally, that it is the religious metaphysic which
alone has made American democracy possible and held it together, I
would enter a qualification. It is the dissenting pluralist tradition in religion, rather than the religious orientation as such, which has been
most strongly linked with American democracy. Religious dissent has
carried along with it the tradition of political dissent. It has fostered the
democratic idea mainly through its stress on the right of the individual to
face and master his own solitariness, according to his own lights. Thus
Americans have managed to remain largely a believing people (far more
than has been true of other industrial cultures) without the compulsion
of imposing their religious beliefs on others—or of imposing *any* religious beliefs, although they hope plaintively that every American will
have a set of "spiritual values."

2. *American Thought: the Angle of Vision*

To MOVE from America's religious belief to its secular thought is less
of a jump than may appear, since the belief became largely secularized
and the thought had deep religious roots. Americans questioned their
gods in the act of believing, just as they retained a substratum of almost
religious belief in their political institutions, despite their refusal to
build structures of theory on them.

This American aversion to intellectual system-building is striking
when contrasted with continental thought. Perhaps those who felt sure
they were shaping in social actuality what Jefferson called an "empire
for freedom" did not hunger for empire building in the realm of the
mind. Daniel Boorstin suggested, in *The Genius of American Politics*,
that the reason Americans found political theory superfluous is that they
accepted the "givenness" of their institutions, and where something is
"given" it needs neither laborious nor subtle definition. In the European sense Americans have had little "grand theory," whether of the
state, the economy, the society, the culture, Nature, or God. In the case
of such towering figures as Jefferson and Lincoln in political thinking,
James and Peirce in philosophy, and Veblen in social theory, one finds a
rich array of fragments rather than an artfully laid out master plan.
Peirce despaired of ever making his philosophical ends meet, and both
Emerson and Whitman flaunted the contradictions in their thinking.

Americans have a fear of rigidifying thought. Believing that forms are empty, they have an antipathy to formal thinking which has caused them to shy away from programs of long-range social change. Thus American thought is tentative, fragmented, directed at the immediate object, and open to change at both ends.

Except for the brief period of the Puritan oligarchy, American thinkers have also been largely free of the appeal to authority and revelation. One of their dilemmas has been to square their basic nonconformism with the stability required by property, investment, and law. When property was riding highest, firm in the saddle of power, the nonconformism almost dropped out of American thought—as it did through much of the quarter century from the Civil War to the Populist revolt. American thinkers have been at their best in their antiauthoritarianism: in the dicta of Jefferson and Madison on freedom of thought, in the pamphleteering of the Jacksonians, in Calhoun's plea for a veto power by which political minorities could hold their place, in Thoreau's doctrine of "civil disobedience," in the thunderbolts of Henry Demarest Lloyd against Standard Oil, in Brooks Adams's gloomy predictions of "centralization and decay," in William James's "pluralistic universe," in Justice Holmes's "can't helps," in Veblen's polemics against "absentee owners." Even the American ruling groups, unlike those of Europe, have relied less on authoritarianism than on the prestige of success and the attraction of the Big Money.

Every generalization about American thought can be offset by a countergeneralization. Suppose you mention the lack of mystical thinkers: except for some of the early Puritan divines you will be on good ground, yet in Poe, Hawthorne, Melville, James, and Faulkner there is a remarkable power in the handling of symbolism. If you note how much of American thought has been secular and rationalist you are confronted in reply by the tradition damning the merely rational, from the divines who denied that it could encompass the mysteries of God's way to man, to the latter-day thinkers who find that the concept of a purely rational man excludes all the half-aberrant, half-heroic ways by which men belie the blueprints of their minds.

If you deny tragic depth in American thought, there are Hawthorne and Melville again to refute you; and Mark Twain, whose comic mask scarcely hides his pessimism of spirit; and Lincoln, whose tragic sense shone through the humorous anecdotes by which he tried to make the ordeal of civil war tolerable. If you say that American thought has a feet-on-the-ground realism you must correct the picture with the millennialist tracts spawned by the experimental communist settlements, and the creative Utopian classics of Bellamy, Donnelly, and Howells. Finally, if you say that American thought—like the American class system—remained pluralistic instead of single-tracked, and was hostile to any scheme of rigid determinism, a minority report would again note the determinism of Frederick Jackson Turner, of Henry and Brooks Adams, of Veblen, and Beard.

Certain historical trends, at least, are clear. American thought has moved from the Utopian and millennialist to a focusing on the calculable future, from a single-factor determinism in history to the more complex multiple-factor view, from religious to secular, from idealist to empirical, from focusing on ultimate goals to focusing on means, from absolutist to pragmatic, from radical to reformist or conservative. On some themes it has gone through cyclical alternations of mood and emphasis. But always there has been the steady beat of change in American life, carrying with it a constant change in the angle of vision of the American thinkers.

In a search for the roots of American thought the first clue is in the interrelations of religion and capitalism. The quest that led to the settlement of America, from the beginning of the seventeenth century to the middle of the twentieth, was a search at once for freedom of conscience and for the El Dorado of the Big Money. Both quests were Utopian in aiming at an ideal community; both were stubbornly practical, responding to felt needs. American social thought was thus, from the start, compounded of conscience and practicality.

The first expression of the American conscience took the form of Puritanism—the fullest amalgam of religion, economics, and politics within a single mold that Americans ever achieved.* Although the Puritan strain came to be watered down, American thought never wholly lost its preoccupation with God's design on the American Continent and with the alternate beat of conscience and acquisitiveness. This suggests a key problem in American intellectual history: how did the early absolutism of conscience turn into the pragmatism of the later period, and how have strong elements of both managed to coexist in the American mind?

A crucial link between the two was individualism. Since a man's conscience was in his own keeping, he had to allow others also to answer to theirs alone. Thus religious *laissez faire* was a strong source of American individualism. It was reinforced by the doctrine of "calling." Puritan thought was dedicated to the City of God and an unremitting enmity to the Adversary. "Calling" started as the reception of grace

* For a discussion of the place of Puritanism in American religious development, see Sec. 1, "God and the Churches." Here I deal with it in the larger American thought pattern. The same applies to individualism, freedom, property, and Natural Rights, all of which have been discussed in their own frames in earlier chapters but are here brought together for the larger frame of American thought.

which marked the commitment to God and the release from the Adversary; it grew into the economic "calling" by which a man's vocation and its accumulated fruits became an outward sign of inner grace. Americans are deeply concerned with private property not because they are made of more grasping human stuff than others but because their culture developed in a climate where a man's individuality was linked with property as a sign of grace, just as it was linked with his conscience as a witness of his identity. The individualist strain was further reinforced by the Christian allegory—the tradition of willingness to incur martyrdom for conscience.

A final link was needed before the chain of thought could be forged joining individualism to property and conscience. This was the doctrine of Natural Rights, with its origins in European thought and a life history of its own in its American locale. It gave a metaphysical basis to the civil-liberties tradition in America, which holds that freedom of thought and utterance, like freedom of worship, is rooted in the "laws of Nature and of Nature's God." Through the link of "Nature's God," much of the emotion attaching to the allegory of martyrdom as well as the doctrine of grace was carried over into the "natural order." Americans came to regard everything related to their individualism as part of that natural order—not only their rights to freedom but also their rights to property.

This freedom-property complex has dominated American thinking throughout the nation's history. It managed to combine the strongly mystical intensity of seventeenth-century thought with the deism of the eighteenth century, the world of transcendence with that of rationalism. To the deeply religious it offered the nourishment of belief, to the skeptical and rationalist it offered secular sustenance. To the nineteenth-century mind it made possible the linking of social progress with individual freedom. For the rationalists it provided a mystique by which freedom, capitalism, and individualism combined to explain the success of the American experiment.

Thus was formed a pattern woven of individualism, Puritanism, conscience, vocation, the allegory of martyrdom, the belief in natural rights, the passion for freedom, and the clinging to property. Within it there have been swings of emphasis—cycles of thought moving spirally in response to the needs and changes of American life.

In its origins, as we have seen, the dominant strain was religious and absolutist. But the sharp advance of science and the democratic impact of the frontier undercut this emphasis. As a result there was a movement toward religious tolerance, the multiplying of sects, and the undermining of authoritarianism, which set the pattern for American religious thought.

In the 1820s and 1830s new winds of doctrine blew westward from Europe in the form of German mysticism and merged with the democratic energies of Western farmers and Eastern intellectuals. The leaders of this "Transcendentalist" movement were Emerson, Brownson, and the Concord group. Strongly idealist in its philosophical roots, it contained within itself the counterpoint to Jacksonian tough-mindedness. Its historians and philosophers saw in the American experience, as in the whole religious experience, the working out of a transcendent idea of good or truth. But some of them began to identify this idea with the good of the common people, the welfare of majorities, and the truth of democracy: from which it was only a step to the reformism which made social gains, rather than a transcendent idea in history, the test of action and thought. As the seedbed for much that was to follow, this strain held within itself the beginnings of hardheaded movements for reform, along with Utopian and millennial schemes. Eventually the discordance within it grew too great to be contained within a single school, and as it burst, the fragments flew in many directions. But during its "Golden Day" its core lay in the strength which the American democratic experience gave to the fusion of German philosophical mysticism with the original intensity of American religious feeling.

Transcendentalism never took root in the formal philosophy of the academies. But it had important parallels in the "democratic vistas" of Walt Whitman, who, in his philosophic base, was idealistic (note his phrase about "the terrible doubt of appearances"). It also had a corollary in the sense of excitement about the energies of the rising nation. Between the Age of Jackson and the Age of Big Business, the driving force in American social thought was the search for a base on which these expanding national energies could build. For a time the struggle over slavery channeled the search into questions of constitutional law and political theory. Calhoun sought a theory to protect the minority rights of the South and the slave-owning property interest without breaking with the basic idea of a Federal union. As Louis Hartz has pointed out, Calhoun did not see that the logic of the Secession movement led to a cult of sections which would be nations in themselves, and which would find a fighting faith in the rightness of their own "peculiar institution." In the North there was a similar groping for an absolutism of individual freedom, which in turn did not dare envisage the cost of a civil war.

With the end of the war two opposing mystiques emerged—Whitman's "leaves of grass" democracy, and the Divine Right of Property.

Each formed a complex of religion, politics, and economics, and around them the forces of radicalism and conservatism took up their positions. It was in the universities, during the entire period from the 1820s well into the 1870s and 1880s, that conservatism found massive support: first in courses on "Mental and Moral Philosophy" which transmitted in diluted form the doctrines of the school of "Scottish Realism" and correlated Christian morality and the "Law of Nature" with *laissez faire* in business and religion; when the Scottish school was overthrown by a "Germanic invasion" of Kantian and Hegelian doctrines, the conservative view shifted its ground and took over the bloodless academic idealism, finding its supreme exponent in Josiah Royce. Just as the realists had insisted that there was no problem as between appearance and reality, so Royce proved triumphantly that all problems, including the crucial one of evil in human life, could be resolved in the larger harmonies of God and man.

When the gap between *laissez faire* and social welfare became too obvious after the Civil War, conservative thought called into play the new popular interest in the Darwinian theories. The jungle character of the economic struggle was frankly admitted, but it was justified and even glorified by Social Darwinism on the ground that Nature had decreed it. The new natural law came to be "natural selection" and the triumph of the "fit" who survived.

The stretch from the turn of the century to the New Deal saw a movement of pragmatism that reached into law, politics, history, education, business, labor, science, and even art and religion. Its seminal minds in philosophy were Peirce, James, Dewey, and Mead. In economics Veblen maintained a withering fire against the abstractions of the English classical school and the Austrian "marginal utility" school, championing a home-grown attitude that studied economic institutions in their whole life context; and Wesley Mitchell applied his insights to the study of business cycles. In law Holmes asserted that "the life of the law has not been logic: it has been experience," asking how the "reasonable man" would assess the customs of his group, and what the "bad man" would be unable to get away with; and Brandeis developed the technique of shaping the judicial judgment less to the logic chopping of "mechanical jurisprudence" than to the community experience. In history James Harvey Robinson and Charles Beard gave new vitality to the relation between social movements and the history of ideas, emphasizing the driving forces of class interest and the ways by which men rationalized these drives. In "progressive" education, Dewey stressed the growth and experience of the child as he "learns by doing."

Through these variations there ran the common thread of the "revolt against formalism" and against fixed principles or rules—that truth did not lie in absolutes or in mechanical formulas but in the whole operative context of individual growth and social action in which the idea was embedded. This movement of thought was, in a sense, the American counterpart to the Marxist and historical schools of thought in Europe which tried to apply the evolutionary process to social thinking. This intellectual base made possible, as it also expressed, the political reform movement from Theodore Roosevelt to Franklin Roosevelt.

The most recent phase of the cyclical swing has been a revolt against the pragmatic revolt. It has taken the form of an attack on the "pragmatic acquiescence," as Mumford called it, including chiefly the phases of American culture that vulgarized the meaning of pragmatism, reducing truth to whatever "works," thereby casting out other standards of value. As in religion, American intellectuals have been groping for a transcendental philosophic belief, turning against the pragmatic on the ground that it ignores the depths of the psyche and the tragic dimensions of life. To some extent this meant a rejection of the humanist matter-of-factness associated with realism in philosophy, law, economics, and politics; but as a repudiation of mass values, it was also a humanist reassertion of the role of the individual personality as against the operation of group interests and the calculus of mass welfare.

Thus the cyclical swing in the history of American thought has moved in a wide arc from the tough to the mystical, back to the pragmatic, and again to the transcendental. To some extent the cleavage between realists and pragmatists on one side and idealists and absolutists on the other has measured roughly a cleavage between the progressive and conservative forces. This parallel can be carried too far. Thoreau and Brownson, each in his own way a radical in politics, were Transcendentalists in philosophy. Veblen started as a Kantian, John Dewey as a Hegelian. The whole philosophy of conservative Big Business thinking, on the other hand, is thoroughly pragmatic.

However much it may be qualified in particular applications, the parallel does hold. The reformist appeal has generally been from social actuality to social possibility, from the facts of poverty and inequity to the potentials of a fast-moving society which can minimize both. Most liberal and radical reformers have made a habit of thinking in these terms of the socially actual and the socially possible. For the conservative, on the other hand, the absolute and the transcendental offer the advantage of being abstracted from the immediate struggles of society, hanging somewhere (as Holmes put it) as a "brooding omnipresence in the sky," never having to be brought down to earth.

Unlike the European societies where the radical movements have a Marxist intensity, in America it is the conservative movements that have carried the sharper edge. They have appealed to the absolutes of economic freedom and the sanctity of property, while the reformers and liberals (in whose minds the Marxist systems never struck deep roots) have appealed mainly to the moderate goals of progress and the common welfare. This is not to say that American political thought has been dominated by the holders of power. Even with the advantage of power on their side, the conservative thinkers have thought of themselves as fighting a rearguard action, just as the reformers seem forever to be defending civil liberties and are ridden with a sense of ineffectiveness. The trait common to both is a Promethean sense of waging an unequal battle to overthrow the reigning divinities. This may shed some light not only on the American character but on American political society, suggesting that power is distributed more diffusely in it than the contending groups are willing to admit.

I do not mean to say that American thought has always or primarily had a political angle of vision. If anything the philosophic tradition in America has been less directly concerned with politics than in Europe, although it has been more directly concerned with the ethical and other problems of society. It is worth noting that George Santayana, Spanish in descent but brought up and for a time rooted in the American intellectual soil both as student and as teacher, left his greatest mark upon American thought as a moral philosopher as well as a literary stylist. The central stream of American philosophy has probably been that of Peirce (with Chauncey Wright as a forerunner), William James, and John Dewey. Yet in the recent decades there has been a strong critical reaction against this strain, especially against Dewey. It has come not only from what may be called the philosophic "Right," which is to say Niebuhr in religion and Hutchins in education, but also from the empiricist and analytic "Left." In the philosophy of science, in the sociology of knowledge, in metaphysics and ethics, American philosophic thought has become more disciplined and exacting in its analysis: it has also become more fragmented in its concerns and more insulated than the James-Dewey tradition was from the currents of social striving. Through the European refugees from the totalitarian regimes it has also been enriched with elements of continental thought, especially from two Vienna circles—that of the Freudians in psychology and that of the "Logical Positivists" in philosophy.

Despite these new strains of thought, the great intellectual tradition in America has been close to the concerns of social reality, and the political camps have reached out and made use of the academic currents of thought whenever they could.

Of the great political angles of vision, the radical tradition has fared hardest. Its handicap at the start was the fact that the American Revolution was colonial and not social. Once it was over and British imperialism pried loose, the radicals had no enemy target left. Since there had been no social revolution they could not, like the French after 1789, fight to maintain its gains; with no dictatorships on the American scene there could be no resistance movements; with no tyrannies there could be no conspiracies of tyrannicide. Except for the limited episode of Dorr's Rebellion, there were not even—as with the Chartists in England —any grand failures of radical action to be retrieved. As a result American radicalism remained a series of sporadic and sometimes eccentric flare-ups which kept alive the equalitarian dream but had no sustained program, no continuing party, nor even a body of common doctrine.

That was why it did not serve as the intellectual Left Wing of the effective liberal movements of the nineteenth and twentieth centuries. In this sense it fell short of the role played by some of Jefferson's circle who as agrarian radicals attacked the newly rising capitalist class, but whose ideas proved usable in a later industrial era. There was also a Jacksonian Left Wing which saw the worker and farmer as protagonists in the struggle against the tyranny of money. The antislavery Left Wing was formed by abolitionist thinkers like Garrison, Wendell Phillips, and Theodore Parker, who prepared the ground for the slavery struggle, and by the Radical Republicans who laid down a devastating fire against Lincoln's compromises with the slavery issue and the South. In the 1890s Left Wing thinkers like Henry Demarest Lloyd gave form to the Populist drive against railroads and trusts which made Bryanism possible; nor could the victory of Wilson's "New Freedom" in 1912 have taken place if it were not for the novelists David Graham Phillips, Howells, and Frank Norris, the muckrakers Lincoln Steffens and Upton Sinclair, and the constitutional critic J. Allen Smith. Finally the New Deal had intellectual roots in Veblen, Beard, and Parrington, as well as the earlier Populists, and Roosevelt's Left Wing critics proved as troublesome as Lincoln's.

There were also more cantankerous intellectual movements which spent their energies in isolated radical episodes—the Fourierists and other experiments in communal living, the movement for "People's Banks" in Jackson's era, the schemes for currency reform, the blueprints for salvation through Henry George's "single tax" or other creeds, the "twenty-four-hour violence" of mass episodes from Shays' Rebellion to Coxey's Army and the Bonus marchers, the sustained violence of the IWW "Wobblies" and their Syndicalist dream of "one Big Union," the succession of third-party movements, including that of La Follette in 1924 and Wallace's in 1948. Despite their crotchety character, the radical thinkers released some of the sturdier energies of American striving. If we may take Henry George as a symbol for the rest, his Single Tax movement was in itself unworkable and sterile, yet it came from a larger intellectual context—Henry George spoke for a "reforming Darwinism" which saw the social order as the outgrowth of evolution but wanted to use it deliberately in a humanizing effort for the weak as well as the strong; and despite the failure of the Single Tax movement, it did have some effect by liberating the social imagination.

What then accounts for the final failure of the American radicals? Some clues will be found in the pace of social change and the constant sense of dynamism, the moving "triple frontier," the persistence of the open-class system. Most important is the folk belief in the going economic and social system. Labor support, without which there could be no class base for radical thought, was given not to the radicals but to the liberal reformers. The Socialist party, which was bidding for popular support as late as 1920, failed because its dogma of the future commonwealth and of "pie in the sky" seemed unreal to workers who were finding life better here and now. The Communists reached their peak of influence in the Great Depression and the early New Deal; from the late 1930s to the mid-1950s they became entangled in the net of Party conspiracy, moral betrayal, the gyrations of the Party Line, and the world adventures of the Soviet Union, and dribbled away what little remaining support they had.

The radicals could not compete with the liberal reformers in an immediate concrete program, yet they had no long-range program. They could not preach "revolution" effectively in a society where actual revolution—in the form of continuous technical and social change—was taking place all around and its products were being distributed at least tolerably well. Nor could they rally the embittered, since even the hopeless retained a shred of hope for their children's future. They could find no rich soil for their dogma in the minds of people who were turning more strongly every decade toward immediate goals and pragmatic means.

What the radicals succeeded in doing was important: they reaffirmed the equalitarian impulse by fresh challenges to swollen power, injustice, human indifference about suffering. Denouncing corruption, plutocracy, and the vested interests, they were obsessed with a dualism between the angels of light and the princes of darkness. They tried to measure American institutions against the original vision, harking back to an American Eden before the Fall. Not content to gloss over class difference and struggles, they saw that all exercise of political power involves conflict. What they did in their episodic attacks was to feel out the strength of the dominant economic minority, testing whether it had gone slack or retained its creativeness. The answer they got was a double one: from the managers and technicians the wavering evidence that they could continue their revolution of production, and from the liberals the resolve to organize this production within a system of controls which could raise living standards for all.

Thus the fragmented American radicalism, little more than a succession of spasmodic local movements of protest and passion, served to keep both the conservatives and liberals alert. Despite the low estate of radical thought during the Cold War era, an intellectual pattern so constant through American history is likely to find renewal.

The conservative intellectual tradition, while it lacked the Thoreaus, Whitmans, Debses, and Dreisers that radicalism had, exerted a stronger hold on the American mind. Unlike their European parallels, who relied upon tradition and authority, religion, state worship, family, and order, American conservatives boldly captured the citadel of the liberal enemy by taking over its high ground of individualism and natural rights. They asserted that men possess inherent natural rights but insisted that there can be no fulfillment of these rights where the state intervenes in individual economic choices. Thus they appealed to the position of the individual in an indestructible order of Nature that precedes human history. They attempted to build a solid intellectual support for property by invoking the same humanist and individualist symbols which sustained the liberals in their attacks on property. Like them, they refrained from too explosive a discussion of ends. They took for granted the same goal as the liberals—that of the "American dream"; but, in rhetoric at least, they almost appropriated the symbol as their own, and once in their hands, it has been stripped of its equalitarian emphasis and given property overtones.

But the conservatives could not maintain this position without making serious concessions on concrete issues—trade-unions, minimum wages, child labor, social insurance, public control of power sources, corporate monopoly. While retaining the catchwords of individualism and freedom, they cemented their hold on men's minds by promising a natural order presided over by neither God nor justice nor even equality of opportunity, but the brute struggle of the market. It was against this conservative tradition that the progressive reformers of the turn of the century directed their assaults. For under the guise of freedom, conservative thought built an iron trap in which there was no escape from the ruthlessness of brute struggle and survival, including the changes and chances of the business cycle. More than anything else this furnished the emotional drive behind the reformism of the New Deal, and it also explains the intellectual impact of Holmes and Brandeis, Dewey, Veblen and Beard better than any philosophical rationalization.

In another sense also the conservatives became too rigid—in their view of the human situation as a constant. ("You can't change human nature.") This pessimist determinism was at the opposite pole from the perfectionist and plastic view of the human situation which the radicals had. The conservative view was reinforced by the sense of sin in the tradition of evangelical religion. But it could not be maintained in a shifting society and an expanding economy where the individual was always re-creating his career, and where the evidences of the transformation wrought by man's will and intelligence were witness against the overrigid view of human traits.

The deepest source of the strength of conservatism has been its succession of social mystiques. The earliest was the cult of the ruling aristocracy—or (as Fisher Ames put it) the government of "the wise, the rich, and the good." This was followed by the cult of the Constitution, to which Marshall and Story so powerfully contributed. This in turn was followed by the cult of property in the natural order, of which the appeal to social Darwinism was a phase. Property came to be seen as something sanctioned at once by "Nature and Nature's God," and further fortified by being linked with the worker who was worthy of the fruits of his labor, and the businessman who had mingled his managerial skill with the products of industry. The most recent mystique for conservatives is that of an antiliberal nationalism, especially powerful in an era of war and cold war. The premise is that American power rests on its property institutions and that attacks on the sanctity of property become subversive of the nation itself.

With all this intellectual panoply, America has nevertheless no articulate conservative philosophy and no outstanding conservative thinkers who can rank with Hamilton, John Adams, and Calhoun among the earlier thinker-statesmen or with William Graham Sumner among social scientists. In political action rather than formal thought the best of the recent conservatives have been men like Chief Justice Hughes, Henry Stimson, Wendell Willkie, and Dwight Eisenhower, who held fast to what was best in the tradition but yielded generously to necessary changes. Unfortunately, in the postwar decade the center of the stage in conservatism was captured by the racist, repressive, and ultranationalist reactionaries who in every generation produce demagogic figures that strut on the political scene for a brief space and live out their transient and paranoid existence. Partly out of recoil against them and partly to fill a vacuum in American political thought, a "New Conservatism" cropped up in the 1950s to challenge the accepted creeds. I have discussed it briefly earlier;* here I want to add only that a reasoned con-

---

* See Ch. I, Sec. 6, "Tradition and the Frame of Power."

servatism is likely to have a difficult time finding a stable intellectual base amidst the tensions of the years ahead.

It is in the liberal intellectual tradition that American belief has characteristically expressed itself. "The earth belongs to the living," said Jefferson, striking the grand theme that liberalism has since followed. Its credo has been progress, its mood optimist, its view of human nature rationalist and plastic; it has used human rights rather than property rights as its ends but has concentrated on social action as its means. It has made "expedient change" an integral part of its methods and has taken from science the belief in the tools of reason and the tests of validity. It has kept its fighting edge through the emotional force of the reformist impulse. Latterly the liberal tradition has come in for drastic criticism from liberals whose new intellectual posture, especially in the academies, seems to be a strain of habitual self-deprecating irony. Much is said of the failure of liberal thought. Certainly there is a need for redefining it within the psychological realities of our time.

The weaknesses of the liberal tradition are clear enough. First, it is indebted for its individualism to the atomistic thinkers like Locke, James Mill, and Bentham, who could reduce a society to its members but could not link individuals with each other to form a society. It has had to resolve the contradiction between this atomism and the theory of strong state action with which it has allied itself. Even the Christian allegory has not repaired this weakness: its willingness to sacrifice came to mean in the American context mostly sacrifice for one's own freedom or identity and not for others, and did not issue in a sense of society. Thus liberalism built a trap for itself with an atomistic philosophy which strengthened the hold of jungle individualism on the American mind.

The second weakness flows from the alliance with pragmatic thought. The strength gained by this alliance enabled liberalism to focus on concrete situations for reform, undeflected by dogma and abstraction, but made it also vulnerable to the changes and chances of history, squeezing it dry of definite goals and standards. The "open mind" sometimes became a drafty cave of the winds, the questioning spirit became merely ironic, the revolt against past codes became an extreme relativism which left no standards by which to measure values. Eric Goldman has pointed out how this relativism, a scourge with which to lash the conservatives of the 1890s, turned into an engine of disillusionment in the 1920s. "The trouble with us reformers," said J. Allen Smith, "is that we made reform a crusade against standards. Well, we smashed them all, and now neither we nor anybody else have anything left." This was also the theme of much of Randolph Bourne's criticism of the liberalism of his day.

Finally, the liberal's view of human nature stressed the aspirations of the American dream and the supremacy of reason. The more sophisticated thinkers—notably Reinhold Niebuhr—recognized the irrationalism of the human mind and the limits of willed human action. But most liberals assume (as did the sociologist Lester Ward) that men can transform their environment and fashion their society as their own work of art. Thus one may say (leaving out thinkers like Holmes, Veblen, and Dewey) that the liberal tends to reduce everything to environment, including human nature itself, which becomes plastic material to be molded by reason, without allowing for the stubborn propensities of men.

However vulnerable, liberalism has nevertheless emerged as the central expression of the American democratic faith. It is no longer tied to the blind worship of experience, of which it was guilty in the past half century. It has proved intellectually flexible, capable of enrolling determinists like Turner and Beard, and even Darwinists like Holmes, but is more at home with the more fluid thinkers. It has absorbed both the optimism of the idealist thinkers and the cynicism of the materialists. But it could evoke from Morris Cohen equal scorn for "those who spin the world out of ideas, and those who look to earth, air, fire, and water to explain all human phenomena." Its best philosophic expression has been in thinkers like Charles H. Cooley and George H. Mead, who saw the levels of meaning in the "self" which interacts with the "group" and also saw how complex the web of causation is. It has drawn upon the currents of religious faith and at the same time based itself strongly upon the ground of scientific method. Eric Goldman's *Rendezvous with Destiny* traces the strands of thought that unite figures like Carl Schurz, Henry George, Richard T. Ely, Tom Watson, Bryan, Terence Powderly, Lincoln Steffens, Ida Tarbell, Clarence Darrow, William Allen White, Parrington, Harold Stearns, Herbert Croly, La Follette, and even H. L. Mencken. Add to these the line of statesmen-thinkers from Jefferson, Madison, and Lincoln to Wilson and the two Roosevelts, and it is apparent that liberalism has furnished the dominant political and intellectual climate of America.

Its strength lies in providing an angle of vision for viewing America and a fighting faith for the freedom of the person, higher living standards and a more spacious way of life. As Maury Maverick phrased it with a perhaps oversimplified pungency, liberalism has always meant "freedom plus groceries"—not only (one may add) for some of the people but for all, not only sometimes but all the time.

Given this angle of vision, it has developed in its concrete struggles an armory of facts and argument and a passion for battle—against the "octopus" of the big corporation, against rate discrimination by railroads, for free public education, for civil liberties, for Negro equality, for religious freedom, for land conservation, for trade-union organization, for aid to farmers at the mercy of a shifting market, for state control of public utilities, for public use of natural resources, for public development of hydroelectric power, for wage-and-hour legislation, for women's rights, for social security.

These are, of course, piecemeal reforms which do not add up to a unified program. The radicals have also expressed their disdain for liberals because of lack of toughness in fighting their big enemies. The charge strikes home. Yet the radical movements that sought to supply the long-range plans and the tough means sputtered fitfully and died, while the conservatives who scorned the liberal vision found that, without it, they had to rely mainly on social power rather than on intellectual persuasion. American liberalism is one of the few movements in history which has not been based on authority or force, yet has held its dominance in the empire of the mind. Its basic premise has been in a majority will capable of organizing itself effectively when the obstructions are blasted away by the dynamite of facts and ideas. The failures to reach the goal have been frequent and glaring, but they have been recognized and taken in stride.

This does not mean that liberalism has been free of the tensions of constant struggle. Actually one of its emotional drives is a flagellant sense of guilt over the gap between the democratic rhetoric and the social reality. With it there is a too credulous hope that all would be well if only some obstacle were removed, some enemy overcome, some reform achieved. It has been one of the illusions of liberal reformers that the only changes required to build Jerusalem on America's green and promised land are changes in social mechanisms: if only the newspapers were in the hands of the right people, if only there were a third party, if only there were currency reforms, if only the press allowed a free play of opinion, if only the schools paid their teachers enough and adopted progressive techniques, if only the movies showed fewer crime pictures and TV reduced the violence of its programs. . . . This "heart's desire" liberalism has a counterpart in the breakdown of a perspective among paranoid liberals who feel surrounded by reactionary Devil figures. Perhaps with greater maturity and a psychology that cuts deeper the liberals will manage to achieve a long view without losing their militancy.

One cannot imprison in a single mold the thought of a culture stretching over more than three centuries. What is true of American living, however, is true also of American thought: both have characteristic patterns that mark them off from the patterns of other cultures. This is not to deny the influence of Europe. American thought may, in one sense, be viewed as Western thought with a distinct bent of its own which reshaped British, French, and German influences to the American context. Puritan thought derived from the English divines and Calvin; the revolutionary thinking of Jefferson was the product of his friendship with the French thinkers; the Transcendentalists borrowed from the German mystics and from Asiatic thought; and in the era of Hitler and Stalin, America became a haven for European scholar-refugees whose fertilizing influence proved important. Yet when this has been said, it remains true that the foreign influences have been submerged in the main American stream, and that in the process of reshaping their borrowings the Americans have added more than they have taken.

3. The Higher and Lower Learning

IN PRIMITIVE CULTURES the teacher-priests transmit the cultural tradition in the form of ritual shrouded in mysteries. When the teaching function is separated from the priestly function, it becomes secular education. The American school system telescoped these changes: at the start it had strong if residual connections with the church and clergy but it became basically secular. Except in the parochial schools it is now free of control by the churches and is controlled by local and state governments.

The difference is important. Education always aims to some degree at instilling beliefs in the plastic minds of the young. A secular school system in a democracy is bound to throw its sanctions behind the existing institutions, and to that extent it may, like a religious system, discourage skepticism and protect illusions by Platonic myths. But since the secular tradition in the Western world is linked with free inquiry, its prime purpose (unlike the religious tradition) is to teach the student how to use his mind for himself. The controls by government units and by the community spokesmen may set a too-rigid frame for the teaching process, but within that frame there is a secular process which does value free inquiry.

In this sense of imperfect freedom within a frame of institutional control, the school system follows the characteristic American pattern to be found in business, the trade-union, the family, and the church denominations. Like them the school system is untidily pluralistic, with some schools and universities privately endowed, but most of them part of the governmental apparatus. Some of the universities are narrowly practical and technical in character, and some devote much of their energy to specialized research. Thus American education looks like a crazy quilt, with no consistent principle either of authority or philosophy. There are those who lament so sorry a patchwork, urging unity of aim and consistency of method and control. The German educational system is clearer in its lines of authority, the French more orderly in administrative terms, and any system of church-controlled schools lacks the ragged edges of educational philosophy the Americans betray. But seen historically, the growth of the American school system is the product of impulsions that have come from within instead of having been imposed from without. It is an organic expression of American life and character.

Americans have an extravagant reliance on education. It is a piously repeated truism that some concrete social problem—capital and labor, Negro-and-white relations, anti-Semitism, juvenile delinquency, war and peace—"can only be solved by education." Beyond this there is the hope for individual advancement which education holds out to the lower economic groups. It was the Workingmen's Associations that pushed free public education in the 1830s, not only on the Jeffersonian theory of creating an "aristocracy of virtue and talent" in the Republic, but even more with the practical aim of securing better income and status. Most colleges today offer scholarship aid, and rich men who were once poor boys contribute to endowments which help educate poor boys who will in turn become rich men. The significant line of relation runs between education and social mobility. Education, it is held, pays off.

Americans make a distinction, however, between the school learning which increases a man's earning power and the newfangled, dangerous ideas which unsettle his thinking. "Education spoils a good field hand" was a remark that American farmers used to make even while they celebrated the virtues of the free school system. A textile mill manager may still have the same lingering attitude toward his mill hands, or a guardian of White Supremacy toward a Negro college graduate. Many employers used to wonder whether book learning might not spoil a boy for business, preferring an exposure to the "school of hard knocks"— although the recent growth of professional schools of business administration shows this to be an archaic attitude.

All through the American experience there has been an anti-intellectualism running alongside the belief in education. Under the New Deal it expressed itself in Congressional contempt for "brain-trusters" who had "never met a pay roll." It takes the current form of a fear of ideas, ranging from the good-natured epithet of "egghead" to the un remitting hatred which some Congressmen and newspapers express for any liberal intellectuals. Actually there is a strain of anti-intellectualism inherent in the American belief in education: Americans emphasize not so much the training of the intellect as they do some marginal value such as vocational skill or "citizenship" or becoming an "interesting" person—or almost anything except creativeness. While most Americans value education as the road to "know-how" and business advance, they suspect it when carried into political action or expressed in social attitudes. The Congressional investigating committees in the mid-century climate of McCarthy, Jenner, and Velde, who made forays into the colleges to ferret out signs of Communist conspiracy, betrayed a Caliban fear of men trained for independent intellectual judgments.

Despite this anti-intellectual strain, the American belief in education has not only persisted but grown, as is shown by the influx of high-school graduates from every social level into the colleges. Between 1900 and 1950 the college enrollment increased tenfold, moving from a quarter million to two and a half million (by 1957 it was three million, and was expected to reach five to seven million by 1970), while high-school enrollment grew at the same pace, from 650,000 in 1900 to six and a half million. In 1950 there were thirty-three million young Americans enrolled in all types of schools and colleges, public, private, and parochial—which gives some notion of the burden that education has to carry in a mass democracy.

Seymour Harris has documented the trend which is saturating the "market for college graduates" and cutting the income differential between the skilled noncollege employee and the unspecialized college graduate. Yet young Americans continue to stream into the colleges. The lower-middle-class or worker's family will scrimp to give its sons, and more recently its daughters, a university training. Partly this is because it provides them with a better social standing even on the same income level, giving them the established insignia of a new kind of class rank. But it is also because they feel that education will open the door to a better and more productive life.

This makes it all the more difficult to account for the financial neglect of education in many areas of America. While new schools are continually being built, a shocking percentage of the school plant is run-down, its equipment archaic, the teachers badly underpaid when compared with the pay of skilled or even semiskilled workers, the class-rooms overcrowded, the textbooks often badly out-of-date. In a typical recent year Americans spent eight billion dollars on liquor, nineteen billion on automobiles—and five billion on public education. Between 1932 and 1950—a period when the student enrollment doubled—the percentage of the national income spent on universities from both public and private sources was cut from 1 to ½ per cent. Since education is largely under local control, the public expenditures vary greatly from state to state. While New York in 1950 was spending $312 a year for each child in its school system, Mississippi was spending $73.

The Commission on Higher Education appointed by President Truman recommended a system of federally subsidized scholarships and a network of "community colleges," with local and Federal funds. The Federal government spent fourteen billion dollars over a span of seven years after World War II for the education of eight million soldiers under the GI Bill of Rights. A notable step forward was taken by the Ford Foundation when it set aside 500 million dollars to establish national competitive scholarships for American colleges and universities, and offered to match contributions from industry for the same purpose Thus American public and philanthropic policies stand at least partially committed to educational expansion. But the hostility to Federal aid continues to be buttressed by religious differences and by a fear of its political consequences.

The continuing local control of the schools has given the big tax-payer groups a stake in holding school expenses down, and a strategic position that helps them keep the winds of dangerous doctrine out of the schoolroom. It accounts for much of the constriction of opinion, the seediness, and provincialism to be found in the school systems of many smaller American communities. It accounts also for the exodus of male teachers from the profession, since an ill-paid teacher is not a free man—hemmed in by narrow community mores and a vigilant censorship of his every move—and has little standing either with his pupils or the community.

With these trammels the American school system has had to assume one of the most massive tasks in history. It has had to take a polyglot people, thrown together from every ethnic strain and culture in the world, and give it a common body of symbols to serve both for communication and cohesion. When an Englishman remarked after the passage of the Second Reform Act, "Now we must educate our masters," he described what education must achieve in any mass democracy. Horace Mann, who devoted his life to building the public-school system of Massachusetts, had earlier put the idea in his own language: "In a Republic, ignorance is a crime." In America, with its constant stream of new immigrants, the schools had to add a second function to that of book learning. They had to take human material from many diverse cultures and teach them the whole body of what is believed, practiced and taken for granted in America. Considering the task of bringing cohesion into such widely different groups, the miracle is not that it was done imperfectly but that it was done at all. Nor could any part of the task be escaped, as in countries which have accepted a cleavage in education between the "gentleman" and the "common man." The American public schools had to accept whatever human material was offered to them and make it part of an equalitarian society.

Two secession movements have merged to challenge the public-school system. The children not only of the wealthy classes but even of moderate-income professionals have increasingly been sent to private schools, while at least five million American children are in the Catholic parochial schools, and a considerable number in Protestant and Jewish. In James B. Conant's terms, a split is emerging between two school-nations that is unhealthy in a democracy. The secession of the parochial groups, who train into the student their own body of civic premises along with their religious norms, is not likely to be healed; the spread of the movement will probably be limited only by the financial drain it imposes on the churches. The secessionists in the private elementary schools might possibly be won back by improved standards in the public schools.

There is a deeper class lesion in the school system which cannot be healed even by such reforms. There are scars of segregation and discrimination which ravage the whole premise of equal educational opportunity. Sharpening the classic question of Warner and Havighurst, "Who gets educated?" one must ask, "Who gets educated how?" The Negroes, not only in the South but even in the North, are still—even after the Supreme Court school decision—largely excluded from adequate education by racist hostility and fear. Their schools are scantily equipped, inadequately prepared. As for the Jews and Catholics, they go to college in large numbers but their range of choice is restricted (especially for Jews) by an operative though silent quota system in many universities and professional schools. The fear in every university is that if the bars are taken down they will stream in and frighten away other groups, thus making the institution "unrepresentative." This bias, however disguised, makes a hash of the principle of equal access at the core of an open society. It infects the atmosphere of the classroom and the campus, and turns the college for many young people into a Heartbreak House.

It would be wrong, however, to conclude that America has a racist or class system of education. The doors to the intellectual life are slowly being forced open even for Negroes. On the level of class obstacles, the Holinshed Report documents the fact that there are still large numbers of high-school graduates equipped for college who cannot enter because they lack the means: even scholarship aid fails to solve their problem, since it rarely covers living expenses, nor does it fill the gap of their earning power in the family income. For such the free school system offers only dusty answers to their hunger for training and knowledge. Yet the big fact remains that a steadily increasing proportion of young Americans gets drawn into secondary and higher education every year. The percentage that gets to college is now something like 15 per cent. Despite the 85 per cent who don't get there, the Jacksonian ideal that every young American shall have a college education is on the way to fulfillment.*

The real issue about the Jacksonian goal is how badly it pulls down educational standards all along the line. Much of elementary and secondary schooling is little more than assembly-line processing with mechanized teaching methods and an intellectual level rarely rising above mediocrity. Since American power rests on its technology, the trend has been toward the technical and vocational, with little stress on the capacity to handle general ideas and sift irrational from rational. Given the boredom of high-school pupils and the pull of jobs and spending power, it has been found necessary in some big-city school systems to weight the high-school curriculum toward the vocational in order to keep the boys at school a few years longer. While this helps produce skilled manpower, it ignores the fact that the problems which will make or break America are no longer technological but social and cultural.

In the face of these problems the rate of contemporary illiteracy among Americans compares badly with the culture of Jeffersonian America, which had an almost complete mass literacy. Recent surveys show also that many Americans who can read have little competence or interest in the public issues on which as citizens they are supposed to reach decisions. This political illiteracy, more serious than the technical brand, is the greatest liability of American educational practices. For education has to perform a dual function in any civilization: it must transmit the cultural heritage, and it must also provide each generation with the intellectual and moral tools for assessing itself, calculating the forces that confront it, and making the necessary changes. In this sense it must be at once conservative and innovating, transmissive and unsettling.

The task is complicated by the extraordinary pace of American social change. It is hard for the teacher to step twice in the same stream. The

* I develop at greater length, later in this section, the contrast of the Jacksonian and Jeffersonian goals.

constant flux requires him to be alert to often subtle changes, capable of assessing them without becoming bewildered and lost in the maze. To add to the difficulty, the school system is only part of the constellation of educational forces. The mind of the young American is also under pressure from family, street gang, and peer group, bombarded by a clamor from all the Big Media around him—movies, radio, TV, and the comics. The hardy teacher who tries to shape the mind and character of his charges thus has access to only a small segment of their attention. He has the despairing sense of wrestling with massive demons for the child's still plastic personality, knowing that whatever brief spell he may have with him in the schoolroom, they are assaulting the child's mind everywhere else the rest of the time.*

To attack the American school system, therefore, as part of the "crowd culture" is to miss at least half the point. The strongest pressures of the crowd culture come from outside the schoolroom, which must itself combat them. To the question "How well does the school express the culture?" some critics have answered sardonically, "All too well." The schools do express one phase of the crowd culture—the spread-eagle rhetoric of nationalist pride mistaken for the democratic idea, the uncritical embrace of the life goals of success and power and prestige, the slack acceptance of questionable means alongside a hackneyed moralism. Yet there are also teachers who are the only counterforce the growing child can invoke to oppose the crassness of the crowd culture. By instilling a love of books, a hunger for experience, a critical attitude toward the prevailing idols of the tribe, a generous one toward foreign peoples and alien cultures, such teachers have a disproportionate impact on each generation. They unlock for each the treasures of history and science, literature and the arts, and place in its hands that key to whatever has been felt and created which makes every educational system potentially revolutionary and every good teacher by necessity an insurgent.

This may explain why the American school system has been under constantly increasing attack by vigilantist groups of super-patriots. Where they have not taken a lethal toll of their victims, they have succeeded in leaving timid men and women more timid than they found them.

The American school is itself a subculture, almost on a level with the family in its importance. It forms a little segregated society, with its own customs, its loyalties, its network of interpersonal relations. Its

---

* For the Big Media as contenders for the minds of children, see Sec. 5, "Revolution in the Big Media"; also Ch. XI.

image is that of an extended family, with most of the elementary teaching assigned to female teachers who act the role of mother for the larger brood. This female domination of the schools goes back to the village "school marm." It is also partly economic, since the men are drained off into jobs that offer better income and social standing and only the women remain—sometimes out of a sense of vocation, often because there is no alternative. In most cases they fail to act as effective authority symbols, nor can they serve as models for role-learning by the boys in their classes. It may be hard for many of them to understand the sexual and emotional urgencies of adolescent boys in their charge. Thus they often treat as instances of delinquency what is usually only evidence of normal sexual development under stress. The reverse facet is also true—that many of the teachers find in their schoolroom an outlet for long-dammed-up emotions.

The teachers themselves, along with the parents, have grounds for anxiety about the shaping of mind and personality among their charges. A 1954 study estimated that 15 per cent of the high-school enrollment in New York City was "emotionally disturbed"—a phrase that covers a wide variety of symptoms, from retarded study performance to school vandalism and sexual offenses. This is, of course, partly a reflection of similar disturbances among the adult population. What happens is that the school is made the dumping ground for tensions and problems which the family and community failed to solve. It has been found that nine out of ten of the "disturbed children" come from homes that are broken by divorce, parentless, scarred by parental conflict, or emotionally bleak because of parental neglect. Thus the schools get the harvest of family failure. The old school task of making the pupils literate has been replaced by the new task of enabling them to cope with the problems of emotional health. The principal difficulty is no longer with the three Rs and with laying a base for an effective technical culture: it is with the student's understanding of his own drives, and with his discovery of his identity, with guiding him through the curve of his emotional growth.

The growing number of cases of juvenile delinquency, both in and outside the classroom, is evidence that the schools are not succeeding where the family, the church, and the community have thus far failed. For many children from slum areas or from homes of emotional tension or deprivation, the school is the only bright spot in their lives. But for many others it remains a bleak place where their difficulties are hardly recognized, and where the necessary resources in the form of counseling and psychiatric help are available to only a minimal degree. It is true that the American school system is almost the only one which provides any psychiatric services at all, but what it does provide does not come near meeting the need. A report by a teachers' group in New York points out that "an average of three children in each class will sooner or later require institutional care because of emotional and mental breakdown, but the educational budget allows three minutes of guidance per child during an entire term." The teachers themselves try hard to fill the gap, but the burdens on them are too harassing, the classrooms are too crowded, their own economic and emotional problems too urgent to allow them to play the role of surrogates for parents and community. Somehow this task will have to be fulfilled, since the schools now occupy the strategic situation between the tensions of the family and the tensions of society.

In addition to the emotional tensions, there are class lines and cliques within the school which also mirror those of the culture. It acts as a common meeting ground for children of diverse class and ethnic origins, where each finds an increment of experience his home has not offered him, and where he feels out the personalities of his peers, measures his strength and vulnerability against them, and begins to find his identity. Important in any society, this is particularly important in a mobile one. Even as some, at the end of the educational process, find the transition to the world of social reality too abrupt, for many of them the school does offer a tolerably insulated "separate culture," with a period of eight to twelve formative years in which they can find themselves and prepare to cope with the rough ways of the culture outside. Perhaps, as some believe, Americans don't expect much more from their free elementary schools than the combating of illiteracy, the Americanizing of the children of the foreign born, the elements of literacy required for work and trade, and the preparation of technicians, laboratory research workers, inventors and scientists. Yet as a culture in miniature the school also performs a more important function.

To understand this is to see in fresh perspective the old battle of concepts that raged for a time between the "progressive education" champions and the "Essentialists." The way the issue is generally put is whether the community is best served when the children are equipped with a precisely drilled knowledge of the essential studies and tools (based on the three Rs), or whether they learn best by relating their learning to the culture and developing their capacities for growth in the context of the living problems of their day. There is nothing wrong—in fact, there is everything right—in teaching the "fundamentals" with precision, although it must be observed that even in the schools that focus on them there is a vast ignorance of geography, American history, and contemporary events. But all that a school can ever hope to do is to equip the student with tools which he can later use to become an educated man. How he will use those tools depends on the kind of person he becomes, and this in turn depends on how his plastic mind and personality are shaped within the school-as-culture.

For the schools do form a separate culture: the question is what kind it will be. A formal school, focusing rigidly on certain "essentials," is likely to carry over into its emotional tone as a culture the accents of authority and subordination: what it will fashion and graduate into the larger society may be not men but marionettes for the crowd culture. A school, in turn, which focuses on the growth of the child, which does its teaching with an eye on social reality and relates the emotional needs of the child to the inherent disciplines of the subject, is likely to develop within its own cultural frame the accents of critical inquiry and generous sympathies.

It is true that much of American education has for some time been operating in the shadow of John Dewey, and his experimental spirit has to some extent carried over into the public-school system. Progressive education, which for a time was based on a too-optimistic view of human nature, seems to have learned from its worst mistakes. It is no longer content to pose questions without offering at least tentative answers, or to underline the relativism of all standards without trying to shape operative standards. It has learned to work within a necessary frame of discipline and responsibility. John Dewey and his followers not only effected a revolution in American educational thinking but offered a characteristic American approach of trial and error and of critical inquiry which has left its mark on the world.

Where this approach seems to have the least to offer is on the level of the college and university, where the problem is not how to protect the beginnings of growth but how to help young people to maturity and shape productive thinking.

The American college did not begin to find itself until the latter decades of the nineteenth century. Founded principally by religious groups—Congregationalists, Methodists, Presbyterians, Baptists, Quakers —it was at first an instrument for turning out ministers, lawyers, and gentlemen, and remained for a time in the shadow of the denominations even after it broke away from their control. The two men who helped transform the college into a university were Daniel C. Gilman and William R. Harper. Asked to submit plans for Johns Hopkins, Gilman placed before his trustees the idea of starting not with a college program but with a graduate school and research center; he sent his faculty to train in the great universities of Germany, and they came back with their booty of European techniques in science, medicine, and historical research. Harper took what John D. Rockefeller had intended as a Baptist college at Chicago and turned it into a university by bringing to it a group of young men—Laughlin, Veblen, Dewey, Mead, Jacques Loeb—such as had never before been assembled on an American campus, and letting them follow their bent. From these sources came the two formative trends of American higher education—the pursuit of specialized research and what Robert M. Hutchins has called the "hospitality to good men pursuing unconventional work."

The danger has been the double one of idolizing the "scientific" and pursuing the specialized and the "practical." The American social thinker, hoping to be a "scientist," tries to emulate the precision methods of his colleagues in the laboratory sciences. In an earlier chapter* I have drawn the distinction between science and scientism—the latter being the belief that all reality is subject to the mathematical methods of the natural sciences, and that everything which does not fit into them can scarcely be relevant to the scholarly life. A corollary has been the cultivation of the narrowly specialized field, which can be reduced to compositable study and subjected to intense "scientific" inquiry. Still another corollary, although—like specialization—by no means a necessary one, has been the cult of the "practical." What scientism and the "practical" have in common is an impatience with whatever is elusive or subjective or in the realm of ethical values—that cannot be pinned down and measured. In pursuit of scientism and the practical, American university life has become a close ally of corporate life and the "organization man," who is dedicated to both these ideals.

Thus a new provincialism has replaced the earlier sense of inferiority that American thinkers had in the shadow of the great European intellectual tradition. It is ironic that the European thinkers themselves —Comte and Hegel, Marx, Spengler, Freud and Jung, Weber, Toynbee, Whitehead—never aped specialism or laboratory method, being philosophers who took human knowledge as their arena. At once cockier in aim and less secure at heart, the American professors seek to build faultless structures inside a narrow domain and are apologetic when they wander afield.

The American university becomes thus less an intellectual community than a collection of professional schools and graduate or research faculties, each of them a small principality. American scholars have excelled less in theory than in empirical studies, such as business fluctuations,

* See Ch. IV, Sec. 6, "The Culture of Machine Living."

personnel management, medical research and techniques, applied physics and engineering, administrative processes, attitude measurement. The tendency toward specialism and practical studies is reinforced by the availability of research funds, especially when they can be shown to "pay off." Recently there has been a drastic shift of subsidized university research to military projects, turning large segments of the universities into satellites of the Armed Services. There has also been a cry for the recruitment and training of increasing numbers of engineers to keep pace with the Russians—as if the problem were one of numbers rather than of social intelligence and humanistic training.

I do not mean to oppose the specialized forms of teaching to the generalized ones, or to imply that intensive university courses are necessarily narrowing ones or that "general education" studies are necessarily liberating ones. Charles Frankel has well pointed out how misleading it is to contrast "liberal" education with "specialized" education. Specialization may be narrow in its tendencies, but it does not follow that failure to specialize brings a humanist view in its wake: it may actually encourage a dilettantist approach to thinking and learning, with the superficiality of cocktail-party conversation. What is needed, as Frankel puts it, is a humanist and philosophical approach to whatever the subject matter may be—an approach that will emphasize the intellectual methods and the moral and aesthetic choices that govern thinking and let the student discover the setting of his particular fact in the large context of life. Seen in these terms the best kind of research may be specialized in the sense that it deals with some problem gnawing at the scholar, but it can yield fundamental results only if it moves from the special problem to broadly theoretical questions. In the ordinary sense of the term such inquiry will never be "practical," although it very often—to the delight of corporations and government agencies —ends with empirical and profitable results. It has even been possible for American physicists and other scholars, subsidized by funds from the defense services, to do fundamental theoretical work of their own choice.

As an instrument of national policy, the American university has broken with its earlier tradition. Although the great university leaders took their scholarship standards from the German institutions of their day, they did not carry over the German idea of the relation of the university to the state. Themselves the product of the state, the German universities were responsible to it, and the professors who governed them were in effect its officials. The American universities, on the other hand, followed the British tradition as voluntary associations supported by endowments. In the mid-nineteenth century this situation was changed by the "land-grant" colleges which became state universities and operated with government funds. Some of them—notably Wisconsin, Ohio State, Michigan, Illinois, Pennsylvania State, Indiana, California—have been colossi with a towering place in the education of a democracy. Yet it remains true that prestige still attaches to the older universities and smaller colleges which continue to operate under voluntary grants of individual funds. These have flowed from Maecenases who, having made their fortunes by single-mindedness and resourcefulness, feel expansive in making princely gifts to the colleges commanding the nostalgic memories and loyalties of their impressionable days. Latterly the privately endowed colleges have come upon lean years, their fixed income from investments cut in value by inflation, and the sources of their gifts being dried up by heavy taxation. Faced with dwindling funds, university heads have sometimes had to become traveling salesmen and have grown pessimistic about the future of free education. But their pessimism seems exaggerated. Even with the heavy tax system, as long as the Big Money flows freely into industry a portion of it is bound to end up in the universities.

The gloomier question is posed by the issue of control. In the growth of the universities several fateful decisions were made. One was to entrust the university to the control of laymen rather than its own faculty. The other was to choose the laymen principally from the corporate masters of business enterprise. Neither decision was inevitable. The British universities, also privately endowed, are controlled mainly by nonbusiness laymen; the German universities, creatures of the state, are controlled by their faculties. The American state universities are supervised by a committee of regents, behind whom are the legislators and the economic and political rulers of the community. The private universities are under the control of boards of trustees—a fact summed up in oversimplified terms by the title and subtitle of Veblen's book: *The Higher Learning in America: A Memorandum on the Control of Universities by Businessmen*. Generally speaking, the administrators of American universities have stood up well to the state, but not so well to the businessman armed with economic power.

But the issue is less clear-cut than Veblen saw it. Paradoxically, a body of liberal university thought developed under the control of the very men who were the targets of liberal attack. When Harold Laski, as a lecturer in history at Harvard, ran afoul of state authorities and corporate groups in the Boston police strike, President Lowell stood by him until he left for a better post at the London School of Economics. When Roscoe Pound and Felix Frankfurter of the Law School displeased the rich alumni by their views on law and (in Frankfurter's case) on the Sacco-Vanzetti case, the university again stood by them. These instances were, of course, more than matched by cases of dismissal at other institutions more intolerant than Harvard or less able to ride out storms. I cite them mainly as evidence that even within the frame of business control there are broad limits of freedom, if only the college administrators have the daring to explore them and enough mastery of men to deal creatively with their trustees. As Chancellor of the University of Chicago over a span of more than twenty years, Hutchins carried his trustees with him, appealing to their sense of innovation and their pride in the University's achievement and prestige. Harvard, under President Pusey, rode out the tide of McCarthyism with a tenacity that cried for imitation by others.

Much depends on the character of the university president. Veblen derided him as a "captain of education"—a minor captain of industry who has transferred his base of operations to the college campus. To document his indictment there are case histories of presidents who have run their faculties as they might run corporate employees, hiring and dismissing them as if they were interchangeable parts, measuring their intellectual productiveness by page of output, fearful of any heretical utterance that might slow up the flow of funds. They have displayed qualities that might have equipped them as easily to head a corporation, a newspaper, or an Army division—except that the last requires courage under fire, a rare quality among college administrators. Usually it is the pliant man, the diplomat with a good public face, who runs the university "smoothly," getting funds and staying out of trouble over "controversial" teachers.

The heads of the great universities are more than college presidents: they are the only quasi-official intellectual leaders America possesses. What is said by the president of Harvard or Columbia, Yale or Chicago, carries weight. The best presidents are trained craftsmen with an ability to handle issues on a big scale and to use judgment in crises. The successful ones often move into diplomatic posts. Sometimes, in turn, men trained in strategy (like diplomats and generals) move into a university presidency—but usually this ends in disaster for the president and the university alike.

The sharpest crisis in their history hit the American universities in mid-century—not a financial one but a crisis of freedom. For many parents education seems to threaten the religious values and the moral conditioning that the family has sought to instill. How many parents, forgetting that the college years are those of adolescent rebellion, show dismay when sons and daughters come home for the holidays with "half-baked" notions in economics and philosophy, and how many a battle has been waged to save the soul of the heretic. These traditional anxieties merged with political ones during the cold war when the colleges were attacked as "hotbeds of Communism." Test oaths for teachers, Congressional investigations, and faculty purges confronted the colleges with an unparalleled danger to free inquiry.

A few strong voices were finally raised to challenge the attack on the Republic of Learning. The more courageous ones agreed that Communist teachers, in following Party Line truth, had forfeited their intellectual integrity; but they added that test oaths and purges did a damage to American education far greater than the shabby handful of Communist teachers could have done; they insisted that the judgment of a teacher's record, character, and worth must in every case be the judgment by his peers and not only by a group of power-hungry political adventurers, or of post-card scribblers who suspect all teachers and hate all ideas.

The impulses toward social timidity, never absent among teachers and students, were strengthened by the crusade of anti-intellectualism. More than ever the teachers tended to play it safe: and the image of courage which a teacher ought to offer as an example to his students was obscured. Every educational system must learn how to present the claims of rival social systems without fear and without propaganda. But the critical sifting of competing claims became more difficult as the courses dealing, for example, with Marxist thought and the nature of Communism grew scarce. Americans had not yet developed the quiet belief in their own social system that would enable them to regard intellectual nonconformism with calmness.*

Like the public school, the American college is itself a culture, with an inner structure of authority and an internal moral and emotional climate. The professors, who have become in contemporary America the counterparts of the clergy in earlier English and American society, are allowed to arrange curriculum matters; but the worldly matters are left to a new college managerial group. It is usually the managers rather than the faculty who make the final decisions even on educational issues. In a historic case at the University of Nevada, a professor critical of the educational policies of the president was ousted after a public hearing: he found it hard to explain to the substantial citizens why the running

---

* I deal here only with academic freedom. For other aspects of freedom, see Ch. VI, Sec. 10, "The Struggle for Civil Liberties."

of a college should be different from that of a business organization by the "boss" or a football team by the coach.

The role of college athletics has continued to be primary, conferring prestige on the victorious universities and the hero-players even though it is widely known that college athletics are in effect subsidized. In the college novels, starting with the classic *Stover at Yale,* the dramatic touchdown made by the hero at the crisis of the football game furnishes the climax both of plot and character. The formula of these novels, with its mingling of football games, college heroes, town-and-gown rivalries, and caste divisions between the inner circle of social fraternities and honor societies and the excluded pariahs, is with all its distortions a meaningful mirror of the college culture. Scott Fitzgerald's *This Side of Paradise,* portraying the Princeton of Amory Blaine, is, however, less an authentic version of the undergraduate world than it is a special case history of the flapper era of the 1920s. The more typical college culture of today is that of the big Midwestern university, so vast and impersonal that the student is isolated and almost forgotten in it, finding his sense of loyalty in the totemic rivalries of athletic events and his sense of warmth in the more compassable fraternity groups. The state universities have transformed American higher education by introducing the type-figure of the female coed. The coed has converted the American college culture from an all-male fellowship, with its legendry of masculine heartiness, into a society in which dating, petting, convertibles, fraternity and sorority dances, campus hairdos, and the latest campus fashions in women's clothes are themes that overshadow scholarship.

The decline in university standards, however, is not explained by the invasion of the women. Simon Flexner made a classic attack on universities that offer courses in poultry raising, clog-dancing, and hotel administration, and every critic of mass education in America has followed him in his indictment. It is easy to ridicule the university offerings which reflect the utilitarian nature of American culture. If a university wants to meet these community needs, it can segregate such courses into extension departments, where they will not affect the more exacting intellectual work. This still leaves the destructive slackness which prevails at the core of a university. This is the twilight world where underpaid teachers, unsure of their standing and feeling themselves failures, talk at cross-purposes to students who go listlessly through a college to the "practical" life goals of the world outside.

In reaction against the mediocrity of college standards, some educators have insisted on rigidly high standards of specialized university research. There are others who contend that research in itself does not add up to education—that it may fragment the individual student and teacher, moving away from the view of an educated man as a rounded one who lives with awareness within his culture and who brings to bear on it the humanizing influence of a productive intellectual and emotional life. The "research" ideal, dependent on large grants of funds and carried through with a large-scale division of labor, reflects the values of a technological culture and can be mutilating to the personality. Caught between the poles of the vocational and research emphasis, the American university has vacillated between the slack and the sterile. Here again, as I have suggested earlier, the crucial question is not one of specialized or general education but the humanism or the narrowness with which both are carried on.

There are, as Robin Williams, Jr., suggested, two ideals in American education—the Jeffersonian goal which would make higher education accessible to all but insists on demanding standards, and the Jacksonian goal which would treat every mind as equal and open the state university to every high-school graduate regardless of capacity. It is against the Jacksonian ideal that Robert Hutchins directed his most effective attacks. The Hutchins group may be too self-consciously intellectual and has laid itself open to the charge of a nostalgic archaism. But its critics are in danger of forgetting that the transmission of the cultural heritage may itself become a radical instrument for a new approach to education in a mass democracy. By invoking the comparison of American culture with the great cultures of the past, possessed of different standards of value, it leads to a critical re-examination of the common ends which give meaning to a culture.

The teachers in contemporary America must conduct their teaching on the edge of an abyss. It is not only that many students are drafted before they have finished high school. Beyond that fact they are part of a generation that has learned something of the power of both evil and heroism, and of man's heart as the source of both potentials. The common ends of education have become those of making power responsible, insuring the survival of free inquiry, and humanizing man in a dehumanized technology. These cannot be attempted without the effort at educating the whole person-in-growth, evoking a sense of generous emotions and of the tragedy of life along with the possibilities for happiness.

This involved the fashioning of belief as well as the sharpening of knowledge. But to aim at it by turning the schools back to a religious or moralistic emphasis is to take a mechanical view of how the training of belief can be achieved. The problem is not to close off divergent views of life by the hot certainties of theology and the dusty answers of dogma but to open every possible door to productive living. Meanwhile it is important to remember that of all the techniques for creating a sense of society, education is the most effective tie for binding men together.

4. Profile of the Press

THE EAGERNESS for news is organic to American culture. "What's new?" as the American greeting puts it, conveys an avidity for fresh impressions which makes the American the largest consumer of newsprint in the world. The news thus becomes for Americans the outward garment of reality. On waking, you turn on the radio news broadcast or the TV "morning show," or run through the paper at breakfast, or scan the sports or market news while crowded in the bus or subway or commuter's train. While you have been asleep you have missed the reality and must catch up with it.

If news is the carrier of reality, it is a rapidly shifting one and must be caught on the wing. The American feels that "time is money." He also feels that each new increment of time carries with it a possibly precious freightage of new events. This passionate time sense is a natural accompaniment for the rise to power of a young people still on the make, oriented not toward an inner life but toward an outer world in which almost anything can happen to give a decisive turn to life. Since anything can happen and may affect him crucially, the American wants to know about it quickly. That is why a "news beat" is important for a wire service like the AP or UP or for the news staff of a broadcasting chain. That is also why "exclusives" are important: the urge to be on the "inside" is linked with the urge to be in on the kill first.

But it is equally true that news must give way to news. As a newspaperman put it, "What is hot stuff today is shelf paper tomorrow." No one wants to be stuck with an old piece of news. There is nothing more ridiculous to an American than to be caught reading a copy of last week's newspaper. All items in the democracy of American news are born free and equal—the trivial and the world-shaking alike. Their viability is contained within the bounds of their time unit. Like one of the species of fruit fly, each of them has its appointed span of life: it is spawned and lives for a day—sometimes only for a fraction of a day, an edition. It buzzes briefly, dies unmourned, is replaced by its successor, and the next day it is sunk in oblivion. In Waldo Frank's phrase, for the American "news is a toy." Every toy has a glittering fascination for the child—to be forgotten when the next toy appears.

Two corollaries follow from this conception of the nature of news. One is that news items are "facts," to be sharply distinguished from "opinion" or "interpretation." The second, related to the first, is that since each news event is fresh and new, it exists independently and derives its meaning from its own innards, rather than as a part of a pattern.

The truth is that the method of reporting news events does influence and mold belief. But the American hugs the illusion that he is not influenced by anything except "facts." When an editor is worried about a piece of vigorous, candid reporting, he is likely to red-pencil it as "interpretation." Very few commentators who fit the news into a pattern of meaning—the exceptions are writers like Walter Lippmann and Joseph and Stewart Alsop—have any prestige. If the pattern of interpretation is based on liberal premises, then—whether in the press or on the air—it is doubly suspect, for to the perils of distortion are added the perils of "Left-Wing slant." The most successful columnists are those who have made colorful characters of themselves, or have fed the appetite for gossip and "inside stuff" but have stayed clear of dangerous interpretation.

As a result, the American tends to be spottily informed and basically bewildered. He has had thrust on him the burden of making sense of his fragmentized world. He listens to the radio "news summaries," buys the "news magazines," which provide the background and setting to give meaning to the news—and in the process often impose their own pattern of meaning on it. They are popular partly because they pick up from the national press many items that the local press ignores, but mainly because the daily newspaper—with all its bias—offers the American few patterns of meaning.

Nietzsche's phrase about "manifold man, the most interesting chaos, perhaps, that has existed to date" describes the American. He overworks, overplays, overeats, overdrinks, drives himself too hard, reads too much newsprint, lives under an overwhelming flood of stimuli. Each news event adds another stimulus, batting him this way and that. He becomes finally only a receptacle into which the floods pour and from which they flow out in energy—a receiving and transmitting agent but not a valuing agent. He sees small and large items given the same sensational importance in the "daily disaster diet"—murders and wars and massacres, sex cases and strikes, personal incidents and revolutions. The result is a debauchery of the meaning and relation of events. The only pattern into which he can fit the unrelated items is the pattern of the stereotypes he already possesses. This is a pattern mainly of strife and combat, with the good and evil symbols taken for granted. As a result the process of history becomes for the newspaper reader a series of raging yet meaningless and impenetrable battles.

The atomized quality of the news sets the American press off from that of continental Europe, where an interpretive political slant is given to the leading news items. Not that American papers refrain from political slanting. But the distortion is implicit, rather than politically explicit, in the process of selecting and headlining the news items and assigning them space. It may be argued with considerable truth that the atomism of the American papers is healthy, since it helps guard Americans against too sharp an ideological cast of mind and prevents the clash of fanaticisms. But in the process it also retards growth toward political maturity.

Every important newspaper has its characteristic profile, which is related to the profile of its culture. A newspaper like the London *Times,* which reports the award of the honorary degrees at Oxford by giving the original Greek quotations inside the Latin citation, would be hard to imagine in America. The graceful and cultivated political essays that appear on the front page of *Figaro* could not find a parallel in the American daily press, nor could the ruthlessly rigged political propaganda of *Pravda* or *Izvestia* or *Borba,* nor the heavy economic emphasis of a German newspaper.

The profile of the American press is made up of murder and sudden death, infractions of the sexual and moral codes, conflict whether in war, diplomacy, labor troubles, politics or sports, and always—people. It is the emphasis on people that makes home-town news, gossip, and social events so important an ingredient of the formula. "One human, earthy story," says Marvin Creager, a Milwaukee newspaperman, "about something being done or happening to someone in our own city, is worth a dozen from the press association wires." It was the intense localism of the American "home-town mind" that made the war correspondents from Des Moines or Dallas papers visiting a front-line battalion in World War II pay more attention to the names and addresses of the "local boys" than to the strategy of battle.

Thus the double visage of the news in an American paper is that of the violent and the familiar. But news, whether international or local, is only one of the reader's interests to which the press ministers. It also gives advice to the lovelorn, provides hints on cooking and homemaking, runs presumably expert hints on how women can reduce and stay young, provides spelling and vocabulary-building exercises and crossword puzzles, gives tips on horse racing, sometimes serves the gambling propensity by publishing the Treasury or racing figures on which the "numbers game" is based, runs stock market quotations, provides readymade comment on news and personalities by columnists, advises on how to bring up children, gives horoscopes, runs advertisements telling where you can buy what for how much and how to get a job and where to hire a domestic or have your Venetian blinds repaired.

Thus, news as reporting on "the glut of occurrences" (as Benjamin Harris, an early American newspaperman, put it) is only a part of the raw material of the newspaper. The American newspaper has had the same experience as the drugstore: its original purpose has been swallowed up by its accretions. So many embellishments have been added that it is hard to remember what the original function was. The emphasis has shifted away from the news itself, so that in making up a ninety-six-page or sixty-four-page tabloid or a forty-eight-page paper of conventional size, there are usually only a handful of front pages left free after the departments, features, and ads have been laid out. This is less true of papers like the *Times* and *Herald Tribune* of New York or the St. Louis *Post-Dispatch* or the *Christian Science Monitor* of Boston, which take pride in having not yet become vendors of sweets and spices. But some inroads are being made even into these fortresses by the barbarians. As in the world of drugstores, where few establishments remain pharmacies rather than emporia for miscellanies, the over-all pattern and trend are unmistakable.

At its best the American press canvasses the news of the world with an unparalleled thoroughness and competence. With their resources, their skilled man power at the shirt-sleeve and leg-man level, and their genius for organization, Americans are unexcelled at the job of news-gathering. The wire services have a world-wide staff—and use their member newspapers as part of their machinery for collecting domestic news. But what they gather at the big end of the funnel is often hardly recognizable when it emerges at the narrow end in a typical small city newspaper. A double process of selection takes place: first by the wire service editors when they decide what news to get, to hold out, to send out; by the publishers and editors when they decide what to print, given their readers and the available space. At both stages a good deal of skill and experience is invested; but at both stages also timidity, unimaginativeness, the sacred cows of the editorial office, political loves and hates, and the conscious and unconscious drives of distortion often play havoc with the final product.

A handful of newspapers, not content with the wire services alone, maintain their own foreign and Washington staffs. The foreign staffs of the New York *Times* and *Herald Tribune,* the Chicago *Daily News* (less today than earlier), the Baltimore *Sun,* the *Christian Science Monitor,* work on the assumption that the press association men will cover the chores, allowing them to concentrate on their own stories. Some of these

men have made the good American foreign correspondent a world symbol of the adventurous and tenacious newspaperman, but some have
been police reporters abroad. In the case of Washington coverage, the
papers named above along with others like the St. Louis *Post-Dispatch*,
the Chicago *Sun-Times* and *Tribune*, the Louisville *Courier-Journal*,
the San Francisco *Chronicle*, the Providence *Journal*, the Milwaukee
Journal, the Denver *Post*, maintain their own staffs. Yet it has been
estimated that the combined circulation of the papers with good foreign
and Washington coverage is less than the combined circulation of the
two McCormick-Patterson papers, the Chicago *Tribune* and the New
York *Daily News*.

Moreover, the quality of the reporting depends on the disinterested-
ness of the publishers in the theme being reported. The Washington
staffs may take on the protective coloration that will enable them to
thrive in the newspaper house built by the publisher, and some even
become his political errand boys. Yet the White House correspondent
can be a powerful force for political illumination, as witness the fact
that the Presidential Press Conference is the only American institution
which subjects the Executive to a cross fire of questioning, as in the
House of Commons or the Chamber of Deputies: it has thus become in-
formally a working part of the governmental machinery. The foreign
correspondents have an independence of their own because they are further away from the scene of intense domestic, economic, and political
conflict.

The product of the American press which most clearly reflects the elements of dream and reality in the culture pattern is the reporter. Like
the other American power men, he is at the opposite pole from the
eighteenth-century European man of sentiment as drawn by Rousseau or
Laurence Sterne. His "hard-boiled" quality may be seen as a mark of the
desensitizing of a competitive society in which one rarely confesses to
being caught off-guard or being "played for a sucker." Under such a
sun and sky the American reporter has flowered. An urban paper tends
to take its stamp from him, and the good city editor or managing editor
never loses the qualities that made him a good reporter. He invests the
whole newspaper world with his qualities: unsentimental, brisk, shrewd,
resourceful, imaginative as to means but not as to ends or sensibilities,
imbued not so much with a curiosity about ideas and value as with a
restless desire to know what's going on and what's new, possessed of an
intrusive quality which readily disregards privacy and exploits human
tragedies as sacrifices for the Moloch of the paper.

Above all the reporter is guided by two drives: never to be "scooped" and rarely to let a conviction take hold of him. To be scooped means to confess a lesser access to the "inside" and an inferior swiftness in getting to the spot first. To be seized by a conviction means a denting of the armor of insensitivity. This armor is the uncapturable part of the American mind, and nowhere in business is the uncapturable more important than on a paper. In the reminiscences of the best reporters one finds their Golden Age going back to the city room and the police court beat, with their deepest affection reserved for city editors, who are portrayed as desensitized, ruthless, and even sadistic men. The gallery of hero portraits tells a good deal about the values of the hero worshipers.

There has been a good deal of controversy about the emphasis the press gives to the sensational aspects of sex, crime, murder, war, politics, sports, and gossip. One school says the readers demand it, while another says they have been taught to like it by the editors and publishers. One may be called the demand theory of the vogue of newspaper sensationalism, the other the supply theory.

Of course, readers, publishers, and reporters alike are part of a larger culture pattern, sharing its traits, which are based on universal human traits but selected and strengthened by the climate and conditionings of the culture. That is why the most popular themes of the successful newspaper have the common elements of sex, violence, power, and—above all —trouble. In a culture at once Puritan and Babylonian, there is a widespread desire to see others implicated in some kind of web, whether of sexual waywardness, or the corruption of politics, or accidental or planned death. What the newspapers do is to whittle the tragic down to manageable (even caricatured) terms within which the popular mind can handle it.

The sensationalism of the "tabloids" has led some critics to condemn stories about sex, crime, divorce, and the foibles of Hollywood as pandering to the depraved tastes of popular culture. The more conservative newspapers that frown on using the press as a calendar of the passions no doubt deserve well of the commonwealth, but they are only a small and marginal part of an institution which can scarcely help expressing with immediacy the primary human impulses in the culture. The important issue is whether the press shall seek to stand above the culture, giving an elite view of it for the elite, or exercise its critical and creative functions from a position inside the culture, surrounded by the sweat and smell of humanity. There is rarely much criticism of the sentimental "human interest" themes: bathing-beauty-contest queens, waiters or clerks who win the Irish Sweepstakes, long lost relatives reunited with their families, "cute" snapshots of children and dogs, cops laboring to rescue a kitten caught on a dangerous ledge. Actually the taste for the sensational and the sentimental are facets of each other. The same newspaper reader who bathes in these saccharine floods also revels in the entanglements of his fellow men in the social jungle.

One other feature of the newspaper profile—the "funnies" (or "comic strip")—forms not merely another department of the paper but in some ways its crucial symbol. For in the comic strip the caricaturing of human relations, implicit but disguised in the rest of the paper, reaches its final expression in open caricature. In reading the comic strip you can let your censor slumber and surrender to unending entanglements and partial releases.

There is a high-flown theory that the comic strip derives from some "folk mind" or "folk unconscious." This is an oversubtle view of a process which—from the success stories of strip creators like Al Capp and Caniff—we know to be a matter of artful craftsmanship mixed with a hard business sense. Another theory traces the vogue of the comic strips to the illiteracy of Americans—both urban and rural—who read them as they read picture magazines, because their verbal level is childlike. This has some truth in it. But while the comic strip directs its main appeal to children and semiliterates, it has been sustained by the enthusiasm of the literates—often indeed of the intellectuals. To read the comics has become a recognized mark of belonging to the American culture.

Some of the early comic strips, like Herriman's *Krazy Kat,* had a wild satiric quality, and the tradition has been continued by Al Capp's *Li'l Abner* and Walt Kelly's *Pogo* among the recent ones. They present a take-off on contemporary characters and trends, deflating the pretentious and mocking the stuffed shirts. They do it all the more effectively because they shape an imaginary world seemingly so irrelevant to the real one that the shafts go almost unnoticed.

But most comic strips are not funny: grotesque, yes, with a kind of Gothic grotesqueness; improbable and extravagant—but not funny. One of the most widely read comic strips, *Dick Tracy,* is funny only if a Lon Chaney or Bela Lugosi movie performance is funny. It is a straight-faced record of extroverted and improbable adventure, with little humor, irony, or astringency. The comic strip offers the entanglements and extrications of a continuous cast of characters in a series of alarums and excursions linked in daily episodes. Above all, it offers recognizable virtue and derring-do on one side and recognizable villainy and skuldug gery on the other. It is at once outlandish adventure and a caricatured morality play, in an imagined world in which every emotion is blocked out in stereotyped form. Thus the comics are not only the American's Gothic romance but also his Plutarch and his *Everyman*.*

Through comics and crime, sex and scandal, local items, columns and features, the newspaper achieves the steady reader loyalty on which it depends for survival. It reaches the reader because it approaches him at his most expressive level, a good deal lower than the angels. James Wechsler, editor of the New York *Post*, has suggested (not wholly with tongue in cheek) that the tabloid readers were better prepared than the readers of the staider "family newspapers" for the findings of the Kinsey Report, and that "the preoccupation with sexual behavior . . . is several thousand times greater than a casual reader of the *Times* would ever guess." The valid point here is that the press, which is still the crucial big-audience medium, must try to reach the whole man within the whole culture.

In doing so, however, each newspaper must be judged by the quality of its taste and humanity. The treatment of news involving sexual entanglements or offenses can be prurient and nasty, or it can be done with honest objectivity. The news of crime can be done sadistically, carrying a love of violence for its own sake, or it can show an effort to get at motivations. A divorce scandal can be treated for the bedroom farce laughs and the Peeping Tom thrills of invading the privacy of the victims, or it can light up some of the blind alleys of American life. The trouble with the old "yellow journalism" was not that it dealt with the violence and drama of life but that it dealt with them degradingly. "Human interest stuff" need not be treated in an inhuman way, callous of human costs.

"Yellow journalism" had one trait which need never have been discarded—the editor's willingness to call a lie a lie even when uttered by a powerful public figure. The contemporary papers (with an honorable roster of exceptions that include the St. Louis *Post-Dispatch*, the Milwaukee *Journal*, the Providence *Bulletin*, the Washington *Post*, and the New York *Post*) have tended to replace crusading with an "objectivity" which often becomes timidity. This has meant in great part an abdication of the critical function inside the profession and the culture. There are still crusades left for the papers that take their craft seriously; crusades against slum housing, polluted bathing beaches, water-front crime, corrupt police and minor politicians, conditions in state welfare institutions, clogged traffic, reckless driving, inadequate or unsafe parks. It would be unfair to call these safe crusades, because usually they require

---

* I have discussed here the daily comic strip. For a discussion of comic books, which have largely broken away from their newspaper origins and become an industry and a problem in themselves, see Ch. XI, Sec. 2b, "The Reading Revolution."

courage as well as research. But most of them involve crusading in a minor key when compared with the great newspaper tradition of the Progressive Era. The press giants of the 1890s and the turn of the century were not loath to attack one another's politics, policies, and personalities with quill pens tipped with a searing flame. But much of their gusto has gone, diluted by an era which fears to take any chances with alienating either readers or advertisers. In the early 1950s most papers were reluctant to nail down the bullying tactics and the Big Lie technique of Senator McCarthy.

Some of the reasons for the muting of the crusading note may be found in the forms the press has taken in its organization and power. In the era of Jefferson or Jackson the paper was shaped by the individual editor, who may have started as journeyman printer, typesetter, or schoolteacher, who came to know his community well enough to guide its growth and express something of its conscience. His fault was to be too closely attached to a political party, dependent on it for funds and political favors and inclined to turn his paper into a party organ.

The rise of the big-circulation papers gave the papers an independence of parties if they wished to exercise it: but it also linked them with the dynastic fortunes and economic credos of men who did not need to be the hangers-on of political machines because political machines had become their hangers-on. These empire builders of the newspaper world were cut of the same cloth as the empire-builders of other industries and of finance. Men like Bennett, Dana, Pulitzer, Hearst, Medill, Scripps, were as daring, imaginative, and ruthless as their industrial counterparts. They ushered in the era of the Barons of Opinion. After their passing the publishing formulas they had developed and their agglomerates of money, plant, and circulation became entrenched in corporate form. The Barons of Opinion gave way largely to the opinion industries.

Whitman's line—"I sound my barbaric yawp over the roofs of the world"—might have been spoken of some newspaper Titans who were cutting each other's throats in order to build their empires more securely on the popular passions. Some of their energy may still be found in the newspaper battles that go on in a few big cities—in New York and Chicago, where Colonel McCormick and Captain Patterson set a pattern of ruthlessness almost as legendary as that of Hearst's, in San Francisco and Denver, Atlanta and New Orleans, Washington and Boston, Milwaukee and Cleveland and Buffalo. In such cities there is competition for circulation and advertising and a calculation of what headlines will catch the eye and stir the blood: a half hour's margin of priority or the choice of a headline theme which engages group emotions may make a difference to the telltale graph of newspaper sales. There is also competition in building up columnists and feature writers or enticing them away from competitors. A good editor and publisher can make the rivalry infect the news pages and copy desks, and thus retain some of the haze of romance that once invested the reporter's job.

If there are a few cities left where competition is in force, the rest of the nation is becoming a desert of monopoly. Morris L. Ernst has effectively gathered, in *The First Freedom,* the figures on the growth of newspaper monopoly cities and the diminishing number of competitive cities. One of the reasons the American press does not fight against monopoly in other industries is that it has itself largely reached a monopoly position. In the case of most American cities, as is now abundantly known, there is only one newspaper; or if there are two—one for the morning field and one for the evening—they use the same presses and are controlled by the same company, though they may have separate staffs and operations. The newspaper chains, the press associations, and the feature syndicates represent concentrations of investment and economic power in no substantial respect different from concentrations in steel or autos or cigarettes, transportation or aviation, machine tools, aluminum, or the public utilities.

The important difference is in impact. As E. B. White has said, "Structurally, American business . . . tends to corner thought, hoarding it and exploiting it as it would hoard and exploit any other merchantable stuff." But the effect of a shrinkage in the steadily vanishing market place of ideas is far more serious for a democracy than the effect of a shrinkage in aluminum or rubber tires. The Hutchins Commission on Freedom of the Press gave the figures on the thinning of the pipelines of communication. In 1909 there were 2,600 daily newspapers in America; in 1945 they had been reduced to 1,750, published in about 1,300 cities. Only 117 of these cities—one out of twelve—have competing papers; which means that in eleven out of twelve cities there is only a single newspaper. In ten states there is not a single city with rival daily papers.

The technological and economic forces behind this process are clear. Since the newspaper to be popular must be kept cheap in price, the burden of keeping it going under conditions of rising labor and newsprint costs falls on advertising revenue, which in turn depends on large circulation, which in turn depends on heavy investment both in plant and features and distribution and on the capacity to bear losses until circulation can be built. This gives the competitive advantage to the big corporation. It means also that the competition becomes intolerable to the weaker papers, and they drop out or are bought out. In the Kansas

City area, serving about a million people, there is only the *Star* as a survivor of this process. In the 1840s in New York, when Greeley and Bennett and Walt Whitman were editing papers, there were sixteen dailies serving a population of 400,000. In 1950, there were seven papers for a population that had increased twentyfold to almost eight million. The New York *Sun*, which had in its lifetime resulted from the merging of five newspapers, was bought up by the *World-Telegram,* which was itself the result of the merging of three newspapers. Thus the process of newspaper cannibalism has meant that eight papers have been swallowed up in one. The facts of newspaper life—lesser competition where there had once been greater, and none where there had once been some —grew out of the strong inner currents toward bigness in all forms of American industry.

Even more than with other small business, the problem of a small newspaper is survival. "The advertisers," Max Ascoli has said, "strengthen the papers that are already strong, while the labor unions weaken those that are already weak," so that merely to stay alive becomes a form of triumph. Caught between the rising costs of newsprint and the pressure of the unions for higher wages, only the papers with growing advertising revenue can continue to publish—and they prosper and wax fat and rich, on the Biblical proposition that to them that have shall be given and from them that have not shall be taken away. In cities where the same owners run a morning and afternoon paper, they may help out the Biblical law by the "tying device," or rejecting advertisements in one unless they are also placed in the other, thus crowding out a hapless competing newspaper in one or the other field. To cut overhead costs a number of newspaper "chains" have bought up papers in city after city. The recent trend, however, has been toward the decline of the chains, since a paper cannot be run effectively by remote control, with an absentee owner or managers sitting in a tower far from the needs and tastes of the local community.

A cynic may say of the press that we have mistaken the commodity it deals in. It does not primarily sell news, features, or entertainment, but advertising space: the news and entertainment are subsidiary industries, designed to support the sale of advertising. He would be essentially right—with several crucial qualifications. One is that even the dependence between advertiser and publisher is not a one-way street but runs both ways. A powerful publisher cannot afford to alienate a large section of his advertisers, but if he can hold his circulation he can thumb his nose at any particular advertiser, no matter how big. The idea that advertisers call the tune of what goes into the newspapers is an overdrawn cliché. The newspapers that support Big Business do so not because the advertisers demand it but because the publishers are themselves Big Business and are affected by its interests and mentality. The real impact of advertising is its drive toward newspaper monopoly, not its creation of newspaper puppets.

There is another qualification: the economic motive operating with greater or lesser purity throughout the business world is not the only motive in the newspaper business. In other industries the stockholders give the managers the job of making the product and showing a profit, and pretty much leave them alone to do so. The split between ownership and management control applies far less to newspapers. Editors and staff are hired to show a big circulation, get a big advertising revenue, and bring in a profit; but the publisher reserves the final voice on the editorial and news policies to be followed. In fact, the Hearst and McCormick empires are evidence that a publisher may place profit second to partisanship, risking circulation in order to destroy an Administration which he hates. The rule of managerial independence is here sharply broken. Much depends, of course, on the regard the publisher has for the tradition of newspaper craftsmanship and on the relative strength of personality of the publisher and his top staff. Sometimes there is an internal staff struggle between the editorial and business executives.

Since the Barons of Opinion occupy the strategic approaches to the American mind, they can, like the feudal barons of old, exact their toll. The toll is not only profits but power—primarily in the effort to entrench the existing structure of economic forces and to resist programs, parties, or leaders whom they fear.

There is, of course, a strong defense for press centralization. E. B. White put it vividly: "A giant can make out a pretty good case for giantism; he has the showy muscles to flex, and he has the appearance of robust health and the air of being a benefactor in the community—which he often is. . . . The facts and figures can be turned to show that the steady tightening of the lines, by mergers and combines, actually enlarges the stream of published ideas." But one must agree with White, as also with Ernst, that this is only appearance. The reality is different.

The impact of press giantism has been a triple one. First it has led to the concentration of power in the hands of a few imperial aggregates. This power places the big publishers among the crucial "lawgivers" of America, using that term in Machiavelli's sense of power figures with a decisive influence on opinion. They might say that they care not who makes America's laws provided they can make its myths. I include in this group the publishers of big-audience papers; the heads of newspaper chains, feature syndicates, and press associations; and the heads of the magazine empires that mark a new phase in the history of the press —news magazines, picture magazines, peptonized digest magazines, along with the mixed feature magazines of the older style and the big-audience women's magazines. Anyone seeking to define the landscape of American power today would have to reckon substantially with the power aggregates contained in the Hearst, McCormick, Chandler, Cowles, Luce, DeWitt Wallace, Howard, Curtis, Knight, and Gannett publications.

This press giantism has led to the standardization of the product, whether through the syndicates that sell comic strips, columns, and other features, or through the "boiler plate" furnished to hundreds of small-town dailies and rural weeklies, providing canned editorial opinion as well as quaint items to fill out the page. Since it results in a shrinkage in the number of sources from which opinion flows and the channels which shape its flow, it brings about a tighter power relation inside the press organization. Here again E. B. White reached the heart of the matter: "The vital question . . . is not how many reporters and commentators we have, it is how many *owners* of reporters and commentators we have. . . . If you believe in private ownership, then make sure there are plenty of owners."

The relation between master and man in the structure of press power is harshly illumined by the case of Reuben Maury, who writes for the New York *Daily News* a brilliantly simple editorial page which is perhaps simpler than the truth. When John Bainbridge pointed out in a *New Yorker* profile that Maury has written "out of both sides of his mouth" on the issue of providing American money for feeding Europe, being against it in the *News* and for it when writing articles for *Collier's*, Maury clarified his plight in a letter to a newspaper craft journal: "When a hired editorial writer is writing editorials he is not writing out of either side of his mouth. . . . He is acting as mouthpiece for the publication for which he works. His job is to express the publication's policies with all the force and skill he can summon up, and without regard to his private opinions. . . . It is merely a phase of the editorial writing job."

The pathos of the craftsman-as-hireling could scarcely have been better expressed. It is a relation one finds throughout industry and government and in the arts of salesmanship and advocacy. But when it is also applied to the craftsman in ideas it turns his nature topsy-turvy. The integrity a writer owes is not to the man who pays him but to the idea. To a greater or lesser degree it is true that most newspaper writers have to stay within limits of tolerance set by those who own and control the papers. The lucky newspaperman works for an editor and publisher whose ideas coincide with his own, or who believe in expressing a diversity of viewpoint. But these are marginal, and not the rule.

It is in the political arena that the power of the press barons is most dramatically illustrated. Since the 1936 Presidential campaign, when Franklin Roosevelt battled against overwhelming press opposition, the Democrats have gibed at the "One-Party Press." They have had evidence to back up their attack. In the campaigns from 1936 to 1956, when Roosevelt, Truman, and Stevenson ran as Democrats, newpapers holding from 70 to 87 per cent of the readership of the country supported the Republican candidate. In some cases (notably the New York *Times*) the newspapers—whatever their editorial commitment—did not let it spill over into the news columns; in most cases they did, as Irving Dilliard has shown with documentation in a notable study of the 1952 elections. In the heat of campaigns the newspapers of both parties display their whole armory of weapons—distortion, suppression, unequal coverage and headlining, highly selective emphasis, the black magic of inflammatory stereotypes. Despite the American's traditional fear of propaganda, he remains vulnerable to the verbal manipulations of the press.

Ernst Cassirer pointed out that magic achieves its purposes in any culture by the dislocation of the function of language. By naming something and then putting it into the universe of magic, it takes it out of the area of communication and places it in the area of the unknowable and unarguable. Epithets like "Red," "Communist," "Marxist," "Socialist," "Fascist," "Totalitarian," "reactionary," "foreign," "subversive," "disloyal," "un-American," label the idea or measure which is attacked and cast it outside the pale of discussion. By a black magic they place a taboo on it. This is the technique of any group that refuses to share power with anyone else and will therefore not allow the competition of other ideas. It mocks Justice Holmes's words in his classic *Abrams* dissent, that the "ultimate good desired is better reached by free trade in ideas—that the best test of truth is the power of the thought to get itself accepted in the competition of the market, and that the truth is the only ground upon which men's wishes can safely be carried out."

Some observers believe that this is bound to evoke a recoil in the opposite political direction. Liberal newspapers, like the St. Louis *Post-Dispatch* and the Washington *Post*, have thrived and even managed to buy out competitive papers. The New York *Post* has also prospered with a militantly liberal policy. From 1932 to 1952 the New Deal and Fair Deal administrations held on to popular support despite almost unanimous press hostility. As Roosevelt saw it, the problem was one of oppos-

ing the "propaganda of the deed" to the "propaganda of the word": he
gambled that what he did would speak more loudly to the people than
what the press said. The 1948 Truman victory was similarly based. But
if the Democrats hoped that they could continue to profit from this
counterforce, they had their hopes deflated in the 1952 and 1956 Presidential elections, when the popular loyalties and identifications were on
the same side as the big battalions of the press.

The job of publishing a newspaper has three aspects: it is a business
run for profit; it is an instrument of political power and therefore part
of the power structure of the society; finally, it is a craft, with a great
tradition of workmanship. An example of the continuity of the tradition, even in a structure of wealth and power, is the New York *Times,*
which must be reckoned one of the great newspapers of the world. It
maintains a corps of correspondents in world capitals; as a "newspaper
or record" it reprints important documents of contemporary history in
full; it retains an austerity of view that does not veer with popular
fashions or passions. Louis M. Lyons has noted that there are a handful
of American cities which are today in a healthier newspaper state than
they were a generation ago—among them Denver, Minneapolis, Washington, Providence, and perhaps even Chicago. The uneasy stirrings of
the conscience of newspaper craftsmanship were also for a time reflected
in the astringent appraisals of press performance by A. J. Liebling in
the *New Yorker,* by the establishment of the Nieman Fellowships for
newspapermen at Harvard, and by the Hutchins Commission. How
much impact they have had is still difficult to estimate.

One of the principal recommendations of the Hutchins group was
that of continuing appraisals of press performance and a self-policing
system by a panel of men whose prestige would be beyond question.
Another measure that has been discussed is some means for reversing the
trend toward fewer papers by encouraging the launching of new ones.
A one-newspaper situation in any sizable city is a disservice to everyone,
including the advertisers. While it may enable them to reach their buyers more cheaply, it puts them at the mercy of a single power, leaving
them without recourse to any competing advertising channel.

The problem of ways and means for achieving this goal presents obvious difficulties. The days when James Gordon Bennett could start the
New York *Herald* with a capital investment of five hundred dollars are
in the dim past. To launch a metropolitan newspaper effectively today
would take at least ten million: even in a moderate-sized city it requires
wealth. Direct government subsidies are too dangerous and would be
bound to boomerang. But it should be possible to create a revolving

fund, perhaps contributed by foundations and run by a disinterested group, to help competent newspapermen set up newspapers in areas where competition is most badly needed. If this be attacked as a form of indirect subsidy, one may point out that a large part of the press—and especially the big national-circulation magazines—today flourishes by virtue of indirect subsidies from taxpayers. These publications are sent through the mails at rates far below cost, which enables them to keep their circulation high and get the advertising from which their costs are paid and their profits come. These are indirect subsidies to publishers and advertisers alike. If this is in the national interest, it is even more in the national interest that the press maintain a competition of ideas.

The most dangerous prospect is the development of a cynical disbelief in most papers. In the old small-town newspaper, like William Allen White's Emporia *Gazette,* there was no gap between press and people because the town knew and loved the man who got out the paper. In the power aggregates of the modern press, the face-to-face knowledge and the love are no longer possible. Trust is still possible, and in many cases it remains; but, tragically, that too is being dissipated. In its place have come indifference and skepticism, like an armor of immunity the reader has assumed.

5. *Revolution in the Big Media*

IN SCARCELY MORE than two generations the other big-audience media went through a revolutionary change much like that of the press; in the process they transformed much of American life. Most Americans associate the magazines, movies, radio, and TV with the arts of living rather than with the molds of thinking, with entertainment and the uses of leisure rather than with attitudes and beliefs. Yet after dealing with the churches, schools, universities, and press, one cannot stop short at the newer forces that have assailed the minds and imaginations of Americans.*

Revolutionary changes took place almost simultaneously in a number of big-audience media. What made them come where and when they did, fusing them into a continuous multiple revolution, was the convergence of three important forces. One was a big audience equipped with purchasing power, not confined to one class but including all of them. The second was the emergence of leisure time needing to be filled. The third was the contrivance of inventions which filled that

---

* I deal here with the impact of the Big Media on opinion. For their impact on popular culture, see Ch. XI, Sec. 1, "Popular Culture in America," and Sec. 9, "Artist and Audience in a Democratic Culture."

leisure by spanning the continent, pulling the far places of America together, assaulting and capturing eye and ear—and doing it cheaply enough to make the new inventions accessible to all.

Of course this makes it sound too pat. Actually the history of the revolutions in the big media—of which the first were the big press, the big-audience magazine, the movies, and the radio, and the most recent have been paperbacks and comic books, color television, long-playing records, and three-dimensional movies—is the history of blundering struggles and experiments that often ended in blind alleys. It is also the history of pitched battles waged on the fields of business combat between giant industrial empires. The story of the radio industry alone would demand of the historian a talent for epical military description, in depicting the battles of patent pools, antitrust suits, consent decrees, and color television. The crucial fact about most of these big media, viewed as industries, is the big initial investment and the high cost of plant, transmission, and distribution. Thus the big media furnish no groves for dreamers to wander in, no secluded nooks in which individual talent can flower. As in the case of the press, their management and operation move steadily into ever fewer hands.

The impact on opinion follows from this fact. Those who control the media come to hold the strategic passes to many American minds. To be sure, the main function of the media is usually held to be not opinion but entertainment. But this only gives added weight to our concern with their effect on opinion. Reaching the mind, ear, eye, and imagination, their impact is all the greater because it eludes the inner censor that alerts the American against "highbrow stuff." Operating through the emotions, it leaves the more enduring image on the mind.

The customary phrase "mass media" implies that they are instruments aimed at targets. The target is presumably the mass of the people and the aim is to "reach" and manipulate them. Whether or not they include advertising (the movies, popular books, and records do not) the shadow of advertising hangs over all of them. Each medium must reach a big audience to provide the outlay needed for the kind of entertainment that will succeed in reaching such an audience. Thus the circle turns back on itself like a snake biting its own tail. The "masses" are the target both of the advertising and of the art, and in the process of providing the medium with an audience and a profit, they afford it also a chance to shape the furniture of the people's minds.

I make no assumption here about the docility and inertness on the part of the audience whose stereotypes are being shaped. The term "mass media" is in itself a dubious one, since it seems to imply a "mass mind" belonging to the faceless and undifferentiated crowd. It carries over the fallacies of the "crowd psychology" concept dominant at the time the new media emerged. There are "faces in the crowd"—the faces of persons who fall into many categories, depending on the handle by which you may wish to grasp their reality, yet remain individual persons.

I prefer the phrase "big-audience media," after the model of the "big-circulation magazines," or, better still, simply "big media." My point is that they have now gone beyond any limitation to a particular class or mass, or even to any particular audience. For an audience is the aggregate of individuals drawn together by a common interest and concern; when the episode that brought them together has run its course, the audience dissolves into its individual parts, only to reassemble in new clumps and aggregates around some different occasion. The editors of the big papers and magazines, the producers of movie, radio, and TV shows, the publishers of paperbacks and comic books, and of popular records, fall into the habit of abstracting some common denominator from all these audiences. I suppose they have to in order to keep from going crazy. Yet these hardheaded, sharp-featured men must know that those whom they have thus abstracted continue to be individuals with a variety of tastes. If they forget this they forget it at their peril, for an audience whose varied and changing taste is neglected will dissolve into thin air. Hence the continuous nerve-racking search for "fresh ideas," new "formulas" and "formats." If the "mass" of the "mass media" were uniform, passive, and plastic there would be no need to woo it by novelties or to watch the fever chart of the changes and chances.

Actually the editors and publishers, directors, producers, and the "idea men" on whom they draw, usually go to the other extreme of assuming that the audiences act as legislators and that their own function is merely to register the convulsions of popular taste like seismographs. Impressed by the vacillations of a curve of taste they cannot understand, they end by playing it safe. To play it safe means to exploit the easiest strata of taste in their audience, to avoid the "highbrow" and "controversial," to abdicate their own creative function by feeling the pulse of "audience response," and to rationalize the result by pretending only to furnish "what the people want." Thus the self-censorship codes of the movies, radio, and TV express a fear of alienating any section of the audience by offending its sensibilities. It is hard to reconcile the fears of these timid men who live in the shadow of the Big Audience they have made into a graven image, with the picture of them as a group of manipulators shaping the malleable material of the "masses" according to their interests and whims.

I suggest that neither of these images is wholly valid. The Big Audience is not an idol to be worshiped by its priesthood, nor is the priesthood a group of calculating knaves who use the idol as a shill. It is better to assume that while an audience retains its individual variations of taste, and while its changing styles are incalculable, it has common impulses and characteristics which do make it plastic to a degree. Put in another way: while in the long run the audience possesses a legislative power over its own tastes and ideas, there is at any time a frame of permissiveness within which the technicians of the Big-Audience media can work either creatively or destructively, either to degrade and corrupt what they find or to evoke its potential.

There is some current tendency to see these media as forms of "mass communications" but it is doubtful whether this gives much meaning to the term. As Norbert Wiener put it, communication is a dialogue between people united against the common enemy, whether we call it entropy or chaos. This implies a two-way conversation instead of a monologue with one person as performer and the other as passive target. Despite studio audiences and "reader response" surveys, it would be spurious to view the outpourings of the mass media as real dialogue. They remain, not communication that clarifies, but a technology of appeal that, for better or worse, shapes the minds and tastes of millions.

Since I treat the big media as part of the apparatus shaping belief and opinion, thought and taste, I must note another respect in which they differ from other parts of the apparatus, like church, school, and universities. However large the congregation or the class, the pastor and teacher never break the personal relation with parishioner or pupil. They too, of course, must make an abstraction of their audience, yet having made it they restore the vitality of the relation by treating each person as a person. This the directors of the big media cannot do. The abstraction remains one. The element of dialogue, which persists in the teacher-student and pastor-parishioner relation, is here broken; the creative process which depends upon the two-way circuit is to that extent truncated. It is true that experiments have been made with church sermons and classroom lectures on radio and TV, and they are likely to prove fruitful in their own way. But the distinguishing mark of the big media remains the one-way transmission. Once the audience rigidifies the habit of listening without answering back, it will become increasingly inert.

There remains the question of the role the big media play in the culture, and what ties them together. If, as W. Lloyd Warner suggests, "they function as distributors of symbols with common meanings to mass audiences," then they are shaping a new language. But every language evolves verbal symbols which convey images and overtones. What distinguishes the language of the big media from the rest of American thought and expression?

The reflective individual uses images that distinguish him from others, but a society as a whole lives by asserting the common symbols that tie it together. Language itself attempts such a function. In a complex society, where persons of disparate backgrounds fumble for a means of breaking through the walls of experience that separate them, a special social language is required. Durkheim spoke of it as "collective representations." They may take the form of religious symbolisms and rituals, or of "mysteries" embodying the religious myth, or of epics or dramas or great celebrations for the populace like the Roman games. American popular culture offers parallels to these forms, except that the "collective representations" have become secularized. Instead of the religious myths there are the myths of national uniqueness; instead of the Roman games there are baseball and football contests; instead of the Greek tragic plays there are Hollywood movies and TV horse operas; instead of the religious mysteries there are the more secular "mysteries" of the whodunits; instead of the English Morality play and the *commedia dell' arte* of the Renaissance cities there are the comic strips, comic books, and musical comedies.

The question remains as to why these particular collective forms of popular symbolism should have flowered in American culture. As one clue I have pointed to the convergence in America of a rapid pace of technological change, a multi-class audience with purchasing power and (for the first time in history) leisure available to the people as a whole rather than the monopoly of a leisure class. There may be another clue in the ethnic and class structure of American society. In his *Essay on Man,* Cassirer cited the Babylonian experience with symbolic algebra, taking it from the historian of mathematics, Otto Neugebauer. They suggest that Babylonian civilization marked a meeting and collision between the Sumerian and Akkadian races and languages, and became involved in a strong emotional effort to find common symbols that transcended these differences. Out of the climate of this straining there developed the energies from which a symbolic algebra was born.

Dare we apply a similar approach to the American case? There is no comparable record in history of the meeting and collision of so many ethnic strains and diverse experiences in a common cultural arena. Societies like the Latin American and the Asiatic, where many such strains have also met and collided, have lacked the impulse both of the free market and of democracy to move them toward a fusion: a solution of a sort has been struck in a system of caste and hierarchy, which recently

REVOLUTION IN THE BIG MEDIA   769

has had to admit a revolutionary nationalism as a common symbol system. In the American case, out of the social climate created by the striving to break the walls of ethnic, regional, and class diversity, there has come as by-product a readiness to accept the common symbolic and emotional systems afforded by the big media.

We may lament the clichés and formulas of these media and the absence of elite standards of taste, but to do so is to lose sight of their social function. They came into existence not to break cultural molds but to form them, not to shatter a symbol language into fragments but to shape a new one. Every language standardizes its forms, and this one is no exception. But every living language also, in its growth, gives scope to great variety and richness. This has proved true of American popular speech: there is no reason why it should not prove equally true of the new symbol language of the big media which speaks so powerfully to the media audience.

The question of media control is a tangled one. The historian of American culture will note that there was a fateful moment in the history of both radio and TV when the choice was presented between control by the chains and sponsors using and playing upon media symbols, and control by the universities and state educational authorities in the interest of traditional social intelligence. The issue was not decided overnight. During the whole decade of the 1930s a little group called the National Committee on Radio strove to save a limited number of educational channels from being cut down by the commercial interests, but to no avail. A similar group was active in the TV field in the 1950s. In both cases they urged that programs conducted for profit are bound to depress intellectual levels and taste standards. They had in mind as a model the standards of the BBC in England, which has made less of a tin god out of the Big Audience. University presidents, school superintendents, teachers, parent groups, liberal industrialists, and trade-union officials joined in these movements. They caused enough stir to compel the appointment of investigating commissions in several states. But the hearings came to naught, partly because of the entrenched power of the chains and advertisers, mainly because of the prevailing conviction that radio and TV should be concerned with "entertainment," not ideas. The contempt of the "practical" men for "highbrow" tastes, and for "do-good" aims in education, gained the victory because it was a contempt shared by many Americans, some of them inside the besieged city of education. The rulers of the empire of the air pleaded their case, in effect, on the theory that the big media exist to reach the Big Audience, and that any other purpose is a dispensable luxury. They are content to let Plato and Newton and Pascal rest where they are while they create new symbolic heroes in the form of Jackie Gleason and Phil Silvers.

A primitive defense of business control, as against that of the educators and technicians, was blurted out most clearly by J. Harold Ryan, President of the National Association of Broadcasters in the 1940s. "American radio," he asserted, "is the product of American business. It is just as much that kind of product as the vacuum cleaner, the washing machine, the automobile, and the airplane. . . . If the legend still persists that a radio station is some kind of an art center, a technical museum, or a little piece of Hollywood transplanted strangely to your home town, then the first official act of the second quarter-century should be to list it along with the local dairies, laundries, banks, restaurants, and filling stations."

The more sophisticated form of the argument avoids this crudeness. It talks of "giving the people what they want" and cites the audience demand for certain programs of high entertainment and low intellectual content as proof of what Frank Stanton called a kind of "cultural democracy." To which Charles Siepmann replied that such a "theory of retailing makes as much sense as if a large department store were to clear its shelves of all commodities except the best-selling lines." It should be clear that there is no strong movement in America to displace the "American system" of private enterprise in the big media in favor of a system of public control like the British. Siepmann and others asked not for the replacement of private enterprise in entertainment and opinion but for a policy that would consider the quality and variety of the product and not only the size of the audience.

In what ways do the other big media follow or depart from the press pattern, especially on the score of the stereotypes of opinion and the struggle for power?

The case of news and picture magazines—which are also opinion magazines—is best discussed by examining the magazine empire of Henry R. Luce. *Time* is edited for the literate middle classes, helping them establish a pattern of meaning in the chaos of events. Within its own pattern-breaking mold, it avoids the more obvious press sensationalism and presents the necessary human diet of conflict, sex, gossip, and human interest indirectly through the summary of news and trends. It appeals to the same universals of human nature as do the newspapers, radio, and TV shows, but by a more decorous approach, as befits a magazine founded by two Yale men who were literary luminaries at college. Luce represents a different kind of "tycoon" of the opinion industries from Hearst, Scripps, or Pulitzer. He is the cultured, reflective man, son of a China missionary, who saw what the big media could do to shape minds in a democracy. He managed to build a circulation empire by serving as an intermediary between the classes. In *Time* and in *Life* he and his editors sought a way of interpreting the outlook and values of a business civilization to the people, while in *Fortune* they tried to interpret some liberal ideas to the managers of the corporate empires. They had more success with the first function than with the second, largely because the first is easier within the cultural frame of the freedom-property complex.

The case of *Life,* involving the first successful American use of the nonverbal symbolism of the action photograph as the heart of the big-circulation magazine, marked a revolutionary phase in the history of the big media. It was followed by *Look* and other picture magazines, each with its own variant of the basic formula. Later some cultural commentary found its way into the pages of *Life* in the form of long essays, so that the literate reader as well as the one who was tired of grappling with words could find his own intellectual level in the magazine. The number of novels and short stories which used the *Time* and *Life* editor as a symbol, much as earlier novelists had used the war correspondent, is testimony to the impact of these new forms upon the American imagination.

Henry Luce's example underscores the fact that the term "mass media" is accurate only if "mass" means big circulation rather than the underlying population. The middle classes comprise the bulk of this "mass" audience, nor does it exclude the highly educated groups. The success of the Luce power suggests that those who think of the big media as the mass-feeding of morons have been misled by old stereotypes. Luce's success lay in the fact that he made one group of his readers feel they were getting educated, and another feel they were learning about life in the raw. He gave very disparate audiences a body of symbols to hold them together in his Big Audience. His two big magazines, edited by young men who spanned the distance between the world of intellect and the world of affairs, were able to market a blend of literacy and sophistication to the Big Audience.

A similar moral is implicit in the case of the big-circulation women's magazines, of which Edward Bok's *Ladies' Home Journal* was the most successful illustration. Lloyd Morris called Bok "the grand Lama of the matrons." Certainly the formula he helped shape, continued and adapted by Bruce and Beatrice Gould, has persisted with some changes ever since—the interest in the world of the home, in fashions and child-rearing, in the dream world of fiction, and in the reform causes with which American women have identified themselves. This mingling of home features, daydream, and uplift has ever since comprised the material of the women's media. In addition, the American woman's role as organizer of spending and consumption made the big-circulation women's magazines a paradise for the advertisers. Finally, the rise of women to political importance made the women's magazine a political instrument even when its material seemed least so: it had the power to reach women's minds through their dreams. I should add that the current women's magazines have moved more boldly into the area of medicine, mental health, psychology and psychoanalysis, and sexual problems than their predecessors would have dared do or thought possible.

A third development has been the radio and TV news-analyst-commentator. Although liberals usually lament the murder of liberal commentators by advertisers and pressure groups, while conservatives charge a conspiracy to keep their own champions off the air, the typical commentator is neither one nor the other but a middle-of-the-road man who presents controversial issues guardedly. Through radio and TV news coverage the ordinary American manages to get a more rounded view of an issue than he can get from his single local paper. While only a few commentators with integrity are able to reach the high audience ratings, political influence is not a matter of counting the heads of the audience, as if they were eggs or pins or carrots. The political literacy generated by men like Elmer Davis, Edward Murrow, Eric Sevareid, Howard Smith, Cecil Brown, and Martin Agronsky can in time be diffused through the body politic. It is the national scope of the radio that gives it the important, if small, leavening of politically literate commentators: in a single city they might be boycotted by pressure groups; on a multi-city network they find an audience that makes them less vulnerable.

The radio and TV discussion program, by its controversial nature, must risk lighting little fires of hate and fanaticism among the politically dedicated. The periods of crisis which bring such programs into demand are also periods of psychic intensity that stir the adrenalin flow of the zealots. The popular taste for blood puts a premium on dramatic conflict even in discussion of public issues—an instance of how the motifs of the entertainment programs, filled with violence or sentimentality, have carried over into the discussion field. TV has also brought into play the powerful medium of the documentary, whether in the reportage of the world-crisis type presenting the background for some important news event or the edited movie and newsreel clips that condense a chapter of history such as the Hitler era or the American 1920s, or the filming of a child's delivery or a psychiatric interview. The most dramatic instances have been the extended documentaries of the Kefauver Crime Commission, the McCarthy-Army hearings, the Presidential conventions. The televising of Congressional investigations raises grave issues not only of the right of privacy but even more of the uses to which political demagoguery can put them. It would be foolish, however, to abdicate the use of an instrument whose potential for healthy political opinion is even greater than for destructiveness. The documentary is an illustration of what gives an almost incalculable power to the media which fuse an appeal to ear and eye and the imagery of both, as TV and the movies do.

A greater danger lies in the economics of the big media which, while making the Presidential conventions of both parties available under advertising sponsorship, sold time directly for the campaign speeches themselves. This throws the emotional force of the big media of radio and TV behind the political party which can better afford the steep expense—which currently means the Republicans.* Thus the economics of the big media strengthen the inherent advantage of conservative forces under a business system and add to the armory of powerful symbolic weapons they already possess in the newspapers and magazines. Frank Stanton's suggestion for free TV time to the major parties in the Presidential campaigns would remedy this inequality, but it would involve a decision to abandon the idea of giving equal facilities to fringe parties as well as major, and therefore Congressional action changing the "equal time" provision of the FCC Act.

The economic factor is, however, not always decisive in the battle of opinion, which pits one pattern of political mythology and social folklore against another. It is on the plane of competing mythologies and folklores that the big media play their more profound role. In a perceptive study of the underlying movie themes, Martha Wolfenstein stressed that of the "good-bad girl," seductive by reason of her apparent badness but turning out in the end to have been a good girl and receiving the reward for her intact virtue in marriage and happiness. In his study of the *Big Sister* radio serial, W. Lloyd Warner found a theme of contrast between the woman who has made her transition to married life by sublimating her dissatisfactions and remaining an attractive "nice person to know," and the uncontrolled woman, impatient of such restraints, who demands more direct emotional satisfaction. Using the T.A.T. projective technique, Warner found most of the program listeners identifying themselves with the first woman rather than the second. The fact that the radio daytime serial ("soap opera") thus

* See also, for the "one-party press," Sec. 4, "Profile of the Press," and for the political aspects, Ch. VI, Sec. 4, "The Party System and the Voter."

bolsters the listener's acceptance of the emotional poverty of her life points up its social meaning and function.*

The daytime serial is not like the magazine serial, an unfolding narrative with some progression in plot and character: it is a number of episodic beads on a string, with the same stereotypes repeated in each. This fact gives them an added symbolic force. Thus the big media may be as telling politically when they deal indirectly with the emotional symbols of the daytime serial as when they deal directly with political ones. In fact, their nonpolitical aspect gives them an entrance into the mind more readily than direct propaganda could achieve. The same need for a common symbolic language which gave the big media their success operates also to stress the themes of acceptance rather than rebellion and of social emulation rather than individual dissent. An audience that accepts the ambivalence of the good-bad girl will also be prepared to accept the paradox of the good-bad corporation or trade-union, which, despite its dubious practices, remains in the end a champion of public virtue; the same may apply to the good-bad government. An audience that identifies itself with the triumph of the superego in *Big Sister* will become the better target for the techniques of psychological conditioning which are looming ever larger on the political scene.

Thurman Arnold had little difficulty in showing that the "symbols of government" and the "folklore of capitalism" have scanty correspondence to the realities of the American political and economic system. The prevailing social folklore does contain some elements of truth: that American society is mobile, that great fortunes and careers have been made in it, that freedom from government controls is an important freedom. The folklore also contains elements of fiction half believed by their propagators, and some elements of doctrine which are not true but continue to be spread in the big media—just as Plato believed in the spreading of myths by the rulers for the underlying population. Whether true or untrue or partly true, such myths are the projection of the spirit of the culture as its people like to think of it. They dress themselves and their institutions in dramatic garments, as freemen capable of achieving anything in an open society, because it gives a heightened value to their lives. To call this "folklore" is an ironic literary device which should not obscure the fact that these beliefs have their roots in popular experience and are indirectly strengthened by the symbol stuff of the big-audience media.

I have tried to trace critically the profile of American belief, the gods

---

* For more on radio serials, see Ch. XI, Sec. 6, "Radio and TV: the World in the Home," and for more on the "content analysis" of the movies, see Ch. XI, Sec. 5, "Dream and Myth in the Movies."

Americans worship, the transmission of their heritage through education, the ideas their thinkers have evolved, and the channels through which belief and opinion have been shaped by the traditional media and the new ones. The big media present dangers to the society, but a democracy must embrace the kind of communication system which its technology has evolved, grappling with the new media as with the old, counting on being able to turn the power of camera, screen, and microphone to the uses of the culture.

I turn now to the popular culture of which these media form a part, and to the standards of taste and the quality of cultural life which it embodies.

CHAPTER XI

The Arts and Popular Culture

IN WHICH we examine the forms Americans use to express their imaginative and artistic life, and the new modes of communication and recreation that tie regions and classes together in the Big Audience of the Big Media. We ask what America has added characteristically to the great tradition of the elite arts that it inherited from Europe. But our emphasis is on "popular culture" and the folk arts—the first in the sense of the arts intended for and accepted by the Big Audience, the second in the sense of the arts that grow out of the energies of the people and are shaped most often by anonymous craftsmen (Sec. 1, "Popular Culture in America").

We first examine American literary creativeness, focusing on the novel in its relation to contemporary needs and experience, and noting the current reading revolution in America (Sec. 2, "Writers and Readers"). We move then to some of the crucial products of the folk culture, including the new types of American folk heroes, the old and new legendry and folklore, and the most impressive product of all—American speech and language (Sec. 3, "Heroes, Legends, and Speech"). Standing between the folk culture of myth-making and the popular culture of the Big Media are the spectator sports, embedded in the American passion for athletics but expressing increasingly the commercialization of that passion (Sec. 4, "Spectator and Amateur Sports"). We then examine the Big Media again—movies (Sec. 5, "Dream and Myth in the Movies"), radio and TV (Sec. 6, "Radio and TV: the World in the Home"), exploring their inner structure of power, their standards of taste and artistry, the revolutions they have brought about in American habits of thought and living, and their rivalries and interconnections. Moving away from the Big Media, we discuss American folk songs, popular music, and dance, focusing on jazz as the most expressive idiom of the mood and tempo of American living (Sec. 7, "Jazz As American Idiom"). We then analyze what the machine has done to the traditional arts, including painting, sculpture, and the theater, but we pay special attention to the contemporary forms that architecture and design have taken in an urban industrial culture (Sec. 8, "Building, Design, and the Arts").

Throughout this chapter there runs a double theme: first, the effort to trace the lines separating the elite arts from popular culture, and the vernacular style from the cultivated style; second, the question of how creative the standards of taste and achievement can be within a culture frame that stresses profit, vendibility, and the mass audience. We end with an analysis of the frustrations and productiveness that mark the dialogue between artist and audience in the American culture, asking whether America has been able to achieve a "democratic aesthetic" and what kind it is (Sec. 9, "Artist and Audience in a Democratic Culture").

The Arts and Popular Culture

1. Popular Culture in America

IS THE kind of civilization America has developed hospitable or hostile to creativeness in the arts? What has the dominance of the popular arts over the elite arts—of the low- or middlebrow over the highbrow—meant in the total pattern of artistic achievement?

Behind both questions is the assumption that what a culture does in its arts betrays its inner quality. The artist may see himself working in a self-sufficient realm, timeless and placeless. Yet what he does and the way he does it tells almost as much about his civilization as about himself. Spengler chose the statue of the Greek athlete and the Gothic spire as his symbols of the Apollonian and Faustian cultures. In every culture one gets glimpses of the inner culture style from the way its artists go about the process of creation and the way their audiences respond or do not respond to them.

For some insight into the relation of the artist to the culture style, one could do no better than turn to Walt Whitman. In the preface to *Leaves of Grass* (1855) he described with splendor the function of the poet in a great democracy. Using "poet" as abbreviation for the artist, as his masters Carlyle and Emerson had done, he sought the relation between the American artist and the cultural life of the people. Some fifteen years later, in *Democratic Vistas* (1871), after a civil war had intervened and in a bleak period in American culture, he came back to the same theme, saddened but holding to his insistence on the artistic strength a democracy required.

> Our fundamental want today in the United States [he wrote] is of a class of native authors, literateurs . . . far higher in grade than any yet known, sacerdotal, modern, fit to cope with our occasions, lands, permeating the whole mass of American mentality, taste, belief, breathing into it a new breath of life, giving it decision, affecting politics far more than the popular superficial suffrage, with results inside and underneath the selection of Presidents or Congresses—radiating, begetting appropriate teachers, schools, manners, and, as its grandest result, accomplishing (what neither the schools nor the churches and their clergy have hitherto accomplished, and without which this nation will no more stand, permanently, soundly, than a house will stand without a substratum) a re-

ligious and moral character beneath the political and productive and intellectual bases of the States. . . . The problem of humanity all over the civilized world is social and religious, and is to be finally met and treated by literature. The priest departs, the divine literatus comes.

Whether or not the "divine literatus" has come, there is little question that other emissaries have—the gagsters and comedians, the dramatis personae of the comic strip and comic books, the "Kings of Swat," the super-sleuths and "shamuses," the crooners, the god and goddesses of the movie marquee and the fan magazines whose profiles, hairdos and kissing techniques have become the legislators of American mores.

These legislators have come to America, but regardless of whether Whitman would have welcomed them, most of America's literary people have shrunk from them. "The proof of the poet," Whitman wrote more hopefully than prophetically in his 1855 preface, "is that his country absorbs him as affectionately as he has absorbed it." Absorption of this sort there has been, but not between the people and their poets and artists. It has been, rather, between the people and their heroes of the popular culture. From Fenimore Cooper to Van Wyck Brooks, American critics have awaited the coming of a great national art and have lamented the failure of the culture to provide the artist with a warm response and audience. Now the critics find the response warm enough and the audience more than generous—but for the wrong kind of artist.

There has developed in America a double relationship between the arts and the public. The feeling between the elite artists and the "general public" has until recently been one of neglect or even contempt; but in recent years writers like Hemingway and Faulkner have been read in paperback editions by millions of readers, and their books have been turned into movies and plays, so that they have become almost popular figures who could not maintain their isolation even if they wished to. This is less true of painters, sculptors, and composers, where there is still a cleavage between public and artist. Within the popular culture itself there is, on the other hand, an uncritical hero worship.

In every civilization there is an educated culture and a popular culture—an art of the classes and an art of the masses. Matthew Arnold defined the first (*Culture* with a capital C), as the best that has been thought and said by the few in a civilization. The other conception refers to the run of what is thought, felt, and liked by the many. Both are included within the broader anthropological use of "culture" as the total design of the life and thought of a people.*

* For a discussion of my use of the term "culture" in this book, roughly in the anthropological sense, see Ch. II, Sec. 1, "Figure in the Carpet."

Using popular culture in the second sense above—as the culture of the many rather than the few, often deliberately differentiating itself from elite culture—there are some who claim for it the only valid elements of truth and beauty in a civilization. The cult of "folk art," like the cult of the "folk mind," goes back to the discovery of the creativeness of the innocent by the weary sophisticates of the European Enlightenment. It is true that creativeness is not the monopoly of the professional artist. An untutored talent in poetry or a "primitive" in painting may come up from the underlying population; and much of the energy of art comes from the experience of simple, anonymous people. But the "folksy" art of America, associated with the Negroes and with some of the white mountain communities, is mostly pseudo-folk. The dangers of an uncritical cult of the people are contained in Franz Boas's remark: "I should always be more inclined to accept, in regard to fundamental human problems, the judgment of the masses rather than the judgment of intellectuals. The desires of the masses are, in a wider sense, more human than those of the classes." I suggest this is the kind of sentimental thinking which is a dubious base for a theory of popular culture, although it may have some validity in the case of a cultural idiom like jazz.

The fact is that the elite arts and popular arts have different functions in a culture. Whether it be Henry James or Sargent, Virgil Thomson or Charles Griffes, Wallace Stevens or Frank Lloyd Wright, the drive of the elite artist is part of the sustained effort of individual creators to express their vision of life. The drive of popular culture (I am speaking here of the genuine folk culture and not of the synthetic and manufactured type) is mainly to find release, in performers and audience alike, for the energy, humor, and self-assertion of the people. Each is a valid form of American creativeness. The characteristic weakness of the elite arts is likely to be found in condescension of spirit, arrogance of intellect, contempt for mass culture. That of the popular arts—and, in America, what may be called the middlebrow arts as well —is found in cheapness of taste, slackness of discipline, the glossing over of real problems, a fear of depth.

The big media and the arts of reproduction have, of course, brought the high achievements of elite musicians, painters, and writers to millions who never before had access to them. But the strength of American popular culture does not consist in its spreading of elite material but in its creation of new popular material. Its relation to the elite arts is not subsidiary but imperialist: the popular arts absorb the work of even the playwrights, composers, and great novelists by a powerful suction force.

The student of the American arts must strip himself of the assumptions he is tempted to carry over from the European tradition. The Greek hero of the year was the prize-winning tragic dramatist; the Renaissance Italians turned out into the street to honor the creator of a new mural masterpiece; in Goethe's Germany the poet graced the courts of princes; in Wagner's time the composer was a national hero; but in contemporary America it is not poet, painter, composer, or tragedian who receives the accolade of the people. To move from the artistic climate of western Europe to that of New York and Hollywood is to experience a Copernican shift in values and assumptions. With the exception of some first-rate novelists who are also "best sellers," the elite arts, which have been and are still the creative categories of European civilization, are not the center of the planetary system of the arts in America.

Not that the Americans recoiled from everything European. Jefferson as architect translated Greek forms to the Monticello terrain, just as Jefferson as political thinker adapted the French Physiocrats and *philosophes* to the American revolutionary struggle. The American stonecutters carved out Greek forms with a Yankee strength and cunning of hand, just as the American shipbuilders fashioned their clipper ships with a tautness of design as economical as any design of the Greeks, yet geared to swiftness and nervous energy. Cooper and Washington Irving copied European forms even while they poured into them the content of a new continent. Emerson was a Platonist who fused the absolutism of the Greek philosopher with a Yankee astringency, and who translated the mysticism of the Eastern sages into terms of Yankee common sense. Longfellow, Whittier, Lowell, Holmes, were a bookish circle who borrowed their poetic ideas from the library stock of European memories, even when their material was native. The poetry of Poe was the inner flash of a tortured mind whose intellectual home (like his acceptance) was in European romanticism.

Yet to measure America thus by European standards is like measuring the Russians of the Czars or the commissars by the standards of the Athenian city-state. While contemporary American writers like Faulkner and Steinbeck are read in Europe as models, America is not a European civilization. Rightly or wrongly, many Americans feel that the elite arts of Europe are the products of dead-end cultures: they feel like the barbarian who, having conquered the traditional empires of power, will not bow down to the traditional empires of the spirit. This is true although contemporary American poets can compare with any in the world, and American abstract artists have created a ferment of excite-

ment everywhere. The question is not how good the American elite art
is, but what is the natural art idiom of the culture as a whole.

Despite a good deal of nonsense written by the glorifiers of the popular arts and the champions of the mucker pose, there is a genuine strain
of rebellion which they express. When William Dean Howells spoke
out against salon writers in the America of the 1880s he spoke as a
vigorous champion of the novel but rejected whatever was prettified and
derivative because it was weakening the traditional elite art. His protest was followed by the work of Frank Norris, Stephen Crane, Jack
London, Ellen Glasgow, and Theodore Dreiser—the group of "rebels
and ancestors" (as Maxwell Geismar called them) who ushered in the
great period of the naturalistic American novel. To be sure, the creativeness of the American novel counts as part of the elite tradition: in the
procession of world novelists, the Americans succeeded the Russians, as
the Russians were preceded by the French, the French by the British,
and the British by the Spaniards. But it may serve to underline the fact
that even an elite art form neglects the popular energies at its peril. The
feeling which the rebels of the American novel had, of looking at native themes and popular energies in the face of an exhausted tradition,
is much the same attitude that Gilbert Seldes brilliantly expressed in
his early championing of American popular culture in *The Seven Lively
Arts*. In the mid-1950s, in *The Public Arts*, Seldes had to confess that
the masters of the big media had betrayed many of the potentials of the
lively arts; yet this does not subtract from his original insight.

It may be that the popular culture of today, for all its vulgarity and
excesses, will prove to have contained the seeds of the elite arts of tomorrow. But for the present the Americans are taking the cash and letting
the credit go. They devote themselves to costume-designed best sellers,
mystery fiction, "true-story" pulp writing, terror comic books for those
who are children in years or in mind. Their jazz has more passionate
cultists than any community cult since the Dionysian mysteries. They
are less concerned with casting a flawless athlete's figure in undying
bronze than with action shots of sports heroes as they perform for millions of stadium, radio, TV, and newspaper followers. They care less
for the epics of Roland or Don Quixote, of Aeneas or Mr. Bloom, than
for the very different epics that the radio "daytime serials" bring
American housewives every morning.

Thus, whatever the artistic merit of its products, American popular
culture must not be viewed as a marginal aberration to be corrected as
the nation's taste improves and some of its barbarisms are worn away

but as part of the American cultural main stream. While much mawkish nonsense has been written about the popular arts, there is little danger that the big media will supplant the great intellectual tradition of the American elite arts. This does not mean the superiority of popular culture over the elite arts, which will continue to assert themselves even while there will be an autonomous realm for the arts of the popular culture.

That is why the student of American expression in the arts must look not only to the painters who work on rectangular strips of canvas but also to the army of amateurs carrying "candid cameras" as their passport to a photographer's Elysium. The history of building and design will fix on the webbed frame of Sullivan's skyscrapers and on Frank Lloyd Wright's poetic constructions of wood and stone, but it will also fix on the American kitchen, the American bathroom, the profile of automobiles and airplanes, and the split-level suburban house. American composers from Chadwick, Ives, and MacDowell to Aaron Copland have fashioned good symphonic music, yet the American musical idiom is probably better expressed in the haunting blend of traditional and vernacular in Gershwin's *Porgy and Bess* or in the sequence of jazz from the New Orleans brothels to Duke Ellington and Benny Goodman. The historian of the theater will trace the great tradition from O'Neill to Tennessee Williams, but he dare not neglect the musical-comedy stage which brought some of the best energies of music, lyrics, comedy, and dance into an amalgam like *Oklahoma!, South Pacific,* or *My Fair Lady.*

"There is a sub-department of American style," as Alistair Cooke has said, "which is enthusiastically saluted abroad: it is the extraordinary transformation of a bunch of hat-check girls with floppy bows on their shoes, who were formerly known as the *chorus,* into a modern ballet—a specifically American impulse which has been taken over in Sweden, France, England." This transformation could not have taken place without a disciplined treatment of the folk material of the frontier legends and the badman balladry, along with the rhythms of the popular dance hall, by choreographers and composers willing to brave the corruptions of Broadway. Similarly, the comic antics of the Keystone Cops were in themselves no great shakes, but out of them developed an element of the style of Chaplin as one of the great figures in the history of mimetic art. American "cheesecake" and the millions of publicity handouts of "pin-up" girls lack the calm beauty of the Greek Venus, but when Anatole France saw the girls in the American cheesecake art of his own day he remarked that any civilization producing them had a strength in it which could outlast the fears of its intellectuals.

American artistic expression has rarely followed the mold set by the professional arbiters of taste, who have often ignored what they were too close to see. It was Fernand Léger who made out the strongest case for American popular culture. "Thank God for the badness of American taste," he wrote after several years in the United States ". . . I always hate to see 'good taste' come to the people. . . . Still there is no need yet to worry. One only has to study the hand-painted ties on Broadway —a locomotive and four pigeons on a violet and black ground, or a buxom nude on a saffron ground—to realize there is still a vigorous survival. . . . Fourteenth Street may be ruined by the taste of Fifth Avenue, but Avenue B is still rich. And in spite of the fact that people run to good taste as soon as they discover they have bad taste, there will always be another Fourteenth Street or Avenue B while America keeps young. . . . Bad taste, strong colors—it is all here for the painter to organize and get the full use of its power. Girls in sweaters with brilliant colored skin; girls in shorts dressed more like acrobats in a circus than one would ever come across on a Paris street."

This suggests that some of the critics of American popular culture have failed to distinguish between what is in bad taste, judged by the standard of the leisure class and the Academies, and what is false and corrupted by any standard. Conversely, they fail to see that the strength of popular culture is not wholly erased even when it is corrupted by the pretentiousness of the pseudo-folk or cheapened by commercial greed. Much of American criticism of popular culture is riddled by what I should call a media fallacy, which fails to distinguish between the sins of the big media and the material of popular culture which they use and so often distort. W. H. Auden is sounder in suggesting a useful distinction between the popular culture that comes "out of the people," deriving its strength from them, and the popular culture that is merely the kind of art most people like. In the first sense it is folk art, in the second it is "lowbrow" or popular art. In both, according to Auden, it would exclude the courtly or salon art of the elites, although it would not exclude "classical" music or academic art or "serious" literature, all of which get wide popular acceptance through the new big media.

In my own definition of popular culture I should be inclined to cut across Auden's two categories. The art of Al Capp, of "Satchmo" Armstrong, "Jelly Roll" Morton, and of Chaplin, does not come "out of the people" in the sense that the great folk tales do or the Negro spirituals; yet, like them, it must be included in popular culture because it takes a vernacular form, shaped by popular taste and everyday life. Nor does everything that is "popular," in the sense of selling well and being widely accepted, fall within popular culture: when Faulkner's *Sartoris* sells in a paperback edition of a quarter million copies, it is still as much a product of elite art and the literary tradition as it was when it sold only a few thousand; when grand opera or symphony music is broadcast anew to millions, it remains part of the courtly tradition; when a historical romance jacketed with a full-bosomed heroine is adopted by a book club, it does not by that fact become a genuine part of popular culture, but is its own kind of middle-class trash. What counts is whether form and idiom are shaped by everyday American life, breaking the traditional molds of writing, music, theater, painting, architecture, and the dance.

This is not to underplay the role of the Big Audience in popular culture but only to warn against being distracted by the bigness of the audience and making it the crucial test of popular culture. The Big Audience can be drummed up by the media masters if they believe strongly enough in what they are doing and muster resourcefulness in presenting it; the Big Audience can also go by default if there is no such conviction and creative active will. The crucial fact is that the potential audience is there: the revolutionary arrival of leisure has brought such an audience into being, and the big media have made it technically possible to reach it. Like Virginia Woolf's "common reader," there is a "common listener" available. He is not the "average man," since he may range from millionaire to day laborer, from pastor to sex offender; he is not always an educated man, because American education is wayward and spotty in its expressions. It is better to say that he is the "majority man"—or woman or adolescent. The best assumption is that he is open to fresh impacts, is not manacled by tradition, is willing to give much that is new a try, provided that the sponsors and box office will expose him to it.

It is hard to find social or historical laws of general enough application to explain why a culture does well or badly in the total tradition of the world's arts, or why periods of artistic ferment or of desert stretches come when they do. The period after the French Revolution produced very little in French literature, tempting the generalization that an era of social turmoil is paralyzing to art—until one recalls (as Lewis Galantière does) that in England and Germany the same period produced some of the greatest of Europe's lyric poets. This does not mean that we must abandon the effort to find the social correlates of artistic creativeness, but only that no single formula will be adequate.

The most productive approach would see both the strength and confusion of American popular culture as flowing from the nature of the open-class system in America. In more rigidly stratified societies we are likely to find a split between elite and folk art, while in a class system as fluid as the American the boundaries between the two break down. Academic art breaks out of the academies to seek the market place; writers who start with a coterie reach a mass popularity in their lifetime; "best sellers" may turn out to be either slick or exacting; the cult of the comic strip spreads to intellectuals; symphonies find millions of listeners, while musical comedies may achieve a classic permanence almost overnight; jazz and abstract painting may develop cult proportions not only in Bohemia but among the middle classes; "little theater" groups spring up across the map; pockets of literary creativeness emerge in unlikely places in the West and South and Midwest instead of being concentrated in Eastern cities; the people become a nation of amateurs.

There are many ways of explaining this but none that can omit the ways in which Americans live. A people breaking the class mold is in a position to break also the artistic mold. In a fluid middle-class society, education of a sort becomes available to all, leisure is spread, and the dominant interest in life for many becomes access to new gradients of cultural experience. In such a society the distinction between popular and elite culture becomes murky, and the same forces which create a Big Audience for the products of the arts tend to envelope both forms.

There is also another way of seeing the same pattern. It is to see that a civilization which in many areas broke radically with the European past cannot cling to it in the arts without violating the principle of wholeness. Most of the great art forms of the Western cultures—painting, sculpture, the drama, sacred and secular architecture, the ballet, the symphony, grand opera, the epic and lyric poem—arose in largely stratified societies. They subsisted on the patronage of the rich and powerful few; and they celebrated either feudal honor and gallantry—the traits of a society of status—or the cementing power of religious belief. Only the novel as a great art form came out of a rising system of industrial capitalism and sought to meet the needs of the emerging middle classes. Except for literature, all of them assumed a tightly knit community that could assemble in a single place to see or listen, or to celebrate a collective ritual.

Americans are not tightly knit but vast and sprawling; they have not one center but a center in every city; they have a middle class with money enough to pay for new entertainments and leisure enough to be bored unless it gets them—hence the revolutionary techniques of movies, radio, sound track. They are a people with such varied ethnic origins that no one tradition could retain a hold on them for long—a people in constant motion, physically and symbolically, requiring arts that are swift, brisk, cohesive. With an economy dominated by big industry, they have naturally made their arts into big industries, through which some of the arts have found a new social support and a new economic base—but at a heavy cost in aesthetic standards which I shall consider in the sections that follow.

Unlike the material culture, the popular culture runs not in terms of what people *make* but in terms of what they *make up*—speech and rhythm and idiom, joke and plot, fable and song and dance, mimic battles of sport, movements across the stage, shadows on a screen. In what they make up they may reveal themselves more truly—because less warily—than in their more purposeful thought and action, their working or fighting, money-getting or rationalizing. It is in the more innocent and imaginative phases of their life that a people's cultural style is best revealed: for here we can catch them, so to speak, with their culture censor off-guard.

2. *Writers and Readers*

a. *The American Novel*

IN ONE OF his later books, *Faith, Reason, and Civilization,* Harold Laski paid tribute to American achievement in "its sudden creation of a literature which became, as at a bound, part of the main stream of civilized thought." But did American literature actually come into the main stream of world thought so suddenly? The historians of American thought and letters, notably Parrington and Van Wyck Brooks, give an answer involving a slower and more organic growth. What may have misled Laski was the case of the American novel, whose more notable achievements are scarcely more than a century old.

Why should it have flowered in the American soil? In its European origins the novel appealed to a middle class emerging from the Industrial Revolution and anxious to explore the reaches of a new universe. The same process happened in America on a new economic level and at a heightened pace. The varieties of experience that opened for all classes in a feverishly mobile society gave the novel at once a body of material and a reading public. The clash of old ways of thought with new ways of life found literary form in the novel of protest against emotional repression and starvation. New currents of tendency, flowing at one time from Darwin and Marx, at another from Balzac, Ibsen, Schopenhauer, and Freud, gave an impetus to fresh delineations of situation and conflict.

One can follow changes in the inner climate of the American novel by tracing that succession of its major themes. In the time of its Founding Fathers, Hawthorne and Melville, the great theme was the struggle of the individual to free himself from the burden of his original nature. Both of them master allegorists, they traced with powerful symbols the ordeal of a conscience no longer certain of Providential design. Hawthorne's obsessive sense of loss expresses itself in terms of the indelible stigma of sin and in the restless query as to whether the whole of life is not the shadow of a substance of which man has been deprived: in fact, one suspects that the Hawthorne of *The Scarlet Letter* may have been an underground believer in the forbidden sensuous joys of life, as Melville also was. In Melville's earlier period, when he writes of his voyages, there is a robust assertion and a feeling of stripped action and adventure which the Americans were to make their own. But of the later novels, one gets in *Pierre* the sense of being implicated in some crucial and inescapable guilt, in *Moby Dick* the wrestling with the Leviathan of one's inner bondage, in *Benito Cereno* the impact of violence upon innocence, in *Billy Budd* and *The Confidence Man* the betrayal of man's best energies by a lurking evil.

In the middle period of the American novel the giant figures are those of Mark Twain and Henry James. *Huckleberry Finn* and Twain's other great novels of boyhood in a Midwestern small town are the record of a lost Golden Age on the frontier, as is also his nostalgic account of *Life on the Mississippi*. When he turned from the wholeness of this remembered Eden to the adult world as he knew it, with its moral confusion and its hypocrisy, the result was a volcanic upheaval which set him to brooding over the ways of the "Mysterious Stranger" and almost shattered his sanity. In James the American novel turned on itself, exploring the nuances of sensibility in a social system being rapidly transformed. James depicted a gallery of representative Americans in a European setting (*The Ambassadors,* to use his own symbolic title) studying the American character when it was dislocated from the American scene, and dissolving it in the onrushing flood of his perceptions and insights. But the crucial aspect of James is to be found less in his insight than in the drama of the moral dilemmas his characters face and the decisions they make: this was the James of the "middle period," especially of *The Bostonians* and *The Princess Casamassima.*

In Theodore Dreiser—the most massive figure in the realistic movement that counted Howells and Jack London, Crane and Norris and perhaps Ellen Glasgow as forerunners—the realism of method seeks to come to grips with a society which Dreiser wanted to describe nakedly, without in any way prettifying it. Stumblingly he searched for some pattern of order, something other than a theological, romantic, or idealistic one, in the prevailing chaos. Himself only a rudimentary thinker (or better, a feeler) he tried to patch together a philosophy borrowed from Nietzsche, Darwin, and Marx—and from Catholic morality as well, since he was bound to it even when revolting against it. He was in essence a dramatist of ideas, casting them in a literary mold. There was a phase in his development when he felt that the man of power and genius can create his own cosmos, and another when he saw the in-dividual caught beyond help between the tropisms of his animal nature and the pressures of his social environment. In Sherwood Anderson, the theme of alienation becomes obsessive, with most of the characters try-ing to find their way back to an instinctual nature that has been over-laid by the crust of business, the machine, and the small-town moral code. Farrell's *Studs Lonigan* depicts the expense of generous impulse and spirit in a waste of shame. Dos Passos's trilogy, *U.S.A.*, interweaves unfulfilled drives that have no organic relation to each other, related only because each is driven by social (not instinctual) forces of which he has little inkling and over which he has no control.

In this sense some of the important novels before the contemporary period may be seen as cultural documentaries, bearing witness to the emotions surging through the civilization and the splits rending it. They suggest why European and some American critics regard the American novel as a reflection of the grandeurs and miseries of life in America. Using the premise that the fiction stereotypes of each period are part of its social and emotional weather, Malcolm Cowley notes an inter-esting succession of dominant American story themes since the turn of the century. In the early 1900s the story was about man and Nature—how a Darwinian hero of the Jack London type, thinking himself a weakling, found his true stature in the frozen Arctic wastes or in the jungle or at sea. In the generation of the 1920s the story was about the conflict between artist and Philistine, as witness *Three Soldiers, The Genius, Main Street:* this theme can be traced back to the turn of the century in Henry James, Edith Wharton, and Ellen Glasgow, but it became a generalized one in the 1920s. Another theme in that decade was the American Byronic hero of Fitzgerald and the early Hemingway. In the 1930s the stereotype was that of the martyred strike hero of the proletarian novel, although a close study of the period shows that there were fewer instances of it than there appeared to be at the time. In the early 1940s it was about the American soldier finding fresh adventures abroad, or the James Jones reluctant soldier seeking to find himself through the cynicism of his army experience or the disillusionment of the brothel. In the 1950s Cowley finds a number of major fictional themes, including the artistic young men ruined by a possessive mother and the adventure story in which "the author is trying to find symbols, symbols, symbols, for the moral chaos of the modern world."

If we take the four recent novelists who have most impressed European writers—Fitzgerald, Wolfe, Hemingway, and Faulkner—we find that the prevailing mood is the sense of being ravaged and lost, yet of finding some characteristic assertion of life meaning. Fitzgerald deals with lives of individual exploits—on the margin of racketeering (*The Great Gatsby*), or in the dream world of the Hollywood power man (*The Last Tycoon*)—or with individual deterioration, as in the account of schizophrenia in *Tender Is the Night* that may be read on both a personal and cultural level. In Wolfe's case the titles of the novels (*Look Homeward, Angel* and *You Can't Go Home Again*) suggest the prevailing theme of deprivation and search that echoes in the repetitions of "Lost, lost"; the readers of Wolfe's letters know of his tortured quest for an authority principle in a world of unremitting flux. In Hemingway's work the accent on fortitude implies a world so awry that only stoicism and "grace under pressure" count enduringly. The best escape from the trauma of an overcivilized world—expressed in repeated symbols of mutilation and psychic deprivation—is found in the heroic encounters of the natural order (the big hunt, the bullfight, the struggle of the Old Man and the shark) or of revolution and war: even over these there hangs always the heavy sense of loss, for in Hemingway's world, happiness lies only in what might have been. In Faulkner the critics have traced a celebration of the bonds of soil and of family kinship with an elaborated legendry tied to a localist tradition. Faulkner is ridden by the sense that the Southern land can never get free of the curse laid on it by slavery, yet he embraces the qualities of gallantry and arrogance under a feudal order, which—for all their self-destructiveness—shine in contrast with the psychic corruption of the parvenus who have displaced them.

Vernon L. Parrington, who in his *Main Currents in American Thought* tried to place American writers in their setting of time, society, and ideas, emphasized the strain of the novel that started with Mark Twain and went through Howells, Norris, London, Dreiser, and Sinclair Lewis, coming to its fullness in the 1920s. Characteristically, in stressing this tradition, he did less than justice to the counter-strain of Hawthorne, Poe, Melville, and Henry James. Lionel Trilling refers to the Great Debate running through the history of the American novel as a dialogue between Henry James and Dreiser. Yet he rightly adds that even with the naturalists whom Dreiser represents there is a strain of individualism, a rejection of society amounting to the asocial, which marks off the American novel from the British and perhaps the French. As the 1920s and 1930s receded, taking their place in the longer historical pattern, it became clear that even Dreiser and Sinclair Lewis as naturalists worked within a frame different from that of Dickens and Thackeray in England or of Balzac and Zola in France.

The American novel has a longer and richer tradition as a vehicle of social protest and reform that is usually recognized, stretching from H. H. Breckenridge to Nelson Algren. Yet once this has been said it remains true that the stronger tradition is one I have traced in terms of alienation from the society and the lonely debate within the writer. This is the more striking because one might have expected the American novelists to reflect the pragmatic and optimistic stress in the culture, the preoccupation with the concrete, the brashness of social construction. It points up the fallacy of seeing literature only as a mirror reflection of social forces. The relation of literature to American culture is far more indirect and subtle, although the fact of relationship is clear enough since the life of the arts is not carried on in a cultural vacuum.

The climate within which American novelists wrote was one of individual dissent, deriving largely from the religious and political tradition. This dissent might have expressed itself in a drive to use the novel as a weapon for social change, yet the novelists whose primary impulse was reform, like Harriet Stowe, David Graham Phillips, and Upton Sinclair, were only marginal as craftsmen. America as an open society allowed a more direct attack on social problems, through politics and organized groups. Hence when the novelist turned to society, it was not to change it but to reject and transcend it: to do this he turned inward on himself, exploring his moral and psychological dilemmas.

By the time of Henry James, it was clear that the orderly world of the New England elite had slipped beyond their control, and that the traditional values had lost their hold. This was accompanied by a change in the social order—handicraft transformed into a machine culture, a closed order of status into a mobile one of effort and acquisition, a cohesive hierarchy into a new rampant individualism. Between the society of the Old Republic and that of contemporary mass democracy a break occurred—one which is perhaps best reflected in Howells, who sensed and acted it out in his novels. Thus the American case embodies the extremes of individualism in thought and dislocation in society: both conditions are the characteristic ones for the modern novel. The American novel flowered at a time when men saw that they had been cast out of the theological order of design into a natural order of chance and tragedy.

If the novel is the epic of the modern world, it celebrates "schism in the soul." The American novel has a continuing strain of the somber, tragic, guilt-laden. Unlike the painters, American novelists rarely go abroad as apprentices to learn their insights or techniques. They take their burden and theme directly from the Puritan and Calvinist tradition, from the marks left by slavery and civil strife, from the contrast between the American promise and the realities of a power civilization, from the gap between the vaulting idealism with which the American experiment began and the tawdry glories that now bedeck it. The novel thus contains the deposits of the psychic past of the civilization from which it derives.

In the closed societies of the ancient world or the Middle Ages the hero's tribulations and achievements express the collective experience. The hero of the epics of those periods is thus a symbol of tribal victories (the *Iliad*) or wanderings (the *Odyssey*) or of a common religious experience (*Divine Comedy*). Modern man must, however, be his own hero and carry his own burdens, and from that truth the novel takes its shape. Most novels are built around the encounters of love, the pursuit of happiness, the career of a mind, the pilgrimage of a spirit. They may be success or deterioration stories; they may end in wedding bells or be as ravaging as Faulkner's tales of guilt and incest; but always the question is what the main figure achieves or is deprived of ("What happens to him?"; "How does she come out?"). Since the novel operates on two levels—an outer one of social experience and an inner one of psychological exploration—it expresses the ambivalence of the culture. It gives a chance for the portrayal of variants from the cultural norm and is a literary form into which the novelist can pour dreams, frustrations, and obsessions.

In the Middle Ages and their world of authoritarian faith, where the individual had minimal decisions to make on major issues of morality and belief, the novel would have been a meaningless form. There is little evidence of its thriving in any authoritarian regime of today. It is the genre of a relatively open mobile society, like the eighteenth-century European society in which it emerged, where the individual must flounder on his own and find his own stability. Thus it is idle to discuss the charge that the American novel of today is "decadent" because of its pessimist theme and symbolism of method. Hawthorne and Melville were notable for their brooding bent and their inward-turning command of symbolism, yet their society was scarcely in decay—even if it was in the process of radical change. F. O. Matthiessen and Harold Laski said of both these novelists that they turned away from Emerson's easy harmonies because they sensed the night ahead. But this is scarcely adequate as an explanation. They wrote not with a prescience of the future but with a sense of their own plight in a frame where each man must make his own decisions, carry his own psychic burdens, find sympathy and identification with others not through a network of established relations of status but by exploring their common humanity. Henry James's emphasis on the individual moral decision—sometimes a startling one—was the product of a similar plight, and the impact of James was on the intellectuals and the new middle classes of a society which felt the same plight.

Thus the American novel is the product chiefly of dissidents and rebels writing in a relatively open social system where there are no authoritarian short cuts to the problems of the individual life. To be sure, not all novelists have the strength to be true dissenters and autonomous personalities. Yet every group tends to shape its own patterns: in America the young man on the margin of the culture, who rejects the life goals of his contemporaries and is thought a misfit by them, is likely to turn to fiction. In many cases he has a small but salable talent and eventually fits himself into his society. But during a phase of his life he enacts the gesture of rebellion and tussles with the Adversary through a literary exploration of his life and time.

I have said that the novel is a fluid form for a fluid society. The problems of hunger for love, of sexual bewilderment, of the struggle of personalities within a marriage, of the clash between old moral codes and new operative norms, of the search for a personal and social ethic, are questions for which American society offers no fixed solutions. Even where the majority has evolved accepted goals and standards the young novelist feels impelled to challenge them: to write about failure rather than success, the world of childhood rather than the urgencies of manhood, wayward impulses rather than power and money.

Some critics have complained, for example, that the American novelists have failed to do justice to the businessman in their portrayal of him. The complaint has a base, but it misses the main point, which is that the novel was never intended as an instrument of balanced appraisal. The novelists wrote as they did about businessmen not because they were infected with radical and Marxist heresies but because they were driven to be critical of the values of practicality and power which the culture sought to impose on them. By challenging the gods of their culture they tried to find the measure of their own personalities.

The same point is made from another direction by Trilling when he speaks of the striking difference in social attitude within the two best-known boy's books of American and English literature, Mark Twain's

Huckleberry Finn and Kipling's *Kim*. Both of them "delight in their freedom from all familial and social ties." But where Kim carries with him carefully the evidence of his father's identity, Huck is relieved by his brutal father's death. Where Kim adopts surrogate fathers who are symbols of authority, Huck has only the guidance of Jim, the Negro slave. Trilling does not stop short at the theme of "alienation from society": he goes on to show that in the American case this assertion of independence is the prelude to an assumption of responsibility, and that it underlies a social universe of difficult but open human and moral choices.

In this sense the American novelists play the role of keepers of the social conscience. In exploring personality and telling how people have tried to find their bearings, they practice "philosophy teaching by example." To shopgirls and stenographers devouring the novel-of-the-month on subways and at lunch hour, to the young wife consuming novels while her husband is at the office, to the college student getting an initiation into society through a paperback reprint of a fictional classic, the novel—good or bad—is a form of popular psychology teaching by example. The psychology it uses is not necessarily good. It reflects the tensions and splits of the society, and too often it expresses the poverty of philosophy and absence of depth it is meant to remedy. Which only means that the novel is the art form of an open society at its best and worst.

The assumption behind the novel is that answers can come only from the natural world of experience and not from a deductive system. Without this assumption the novel could never have flowered. There are torrents of experience pouring through the pages of American fiction. The dust jacket of every first novel is an absorbing study in the apprentice years which the young novelist serves while "getting material" for his novel—that is, getting the varied feel of American life. If one compares the allegorical tales of Hawthorne with the most recent best seller, there is a striking contrast in mood and tempo. Inevitably the big-audience media have left their mark on storytelling, putting the emphasis on a swift pace which keeps the "story line" moving, authentic detail, and a "clean" style—meaning one uncluttered by excesses of phrase or difficulties of thought. For a story to be swift, authentic, cleanly contrived, and to "pack a punch" becomes the culture form for literary success. The characteristic American "know-how" approach is thus applied by the fiction writer, who tailors his product either to the sentimental or to the hard-boiled note, depending on demand, and injects the proper modicum of violence and sadism for the market. At the other extreme is the novelist who is preoccupied with anxiety-ridden psychiatric themes and with symbols that serve as a substitute for thought.

Thus while the American novel shows no signs of being "doomed," it is caught between the dangers of a slick mechanical facility and the pretentiousness of the coteries. The seductions of the big-audience media do not keep the well-heeled writer from continuing to dream of the legendary "great American novel." But the fact is that no single American novel can be the "great" one, since all of them together portray the shallows and reaches of the American spirit.

I have concentrated here on the novel because in it American achievement is most marked. I have had to omit the short story, which is probably more characteristic of the future trend in a culture where time is measured out with such precision and where there has been (in Clifton Fadiman's phrase) a "decline of attention." In lyric poetry the American record is surprising when one remembers that the main cultural impulse is toward what is useful and salable—and poetry is neither. In Poe and Emily Dickinson, in Whitman, in Hart Crane and Eliot (if he be considered an American), in Frost, MacLeish, Pound, Robinson Jeffers, and Wallace Stevens, American poetry has shown a range and lyric power which belie the usual stereotypes about the American mind.

In the nineteenth century, American poetry was to some extent a popular art and entered the popular consciousness, as witness the poems of Longfellow, Whittier, Lowell, Poe, Bryant, Eugene Field, and James Whitcomb Riley. But these poets have no standing with contemporary critics. In the twentieth century, even when it drew heavily on folk material—as in the case of Carl Sandburg and Vachel Lindsay—American poetry was largely an elite art, with an appeal only to the literate minority. America did not produce a Burns, a Wordsworth, or a Kipling who could be embraced by both audiences—unless Frost is the exception. It is as if the young American poet, searching for an idiom, could give himself individuality only by walling himself off from the rest of his society. The people, in turn, are cut off from the poet and feel something close to contempt for him. The universities find room for poet-in-residence, but as Norman Pearson put it, "The student avid to sit under him in a course on creative writing turned into a citizen who refused to buy a volume of verse after he left the university."

Even in so sketchy a survey I cannot omit a brief word about American criticism, which had a kind of flowering in the quarter century between the mid-1920s and the 1950s. It was a sign of American literary maturity that the critics could not be fitted into any one school, whether one spoke of Edmund Wilson, R. P. Blackmur, Van Wyck Brooks, Constance Rourke, Malcolm Cowley, Allen Tate, F. O. Matthiessen, Lionel Trilling, Maxwell Geismar, Kenneth Burke, Yvor Winters, or Alfred Kazin. About all of them, and a number of others as well, there was an adventurous searching for the relation of forms and meaning, and sometimes ideas and values, which expressed on another plane the restless quest within American society. If Matthew Arnold was right about the alternation of periods of critical and creative effort in a culture, the current "age of criticism" augurs a new creative flowering to come.

b. *The Reading Revolution*

IN THE LAST GENERATION something like a revolution in reading has taken place in America in the form of low-cost paper-bound books, making of Americans a nation of readers. With this has come a rise in publishing costs which makes books that are destined for a very limited audience a luxury few publishers can afford. Thus there has been simultaneously a dwindling of the Small Audience for reading and a vast growth of the Big Audience.

The "best seller" has been chronic throughout the history of American publishing. Defined by its closest student, Frank L. Mott, as any book which a decade after publication had a sale equal to 1 per cent of the population, the best seller would include in the seventeenth century Michael Wigglesworth's poem, "The Day of Doom," with the sale of a thousand copies in 1690, and Mary Rowlandson's story of her Indian captivity; in the eighteenth century *Mother Goose* and Tom Paine's *Common Sense;* in the nineteenth century Parson Weems's *A Life of Washington,* Harriet Beecher Stowe's *Uncle Tom's Cabin,* and Mrs. Southworth's novels; in the early twentieth century Gene Stratton Porter and Harold Bell Wright. In more recent decades the best sellers have been books like *Gone with the Wind, Forever Amber,* the Perry Mason mysteries, and almost any book of popular religious exhortation. To regard this list as revealing the furnishings of the American mind would be to ignore the ephemeral nature of best sellers, which the reader treats much as he treats magazine fiction or radio soap opera.

Despite the best-seller figures, "reading a book" is still felt to require a special effort and a ritual frame of mind. It is well known that President Eisenhower read few books, partly because of his crowded life, but mainly because—like other American men of action—he preferred to absorb through the ear and the eye rather than through the printed page. The estimate is that half the American adults buy no books at all, and most of the rest buy very few. The inroads of TV have threatened even the big-circulation magazines, since there is some evidence that TV viewers read less than the others. Even the college students coming from reading families are fewer than those from families where books are alien intruders.

The emergence of the paperbacks, along with the book clubs, has had a revolutionary impact on American reading habits. The clubs have served not only as large-scale distributors but also as reading counselors, and through them millions of Americans have shaped new reading tastes and habits. The book industry had been more backward than most American industries in developing large-scale merchandising through retail outlets. There are 1,400 bookstores in America, compared with 500,000 food stores, 350,000 restaurants and bars, almost 200,000 gas stations, and over 50,000 drugstores. The revolution of paperbacks has been accomplished by mass-production cuts in cost, by a shrewd editorial selection of titles suggesting sex, crime detection, and violence, along with a number of classics, and finally by a revolution in distributing techniques. This has been achieved mainly by adding drugstores, newspaper stands, and even food markets to the bookstores, thus bringing the reading habit to the ordinary American in his everyday haunts.

At mid-century Americans were buying almost a quarter billion paperbacks a year, with about a thousand titles appearing annually. Freeman Lewis calculated that the five most popular authors have been Erle Stanley Gardner, Erskine Caldwell, Thorne Smith, Ellery Queen, and Mickey Spillane. Three of the five are murder-mystery writers, and Spillane's books embody the worst fusion of violence and sexual exploitation in American writing. Yet a different kind of book, including some of the classics of social science and literature, has also found its way to a mass reading public. The long-range consequences of paperbacks are likely to include the popularization of the best in literary achievement. Whether this will counterbalance the shoddy and sadistic stuff is an unresolved question. It should also be added, for perspective, that despite their astronomic sales paperbacks are bought by something less than 10 per cent of the American population.

The most depressing part of American reading is in a category far below the paperbacks. It is what may be called the cloacal literature, with which street newsstands are filled. It falls into a number of broad divisions—the grotesques (comic books, horoscope sheets, cultist magazines), mystery and adventure (whodunits, terror stories, "Westerns"), romance (love story, "true experience" confessions, and movie magazines), the "Confidential" magazines (battening with enormous circulation success upon the "revelations" of moral lapses in the sexual behavior of movie and TV stars and other public figures), sexual exploitation (joke books, leg-and-breast cartoons, pornography), betting sheets, the how-to-do-it vade mecums (how to comb and feed your dog, how to play mah-jongg, how to improve your golf scores). Examine a newsstand thus weighted down in any American city, and it will be hard to suppress a shiver of apprehension about the American future.

It is important to understand that the corrupting principle does not lie in the machine principle—itself only a duplicative force—nor in the popular standards of taste, which are product rather than source. At the core is the apathy of people who have never been exposed to quickening ideas, and the slackness of thought which makes them victims of cynical and greedy men. In this sense there is no great difference between the sleaziness of the "comic books" (a hundred million copies of which flow into the American market every year) and that of the "slick" magazines produced on coated stock and selling for much higher prices. They have in common the assumption of an inert reader who will respond to a formula. In both cases the situation is contrived and the solutions are easy. The difference is largely that the comic books contain stronger ingredients, including violence and sadistic terror, that they take less pains at simulating plausibility, and that they mainly reach young readers.*

It is this latter fact, striking home at the conscience of Americans as parents, which has recently made them uneasy about the spectacular increase of the worst types of comic books. In the mid-1940s the crime-and-violence comic books formed only a tenth of the total sold; a decade later they were over a third. Part of the comic-book formula is to combine sex, crime, and horror, thus intertwining these themes in the fantasy life of growing children. The serious impact of comic books is therefore not so much on the abnormal children who become delinquents for a variety of reasons, of which comic-book addiction is only one, but on normal children who get much of the furnishings of their mind from this source. Some students regard comic books only as an extension of the realm of make-believe, much like the classic folk tales and children's stories; while others think they leave a traumatic deposit of anxiety and terror. The difference may lie between those children who pass through the comic-book stage as a phase in their imaginative development, moving on to good romantic reading and then to the writers who deal with some of their own life problems, and those children who never move on but remain perpetual adolescents with a comic-book mentality. The experience of the Armed Forces shows that a sizable number of the young American soldiers fall into the second category, frozen at the level of comic books and whodunits.

Possibly the "reading revolution" of paperbacks may break down the

* For the newspaper comic strip, see Ch. X, Sec. 4, "Profile of the Press."

division between elite reading and moronic reading. The fruits of the experiment in popularization will not be known for several generations. But they cannot be productive unless there is a creative impulse within the reading industries which will offer the public good books to place alongside the shoddy ones.

3. Heroes, Legends, and Speech

THE MYTH-MAKING faculty is still active in contemporary America.* Its expression may be found in the folklore deposits left by the past and it is still operative in the legendry that grows up around the type-figures of popular stories and songs and in the changing forms of American speech. The common element in all of these is in the energies of the people, at once anonymous and collective, working spontaneously to produce their record.

Anyone who studies American folklore, keeping his eye not only on the past but also on the vivid facts of genuine folk interests in contemporary American life, is bound to be struck by the threads of continuity between them—but also by the extent of the break. The continuity is there in the sense that the legend-creating faculty continues active, using whatever materials are at hand. But the break is also there. The American schoolboy, whether from city or country, will know far less about Casey Jones than about Joe DiMaggio. The continuing mobility of Americans, along with the constant succession of newly arrived ethnic groups, has led to a break between the legendry of past and present. Since the traditional heroes are not readily available to tie these groups together, the need for new ones is the more urgent.

When I speak of American heroes I think of two kinds. One is the *history-book hero:* like the *heroes* of Greek civilization, he embodies the accepted culture traits and the collective achievement. A Washington, a Lincoln, a Roosevelt, a Grant, an Eisenhower, he is the man with a halo who gives Americans a satisfying sense of national stature. But he is overshadowed by the second hero type. He may be called either the *vernacular hero,* in the sense that he comes out of the everyday life of the people, or the *archetypal hero,* since he serves as a bigger-than-life figure around whom young Americans weave their wish-fulfillment fantasies.

This hero is likely to be a less imposing person than the history-book hero—probably an ordinary young-man-with-a-horn, or a crooner who

* For an earlier discussion of American folk myths, see Ch. VIII, Sec. 1, "The Personality in the Culture." For children's literature, see Ch. VIII, Sec. 3, "Children and Parents."

evokes exciting sounds, or a small-town girl who is no Joan of Arc and has seen no visions except her name on the movie marquees, or a King of Swat with hefty muscles and the ability to swing powerfully at a baseball. This hero's day of glory is brief and his fame is precarious and transitory, like the spurt of a lighted match, for the hero symbols of each generation seem eccentric to the next. But his hold on the popular mind, while he has it, exceeds in intensity the hold of the military and political figures. The living little hero is more important in understanding America than the dead big hero.

In some cases the hero spans both types, acting both as symbol of national achievement and projection of the individual life wish. The businessman hero will serve as an example. In earlier generations he might have been a Gates, a Drew, a Yerkes, a Vanderbilt, a Rockefeller, a Morgan—hard, acquisitive, honed to a sharp edge of predation; yet he received from the young men the final honor of imitation. It was not—as it was with the Greeks—the man of public virtue who was honored but a very imperfect man who embodied a particular strain in the social striving. A Carnegie who broke strikes or a Rockefeller who crushed his competitors was not limited in his prestige to the role of a class hero—as with Gene Debs or Big Bill Heywood—but was accepted as a national hero. Since the people identified themselves not with him as a person but with what he amassed, he did not have to be either likable or virtuous. The business Titans were accepted as almost Plutarchian models because their tenacity, resourcefulness, and single-mindedness in pursuing profits were also the traits of a power civilization. In contemporary America these picturesque pirates have been replaced by corporate managers whose names are scarcely known outside the trade journals. The new business hero is institutionalized: in an impersonalized society he has become A.T. & T. or General Motors.

It is in the archetypal heroes of movie and TV and baseball diamond that Americans seek the sense of human warmth they fail to find in their depersonalized business heroes. In Leo Lowenthal's phrase, the "idols of work" have been replaced by the "idols of leisure."

When one moves into a third hero realm—neither the public figure of politics and business nor the idol of the Big-Audience media—the processes of popular myth-making stand most clearly revealed. Here one finds the folklore hero, who may be drawn from some actual person and expanded to legendary proportions or may be a wholly fictional product of the collective imagination.

The first such folk type was the legendary Yankee who emerged from the American Revolution—slow of speech, with a high-pitched voice, homely in expression, perhaps a traveling peddler, perhaps a sailor or a farmer, full of shrewd wit and homespun resourcefulness. As the type-figure around which American folklore clustered, the Yankee was succeeded by the backwoodsman of irrepressible spirits—the "gamecock of the wilderness." He might be Colonel Nimrod Wildfire, the hero of *The Lion of the West,* a play which swept the country in a number of versions, in all of which he was (in Constance Rourke's words) the "early backwoodsman, leaping, crowing, neighing, boasting, dancing breakdowns and delivering rhapsodic monologues." Or he might be Davey Crockett himself, from whom Nimrod Wildfire is believed to have been copied, or Mike Fink or Sam Slick or Sam Patch or any of the other figures, part hero, part buffoon, who were described in the tall tales that Americans spin.

Later, as the forests were felled and logging camps sprang up, as steamboats appeared on the torrential rivers, as railroads were laid and spikes driven into steel rails, new accessions of folklore were added. The heroes who had already become in great measure boasters were transformed further into giant-sized myths of miracle workers, signalizing both the pathos and the achievement of the opening of the continent—Paul Bunyan of the Big North Woods, the demigod of the shanty boys and the loggers; and Pecos Bill, who has been called the culture hero of the cowboys; and John Henry, the giant hero of the rock-tunnel gang; and the "badmen" and "rip tail roarers" of the cowboy country; and killers like Billy the Kid and Jesse James; and Joe Magarac, pourer of molten metal.

Stories were told of these men and ballads were written about them: there were tall tales and braggart lies. In time the Americans built up a body of legendry about every phase of the continent's expansion—the mountain men, the covered wagon that crossed the plains, the Mississippi steamboats and their epic trails of speed, the river gamblers, the lumberjacks and shanty boys, the Pony Express teams, the gold miners, the cowboys, the frontier-town outlaws, and even—as in the ballad of Casey Jones—the railroad men. These yarns were the literature of the bookless world. For the most part they were organic to the growing energies of the South and West, although some of them were the detritus of a kind of Lumpen-campfollower of the country's growth. At its best this folklore had a braggart quality that never took itself seriously and a humorous ferocity that stopped short of the sadistic. There are also mountainous masses of other material that consist mainly of ghastly idiocies, smart-aleck cracks and synthetic jokes. It was not all pitched to the same key. There was an astringency in the talk of the Yankee characters as against the spread-eagle, rhapsodic assertiveness of the backwoodsman, or the wild fantasy of the "strong man" legends, or the saccharine sentiment lavished on the outlaw killers. But in whatever key, American folklore was the noise an expanding culture makes as it struts and boasts, puffing its chest a little out of cocky assurance and overbrimming energies, and a little out of the insecurity that needs reassurance.

The material out of which this legendry was shaped was the everyday stuff of living; the form it took was the yarn and ballad; the setting was local, in hamlet or county, logging camp or ranch or mining town; the proportions were heroic; the mood was mock-epic; the type image was the hero who was also a bit of a charlatan and a cutter of corners, conscious of his own comic vulnerabilities; the audience was an assemblage of whoever happened to be around, but there was little dividing line between audience and performer, with the roles shifting easily and the observers becoming participants; the method was that of continual change by improvisation of the stories, ballads, and folk themes until the original text was submerged by the successive waves of change.

Since American legendry is notoriously short-lived, it is almost wholly forgotten—or, what amounts to the same thing, enshrined in scholarly books and antiquarian journals. Every so often, as happened in the 1950s with the Davey Crockett boom, one of the legendary figures of American history and mythology becomes a contemporary folk hero. When this happens, the boom takes on runaway proportions and becomes a kind of hysteria sweeping through the country, bursting into the newspapers, the movies, comic strips, and TV, inflaming the imagination of children, and spawning whole new industries, as with "Davey Crockett" hats, suits, pajamas, toys, and souvenirs. Then just as suddenly as it came, the boom subsides—and is replaced by another. In the 1950s the Davey Crockett hysteria was followed by a teen-agers' cult of James Dean, a movie star who had died in an auto crash only a few months earlier but was quickly given immortality by a young generation which formed "James Dean Clubs" and refused to believe that their hero was dead. The true nature of these booms must be left to the social psychologist who studies fads and social hysterias as well as legendry, and the clue to them must probably be sought in the psychic hunger for a compassable legendary figure in an era of the mechanical and impersonal.

Yet, quite aside from these temporary booms, American legendry has left a deposit on contemporary American character. You will recognize in Abe Lincoln's talk some of the comic bravado of the folk tales, with a new dimension of depth; and Lincoln was himself to illustrate after his tragic death the mythologizing process. The reader of Mark Twain also knows that his achievement would never have been possible unless his roots had been in the folk memory. Even in novelists as sophisticated as

Henry James, as Constance Rourke noted, there is a conscious shaping of his figures in terms of the archetypal mold of the American character, as if he meant to show triumphantly that the folk theme can permeate even a craftsman seemingly furthest removed from it. In Steinbeck, Faulkner, and Caldwell, Sherwood Anderson and Ring Lardner, the folk material is like a network of underground streams bursting through the landscaped surface.

One can see the myth-making process still going on, pouring new substances into essentially similar molds. The Western heroes and the dime novels have been replaced by the dramatis personae of the comic strip; Paul Bunyan and John Henry, who were themselves cast in the image of a frontier Hercules, are now Superman or Dick Tracy; the backwoods hero, in a modern burlesque version, has become L'il Abner; the animal tales of the Tar Baby and Br'er Rabbit have become Pogo and his companions; the yarns of the Jumping Frog have been transformed into the modern legendry of Henry Ford's Model T; the badmen of the frontier have taken more recent shape in the exploits of Dillinger and Willie Sutton; the local cracks and gibes are now radio gags or "little moron" variations; and the earlier American boy's storehouse of traditional lore has become the contemporary boy's precise knowledge of the team standing and batting averages of Big League baseball.

To say that the modern material is inferior to the earlier, or less glamorous or more synthetic, is to lose sight of the fact that the basic myth-making needs arise from the people themselves, and that they feed on whatever the culture presents them. There are figures in every era who attract the myth-making power of the people, around whom legends cluster; there are also symbolic events in every generation—inventions, wars, disasters, new media for communication. In the case of societies which have relatively stable habits of life over a long time-span, the folklore consists of traditional collective memories, as is still true in the pockets of cultural isolation that persist in the "Down East" communities of New England or the backward reaches of the Appalachians. But these are only marginal for America. In the foreground there is a process not so much of folk memory as of continually fresh hero-creation, word-coinage, stories and jokes, cults that take almost overnight possession of the people, whether in games or sport or amateur activities. A culture like the American, cutting itself off from the older mythologies, has felt freer to generate new ones. As I have suggested, the presence of so many diverse ethnic and regional groups helped the process by making a fresh start necessary in almost every generation. Yet Americans did not always cast out the importations from the foreign cultures. As in the case of Scandinavian, Jewish, or Negro myths, the myth-making process was enriched by absorbing the tributary streams of mythology that merged with the main current.

How creative have the American myths been? Have the folk heroes expressed the strength and depth of the American character? Have the stories and ballads poured into them the emotional intensity of the American experience or have they tapped only shallow springs?

It may be too early to answer these questions for a culture still young when compared with those out of which the Greek and Norse mythologies came, or the ritual celebrations of the Dionysian cult, or the great myths of the "White Goddess," or the folk material underlying the Greek tragedies, or the Homeric and Arthurian legends, or the myths clustering around a Moses or Joseph, Faustus or Siegfried. American legendry lacks the archetypal depth of these great mythical themes, nor will it offer to the imagination of individual artists the rich opportunity these themes have offered. Partly the reason lies with the nature of the American character, which has been aggressively of a debunking and deflationary turn, partly in the unwillingness to surrender to the imagination when there is so much danger of appearing merely gullible. But mainly it seems true that the tragic dimensions of the American character were contained in its religious brooding and in its great novels, and the folklore—from the impetus it got in frontier expansion—took a more expansive turn but one with less emotional richness.

The collective imagination has operated with the greatest fertility in the continuous re-creation of the inherited language. American speech is surely one of the richest products of the American experience, at the base of much else that is creative in American popular culture. Abrupt, inventive, muscular, irreverent, it expresses with striking fidelity the energies and rhythm that have gone into the making of the national experience. Rarely has a new civilization taken the mature language it has inherited and adapted it so radically to its purposes. American spelling diverged sharply from British at the end of the eighteenth century, and the efforts of men like Noah Webster gave Americans the courage to break free from their cultural colonialism and assert their independence in spelling and pronunciation. While grammar and syntax in American speech have been slow in changing, the process of vocabulary-making has been a daring one: the creation of new words and expressions in the American common speech accompanied the opening of the continent. For a parallel in linguistic inventiveness, one must go to the England of the Elizabethan Age, when the speech of the common people and that of the dramatic writers burst into a new flowering, each of them affecting the other.

With all its richness, however, American speech is strikingly uniform when compared with its mother tongue. The English developed dialects so sharply divergent from one another that a traveler from one region could scarcely understand the dialect of another: it was the Midland dialect, more progressive than the archaic Southern one but less daring than the rapidly shifting Northern dialect, which came to be established as the basis of "standard" or "general" English. The Americans had no such difficulty and no need for a standard or general American speech, since a man can travel from the Atlantic to the Pacific and encounter no difficulty in being understood. The clue lies in American mobility: with so constant a turnover of people there is no chance for the hardening of local speech peculiarities. With the big media every fresh coinage or usage or pronunciation found a vast, capturable audience with which to make its way throughout the nation. Especially through TV, where the spoken word is memorably associated with a screen image, the big media have had a standardizing effect on American speech. The uniformity of speech must not, of course, be overstressed. In his "Second Supplement" to *The American Language*, H. L. Mencken gives a state-by-state roundup of homespun terms which are so local that they sound like gibberish to the rest of the nation; but the fact that this was considered a labor of affectionate erudition is in itself proof that the local diversities are marginal rather than central.

One can also overstate the separateness of the "American language" as a whole. The structure of the language spoken in America is very much like the structure of English. The basic vocabulary is the same and there is a common freightage of literary association. The differences of pronunciation are considerable, but no greater between Americans and British than (let us say) between Americans in Mississippi and in Brooklyn. Where then do the great differences lie? They do not lie in the language seen as a structure or as an instrument of literature or ideas. There is still a common literary vehicle, in which the American of John Dewey differs little from the English of Bertrand Russell, and even the American of Sinclair Lewis differs little from the English of H. G. Wells. The chief differences lie in the idiomatic vocabulary that makes up a large part of the spoken language, especially as used in the big media. They lie in rhythms and inflections, in energy intensity, in the everyday (nonliterary) associations of everyday words. What is chiefly different between the English and American languages is the common speech in its everyday usage—American speech viewed as an expressive emotional instrument.

A people's speech is the skin of its culture. It contains the indigenous vocabulary, the inflections of meaning, the tricks of rhythm, the nuances of association, that give the members of the culture the sense of belonging together and being marked off from those who use different words, rhythms, inflections, connotations. It contains—to use a military figure—the symbolic strategies that make the "we" seem superior to the "they" —a superiority that is part of the psychology of cultural nationalism. The language of American speech is, as I have said, not separate enough from the English to be called with justice an independent language. But the whole complex bundle of intangibles, which are not so much a language as a speech, forms something as distinct from the parent English as American culture is distinct from the parent culture.

Nor is it hard to see how the separateness came about. The Americans had the English language and literature to start from, yet the heritage came from a culture to which they owed no allegiance after the Revolution. Thus American speech started off with the ingredients at once of tradition and innovation, of discipline and freedom. The political release from colonialism demanded a cultural release too. Frontier farmers and backwoodsmen, land prospectors and speculators, preachers and teachers, promoters and lawyers, peddlers and country storekeepers, forge workers and innkeepers, canal bargemen, steamboat pilots, and railroad construction gangs, country editors, newspaper reporters, shrewd young men making their fortunes in the cities, storytellers—by mid-nineteenth century all of these had built a speech with an idiom, a rhythm, a pace, an inflection, a vigor and tang of its own. It was separated by more than an ocean from the speech of the England of Anne and William and Victoria. The Americans sensed that they were shaping something with a fertility and energy of its own and treated it as a plastic instrument rather than as a classical heritage.

The homespun quality of the speech found its way into the newspapers in the late eighteenth century, into the country stores and the city streets, into Andy Jackson's talk and Abe Lincoln's anecdotes. Royal Tyler's play, *The Contrast,* depicted the gap in character and dialect between the British and the Americans. Some forty years after Tyler, Augustus Longstreet was among the first who made the spoken everyday language of Americans into a first-rate sensitive literary instrument. Lowell's *Biglow Papers* and Harriet Stowe's early short stories put New England dialect into literature. Dialect became a kind of fad in the 1880s: Mark Twain wrote the whole of *Huckleberry Finn* in dialect. But while it was amusing to the buyers and readers of books, it was not a fad for those who used it; it was their speech. Yet the writers had a function to perform. Once they had done their work, it was clear that victory had been won and that the decisive battles would never have to be fought again. There was no longer the danger that America might suffer the fate of Europe at the end of the Middle Ages, when men wrote and read in the language of the educated classes but spoke in the plebeian tongues of the new nationalities.

To be sure, some of the greatest writing by Americans was still to be done in the classical English literary tongue, and men like Henry James could make a supple literary instrument of it. Among the academic thinkers and editorial writers, political orators and literary Brahmins, the official literary language and rhythm (the "mandarin style") continued to be used without much infiltration from daily popular experience. This was more than made up by the way the popular arts embraced the new vigor of the American speech. The short story, the movie script, the vaudeville skit, the musical comedy, the newspaper column, the mystery thriller, the crime and sports reporting, the radio gagster—all came under the spell of the new idiom that had been shaped by the rhythms and mintage of American speech. Without this richness, the popular arts could not have gained their hold on Americans. Even the formal art of the novel was transformed, as witness Anderson, Lewis, Lardner, Hemingway, Farrell, Faulkner, Steinbeck, O'Hara, James Cain, Nelson Algren—to name writers widely removed in method and artistry, yet all of whom have become masters of American speech. From other genres one thinks of Hammett and Chandler, Odets and Arthur Miller and Kober, Mencken and Don Marquis, Sandburg, Broun and Damon Runyon, of Cole Porter and Hammerstein, of Ogden Nash and Perelman, and one gets a sense of a remarkably plastic language instrument that need not be cut away from the speech of the people in order to be of use to the literary craft. For American speech does not have to be split into fragments and recombined, as Joyce tried to do to the exhausted literary language of his culture in order to squeeze a desperate freshness from it. New words have cropped up out of American speech faster than they could be absorbed, so that many of them (as witness the researches of Mitford Mathews in his *Dictionary of Americanisms*) have been stuck in historical blind alleys. But every word that has survived has borne a fragment of the great hyperbolic myth of the American experience.

These accessions of richness came at first from frontier living and from the savage exaggerations and the bragging stories that grew with the opening of a continent. Then they came from the life of the growing cities, from miners, steel workers, and lumberjacks, from casual workers and stevedores, from war and the Armed Services, from the criminal rackets and from the lawless margins of business. Finally they came from big-audience sports, from the stage and the movies, and the radio, from popular music and jazz and the dance, from the stock markets and the trade-unions. The new words (and the new uses of old words) generally emerge from the routines of some pursuit, or from some sport or art which a few people follow with the devotion of *aficionados*. They may at the start form only a sort of jargon. But by an osmosis the jargon seeps through the general popular language to people who would never dream of mingling in the activities (crime, racketeering, gambling, vaudeville, burlesque, hot music, prize fighting) from which the new words or new uses first came.

The secret of the vigor of American speech is that the physical and social fluidity of American life have opened the sluices for a similar fluidity of American speech. In hierarchical societies the class strata operate to split the language of the culture into layers of language—clerical and secular, literary and vernacular, aristocratic and plebeian. But the openness of the American open-class system kept such divisions from rigidifying. Here was one creative activity in which even the humblest man could take a hand. The fashioning of American speech is the most popular of the popular arts since it admits of the widest participation, with no admission fee charged except a questing tongue, a feel for metaphor and color, and a bit of boldness in experimenting. Whatever other genius may be denied to the collective American spirit, the genius of the language surely belongs to it.

I do not mean to underestimate the conservative influences that have operated on American speech. The strongest is that of localism. Despite the great geographical mobility of Americans, the speech habits of the region and even the locality into which they move will in time shape the phrasing and pronunciation of the newcomers. A New England family settling in the South takes on the Southern dialect and intonation. It is surprising how clearly many of the contemporary American dialects can be traced back to England, and how little influence the large, non-English-speaking immigrant population has had on them. The American local dialects have been less tenacious than the English, partly because English history over a thousand years has covered a period when roads were bad and communication difficult, while American speech has been shaped for the greater part of its history in an age of rapid communication. As Donald Lloyd puts it, it has "leapfrogged" its way across the continent—yet, he adds, so great is the strength of localism in speech that one can draw lines, especially with respect to vocabulary, around California towns that are less than a half century old. Pronunciation is also largely local or regional.

The concept of American "speech communities," which Lloyd and Warfel have suggested in their *American English in Its Cultural Setting,* sheds a good deal of light on the differences within the larger structure of American speech. One can see America as a cluster of speech communities set apart from one another, each using subtle clues of language to detect and exclude outsiders and to make the insiders more cohesive and more comfortable with one another. Cutting across them, one should also distinguish professional (as on radio and TV) from conversational, and literary speech from the functional speech of people who must find a language for the material they deal with. One must reckon in addition with the conservative influence of the schools, which continue to resist innovations whenever the teacher can spot them. The "educated" American has a "correctionist" bent, both for his own speech and that of others: in the language democracy of America every man is a judge of language, yet if he pretends to an education he is a bit frightened about his judgment. As Americans move up the educational ladder, they move further away from the speech of ordinary people. Yet that speech has entered their lives nonetheless. They have no way of knowing what words that come to mind as they speak come from the literary tradition and what words from the speech community in which they move.

One clue to the strength of American speech is found in the relative absence of rigid principles of "correctness." There is an illustration of this in the animating spirit of the three great volumes of H. L. Mencken's *American Language*. Mencken had two basic principles in his work: that of studying American speech inductively, to find how it was actually spoken instead of how it ought to be spoken; and to scorn any notion of authoritative standards in language, other than the actual usage of the common speech. It was a curious paradox that the writer who had fought a crusade against popular democracy in politics and economics should have embraced in linguistics the principles of *vox populi, vox dei*. Since his time other students of American speech have followed the same emphasis, although one detects in them (as indeed in Mencken also) a certain snobbism in the ironic way in which they celebrate the victory of the barbarian mass. Most Americans have rejected authoritarianism here as elsewhere and have followed in the language wherever their daily experience, their image-making impulses, and the deep currents of their striving have led them. If they have thereby missed achieving an Alexandrian purity of speech, they have also largely avoided the film of gentility which after some centuries of history covers a language and presages linguistic and cultural stagnation.

There remains the question of the standard to be followed in appraising the validity of new coinages of speech even when academic standards are rejected. One can say that some change in grammar and syntax or some new word has met the inductive standards when it has come into general use. The final test is the naturalistic one of survival. Many new coinages never achieve currency and die from disuse. Among others that do, there are often shoddy or clumsy, pretentious or synthetic words. Mencken has some delightful passages on what he calls "scented" words

—such as, *realtor* for real-estate agent, *mortician* for undertaker, or *sanitary engineer* for plumber. Similarly, salesmanship has introduced the use of *contact* as a verb, while advertising has contributed *cost-wise* or *audience-wise*. These are the product of the streams of argot that flow into the language from every American activity. They are often adopted most quickly by those who hanker for gentility in speech or who pick up every linguistic fad in the hope of seeming sophisticated. What are usually called "vulgarisms," such as *it's me* or the use of the double negative, represent strong undercurrents of popular impulse which are bound to triumph despite the resistance of the educated classes. But the scented words and the pretentious argot of the genteel or the self-conscious (take, as a recent instance, the use of "fulsome" in the sense of "abundant") give American speech a quality of phoniness as the price it pays for opening its doors to all inventions. There are signs of the emergence of a new language of gentility, befitting an overwhelmingly middle-class society, in which workers have been replaced by salesmen and the insecurities of status make the newly successful people anxious to wear their words as badges of belonging.

We may speak of three classes of additions to the language: there are *functional words*—technical, occupational, or scientific, which make their way as effective short cuts to meaning, like "megabuck" from the new science of atomic production; there are *exuberant words,* notably in the coinage of the teen-agers and the jive and hepcat set; finally, there are *synthetic words,* the product of cerebral inventiveness rather than of life energies in the culture. The scented words and other strainings for gentility of effect belong in the last of these categories.

This raises the question of how long American speech will maintain its vigor and its principles of growth. The fact that it still has them is shown by the way the language has spread its influence to the twelve corners of the earth and attracted the imitation of young people everywhere. There is scarcely a non-English-speaking country, whether in Asia or Africa, Europe or Latin America, in which the desire to learn English has not become an urgent one: it is as if the legend of America's wealth and influence had made it a kind of *lingua franca* over a large part of the globe—a "second language" for the educated, an aspiration for young people who have not had a chance at it.

But as the big media become the principal carriers of linguistic invention, an element of falseness far more dangerous than vulgarity of taste is coming to pervade that invention. Like the eighteenth-century court ladies in France who affected the simplicity of Rousseau's milkmaids, the grandees of American cultural commercialism are trying to make a good thing of the phony posturings. They affect a nativist mucker pose or cultivate a racy extremism of jargon which often makes them unintelligible as well as synthetic. Listen to what some of the highly paid script writers dream up for the big radio comedians. Try to follow a disk jockey on the air dishing out a "hot" record with the faded remnants of the Basin Street patois. Pick up any of the "hard-boiled" mysteries, its pages larded with the effort to duplicate the staccato mouthings of a down-at-the-heels sleuth. In all these you will get a febrile jargon contrived for money, loaded with the artificiality of a literary language but without its discipline and taste.

I do not mean to overestimate the effect of the big media on American speech. To be sure, writers, announcers, actors, and commentators working in these media are deeply affected by each other. But most of their listeners are less affected by what they hear than by the usage which is rooted in their daily life and work. Isolated words and phrases are given rapid and vast currency by TV, radio, and movies, but pronunciation and idiom grow out of conversation, and you cannot converse with a TV set. The real danger is that the synthetic may be substituted for the authentic roots of popular speech. American writers are in danger of forgetting that what gave strength to Longstreet's *Georgia Scenes* or Mark Twain's *Huckleberry Finn*, George Ade's *Fables in Slang* or Ring Lardner's *You Know Me, Al* was that the language of each had been lived by millions of people before it was re-created by the individual artist. Many of the literary artifacts of latter-day America seem to have been lived by no one. Their world is of cardboard and paste, flimsy and uninhabitable; there is no smell of earth in it and no commonalty. It is contrived without ever having been experienced, and its only life is the hothouse and penthouse life of those who, in their eagerness for the sophistication of the moment, seek pathetically to imitate the imitators.

The fault does not lie in popularization. Actually the brashness, the tongue-in-cheek satire, and the quality of wild and unashamed hyperbole are exactly what gives strength to a language. What is wrong with many of the recent affectations in American speech is not that they are too much but that they are too little the speech of the people.

4. *Spectator and Amateur Sports*

SPORTS DO FOR the popular culture of America what "circuses" did for the Roman culture at the height of the Empire. They let the populace take part in a crucial ritual that binds them to one another and to the culture. Every people, no matter how civilized, must have a chance to yell for blood. Americans express this barbarism daily in their gladiatorial arts—in acting as spectators and psychic participants while other men fight, wrestle, and race with one another, break through human walls to make a goal in football, on ice, or in basketball arenas, hit a ball hard and race out its return.

Compared with some other historical civilizations, the ritualized violence of the American gladiatorial arts is pretty thin. There are no Carthaginian or Aztec human sacrifices to watch, no Latin bullfights, no guillotinings such as once sickened Tolstoy in Paris, no public hangings such as the British once had, no cockfights or bear fights (except on the early frontier or as survivals in the mountain areas today), no battles to the death between Roman gladiators, no mangling of men by lions. What cruelty there is in American culture is reflected less in its spectator sports than in any other of the pugnacious civilizations of history. Only wrestling, boxing, and (to some extent) football and ice hockey remain brutal, and the most ruthless of these—wrestling—has been converted into a TV buffoonery. The prize fights have had their murderousness muted since the days when frontier bullies fought catch-as-catch-can or two toughs pounded each other with bare knuckles for as many as fifty or sixty rounds. As the gladiatorial arts have become big industries, the brutal in them has been diminished and the spectacle accented.

But these spectator sports are balanced in America by a network of participant sports in which people pursue their amateur skills actively and almost obsessively. This requires leisure, with whose development the history of American sports has been tied up. In earlier America, while work was still a life goal, fun was largely restricted to recreation at working-bees or the amenities of church socials, while on the frontier it took the form of heavy drinking and rough games. In a culture where farming exacted a round-the-clock attention to chores and factory hours were long, leisure for organized sports was rare. "Pastimes" imply that there is time to pass with them; spectator sports require purchasing power for admission—that is to say, a surplus after the necessities of life have been met. The increasing industrial productivity, by cutting down the working day and raising living standards, made both possible.

But before the big audience could find sports to watch, or the mass armies of amateurs could find sports to pursue, there had to be games carrying prestige that would furnish pyschic pleasure. This happened when the American wealthy lost their sense of guilt about "conspicuous leisure" and began to develop horse racing, polo, yachting, and golf as the sports of aristocrats. One of the early games the rich took up was baseball. But they could not keep it long as their coteried possession. By mid-nineteenth century baseball became a mania, by the 1880s a big business. The same thing happened to football, which started as the monopoly of the Eastern colleges. Fishing, hunting, bowling, lawn tennis, golf, all went through the sequence of being started by the fashionable and genteel, then becoming a diversion of the middle class, and finally a popular sport.

How far America has come away from sports as a leisure-class pursuit may be measured by the fact that Veblen's *Theory of the Leisure Class,* at the turn of the century, spoke of sports as an upper-class obsession, uncherished by the working class. His contention was that sports are a form of arrested emotional development, a survival of barbaric prowess, consisting of a "proximate workmanship and an ultimate futility." The fact is that the gladiatorial arts have become more necessary to the middle and lower classes than to the rich. The rich still have their exclusive sports—fox hunting, yachting, polo. But the elite sports of yesterday are becoming the mass sports of today: golfers swarm over municipal links, tennis is played everywhere, horse racing and greyhound racing have been taken over by the pari-mutuel betting system, and even sailing has now been opened to a large middle class. As the lower and middle classes got money and leisure they used it on entertainment to get a direct or vicarious sense of bodily prowess. What they want in a spectator game is action, excitement, speed, and power. By these standards racing, basketball, and ice hockey are the sports moving up, and even the "national game" of baseball is stodgy by comparison.

The change of scale in the mass spectator sports has brought with it also a change of phase. Much the same thing has happened to sports as to the big media: they have become adjuncts of Big Organization and the Big Money. It has proved difficult in games like football, basketball, and tennis to retain even the outward forms of amateurism. Whole industrial hierarchies have been built around the national reputation of some tennis or football star—outfitting firms, sports equipment, auxiliary children's souvenirs, the newspaper sports pages, and the new profession of sports writing. In the case of college football, what was once a contest of prowess between young players has been transformed into a struggle of strategies between highly paid coaches who instruct their players on every possible move, leaving them only the refinements of execution. In professional baseball, what the "fans" regard as the triumph of particular stars is often the result of an elaborate system of baseball "farms" and a heavy money investment that makes the assemblage of talent possible. Thus the repetitive pennant and World Series triumphs of the New York Yankees may be seen at least in part as the triumph of Big Business organization applied to the task of developing pitching and hitting power.

The fun industries (not including betting) are estimated to cost about ten billion dollars a year, and the figure may be low. The amount spent on minor sports like golf and motorboating equals the box-office receipts of the movies. On bowling alone the estimates vary from a quarter to three quarters of a billion, spent by twenty million bowlers. As for horse racing, the important figures relate to betting. The estimate is that six billion dollars a year is bet on the races, and almost an equal amount on baseball, especially on the World Series. Clearly, this is a big jump from the little groups on the frontier that gathered around the bear pit or the cock pit, or the aristocratic spectators who gathered at their watering spas or watched horse trotting. The sports themselves have become the narrow base of a top-heavy structure of the box-office and the betting industries.

The striking fact about this is that the commercialism of the spectator sports does little to trouble the American public, who take in their stride the fact that baseball, football, basketball, and boxing have become Big Business. In fact, they are the more inclined to value them for that reason and are pleasurably excited when a popular idol like Di-Maggio receives a salary running into six figures. This gave him a standing in the Pantheon, just as Eddie Arcaro got it by the purses he brought in as a jockey, or Joe Louis by his winnings as a heavyweight fighter.

One of the instructive episodes in this connection is the history of the futile attempts to ban the "reserve clause" in baseball contracts as a vestige of the preindustrial peonage system on which baseball as a big business is built. In the Gardella case, which came to the U.S. Court of Appeals in 1949, Judge Jerome Frank commented wryly that "if players are regarded as quasi-peons, it is of no moment that they are well paid; only the totalitarian-minded will believe that higher pay excuses virtual slavery." But little emerged from the efforts to restrain this throwback to a feudal system under the antitrust laws—although in 1957 the Supreme Court, in a decision involving professional football, hinted that it might have second thoughts about the whole subject. The baseball fan does not seem shocked by the fact that his favorite sport rests on a system of chattel contracts by which players lose their right to bargain in a free labor market, being "bought," "sold," and "swapped." Sometimes this even cuts the deeply ingrained loyalties of the fans, as in 1956 when Jackie Robinson was sold to the New York Giants and his devoted Brooklyn Dodger followers had to contemplate either abandoning him or transferring their allegiance to a hated enemy. When Ty Cobb appeared before the Celler Congressional Committee to defend peonage in baseball, no Congressman dared challenge him, for Cobb as hero symbol embodied the whole array of sentimental loyalties—of the players, the fans, and the bettors—which give the spectator sports their mass hold.

The psychic basis of American mass sports is tribal and feudal. Baseball is a good example of the modern totem symbols (Cubs, Tigers, Indians, Pirates, Dodgers, and Braves) and of sustained tribal animosities. The spectator is not *on* the team, but he can be *for* the team; he identifies himself with one team, sometimes with one player who becomes a jousting champion wearing his colors in a medieval tournament. Hence the hero symbolism in American sports and the impassioned hero worship which makes gods of mortals mediocre in every other respect, and gives them the place among the "Immortals" that the French reserve for their Academy intellectuals.

There is a stylized relation of artist to mass audience in the sports, especially in baseball. Each player develops a style of his own—the swagger as he steps to the plate, the unique windup a pitcher has, the clean-swinging and hard-driving hits, the precision quickness and grace of infield and outfield, the sense of surplus power behind whatever is done. There is the style of the spectator also: he becomes expert in the ritual of insult, provocation, and braggadocio; he boasts of the exaggerated prowess of his team and cries down the skill and courage of the other; he develops sustained feuds, carrying on a guerilla war with the umpires and an organized badinage with the players, while he consumes mountains of ritual hot dogs and drinks oceans of ritual soda pop.

Each sport develops its own legendry, woven around the "stars" who become folk heroes. The figures in baseball's Hall of Fame have their sagas told and retold in newspapers and biographies, and the Plutarchs who recount exploits become themselves notable figures in the culture. Some of these sports writers later become political columnists, perhaps on the assumption that politics itself is only a sport riddled with greater hypocrisy and that it takes a salty and hard-hitting sports writer to expose the politicians. The sports heroes become national possessions, like the Grand Canyon and the gold in Fort Knox. It is hard for a people who in their childhood have treasured the sports legendry as a cherished illusion to surrender it when they grow up.

Each sport also forms a kind of subculture within itself, which a curious anthropologist could profitably study. The stars become life models for Americans who have played sand-lot baseball as kids and dreamed of striking out Babe Ruth or hitting like Ted Williams. This is important among the ethnic groups in slum areas where boxing and baseball give Irish, Jewish, Italian, Polish, and Negro boys a greater chance at a career, and where a boy who has made good in the ring or at Big League ball becomes the focus of the role-playing of all the neighborhood youngsters. The street-corner gangs in the tough neighborhoods serve as training and recruiting grounds for pugilists, and boxing—and to some extent baseball and football—become not only ways of getting into the big money but also of channeling the emotional tensions of lower-status groups in the society. This is especially true of

Negro players who have finally been admitted into Big League baseball and the bowling tournaments but are still kept out of golf and tennis tournaments. Negro sports figures like Joe Louis and Jackie Robinson become not only national heroes but ethnic symbols of prowess and progress.

The point at which mass sports have violated the ingrained mores of the public is on the question of bribery. Americans have long been accustomed to the crookedness of the Yahoos of wrestling and have written it off as a serious sport. In the second decade of the century there were several scandals involving the "throwing" of games by bribed baseball players which led to a rigid supervision of the morals and public relations of the teams under Judge K. M. Landis as baseball "Czar." This system of internal policing enabled Big League baseball to survive and thrive. In the 1940s similar episodes developed in big-college basketball, with evidence that players had been bribed to rig games. Actually corruption of this kind is only marginal to the betting industries, which on the whole do best financially when the games are honest. But what is not marginal is the fact that even where everything is "straight" the fun and excitement of sports have been largely crowded out by commercialism. The capital investments not only in Big League professionalism but even in the college stadiums, the clinking of gate receipts, the noise the totalizers make, have all become too insistent to be ignored.

A realistic sports writer, hearing for the thousandth time about the "clean ideals" and "manly virtues" of sports, will reflect that even in the colleges the rhetoric of amateurism has given way under the steady pressures of "big-time" spectator performances. President Hutchins made a sardonic guess that his quarter-century tenure as head of the University of Chicago would be remembered chiefly by the fact that he banned college football. A number of colleges have a structure of hidden subsidies for recruiting their football players and maintaining and tutoring them while at college. When one former college president, Dexter Keezer of Reed, ironically proposed that the college convert the hidden subsidies into open ones and hire the best football team it could get, paying the players as well as the coaches, he was taken seriously and swamped by applications. There is a logical progression from these subsidies to the game-throwing episodes: if you are furtively recruited and bribed to play well, it is only a step to being bribed to play badly. What is striking is not that so many but that so few young Americans succumb. This is a tribute to the hold that amateur sports still have on the imagination of the young. After the pattern of Ring Lardner's biting short stories, the baseball player has been depicted in fiction chiefly as a zoological specimen whose brawn exceeds his intellect. What is more impressive, however, is the degree to which the player becomes emotionally involved in his pursuit, so that a loose collection of raw-bound young men is forged into a smoothly functioning team unit.

Moralists and psychologists have made too much of the passivity of spectator sports. America has been treated by them a little like a "condemned playground," doomed as Roman culture was doomed by the mass pursuit of pleasure for its own sake and by its passive spectator role. True, the people in modern societies preferred to seek external entertainment rather than to explore their inner resources. True also, the cult of American sports may delay maturity, keeping many of its devotees frozen as eternal juveniles. But there are few parallels in history to an American culture which was presented overnight with the gift of leisure, not just to one class but to almost the entire culture. Americans have found in sports a set of loyalties that in past cultures have been linked with more destructive pursuits. They have also found in it a kind of substitute for an urban culture's loss of relation to the natural environment.

One may argue, as Plato did, that the youth of any society carries on in its civic life the modes of behavior it learns in its sports. In that sense Americans have come to view politics and war as games after the image of competitive sports. The image of the team whose players work together under a captain or quarterback has been carried over into the popular thinking. One may assert, on the other hand, with Aristotle, that the real function of sports is not emulative but purgative. It is a familiar theory that spectator sports strengthen American democracy by serving as a safety valve for tensions and emotions that might otherwise have broken into flames of violence.

Beyond these theories is the fact that American sports express the energies of the culture as a whole and the will-to-youthfulness of its people. Sometimes this takes ugly forms of expression, as with bullying and bottle-tossing fans. Sometimes it is expressed in a manic ferocity, as with Branch Rickey's description of the ideal ballplayer as one who "will break both your legs if you happen to be standing in his path to second base." Again it may take on the tinny values of the box office or the press agents. Sometimes it gets mixed up with gamblers, racketeers, and crooks, or with the fake heroics of what has been called the "grunt-and-groan business" in wrestling. Yet spectator sports are saved by a cultural vitality which both audience and players express.

The most hopeful fact about American sports is that they have reached their saturation point as passive spectacles, and that their growing point is now in the area of amateur participant sports. In sports, as also in writing, painting, photography, theater, carpentry, crafts, cooking, and dressmaking, America is becoming a nation of amateurs. The recruits for Rose Bowl football and for Big League baseball are taken from the sand-lot ball games of the kids and the skeleton football scrimmages at school and on the city streets. In the social climate of the mass sports, young Americans wrestle, race, swim, fight with their fists; in many localities high-school basketball has become a community passion. But beyond this recruiting base that the culture gives the spectator sports, there is also a new emphasis on direct participation of adults in forms of organized play and fun. The new leisure has made the beaches swarm with swimmers and sun worshipers; in winter the ski trains carry middle-class groups who never before had taken part in winter sports; golf has been largely transferred from the private links to municipal courses which make it available to almost any income group; with the automobile to transport them to formerly inaccessible streams, fishing has become possible for many new millions; in terms of the numbers engaged, bowling has become the top American national sport, reaching into the factory and offices of the corporations, each of which has bowling teams belonging to the industrial bowling leagues.

This has given sports amateurism a new meaning, broader than the earlier sense which made an amateur a steady contestant who could afford not to sell his services. Amateurism in this older meaning has been declining rather than increasing in the commercial context of big American sports. The true amateurs have become the men and women who pursue sports in their leisure because they love them and find in them new accessions of experience and a play of bodily skills which the machine culture fails to use. This may bring a psychic fulfillment more far-reaching than is involved in the theory of the spectator sports as a safety valve for tensions and frustrations. A people that finds an expressiveness at play too often denied on the job is less likely to be capturable by mass emotions. Thus the growth of sports amateurism acts as a counterforce to the more synthetic entertainments and hero worship engendered by the spectacle sports.

It is probably true that Americans will never develop in their sports the kind of ritual meaning and religious symbolism that makes the bullfight in Spanish cultures express the tragic meaning of life. The genius of American sports is a different one. It expresses exuberant energies rather than a killer instinct or a death obsession. It is suited to a people who feel that careers are open for skill and resourcefulness, and that life with its unlimited possibilities yields both the big prizes to the professional and a quieter satisfaction to the amateur.

5. Dream and Myth in the Movies

NEVER IN HISTORY has so great an industry as the movies been so nakedly and directly built out of the dreams of a people. Any hour of the day or the evening you can go into a darkened theater (the darkness is in itself like a dream withdrawal) and as the figures move across the wide screen you sail off on storm-tossed seas of sex, action, and violence, crime and death. The "super-colossal" is at your disposal. The loveliest girls (voluptuously feminine), the most "romantic" men (blatantly masculine), the most stylish clothes, the shapeliest legs and most prominent bosoms—these are yours with an explicitness that leaves nothing subtle to be supplied. When you come home to sleep, your dreams are woven around the symbols which themselves have been woven out of your dreams, for the movies are the stuff American dreams are made of.

New standards of living and taste have leveled up the masses and leveled down the elite into a vast movie-going audience that is more complex emotionally than the movie makers suspect, but homogeneous enough to serve as an abstract "average man" in their calculations. This audience has the thin taste of experience that marks the new American middle classes. They go to the movies not so much to get a compensation for what they have lost emotionally as to get a surrogate for what they have not yet achieved but know to be possible in their world. Thus, the movies are dreams but not necessarily "escape" dreams; they may also be ambition-and-attainment dreams. It is impossible that a people should reach for new living standards without at the same time reaching for new emotional experiences.

The trouble is that emotional richness and depth cannot be attained mechanically, especially in a civilization dominated by the practical and the pecuniary. You cannot distribute it as you might distribute Pepsi-Cola, the electric light, radio, comic books, or universal suffrage. The thirst for it is there, and when thousands of screens offer to slake the thirst the people are receptive. But they are not "escaping" from anything; they are reaching out. By their essential technique the movies make this possible: the camera picks out for the audience the elements of a scene, getting its emotional effects by selection and sequence of shots and by their pace and rhythm as they unfold a story; it can weave together past and present, annihilate time and bridge space; by varying "close-ups" with long shots, by showing the individual face and framing the total scene, it builds up tension and evokes a continuous flow of absorption; it reaches to the instinctual in man, cutting across nations and cultures; it appeals to the emotional and imaginative elements in our make-up as no other popular art has ever done.

This is what makes the movies a crucial American popular art, although in economic terms the industry is slipping. The press is stronger in shaping attitudes, the radio in reaching more people more quickly, TV in bringing a more varied world into their homes. But because they alone deal in a sustained way with dreams and fables, the movies maintain their role in America. If TV is to displace them it must first take over this dream function they possess.

The movies started as a peep show in the Edison slot machines that were housed in penny arcades. They shifted to the status of lantern slides in illustrated lectures, and finally won an independent audience in telling a connected story with the "nickel madness" of the "nickelodeons" that swept America in the first decade of the century. The Founding Fathers of the new industry were men who, by an historical accident, came mainly out of the clothing industry of the Eastern cities, largely Jews of lower-middle-class virtues and energies, intent on success and wealth. Almost at its start the new medium brought into the studio the central figure of the great directors, like D. W. Griffith, and a technical inventiveness which included the resourceful use of the camera and lighting, the crucial "close-up" bringing the actor into immediate relation with the audience, and the technique of film cutting, enabling the director to shoot his picture out of sequence and then put it together as a writer might put a novel together with structure and flow and climax.

From the start the pace of innovation in the movies was exacting. The crude early sentimental "drama" was converted into a full-length "feature," the one-reel thriller became the double-feature evening's entertainment, the slapstick comedy grew more subtle, the "star" system was introduced, with actors and actresses who became popular idols, the silent movies were revolutionized with sound, an elaborate system of distributors and exhibitors was developed, color was introduced, and under the spur of TV rivalry the movies turned to three-dimensional gadgets and the wide screen. At each stage the movie makers were obsessed with a sense of crisis, and—once successful—each step brought with it an elation which in turn gave way to another depth of despair. The movies have thus in their brief history had an almost manic-depressive succession of emotional states, feeding on the pressure of technological change and on the need to outdistance the competing big media, feeling the audience pulse, taking the temperature of an often hostile public which regards Hollywood as the seat of Satan.

What Justice Brandeis called "the curse of bigness" afflicted the movies as it afflicted the other big media. Since the industrial problem in the movies was largely one of distribution, the bigness showed itself mainly in getting control of the theater outlets. The first big "film exchange" was dissolved by the Federal courts in 1915. In the 1920s the producing companies achieved control of the theater chains and in turn became "integrated" with the manufacturers of sound equipment and the big banking houses who could find capital for the pictures which poured out inexorably at steep production costs. The Federal courts again stepped in to effect a degree of separation of the producers from the theater chains and to ban "block booking." Yet the movies differ from the press and radio industries since they do not pose primarily a problem of monopoly and its control. Although the giant producers have dominated the industry, the competitive struggle between them has been genuine, and there has always been a chance for the rise of "independents" and recently for the competition of foreign-made films.

The problem of the movies is not the power of the producers nor the silencing of competing voices, but the content and emotional level of the product. This in turn is linked with the quest for profits and the evaluation of the tastes and demands of the audience. The makers of the movies may consider them an art form, but even when they do, they think of it as an art that must be mediated through an industry that produces and sells a commodity. Whatever their origin, the movies have become one of the nation's biggest industries, with high salaries for producers, directors and stars, with experts for production, processing, distributing, selling, advertising and promotion, with a network of theater outlets reaching into city and village, and with a huge apparatus for exporting American movies to every corner of the globe.

The aim of the movie makers, as in other industries, is to make a profit on their investment. When a first-rate movie, *The Treasure of the Sierra Madre,* got an Academy Award but failed to gross even half of what a Betty Grable picture achieved, its producer said decisively, "From now on, art is out." There are undoubtedly some producers and directors who think in terms of exacting art standards. But when they do, the clinching argument they use for their view is that good art pays off. When good movies are produced—and an impressive number of them have been—the masters of the industry must be convinced that they will pay off, and enough of them must do so before the directors are allowed to attempt others. The great Hollywood problem is to integrate money-making with creativeness: where the process of integration seems silly to the greedy, or difficult to the lazy, or beyond the reach of the uncreative, money-making stands alone and unashamed as a motive.

Despite the glamour that attaches to the stars, there is a deadly assembly-line monotony about Hollywood. The qualities of the industrial process in Hollywood are the qualities of any big American industry: machine-tool technology, division of labor, mass production, bureaucracy, hierarchy. The work is infinitely subdivided, specialized and mechanized as far as one can mechanize a process where the basic material is not molten iron and rivets and sheet steel but human beings and the pantomime and inflections of human emotions. The mechanization extends even to the writing of most scripts—galling as that may seem to writers who are attracted by Hollywood prizes but outraged by the Hollywood methods that put the prizes within their reach. For the original novel or play must be "licked"—that is to say, revamped and sometimes butchered to fit it to the demands of the screen and its market. It must be reworked by many hands until it contains the exactly right formula ingredients. The scenes must be broken into manageable units, each of them acted and re-enacted until it suits the director's taste, then cut and fitted together into the final product, embellished, embossed, labeled, and packaged. This is the process that gives the Hollywood movie the qualities for which it is noted—the precision, the attention to detail, the assembly-line smoothness, the pace, the feel of collaborative effort under a central direction, the gloss, the sensuousness—and the sameness.

Given this setup, it is not surprising that the principal creativeness emerging from Hollywood is that of the director (sometimes the director-producer). He is the interweaver, manipulator, and synthesizer of everything else. I am thinking of men like Kazan, Huston, Zinnemann, Stevens, Mankiewicz, Wyler, among the directors, and among the producers men like Thalberg, Goldwyn, Schary, and Zanuck. The director, himself doing none of the specialized work, stands outside the process yet somehow at the center of it. He pulls together the strands of what others have done, keeping in mind the mood and effect he is aiming at. He makes the decisions on theme and story, scope, expense, actors, treatment, pace, mood, emotional quality. He must assess the drawing power and staying power of the "stars" and take care of their temperaments, love affairs, and marital headaches. He must tangle with the censorship, determine the strategy of promotion, watch the publicity. The producer-director is the general who, unlike Kutuzov in *War and Peace,* genuinely believes that his generalship shapes the outcome of the battle. Scott Fitzgerald saw this when he wrote his novel about Hollywood, *The Last Tycoon,* and chose as his central character Monroe Stahr, a director-producer cast in the mold of Irving Thalberg.

This line-and-staff hierarchy of Hollywood, with its pyramiding of power and its constriction of creativeness for most of the people in-

volved, represents the greatest weakness of the Hollywood system. Fitzgerald's study of Stahr is on heroic lines: he invested the movie mogul
with a Napoleonic imagination and with a half-lyrical, half-theatrical
amatory life. He had a feeling of pity for Stahr, showing him caught
between labor troubles and financial conspiracies, yet he gave him a
touch of nobility as well as the grand manner. But Fitzgerald failed to
show the curious quality of Hollywood as a way of life, built Versailles-
fashion around a set of *grands monarques*, each surrounded by cour-
tiers, jesters, parasites, and favorites—a court where men rise by predacity and live in fear, half harem and half jungle. Hollywood in
this aspect is more nakedly shown in Budd Schulberg's *What Makes
Sammy Run?* and in Nathanael West's *The Day of the Locust*, whose
George Grosz portrait was, however, meant to apply more to the movie
audience than to the movie makers.

The pictures these men make tend to run in "cycles," for Hollywood
—being attuned to shifting audience moods as sensitively as a stylish
American woman is attuned to the changes in fashion—is a place where
successes and failures are contagious. The producers are anxious to
cash in on the winds and moods of the current taste, using always the
test of what has made a killing for others. Thus there was a gangster
cycle, an anti-Nazi cycle, a G-Man cycle, a Negro and Jewish antiracist
cycle, a cycle of sophisticated "Westerns," a war action cycle, an anti-
Communist cycle, a cycle of big Biblical panoramas, a musical-comedy
cycle, a cycle of "problem" movies on juvenile delinquency and dope
addiction. The idea men tap a vein of public response, and the imitators rush in to exploit it until the ore runs thin. Recently the emphasis
has come to rest on the musical and the spectacle. Both are safe, both
nonpolitical, both appeal to the young audience that frequents the
movie houses. Girls' legs, battle scenes, catchy tunes, dream-ballet se-
quences, Samson and Delilah, and the decadent days of the Roman or
Egyptian empires are material on which it is hard to go wrong.

Recently the impact of high taxes has led to a reversal of the trend
toward concentration in movie making. A number of new producing
units have emerged, built around one or several movie stars or a talented director. But the economics of the movie industry put pressure
on reducing the number of pictures and making only the "big" ones.
A picture must now reach into small cities as well as large ones, which
means that there must be a heavy concentration on advertising and
promotion. Thus the "middle bracket" pictures are being squeezed
out, and the studios operate increasingly on the "jackpot theory"—
either you hit the jackpot or you take a loss. The low-budget pictures,
the "sleepers," and the modest experiments of the independents still

have scope—enough, at any rate, to show that a movie addressed to emotionally mature men and women may also bring in profits.

The movie industry is at its best in its technical skill. Lighting and sound, cutting and editing, the building of sets—all of these command admiration. Wherever Hollywood offers a chance to do an honest job, it can be fulfilling. Every few years some team of youngsters shows up in Hollywood with an idea of how to make good low-cost pictures and brush aside the cluttering idols. But in time the young man who came with a fire in his belly comes under the spell of the practical men and grows accustomed to astronomical figures and comfortable living. He gets cut off from the original sources of his strength and ends by offering sacrifices to the fire in the belly of the Moloch of success.

Like other forms of American popular culture, Hollywood is a little world in itself—a subculture of the larger society, but with marked mirror distortions. It has strata of prestige and power, narrowing to a small top group who sit at the peak of the pyramid. They are the studio executives in charge of production. A mass of legendry clings to each of them, and what passes for conversation in Hollywood is likely to be anecdotes, gossip, and malice about them. Their royal position casts a deep shadow on Hollywood, for independent critical judgment is impossible where the employee must also be a courtier. A Hollywood "big shot" is surrounded by yes-men whose function is to give Number One the heady sense of being right. Where one man has the power of life and death there can be none of that responsibility which must mean taking risks in order to make independent choices. No one feels secure in his tenure—not even the top executives, who fear the intrigues of their rivals and the power of the bankers, and these in turn fear the whims and hostility of the movie audience.

The final decisions that affect creativeness are made in the "front office," with an eye on picture budgets that may run into millions of dollars. Everyone connected with a picture, including the director and script writers, knows that two or three million dollars may be at stake: as a result, no one takes risks with ideas, theme, treatment. The phrase "venture capital" has an ironic meaning when applied to Hollywood: since the capital being ventured is big, nothing else can be ventured. This is the nub of Hollywood's timidity. And timidity joins with bureaucracy and the money yardstick to form Hollywood's deadly trinity.

The movie colony is always in feverish motion, always coming up with "terrific" ideas for "colossal" successes; yet for all its febrile quality, it is always in danger of becoming stagnant. It isn't a metropolis, yet it feels too important to be content with the life of a small town

—nor could it even if it wished, since it is torn away from all the normal activities of a town. Thus Hollywood is one of the loneliest places in the world. The Communists were able to exploit this loneliness in the 1930s and early 1940s by offering the young writers and actors a continuous courtship and a cause to hang their hearts on.

To create what it does Hollywood has to draw young people, often of unstable temperament, from all over the world. It plunges them into exacting work, surrounds them with a sensuous life, pays them fantastic salaries, makes them truckle to their bosses or smothers them with the flattery of their hangers-on, cuts them off from the sources of normal living. Thus the men and women who manufacture dreams for other Americans find that there are few they can snare for themselves. The Hollywood heartbreak is of two kinds: that of not getting where you want to get; and that of finding, when you have got it, that it was not worth wanting. Gilbert Seldes hit it right when he spoke of the "high potential capacity for disaster" in Hollywood.

The most publicized and glamorized figure in Hollywood is, of course, the star. Few stars have more than mediocre acting ability. They are rather heroes and heroines—men and women who by their native endowment of figure, stature, and looks, some trick of grace or radiancy of personality, or by benefit of cosmeticians and publicity "build-up," have become the dream image of movie-goers. Among the icons in Hollywood have been Pola Negri, Mary Pickford, Rudolph Valentino, Douglas Fairbanks, Jean Harlow, Carole Lombard, Clark Gable, Humphrey Bogart, Rita Hayworth, Marlon Brando, Marilyn Monroe—and, of course, the greatest of all, Chaplin and Garbo. Below them in the hierarchy are the minor stars, the temporary "rages" who last for only a few seasons, the "starlets," the hopefuls. The radiance that invests a star has come to invest the whole of Hollywood with a career dream atmosphere for millions of young Americans.

The justification sometimes made of the star system is that the movies are not theater, and that the great movie figures may know how to act but they don't have to know, since the character each creates is not something out of a script but himself: it is with him, and not with the character he portrays, that the audience identifies itself. There is truth in this, and it applies equally to the clowns and heroes of radio and TV who enter familiarly into the American home. What the movie screen adds, with its annihilation of time, its illusions of space, and its selective weaving of dreams, is an emotional identification through the star with those dreams and with the magical world spun out of them. This gives the star system its hold on the audience—and on the star too, since it is a heady wine of adulation he drinks. One must add, however, that the younger Hollywood stars are not content to be symbols: a number of them have found on the Broadway stage the kind of craft satisfaction which the studios have failed to offer them, and some have preferred miniscule salaries on or off Broadway to the fleshpots of Sunset Boulevard. A number of them have been trained in the Actors Studio, have thought a good deal about acting, and care about the suffrage of their fellows and the critics even more than they do about their popular image. The greatest of the stars, like Chaplin and Garbo, or even Muni, Fredric March, or Edward G. Robinson, have also been good actors, although Garbo carried with her always the fringes of failure and was always promising more than she achieved. An illustration of how hungry the public is for a Hollywood image to worship may be found in the curious cult that developed after his death around James Dean (as it developed once around Valentino), although Dean starred in only three pictures before he was killed in a racing car on the California roads. With a wild but still unformed talent, he was a searching, puzzled, unhappy boy: his meteoric rise and his death were a life symbol, phoenix-wise, for many young Americans who shared his frustrations as well as his dreams.

But the prizes are few and most of those who are drawn to Hollywood and do not drift home again remain to work as "extras" on the Hollywood sets, or as waitresses or soda clerks or hat-check girls—in the hope that someday the lightning may strike. However foolish their dreams may seem they are not wholly foolish, for the movie arts are among the few remaining areas of American industry where talent can reach for the big money without a heavy prior investment. Yet this fact makes the competition ruthless: nothing is more pathetic than a fading star, like a faded mistress, striving to hold attention by ingenious wile and seductiveness. The Hollywood constellation is like a crowded streetcar, and every time a new luminary pushes its way on board it pushes a declining one off.

This may explain why Hollywood, with a tiny fraction of the nation's population, supports a large percentage of the nation's psychoanalysts. The sense of personal frustration along with public success takes its toll, especially among the actors and writers. The whole atmosphere is that of demonstrative sex. Bent on careers, some of them use their looks and magnetism as a way of getting a start, while the power men are ready to offer a chance at success in return for favors. Simone de Beauvoir's *The Second Sex* uses the Hollywood actress as the prime contemporary example of the hetaira. The American people, many of whom regard the movie colony as the Jezebel of America, eagerly consume the newspaper headlines about Hollywood divorces, suicides, marijuana parties, drinking, and premarital sex relations. In his survey of the social structure of Hollywood, Leo Rosten showed that while the Hollywood divorce rate is probably higher than the American average, the gap is not great. The public-relations men, who hover over their charges like male governesses, are anxious to play them up as spotless Sunday-school characters with every private and civic virtue. They err in this effort: the attraction that the Hollywood heroes have for movie-goers is not that of small-town Catos and Brutuses but that of flesh-and-blood men and women whose lives outwardly match the glossy lives on the screen.

There is obviously a strong relation between the themes of the American movies and the psychological drives in American life. Certainly the masters of Hollywood have tried to probe into the American personality pattern, playing up whatever gets a deep response. Unfortunately, while they mirror well the life values of the culture, they present them often with only a surface fidelity and repeatedly fall into stereotypes which can appeal only to the immature. All the traits of the culture are there in the movies, but dressed up, foreshortened, softened up, made more contrived by indirections and glossiness.

To start with, of course, the movies mirror the value and power of money. "There was money in her voice," said Scott Fitzgerald, and money continues to speak through most of the Hollywood products. There is money in Hollywood's voice, in the way the camera dwells on surfaces and textures. There is money in the lavish settings, whether of estate or hotel or penthouse suite: every picture says dutifully and explicitly that money is not everything, that money (in fact) doesn't count, that love and self-respect and happiness are better than money; but every picture continues to say implicitly, by all the things it takes for granted and by its own example, that nothing really counts quite as much as money.

As for sex, what the movies express (as Gilbert Seldes documented it) is not sex or love but sexiness. In formal terms an elaborate contrivance of self-censorship, called "The Code," bans the exposure of too large a surface of the female breast, or a male and female embrace in a horizontal posture. Yet obviously there is ample leeway for blatant sexiness set against provocative backdrops, or subtle sexiness encased in the silkiest adornments. Sometimes the battle of the censorship makes the producer ingenious in suggesting more than the picture seems to say, and inventive in seeing what he can get away with. The movies rarely express the passionate attraction of mature people for each other, such as may be found in some of the foreign films. This would be difficult in a Hollywood product, extramarital liaisons being forbidden on the screen. Since movie characters cannot be caught in any strong passion, since they have babies only for humorous effect, since divorces cannot be carried through and cannot be shown as having a valid base, since marital difficulties cannot be described in the full-blooded terms of people grappling with the genuine problems of a marriage, the result is that life is presented as a series of pretend entanglements which are resolved by pretend solutions, both of them applying to people whose lives are drained of emotional meaning.

In the absence of three-dimensional figures with strong emotions, the movies must turn to action as substitute. The movies do move fast. The art of cutting sees to it that each scene slips into the next and there is never a pause for contemplation. Things must be happening all the time—threats, quarrels, dangers, traps, narrow escapes, flights, reconciliations, falling in love, misunderstandings, courtroom scenes, gun battles, mob scenes, barroom brawls, escapes from moving trains, shipwrecks, death in the skies, automobile chases, the discovery of unexpected corpses, conspiracies, skulduggery, the confusing and unmasking of identities, deathbed confessions, the triumph of virtue. Rarely do they offer an internal exploration, and then it may be the tracing out of a split personality in connection with some mystery thriller. The American conquers as a man of action, he puts his faith in action, and he expects action in his movies.

To these ingredients must be added violence. It may be that the movies reflect the strain of interior violence and tension in the culture, yet it is grotesquely inflated. When genuine love and sexuality are crowded out of any literary or dramatic production, whether by censorship or timidity, violence comes in to fill the vacuum. Where there is no mature expression of the relation between the sexes, the "battle of the sexes" is presented in a bantering way, with strong overtones of masculine dominance. The earlier movies had treated women mainly as prize and idol, as temptress and siren. A landmark in the history of the movies came in the classic episode in *Public Enemy* when James Cagney pushed a grapefruit into the face of his girl. It was greeted as the reassertion of manly power in a society beset by female values. The violence theme also finds other outlets—the tyranny of a hard parent, a sadistic jail warden or ship captain, a gangland leader.

The strain of violence is reinforced by the toughness of the detective-hero in the crime and mystery thrillers, where the girl—although spoiled and sophisticated at the start—recognizes his strength in the end. The ingredients of the murder thriller, as of the racketeer or prize-fight movie, are slickness, pace, fast dialogue, and continuous violence. The movie detective does not have to be a mastermind. His story has become that of a hard-boiled Tom Jones who is no great shakes as a detector but who shows he can take whatever punishment is in store for him. Even his ordeals are physical rather than psychological. He meets with a succession of adventures that crowd in breathlessly, he is warned but persists, he is ambushed, slugged, kicked, tortured, given up for dead, he endures all with fortitude, and in the end he gets his man and—in another sense—gets his girl. His story is a picaresque of death. In the course of his adventures he discovers or creates as many as a half dozen corpses. Every death is an unevocative event—an item rather than a tragedy. It has neither psychic roots nor psychic consequences, just as the crimes themselves have no moral roots or consequences. This pervasive violence, with its need for ever stronger stimulation to produce a "thrill," may be a portent of the desensitizing of the society itself.

Wolfenstein and Leites, in their *Movies: A Psychological Study,* did a content-analysis by searching out not the overt but the covert meanings of American movies, not what was manifest in them but what was psychologically latent. While this can be stretched to the point of burlesque, it does rest on the sound proposition that the important relation of the movies is to the daydreams and the fantasy world of Americans. The producer may guess only blunderingly at these daydreams and is severely limited by censorship and his own timidity, so that the pattern that emerges may not represent his considered judgment of what the audience is like. He may not be knowing or cynical, but only a man who wants to make a lot of movies and a lot of money, and is deeply troubled—as David Selznick was—because the movie critics approach films as an art form. To succeed, Selznick argued, a movie producer must aim not only at the "common denominator" of the people but at their "lowest common denominator."

This does not mean that the movie industry has not produced some great pictures. Actually it is the only one of the American popular arts which has thus far built up a heritage of great artistic products to leave to future generations. One may include among these classics such diverse pictures as Griffith's *The Birth of a Nation,* Chaplin's *City Lights, Monsieur Verdoux,* and *The Gold Rush,* the Westerns like *High Noon* and *Bad Day at Black Rock,* comedies like *Born Yesterday, It Happened One Night,* and *Nothing Sacred,* detective mysteries like *The Thin Man,* and *The Maltese Falcon,* murder stories like *Double Indemnity,* gangster pictures like *Public Enemy* and *Earl of Chicago,* terror movies like *Night Must Fall,* documentary pictures of urban life like *The Asphalt Jungle,* war pictures like *Hell's Angels* and *The Red*

Badge of Courage, social documentaries like *Home of the Brave, The Men, Not as a Stranger,* and *The Wild One,* movies of character and adventure like *The Treasure of Sierra Madre* and *The African Queen,* character studies like *The Informer* and *Citizen Kane.* The list could be greatly extended without lowering the quality of what it includes. And no list would be complete without the inclusion of the wonderfully inventive cartoon pictures of Walt Disney, one of the geniuses of the popular arts, who created a world of his own in his nature studies as well as his animated cartoons.

It is curious that a medium capable of such work should be confronted by the fact of a declining audience. Yet thousands of movie theaters have recently had to close up, and the audiences are heavily weighted toward those under thirty-five and especially adolescents. A number of critics put the blame on the movie products, saying that movie fare presented on a higher intellectual and emotional level would tap an unreached audience of adult minds. David Riesman feels, however, that the older people may be staying away from the movies because they don't understand them and have not yet caught up with the younger ones who do. The argument is that recent changes in American society have changed the nuances of living together, bringing in new aspects of social experience which the movies express and which the young can grasp but the old must sweat for, since their minds are turned toward the past.

I agree that young Americans go to the movies not just to be amused but (more or less consciously) to get guidance in "interpersonal relations." But this only makes more urgent the question of what kind of guidance they get. It is hard not to conclude that the worlds of feeling and thought presented to them are imaginary worlds, using that phrase in the synthetic sense. There is little feeling for growth of personality and the painful groping for identity which the best novels give, and from which young Americans do get clues to their dilemmas. I suspect that the movies stereotype not only the solutions but even the problems, and that the young people who see them get even their dilemmas from them. In time such a process could result in real emotional matching of movies and audience, but it would be one in which the audience had been first corrupted and conditioned into such a matching.

The validity of Hollywood's view of man's nature and man's fate would not be so important if it did not rule an imperial domain. What Hollywood does, and how, becomes a way of life for millions throughout the world. Hollywood produces, distributes, exports, more than pictures. People take their philosophy, their clothes style, their manners, their walk, their talk, their worldly wisdom, from the pictures they see and the Hollywood fan magazines and gossip columns they read. For the movie fan, what is called the "entertainment" value of the movies is an inextricable mixture of magic, mores, and morals. The lavishness which is meant to dazzle him remains to guide him. The action and power that are meant to thrill him remain to set his tempo. The sexual glamour that is meant to lure him remains to embellish his dreams. The violence that is meant to give him "a wallop" remains to desensitize him.

There have been great movies and movie directors, as I have noted above, who have gone against the grain and tried for different values. I hold firm to my belief that the movies as art form—despite the cynicism of some of the Hollywood businessmen—have achieved a far higher level than any of the other American big-audience media. My criticism of the movie makers is based on the gap between the reality and the potential. However great this gap is in the case of the movies, it is a good deal greater—as we shall see—in the case of the popular arts of radio and TV.

6. Radio and TV: the World in the Home

IF THE MOVIES are the art of glamour and the dream, radio and TV are the arts of the home.* They make the world accessible to almost every American. By the twisting of a dial they also make him, alas, accessible to the masters of radio and TV. While the American family is strategically trapped in its living room, they make it the victim of soap operas, horse operas, crooners, comedians, husband-and-wife breakfast shows, quiz shows, big money give-away shows, audience participation shows, variety shows, housewives' chatter, news commentators, forums, sermons, political campaigners, hot jazz and disk jockeys—and, above all, commercials. The sights and sounds that come pouring in comprise what must be the weirdest mixture history has witnessed.

There is human and social meaning in this cacophony. Radio and television are more than a potpourri of entertainment. They form one of the great tying mechanisms of American culture, bringing every part of the nation together instantaneously. They are thus the crucial arts of communication since they focus the attention of millions on the same thing at the same time. Americans are lonely people. If they cannot have a community of collective effort, they can at least form a cohesive "unseen audience." And a standardized one too: for it listens

* I deal here primarily with radio and TV as popular arts. For a discussion of their relation to the shaping of opinion and belief, see Ch. X, Sec. 5, "Revolution in the Big Media."

to the same tunes, the same gags and jokes, the same advertising slogans, the same commercial jingles, the same variations of the same stale plots, the same hackneyed arguments. This standardization drives the intellectual and taste levels downward.

Radio and TV form a single broadcasting art whose common element is that both are forms of broadcasting from a central point of origin to millions of receiving sets which pick up the material with their antennae. Both of them also make use of the electronic vacuum tube as their basic means of transmission, instead of the printed word as in the case of the press or the camera image as in the case of the movies. The differences are that TV transmits to a screen, and that its techniques of broadcasting are more elaborate and expensive. Yet the continuity was maintained: the radio broadcasters generally became the entre-preneurs of TV, and the same homes that had radio sets added TV sets. In both cases there is no intermediary public exhibition, as with movies or spectator sports. And since they do not rely on the printed word, literacy is not essential to them as it is with newspapers, magazines, and the other reading media. Radio and TV, as broadcasting arts, can reach wherever the spoken language is understood by the ear and wherever the eye can grasp a picture. They are thus the arts of sight and sound and the images raised by the spoken word. In this sense they parallel the movies.

But what they add, in the form of the electronic tube, makes it possible for the radio listeners and TV viewers to get their entertainment without ever stirring from their homes. Moreover, they get a highly diversified bill of fare, so they need never stay committed to one program or station but move as taste-shoppers and dial-turners over a number of available shows and arts, including movies, theater, musical comedy, vaudeville, dance, jazz, and sports. Thus in a sense radio and TV became the synthesizers of all the popular arts. They bring the world to the home, wrapped up in a single gleaming febrile package whose contents change magically and continuously on the quarter and half hour.

The early development of the radio belongs to the decade of the 1920s, when it was a boom industry in a boom decade. Radio first burst upon the nation when it transmitted the results of the Harding election in 1920; it reached its first climax of popular acceptance in the *Amos and Andy* show in the late 1920s. In its first phase the programs were broadcast as a public service, without advertising sponsorship and with an eye mainly to profits for the equipment companies from the sale of sets. In the next phase, the late 1920s and early 1930s, advertising came to stay as the principal source of revenue, and the same centralizing force which operated in the other media brought the big broadcasting chains into radio. Because of the limited number of available frequencies for radio and of channels for TV, this centralizing force has had a physical basis as well as an economic one. By 1934, when the Federal Communications Commission was established, the three big features of broadcasting—private enterprise, advertising sponsorship, and public regulation within broad limits—had become accepted. After that, Frequency Modulation (FM) seemed a revolutionary development that promised to give a clearer reception and make more frequencies and stations available, and was hailed as "radio's second chance." But it proved (as Trevelyan remarked about the 1848 revolution) a turning point at which history failed to turn, and it was taken over by the established networks. The two later technical revolutions, however—TV and color—proved to be genuinely revolutionary.

Unlike radio at its start, TV came into being when the principles of private ownership, advertising sponsorship, and government regulation were already accepted. Its original impulsion came from the radio broadcasters, aware that TV would cut into the radio listening audience and might even displace it, but forced to make heavy investments in their own executioner. Each chain took part in this technological race because it was anxious not to be isolated by a forced march its rival might make, and wanted to occupy the strategic high ground from which it could command the whole terrain of the popular media. The struggle between the two major networks over color television illustrated how big corporations in the big media find themselves compelled to create the obsolescence of their own plant and equipment—a compulsion through which the broadcasting media move ahead technologically to new revolutionary changes. In the process the other big media found their audience diminished, but after TV sets had their initial effect in cutting down reading, movie-going, and radio listening, the truants tended to return. The net result was the accession of a new audience to the new popular art and an increase in the total audience for all the media that TV synthesized and popularized.

There is a unique situation in broadcasting that determines who shall control the programs. One may speak of a Big Four who dominate the industry and the art: the broadcasting stations and chains, the equipment companies selling sets, the advertising sponsors, and the audience. Between them there is a chain of relation which runs somewhat as follows: when more radio and TV sets are sold, there is a profit to the equipment companies and also an increase in the audience; with a larger audience there is more for the broadcasters to sell to the advertising sponsors of the shows, which means a greater profit to both; with more money available, bigger and better programs are possible; as the offerings grow in coverage (witness the Presidential conventions or the Congressional hearings) a new audience is won, creating in turn a greater demand for radio and TV sets—and the chain reaction starts again.

This dramatizes how central the relation is between audience and advertiser. Since radio and TV are arts of the home, no admission price is charged, although in the mid-1950s the idea of a subscription radio system and of phone television was broached and debated. Business must thus levy its tax at another point. It does so through advertising. The broadcasters have chosen to take the subsidy largely on the advertiser's terms, giving him control not only over his advertising time and commercials but over the nature and even the content of the program. This was a fateful choice and an avoidable one. As a result the broadcasters not only sell advertising time but sell the audience as well —and themselves.

By that fact they have altered the axis of emphasis. In the case of the movies and press the content of picture or paper is the product of men who are themselves primarily craftsmen even while they are producing a product for sale and profit. In the case of radio and TV the content is chosen and tailored by a group of businessmen (generally advertising and sales agents) in order to *sell another product.* In their own circles their effectiveness is not judged by the artistic merit of their program. Their concern is to keep the largest audience tuned in, to lure them away from other programs advertising other products, to annoy as few as possible and outrage none, to make few experiments, to take little risk. They are judged not by the merit of the program but by its "rating." It is this "rating" that is sold to the advertiser-sponsor. In the case of a movie, the product must be entertaining enough so that the movie-goer will pay to see it. In the case of radio and TV it must catch audiences that will watch it for nothing, so that the station can sell the program to the advertiser, who buys it to sell soap, soup, razor blades, cigarettes, cosmetics, beer, refrigerators, or cars to the listener.

The listener, who is the potential buyer of these products, is not the buyer of the shows: *it is he who is being sold.* So long as he can be delivered to the advertiser, it matters little what the program does to his taste and values. This is the art of the market place brought into the living room. It is entertainment not as art but as advertising.

This gives meaning to the commercial—a sales talk, unctuous, hyperbolic, and persistent, which flanks the program and breaks into it, is usually delivered in a tense and feverish tone and is itself punctuated and capped by a slogan. When the slogan is a jingle, the result is a "singing commercial" which is turned out by highly sophisticated specialists but itself often becomes part of the musical folklore of the culture. Thus the advertiser succeeds beyond his wildest dreams in getting his product into the subconscious of his audience. There are many who are depressed by the chatty ladies selling gadgets, lotions, and household appliances in between their discourses on books and world affairs, or their interviews with famous people. But there are others for whom the agony of having to hear the commercials, as the admission price for the program, becomes a form of torture, like the drilling of a nerve. The most terrifying form of the commercial is the agency man especially detailed to do the "hard sell" or the "relaxed sell"—a long solo performance on the merits of his product, with demonstrations of its use and enjoyment. During the sales talk, there are animated cartoons on TV: as Thomas Whiteside described them, a "panorama of flying beer bottles, zooming candy bars, exploding containers of breakfast foods, singing cough drops, and animated coffee cups." The great innovation that Disney started in the movies has ended in TV advertising. If everything in the "relaxed sell" is smiling unction, everything in the accompanying cartoon seems to be bursting with an explosive purposiveness. Even ex-President Herbert Hoover, not notable for his anti-commercialism, found the commercials intolerable. To deal with this "periodic interruption of huckster chatter," Hoover proposed the invention of "a push button by which we could transmit our emotions instantly to the broadcasters."

Despite this resistance of a portion of the audience, TV has revolutionized the marketing of goods in the American economy. For the first time, you not only hear about the product but see it and almost smell and taste it. Whether it is a washing machine, a kitchen range, beer, an automobile, or a baking powder, the advertiser has seen his dream come true—the dream of being able to demonstrate his product before millions of people with the powerful aid of cartoons, jingles, and rows upon rows of shapely legs.

The broadcasters tend to regard the commercial as a necessary evil, although M. W. Loewi, director of one of the TV networks, was candid enough to say that "we are selling TV short when entertainment is allowed to dominate the schedule to the exclusion of a sales message well presented." Loewi's appeal has a certain logical consistency. Since the advertiser buys not so much the "show" as an audience for the merits of the product, the commercial which is so widely regarded as an intruder on the entertainment is actually the intrusion of reality into a system of make-believe. That indeed is why it is resented, for we are always resentful when somebody breaks into our fantasy world. The commercial awakens the listener from his belief that the resources of the entertainment world are at his command without any cost on his part. Like Dr. Faustus, bemused at having been able to call up the beautiful body of Helen, he forgets about his bargain with Mephistopheles until that personage breaks in to exact his price in the form of the commercial.

To the sponsor the commercial is not marginal to the program but the thing itself: if anything, the rest of the program is marginal to it. In this spirit he decks out the commercial in all the frumpery he can buy, lavishing his best creative energies on it. He hires the brains of young men with an expensive college preparation who have ransacked literature and philosophy, psychology, and art in order to work for an advertising agency. These young men, febrile, conscience-stricken, torn, are the "hucksters." They form a lost Foreign Legion of desperate spirits who sell themselves for a term of years into a strange country to take part in fantastic drills and meaningless adventures. The psychic cost falls first of all on the program, since the emotional tone of the whole show is set by the commercial and the men responsible for it. It is hard for either script writer or performer to slow down his pace or mute his tone when the hyperthyroidal extravagance of the advertising message permeates everything. It falls also on the whole culture, since a mass art in which everything is overvalued (as it has to be in the atmosphere of the constant radio advertising) cannot help communicating its contagion to the culture which feeds on it.

Added to this pervasive atmosphere of hyperbole there is the fact that the audience is both vulnerable and changeable. For any particular program the TV viewers are not a captive audience. There is always the chance that a competing program will lure them away by its more seductive promise of entertainment pleasure or thrills, and that the customer will flick his wrist and twist the dial to another channel. Important as it is throughout American culture, the element of time is crucial in the TV business. The researchers seem to have established that unless there is a strong counterattraction elsewhere, something like 60 per cent of the audience will stay on the same channel when the show is over, and where one "big" program follows another of the same type the legion of the loyal may be as high as 80 per cent. Hence the somewhat monotonous "back-to-back programming" of similar attractions, such as mysteries, giveaways, and comedies during the important evening hours. Along with this there is a fierce competitive effort to win away the audience from the other channels, in a wearing psychological warfare. The crucial minutes are those at the opening of a new time period: hence the tense, almost hysterical, opening gambit in any radio or TV show and the trip-hammer recurrence of intensity at crisis moments until the end.

Hence also the "rating" system which (highly unreliably) measures and remeasures on a continuing graph the size of the audience for each program. Related to this is the "research survey," where listening and viewing habits of an audience are studied in more intensive detail, and which is used to predict future trends in audience taste. The rating systems perform the function in the American media that the priests who consulted the oracles and omens performed in the Roman Empire—and by any rigorous standards of statistical technique their scientific validity is just about the same. Yet they determine whether a program shall survive or die, and a change of several points in the weekly rating may drive an agency executive to drink, ulcers, or suicide, or it may raise him to dizzying heights of joy from which the next week's drop may dash him to despair.

As for the TV programs themselves, they form a potpourri of everything the big media have developed. Here, as in the movies, there are cycles of taste that mark the birth and death of countless shows. There was a time when the discussion forum ranked high in radio, but it fell away in popular interest, and when it was transferred to TV it took on the more dramatic form of a "press conference" show, assimilating another of the big media. The news commentator is more at home on the radio than on TV, where the continued concentration on his face makes both the audience and him uneasy, and where he usually backs up his script with feverish picture clips from news photographs: easily the best of the news commentaries on TV has been *See It Now,* which relies heavily on an editing of specially prepared photographic shots around a single subject. It was on this show that Edward Murrow presented his version of McCarthyism in action—the most important single program in the history of TV thus far.

The panel of experts, which flourished on radio in the form of "quiz" programs, was transformed on TV into games where the "experts" try to unravel riddles whose solution is already known to the audience: the panels quickly hardened into a formula, usually with a moderator and four panel members, carefully distributed among glamour, wit, and celebrities. One of the ideas that swept the media for a time was the "audience participation" show, part quiz, part interview of members of the studio audience to heighten local interest and furnish a flavor of the common man. The most successful show on both media was the big "giveaway" for answering difficult factual questions:

when Louis Cowan dared to set the giveaway sum staggeringly high in his *$64,000 Question,* it broke through previous barriers and set a new level for munificence which had TV in a furor for a time—until other programs came along raising the sum even higher. Murder mysteries and crime thrillers were more successful on radio than on TV, since the concentration on the ear heightens the suspense; but TV took over the showing of mystery films as an effective ready-made substitute. Soap-opera dramas seemed equally at home in both media. The variety show, featuring an array of vaudeville talents built around the "big-name" radio comedian, came into even greater glory on TV: but in both media the comic talents of a Jerry Lewis or a Jimmy Durante, depending on rapid improvisation in the intimate atmosphere of a night club, be-came mechanical; and in some instances the TV comedian—at once obsessive, trivial, and epicene—proved one of the worst products of the media. Less objectionable was the female performer, sometimes chatty, usually with no particular voice or wit but with a certain conspicuously displayed sexiness. A whole separate TV realm was set aside for children, with shows which sometimes (as in the case of *Kukla, Fran and Ollie*) had a quality of fantasy and charm that "adult" shows usually lacked. Also an outgrowth of the children's audience was the vogue of the sci-ence-fiction "space" shows, which charted the imaginative worlds with such mechanical thoroughness that nothing was left to the imagination. The "crooner" shows continued their special appeal in both media, and —along with the comedians—furnished the largest number of TV idols. The broadcasting of classical and symphonic music remained an effec-tive function of the radio even when it was overshadowed by TV. The most productive area for TV to exploit was the documentary, including not only political spectacles like the Kefauver crime investigation and the Army-McCarthy hearings, and sport spectacles like prize fights and football and baseball games, but also demonstrations of new techniques in medicine, science, and psychiatry.

This bill of fare of the media is necessarily a transient, since fads de-velop, fashions change, and new areas open up for exploitation. I have given it in detail to document the role of radio and TV (especially the latter) as the synthesizing arts of the popular culture. There are few things that happen in the real world of events, science, and political conflict, or in the make-believe worlds of sport and movies, theater, dance, music, that cannot be projected on a TV screen. This suggests the breath-taking potential of the broadcasting arts.

What both media have at their best is vitality, pace, timing, and an imaginativeness about technique. Without being in themselves dis-tinctive arts, they combine a dozen different arts but are somewhat more than their passive carriers. For whatever the art may be—theater, dance, sports event, jazz, news documentary, variety show, domestic skit, mystery—it poses special problems and acquires a special tension when transferred and transformed into the new medium. It also acquires, especially on TV, a sense of immediacy. The characteristic quality that TV has is the feeling it conveys to the audience that something is happening at that very moment before their eyes. Neither medium possesses the capacity of the movies to transfer the audience back into time through the flashback nor to get inside the mind of the character by an interior monologue. Yet the capacity to bring all the arts together into one gives TV an advantage over every other communication technique thus far.

It means, however, that the men who run both media, and especially TV, have to keep their Moloch appeased by a constant stream of material—scripts, "angles," gimmicks, jokes, formats, routines, variety-show combinations. There is an insatiable cannibalism of material on TV, a constant drain on talent and ideas, on available "names," on stories and plays which can be rewritten and adapted to the new media. This does not nourish artistic creativeness. But without having in themselves much generative power, the broadcasting arts have a duplicative power such as no popular art has ever had. When well used they can insure the horizontal spread of whatever creativeness the culture develops: they can reach the subconscious of the audience, get into the crevices of their minds, hit them with an immediacy and continuity of impact denied to any other technique.

In the mid-1950s the big movie studios, which had held out against supplying TV with their storehouse of movie prints because of their fear of TV competition, finally succumbed to the lure of the big money and made almost the whole past repertoire of the movie arts available. The fear that audiences would stay away from the movie theaters was not fulfilled, and the quality of the films on TV was decisively improved. Looking ahead, we find that it is not clear whether TV will eat the movie industry, cannibalwise, or whether the movies have found a new outlet for their commercial product and their artistic creativeness, transferring from the public theater to the home. Probably both are true, and neither wholly, since each art has been enriched in the process. It is likely that TV will emerge as the dominant carrier form of the big media, combining all the rest, while the movies retain their position as the creative form.

As with the movies, there has been a continuance on TV of the system of "big name" stars, who are given long-run contracts with staggering salaries. The glamour of these heroes does not depend on the sense of distance between them and the public. Even the movie heroes and heroines are somewhat further removed. What the TV stars sell is a quality called "personality": in fact, they are usually called "TV personalities" by the same people who would never dream of calling one of the heroes or heroines of the screen a "movie personality." The difference lies in the greater familiarity of those who have become part of the domestic circle. The heroes of TV are everyday fare, entering the home weekly or even daily and becoming familiars in the household: the fact that their glamour still holds up marks the emergence of a new kind of hero-type:

> A creature not too strange or good
> For human nature's daily food . . .

and is evidence of a remarkable inner harmony between the performers and their audience. This harmony persists despite the shoddiness of much of the material the performers present and marks a triumph for their infectious personalities over the context in which they appear. Thus the big-name system not only helps sell the sponsor's product but furnishes the human continuity which makes tolerable the barrage of whirling images and exploding noises.

This may shed some light on the question of the role of laughter in the communication between star and audience. While very few of the great movies (except for the Chaplin series) have been comedies, TV would almost cease to exist without the comedians. Some of them have come from the vaudeville stage, others from the night clubs, still others from the radio. When they "arrive" on TV, they become important properties, are given teams of script writers to prepare their material, and are surrounded by pretty girls and other talent in order to keep the attention of the audience from wandering to a competing show. When the audience shows signs of growing bored with them it is not unusual for the publicity men to think up a "feud" between several of the comedians the element of hostility seems to invest them with greater appeal, like a dark curtain against which their wit may flash the more brightly. But always they are expected to get laughs. This laughter-compulsion on TV (it spills over into the noncomedy shows as well) parallels the fun-imperative in American morality which I have discussed earlier.*

Several explanations of the demand for comedy have been suggested —one of them that since no smutty stories are allowed on the air, laughter becomes a form of emotional release, while the other stresses the sense of well-being in an America of high living standards. But othei

* Ch. IX, Sec. 6, "Morals in Revolution."

explanations seem to make more sense. On the emotional level the lonely American finds in TV a sure method of getting away from the confronting of his own image, with all of its anxieties: laughter furnishes their solvent. On the social level, the fact is that most people usually watch TV not as one or two people sitting in a large audience but as a little cluster of family or friends around the set: laughter is a good way of tying this cluster together and giving it an ease of relationship. Finally, on a practical level, the advertiser who sponsors the show wants the potential purchasers of his product to associate it with something pleasant and sunny rather than with the unpleasant and the tragic. Thus TV is mainly the art of comedy because it is the social art and the advertising art.

Something of the same approach may be useful in assessing the standards of taste and intellect, courage and morality, that prevail in both radio and TV. The gap between potentials and actuality was poignantly put in a letter written to the National Association of Broadcasters by Lee De Forest, inventor of the Audion tube which was the crucial technical element of radio, on the occasion of its fortieth anniversary: "What have you gentlemen done to my child?" De Forest asked. "He was conceived as a potent instrumentality for culture, fine music, the uplifting of America's mass intelligence. You have debased this child, you have sent him out on the streets . . . to collect money from all and sundry. . . . You have made him a laughingstock of intelligence, surely a stench in the nostrils of the gods of the ionosphere. . . ." And John Crosby, a perceptive critic of broadcasting, has listed the "deadly sins of the air": among them that radio "sold its soul to the advertiser"; that it "pandered to the lowest tastes and almost ignored the highest"; that it was "avaricious and cowardly"; and that it "created an insulting picture of the American people." Most signs indicate that TV is following essentially the same road.

The way in which violence is treated on the air may illustrate these comments. There are probably at least eighty programs of horror and mystery thrillers a week on the air. Within a span of five hours on Sunday evening the three big networks during one year had nine mystery shows. On that night, in a total of perhaps twenty million homes, there were enacted a dozen violent deaths whose victims, as *Life* summed it up, were "stabbed, poisoned, shot, blown up and thrown out of windows, plus one exceptionally messy suicide."

There is little question that TV had an impact on the lives of children. A 1950 study showed pupils of junior-high-school age spending twenty-seven hours a week at it—about equal to the time they spent in the classroom; the average for children from seven to seventeen was three hours a day; in the case of five- and six-year-olds, the figure was four hours a day. Only one child out of five failed to become a regular member of the TV audience. They watched not only the children's programs, including puppet shows, circus-and-clown shows, and space shows, but many also got the nightly "adult" spell of murder, robbery, mayhem, blackmail, and kidnaping. This produced a pervasive anxiety among parents and educators who were caught between a reluctance to deprive the children of culturally accepted entertainment and a fear of the scars it might leave.

For good or ill, TV became the "unacknowledged legislator" of the minds of American children, carrying into those minds the sex and the fripperies, the silliness and stupidities and terrors of the "adult" shows. In some cases it made the children smart and cynical before their time, with the shallow smartness of those who have seen sophistication and violence but have not experienced either of them, whose imagination has been excited but not nourished. At the best it enriched the child's visual and imaginative experience faster than ever before in history. At the worst it desensitized the child while it burdened him with a heavy load of anxiety. Yet those who feared that it would produce a generation of little monsters allowed their own anxiety to overcome their good sense. Just as children have for centuries been able to absorb the terror and sadism of some of the classic fairy tales, so TV added its own contribution to the violent world of the children's imagination. An American generation brought up on comic books was able to take TV in its stride. What the children themselves get from it is much what the grownups get—a long look at the outside world, with all of its buzzing, booming confusion. Children have to visualize this world with pictorial images and not only with words. If, as some psychologists have suggested, Americans tend to keep too tight a rein on the primary impulses of their children, TV may prove a safety valve for their gathered frustrations and aggressions. A study made of children whose parents had banned their watching TV showed a disproportionate number of them ridden by the very anxiety which the ban was presumably meant to prevent.

The debate on the psychic and cultural deposit left on young and old alike by the broadcasting arts is not likely to be resolved easily. Harriet Van Horne, a TV columnist, lamented that "our people are becoming less literate by the minute. . . . As old habits decline, such as reading books and thinking thoughts, TV will absorb their time. By the twenty-first century our people doubtless will be squint-eyed, hunchbacked, and fond of the dark. Conversation will be a lost art. People

will simply tell each other jokes. . . . The chances are that the grand-
child of the Television Age won't know how to read this." This is
bright writing, but it seems oversold on doom. The history of the big
media offers proof that every new medium has been hailed as a worker
of miracles and dreaded as a destroyer of the ancient virtues. Neither
the salvation nor the doom has been fulfilled. The residue depends on
how and for what purpose the medium is used by its masters and its
audience. It also depends on the nature of the society and the culture
into which it is introduced. Harold Innis, in a broad historical survey,
has shown that every revolution in the techniques of communication
brought with it an equal revolution in society and culture. It would
be surprising if this were not proved true of the electronic revolution
which has largely replaced the printed word by the visual image conveyed over sound waves, and which is bound to transform American
society—and others as well—in ways still undreamed of today.

One of the important transformations is in the area of social power.
It should be obvious that those who control the images that reach into
men's homes and also into their minds will have a good deal of at least
indirect control over those minds as well. Hence the question of how
the structure of this power shall be organized.

The issue of the control of radio and TV is no longer one between
private and government ownership. Private enterprise in the big media
is now established in America and is not likely to be disestablished.
The British, who ran their broadcasting under a government corporation, did a better job with intellectual and taste standards: yet they too
found that government control narrows the choice of viewpoints presented on the air, just as control by advertisers narrows it in a different
way. One must doubt whether the American government is mature
enough to handle this kind of power without abusing it. In the mid-
1950s even the British turned to commercial sponsorship of TV, per-
suaded that it provides the audience with an array of good as well as
shoddy choices such as no other system had thus far offered. Yet the
current British arrangement improved on the American in at least one
respect: the British competition in TV is not just between one commercial chain and another or one advertiser and another but between
a commercial and government service, between private and public.

Where the system falls down, as I have suggested, is in its sleaziness
of taste standards and its pandering to greed and timidity. Raymond
Rubicam, who learned to know the advertising agency from the inside,
wrote that the reason for the failure of radio to serve the public interest lay in "the domination of radio by the advertiser . . . what amounts

practically to a monopoly of radio and TV advertisers to the point where the public's choice in program is more of a theory than a fact." This challenges the usual defense of advertising control as representing a democracy of audience choice. The trouble with this defense is that the audience chooses only from what is made available, which is limited by the calculus of the advertisers. Senator Benton's suggestion for a citizens' group to appraise annually how radio and TV have served and failed to serve the public interest was never acted on—which may be just as well, since it would have meant the appointment of a group of private citizens by the Senate, and therefore the vesting of consider-able power without responsibility. Another suggestion, by Frank Stanton, was the launching of a research study on the kind of anxieties and questions and answers that Americans have about TV. But this would have meant only another attitude study rather than the "dialogue" be-tween broadcasters and public which Stanton seemed to envisage. Nor has anything been done about the suggestions for turning a TV channel over to creative people who would develop new programs without the benefit of advertising, but with public or foundation subsidy. Programs like *Omnibus,* first subsidized by the Ford Foundation and later moderately successful in finding sponsors, indicate that the commercial sponsor and the advertising agency suffer less from an anticultural bent than from a poverty of imagination, which leads them to seek the easy way to win and hold an audience. A method of subsidizing new program ventures until they could prove their appeal, a noncommercial channel for use as a yardstick, a more rigorous enforcement of the provision for "public-service programs," the use of an advisory board of technicians and laymen for a continuing reappraisal of the media—these are a few steps that might help.

This is another way of saying that the core problem is one of ma-turity. Just as important as the consequences of TV for American society are the consequences of the society for the art of TV. Just as serious as the question of what TV does to children is the question of what chil-dren do to TV. It is not that the programs are geared deliberately to catch them but that they are shaped so as to appeal to the child's mentality in children and adults alike. Since you can listen to radio and TV free, without budging from your living room, twisting programs on and off with the flick of a dial, this means a huge audience but also a fluid and slack one. It places a premium on the slick and the quick, the noisy, the flashy, and ephemeral. It means pampering the audience, treating it as one treats a child whose attention span is short, whose interests are sensuous and surfacy, and whose fancy is a wandering one. Perhaps nine tenths of the brains and energy in radio and TV are directed toward finding somehing gaudy to catch the attention, something wry to evoke laughter, something new and ingenious to tickle the fancy. This makes for a somewhat bizarre sprightliness and a sense of alertness and tension, but not for substance and emotional depth.

To defend this on the score of "audience choice" is to set up a new and more imperfect Benthamite calculus. In measuring the greatest happiness of the greatest number, the Calculus of Bentham sought at least to take account of pains as well as pleasure. The Calculus of TV has no clear way of determining how much pain is mixed with the pleasure of a particular program—except that the pleasure out-balances the pain enough to keep the listener tuned in. To accept this critical standard is to abdicate all others. It is as if one were to accept the suffrage of the largest number in judging the value of books, which would mean that trashy best sellers and comic books would have to be crowned with an accolade. In the world of books a number of audience taste levels are given a chance to operate, with none shut out, whether it be symbolist poetry or the dregs of the newsstand pulps. Until radio and TV find some means for providing a comparable set of choices for varying audience levels, with no significant level shut out, there can be little valid talk of a cultural democracy of audience choice.

There remains the question of the impact of TV not on the cultural level but on the social structure. Studies of the distribution of TV sets show TV to be the poor man's luxury because it has become his psychological necessity. While TV flowers best in the middle-bracket income groups, its importance for the lower income groups is far out of proportion to their numbers and purchasing power. This can be verified by the sky line. Wandering about in the poorer quarters of the cities you will find the greatest concentration of TV antennae—exactly in the areas where people live hemmed-in lives, economically and intellectually. This is true of the Negro areas of Harlem and Philadelphia, Detroit and Chicago; it is true wherever ethnic groups are crammed into ghettos. In the housing developments for middle-income groups, such as the new Levittowns and Park Forests, TV sets come built in with the equipment, and have become as routine a part of the household as the phone and the refrigerator. For those who during the day are shut inside factories or stores or offices, or for housewives who stay home with small children, TV furnishes an unparalleled release by night and day.

For those who are excluded from many forms of direct experience by the bars of discrimination, TV is a way of breaking the bars, so that they can watch the glamorous figures of make-believe and the weighty figures of the world of power. For the Negro the big fact about TV is that Jim Crow has no way of policing a man's eyes and ears as he watches the set in his home. He can turn to TV to make what is unavailable to him in the world outside available for the fleeting moment as he watches it in a world of sound and sight where everyone is equal. Another big fact is that, for the radio and TV sponsor, the purchasing power of a listener counts the same, whatever his skin. Hence the appearance of Negroes, picked for their skills on the big-prize shows like *$64,000 Question*—with far-reaching consequences in changing the earlier popular stereotypes.

If it be said that the TV audience is one of only passive watchers, the same is true of the movies and the spectator sports. Short of arranging some kind of genuine forum, accessible to thoughtful leaders of opinion and the rank and file as well, where the audience could take pot shots at some of the most revered institutions and practices of TV, the medium can do little in creating the dialogue which is the essence of communication. TV cannot transform the passive into the active, but it does bring all the spectator arts together on a single screen. It does so with a technical mastery so great that the sports promoters fear the audience will see the prize fight or football game better on the screen than from the field or arena; as a result the sale of radio and TV rights has become important in the financing of these events. From the prize fight to the movie to the Presidential convention, spectacles which were once meant for their own immediate audiences are being tailored to the TV audience.

This must have incalculable effects on the emotional cement of a democratic society. While the broadcasting media present their own internal problems of privilege and power, they will inevitably help erode the landscape of social privilege. They do not decrease the economic distance between the classes, nor can they level the walls of segregation overnight. But they can help create a common sense of belonging and provide access to the common experience for many from whom it was formerly withheld.

7. *Jazz As American Idiom*

THE KIND OF music, song, and dance a people generates, with their characteristic rhythm and beat, forms one of the best indexes of its cultural style. In America the national musical style is more closely related to the tom-tom than to the organ. It is not the style of church music, nor of the symphony or sonata, the madrigal or the morris dance, the ballet or opera. The dominant American musical styles are those of the "blues," "swing," and "jazz."

Every civilization finds also the musical instruments that express its idiom. In America they are brass and percussion—the trumpet and saxophone, capable of expressing both a melancholy moan and a triumphant blare like the exultant cry of an animal; the drums with their rhapsodic deafening beat; and the piano, which beat out ragtime in the 1920s and still beats out the foundation rhythm incessantly, lest tension and attention lapse. Add to these four instruments a young female voice, husky and throaty, to express the melancholy of the "blues" and the sultry sexiness of "torch songs," and you have the basic American musical unit. Around this unit there cluster the characteristic accompaniments of American musical life: the "name band," night club, blues singer, dance record, disk jockey, tinpan alley, dance hall, jam session, musical comedy, crooner, juke box, and the bobby-sox brigade of youthful music worshipers.

More than in any other popular art Americans express in their music both a mood of melancholy and the beat of Dionysian impulse. In a culture that regards sadness and pessimism almost as crimes against the Republic, the American popular songs have given expression to the plaintive along with the boisterous. The songs and ballads form one of the sources of contemporary jazz, but they are even more important in mirroring the sequence of folk experience in American history. Every aspect of the building of the country is represented in them: in the marching songs, the work and road-gang songs, the cotton-picking songs ("Oh, de boll weevil am a little brown bug"), the cowboy songs, the badman frontier songs:

Roll me over easy, roll me over slow,
Roll me over on my right side 'cause my left side hurts me so . . .

the trail songs, the plantation songs, the hillbilly mountain songs, the spirituals and the sinfuls:

When dey let my baby down in de groun'
I couldn't hear nuffin but de coffin soun' . . .

Sometimes I'se up, sometimes I'se down,
Sometimes I'se almos' to de groun'.
Nobody knows the trouble I've seen,
Nobody knows but Jesus.

In some, especially in the work songs and frontier ballads, there is an element of tongue-in-cheek exaggeration, but also a deep strain of sadness which is found wherever the Negro influence has touched American song. The work songs were intended to make the burden of manual and field labor more tolerable: Alan Lomax has called it a "spiritual speed-up." Its roots may be found in West Africa, but it developed on the American plantation system, and its call-and-response pattern is similar to the same pattern in Negro spirituals, with the work leader improvising the call and the work crew giving the chorus response. It was only a step from the cotton plantation to the railroad section gang ("I've been workin' on the railroad"), and another step to the chain gang in today's South, where forced manual labor still survives and the machine (which kills the work song) has not yet entered.

The deepest expression of the strain of sadness may be found in the "blues," born in the Negro quarters of Southern cities, drenched with the melancholy of the West African slave-serf-alien in America. It is a dithyrambic melancholy, a lament over a turn of fortune that has left the singer penniless and shorn of a lost love-object; but also an undaunted melancholy, with the quality of resilience in it. Of all the early strains in American folk songs and ballads, it alone survived as a strong shaping force in American musical culture. It alone seems to have emotional depth and an unashamed passion. The "blues" tradition reached its greatness in the genius of W. C. Handy and in the singing of Bessie Smith, Ma Rainey, Jimmy Rushing, Dinah Washington, and Billie Holliday. While it is still popular, especially in Negro night clubs, it is largely nostalgic. Its creative strain was carried on and in effect replaced by that of jazz itself.

Related to the "blues" is the spiritual, which is the most general term for the religious music of the American Negro. It goes back in its origin to the beginning of the nineteenth century but did not become known to the white community until after the Civil War. Sometimes it takes the form of gospel songs, sometimes of the closely related "jubilee," sometimes of the longer-sustained melody permeated with a sense of reverence ("Go Down Moses" and "Swing Low, Sweet Chariot" are among the best-known examples). To some extent the spiritual arises out of the church hymn, drawn from a European context and transplanted into the Negro church and revival meeting. To some extent also it comes from the African musical tradition. When the African slaves came to America they found folk hymns which had themselves been transplanted into the South from England and New England. What Negro religious life added was the "praise meeting" on the plantation and later the revival meeting, both of them using the song sermon and the "ring shout." Marshall Stearns has skillfully traced the development of these steps into the jubilee ("When the Saints Go Marching In"), with

its lengthened melody, and finally into the spiritual, with its crystal-
lizing of the original improvisations. However carefully we follow these
steps, we must not lose sight of the relation of the spiritual as a total
form to the Dionysian rhythms of jazz itself. Even today much of the
new jazz takes its emotional source from the religious spirituals.

The younger and more secular cousins of the blues and the spirituals
—the songs of the crooner and torch singer—have a different quality, as
have most of the tin-pan alley songs and the synthetic hillbilly ballads.
The emotion in them is likely to be prurient and sentimental, appealing to the moon-struck: the melancholy has become a masochistic accompaniment to teen-age. There is the cry of loneliness ("All alone
on the telephone") and the confession of unworthiness ("And when I
tell them how wonderful you are, They'll never believe me") and the
pathos of self-pity ("I'm nobody's baby," "I'm always chasing rain-
bows"). Out of jingles like these and thousands of others—Mammy
songs, nonsense songs ("Yes, We Have No Bananas," "Barney Google,"
"Mairzy Doats"), songs of regional nostalgia (longings for the Wabash
or the Sewanee or the Blue Ridge or the heart of Texas), songs of
rustic love, songs of erotic innuendo, songs of sexual dream-fulfillment—
a music-sheet and song-record industry has been built which seems to
bring either thrill or anodyne to millions of young Americans. A
diaspora of juke boxes all over the land grinds out tunes played by
"big-name bands," a nickel or dime at a time, at roadhouses, saloons,
restaurants, crossroads cafés. The lilt of these tunes is sweet to the taste
of the youngsters, and lachrymose singers like Johnnie Ray and jaunty
singers like Bing Crosby and Frank Sinatra become the objects of adolescent worship. The words ("lyrics") perform the same function for their
imaginations that the lyric poem did for middle-class England in the
century between Burns and Tennyson. They are, in fact, all the poetry
that most young Americans know. Their effect on American taste makes
the juke boxes a greater danger to American life than the Jukes.

The more important musical idiom of America was the "ragtime"
and "hot jazz" of the twenties, the "swing" of the thirties, the "cool
jazz" of the forties, and the "rock 'n roll" of the fifties. These terms imply complex beat and rhythm, improvisation, and musicianly teamwork.
The element they have in common is a disciplined Dionysian excitement and a thinly sublimated eroticism. Starting among little groups of
local musicians, this idiom—in more or less diluted form—reached the
larger public through night clubs and concerts, radio, TV, big-name
bands, and dance records. It thus became a new folk language of American music. While very few of its creators got much income from it, many

of them remaining in poverty and even obscurity until their death, their work achieved a greater popular acceptance than the language of literature.

The origins of jazz lie hidden in the folklore of lowly groups of musicians in New Orleans, St. Louis, Chicago, and other centers where American Negroes were forced to lead a segregated life but were exposed—despite the segregation—to influences from the musical traditions of every part of the world. Thus jazz had more than an African origin: there was much in it from America, and much from the Latin cultures of Europe and the Caribbean. Alan Lomax speaks of New Orleans as having "absorbed slowly over the centuries Iberian, African, Cuban, Parisian, Martiniquian, and American musical influences." The result, as he puts it, was a "musical gumbo." But the energizing force was that of the Negro musicians in the big cities, especially New Orleans. They took the syncopated ragtime developed in the honky-tonks and saloons of Sedalia and St. Louis, and turned it into the two-beat Dixieland jazz that was given shape by the "jazz professors" of the Storyville bordellos and by the marching bands that followed so many funerals through the New Orleans streets. The ragtime of the first two decades of the present century was beaten out on the piano: when the brass and wind instruments were added, it became the jazz of the 1920s.

No one has resolved the cultural mystery of how a harvest of musical talent seemed to flower in a few brief decades out of the unlikely soil of brothels and funeral rites in the Mississippi delta. With musicians like Buddy Bolden, "Jelly Roll" Morton, and Louis Armstrong, there was an authentic musicianal passion that entered the life of America and never found its like again. From the Gulf Coast the contagion spread northward to St. Louis and Chicago and eastward to New York and the other big cities there. Here it suffered a change of phase. The impoverished musicians who had improvised in the cribs and bawdy houses became the leaders of big-name bands and best-selling records; a new economic force came in which made music a nation-wide commodity and eroded the folk and regional sources of the original impulsion; the primitive music grew sophisticated, and the "hot jazz" turned into "cool jazz"—polyphonic, with an unaccented beat, and with borrowings from Hindemith and Bartók.

This summary telescopes almost a half century of jazz in America. It does scant justice to the passions and rivalries that beset the struggle of conflicting styles of musical execution. These musical wars arose not only from local rivalries but from the inherent nature of jazz. For in early jazz the composer was of little importance compared with the execution. The musicians took almost any tune, and what came out of the instruments was a miracle of transmutation—a delicate lacework

of magic that intoxicated the senses and was especially tantalizing because it depended entirely upon the improvising of the moment and the
interweaving of instruments caught in a common excitement. Since
good jazz is evanescent, it must be captured and treasured in the memory. Hence the cult of jazz records, in which the *aficionados* feel that the
accents of greatness, whether of some star performer or a "side man,"
have been caught forever. Hence also the lore that develops in the cult
—the arguments about who played what with whom, and when and
where. Jazz developed in a brief time a history and a tradition, with
"great dates" and legendary figures.

The Pre-Raphaelite Brotherhood of young Americans is more likely
to be found in hot and cool jazz than in the elite arts of poetry, painting, or the novel. In the 1940s, Harry James meant more to most young
Americans than Henry James or William James. Negro and white
trumpet players, saxophonists, and pianists were heard and appraised
by the young American elite with a critical fierceness that few of them
applied to poetry or philosophy. The whole structure was in some ways
reminiscent of the Christian Church in its earlier phases. There were
raging rivalries as to which style is orthodoxy or heresy, but there was
agreement that salvation can only be found inside the musical church
of jazz. There was the basic religious nostalgia for the lost Eden, the
Golden Age when the church was founded amidst the apathy of surrounding heathendom. There was the rivalry between the adherents of
St. Louis and the adherents of New Orleans, of Beale Street and Basin
Street, for the nativity of the cult. There was the mythology growing up
around the Early Fathers.

A passage in John O'Hara's novel, *Butterfield 8,* about young men in
New York at the end of the 1920s, gave a taste of the hero worship:

> They . . . would have their jam sessions, and some night when they did
> not play they would sit and talk. The names they would talk: Bix Beider-
> becke, Frankie Trumbauer, Miff Mole, Steve Brown, Bob MacDonough,
> Henry Busse, Mike Pingatore, Ross Gorman and Benny Goodman, Louis
> Armstrong and Arthur Schutt, Roy Bargy and Eddie Gilligan, Harry Mac-
> Donald and Eddie Lang and Tommy and Jimmy Dorsey and Fletcher
> Henderson, Rudy Wiedoeft and Isham Jones, Rube Bloom and Hoagy
> Carmichael, Sonny Greer and Fats Waller, Husk O'Hare and Duilie
> Sherbo, and other names like Mannie Kline and Louis Prima, Jenney and
> Morehouse, Venuti, Signorelli and Cross, Peewee Russel and Larry
> Binion; and some were for this one and some for that one. . . .

O'Hara, a faithful social historian of his era, caught in this reverent
catalogue the right dedicated accent. One should be wary of using the

analogy of the Early Church, since there is little of the Orphic element in jazz, and therefore far less of the Christian than of the Dionysian. Yet the lives, exploits, and sufferings of these men are discussed by young Americans in the same terms as those of the saints were discussed in other centuries: there is the same discovery of vocation, the same dedication to the new work, the same revelation of a special gift, the same entrance into the mystery, the same epiphanies, the same final state of grace.

In the gallery of the saints of jazz there is a central figure whom the worshipers call "Bix"—a Midwestern youth whose name was Leon Bix Beiderbecke, from Davenport, Iowa, who first heard jazz as a boy on the river boats of the Mississippi, met Louis Armstrong, and established himself quickly as the leader of the "white" jazz movement of the 1920s, dying at twenty-eight after a brief career of legendary excesses which—along with his inspired playing—became the core of a cult. Bix haunted the night spots of the Negro quarters in Chicago's South Side, where he absorbed the trumpet playing of Joe "King" Oliver and the blues singing of Bessie Smith, and took part in "jam sessions" and "cutting contests." In New York he played with Paul Whiteman's band and spent much of his time in Harlem, where he was a pioneer in the crossing of race boundaries. But mostly he was a musician's musician, the dimensions of whose power and glory are used by his worshipers as standards by which to measure everything mortal. His achievement lay neither in volume of tone nor in frenzy of playing but in a purity of note which was the product, as Wilder Hobson has put it, of "what the imagination presents to the instrument." E. M. Forster has noted that a critic's function in music is different from his function in literature: he cannot presume to tell the musician what to do or even where he is going. This suggests the overtones of fatality in the world of connoisseurs of jazz—a world of absolutes and of "can't help's" in which one either understands or does not. When Fats Waller was asked for a definition of jazz, he answered, "Man, if you don't know what it is, don't mess with it."

Obviously this forms an ideal medium for an art which is at once part of the popular culture and also of the domain of the aesthetes and intellectuals. In the era of Bach there was, to be sure, a gap between the musical language of the man on the street and of the creative artist, but in contemporary America there is more than a gap—there is an abyss. It applies less, however, to jazz and swing, where the cult has a genuine mass art as a base. In Bach's day the works by anonymous composers used the same musical language as did Bach himself. In contemporary America any "young man with a horn" who plays all day and most of the night is—even though an amateur—part of the same milieu, using the same musical language, as the virtuoso performer: and both the amateur and virtuoso are understood in a considerable segment of the culture and express its rhythms.

The "lyrics" that go with this music are often mawkish and sometimes nonsensical, but often they also embody a wild and earthy humor or (as in the case of the blues and the spirituals) a sad and tragic strain. American hot music is not written to be danced to, as distinguished from American popular tunes, which are primarily danced to. In fact, in most of the country's principal jazz clubs, like Birdland and Basin Street, there is no dance floor at all: more and more jazz is being played in concert halls, where the separation from dance is complete.

Yet there is an internal beat in jazz which relates it deeply to dance: the movements of the body interpret its intent better than words can. When there is dancing, the dances break away from a formal pattern and at their best they take on a fluid, improvised character in keeping with the improvisations of the music. Unlike the earlier American folk dances, which are collective, so-called ballroom (really dance hall) dancing is couple dancing, since to take a girl dancing is an integral part of courtship and you don't know the others well enough to join with them. But as the music mounts in the more adept swing dancing, the partners break away to execute complicated solo variations and then rejoin each other. The musicians are at the same time vying in improvisation, and as the jam session approaches one of its climaxes the dancers pay the players the tribute of gathering around to cheer them on. In the organic fusion of popular dance and music Americans reach closer to a mass exaltation and a native idiom of religious feeling than in any other aspect of their lives.

The history of the dance in America illustrates the same fusion of the elite and the popular. Unlike the religions of Asia and Africa, the Christian tradition banned dancing from its religious rituals, and as the inheritor of that tradition, Puritan America placed its dead hand on the expressive use of the body. The frontier dances broke away from this for a long time, but it was not until American students rediscovered the classical and Oriental religious dance that American dancing came into being as an elite art. Its renascence came through Isadora Duncan, Ruth St. Denis, and Martha Graham, who created an interpretive "modern" dance art. It did not reach popular audiences, however, until it was incorporated into the Broadway "musical," after being fused with the ballet and the folk dance. The turning point came with a musical like *Oklahoma*, where the dance forms of Agnes De Mille succeeded in achieving the fusion I have described.

The American "musical" is a remarkable example of how the genius of the culture forms a new entity out of scattered and seemingly discordant elements—a light opera containing a thin "story line" (sometimes taken from a play or novel) with vaudeville woven around it, a sequence of popular songs which yield the big money through dance and radio records, and a central ballet pattern created out of regional, folk, or topical material. How deeply the jazz idiom has permeated musical composition for the stage is shown in the dance and music of light opera, like *Porgy and Bess,* as well as in the musical comedies that are in a direct line of descent from *Oklahoma.* There is a strong probability that the musical direction of the new American future will lie with the popular theater and its dance, opera, and jazz forms, rather than with the "serious" composers who can write symphonies.

This is not to undervalue the receptivity of America to "serious" music. Through radio, TV, and the "hi-fi" long-playing record, the masterpieces of the classical tradition became widely known. America in the 1950s was in a Golden Age of orchestra performance, with a symphony orchestra in every big city and a large audience (mustered with brilliant business skill by experts at the job) available for first-rate traveling orchestras and musical virtuosos. This was partly due to American wealth and to the historical accident of the great European orchestra leaders who came as refugees from Fascism. But mainly it was the awakening interest of the American middle-class "middlebrows" to the treasures of the world's musical tradition which created a literate musical audience and made Americans a nation of musical amateurs. The role once played by the proud capitals of music—Milan, Munich, Dresden, Vienna, Berlin, Amsterdam, Prague—was taken over by America. Out of this receptivity came a vigorous school of contemporary American composers who felt somewhat dwarfed, however, by the historic giants who were being eagerly rediscovered. For a time there was an effort to create a school of native composers using "American themes," but it proved ineffectual, since "native" music cannot be created by will. American composers studied largely with Stravinsky, Hindemith, and Schönberg, and a number of them since the 1920s served an apprenticeship in the Paris salon of Nadia Boulanger. In the mid-1950s the names of Copland and Barber, Sessions and Schuman, Piston and Shapero, were evidence of an American composer's art that was becoming part of the great tradition. They gave themselves a freedom and a largeness of scope as did the composers in the elite societies of the past, and left the expression of popular cultural forces to the "popular" music and dance.

Like all true popular arts, jazz attracted its camp followers of pseudo-folk art. There were "Mammy writers" who tried to imitate Stephen Foster, himself a native of Pittsburgh who celebrated the Southern folkways. City youngsters who had never been south of Brooklyn wrote countless songs about "Dear Old Alabam'" or "Back Home in Tennessee" or the Sewanee River, and vowed that "nothing could be finer than to be in Carolina in the morning." What happened here was a cultural hybridism in which the ethnic accents of the Old World were grafted on to the regional traditions of the New: when Al Jolson sang his famous *Mammy,* using the black face of the American minstrel tradition, it was the Jewish mother of his own ethnic tradition he was invoking. Much more indigenous to the Southern soil were the "rocking, rolling, shouting blues" of the great blues singers.

What saved many of the tin-pan alley tunes, despite their cloying sentiment and artificial garments of a borrowed culture, was the vitality they carried over from the days of ragtime. It was this vitality that gave impetus to the Big Five among the contemporary popular song writers—Irving Berlin, Jerome Kern, George Gershwin, Cole Porter, and Richard Rodgers. Of these, Berlin was closest to the popular mind, Cole Porter was the most literate, with his combination of wit and bawdiness, while the team of Rodgers and Oscar Hammerstein II fused best the lyricism of the popular song with the virtuosity of the Broadway musical. Today the music makers, having left tin-pan alley behind, are caught between the high pressures of the radio "Hit Parade" and the timetable of Broadway and Hollywood productions. The old art of song-plugging was never quite lost but was reinforced by the microphone and movie, and became part of the "Big Time" of a mechanical culture.

This leaves jazz itself, rather than the melodies of popular music or the synthetic hillbilly ballads, as the true musical idiom of America. In fact, jazz is the most indigenous of all the American popular arts. It moved from the early New Orleans musicians, who could scarcely read a note, to the atonal "cool" jazz of a number of highly cerebral young men, each of whom had his brief spiel as the reigning divinity among the knowing. But throughout its course it was informed by a demonic response to the violent inner rhythms of the American culture. One could be wrong to attribute this wholly to the Negro influence, although that has been substantial ever since the days of the New Orleans barrel houses which Vachel Lindsay celebrated in his poem, "The Congo." Jazz has evolved from a segregated Jim Crow art into a pervasive interracial culture, which has spread over western Europe, has reached into Asia, and has penetrated even the barriers of Communist censorship in Russia. What remains primitive in it is the generic human impulses breaking through the strata of Western machine living which have threatened to overlay the instinctual life.

The breaking through of the dance beat is the triumph of the instinctual life over the institutional crust. To a foreign observer like Sartre, who described American jazz as a cultural expression, its initiates seem a new kind of possessed men, taking the place of the possessed men of the medieval religious frenzies. Not many of the young American jazz devotees are technically "hepcats," but there are few who do not yearn to be "hep"—that is, to be insiders rather than outsiders, to take part in the mysteries of abandon and possession which link them with one another. Thus jazz and swing and, more recently, "rock 'n roll"—a febrile and probably temporary variation which has its own cult and deities and does not please the true jazz men—are more than the expressions of the charged tension of American living: they are a recoil from the loneliness of an atomized culture, a not inconsiderable effort to use music to heal the psychological alienation of person from person.

The traditional elite music tends to make passive listeners out of its audiences. It is the music of the popular culture, with its widespread singing, dancing, and improvising jam sessions, that turns audiences into participants, bringing them closer to a dynamic and communal activity. This was true also of the traditional music in its origins. "Virtually up to the seventeenth century," writes Wilfrid Mellers about the English Tudor period, "all music was communal and contemporary, and either religious or domestic. It depended upon active participation between composers, performers, and audience. . . . The idea of sitting solemnly in rows and listening to music (for its own sake) would have seemed absurd to Byrd or Palestrina; either one made music oneself or listened to it as homage to God." American contemporary music and dance have captured much of this spontaneous and even devotional spirit. The hepcats and jitterbugs do not dance and sway out of devotion to any gods the churches would recognize. But they do pay homage in their own way to the Dionysian in American life.

8. Building, Design, and the Arts

IN AN INDUSTRIAL culture like the American, one would expect the great elite arts of the past—painting and sculpture, theater, architecture, and design—to be transformed in the image of what the machine can do with the materials of plastic form. For the most part, this has happened.

Sculpture is an instance of an art falling into disuse when the mode of life no longer makes it meaningful. In the civilizations of the Nile, the Euphrates, and the Mediterranean, it was a crucial art. But the carving of figures out of stone required for their display the public square, the public building, the public occasion, and a ruling class that lived by all three.

Americans once built their city life around a public square but do so less and less. They retain the park and the courthouse, and they have sculptured figures of soldiers in the one and of jurists and statesmen in the other, yet these are products of habit and nostalgia rather than of living belief. Here and there, as with the colossal seated figure of Lincoln by Daniel Chester French in the Lincoln Memorial, belief breaks through. But mostly sculptors either make their livings by getting commissions for fountains and playground figures or experiment in the new abstract international styles. Since the product of sculpture is unique, not to be reproduced in millions of copies or transmitted by the big media, it offers no jackpots. To be sure, America presents, in the grace of athletes and the beauty of women, the living material to be celebrated. But sculpture cannot compete as a mass art with photography: the sports pages are filled with action shots of athletes that make most Americans regard sculpture as static, and magazine covers and advertising pages, as well as movies and TV, are filled with the American girl in every pose of glamour and glory. The sensitive sculptor, like the painter, has to move away from the portrayal of the human body to the symbolic distortions and abstractions of it. The result needs no justifying, especially in the work of someone like Lipschitz, yet there is more of a gulf between these sculptors and the cultural experience than had been true of the sculptors of the past. An even greater departure from the general dictates of American taste was achieved successfully by Alexander Calder, whose development of abstract mobiles has become internationally known and accepted.

America has had painters of considerable talent and varied schools, but they lacked a sustaining audience and environment. They also lacked a myth to celebrate, such as the Christian myth which the Italian and Flemish painters of the Middle Ages and Renaissance had; and buildings to house that myth, like the Sistine Chapel, whose walls are there to be covered with symbolic figures. The French, Belgians, Spaniards, Italians, who produced the great schools of painting in modern times, had largely escaped the main currents of Protestant capitalist power and still had residues of the great religious tradition. The two great postreligious themes of modern times, Nature and the individual, turned painting to landscapes and portraits. Yet on the score of fidelity to the subject the arts of photography were hard to rival. To differentiate themselves from such a competitor, and also to express the confusions of contemporary life, the painters adopted a style of symbolism and expressionism which produced great work in France and Germany but was late in coming to an America that was too purposive and optimistic for it. Realism flourished with Sloan and Hopper, and it was natural in a rich economy that the painters of the rich and their women —like Sargent—should catch the burnished surface of American power and assurance. When the critics lamented the lack of an indigenous school, painters like Wood, Curry, and Benton tried to create it by using American "folk" themes. But even the talent of these men rarely dug far beneath the flat surfaces of the American character.

What was needed was a sharper probing into the inwardness of the civilization through the inwardness of the painter's own vision. This was achieved in an earlier generation by Hartley, Marin, Maurer, and Weber, and in a later one by Shahn, DeKooning, and Pollock. What took place in painting was an easing of the provincial self-consciousness which had seen Europe as the sum and source of all sensitivity: when Americans no longer felt like gawky schoolboys, when power and anxiety and the Freudian vision had moved westward across the ocean and one no longer felt guilty to be daubing a canvas with seemingly aimless shapes and splashes of gaudy color, American painting found itself. The painters broke through, discovering an idiom at once symbolic beyond place and time and yet somehow expressive of America's energy and its unceasing quest, as Melville's idiom was in literature. Since paintings could be reproduced in the era of Malraux's "Museum without Walls," they cropped up everywhere in magazines and books and were bought or rented by young couples furnishing their new homes and apartments. The new middle classes began to discover new levels of taste and enjoyment. While most of the reproductions were of the Old Masters, there was an increasing awareness by Americans of the achievements of their own painters, and contemporary American paintings began to be exhibited even in the big department stores which catered to a mass audience. American painting achieved something of an economic base.

The new art whose imperialism corroded painting and sculpture was photography, both as an obsession of amateurs and in its big-media forms of the movies and TV. Allowing light to enter an opened shutter and be inscribed on a sensitive plate, the camera as an art form was quick, faithful, fluid, mobile, infinitely reproduceable and transmittable, conquering at once time and space, and was bound to become the prime visual art of a technical civilization. Americans with cameras roamed the nation and the world. There were numberless photo clubs, photo magazines and annuals, photo contests and prizes. The art had its pioneers, like Brady, and its great prophet in Stieglitz; after him, Americans lavished on the photograph the careful and devoted artistry which other cultures had lavished on paintings and sculpture. The importance of the picture magazines like *Life* and *Look* meant that talented photographers from all over the world were drawn to New York as the arena of fame and the big prizes. In their hands photography became a form of painting, in which the material of Nature was caught in forms and designs that went beyond realism to suggest the symbolic. As a mass art form, it still expresses the main preoccupations of the culture—"human interest," dramatic action, dynamism, surface, and movement.

Many inquests have been held on the case of the "vanishing theater" in America. The premise underlying them has been that, compared with the Periclean and Elizabethan periods, or the era of Ibsen, Chekhov, Strindberg, and Shaw, in the European theater, the American experience has not proved creative for the theater. The traditional indictment is familiar enough: that the American theater has too narrow a base, being centered on Broadway, in a single area of a single city; that its economics are burdensome, involving a large capital investment, expensive contracts with the trade-unions, and the necessity of getting a "hit" in order to survive; that a tiny group of critics rules over the destiny of the play and tends to be hostile to the unfamiliar; that the theater in America is a middle-class art, written and produced for middlebrows and invested with middlebrow values; that the temptation is strong to avoid the experimental and to play it safe with a tried formula and popular stars. Finally the theater is dismissed with the remark that it depends for its material on the novel and is tributary on the other side of the movies.

However much truth there may be in any or all of these judgments, they do not reach to the heart of the matter. By the kind of logic I have traced above, the American theater *should* be a vanishing art—but it isn't. It had a remarkable upsurge of creativeness in the 1920s with Eugene O'Neill, in the 1930s with Odets, Saroyan, Lillian Hellman, and Sidney Kingsley, in the 1940s and 1950s with Tennessee Williams and Arthur Miller. Add to these the remarkably creative work of the music-and-lyrics teams in the musical comedies and dramatic operas. A record of this sort, stretching across forty years from the days of the Provincetown Theater until today, is not a mere episode but a sign that American energies have found a characteristic expression in the theater in the present century, as they have in the novel. An objective historian of theater arts would have to say that since Ibsen and Strindberg and Shaw, the focus of creativeness has tended to shift across the ocean, and that Broadway—which once depended wholly upon importations from Europe—can now hold its own with London and Paris, and even create some twinges of envy.

The fact that the theater is closely linked with TV and the movies is not in itself an element of weakness. It is true that Hollywood and Madison Avenue exploit Broadway by buying its plays and offering jackpots to the successful playwrights, hiring them much as the Roman conquerors hired the Greek intellectuals to teach them philosophy and art. But despite the swagger and brashness of the Hollywood money, one may question which is the main stream and which the tributary. There is a wholeness in a play which neither the movies nor TV offers— a wholeness of experience for playwright, actor, and audience alike.

When several arts are linked together, as is true of the theater, the movies, and TV, they may fertilize one another, and each of them may profit from the connection. The era of dramatic creativeness in America coincides curiously with the emergence of the movies and TV. I do not say that these are the only forces at work, but they help. The knowledge of a playwright that his play, while first produced on Broadway for a limited audience, may ultimately reach millions of people, must prove a stimulus to his imagination. Some of the people he ultimately reaches may lack sensibility, but this will not be true of all of them. The fact is that an Elizabethan audience showed a sense of excitement even when the crowd in the pit applauded and derided at the wrong passages. They sensed that new things were happening in their world, and the theater gave a concrete dramatic form to this awareness. The Americans too have an awareness of new things happening. And although millions of them flock to the movies and watch TV, while only the thousands go to the theater, the fact is that, for writers and actors alike, the prestige attaches to the theater and not to the big media. No great theater is possible in any culture unless the people consider it a great art—a place of great writing, poetry, and mime, and a place for the enactment of ideas and passions.

Much of the experimental work in the New York theater is done in the "off-Broadway" theaters that are smaller and more informal and therefore less subject to heavy overhead and production costs. Yet even the concentration on Broadway need not prove the hindrance that it has been portrayed. There was a similar concentration on a short radius inside London at the time of the Elizabethan tragedy, and the same applies to Athens. Broadway has become a convergence point for play-goers from every corner of the country. Replicas of the Broadway effort are to be found in "Little Theater" groups which crop up in surpris-ingly out-of-the-way places. And the lure of Broadway is even stronger for playwrights and actors than for playgoers—stronger, in fact, than the lure of Hollywood. The theater serves as a kind of recoil from the big media—a chance for a playwright to do some probing and exploring in depth as he may not be able to do in the other media, a form in which he does not have to express the optimism of American life or its surface values, and where he is not dependent upon big sponsors or a mass audience. Since he is writing in the first place for a relatively limited audience, he can become part of the countercyclical force, reversing old trends and creating new ones, becoming a molder who in turn will be followed by the big media.

Thus the theater has thrived in America and may continue to thrive, because it does more than serve as a supply base for the big media. Like the novel, it represents the best opportunity that America has for a dissection of motive and personality, at the same time that it expresses in heightened form the tensions and the sense of power of contemporary American life.

In the case of American domestic architecture, the product is likely to emerge from an unequal struggle between an impulse to utility and beauty on the one hand, and on the other the building codes, the high price of land, material, and labor, and the crushing of imagination by conformism. In the big income groups, the taste displayed in the showplace resorts of Newport and Saratoga Springs, and in the mansions built by New York and Chicago industrial kings at the turn of the century, is a matter of history: some of it, judged by modern standards, was garish; but the work of Hunt, McKim, Stanford White, Platt, and Halsey Wood at the turn of the century was among the most interesting in the record of American architecture. It is true that there was also display for the sake of display. Having made their money from machinery which expressed a strict fitting of means to use and was therefore beautiful, the industrial kings spent it mainly to show they had it to spend, with a resulting ostentation that violated taste because it had little relation to either use or beauty. The ostentation has been reduced in recent years, and the middle-class "homes" loom larger in the American architectural scene as in the whole life scene. There is still showiness in some of the "palatial homes" of tycoons in Florida or movie stars in Hollywood. Yet the shaping fact about domestic architecture is the large number of moderately well-to-do families who seek to express in their homes their desire for comfort and their sense of well-being. It is notable that Americans, so confident about machine tools, automobiles, bridges, and highways, are still fumbling for an architectural style—or perhaps a diversity of styles—which will express the way they feel about life and about themselves.

They have a number of styles out of their past to draw upon, each of which had meaning in its time and region. The New England colonial house had a strong and simple design which expressed the angle of vision of men and women who believed in a life ruled by orderly divine and human law: whether it was farmhouse or town house, church or school, there was a sharpness of view that the New Englander communicated to the wood he used. He showed it equally in his household furniture, and especially in the great and graceful clipper ships such as those by David McKay, which were among the best achievements of American design.

The Southerners also had their characteristic modes of building, their best early production being the Georgian style that flourished in Virginia, Maryland, and the Carolinas in the eighteenth century: its products may still be seen in the reconstruction of Williamsburg and in the great Georgian houses of Virginia, including Washington's house at Mount Vernon and Jefferson's at Monticello. The big sugar and cotton planters of the nineteenth century built their dreams into columned plantation houses in the style of the Greek Revival, made of wood and of the stuccoed brick obtained from the clay and river sand of the Mississippi. In the Southwest the settlers borrowed from the Spanish tradition, just as those on the Atlantic Coast had borrowed from Inigo Jones and Christopher Wren; and the influence of Indian and Spanish elements, along with the environmental setting of desert and vegetation, resulted in a sharply regional style which survives even among the new modern forms. The Western region has given American building the "ranch house," expressing an informal rustic theme and combining a sprawling comfort with the suggestion of outdoor simplicity.

I have omitted an interesting American contribution to home-building—the "salt box," which started in the Middle West in the 1830s and was linked with the "balloon frame." This was a new way of building the basic skeleton of a house—quick, light, inexpensive, effective even against prairie storm, and ugly. Its bareness and utility persisted into the twentieth century, dominating the lower-middle-class house in the small town and city. It is a characteristic dwelling made for people who have never known, from one generation to another, where they would be settling down to live. For such people houses are not built to last over generations or transmit a family heritage and sense of place, but for the here and now, out of available materials and skills. Americans built their houses as they built their railroad tracks and locomotives, their plows and firearms and cotton gins—for utility. When they grew wealthy, they still gave the prime job to the structural engineer and then called in the architect to add the decorative touches and the grace notes. Thus the Americans were led, by their feeling for structure, to draw a false line between the engineering and architectural phases of building. Hence the foliation of what came to be called "American baroque," and the lavish distortions both of form and function in the Brown Decades of the 1870s and 1880s.

One of the merits of what came to be known in the 1930s as the "International Style" of architecture, with the emphasis on geometrical planes and angles, on the use of steel and glass and concrete, and on the maximum access to light and openness, was that it lent itself to big public-housing projects. The members of this school, especially Le Cor-busier, Gropius, and Mies Van der Rohe, stressed the close relation between form and function. Their opponents delighted in mocking Le Corbusier's epigram that houses must be "machines for living"; and it is true that the American functionalists developed a spare and cold style which made many uncomfortable, especially when separated from public housing and applied to the individual dwelling. In contrast, Frank Lloyd Wright continued with his poetic strain, calling for a close relationship between interior, exterior, and environment, using warm-colored woods and bricks and rough stone, and building houses which hug the landscape and sometimes seem to grow out of it. He professed to care less about men's daily needs than about their aspirations, less whether the house served their purposes than what living in it did to them.

The recent trend in American building has been toward a fusion of style, with some borrowings from the historical forms of Colonial, Georgian, and Southwest, with the use of whatever materials are most accessible, with a strong leaning toward regional styles: it has enough of the functional to show its impact, yet it retains the warm and informal qualities which most Americans regard as "livable." In essence, it is fluid and mobile in form, the living memorial of the fact that Americans are a composite product of many cultural strains, and that they are as little didactic in their housing as in their political ideas.

The big fact is that the battle cry of "houses for the people" which haunted the European architects at the turn of the century did find ful-fillment in America, where tradesman, worker, or farmer could have a house of his own for his family. With the growth of the big city a new problem arose about housing the workers and white-collar classes in the congested areas. This seemed to leave the large mass of the population doomed to crowded and ugly living quarters. An eventual solution was indicated in the development of mass-produced housing projects in the suburbs, with the basic heating and service units prefabricated and with the arts of pouring the foundations and putting up the walls reduced to standardized procedure.* In 1910, as Peter Blake points out, an automo-bile and a one-family house cost about the same to build: today the house costs ten times what the automobile does, while the automobile is a good deal larger and the house a good deal smaller. This is to say that even with the new developments, the Industrial Revolution in building has not yet carried through as it has in the mass-production industries.

It has remained for the recent low-cost housing on a mechanical model to generate again the energy for town planning which American

* For a discussion of these projects, along with the whole question of American housing (as distinguished from architecture), see Ch. III, Sec. 6, "The Sinews of Wel-fare: Health, Food, Dwelling, Security," and Sec. 10, "The Suburban Revolution."

building once possessed, especially in Connecticut and other New England towns in the Colonial period. The planning impulse in the big American cities today comes either from the shift in dwelling patterns as the "less desirable" ethnic and income groups press against the "residential" areas, or from the problems of traffic congestion. As dwelling units grow less desirable and fall into neglect and disuse, a chance is provided for rebuilding and replanning whole sections of a city, as if it were sloughing off its old skin and growing a new one.

Great architecture is based on belief. Americans have not yet developed a way of domestic life sharply enough differentiated so that a body of belief can be built on it and in turn give rise to a distinctive architecture. But they do believe in their system of technology. To put it differently, Americans have had greater success with the arts of consumption and comfortable living than with the problem of their life purposes. Wherever they have built structures connected with production—factories, office buildings, hydroelectric dams, power generators and transmission lines, road networks—there has been a sureness about them absent from the recent fumblings with domestic architecture.

To the balloon frame for the wooden house, which I have mentioned, the Americans have added as a more lasting contribution the steel frame for the big industrial and office structure. That too emerged from Chicago, which had to be rebuilt after the Great Fire, and offered a new start for new ideas. In what may be seen as the great Renaissance period of American architecture a little group in Chicago—notably Dankmar Adler, Louis Sullivan, and William Le Baron Jenney—evolved the skeleton of the commercial skyscraper and filled the steel frame in with stone and cement.

The American skyscraper is a good illustration of John Ruskin's thesis about "The Lamp of Power" in his *Seven Lamps of Architecture*. I use skyscraper as a term for any of the tall office buildings that tower above every American city, at once an instrument and monument of American industrial genius. It may be the *Tribune* Tower in Chicago, or Rockefeller Center or the Empire State or Chrysler buildings in New York, or the *News* Building in San Francisco: almost always it is the power projection of some man, family, or institution. It is meant in theory to conserve valuable ground space in the badly congested areas of New York, Chicago, Cleveland, Detroit. But those who have seen a twenty-story office building jutting out of the flat spaces of a Texas or Oklahoma landscape, with plenty of elbow room immediately around, will understand that with these massive piles of masonry, steel, and cement built on the smallest possible plot, the congestion is not diminished but increased. There is in the skyscraper tower what Ruskin, Henry Adams, and Spengler saw in the Gothic spire—an aspiration toward stature which is as strong in an oil boom town with plenty of building space as it is in New York with little.

But even in crowded city quarters, where every foot of space counted, the problem of light persists. The new urban trend, largely influenced by the International Style, is toward buildings which use enough surrounding space so as to make their geometric designs visible. It is as if Americans had grown sure enough of themselves to afford a setting for their sense of power. Something of the same has happened with their bridges, as notably in the case of the George Washington Bridge over the Hudson: the original plan called for a "decorative" concrete sheeting around the steel towers at each end of the bridge; the structural design itself was so striking that public protest against any decorative additions left it standing "unfinished."

There is more to the skyscraper than height: there is also an economy of structure and a simplicity of line which are true of other forms of the architecture of power in America. They are true of the modern factories, bridges, parkways, auto highways, aqueducts, tunnels under rivers, railroad stations, airfields, air hangars, hospitals. Whether publicly or privately owned, these are the public buildings of America in which functions are carried on that have validity in American eyes. This cannot be said in equal degree of American colleges and schools, nor of the churches and cathedrals. Unlike the early New England village churches, which had simplicity, solidity, and harmony with the religion and the community, the current church buildings in America look hollow and derived, evidence that the true gods of America are housed elsewhere. The American state capitols tend also toward the ornate, as if their grandiose lines were a way of saying that the real power is not in the government but in the technological frame of society.

My underlying assumption here, like Ruskin's, is that it is hard to tell a lie in architecture since it will show through. The convincing buildings are those with belief behind them. The style a people develops in wood, stone, and steel is as much an expression of its inner being as the style it develops in words and music, in line and color.

Closely related to industrial building is industrial design. Americans have rediscovered the effectiveness with which the early settlers fashioned articles of daily use, giving them a simplicity later lost in the decades of the "American Provincial." Writing with a passion for what he calls the "vernacular" as against the "cultivated" tradition, John A. Kouwenhoven sang the praises of the Revolutionary rifle, the lowly manure fork, the plow, the railroad locomotive, the sewing machine, the clipper ship, the machine tool, the Model-T Ford. Certainly Americans have been at their best at industrial design when they have been least self-conscious and least "arty." Equally, as a machine culture, they would be out of character if they scorned the products of the machine process. Although skilled with their hands, their genius does not lie—as it did for the Renaissance craftsmen or for the artisans in rural and still primitive communities—in the laborious handicraft which is transmitted from generation to generation. The Americans achieve their effects by making machines which in turn produce standardized products that, at their best, have precision and cleanness of design and utility for their purpose. There is no longer any need to refute the argument that what is machine-made is inferior in either use or beauty, and what is turned out for a mass market loses the distinctiveness it would have if only one example of it were available.

The illustrations of this thesis surround American life everywhere: among the lasting contributions of American domestic architecture are the bathroom and the kitchen. Both express the American belief in sanitation and in utility. Similarly, a new profession has arisen—that of the "industrial designer," whose function is to give attractiveness of outline and packaging to the mass-produced commodities. The result has been the focusing of new attention upon cigarette packages, soap and soup wrappers, knives and forks, flatirons, automobiles, dining-room chairs, washing machines, typewriters, radio and TV sets, whisky bottles, refrigerators, electric ranges, waste baskets, perambulators.

The design of machine-made, useful American products has not always been a happy one. The case of the mass-produced automobile underscores the difficulties and compromises. Wholly in engineering terms, the automobile has many unnecessary features that the trade calls "chromium razzle-dazzle." This violates directly the principle that design which adds decoration and has no meaning for use makes little sense as design.

The American automobile industry has come a long way since the Model-T Ford, which made no concessions to gadgeteering and refused —as Ford put it in 1923—"to change designs so that old models will become obsolete and new ones will have to be bought." A self-respecting automobile owner would be terrified at the idea of holding on to a model more than two or three years old. Each year's model must seem more lustrous and dazzling than the previous year's—which in its turn was presented as the ultimate. The situation, both with respect to obsolescence and to fashion, is much as with women's clothes. Like the clothes, the automobile must set off the personality of the owner and must take not too long to wear out and be replaced. Given the conditions of city traffic and bumper-to-bumper auto roads on week ends, the swollen fenders—vulnerable to the slightest dent and abrasion—make no sense in design: they make sense only in obsolescence and show. Similarly, the size and unnecessary extra engine power of the American car are intended to nourish the feeling of magnitude rather than to serve ordinary users. These are all phases of a civilization which has a margin for waste and which has come to regard the luxurious as the necessary.

In contrast to the auto, the American airplane illustrates the best in American design. Every element of it is shaped and built for speed, engineering, reliability, and safety. There are no frills or unnecessary gadgets. Yet—or perhaps therefore—the beauty of the airplane has scarcely been surpassed in the history of industrial design. The crucial difference between the plane and the auto is that the auto is produced for a mass consumer's market while the plane is not. The pace for selling autos is set by their production. The problem in planes is to supply the demand, not to create it.

Thus the thesis that the vernacular* is always right cannot be sustained. The elements of taste that enter into design through high-pressure salesmanship and conspicuous display do not always make for simplicity, economy, and beauty. When the vernacular style wages a battle against the merely decorative elements of elite art, or against the stodginess of traditional art, it is likely to triumph through its vigor and directness. But when it becomes itself associated with the emulation of elite values, while staying in a mass-production market—as in the case of most automobiles, with the honorable exception of the "jeep" and some of the simpler station wagons—it falls foul of its own principles. Finally, the vernacular style runs into trouble when it sets up a false standard of nativism. The International Style in architecture has its own strengths and defects, but the fact that it is an importation from European experience has no relevance to its merits. American art, building, and design have throughout their history borrowed ideas from foreign cultures and have in turn had an impact upon them. America has shown a hospitality to artists and designers from abroad that has kept its indigenous elements of strength from becoming too ingrown. While there are nativist outbursts from those who resent the influence of foreign architects and designers, these are passing episodes. There is remarkably little cultural isolationism as yet among a people who can take pride in having created their own world of machine commodities with a design of their own.

* The terms "vernacular" and "cultivated" as used here need some precision of meaning. The "vernacular" style is associated with the immediate realities of democracy-and-technology; I use "cultivated" to refer to the tradition acceptable to the elites, whether of the arts, of wealth, or of birth. In Europe the vernacular tradition blended largely with the cultivated tradition; in America there has been antagonism between the two.

9. *Artist and Audience in a Democratic Culture*

PERIODICALLY, when the arts in America are in the doldrums, the blame is put on one of the new media. But it is idle to talk of any art as the enemy of the others. The theater lives in the golden shadow of Hollywood, and the novel seems at times tributary to it: but that does not make Hollywood their enemy. Nor is photography an enemy to painting, nor jazz to "serious" music, any more than night baseball is an enemy to the concert hall or the mystery to the novel. Even TV, whose shadow seems to have fallen on movies, radio, and book publishing, can scarcely be regarded as the Adversary. For to think of the arts as rivals is to think of them as flowing from a fixed fund of energy, so that a popular devotion to one of them means anemia for the others. It is true that some of the newer and lustier popular arts display an imperialistic bent in crowding their neighbors, but in its youth each of the elite arts was also arrogant in its imperialism. Actually the movies and jazz, radio and TV, the paperbacks and the spectacle arts, have reinforced one another because their vitality is contagious rather than sterilizing.

I am not talking here of the question of what medium commands a larger segment of the Big Audience. Given limited leisure, it is plausible that a revolutionary increase in the TV audience should have a drastic effect on movie attendance. But such audience rivalry is different from the rivalry in the intellectual and aesthetic standards of the media. Quite possibly American radio may be able to reach better levels of achievement by limiting itself to good music, news commentary, political discussion, and suspense shows, than it reached when it spread itself thin into areas where TV can do better. The movies may discover that TV cannot be surpassed in the histrionic display of sex and violence, or in the presentation of a documentary sense of the immediate moment: by concentrating on emotion and characterization it may perform for TV the kind of generative function that the theater over several generations performed for the movies. There is a big enough audience in America to furnish for each popular art some perceptive portion of the population that will sustain it economically, especially since another popular art may use it as a feeder for ideas and talent.

In thus dismissing the necessity of a Big Audience I do not accept the view that any art which has one is thereby cheapened. This would be to hold that the chief enemy of the arts is their popularization. One may believe that the spreading of an art wide among a mass audience necessarily brings with it a dilution of its standards: "the wider you spread it, the thinner it spreads." But to hold this view mechanically means, for example, to forget the creative achievements of an art like the movies. It implies a curious antipopulism—a fear that the wide support of an art must taint its quality or destroy its fine bloom. This is the Great Fear that one finds in American literary and art criticism; and one can match it only by the Great Contempt that one finds in turn on the part of the Big Audience—a contempt for the elite arts it cannot understand and whose aestheticism it distrusts. The contempt and the fear together split a society into a Big Audience and a Little Audience, driving a wedge between the creative people and those who are needed to nourish their creativeness.

The fear of the "horde" in art undercuts one of the cultural assumptions of a democracy—that the human personality is a bundle of potentials irrelevant to income or social or even educational rating, and that the richness of popular culture will depend on how well those potentials are fulfilled. The Elizabethan theater in Shakespeare's time, the great church music of the Middle Ages, the acting of Chaplin and Garbo in Hollywood in our own time: all have been people's arts. To be sure, the need for reaching a Big Audience has often been used to excuse the trivial and unexacting. But there is proof enough that, if greatly conceived, the popular arts can derive strength from a massive popular base and can reach the many by reducing themselves to simplest elements—that is, to their broadest humanity.

If we take American painting as an instance, we find an art that has never appealed to a wide audience. It has suffered from the twin plagues of the Expensive and the Esoteric. Having made their fortunes, the American captains of industry ransacked European galleries for their best works and brought them home at big prices. Since the dead masters were the object of their pecuniary piety, they stored them in museums; and most Americans came to think of painting as something in a museum or a rich man's house, removed from their lives—and so they ignored it. The painter, in turn, cut off from his audience except for an inner circle of means and sensibility, came to despise those whom he could not reach.

This isolation of artist and audience from each other has been attributed to the machine, which revolutionized the market for art products as for other commodities. Where the product is one of unique workmanship and is not reproducible, as in painting and sculpture, the arts have remained much as they were during the Age of Handicraft. Even in painting the revolutionary techniques of reproduction have made possible a "museum without walls." In the case of the printed and spoken word and of images and movement, the press and film and electronics have made them infinitely reproducible and infinitely accessible. The machine has made possible the widespread appreciation of music, the cheap distribution of literary classics, the enactment of dramatic performances in thousands of movie centers and millions of homes.

The problem of distribution in the arts has been effectively broken. What remains is the question of the conditions of creativeness. I have suggested that in America this problem focuses not on the fact of popularization but on the isolation of the artist. The pushing, successful people among the Americans regard him as an outsider. They do not make a hero of him, as they do of the technical or moneyed genius or the man of power, or even the successful performer in a Big-Audience medium. At best they regard him as a luxury a culture can perhaps afford. Where once the American artist had to wage the Emersonian fight for self-reliance and for freedom from a sense of provincialism, his main fight now is for acceptance in a culture that values the pecuniary. This has led him periodically to flight abroad, especially to France and Italy, where he could thrive in a social climate of acceptance. Sometimes it has led to surrender to the idols of the market, sometimes to a flight into himself. The European apprenticeship has been of value to American artists, but the surrender has been uniformly destructive, and the flight into himself has usually led to obscurity rather than depth. But the American artist has been maturing, and some have achieved the power of synthesis—of exploring their own being without cutting themselves off from the currents of their place and time.

Since the pressures to conform are strong, the artist still works in a difficult environment in America. When he fights against them he runs the danger of joining a coterie which spins out a narrowly private universe with an incommunicable language. He finds it hard to assimilate the rapid pace of cultural change and the vast human deposits of his own culture. He may retreat to the realism of describing one "slice of life" he knows, but he makes no connections between it and the universal values he has failed to grasp. The poet or painter may single out a few crucial items of experience as symbols for the whole, but he soon finds that to handle symbolism as well takes even greater grasp than to handle naturalism. He may concentrate on a locale or region which seems manageable, only to find that the problems of creativeness are not diminished by shrinking the map. Failing there, he almost always turns to the popular arts. Sometimes the Pilgrim's Progress of a writer or artist in America is a progression through all these phases.

The fatal magnetic force is that of the Big Prizes. Given the Big Audience, the prizes are big enough to engender cupidity and enforce timidity. There is no scorn in America more withering than the scorn felt for "the highbrow." The charge against him is not only that he cuts himself off from the people but also from "reality"—which is identified with making money. The easiest way to get at the Big Prizes is by pandering to the culture traits in all classes that will mean a sure-fire sale. The Midas touch which turns everything in American life to gold does not spare the energies that might otherwise go into difficult reaches of the intelligence and imagination.

If the artist decides to take the pecuniary culture in his stride, aiming at a good living without chasing the Big Prizes, he will still come up against another obstacle—the increasing bureaucratization of the arts. He will need an agent and a lawyer to take care of his contracts; or he may go on concert and lecture tours, barnstorming across the country, largely repeating himself but making money enough to let him do the work he loves the rest of the year. If he is a playwright, he must deal with Broadway producers, theater owners, stage-hand unions. If he is a musician he must pay for an initial recital and "paper the house" with free tickets. As a painter he must be *persona grata* to galleries, museums, rich customers. As an actor or radio performer, he must deal with the networks and sponsors, and with their agents and his own. If he is an architect he must tangle with building codes and city officials and the construction unions. As a novelist he must reckon with serial rights, book-club and cheap reprint rights, movie rights. For the novelist, playwright, and actor there is the guild of reviewers to reckon with, who have it in their power to damn an author or performer who has proved a literary or political heretic, slaying him either with abuse or silence. For the short-story writer there is either the poverty of a host of "little magazines" or the Big Circulation magazines that pay well but may exact in return a large measure of conventionality in art and a conformity in politics.

Even the star system, which seems at the opposite pole from bureaucracy in the arts, works in much the same way. The movie star, the boxing champion or baseball hero, the TV comic of national fame—all represent a huge investment in which many financial groups may have a stake. Highly personalized though their lives may seem, they are actually depersonalized since they must move within narrow patterns set by the bureaucracy their public image serves. It is usual for the writer, composer, or designer in the popular arts to remain anonymous while the performer is played up. It is not the creator but the executor whom the public gets to know as symbol—not the novelist or script writer or composer, but the starred actors and perhaps the director or producer; not the radio or TV writer but the gagster or crooner or the M.C. of the variety shows. The folk heroes of popular culture, as is true of all folklore, are not the creators but the protagonists—of radio serial or comic strip, baseball field or movie studio. There is thus an anonymity in the popular arts that does not exist in the elite arts—the anonymity of the creator but not of the hero. This lack of interchange between the creator and his audience may account for much of the isolation of the artist of which I have spoken. It is a tossup whether the anonymity of the creator or the stardom of the performer is more destructive to personality.

Despite these obstacles, the American artist has one advantage the European artist lacks—the sense of cultural hope and dynamism in a people reaching out for new ways of expressing itself. The American feels he has a future, while the European feels caught. Out of this sense of being caught may come a quality, at once mellow and doomed, which will not be found in the American writer, who has new media always opening for him. Thus the American artist has typically a more meteoric rise and a more abrupt collapse than the European. This has proved true of young novelists who start as sensitive recorders of what they remember, catching the characteristic tone of their generation and pinning it down as you might mount a butterfly. But the high expressive moment of the generation passes, and if the young novelist or playwright has no other resources than gaiety and vitality and the gift of transcription, he stops in his tracks as a writer and goes to pieces in his life.

If the career of the artist in America has its dangers, which I have described, it also has its strength. Popular culture has performed a great ground-clearing function by breaking the monopoly over taste that the elite arts held so long in the Western World. But to clear the ground is only a first step toward constructing a new structure of sensibility. There remains the question of by whom and for whom it will be built.

This is not a new problem in America. The split between the "vernacular" and the "cultivated," which I have discussed earlier, started with the long-barreled rifles of the frontier and the economical lines of the farmer's tools. The issues of battle have never been sharply defined: it is not always the mass-produced as against the unique product, nor the popular as against coterie art, nor the "modern" and "functional" as against the academic. Nor can one agree that when the vernacular has won out against the cultivated, as has repeatedly happened in American history, it has always been to the advantage of the product. Yet if it is possible to speak of an artistic culture predominantly phrased in the vernacular—that is to say, a popular culture—

America must be counted its most fateful experimental instance. What some of the younger art historians and critics call a "democratic aesthetic" will either be shaped in America or nowhere.

One question about it is whether it must rest on indigenous art forms alone. If this is taken to mean exclusively home-grown forms and techniques it would be absurd, since it would force each culture to cut itself off from the world and retraverse every step other cultures have taken. Throughout American history there has run a demand for a nativist art, whether in architecture or literature, music or aviation design. In part this has been a recoil from an earlier cultural provincialism, but it has maintained its self-assertiveness and been sustained long after the declaration of cultural independence. At their best the nativists have seen that an indigenous art may and must borrow widely: what makes it indigenous is how it uses the materials it finds at home and abroad, and how it weaves them into a pattern expressing the common experience.

An indigenous art in this sense need not be troubled by the question of the classes from which its material derives or by which its product is accepted. Just as Joyce could appropriate scatological language and make out of it a complex art product intelligible only to the few, so the American language has shown that it can adapt the restricted phrases of the educated classes and integrate them—often with a saving grace of irony—into its own mood and pattern. American ballet has taken traditional dance form derived from the aristocratic societies of St. Petersburg and Vienna and fused it—as in Agnes De Mille's *Fall River Legend*—with the folk material of America, giving it a tongue-in-cheek hyperbole that stamps it as American popular culture. Because these forms have been mixed with the sweat of American experience the lowly do not distrust them as highbrow, nor does the elite despise them as vulgar, but all classes can relax and accept the accents of the universal in the indigenous. These art forms are in turn accepted abroad because they bear the smell of the soil from which they came, yet break through the walls of cultural separation.

Within this frame of the universal the accents of the American vernacular often crop up in very diverse arts. Thus, there are a stridency and exaggeration running through folklore and speech as they do through the comic gag, the radio and TV program, and the spectacle sports—as if the tone of the frontier swaggerers were able to be maintained because the richness of the unbroken wilderness still persisted among the towers of the city. Thus also there is, throughout the popular arts, a blending of the rustic and urban such as will be found in few other cultures. This is illustrated by the blues songs and jazz, whose themes and overtones belong to a preindustrial people but whose beat carries the tensions of the big cities.

To a curious degree the American popular culture, unlike the "Socialist realism" of Marxian cultures, stays clear of the descriptively naturalistic. On the surface it uses the method of realism, but it achieves its characteristic effects in the abstractions from reality. It is a kind of cartoon or gargoyle art, in which everything is bigger than life. This is true of a rich vein of the comic tradition in Hollywood from the Keystone Cops and Charlie Chaplin through W. C. Fields, Harry Langdon, and the Marx Brothers, and of the radio comic tradition which Jimmy Durante expresses. It is also part of the American theater, from the early traveling minstrel shows through the masks of O'Neill's characters and the poetic expressionism of Tennessee Williams. The same abstraction from life will be found at once in movie musicals and spectacles, in jazz and in the skyscrapers (the "jazz of architecture"), as it will also be found in painting. The younger expressionist painters and sculptors who have never won popular acceptance have a quality similar to that of "cool jazz."

This makes hash of much of the "battle of the brows" in the controversies over American taste. I have mentioned in an earlier chapter the amusing discussion by Russell Lynes, in the manner of Thackeray's *Book of Snobs*, on the highbrow, lowbrow, and middlebrow in America.* The truth is that tastes of Americans, like their classes, are hopelessly intermingled. Legend has it that Justice Holmes, a Yankee Brahmin, slapped his knee while sitting at a burlesque show and muttered to his neighbor, "Thank God for our low tastes." The American who likes Jackson Pollock is likely also to delight over the travail of Li'l Abner; the enthusiast for Frank Lloyd Wright may devour cheap mystery stories and roar over the obsessive adventures of Groucho Marx. The fluidity of the class system, the sweep of common experience, and the spread of the big media have done havoc to the hierarchy of the brows, and American society never remains stable long enough for the brows to rigidify in their angle of elevation. Moreover, one can discern in contemporary American literary circles (as Riesman suggests) a separation between the Old Highbrow and the New Highbrow. The Old Highbrow has an attitude of either reserve or hostility toward popular culture, either because as an aristocrat he regards it as vulgar or because as a radical he sees it as a corrupt product of capitalist incentives. The New Highbrow, recoiling both from the genteel tradition and from Marxism, has come to embrace popular culture, finding in it—shoddi-

* Ch. IX, Sec. 3, "Manners, Taste, and Fashion."

ness and all—something of the mystique the eighteenth-century intellectual found in the Noble Savage.

There are signs, however, of a new criticism which will separate the true vernacular from the spurious mob language and combine the best of the vernacular with the best from the elite arts. Such a critic will face the fact that the big media will tend to gravitate toward whatever is flat, stale, and profitable, that the press lords will debase their product and the radio sponsors will narrow the imaginative world of the radio to the compass of their own shriveled intellectual universe. But he will not retreat in despair, but will see the growth of popular culture in perspective, just as he looks back at the history of the elite arts and sees in perspective that they too had the vigor to outgrow their excesses.

Where the Old Highbrow regards every Big Audience as a bad one and the New Highbrow sees the Big Audience as a great one, the critic I speak of will understand that the great audience is only a potential in the Big Audience, and that the potential will not be fulfilled except in an intellectual climate that affirms its possibilities even while it criticizes the actual product. He will not despise the movies and TV because mainly the young are drawn to them, but neither will he count that fact in itself an index of vitality. He will recognize that every form of popular culture has varied levels of audience appeal, and that a mature art will shape its product—as Chaplin did in the movies—to reach each audience on its own terms, yet hold them all in suspension by universals which give each a new dimension. He will respect the subtleties and richness of the American language, and the capacity of the common speech to express the common experience of Americans. He will not scorn the escapist in the arts, since imagination must create a sheath within which to feel secure before it can release its quickening energies. But he will refuse to the popular arts—as to any art—the easy, jerry-built solutions to old human dilemmas, exacting from them the emotional honesty with which a mature man cannot dispense.

This is the final test of a democratic aesthetic, whose parallel will be found in the politics and economics of a democracy. No one expects a general leveling of either income or power, but a democracy does require that the whole personality of every man be valued by giving him access to the common political and economic opportunity. Similarly, a democratic aesthetic will not level intellectual and taste standards; but it will reject the principle of a frozen elite of the arts. It will open a hospitable door to any experience which can be phrased in a universal language of art from which no one need be shut out. It will value the indigenous material not because it is "native" or "American" but because—coming out of the common experience—it can be couched in this common language of emotion, so that the reader or listener is at once source and receiver of the creative process. In this sense a democratic aesthetic, like a democratic ethic, gives dignity to every personality.

The foreigner's picture of American popular culture, whether in Europe, Asia, or Latin America, is often wide of the mark. The Communist campaign against "degenerate" American jazz or the "corrupt" press or "degrading" movies or "Coca-Cola imperialism" sometimes impresses many who are otherwise sympathetic to America and its democratic experience. But Americans are needlessly worried about this obviously ephemeral phase. Foreign cultures have accepted and absorbed American movies—and in some cases gone on to produce better ones of their own; they have picked up the more colorful phrases of the American language from soldiers, travelers, and books; they have been deeply influenced by American jazz, by American design in the items of daily use, by American novelists and playwrights. Whatever proves to be universally valid in American culture will make its way in other cultures.

The idea that movies or jazz or literature is a "weapon" in the international struggle has been overstressed in American anxieties about them. It is foolish to use this as an argument for censorship or for changing the direction of the arts themselves. Movies cannot be prettified merely because they will give Communists abroad a handle for attacking America, nor can the historic fact that jazz originated in the brothels of Storyville be muted because it is used against America. In the domain of artistic integrity, cold wars intrude a dimension of irrelevance. The popular arts will serve American interests best when they express with depth and universality the surging impulses of the common American experience.

CHAPTER XII

America As a World Power

WE COME *finally to an over-all view of America's place in the frame of world power, asking what kind of power it embodies and how much promise or menace it holds for the world (Sec. 1, "Among the Powers of the Earth"). We examine what currents of thought, impulse, and emotion have shaped American foreign policy, what strategies of national interest it has tended to use, and what sense Americans have had of their mission in world history and their role in the world struggle (Sec. 2, "The Shaping Currents").*

Among other things we ask some of the questions that have long engaged students of American life—what are the roots of isolationism in the American mind, and to what extent it still survives, what impact the nation as a social myth has had, what has impelled America to enter the arena of world power actively, what have been the sources and forms of American expansionism, and whether America is basically an imperium—*a power mass content to let alone and be let alone, interested mainly in world order and peace—or also an* imperialism, *throwing its weight around and bent on making its own institutions and its ways of life prevail (Sec. 3, "National Interest and an Open World").*

We try to get a closer look at Americans at war and in a military posture, examining the relations of military to civilian internally and the role of the military elite in a highly technical atomic era (Sec. 4, "Landscape with Soldiers"). We then take a double exposure of the American image, asking first what image the Americans have of the world outside their national boundaries, and then what image of America is to be found in the minds of the other peoples of the world, and in both instances what leads to the distortions and stereotypes (Sec. 5, "The American World Image"; Sec. 6, "The World's Image of America"). Finally we look backward in history for parallels to the present American situation, paying special attention to the often discussed Roman parallel, and we look at the relations of the two super powers—America and Russia—in the world of today and tomorrow, and then we venture a look into the calculable future in an effort to get a glimpse of the destiny of America as a civilization (Sec. 7, "The Destiny of a Civilization").

Thus we end the chapter and the book.

CHAPTER XII

America As a World Power

1. Among the Powers of the Earth

THE rise of America to a position of world power focuses attention on the qualities that underlie so dramatic a rise. When the nascent Americans met in 1776 to declare their independence, they voiced the hope that they would "assume among the powers of the earth the separate and equal station to which the laws of Nature and of Nature's God entitle them." They could scarcely have suspected that these straggling colonies of small population—huddled along a strip of ocean coast, pitifully weak and disunited, with survival their most pressing problem —would assume in less than two centuries a commanding position "among the powers of the earth." To a contemporary observer so daring a perspective of the grandeurs of world power must have seemed a megalomanic fantasy of minds that had dwelt too bitterly on their weakness and grievances.

How explain this mushrooming rise to power? The important clues are less likely to be found in the history of diplomacy or the record of America's wars than in the drive within American institutions and in the intellectual and moral features of American character, helped by a cluster of favoring circumstances.

First among these circumstances was *geography,* which equipped the nation with the resources on which power always rests. It provided the timber that made it a shipbuilding people, and the sea lanes that made it a trading people while severing it by the span of oceans from the centers of world production, giving it thus the impetus to develop its own industries. It furnished the sinews first for a technology of coal, then of electricity, and now of atomic power. Geography made available also a great land mass ready to be rounded out by settlement, purchase, and conquest, giving shape to the ever-present sense of continental unity and providing a striking combination of safety and access. There have been great land empires before and great maritime empires, but it would be hard to cite an earlier land empire with its own available sea lanes, or an earlier maritime empire with so vast an expanse as its land core. The availability of land and access by sea—and later, jobs and wealth, living standards, freedom, and the legendry of America—made America the magnet that drew people from all over the world. Thus *man power* was added to *resources* and *technology,* as the sinews of the American's command over Nature.

This command made possible a high industrial *productivity,* which in turn gave weight to America's voice in peace and arms in war. It led to the repayment of the big European investments when, early in the present century, the Europeans had to call them in. It gave America a favorable trade balance, turning it into an investing nation which exported capital to the world's undeveloped regions. It was *investment* that enabled America to become a mighty engine of world finance gathering increments of power from old enterprises bolstered or new enterprises opened with American capital. It was *finance* in turn that shifted the economic center of the world westward across the Atlantic, making America the axis of power on which the non-Communist world turned.

Thus, geography, technology, man power, productivity, investment, and finance are links in the Great Chain holding American power together. America's world position is not wholly summed up in these terms of economics and geopolitics. It was a fallacy of Marxist thought to assume the inevitable collapse of world capitalism through the weight of its inner contradictions. This involved a blunder of diagnosis. It assumed that the Western World, the scene of a succession of power struggles between capitalist Great Powers, was on its deathbed. Marx and Engels announced the coming funeral, and Lenin read the funeral oration. Spengler unfolded an apocalyptic vision of what was to follow. They failed to see that the Western World, including Europe, might have a greater recuperative power than they had counted upon.

This was linked with a second blunder of diagnosis, which was concerned with America. Every great system of European thought, from Marx to Toynbee, saw America as at best an appendage of the larger "Western" system which was at the mercy of its inner laws of disintegration and decay. They did not grasp the import of this new world power—born out of straggling colonies, at the start a "have-not nation" beset by hostile "have" powers, filling out its continental expanse, sweeping away whatever obstructed it, girdling the seas with naval power, darkening the skies with air power, waxing in strength while other nations were waning, perhaps even *because* the others were waning. The Europe they saw as the center of Western power turned out to be the rim, and the America they saw as the rim turned out to be the center. Nor did they understand the capacity of this new center to extend and re-create the tradition of European power and yet remain its own entity with its own laws of being and conditions of health and unhealth.*

* For an earlier discussion of this failure of perspective, see Ch. II, Sec. 2.

It was not technology or economics alone that accounted for the rise of this new power, nor will they alone condition its decline and fall when the time is ripe. What is crucial about America as a world power is that very mixture of idealism and material power which has evoked many a jibe and has been the substance of almost every "exposé" of the contradictions of American foreign policy. If the Americans have been conquerors in the domain of world power they have come not as conquerors with a sword or a book, but with the machine, the dollar, and the idea of freedom. One of the difficulties with both the economic interpretation and the Machiavellian interpretation of world power is that they neglect intangibles and social myths as in themselves decisive power elements. The fact that America emerged out of a colonial revolution, the first modern symbol of liberation from imperialism, gave it an impulsion toward world power which was worth many Army divisions. It could not, of course, have risen to its present domination through this freedom symbolism alone. Yet it served as a kind of "multiplier," giving an enhanced force to every element of substantive strength derived from geography and economics.

The power factor of freedom can be spelled out on at least three scores. First, it brought some of the best human resources in the world to American shores, through a selective process of emigration by which the restless energies of each nation found an outlet in America. Second, the birth of America in colonial revolt meant that there was never any entrenched feudal class (as in France) against which continuing revolutionary action was needed: America's strength was thus not splintered by internal class struggles on the European model. Third, the legendry of America as the land of freedom has served as a dynamic weapon of political warfare on the side of every American cause, from that of the Northern States in the Civil War, through the two world wars to the present time. Marx's writings on the Civil War are testimony to the force of this legendry; in World War I the *éclat* of Wilson's Fourteen Points and the excitement produced by his appearance in Europe were additional proof of it.

Thus the "revolutionary idealism" of Wilson—and, to an extent, of Franklin Roosevelt—so bitterly attacked by champions of American "national interest," turns out to have been part of the American world strength which protects that national interest. In both world wars, America's role was to help a European coalition whose defeat America feared, just as it feared the victory of the opposing coalition. Later America became the center of a democratic coalition seeking to win and hold allies in the struggle against a Communist coalition. This change cannot be seen in Marx's terms of the weakness and inner disintegration of capitalist power, nor in Lenin's terms of the division of the world among imperialist cartels. It is more intelligible as the radiation of a strong organizing force out from the center into a vacuum left by the decline of the European power system, and into a receptive border zone of colonial countries emerging into their own in the Near East and Far East. Thus America's rise as a world power, far from being a deterioration story of the decay of an old system, marks the thrust of a strong new system into an arena where it has to meet the counterthrust of another new and expanding power.

In the process of its history and the carving out of its imperium, America shows signs of having grown conservative. It has the sense, as the Romans had, of being enveloped by the encroaching forces of the new barbarians, and it is caught within a ring of fears of "alien" and "subversive" ideas. The face it shows to the world is, however, only one aspect of its character. The other, implicit in the historical emergence I have traced, is the aspect of a continuing revolutionary energy. The nature of that energy has great bearing on the destiny and survival power of the civilization pattern I have tried to analyze. There is little question that the present age is one of world revolution, with a ferment of colonial revolt, movements of national awakening, new amalgams of economic and social power, peoples in the breaking and making. The fact that Americans shy away from the concept of revolution should not obscure the more important fact that Americans have had a revolutionary history, and that their rise to world power has itself been the product of a revolutionary era.

The present era of world power is not revolutionary in a suddenly new form: it is the extension into our own times of a long-continuing series of social transformations that have changed the profile of societies and shifted the axis of power from one capital to another. There is no single clue that will unravel the logic behind this shift, whether it be the clue of technological change, or of military vigor, or of the personality of great leaders, or of master ideas and religions. An adequate account would see world history as shaped by movements which are vaster in scope than single nations and peoples, or even continental expanses of resources and armies, but are great energy systems drawing vitality from every source, and organizing armies and ideas, economics and societies, into effective engines of action.

The American revolutionary impulse has not aimed at overthrowing a ruling class or a prevailing system of government. Once the Americans had freed themselves from England they expressed their continuing revolutionary impulse through changes in technology, which in turn have transformed the landscape of American society and culture. That is to say, it has been revolution by indirection, in the sense that the revolutionary changes have been the unintended consequences of actions taken in a matter-of-fact and nonrevolutionary spirit. For example, the demands of a warfare economy and of world power-politics have, by indirection, kept the revolutionary impulse alive in America. For the demands of international politics have in themselves a transforming effect on the internal nature of a social system; and even war is a form of revolution. The structure of heavy taxation, which seems necessary if profits are to be forcibly plowed back by governmental expenditures, was one to which the American business groups became amenable only when danger forced it upon them. The pace of capital formation was also increased by world responsibilities, for while war is one of the great destroyers of capital, the energies of a world power are heightened in the formation of new capital. Thus, far from diminishing as American power was dispersed by new demands around the ramparts of the world, it continued to grow as an energy system.

Curiously, the enlargement of the American world perspective has taken place fitfully, by a process of unwilling advances and forced retreats, almost against the will of the people and their leaders. Faced with the turmoils of a world from which they thought they had safely withdrawn themselves, and with threatening new shapes of crises and power, they reluctantly met the new challenges with new responses. First Europe, then Asia, then the Middle East and Africa were added to the map of American concern. A people that had prided itself on its isolation from foreign entanglements was forced against its will into them. A people that had scorned the wiles of diplomacy and condemned the "striped pants and Homburg boys" and the "cookie-pushers" was forced into a vigorous diplomacy and into developing its own effective type of diplomat. American soldiers, many of whom had never before left their own state, where they had gone to high school or worked at a filling station, roamed over the twelve corners of the earth, reluctant wanderers who resisted the ways of the "foreigners" but would never again be what they had been. In a world where Americans had to hold their coalition together despite the faltering economies of their allies, and where they had to keep undeveloped economies from succumbing to Communism by default, they found new political uses for reconstruction and investment capital and for the export of technical skills and the tools of war and peace.

Hostile critics called this American imperialism; certainly it was, in the sense of an American imperium—a vast structure of military, economic, and administrative power that could be used to override competing structures and achieve its power purposes. But it was also an extension of the same revolutionary process by which Americans had found tools and techniques for whatever was at hand to be done. At every stage, ideas and attitudes lagged behind the new techniques; Americans did what they had to do as a response to the challenge and then grudgingly discovered that their perspective had changed in the process. This was *homo faber,* approaching both peace and war as an engineering problem of finding the right tools. It was not the zealot with a religious idea or the thinker with an intellectual system seeking to transform the work in the image of his dream. If it now built a huge structure of power and commitments in the world, it was as a by-product of its technical drive. The British had once, in Seeley's phrase, "conquered half the world in a fit of absence of mind": the Americans did much the same thing, not absent-mindedly but like a truant schoolboy who stays after hours to dispose of the lessons he should have mastered earlier.

What made the task harder was the fact that, having forgotten their own history as a revolutionary society, they confronted a world in revolution with a sullen bewilderment. The revolutionary techniques that Communists used where they came into power resulted from the welding of Marxist rationalism and predemocratic ruthlessness and were most successful in politically and economically undeveloped areas. The American revolutionary technique was that of technological change in an open-class system, assuming economic development as the prime value, and with a genuine although imperfect commitment to an open society. The question that both America and the world had now to resolve was whether this authentic revolutionary tradition could be applied fruitfully to conflicts of world power and the struggle for men's minds, or whether it had grown into a rigid mold in the process of reaching world power.

2. *The Shaping Currents*

I HAVE SPOKEN of America as the center of one of the great energy systems of history. The thrust of expansionism has been a continuous impulse in American history. Land hunger, power hunger, newness hunger, and bigness hunger, have proved wants that feed on themselves. In the earliest phase of American history it was a question of reaching from the coast far enough into the interior to tap its resources; then the felt need became one of wiping out the Indians in order to use the new resources; and of driving out or buying out the remaining outposts of the British, French, and Spanish so that America would be an exclusive preserve for Americans; then there were exploratory wars fought against Canada and Mexico, to make sure that the neighbors to the north and south were not too difficult to handle and not too imperious as rivals; then the need became that of rounding out the continental expanse and reaching the territorial limits of America's "manifest destiny."

The process was not a matter of course; it took will and imagination. With the image of a continental America in our minds, it is hard to think ourselves back into the mental atmosphere of a period when such an image must have seemed daring. Actually the radical groups of the early period—the Jeffersonians and Jacksonians—were even more eager than the conservatives of the possessing classes for this kind of expansionism. "Manifest destiny" was the rationalization that Americans gave to their expansive thrust and their hunger for land and power, for profits and bigness. Nor has this thrust ended. It would be rash to think that an energy forceful enough to push the frontiers to their continental limits would stop at the ocean's edge.

This raises again the issue of the nature of the American imperium. There can be no question that America has built one of the big empires of history. But to say this is not to carry along with it all the connotations that "imperialism" conveys as a set of drives toward aggrandizement which colors the nature of the imperium. As I have suggested, America did not set out to dominate the world as the Nazis did under Hitler, with a notion that its people were meant to be *Herrenvolk* while the rest were sub-men. There was no ideological fanaticism behind American expansion, as in the case of the Communists. The American case is not even like that of the Roman Empire, which was the product of a similar energy system but which rationalized its expansion as Rome's civilizing function in a world of outworn kingships and barbarian hordes. The Americans come much closer to the British, who had to keep the seas open for their commerce and dressed the need up as "the white man's burden." Even more sharply than the British, the Americans were moved by a drive toward economic power. The business spirit has informed American foreign policy as it has informed every other aspect of American power—the political machines, the legal system, the course of constitutional interpretation, the churches, the press, even the labor movement.

Actually, the American business spirit was for a long time isolationist rather than imperialist. It led Americans to put the development of industry ahead of the quest for territory. That was one reason why the New England shippers and manufacturers opposed the War of 1812 with Britain, while the Western farmers and frontiersmen wanted it. That was also why Americans for a long period cared more about protective tariffs for their "infant industries" than they did about foreign adventures. Once the industries had been built the stream of new immigration provided at once the labor power for exploiting the resources of the country and a vast home market for farm, mine, and factory products. The impulse which did much to shape American policy through most of the nineteenth century was the self-sufficient exploitation of resources and profits within America which Charles Beard, mocking the imperialist phrase, called "the open door at home."

This may shed light on the strain of isolationist thinking which took the form sometimes of the "hermit nation" that could shut itself off from the corruptions and subversions of the rest of the world, sometimes of the idea of defending the American "stockade" against its savage enemies in the surrounding forest, sometimes of the hard-bitten resolve of an individualist nation to "go it alone" in a world of "ungrateful" allies. I want to come back later to an analysis of the nature of the American isolationist pattern. Here I point out that it could prove strong and enduring only among a people with resources, labor power, and home markets rich enough to keep them self-sufficient, and only among a people in a position to profit from self-immersement. America could afford to turn in on itself, away from the world, partly because it was admitting within its borders as much of the world as it could digest and partly because it was already a world within itself. Hence Beard was right in calling the traditional American polity, from Jefferson on, less one of "isolationism" than of "continentalism." It was not so much a question of cutting America off from the world as it was of rounding out and fully exploiting the part of the world that was America.

One can thus trace side by side through the nineteenth century the twin impulses of expansionism and self-sufficiency. Only with the continent rounded out and the home market saturated, when the continental limits of America were bursting at the seams, did American foreign policy encounter a succession of crises. America then had to decide not whether to be a world power, which had been decided for it by events, but what form its decisions about participating in the world struggle were to take. From the 1890s there were premonitions of crisis, but it did not assume its more ominous proportions until the two world wars in the second through the fifth decades of the twentieth century.

Americans had then to reckon with the chance that another great power might not only overshadow them in the world but threaten the stability and survival of their own system at home. In 1914 the danger came from the expanding power of Imperial Germany, threatening to shut off the sea lanes that connected the American industrial system with the materials and markets outside. In 1933 it came from a new ideological force in Germany aiming to consolidate a "thousand-year empire" that would dwarf America or make it vassal. After 1945 it came from a Communist imperium using the resources of a Russian sub-continent and a whole arsenal of ideological appeals to establish Com munism not "in one country" but in the frame of world power. After 1952 it came from a Moscow-Peiping axis that had consolidated a vast Eurasian land mass. In the mid-1950s it came from a set of Communist alliances that aimed to organize the slumbering energies of the under-developed countries of the Middle East, and formed a Moscow-Cairo axis. In all these cases the Americans were moved by the challenge of an opposing structure of power and by both a fear and repugnance for the image of human personality which such a threat conjured up. Through four decades America took part in power struggles whose arena was thousands of miles away, whose other contestants seemed alien and often barbaric, and which burst the continental bounds of traditional American expansion. Once the continental phase was over, the thrust outward and the thrust of concentration could no longer be compatible. In their new form these two thrusts expressed a split which was to dominate American thought and emotion. Yet even in the new form the expansionism—or, as it came to be called, "interventionism"--had little of the traditional imperialist coloring.

There have been various attempts to correlate isolationism and inter-nationalism with political attitudes on domestic issues, but it is diffi-cult to carry the parallel through American history. Actually the Jef-fersonians were expansionists as against the Federalists; the Jacksonians were apostles of Manifest Destiny as against the Whigs; at the turn of the century Bryan's liberals were the custodians of anti-imperialism and therefore of the "Little America" or isolationist position, while the conservatives were behind the Spanish-American War and the Philippine adventure. Yet there were also imperialist liberals at that time, as witness Theodore Roosevelt and Senator Beveridge, and there have been anti-imperialist conservatives like E. L. Godkin, and Senators Sumner and Hoar. In the twentieth century the political battle lines became even more confused. The liberals who had once stood with Bryan against imperialism became "internationalists" and found them-selves the apostles of a concept of internationalism which was equivalent to a Big America trend. Those who had once whooped it up for Cuba and the Philippines found themselves moving toward isolationism, for-saking the turbulent world of power politics. In most cases the forces shaping American attitudes on foreign policy had little relation to the traditional forces shaping their attitudes on the conduct of affairs at home.

One alliance was a rather striking one—the alliance between some of the big business groups (especially the Eastern ones, trained in the Ivy League colleges, with the world outlook of men of finance) with the political liberals of the persuasion of Theodore Roosevelt and Woodrow Wilson. From the time of Wilson on, each group felt it had a stake in the emergence of an active American responsibility in the world: in the case of the business groups, the stake was the maintenance of open world markets, in the case of the liberals the maintenance of a world climate hospitable to the basic freedoms; in both cases there was a belief in an open society, whether for the pursuit of profit or the life of the spirit. Basically it was this alliance against the totalitarians of both Right and Left which became ever more explicit in American policy. For a time it took the excessive and almost paranoid form of a fear of Communism. But on this score the "go-it-alone" groups were far more intense than the business and liberal groups. The same fear of Communism which led the business-liberal alliance to international commitments led in the other case to an antiforeign "go-it-alone" policy.

The question of the regional roots of isolationism is a difficult one. There has been a widespread impression that isolationism is an accident of the Midwestern mind in America—part of a glacial deposit of resentment and suspicion that has descended on that mind, and needing only some urgings of reason to be thawed out. This is too easy, yet there is a core of validity in it. Isolationism is partly a sectional fact, but it also goes beyond geography and has become a social fact. It existed long before the Populists, yet its strongest expression was linked with the Populist mind, where the suspicion both of European cunning and capitalist cupidity for war profits was most deeply rooted. As Populism hardened, these attitudes were transferred to a new social base—that of the heavy-industry reactionaries of the country's interior who feared both the Eastern financiers and the European ideas. The isolationist feeling which had started in the farm granges and among the Bryan anti-imperialists moved into the custody of Colonel McCormick and Senator Taft. Then it made another shift from the Midwestern business and farm groups to the new white-collar classes, the strata of conservative unions and unorganized labor, and the Big Money of newly rich Southwestern oil millionaires. Thus isolationism, while associated with the Midwest, was an enduring phase of the history of power struggles within America. Its base shifted in the last half century from Western Populism through Midwestern conservatism, to a widespread array of frustrated and embittered social groups. Its psychological base was also shifted from distrust for Europe's monarchies and corruptions to a panic fear of "Marxism" and "atheism" in Europe and Asia.

The isolationist forces have thus changed their class base and leadership in each generation. Most recently they were associated in military strategy with General Douglas MacArthur; in Asian policy with Senator Knowland and the "Asia First" movement; and in domestic policy with Senator McCarthy. In no case did they win a Presidential election, but—as was true of the "America First" movement of the late 1930s—they had considerable popular support and affected the foreign policy even of "internationalist" administrations.

The impact of the pressures from the "China bloc" in the 1950s may be taken as the best instance of the effects of neo-isolationism. These pressures operated both on Democratic and Republican administrations. After the success of the Chinese Revolution they prevented President Truman and Secretary Acheson from coming to terms with the new Chinese regime: it would have been political suicide, as Truman saw it, to get in the way of a force which was ready to call its opponents betrayers of America and saddle them *ex post facto* with the loss of a big segment of the world to Communism. When the Eisenhower Administration came into power in 1952, Secretary Dulles—who had previously favored the recognition of Communist China and its acceptance into the UN—was forced to retreat into a position of immobility on this issue. The devastating result in both administrations was that a small group, playing upon the fears and vulnerabilities of public opinion, was able to paralyze two internationalist regimes into a frozen isolationism with respect to Asia. Both administrations lost their power of diplomatic maneuver in this area: and with the loss of this power of maneuver, the danger of a resort to atomic politics was increased, with the constant threat of using nuclear weapons as instruments of "massive retaliation." Thus isolationist politics and atomic politics converged, and the go-it-aloners fashioned their own brand of atomic imperialism.

An illuminating clue to this phase of American impulse and opinion may be found in Josef Schumpeter's classic essays on *Imperialism and Social Classes*. Writing at the turn of the twentieth century within the context of a Europe moving toward the first World War, and wrestling with the problem presented by John A. Hobson's and Lenin's theories of imperialism as the division of the world between capitalist powers, Schumpeter rejected their approach. He saw that the business groups had far more to lose than to win from imperialist wars, and that while they often exploited and themselves succumbed to the tensions of the

super-patriot they were not the driving force behind the great ex-
plosions of popular passions that led to wars. He fixed rather on the
tinderbox of the formless mass, mainly outside of the trade-unions, especially the lower middle classes, which had not found a secure place in
the social structure. This approach, which has never been adequately
adapted to the American case, sheds considerable light on it.

The same fear of "alien" influences that caused the go-it-aloners to
withdraw behind their intellectual stockade can be transformed into
a war fever. As isolationism has been hard pressed by the inescapable
needs and interests of America, it has not succumbed to internationalism
but has moved to a militarist imperialism. Prick the skin of a go-it-
aloner and you draw interventionist blood—but of an interventionism
within a wholly different frame of values from that of the internationalist. For the obsessive fear of "foreign influences" leads to a hatred of
many of the ethnic groups within America whom an unprincipled or
slack mind can link with the sources of foreign "subversion." Thus the
go-it-aloners become the allies of racist groups whose principal targets
are the recent immigrant stocks. Again, the go-it-aloners are ridden by
an intense hatred and contempt for the European peoples, whom they
accuse of begging for American handouts. They lump the non-Com-
munists of the labor and Socialist movements, and the neutralists of
Europe and the Third Force of Asia, with the Communists. Their impulse is to destroy any broad coalition in which America might find
support, and to break away also from the United Nations. But to the
extent that they achieve this, their reliance must be on naked military
force. That is why I link the mentality of the go-it-aloner with that
of the atomic militarist. In fact, almost uniformly (as I have suggested)
it is the go-it-alone group which, in recent years, has clamored most insistently for the use of atomic weapons in a preventive war.

More and more clearly these lines of thinking merged into a pattern
for which Americans have found no name, as they had for the internationalists. The elements of it are clear enough: the repudiation of
the UN and international action for a go-it-alone policy; the substitu-
tion of military and especially atomic weapons for negotiation and diplomatic alliances; the reliance upon the air arm, especially as a carrier
of atomic weapons, rather than upon the infantry and artillery arm;
the shift of orientation to Asia—to Communist China and the Arab
Middle East and equally from liberal democracies as allies to the nationalist movements of the Right; the alliance at home with racist
movements; the reactionary domestic programs; the use of the Congressional investigation in order to unearth "subversives" who can be
linked with liberals and internationalists.

Actually this pattern adds up to a nationalist imperialism of the Right. The Communist propaganda in Europe and Asia has cynically confused this world view of the go-it-alone imperialists with that of the liberal internationalists, attributing qualities of the one to the other: thus, they find "war-mongering" aims in a program of internationalism which seeks to build a liberal coalition and work through the UN. It applies the stigma of militarism to a group which has explored the techniques of economic aid and reconstruction to a degree unparalleled in history. The pattern of Big Empire as practiced by Americans has actually been an empire unknown in the history of imperialism. For where imperial powers in the past have aimed at exploiting the colonial and economically backward areas for their own economic advantage, taking out whatever resources they could and exploiting native labor, American imperialism is the first on record to pour its resources into undeveloped areas and weak economies, exporting capital, technicians, and technical skills to them.

The motive is not altruistic. Partly there is a fear of the growth of Communist world power if such countermeasures are not taken. Partly also there is a fear, on the part of strong business and even labor groups, that the American economic machine will slow down if defense production is not kept going at full blast and if there is no way to dispose of surplus products and investment through programs of international aid. But while the motive is self-interested, the consequences are unlike those of the colonial or ideological empires of the past. This reversal of the traditional imperial pattern was possible only through a recognition—largely by American liberal thought—of the connection between economic health and unhealth and the march of ideas. This, fused with the steady accretion of America's economic power, produced what may be called a Big Empire internationalism.

This brings the analysis back to the dynamism of American world power. I have suggested that the growth of that power has been propelled by the technological impulse of the culture more than by an impulse toward conquest or domination, and that the guiding spirit informing American expansion has been not an exploiting imperialism but a Big Empire internationalism. What appeal is this view likely to have for other peoples? What they have to gain is the assurance that while all small nations are bound to live in the shadow of the big empires, the shadow cast by the American brand is likely to be that of a constitutional imperialism operating within a relatively open world constitutional structure. Americans have talked, often quite foolishly, of their own economic system as the only one that can work: in their eager confidence about its merits they have overestimated its applicability. They have on the other hand underestimated in their own economic pattern the principle of inner mobility which makes it in some degree more revolutionary than the varieties of planned systems. The real persuasiveness of the American imperium, in its world struggle for widespread allegiance, flows from this flexibly changing pattern of an open society, and from the quickening energies of the American emphasis on access to life's goods.

Thus, in terms of the revolutionary Asian situation, America failed to make effective what it had to offer to the new Asian nationalism as the image of a working society. It could offer the example of a successful colonial revolution against imperialism; it could offer the continuing effort to keep many ethnic strains living together in peace in a complex society; it could offer, finally, the image of the independent farmer and of the career still largely open to talent. If the revolutionary world ferment at mid-century was anti-imperialist, anti-landlord, and if it was assertive not only about its nationalist energies but also about ethnic equality, then the American dialogue with these peoples was not doomed to futility.

These then are some of the shaping currents in the history of American foreign policy: the thrust toward expansionism; the impulse to fill out the "manifest destiny" of the continent and at the same time retire within its self-sufficiency; the fumblings, once the old self-sufficiency was broken, to find some means by which America could use a decisive leverage power in world affairs without entering on a series of interventionist adventures; the sense of geographical and ideological encirclement that has replaced the earlier sense of security; the impulse to make America the world carrier of the democratic idea; and the pragmatic limits which the American mind sets around that impulse, keeping it from becoming a messianic idea.

3. National Interest and an Open World

AMERICA IN MID-TWENTIETH century came to recognize itself as one of the two great power aggregates of the world, the other being, of course, the Russian-Chinese Communist bloc. This has meant a revaluation of the national-interest doctrine within the frame of a world struggle for power and a world imperative of peace. The era of Wilson and Roosevelt—that is to say, of World War I and of World War II—was followed by a period of sharp disenchantment with the "idealism" and "internationalism" of both of them. Many Americans began ruefully to add up the cost, in lives and treasure, of the American adventures in the succor of other peoples. The epigram that "America always wins the war and loses the peace" came to express a widespread disillusionment whose roots reached deep in the folk mind. Since America could not secede from the world, the disenchantment led to an insistence on a realistic view of national interest rather than some vague ideal of international good will.

But the idea of national interest no longer ran in the traditional balance-of-power term. It is possible to trace a balance-of-power calculation in American diplomacy from the start. In the early days of the nation's history, when the new Republic was still weak, its leaders knew that their political independence and their ideological democracy were threats to the existing great powers. They feared these powers and made a great show of maintaining their strict neutrality amidst the European dynastic struggles. Yet this did not prevent them, when the occasion offered, from playing off each of the great powers against the others, seeking (as it were) survival in the interstices of the power struggles. In fact, they were saved from being snuffed out in their infancy by the fact that the powers of Europe were at one another's throats: no one of them alone dared crush the new American republic, yet they could not agree to do it together. Europe's distress proved America's salvation. The American leaders combined wisdom and an eye for the main chance along with their luck. They swallowed insults from British and French alike, putting survival ahead of pride. When they felt themselves strong enough in 1823 they announced the bold proposition that the European powers were to stay out of the whole American hemisphere, which was to be the special preserve of America as a great power. Only the hostility of the British and Russians toward each other, and the fact of the British fleet, which stood between America and the vengeance of Europe, saved the Monroe Doctrine from being only a ridiculous scrap of paper. Later the Americans rode out their Civil War, increased their strength and population, stretched their new territories westward and southward until the nation reached its present continental limits inside of roughly seventy-five years. The "separate and equal power" rounded out a truly imperial domain in the New World under the protecting shadow of the power conflicts and ebbing energies of the Old World.

Such a diplomatic recipe, in varying combinations of neutrality and balance-of-power politics, was the strategy of Washington, of John Adams and John Jay, of Jefferson, Monroe and John Quincy Adams, of Lincoln and Seward. When America became itself a great power, the aim of the formula shifted; it became that of preventing any other power from overshadowing America and threatening its survival. This was the logic of John Hay's "Open Door" policy, which tried to keep the Far

East from becoming the private preserve of any one European nation. It was the point of Theodore Roosevelt's balancing of Russian against Japanese power when he made himself a conciliator between the two. It was also the logic of America's entrance into the two world wars, when she joined to prevent a German world dominion.

After World War II, much of American policy continued to follow this logic. Even before America had wholly defeated Germany and Japan a brilliant American political geographer, Nicholas J. Spykman, pointed out that America would have to rebuild German power in Europe and Japanese power in Asia. This appeared cynical at the time, but it was prophetic of the policy that was actually followed. In some posthumously published letters Spykman also backed American support of a UN organization not from idealist or internationalist motives but on the ground that it would be useful as a counterweight to the Soviet network of satellites. Thus, despite the opprobrium the "power-politics" idea carries in the American mind, America has continued to practice balance-of-power politics.

The traditional policy, however, had to be pursued under drastically new world conditions. These new conditions included the emergence of a great power axis stretching west from Moscow to Berlin, east from Moscow to Peiping, south from Moscow to Cairo. Confronted by this new power reality, America had little choice except to build "positions of strength" against it. The span of oceans separating America from Europe and from Asia might have been reckoned as an insulating and isolating element, but the oceans have shrunk to the scale of rapidly traversed airways, while the new colonial revolutions—often with Marxist slogans and leadership—have given Americans a more oppressive feeling than that of geographical encirclement, namely the sense of ideological encirclement.

In meeting this challenge, the Americans had to change their policies along three main lines of direction. One was the arms race, and the testing of each phase of American policy by its impact on America's "military potential"—a phrase whose currency (along with "readiness economy" and "defense posture") attested the new mood. The traditional American fear of standing armies was broken, and American soldiers and air bases could be found in every part of the world. The second change was a new economic diplomacy which sought to strengthen the shaky economies of the areas that the Americans hoped to bring within their sphere of influence. Third, Americans accustomed themselves to think in terms of "psychological warfare"—that is, of a contest of propagandas and a war of ideas. Thus, for all its traditional idealism, the pull in American policy was toward atomic weapons, economic pressures, and political warfare. The aim was to prevent strategic areas from falling into the opposing polar pull, to consolidate their strength and make them an effective part of a structure of collective international action.

Actually the phrase "bipolar world" oversimplified the complex reality. Not only was there an American world and a Communist world; there was also a whole array of peoples in a third world who refused to commit themselves to either. Whenever one of the two "polar" powers strained too hard to hold its allies and dependents within a tight discipline, there were inner tensions which showed that there were many forces of dynamic change in the world that were too insistent to be contained within two armed camps. A number of the newer non-Communist nations of Asia, Africa, and the Middle East were especially determined to stay clear of the bipolar struggle, and the leadership of Nehru furnished them a rationale of noncommitment. It became ever clearer after mid-century that the "cold war" era had itself been only a historical phase, and that whether the world was to witness a cataclysmic war of atomic weapons or not, there was more in the Heaven and earth of world energies than were dreamed of in the philosophy of a bipolar world.

All this meant that the concept of the "national interest" would have to be defined broadly enough to include America's stake in international action and in the building of collective sanctions. In an anarchic world the drive to achieve international order became itself a form of realism. That may be why some of the chief protagonists of the national-interest concept have broken as many lances against the isolationists as against the "tender-minded" internationalists. As typified by Hans Morgenthau and George F. Kennan, what the national-interest school stresses is toughness of approach. It is in the "tough-minded" tradition of Machiavelli's state system, applied to America's situation, as against the supposedly tender-minded approach of Wilson, Roosevelt, and the "global" thinkers.

"I always consider the settlement of America with reverence and wonder," wrote John Adams in 1765, "as the opening of a grand scheme and design in Providence for the illumination and emancipation of the slavish part of mankind all over the earth." There is a literature of the "American mission," as Clinton Rossiter calls it, that stretches from the divines of the Colonial Period to the most recent newspaper editorial proposing a "liberation policy" toward the peoples enslaved by Communist power. Messianism in this sense is not restricted to the liberal internationalists. Yet what gives this weapon its strength is the strength of world belief in the reality of American revolutionary ideal-ism. Nothing shows more clearly the intertwining of the tough-minded and tender-minded, the realist and idealist, in American thinking than this paradox of "liberation." The same editorialists who called Ameri-cans "suckers" for assuming the role of world saviors saw no irony in demanding an aggressive liberation policy which was meaningless unless the victim people believed in the American savior mission.

The messianic element in the American tradition is more complex than is generally understood. It is true that Americans believe in their characteristic institutions—free elections, free worship, free discussion, a free market. Like others who believe in an idea, they don't under-stand why the rest of the world does not adopt it. Yet they are pulled back by a self-critical censor that makes them fearful of all-out causes and disillusioned after they have succumbed to them. There was a strong sense of revolutionary idealism in Jefferson, yet he was fearful of allowing its logic to carry America into foreign military adventures. He had an astringent conviction that America could best perform its historic mission by cultivating its own continental garden. The fact that Americans believed so deeply in the validity of their national experi-ence meant that they rarely made it articulate but took it for granted. One would expect such a people to be chary of ideological Holy Wars. When a Holy War element did enter into their wars, as in 1917 and again in 1941, the result was disillusionment.

American thinkers for a long time stayed clear of the sweep of global problems that interested their European contemporaries and shaped their intellectual systems. It was not until Theodore Roosevelt and his group of intellectual intimates (John Hay, Henry Adams, his brother Brooks Adams, Admiral Mahan) that the self-containment of American thought was broken. None of these men, except for Brooks Adams, was a trained social thinker. Henry Adams's letters are full of acute political insights and a prophetic understanding of world forces which enabled him to gauge the weakness of Great Britain as a world power and the coming strength of Russia and America. Yet his mind was mainly trained in the balance-of-power maneuvering of the great pow-ers, as befitted the descendant of two Presidents and the son of an ambassador. His theory of the coming explosion of the two concen-trated energy systems of world power forecast the doom of all civiliza-tion and had little about America's own world role in the interval. Mahan's mind, less far-ranging and more centered on naval power and its implications, anticipated the interest of later American thinkers in the politics of military strategy and geographical location.

Like Adams and Mahan, Theodore Roosevelt was interested in the techniques of balance-of-power politics. Declaring that "American politics is world politics," he dared to see that America's security lay not in neutrality but in helping give order to the world arena itself, and thus he burst the bounds of self-contained continentalism. His world view, like his New Nationalism, flowed from his cult of the "strenuous life." Inherently belligerent, he gave a tone of belligerence to whatever he uttered. He was contemptuous of pacifists as "molly-coddlers." He infected in this respect the thinking of Herbert Croly, who asserted in *The Promise of American Life* that "if America wants peace it must be spiritually and physically prepared to fight for it. . . . The road to any permanent international settlement will be piled high with dead bodies, and will be traveled, if at all, only after a series of abortive and costly experiments." Croly showed both the juvenile tough-guy posturing and the genuine tough-mindedness that were mingled in the thinking of the internationalist progressives.

With Woodrow Wilson, who has become the favorite target of the attack on legalist-moralist idealism, the juvenile gestures were replaced by an equally synthetic high-minded spirituality, and the tough-mindedness was diluted but not wholly dissolved by idealist doctrine. In the case of Franklin Roosevelt, who was less doctrinaire than Wilson, there was a realistic use of every American resource—economic, military, and ideological—in the interest of Wilson's ruling idea of a collective international will. How resistant Franklin Roosevelt was to the world-savior role may be seen from the fact that America waited until Pearl Harbor before formally entering World War II; but how shrewd he was as a manipulator of symbols may also be seen from the fact that he was not wholly sorry to use the Japanese aggression to resolve his dilemma as a policy-maker—the dilemma of one who understood the threat of Fascist world power but could not count on a unified American public opinion in meeting it.

Reinhold Niebuhr has written brilliantly of the "irony of American history" represented by the thinking and actions of these leaders. Given their horror of war, it was certainly ironic that both Wilson and Roosevelt were entangled by history in world wars. Yet each held fast to the central creative idea that balance-of-power politics and military force were justified only as steps toward a structure of international sanctions. Each of them thus became the symbol of vast movements of popular opinion that went far beyond the American boundaries.

Brooks Adams, who was not a statesman but a student of the materials with which statesmanship has to work, came closer than any other thinker to formulating for Americans the logic of their new power position. In his *America's Economic Supremacy,* which appeared at the

turn of the century, in 1900, he saw the Spanish-American War as marking a "new equilibrium of the world." In an earlier book, *The Law of
Civilization and Decay,* Adams had speculated that the rise and fall of
national greatness followed the shifting of the world trade routes. He
added the theory that geographical imperatives shaped two great centers
of economic empire—one a continental (land mass) empire and one a
maritime empire. The capstone to his theoretical structure was the "law
of centralization"—that in "the new struggle for life among the nations,"
society tends to "become organized in greater and denser masses, the
more vigorous and economical mass destroying the less active and more
wasteful." Like his brother Henry he saw history as an energy process
in which, as in physics, there was an acceleration followed by a slowing
of national energies: the world moved from one equilibrium to another, each interval representing a "phase" of history, each displacement
of an equilibrium being marked by social convulsions, wars, revolutions,
and catastrophes until a new equilibrium is achieved.

However one may quarrel with a theory of history using the metaphors of physics as if they applied to cultural development, Adams had
at least part of a truth by the tail. America's economic dominance came
about at the same time as England's power decay, and America replaced
England as the world's big maritime power just as Russia followed
France and Germany as the big European continental land power. In
both cases there was an unexampled drive toward centralized power
and organizational techniques.

But it is one thing to possess an economic supremacy and another to
use it maturely. Until after World War II America was the Reluctant
Giant, unwilling to measure the full extent of its might. Since that
time it has surprised both friends and critics by an assertive diplomacy
and an almost bristling eagerness to use American power to the full.
This change of policy does not register a basic transformation in
American outlook or character structure. Those are unchanged: the
attraction-and-recoil pattern, the fear of being "taken in" by foreign
wiles, the chip-on-the-shoulder attitude, the demand for signs of affection from the beneficiaries of American largess, the anxious pursuit of
national "security," the belief that the American angel must always
look homeward. What has happened reflects rather a reassertion of the
thrust of American energy whenever it encounters a challenge from
which it cannot escape.

Seen from the vantage point of the sobering problems of American
power in the mid-1950s, the turn-of-the-century phase of American
imperialism a half century earlier had a half-baked quality. The Spanish-
American War and the protectorate thrown over the Philippines,

Hawaii, and Cuba may have seemed impressive steps toward establishing American power in the Pacific and Caribbean seas. But their very closeness to the classic pattern of colonial imperialism should have cast suspicion on how well they expressed the real drives in American life. The turn-of-the-century imperialist champions—Hay, Theodore Roosevelt, Beveridge, Mahan—were intellectuals who were moved by an image of America's Manifest Destiny across the seas. The imperialist adventure was not so much the expression of the drive of tough-minded businessmen as the high jinks of men who saw themselves as the shapers of American destiny. The great anti-imperialists of the day who opposed this pseudo-imperialism—Bryan, Mark Twain, William Vaughan Moody —took it for the real thing and fought it with passionate and generous energies. The wonderful satiric humor of Mark Twain that pilloried the missionaries and their Christian burden, and the majestic rhetoric of Moody's *On a Soldier Fallen in the Philippines,* hit home in showing how the *opéra bouffe* imperial adventure stirred the latent jingoism of Americans and made ninnies of them.

But the whole episode, with its noisy fireworks and the hoopla of Hearst journalism, was marginal to the development of American power. The amassing of American imperial power has scarcely followed the classic pattern. It has operated by the techniques of trade, investment, and profitable sales in foreign markets; it has not been averse toward using "dollar diplomacy" to remove the obstructions in the path of business profits, to start convenient revolutions or quell inconvenient ones, and it has more recently operated by economic and technical aid to underdeveloped areas.

There could be no denial that the fact of Soviet power was real and massive in the mid-1950s, and that the Communist appeal was strong, especially to the colonial peoples and the emergent nationalist movements of Asia and Africa. America found itself having to make strategic and diplomatic calculations globally, for all the continents at once. To focus on Europe, which had once seemed the widest stretch of internationalism, was no longer enough. American thought and planning underwent a drastic shift of axis from Europe to the Middle and Far East, which became the next great continental stakes for the world struggle. Since the Soviet revolutionary appeal to the Middle East and the Chinese appeal to Asia were at once economic and ideological, the Americans had to take stock of their capacity to offer a counterchallenge on both scores.

The economic problem had its setting in the fact that the under-developed areas would need new capital investment and technical aid.

Lenin's classic formulation put the problem as a choice between turning to the capitalist powers for investment or getting it out of the
nation's own resources by a stringent program of economic planning,
by austere consumer sacrifices in the early phase, and by plowing back
into capital formation the whole surplus over bare subsistence. Lenin's
reasoning was that to borrow from the existing powers on their terms
was to become colonial to them. The Russians said in effect to the
emerging nationalisms of Asia, "See, we lifted ourselves by our own
economic boot straps, without becoming colonial vassals of the imperialist powers. You can do the same." As for the problem of industrial initiative and managerial efficiency, they sought to solve it by the
creation of state trusts and farm collectives, by a stretch-out which went
under the name of "Socialist competition," by the creation of a managerial Communist elite within industry, and by the iron "discipline"
of a single party and police state. They used also the persistent propaganda of "capitalist encirclement" and the myth of an inevitable triumph of the Communist cause, which was embedded in the prophetic
phase of the Marxist dogma.

America had a clear answer at its disposal. In terms of its own economic history it had achieved most of its capital formation by plowing
back its surplus into railroads, factories, machines. It had at the start
used British and French capital without becoming a vassal of either
country. In its economic growth it had disproved the Marxist dogma
of decay through the internal contradictions of capitalism. Its rich had
grown richer but they let the state take the larger part of their income
through taxation, and their own consumption formed only a tiny fraction of the total national product. Its poor had not, despite the Marxist
dogma, grown poorer: in fact, they had grown steadily better off. As a
result America had brought into being a nation which was mainly
middle class, and whose middle classes had living standards previously
achieved only by the wealthy of other nations. America had a surplus
of capital and a command of technology which it was ready to put at
the disposal of underdeveloped areas. Its greatest appeal was the example of its own living standards and its basic freedoms. It had the
advantage of being able to show that both the living standards and the
freedoms could be achieved without big state trusts, the rigor of farm
collectives, and the barbarities of a police state.

America labored, however, under two handicaps in making this
counterchallenge effective. One was its own nationalist impulse to think
in military rather than economic terms, to strike alliances with authoritarian regimes provided they were anti-Communist, and dream of a

pax Americana which would impose its own kind of order upon the world. The second and closely related handicap was the recurrence of an internal drive by a minority against civil liberties, using the fear of subversion as its chief source of popular support.

American nationalism during most of its growth had in it the self-assertiveness of a people who had won their freedom and were certain of the dimensions of their destiny. American nationalist loyalties clustered around the Constitution as a symbol, the "American mission" as an evocative myth, and American wealth and prosperity as the visible signs of Providential grace. Except for short periods of hysteria, from the Alien and Sedition Acts to the radical hunt after World War I, American patriotism was of the spread-eagle sort that was swaggering without being intolerant. For the most part it was the kind of good-natured nationalism that flourishes in a democratic society—with a strong pride of place, a we-can-do-it-better-than-anyone assertiveness, and a fierce don't-tread-on-me belligerence. "My country, may it always be right—but, right or wrong, my country" expressed the hold that the nation as a social myth had on the American mind.

The period after World War II marked a transition to a new phase of nationalist feeling. It took two main forms: a militarist emphasis in foreign policy and the increasing anxiety about "security." The two forms tended to become interlocked. The proof of "loyalty" came to be defined by the political bigots in terms of adherence to their own world view and their own political and property attitudes. For a brief interval at mid-century the symbol of this narrow nationalism, which contained elements of police-state Fascism, came to be "McCarthyism." Yet the symbol was less important than the tensions it expressed, and from which other symbols like it might draw their continuing energies. A number of foreign observers made the mistake of identifying "McCarthyism" with the main drift of American energies—a mistake welcomed by the masters of Soviet propaganda, since it distracted attention from their police state. But it was also wide of the mark to dismiss this new bigoted nationalism as irrelevant to the real America—as if there were some way of authenticating America by the standards only of its social health and discarding everything else.

The cult of the nation as social myth has run as a thread through the whole of American history. It started as the revolutionary nationalism of the War for Independence, it became the assertive nationalism of a people in industrial growth, and it reached its newest phase as the bigoted nationalism of an antidemocratic minority pretending to track down "un-Americans" and "subversives." The Marxist analysis which makes this nationalist drive the bond servant of a master class of corporate managers did not stand up historically. There were, of course, ties between the nationalist bigots and some Midwestern businessmen, some Texas oil millionaires, and some of the new economic feudal masters of the Pacific Coast. Yet the main body of American business found itself deeply disquieted by a movement of bigotry which threatened their own position ultimately because it threatened the business and constitutional fabric itself. They welcomed some of the consequences of the new tribalism, particularly in the devastation it wrought among liberals by linking them in the popular mind with "subversives." But they were aware of the final danger of the movement.

More important than its links with the corporate classes were the links the new tribalism had with the formless fears and anxieties of the middle classes and the unorganized workers. The intensity of tribal feeling was all the greater because of the insecurity of the recent immigrant groups, and the social competitiveness every group felt in a society where each man had to make and hold his own place. The chief drive was the striving for respectability, and its linkage with unquestioned "loyalty." Without being a rigidly stratified class society, America forms a kind of terraced society, with each terrace level shaped by one's income level and prestige and by the sense of security within the social group. The older and more settled Americans were less likely to become victims of nationalist bigotry than some of the more recent ones, who found it necessary to prove that they "belonged" by becoming the challengers of other people's loyalty, and who sought to outdo all others in the virulence of their attack on the "alien" element. Thus, among the new feudal rich, among the amorphous white-collar classes, among the failures and those tagging along on the margin of a failure, and among second- and third-generation immigrant groups, the nation as a social myth exerted a powerful force. While its uses were in many cases part of the defensive tactics of Big Property, the roots from which it got its popular strength were not those of class interest but of the psychic hunger to belong. Hence the tribal feeling in America was often more fanatic among those classes and groups who would prove to be its first victims if an authoritarian state were ever to be established in America.*

These inner sources upon which American tribalism fed must be correlated also with the fear of the world outside which neither the possessing nor the middle classes could grasp. Despite the revolutionary origins of America, they were fearful of a new kind of world revolutionary ferment which enveloped them. They did not see that the achievements of America had raised expectations throughout the world

---

* See also Ch. VI, Sec. 10, "The Struggle for Civil Liberties," and Ch. IX, Sec. 4, "Varieties of American Character."

which expressed themselves in new nationalist energies and in the demand for new living standards. The Marxist program was one phase of the Western heritage that had pre-empted the revolutionary challenge. Yet the American experience embodied a more authentic revolution, which could respond more fully to the claims of Asia and Africa as well as of Europe.

Even within the doctrine of national interest there was room for an American world view which would not deny these revolutionary claims. The conflict between the national-interest school and the internationalist was, at bottom, a clash of views about human nature. In the writings of men like Hans Morgenthau and George Kennan there is an underlying premise that in the struggle for world position the great reality is power, that international law and morality cannot be expected to displace power or even fundamentally to affect its exercise, that little can be expected of human nature except self-interest. In the internationalism of Wilson, on the other hand, there is something of the perfectionism of the eighteenth century and its belief that conflict can be resolved by the proper institutional means. The first group share a world view that goes back to Machiavelli, the second a view that goes back to Plato, who believed in the possibility of organized virtue within a frame of traditional ideas. The first view is deeply pessimistic in mood, the second optimistic. The experiences since World War I—the failure of the League of Nations, the broken balance of power, the betrayals of international agreements by both Hitler and Stalin, the tarnishing of war aims in peace settlements after both world wars—disillusioned Americans about international action and created a climate favoring a narrow version of the doctrine of national interest.

Yet there are phases of the American character that are excluded from the world view and the view of human nature implied in this doctrine. There is an inbred optimism in the American which will not let him hold too long to a pessimistic view of human nature as wholly greedy and self-seeking. Even in its Calvinist origins the American mind shaped a doctrine of what may be called practical messianism. The tradition in which Wilson worked was that of the Covenanters—a spirit translated into a doctrine of human rights as the stern imperative of history.

In spite of their tribalists and their advocates of a *pax Americana,* the Americans had the right to face the struggle for world leadership with the assurance that time was on their side, and that their philosophy contained a strong appeal. Their fault was to see this appeal in the negative terms of the dangers and evils of the Communist philosophy. Unquestionably, the Communist doctrine, when translated into action, carried with it a moral indifference to human values, the swollen arrogance of state power, and the nullifying of the individual in the impersonal drive of history. There were inner weaknesses within the Communist societies that promised in time to lead to inner breakdown, since every police state is bound to generate palace intrigues, praetorian conflict, and the murderous struggle of rivals for power, which break it from within.

But America had a more positive contribution to make in foreign policy that corresponded to its contribution in day-to-day living. It went beyond high living standards and even beyond civil liberties. One way to formulate it was to transfer the concept of the open society to the larger sphere of world action. For America has shown in its history that immense structures of economic power, a steady pace of technical and social change, and widely divergent class and ethnic groups could be contained within a society flexible enough to allow for dynamism without tyranny. The challenge was whether the rivalries of nations and the clash of power imperialism could be similarly held within the frame of an open world society.

All through the period since World War I there were fumblings toward such a world view. Since Americans are legalist and humanitarian, these efforts took the form of plans for the League of Nations and the UN, blueprints for world government, and a vague sense of responsibility toward the people in the underdeveloped areas. They were symbolized by such slogans as Wendell Willkie's "One World," the Marshall Plan, Point Four. It does not subtract from them to say that none is as deeply characteristic of the historical achievement of America as is its open society. The logic of American history has been to take one step after another, instead of attempting a broad leap to achieve an abstract idea. Thus what America could contribute in international action is the practice of an open society transferred to the broader arena of an Open World. I have noted above that the idea of a bipolar struggle does not correspond to the realities of today's world, which is too varied culturally and too diverse in the aims of the member nations and the varying phases of their development to be contained within two armed camps. The alternative to a bipolar world might conceivably be a world state, but that has difficulties that have proved insuperable thus far, and it has dangers of rigidity or tyranny. Far more feasible, as well as far more attractive, is the idea of an open world society in which national differences survive and national development is possible, but there is a core of international authority to prevent the suicidal anarchy of war.

The merit of this is that it dictates no imperialism, whether military, economic, or moral. It allows for a wide divergence of cultural forms and national traditions within a common frame of tolerance and constitutionalism. It involves a refusal to foreclose the future against any economic doctrine or social system—whether capitalist or Socialist, democratic or authoritarian, provided it stays within the spirit and codes of an open world society. Nor does it make the mistake of pitting "West" against "East," thereby yielding to the Communists the prescriptive right not to be considered Westerners by the Asiatic peoples. The fact is that there have been fusions as well as clashes between the cultures of East and West, and each has interpenetrated the other. As the best example history offers of a mingling of all ethnic strains within a loose social frame, the Americans had a right to assert that both East and West were contained within their image of an open world society.

Thus America might put its tradition of revolutionary idealism to effective use in the interest of realistic aims, achieving a not impossible synthesis of internationalism with "national interest." Whether it can make this world view persuasive to other peoples depends, however, on the course which its own people follow internally within their own open society. The danger was that Americans might betray this image of an open world by a belligerent go-it-alone policy, by the moral arrogance of expecting other peoples to bow to their superior wealth and strength, but especially by betraying the open society from within. They found that when they had to defend themselves against the growing threat of "McCarthyism" at home, they had also to go on the defensive in the world at large. In this sense the most effective single weapon in the entire armory of American foreign policy was bound to be, in the generations ahead, the image of an open society.

4. Landscape with Soldiers

DESPITE CHARGES of "war-mongering" and the impulses toward military muscle-flexing, America can scarcely be described as a warlike civilization or a military society. Americans make pretty good fighters when they have to fight; and the statue or memorial in the public square of an American town is more likely to pay homage to a military figure than to a jurist, artist, scholar, saint, or businessman. But despite this, Americans don't glory particularly in military feats, don't like wars, don't allow their sense of bigness as a people to depend on the deeds and ordeals of their soldiers. They are combative and pugnacious; the "chip on the shoulder" (as Margaret Mead has seen) is a symbol of one of their basic character traits. But to be pugnacious as individuals is different from being aggressive as a nation or militarist as a society.

How explain the antimilitarist tradition among such a people? De

Tocqueville found a clue in the "principle of equality." In European societies there was little chance to move from one social class to another in civilian life: hence the army as a career offered the main channel for advancement. In America, however, where a man moved up rapidly in civilian life, the military offered few attractions as a permanent career: hence the passion for peace De Tocqueville found in America in the 1830s. He went on to point out, however, that while the American people abhorred war, the regular soldiers—and especially the noncommissioned officers—might be expected to desire war: their big chance for advancement comes in wartime, when the democracy has been turned into a people-in-arms, and the officers of the small standing army are jumped in rank in order to lead the expanded military forces.

But De Tocqueville was hasty in assuming that the "principle of equality" would keep Americans from military embroilments. A decade after he wrote, Americans were involved in a war with Mexico which was an imperialist adventure, aimed mainly at grabbing the rich domain of Texas. They later fought a civil war, still later a war with Spain, fought in two world wars, and then found themselves caught in military episodes in Korea and elsewhere in Asia as part of the struggle with the power of the Kremlin and Peiping. While this is not the record of a militarist people, neither is it the record of one lacking the martial impulse.

What happened was a drastic change in America's world position which forced upon it, if not militarism, then readiness for wars. The American antiwar tradition was shaped in a society which was physically separated from the rest of the world and felt itself safe between its buffer oceans, and which could therefore risk keeping its standing army small and neglect its armed strength during long stretches of peace. But when the oceans were spanned and the rise of new power structures threatened America, the antiwar tradition was drastically eroded. For a time it took the form of a neutralism which counseled America to keep itself disengaged from world struggles. Then neutralism in turn became an ever less tenable position. Three times in the course of thirty-five years, from World War I in 1917 to the Korean War in 1950, Americans found themselves plunged into major wars.

As long as they were neutral the Americans cultivated an indifference to the embroilments of other nations. But as soon as they got into a war they made a "crusade" out of its military and ideological aspects and a "campaign" out of every civilian aspect. It was under Woodrow Wilson's leadership that World War I was turned into the first of the modern ideological wars. The intensity of the original antiwar feeling seemed to be doubled as it reversed its direction. Every war becomes a total war for Americans, unless—like the Asiatic wars—it is too distant and unpopular to take the usual course. The tendency is for American war aims to be phrased in terms of total victory, and for American peace terms to be unconditional surrender. Even—or perhaps especially—the bitterest of the former isolationists become super-patriots in war, and their former apathy is turned into the loudest battle cries.

The difficulty Americans experience in their war behavior is that they cannot apply to it the logic of their peacetime society. Ordinarily they bargain and compromise, and find their goals in the step-by-step course of daily life and work. The traditional antiwar bent has been that of a people whose pursuit of profits, careers, and happiness has made them shrink from anything that might cut these short. Hence the violence of their initial reaction against war involvement. But when they are forced into a war, there is an intensity of recoil from their initial indifference. It is as if they had to overcompensate for their earlier lack of feeling by the total absorption with the war. And this in turn is reinforced by the irrational blood urge which, once set in motion, transforms the American (and especially the civilian at home) into a fire-breathing enthusiast.

The basic contradiction here is that of war itself—the most irrational of all human actions—operating in a society founded in the Age of Reason on the assumption of man's perfectibility. From this crucial contradiction most of the others flow—the almost schizoid alternation between peace-mindedness and war-mindedness, the impassioned cries, and in diplomacy a deep moralizing strain alternating with military pressures and alliances. Americans are likely to wait until the last moment before they fight, but once the blow has fallen they are caught up in enthusiasm. They start by expecting the war to be short, then settle down to a long and weary one. After the peace, the inevitable mood of disillusionment sets in, and the whole cycle is ready to be repeated.

Since they are a technological people the Americans find themselves at home in the new technology of war, which has become warfare by machines, with the soldiers functioning mainly as machine operators. I have said earlier that the American is *homo faber*, the archetypal man of the modern world. The same qualities which have given him primacy in peacetime industrial technology make him feel at home in mechanized warfare. Many of the American war novels are obsessed with the details of how the precision machinery of warfare operates. The same technical bent and engineering skills that enabled the Americans to make the start on atomic weapons also made them adept in the use of flame throwers, napalm bombs, heavy long-range jet bombers, and the range of electronic navigational and firing devices that make the warplane in a supersonic age a complex mass of machinery on which the pilot "goes along for a ride" and (as Hanson Baldwin puts it) "has become an electronics specialist and radar engineer."

This changing nature of warfare has brought about a shift in American strategic thinking. The abrupt realism that led General Nathan Forrest to sum up the whole wisdom of strategy as that of "getting there fustest with the mostest" has been translated into what is now called the science of "logistics": the problems of transporting large masses of men and material thousands of miles from the home base have taken on meaning at a time when no part of the world is outside the area of potential hostilities. But where warfare was once mainly a matter of man power, the American emphasis is now on war technology. There are few military operations which are not preceded by saturation bombing. The emphasis has been shifted from the infantry and artillery to aviation and atomic weapons, and even the naval arm has assumed importance mainly as a set of floating air bases and as a way of keeping the sea lanes open for the transportation of war material. In the infantry itself, mobile tank warfare has most dramatically captured the American imagination. The generals who emerged as heroes from World War II were either tank officers like George Patton or organizers of war administration and war diplomacy like Marshall and Eisenhower.

Arthur M. Schlesinger, Jr., has suggested traditional lines of difference on military strategy between the two major American political parties, with the Atlantic as the "Democratic ocean" and the Pacific as the "Republican ocean"; thus, too, with the branches of the Armed Services: the Army and Navy have been the Democratic branches, while the Air Force has been the Republican branch. The "New Look" in defense, as the Republicans called it in the mid-1950s, put its emphasis on atomic weapons carried by the air arm. Yet the Democrats were capable of taking over the emphasis on the air arm: the emphasis of the Symington Report, in 1957, was on the failure of a Republican Administration to keep up with the needs imposed on military aviation by war in a nuclear age.

At the core of the American attitude toward war was the hatred of using and losing American lives. It led the American leaders to use the atomic bomb in Japan in the hope—wise or otherwise—that they would thus save a million American casualties. Every American political leader knows the value of the slogan "Don't send American boys overseas." The fact that Americans were able to keep their home territory from becoming a battlefield, ever since the Civil War, has led them to think of war as a highly technical operation, fought preferably on distant shores with the minimum use of American troops and with a massive expenditure of materials and money. This may partly explain the American willingness to use massive economic aid in peacetime as a way of averting a war, and even the curious American belief that if you have money enough as a nation you can somehow buy peace. It should be added that, when the test came, Americans spent their own lives profusely in both world wars and in the Korean War. But even while they did so their sense of the sanctity of life and their reluctance to use it in battle were undiminished.

In an era when war is technology the organization of the war economy is crucial. The American tendency is to superimpose the machinery of a war economy and war state upon the peacetime pursuits, yielding reluctantly step by step to the necessity of changing from the "business as usual" pattern. This leads to a mixture of wartime and peacetime attitudes which has baffled many. Thus heavy taxation is found side by side with profiteering from war contracts, often with defective materials. There is always a cry to "mobilize" capital and labor in the war economy. Yet in every recent war the trade-unions have grown in strength and have given up none of labor's rights except that of striking in crucial war plants, while after every war the big corporate units emerge even bigger and more powerful.

Randolph Bourne, a young American radical writer during World War I, used to say ironically (quoting from a German military historian) that "war is the health of the state." Certainly state power feeds on war. The antitrust laws are suspended, and there is a machinery for controlling prices and production and allocating priorities for scarce materials that would not be possible in a peacetime America. There is full employment and a forced investment by which the high profits are skimmed off through heavy taxation and channeled into directed war uses. The businessman is caught between the bonanza of big war contracts and profits on the one hand, and a system of high taxes and military Socialism on the other. Yet the American has not lost his capacity to live with such paradoxes and make the best of both worlds.

A more baffling paradox was presented by the economy after 1945, which did not have to wage total war, yet was unable to return to peacetime standards. It was the economy of the arms race: or in somewhat gentler terms, a "readiness economy." It retained many of the features of the war economy—the danger of inflation, heavy taxes, big war contracts and profits, full employment; yet the sense of pressure which comes from the ordeal of war survival was absent and could not be supplied synthetically, although for a time it was supplied by the "Cold War" and the Communist scare.

The arms race presented America with a difficult problem of social decision. After 1938 the American economy in great measure had to use its resources for armaments, with alternations between a war economy and a readiness economy. In both cases the conditions assumed as necessary for the functioning of capitalism in peacetime did not exist. American businessmen found themselves moving steadily away from the free market for civilian goods toward a market in which the government was at once Big Customer, Big Regulator, and Big Taxer. They watched the steady transformation of private capitalism into state capitalism, with the dangers of military Socialism always present. Thus, despite the Marxist theory of war as the instrument of capitalist groups, it was the businessmen who were most worried by the revolutionary consequences of the war economy. Hence the political outlook of the business groups, typified by the career of Senator Robert A. Taft, with its demand for lower war budgets, less aid to America's allies, fewer government controls, and lower taxes. But it was the ironic destiny of American business to move steadily toward a result it dreaded. Even when the businessmen had a Republican Administration, as after 1952, they seemed powerless to reverse this trend.

American liberals were equally caught between two conflicting impulses—to use the full potential of American strength in preventing a Kremlin world domination which would mean the death of liberalism, and on the other hand to prevent the fatal militarizing of American life in the process. What troubled them most was not only the new role of American generals in decisions extending far beyond the technical aspects of warfare. Even more they were troubled by the evidence of how hard it would be to dissolve the armament economy and return it to a peacetime basis. There are economic historians who assert that the New Deal would have failed if it had not been retrieved by war contracts starting in 1938, and that postwar prosperity would have been impossible without the arms race. One need not go along with this view to recognize how many problems a democracy is absolved from meeting because a warfare economy makes it easier to avoid them. Since it is unlikely that either the arms race or the armament economy will be abolished in the calculable future, the question of what American capitalism would do without war orders is for the present an academic one. The same applies to the question of what the Communist states would do if they did not have military Communism to give force to the decisions of the governing groups and cohesion to a restless people. It is a striking fact that the American economy has survived in the artificial atmosphere of war and the arms race, and has shown an impressive flexibility in being able to move and adapt itself to the alternations of war and peace and to that twilight condition which is neither. It should be added, of course, that an armament economy is not the only solution for the problems of full employment under capitalism: as I have noted earlier* Americans have learned what is needed to keep the economy going without the artificial respiration of armaments, if only they have the will to apply their knowledge.

Even amidst the alarms of a world struggle, the American Army has not become a professional one but remains an army of civilians in uniform. The current standing army of several million men, a large number of them stationed abroad, is mainly a collection of draftees who are rotated through a term of training and service: the number of those who make a lifetime career of it is relatively small. During a period of active war, as in World War II, the larger part of America's young manhood takes part in the war experience. In this sense the American Armed Services are the "nation-in-arms" of Napoleonic times—a far-flung organization of young people who have been civilians and hope to be civilians again, and are determined to survive the strange interlude of war as best they can.

Given this civilian emphasis, it is not surprising that the American soldier judges his Army experience in civilian terms. Attitude studies of the Army, notably Samuel Stouffer's work in *The American Soldier,* found that what the soldier wanted from the Army was: status while he was a soldier, training which would help him in his job or career after he left the Army, the minimum of exposure to the dangers that would make a casualty of him, and the kind of comfort he could not get if he was stationed at a "God-forsaken place" like the Aleutians or Tasmania. These four wishes may seem the desires of men who are not serious about the business of war, but they are characteristic of a society that values the pursuits of peace and leaves them only under pressure of necessity and not from any valuing of the martial virtues.

This makes more ironic the contrast between the relative freedom of civilian life and the highly disciplined and hierarchic society of the Army. Every generation of young Americans must take the traumatic leap from the one to the other. Since many of the draftees come from relatively protected middle-class homes and a family structure that stresses individual freedom, the shock is all the greater. To be sure, there are many men for whom the drastic devaluation of the individual in Army life becomes a value in itself: they find a kind of peace in surrendering themselves to the Army collective. But for most others the transition is too abrupt, and becomes an agonizing experience. Much has been

* Ch. V, Sec. 10, "The Emerging Amalgam."

changed in the structure of the Army: it has moved from a small force of volunteers to a vast conscript organization, and from local and state units to a national one. But its discipline is still rigorous to the point of being Prussian. For those who are not broken by it, the initiation into the Army may be a valuable school of experience. For many others it is a struggle not only for the toughening of the body but for the survival of the spirit—a struggle through which the soldier manages to pass because his pride forces him to show his group that he "can take it." This same group feeling underlies Army "morale," which is based less on any personal commitment to the war or its purposes than upon an esprit de corps.

What gives the American Army its stamp as a society is that it has shaped its ways in relative insulation while the civilian ways were being shaped competitively and therefore more flexibly. The Army fails to make use of civilian society's competitive techniques, with direct rewards for merit and achievement. Instead of the high degree of mobility in American society, there remains between the officers and the men— the leaders and the led—a wall which cannot be overleaped. This separation and its hierarchic structure are present in every army, but they are especially galling to the American democratic spirit. Not only must the soldiers be broken before they can accept it, but most of the officers must also have their earlier habits remolded. The training for officer candidates has been described as an anxiety-ridden experience more severe than college hazing, in which the personality structure of the candidate is first broken down and then is so reconditioned that he finds a relief in taking his repressed aggressions out on his men. Thus the Stouffer study showed that it was easier for the American Negro to adjust himself to Army conditions than for the white, since the Negro had already become accustomed to a situation of status.

The case of the Negro soldier illustrates the influence of levels of expectation upon Army experience. The Negro in World War II felt bitterly about the persisting discrimination and segregation in a struggle whose professed aims were antiracist. Yet on the whole the Southern Negro, with a lower level of expectation, suffered fewer psychological scars in the Southern Army camps than the Northern Negro in his Northern camps. Similarly the soldier who fared best in Army life was likely to be a boy with little education, coming from a farm or a small town. Partly because they were still strongly rural, and partly because of their persisting authoritarian values, the Southern states have played a role in American warfare far beyond their ratio of population. Since the martial values are largely feudal virtues, and since Army resentments are conditioned by the expectations with which the soldier starts and his sense of his worth as an individual, it is the better-educated men from urban and industrial areas for whom the Army experience becomes an ordeal.

Even before warfare became thoroughly mechanized the soldier was cynical of the glory ideal. As a Union private put it in a letter from a Civil War battlefield, "Glory consisted in getting shot and having your name spelled wrong in the newspapers." To be sure, someone like young Oliver Wendell Holmes, Jr., who went through the Civil War and was several times wounded, was later to look back on this period as the most meaningful of his life. "In our youth," he wrote, "our hearts were touched with fire. It was given to us to learn at the outset that life is a profound and passionate thing." Yet even Holmes had to confess that "war, when you are at it, is horrible and dull." Only in retrospect did the passionate part emerge. "The reality was to pass a night on the ground in the rain with your bowels out of order, and after no particular breakfast to attack the enemy." In the Civil War there were more deaths from dysentery than from battle, and the problems of sanitation and diet proved more devastating than those of lead and steel. Today the American soldier is as well fed and cared for as any in history. Yet while American technical efficiency, grappling with the administrative problems of warfare, has achieved triumphs of engineering, sanitation, preventive medicine, and surgery, the American soldier has no real stomach for fighting or glory for their own sake.

What makes it worse is that war has become more destructive as the American cherishing of life and its values has grown more urgent. The old hand-to-hand combat of the Civil War has been replaced by an impersonal warfare in which destruction is wrought by remote control, as with the nuclear warfare. But the impersonality of dealing out death or of facing its chances has, if anything, increased rather than lessened its horrors. A large portion of American war casualties has proved to be that of battle shock, either in anticipation or under the stress of combat. The number of "psychoneurotic" cases has borne testimony to the gap between civilian conditioning and the conditions of war.

The remarkable fact is that the American soldier has fought well, died well, and—where he has survived—become part of civilian life again at home without being shattered. Partly it is because, with a kind of fatalism, he decides that he has a bad job on his hands which he must suffer silently and get over with. All war partakes of the nature of licensed murder, and there is a sense in which it channels impulses that have been repressed in a peaceful industrial society. But none has yet been able to assess the mutilating effect of war on the spirit of the civilian soldier. Every society demands a considerable truncating of emotion, yet the young soldier finds himself subjected to it at a time in his life when he requires elbow room for generosity.

This may offer a clue, however, to the effectiveness of America at war. The civilian premise that the individual counts for something is severely hemmed in by the Army as a society: yet it is strong enough to survive, and carries the soldier—as it carries the whole nation—through the war ordeal. American war strength is greatest just at the point at which an authoritarian society would have used up the impetus of its imposed belief and be ready for internal collapse. Here, as in other phases of American life, the conditionings of an open society reap their harvest of strength. That they should do so in something so barbarous as modern warfare serves to make the triumph more dramatic.

While it is the common soldier—Johnny Reb or Billy Yank or G.I. Joe —who is glorified by the orators and politicians, with their cult of the anonymous common man, one drastic consequence of America's new military era has been the creation of a professional military elite.* In the wartime armies many of the officers are civilians drafted for the Army, who learn the art of command and sometimes show remarkable qualities of leadership; yet the top command remains with the Army professionals.

These professionals have not been able in America, as they have in Latin America, Germany, Spain, Japan, to create a caste which would dominate the society and even challenge the powers of the civilian government. From the beginning of the national experience, Americans have feared control by the military and have insisted on control being retained by the civilian arm. Since the President functions as Commander-in-Chief of the Armed Forces it is largely through him that the control is exercised. The crucial figures in this history of military-civilian relations were Washington and Lincoln. Washington set the initial precedent, both in theory and practice. Again and again he insisted, in letters to his officers and to the Congress, that the civilian authority had to be kept paramount. As for Lincoln, since most of the military leadership talent went over to the Southern cause, he had to find promising young officers and make leaders out of them. The story of his trials, disasters, and final success in this quest is well known. But much as he valued good generals Lincoln reasserted the principle of civilian authority over the military. This does not mean an American acceptance of the principle of political commissars as in totalitarian societies, where the soldier-technician is distrusted and his political reliability has constantly to be guarded. Where Lincoln found a good technician, as he

* See also Ch. VII, Sec. 2, "The Seats of the Mighty."

did in Grant, he gave him complete headway. But he never abdicated his right to appoint and dismiss, nor his right and duty to decide on the larger outlines of strategy which are bound to be as much political as military.

There have been few "political generals" and very little Bonapartism in American history: the most notable cases have been those of General McClellan, who was appointed Chief-of-Staff by Lincoln and ran for the Presidency while the Civil War was still on, and General MacArthur, who saw himself as a man of political destiny throughout his career. In the struggle between President Truman and General MacArthur during the Korean War, the issue was not the merit of the strategic ideas of the two men but the question of where the final decision lay. In this sense the episode marked a constitutional crisis. MacArthur had strong popular support, which made President Truman's challenge to him an act of courage and seemed for a time to open the possibility of civil strife. But the tradition of civilian control proved too strong to be overthrown. There is a difference (contrasting President Grant and Eisenhower) between a military man who turns after a war to the tasks of peace and one who seeks to use his military power and glamour for political ends, and seeks the supremacy of the military over the civilian. The creation of a new elite of generals has thus far been kept within the frame of civilian control, but the question of the future is more difficult.

The new American general, because he must administer an army and often act as a kind of proconsul on foreign soil, is a mixture of many men. Not only is he trained in the history and art of war; he must also be something of a diplomat, and he must know how to move and direct vast bodies of men and material, yet also how to govern occupied territory and maintain delicate relations with his allies in a coalition war. With all this he must remain a politically neutral technician, a little like an American corporate manager who runs a big plant but must take his larger directives from his board. Such requirements involve broad training, and because of this a number of the abler generals have been used in diplomatic and administrative posts. While their sympathies tend to be with business, they form one of the rare power elites in American life that is trained to keep itself free of money as an incentive.

The danger with the military group, as German history has shown, is that it will grow into a professional caste cherishing its own conception of honor, frightened at the infiltration of new ideas, cut off from the rest of the culture, and living by its sense of power. In some respects the Joint Chiefs-of-Staff have tended to parallel the development of the German General Staff, especially in the spread of its interests and the con centration of power in a single person at the top. But the inner differences between American and German society make it more likely that the American general, like the American soldier, will remain basically a civilian, and that the conditionings of democratic life will counteract the authoritarian nature of his task and training. The sharpest challenge, after the MacArthur episode, to the nonpolitical character of the Army came when Senator McCarthy tried in 1954 to use the Congressional power of investigation in order to force the generals and the civilian secretaries to take his lead in their dismissal of subordinates. The failure of this effort showed again that the nonpolitical Army is deeply ingrained in American society.

The burden rests not so much with the military as with the culture itself. Fortunately the Americans have not developed the cult of martial virtues which has paralyzed military societies since Assyria and Sparta. Such a cult is more likely to grow in a society that glorifies feudal rather than industrial qualities, despises human life instead of valuing it, and has never launched on anything like the American quest for happiness. What makes militarism suicidal is the nature of the virtues it celebrates and their deadening effect on cultural growth. The military virtues are subordination, hierarchy, loyalty, clan honor, physical prowess, and above all the habit of mind that regards all questions as settled by authority. Despite their victories and sense of power, the American soldiers have come out of their major wars with a saving distaste for such virtues and for military life. With all its pressures to conformity American society offers an unfavorable soil for militarism. The stress on mobility, on reward for effort, on creative comforts, on happiness and on individual freedom, more than counterbalances whatever glamour the military life has offered in history.

5. The American World Image

THERE IS AN episode in Thomas Jefferson's career that illumines the image which the American has of the world. As President he put through the Non-Intercourse and Embargo Acts to keep America from being drawn into the struggle between the British and French for control of the seas. "I have ever deemed it fundamental for the United States," he wrote fifteen years later, "never to take an active part in the quarrels of Europe. . . . Their mutual jealousies, their balance of power, their complicated alliances, their forms and principles of government, are all foreign to us. They are nations of eternal war. . . . On our part, never had a people so favorable a chance of trying the opposite system, of peace and fraternity with mankind and the direction of all our means and faculties to the purpose of improvement instead of destruction!"

On which Henry Adams commented in his monumental *History of the United States:*

> War, with all its horrors, could purify as well as debase; it dealt with high motives and vast interests; taught courage, discipline, and stern sense of duty. Jefferson must have asked himself what lessons of heroism or duty were taught by his system of peaceable coercion, which turned every citizen into an enemy of the laws—preaching the fear of war and self-sacrifice, making many smugglers and traitors, but not a single hero. . . . Under the shock of these discoveries Jefferson's vast popularity vanished, and the labored fabric of his reputation fell in sudden and general ruin. America began slowly to struggle, under the consciousness of pain, toward a conviction that she must bear the common burdens of humanity and fight with the weapons of other races in the same bloody arena; that she could not much longer delude herself with hopes of evading laws of Nature and instincts of life; and that her new statesmanship which made peace a passion could lead to no better results than had been reached by the barbarous system which made war a duty.

True, it was an Adams who wrote this, with the traditional Adams hostility to Jefferson; and it was written at the turn of the twentieth century about an episode a century earlier. Yet whatever their real divergence of view, it is curious that both men built their intellectual systems on the concept of the elemental principles of Nature. No less than Jefferson's, Adams's appeal was to "the laws of Nature and instincts of life." The difference was that Jefferson lived in the eighteenth-century intellectual universe which saw Nature as an initial harmony disturbed by the destructive artifices of men, while Adams lived in a post-Darwinian world which saw Nature as a cruel, unending struggle. Yet in both cases there was an appeal to a peculiar American consonance with Nature. Adams used it to justify intervention just as Jefferson had appealed to it to justify isolationism. The internationalists of today go back to the same image of America's relation to the outside world which lay at the heart of Jefferson's world view, although they derive from it a directly contrary conclusion: since America is what Jefferson felt it to be, it has the mission of setting the world aright, spreading the gospel of freedom and democracy.

This is the metaphysic of the American world image: America is the New World, while all the rest of the world that is not America is the Old World. The ruling principle of the Old World is artifice and cunning in an arena—as Charles Beard saw it—"encrusted in the blood rust of centuries." To correct this, America was founded as part of an Order of Nature, as distinguished from the Artificial Order. This gives Americans a unique relation to Nature which may justify intervention in world affairs, as it may also provide ground for its isolation from a world embroiled in hopeless quarrels. Thus the role of America as a hermit nation and its role as liberating nation are twin impulses in American history and the American mind; they are inseparable not only from the fabric of the civilization but from each other. They are the thrust and counterthrust which form the seeming paradox of the American attitude to the world.

One finds in this metaphysic a clue to some elements in the American outlook which might otherwise seem contradictory and wayward. A brilliantly acid British observer, Geoffrey Gorer, has managed in his portrait of American world attitudes (in *The American People*) to depict them as perversely juvenile and quaintly imbecilic. If this were true, it would be hard to explain why a people ridden by such idiocies could have risen to world power or could be thriving in a world which does not coddle ineptitude. There is, of course, a quality of mingled innocence and shrewdness in the American world image, as there is in the whole of the American national character. The central element of the American metaphysic is the belief that American institutions are more "natural" and therefore better than those of other peoples. This belief is part of the organic strength of America. There is a childishness in it, but this very childishness strips it of what might otherwise become a cynical imperialism. Using Spengler's symbols, the American world image is more closely related to the "springtime" of a culture than to the twilight "Caesarism" which, in its disillusioned belief in power alone, would use it to put other peoples in an inferior status.

The idols Americans worship are not primarily the idols of power but the idols of their own culture transposed upon the world scene. Since they believe in productivity within their own system, they tend to value productivity in others. The preindustrial cultures seem to them backward: they may also regard them as picturesquely quaint but they reserve their admiration for the cultures that have developed housing, sanitation, and mechanical skills. Similarly, since Americans live by machines they use them in their foreign policy, both in war and peace. Even lethal weapons are for them tools and gadgets rather than death-dealing devices. When they seek some way of aiding a friendly people, they prefer to help them achieve the same weapons and gadgets they have themselves. When President Eisenhower was confronted with the problem of accepting or refusing the method of atomic disarmament, he proposed an "atoms for peace" program to turn technology from wartime to peacetime uses and then an "open-sky" plan. They also make an idol of the dollar. Partly this is a matter of pride in their resources, partly a way of saying that there are better methods of conducting world affairs than the Old Diplomacy. As compared with diplomacy and war the use of the dollar seems to them part of a more rational New Order—saner, more logical, less destructive. They seem to have an inveterate conviction that peace is something they can buy with their dollars as readily as they can buy a house, a car, a TV set, or new clothes for their families. Again there is a degree of childishness in this view, yet it is not wayward but organic to the national character.

The American need for signs of affection from other peoples has often been noted. In part it expresses the overvaluing of love which I have already discussed.* But it also expresses a desire for a mutual generosity in relations between peoples. There is an understandable skepticism about American motives in such ventures as the Marshall Plan, NATO, and Point Four by those who note the expectation of a *quid pro quo* whenever aid is granted. But the truth is not so much that Americans believe they can buy love and affection with the dollar, as that they are bewildered when they do not find in foreign affairs the kind of reciprocity they expect between neighbors in their own towns. Gorer has remarked acutely that for Americans all international relations are interpersonal relations. Believing in their own motives, they are bewildered when—after spending some fifty or sixty billions in military and economic aid to their allies—they reap a harvest of suspicion, fear, and envy.

One of the American traits is the recoil from the unfamiliar. The trouble with the world, Salvador de Madariaga once remarked ironically, is that there are so many foreigners in it—which pretty much expresses the American attitude toward outsiders. The American traveling abroad is likely to be puzzled when he finds that others do not share his ideas on food and clothing, sanitation, work and play, manners and morals. This seems the more curious when one remembers that America is itself a "nation of nations" and contains a multitude of diverse cultural traditions. Yet this fact only serves to increase the bafflement of the American abroad: since he has seen people of foreign extraction in his own country abandoning their customs and becoming "Americanized," he cannot understand why the people of foreign countries should not do the same. There is little xenophobia, real hatred of outsiders, in this attitude. Rather does it express the American's illusion of centrality in his conviction that what he is and does and how he does it are part of the order of Nature.

This attitude turns in part on a distrust of foreign social and political

* See Ch. VIII, Sec. 5, "Courtship, Love, and Marriage."

systems. The original rejection of Europe, based on a recoil from Europe's monarchies and dynastic wars, has been transformed into a fear of Communism and a distrust even of "Socialism." Americans tend to lump under "Socialism" all economic and political forms which differ sharply from their own. Given the constant change of the American social structure, this seems a curious attitude, which can only be explained by the feeling that a "Socialist" system seems to contain not only the unfamiliar but also the subversive. Americans have not learned that they do not have to embrace Socialism in order to accept the fact that other peoples may have turned to it either out of choice or out of necessity.

I have noted in an earlier chapter the rejection of the European father which underlies much of the American attitude toward Europeans.* But something very different is involved in the American attitude toward the Asians. They seem to form a wholly different world to Americans, who speak of the struggle between Communism and democracy as one between "East" and "West." Actually, of course, Communism as a system of thought is as much a product of the Western tradition as is democracy: both flow from the science, rationalism, and industrialism of the seventeenth and eighteenth centuries. Yet by equating Communism with the East the Americans in effect give it a prescriptive claim to the whole of the Oriental world. This does not reckon with the fact that America contains within itself strands from both East and West. The American soldier in the Korean War who called the Asian soldiers "gooks" was only expressing his sense of the strangeness of finding himself fighting for or against peoples so alien to his experience. What the American finds different about the Oriental mind is its tempo, its valuing of the group rather than of the individual life, its slow continuity of tradition. Yet there are stirrings of self-questioning and self-doubt within the American mind which are making Americans readier to open themselves to influences from the Orient. This has been shown recently by an interest in the art and thought of Asia, from the Japanese dance to the temple sculptures of India and by the new understanding of Asian political leaders like Gandhi, Nehru, Magsaysay, U Nu, and by a more sympathetic approach to the foreign polities of the "uncommitted" peoples of Asia.

Americans like to think that their foreign policy is based on "the man on the street." Actually this is far truer in domestic than in foreign policy, whose direction, at least in theory, is in the President's hands. As

---

* See Ch. I, Sec. 3, "The Slaying of the European Father."

Alexander Hamilton put it, he is "the sole organ of foreign policy." By his power to make treaties and agreements and appoint ambassadors to represent him, by his conduct of diplomacy and his role as commander-in-chief, he can shape policy according to his own ideas. He has the power to be not a follower but a creator of public opinion since he can in large measure shape the situations to which public opinion responds.

This power of the Executive can lead to dangerous consequences. While only Congress can declare war, the Executive can by his conduct of diplomacy bring about a situation in which a declaration of war cannot be avoided. The charge that Franklin Roosevelt deliberately induced the Japanese attack on Pearl Harbor has been grossly overstated; yet the point is that it might have happened, and that it is quite possible under the American system. The action of President Truman in ordering troops to Korea immediately after the North Korean attack is another illustration. Legally it came within America's adherence to the police power of the UN and morally it was justified, yet it had the effect of plunging America into a war without any declaration by Congress. Similarly when President Eisenhower, in 1957, asked Congress for a Joint Resolution giving him a "stand-by" power to move troops to avert aggression in the Middle East, a number of Constitutional authorities argued that he had the power anyway and that the request was superfluous.

There is thus no direct relation between American popular attitudes and American policy. When the Cominform in 1948 expelled Tito, it is doubtful whether American opinion was ready to accept the break as genuine and help Communist Yugoslavia. It is also doubtful whether popular opinion supported a similar move to give aid to Franco Spain in return for military bases, or whether there was ever any popular opinion behind the Administration policy of bolstering American oil concessions in the Arab countries by military aid and alliances. In all three cases the State Department acted on grounds of high policy, and the people accepted what they may not have liked. On the other hand, when President Truman proposed the appointment of an ambassador to the Vatican he encountered a storm of protest and had to retreat. Thus public opinion sets the outer limits of tolerance for foreign-policy decisions. The policy-makers need not follow it in day-to-day decisions, but if they move too far from it on matters that seem symbolic, they must draw back or lose Congressional and popular support.

In the functioning of foreign policy the most serious question is the separation of powers between Congress and the Executive. After its honeymoon period, every administration has had to face the rise of an opposition to its foreign policy even within its own party. In time of war a skillful President can carry the country along with him from crisis to crisis, as Lincoln did in the Civil War and Roosevelt in World War II. He must balance the needs of war strategy with the requirements of military and civilian morale. In the midst of war he must think of the next election while he strives to keep the country cohesive in the face of retreats and defeats. But in one sense a crisis of peacetime diplomacy involves even greater difficulties, since the cementing force of a common danger is not present. It was the great achievement of Senator Vandenberg, after World War II, to hold the Republicans in line on a "bipartisan policy" which presented an unbroken political front to the Kremlin. But such leadership is rare and has not been duplicated since. Thus American foreign policy has had to fight constantly a two-front strategic struggle—one with America's opponents abroad, the other with the Administration's enemies in Congress. The call for party discipline, more insistent in recent years, has had scant response, and as a result both the foreign policy of successive administrations and the counterpolicy of the opposition party have been the product of haste and improvisation rather than policies planned and hammered out to represent a collective party position.

Perhaps only the abundance of American power and wealth has provided the margin of waste which has made possible the luxury of the violent expression of American attitudes on foreign affairs inside America. Commentators from countries where the press is state-controlled or where it is held "responsibly" in line with government policy cannot dissociate American press headlines from the government's position. Yet the dissociation must be made. When Colonel McCormick, the publisher of the Chicago *Tribune*, carried on his private war with the British he was engaging in this luxury. The same holds for the tenacious clan of isolationist Senators. The effect is clamorous, but it is serious only when American policy is weak enough to respond to it. If a newspaper, a Senator, or a pressure group can cow the State Department or President into a policy change, then those who forced the change emerge as the real policy-makers. The task of a wise administration is to steer its course according to its principles, but always to take soundings of public opinion in order to re-examine the wisdom of the principles. In short, foreign policy in a democracy is a two-way relation in which the decision-makers never cut themselves off from the people but never flinch from clarifying the alternatives before them and guiding the nation in the choice it makes between these alternatives.

6. The World's Image of America

WHAT THE WORLD thought of them used to be of intense concern to Americans in the days when they were making a bid for their equal place among the powers of the earth. Like every new social experiment, this one wanted to feel itself a success; like every culture coming to power, it sought a mirror to catch the reflection of its crescent might.

Americans got plenty of attention from travelers, visiting luminaries, and foreign critics. In the period before the Jacksonian era the driving curiosity of the foreigner was about the nature of this new comet, whether it would survive, and the type of new man who lived on it. Later the commentators split between Tories who recoiled from the new democracy in action, and liberals and radicals who welcomed it as the world's best hope. In the period between the Civil War and the World War, America was accepted as a successful going-concern, but anxiety fixed upon its machine culture and materialist values. In the era of the world wars and the long Armed Truce the emphasis shifted again. While Europe still sat in judgment on America it was chiefly concerned with the nature and maturity of its leadership in a world of atomic power. With these queries came a new kind of split in the world's attitude toward America.

The earlier commentators had also been split in their own way. To be sure, St. John de Crèvecoeur had the timeless accent of someone writing about Paradise in the dawn of the world. He was a European who, having discovered the charms of America, had become an American; yet he wrote in French and as part of the continental tradition. There was a naïve insight in his perceptions, an idyllic quality as in a painter of the Primitive School. "Wives and children, who before in vain demanded of him a morsel of bread, now fat and frolicsome, gladly help their father to clear those fields whence exuberant crops are to arise to feed and to clothe them all." There is, however, also an Hobbesian view of the frontiersmen "often in a perfect state of war; that of man against man . . . ; that of man against every wild inhabitant of these venerable woods, of which they have come to dispossess them. . . . These men appear to be no better than carnivorous animals of a superior rank. . . . Remote from the power of example, and check of shame, many families exhibit the most hideous parts of our society." But if De Crèvecoeur saw the early settlers of the frontier as a *Lumpenproletariat* of the forest, he felt also that they were quickly civilized by "decency of conduct, purity of morals, and respect of religion." His estimate of the salient American traits of his time (he was speaking of the Middle Colonies) could still stand: "industry, good living, selfishness, litigiousness, country polity, the pride of freemen, religious indifference, are their characteristics." Thus even in De Crèvecoeur, who is held to have presented an American idyl, one finds the beginnings of the split which was to plague the European mind in one form or another for centuries. The hopes that clustered around new American institutions fought with the fears of the untrammeled elements in American life.

De Tocqueville, the deepest of the foreign observers, also felt this split. The young banker and aristocrat, who was in his later years to play a role in French politics and write a great history of the Old Regime in France, came to America to study this new portent in the Western heavens. He was a rare mixture of student and man-of-affairs who refused to read his own preferences into history. He was himself an aristocratic liberal who hoped for enlightened policies to be carried out for the French people by a responsible elite of blood and ability. Thus the principle of "democracy" which he saw in America, and which he did more than any other writer to define as a category of modern political thought, was a sharp challenge to his own values. He sensed the danger that the political principle, "the majority will must prevail," would become the moral principle, "the majority is always right." Yet he did not let his sense of danger distort his capacity for observation. Nor was he dismayed by the fact that the stream of democracy (to use the figure in one of his famous passages) was turbulent and muddy: he saw it cutting a new channel, and he knew that the turbulence and mud were part of the process. In short, De Tocqueville still stands up because he wrote with the humility of a great political analyst.

The same cannot be said for many of the British travelers, like Basil Hall or Mrs. Trollope, who also visited America at the floodtime of Jacksonian democracy and who wrote (as Allan Nevins put it) out of a "Tory condescension" toward an America they still considered a barbaric colony. Charles Dickens, more of a radical than a Tory, who had done his share of attacking abuses in English life, blurted out in *American Notes* and *Martin Chuzzlewit* his home truths about American materialism and dollar worship with an unendearing assurance of the righteousness of his own English values. The greatest contrast to De Tocqueville's spirit was that of Macaulay, who wrote of the putative ruin of America in the future with as much finality as Gibbon wrote of the actual ruin of Rome in the past, and whose famous letter on American democracy moves with a sweep still impressive even after it has been proved dismally wrong: "It is quite plain that your government will never be able to restrain a distressed and discontented majority.

. . . There will be, I fear, spoliation. The spoliation will increase the distress. The distress will produce fresh spoliation. There is nothing to stop you. Your Constitution is all sail and no anchor. When a society has entered on this downward progress, either civilization or liberty must perish." Where Mrs. Trollope found the Americans boors, where Dickens found them money grabbers and Macaulay found them despoilers of liberty and civilization, Matthew Arnold a generation later found them only Philistines. He ushered in a whole school of criticism by asserting that America was simply neither "interesting" nor "elevating."

It was in response to such criticism that James Russell Lowell, his cultural pride goaded to a pitch of genteel anger, wrote his famous *Atlantic* essay, "On a Certain Condescension in Foreigners." Not even the urbane *American Commonwealth* of Viscount Bryce, which helped Americans to a quieter self-assurance about their institutions and their standing in the world, could quite wipe out the memory of the brash men who had come to sit in judgment on America.

There is a touch of unreality today in reading some of these traveled, sophisticated, and wise men of Europe. They came from every European culture. Some came to stay, some only to hit and run. They took inventory of the rough manners, the rich raiment, the fabled wealth of this parvenu who was knocking at the gate of world recognition with an insistence not to be denied. In the earlier phase they passed judgment on America's morals, inns, bedbugs, spitting and chewing, strong drink, factory girls, high society. Later they examined its machines, slums, political corruption, Southern lynching, Midwest isolationism, materialism, absorption in sports, yellow journalism, religious sects, crime and gangsterism, movies and TV, jazz and jive, novels, skyscrapers and bathtubs, businessmen and labor leaders, ways and failures of making love, psychoanalysis and neurotic women, booms and busts. Surely there has never been in history so full and free a concentration on a living culture over so extended a period.

In our generation a radically new phase of commentary on America has begun. Books are no longer written out of an aristocratic disdain for democracy nor out of the enthusiasm for it which was the reverse side of the shield. It is no longer America who knocks at the gate as a newcomer, peddling its wares of democracy, science, technology, high living standards, and asking the world's approval. It is not America that feels itself judged, nor Europe that sits in judgment as the acknowledged keeper of the cultural seals. The comments of the latest British novelist, arriving in New York en route to Hollywood, on American overheated houses or American clothes-horse women or any of the other standard topics, no longer draw blood. Since Americans are conscious of possessing the power, they take better to criticism of their cultural glory.

Even the myth of America, which had exerted so powerful an appeal on the minds of the European masses, has changed. Originally it was the myth of the Western Island—the legend of a bright promise amidst the surrounding darkness of the Old World. It was the place where one went to get away from the rutted stability of vested power and privilege. Many of the European novels, even as late as Lawrence's *Lady Chatterley's Lover*, had as their typical ending the hero setting off for the virile land of America. But the myth went through a number of transformations: the type-figure of the Noble Savage changed into the frontiersman, and that in turn into the commercial traveler, the Western cowboy, the Big Business tycoon, the Chicago gangster, and the devotee of the true cult of jazz. Today there is no longer a single legendary symbol for America. The immigrant's dream of streets still paved with gold is counterbalanced by the nightmare of the Congressional snooper. The "metaphysic of promise" still holds good, and young men and women the world over still long to come closer to the center of world power; but this too is counterbalanced by the image of America spread by the Kremlin propaganda lords.

There has been a double change therefore, in our time, in the world's image of America. One phase of it has been the shifting of emphasis in the appraisal of America: America is being judged no longer as a newcomer on the world scene but as a great power. The other is the civil war that rages in the hearts of those who are both drawn toward American power and dependent upon it, yet—because of the very fact of their dependence—also judge it harshly.

In this civil war raging in the mind of European and Asian man there is a danger of underestimating the pull that America still exerts on both. What attracts them is less the image of American power than of the American personality and social structure. Even many of the Russians—whatever their propagandists may teach them about American "imperialism" and "war-mongering"—are drawn toward the American personality. The case histories of Russian defectors into Germany and Austria, and of Hungarian refugees fleeing to the United States, show a residual sympathy for American society which two generations of Communist dogma have not been able to efface. This is, of course, even truer of western Europe, which shares so many of the basic American values.

But the very closeness of the European and American traditions makes the relation of dependence even more difficult. It is one thing to be conquered by an alien people—an event that can be written off as a combination of catastrophe and the Devil. But to be saved by one's kinsfolk, to be an Anchises carried out of the flames of Troy on the shoulders of Aeneas, bears the sting of humiliation. To the sensitive it implies that they are in the declining arc of their vigor—which is not an easy thing to admit, especially to oneself. They ask themselves why the Americans have been blessed with so much of material goods and they with so little. The answer cannot be American virtues and European vices, nor American merits and European defects. As they see the answer it is partly the luck of natural resources and of being cut off by oceans from the ravages of war. As much as luck it is also (as they see it) the willingness of Americans to pay a heavy human cost for what they have achieved: the willingness to be ruled by gadgets and machines, by business giants and intellectual pygmies, by political demagogues and the corruption of city bosses, by press barons, by advertising slogans and TV commercials, by spoiled women and even more spoiled children. To the European mind, with all its good will, the things that make Americans more powerful make them also more boorish, the things that make them more like giants make them also less like men. Even American aid has seemed the clinching proof that the American is the son who left home to make his fortune and now rolls in wealth while the old folk must hold out their hands for gifts to keep from going to the poorhouse.

Thus the phase of recoil is compounded of reluctant gratitude, envy for American wealth and prowess, resentful pride, and an uneasy fear of how America will use its power in world affairs. Edwin Arlington Robinson, in *Eros Tyrannos*, depicts a woman with pride of lineage drawn to a man from whom she is separated by the impassable distance between the faded aristocrat and the vigorous parvenu:

> *She fears him, and will always ask*
> *What fated her to choose him;*
> *She meets in his engaging mask*
> *All reasons to refuse him;*
> *But what she meets and what she fears*
> *Are less than are the downward years*
> *Drawn slowly to the foaming weirs*
> *Of age, were she to lose him.*

Thus Europe is caught between the need for America and the recoil from it.

This may explain the "Athens complex" which spread among the intellectuals of western Europe in the postwar years, when the shift of power to America became apparent. They were forced to compensate for their dependence by claiming for Europe the role of a cultural Greece to the American Rome—a Greece which, while conquered, takes the conqueror captive. Unquestionably the European cultures are mellower and more mature than the American. Without any overtones of provincialism the American intellectual feels that the British, French, and Scandinavians are extremely civilized people and the American artist continues to find in Italy an emotional haven he finds nowhere else.

Yet it would be wrong for the Europeans to conclude from this that the Americans have a sense of inferiority about their own culture. Except for a small number who are isolated by a cultural self-hatred and feel that nothing American can be good, the strong trend among the intellectuals is toward a critical acceptance of what was called (in a *Partisan Review* symposium) "our country and our culture." I speak of it as "critical acceptance" and not as "celebration": few of the American writers and thinkers have become apologists or have lost the skepticism which marks the craft of the thinker; nor have all of them stripped themselves of the driving impulse toward social and institutional change. But many of them have come to feel that charges born of hatred are destructive and barren and have struck a kind of pact with the basic frame of the culture within which they continue to function critically. They can absorb European criticism as well, since they value the great civilization out of which the criticisms come. If it helps the Europeans to think of themselves as Athens and of America as a less creative Rome, and to see American qualities through a glass darkly, the Americans have won enough assurance to take it in their stride.

It is natural that in the polar struggle for world position America's enemies should strive to exploit the civil war in the European and Asian mind. The Russian image of America is compounded of rivalry, fear, ideological antipathy, and cynically deliberate distortion for both home and foreign consumption. If a global war can be averted this image will in time change, as will happen also to the seriously distorted American image of Russia. In the meanwhile the Communist indictment of America has left its impact on the world's image of America.

The indictment is familiar. It charges that the American economy is riddled with "internal contradictions," that in its declining agony it turns to imperialist adventures and wars, that it is a Shylock lending money to the helpless and demanding its pound of flesh in the form of economic and political vassalage, that its prosperity has been made possible only by wars and armaments, and that as soon as it tries to stand on peacetime production alone it will collapse; that its inherent and feverish oscillation between boom and bust will be ended only by the inner explosion of class struggle; that this explosion is being post-poned through the skillful use of big armaments by a ruling class which uses the war fever to build an increasingly Fascist police state; that its inner savagery shows itself in barbaric methods of warfare, including germ warfare in Korea and China and plans to use the hydrogen bomb when the point of desperation has been reached; that its vaunted free-dom does not apply to those who challenge capitalist power, and that its façade of high living standards conceals the realities of poverty and slum housing; that there is an inner violence in its culture which ex-presses itself not only in lynchings and Jim Crowing of Negroes and in anti-Semitic hatreds, but also in literature, the arts, and the big media; that its materialism is hoggish, its morals reckless and decadent, its men emasculated, its women frigid, and its music and dance de-generate.

The path of this propaganda image is made easier by the widespread fears of American power. The American policy-makers have often given ground for such fears by reckless statements and foolish improvised actions. The growth of America's own nationalism has led to pressures which have cut aid abroad, put obstructions in the way of trade, or ruffled the sensitivities of the "junior partners" in the free-world coali-tion. This feeds the natural feeling that Americans are immature in the handling of their power, like children playing with toys. When the Americans become impatient of the pain and difficulty involved in trying to reach a consensus with their allies, the European answer is the British quip "No annihilation without representation." The Euro-peans feel that, caught in a war between the two polar powers, Europe would become an expendable continent, another lost Atlantis sunk un-der the dread weight of atomic destruction.

Hence the "neutralism" or "noncommitment" of many Europeans and Asians, which helps shape—and distort—their image of America. Hence also the rage of American policy- and opinion-makers at the fence sitters, whom they find more exasperating than the outright en-emy. It infuriates them to have an Aneurin Bevan impale them on an epigram, a Nehru view them with a cold detachment at once anti-capitalist and aristocratic, a Laski challenge the impact of the busi-nessman upon American democracy, a Priestley depict the "new society" as an American nightmare, a Sartre use the allegory of the respectful prostitute to flay the conformism of American public opinion.

Many Americans who are not narrowly nationalist, and who want America's allies to be independent, also want them to carry the respon-sibility of their independence. They suspect that their non-Communist critics are able to enjoy the luxury of hurling barbs at America exactly because it has shouldered the principal burden of democratic defense. They point out that since the Communist coup in Czechoslovakia and, even more, since the crushing of the Hungarian revolution, no one can question what happens to a European regime when Communism captures power. They see themselves not as crusaders against an ideology but as realists determined to keep the world open for a variety of social structures—provided each refrains from aggression.

The image of America current in Asia takes a somewhat different form. The Asian, newly liberated from colonialism or struggling to be liberated, finds in America a Devil symbol which serves to channel both his resentments and his newly felt sense of triumph. When Europeans take America apart, they are taking apart something they have come to regard as close to themselves. The European democrats speak and write acidly about America because they feel involved in the American venture and its destiny. In the case of Asia there is the sense neither of a shared past nor of a common destiny. The great cultural contacts of the Asian peoples have hitherto been either among themselves or with the peoples of Europe. America is viewed as the outsider, the giant who typifies what is held hostile in the Western way of life. Asia has shown a genius for religion-creating, a leaning away from activism, a distaste for materialism and the machine, a preference for refinement over raw vitality, a commitment to the family or the collective village unit as against the individual, a sense not of time but of permanence.

This may account for the fact that the Asians feel removed from the activism and machinism of both the polar powers. Thus far the Russians have managed to avoid the mistake of speaking of themselves as part of the West and thus alienating Asia. They have the advantage of facing toward both Europe and Asia, and are thus able to make an appeal to each. The Americans, who have only recently begun to face toward Asia, have made their appeal mainly as a society of freedom and abundance, of food and sanitation. They have not understood the deep Asian resentments which are further embittered by the image of America as a storehouse crammed with commodities. They have missed the fact that for the people of the Far East the American living standards seem incredible because they are incommensurable in terms of Asian experience. They fail to offer these people a compassable earthly vision, just as they fail to offer in spiritual terms a vision that will sustain the Oriental hunger for renunciation.

Thus the world's image of America is the product at once of American behavior, Communist propaganda, and the civil war that rages in the hearts of non-Communist Europeans and Asians. The result is that wherever Americans travel or wherever their official or unofficial spokesmen present America's case the questions that are asked them are a strange mixture of genuine disquiet and the unconscious echoes of political warfare. The questions are aimed at what is most vulnerable in the American reality—the surviving racist discriminations, the internal attacks on civil liberties, the strain of violence in the popular culture, the loudness with which the reactionary nationalists make their views heard, the jitters felt about "subversives," the power of a business oligarchy, the temptation to throw their weight about which American policy-makers do not always resist.

There have been distortions in the image of America all through the centuries. At the start there were the distorting lenses of hope, then the distortions of the legend of power or of wealth. For a time there were the distortions that ran in terms of gangsterism. Today there are the distortions of the violent political emotions involved in the long Armed Truce. The reality that is America gets lost in a series of fantastic mirror images.

The best answer to these questions is a candid answer. The Americans are aware that they have not struck twelve, that the struggle for an open society is by no means ended in America, that democracy is a continuing process in which every step is a compromise between opposing forces in the movement toward goals themselves in dispute. The mature American does not fear criticism of his institutions from abroad, as he does not hesitate himself to criticize them. If America is to make its qualities persuasive to world opinion, it must expect also to repair the defects of those qualities. If it reaps the advantage of such symbols as living standards, productivity, freedom for ideas, ethnic diversity, educational democracy, it must be willing to be damned for its failure to live up to them. And on a number of scores—on conformity, smugness, the overvaluing of personal security and the jitters about "national security," the resistance still offered by racist thought, and the faltering of leadership on the world scene—the failures have been real and sometimes dismal.

The problem is not one of answering the charges defensively or apologetically. It is one of finding a way of saying, through behavior as well as through words, that democratic society anywhere in the world would find it hard to survive the destruction of American democracy; that America does not seek to force conformity upon any culture; that the world it envisages is one in which diverse streams from every tradition flow into a cultural pool; and that such an open world is the fulfillment of the idea of an open society which alone gives the American experience its greatness of meaning.

7. The Destiny of a Civilization

"EVERY MAN," wrote Thomas Jefferson, "has two countries—his own and France." A young African writer has amended this to read "his own and America." It suggests the extent to which people far beyond the boundaries of America have had their imagination touched and their emotions engaged by the American experience. Only one other civilization in history—the Roman—can match this impact.

The comparison between Rome and America has absorbed many social thinkers. There are some striking parallels. We may, for example, sketch the lineaments common to both civilizations somewhat as follows: a world power span, by land and sea; a pride in republican institutions, with the emphasis theoretically on limited powers even while in practice the Executive is one of the most powerful offices in history; a continuing struggle between an oligarchic and a popular party, with the abler leaders gravitating toward the popular, but with the core of social power in the hands of the oligarchy; the reduction of politics to sloganeering, political recrimination, and charges of conspiracy.

Add some other parallels: a "capitalist" economy (I use "capitalist" in quotes since Rome, with land as its principal form of wealth, was not capitalist in our modern sense) growing strong in its later phases on world-wide resources and selling in far-flung markets, with cyclical swings of prosperity and depression; a distribution of wealth which arrays side by side the extremes of opulence and poverty; vast outlays on public works, an arms economy, and a network of economic controls in order to sustain the system; the piling up of a national debt, and a preoccupation with taxes and tax-gathering; the emergence of landless and toolless classes, at the mercy of fluctuations of prosperity and changes in state policy, absorbed with "bread and circuses"; the succession of ever bigger wars, enriching the nation yet draining its resources, spreading over the world the clamor of its arms; the absorption with the strategy, logistics, and technology of war; the use of military reputation as a road to high civilian office; the increasing domestic role of groups of war veterans; the creation of a remarkable system of administration and law, with armies of occupation and imperial proconsuls enveloping a turbulent world within the protective custody of border armies; the prestige and pride of citizenship in the world's greatest power structure.

To finish the portrait, add the cult of magnificence in public buildings and the growth of the gladiatorial arts at which the larger number of the people are passive spectators but emotional participants; the increasing violence within the culture; the desensitizing and depersonalizing of life; the weakening of the sense of place; the decay of rural life; the uprooting of people in a mobile culture; the concentration of a megalopolitan urbanism. In the area of personal life add the increasing split between moral standards and operative codes; the greater looseness of family ties and sexual relations, and the exploration of deviant and inverted forms of behavior; the Byzantinism of life, the refinements of luxury; the decay of formal religion, the turning toward new religious cults, the feverish search for the sources of evil; the feeling of widespread frustration, the "schism in the soul," the premonition of doom in the distant march of barbarian tribes.

It will be obvious that such a portrait of a civilization and an era might describe equally the Rome of the late Republic or early Empire and contemporary America. The parallel has been pushed hard by those who have sought in it variously a sermon against capitalism, the New Deal, or the public debt, religion or irreligion, materialism or supernaturalism, sexuality or divorce. Sermons aside, however, the question is whether the parallel is actually a deadly parallel or a mélange of striking metaphors, dramatic coincidences, and half-truths that fascinate the historical imagination while they mislead it.

The trouble with historical parallels is that they are selective and omit whole areas of unlikeness. If I may use this as a way of summing up a few of the points of emphasis of this book: there have been elements in American life crucially missing in the Roman: the steady advance of science and technology to sustain unparalleled living standards for every class; an emphasis on productivity, with an almost compulsive drive to raise living standards; a class system without the amorphous Roman proletariat; the heart of the culture in a broad middle class such as Rome lacked, and in an open-class system which dulls the sharpness of class struggle; the long-continuing survival of the constitutional tradition, the exclusion of extreme political philosophies and the minimal role played by political mobs.

Looking at it from the other direction, we find that Rome had only a narrow economic base in the skimpy and impoverished farms of an Italian peninsula not rich in resources. The treasure that gave her power came from the looting of riches in the stretch from Britain to North Africa and from Spain to India. Thus Rome as an empire was top-heavy: the superstructure of tribute and power had no self-regenerating base either in a culture of science and technology or in a fluid class system continuing to produce new talents and offer new rewards to match new hopes. It rested, rather, on the Roman legions and their mercenaries: when the imperial mold was broken, with the consequence of internal dissension and the "failure of nerve," the supports snapped and the civilization fell in ruins.

Turning to the institutions of the two societies America possesses an educational system which, for all its deficiencies, provides a constant stream of new human abilities for decision-making in industry and government. It has spread its national income widely enough to hold the allegiance of its people even in times of the most dangerous inner and world crises. It possesses a popular vigor that shows itself in the American speech, jazz, movies, and other popular arts, and offers proof that the fires of cultural strength still burn intensely. It has opened up to most of the people accessions of new experience in the big media, yet it retains a gusto for living and an earthiness of taste and style which are far from being the signs of a decadent or effeminate people. It renews its strength from institutions of freedom imbedded within the family system and the prevailing religious traditions, as well as within the economy. It has shown a resilience in bearing the shocks of war and depression, and a strength of fiber in meeting the challenges of old tyrannies and new "barbarians." Finally it evinces an inveterate optimism which restricts the prophecies of doom to small groups of moralists and intellectuals, whose experience scarcely touches the experience of the rest of the people.

I do not deny a degree of force in Spengler's contention that inner homologous structures may be "contemporary," even when they are far removed in time and place. They may face the same kind of crises, be subject to the same kind of stresses, traverse comparable life histories, run similar social and moral dangers, and (as so many civilizations have done) fall victim to the same combination of external challenge and internal weakness.

Yet I must reassert that America is not Rome but itself. The learning of all the cyclical theorists, from Vico to Toynbee, gives us no formulas that will explain the unlikely genesis of American civilization, the phenomenon of its growth, the paradox of outer slackness and inner strength, the riddle of why a power structure that by every historical parallel should have destroyed itself has retained not only its vigor but much of the unadorned directness it had in its less complex phases. This is not to say that America as a civilization is imperishable. It will perish, and it may even now be doomed by the destructive force that science has unleashed and man may not be able to control. But if so it is doomed for the ills and by the laws of development of the whole contemporary Western World, and not those of Rome or any other civilization of the past.

If America were Rome, who would be the barbarians? From America's standpoint, they would have to be the hordes of Communism, with the Russians and the Chinese as the leading tribes. The weakness in this analogy is immediately apparent. The Russians, with their tight statism, their rigid doctrinal unity, their ideological obsessiveness, their social conformism, are far from the image of amorphous barbarian bands pushing against the tottering ramparts of the empire. As for the Chinese, they combine the new steel frame of Communist doctrine with a civilization older even than that of the Russians, which in turn is older than the American, and with a highly complex structure of society and an ancient heritage of art and learning.

It is ironic for Americans to search for a "barbarian" image when they have themselves long embodied that image for Europe. Take almost any commentary on America written in the past half century by almost any culturally self-conscious European—let us say Georges Duhamel's *Scènes de la Vie Future*—and you will find in it the overpowering image of barbarians with machines coming to invade the empire of the spirit and preparing to lay waste to the ancient structures of sensibility and personality. There is also a second sense in which the concept of barbarians may be used. Spengler premised a phase of history in which politics and the state had broken down into a formless pursuit of individual greeds. He saw America as a random collection of people drifting from city to city in pursuit of the dollar, incapable of understanding politics in the Spenglerian sense of the arts of disciplined mastery. But Spengler also saw Bolshevik Russia as the same kind of barbarian horde that had "ceased to be a state," its economic man dominant over the political man, its political outlook lacking the dimension of depth. Unfortunately such a definition of the barbarian would include most of the economically developed peoples of the world, leaving only the Caesarist regimes of Fascism to sustain the idea of civilization.

The West European and the uncommitted Asiatic might regard America and Russia as expressing only alternative modes of barbarism. In both there is the abundance of energy that threatens to overwhelm the mellower or more passive civilizations, in both a high degree of organizing genius as the "practical" men seek an engineering approach through the state trusts of the commissars or the corporate trusts of capitalist Big Management. Given the polarizing pressures of the two superpowers, a large part of the world has begun to offer a growing resistance to the "either/or" choice between the two Romes. The struggle is not between a world empire and a number of barbarian outposts but between two great powers who are competing for world power while each insists it desires only its national security, and much of the rest of the world refuses to accept the terms of the struggle or to enroll as a conscript in either army.

One aspect of the struggle is the rivalry between America and Russia for the pacifying and organizing role that Rome played in the late Republic and early Empire. The period of the *pax Romana* was one of relative peace and prosperity not only in Rome but the provinces. There are few periods in world history when, over so wide an expanse, men could go about their business, arts, and pleasures in so undisturbed a way. The real disaster came out of the resulting rigidity and stagnation. Like the Americans and the Russians, the Romans were highly "practical" men who valued things more than they valued ideas: they perished by a failure of the imagination. A single world empire provides no rivalries of power and of values. Rome could destroy Carthage, but it could not overcome its own institutions of privilege and slavery which sapped its productive force and stripped its technology of dignity. It glorified the martial virtues but had not inner strength to give them meaning. When the challenge of the barbarians finally came, Rome had to pay Danegeld to buy off the marauders. The disease of war put the finishing touches to what had been left by the disease of class and underlying both was the disease of social uncreativeness.

What are these two civilizations, each of which is exerting its claim to organize the future by its own *pax Romana?* Their struggle for world influence is not an overnight phenomenon. Here is what De Tocqueville wrote of them:

> There are at the present time two great nations in the world which seem to tend toward the same end, although they started from different points; I allude to the Russians and the Americans. Both of them have grown up unnoticed; and while the attention of mankind was directed elsewhere, they have suddenly assumed a prominent place among the nations; and the world learned their existence and their greatness at almost the same time. All other nations seem to have nearly reached their natural limits . . . but these are still in the act of growth; all others are stopped, or continue to advance with extreme difficulty; these are proceeding with ease and celerity along a path to which the human eye can assign no term. The American struggles against the natural obstacles which oppose him; the adversaries of the Russian are men; the former combats the wilderness

and savage life; the latter, civilization with all its weapons and its arts; the conquests of the one are therefore gained by the plowshare; those of the other by the sword. The Anglo-American relies upon personal interest to accomplish his ends, and gives free scope to the unguided exertions and common sense of the citizens; the Russian centers all the authority of society in a single arm: the principal instrument of the former is freedom; of the latter, servitude. Their starting point is different, and their courses are not the same; yet each of them seems to be marked out by the will of Heaven to sway the destinies of half the globe.

It took a remarkable insight to discern the destinies of Russia and America at a time when Russia was still a preindustrial despotic monarchy and America, just beginning to look across the Mississippi, was still a small agrarian society and had only just proclaimed the Monroe Doctrine. But De Tocqueville sensed that there were common elements in these two societies and comparable resources for them to develop, which would one day make them the polarizing forces of the world. Each had a massive continental stretch that could be exploited as a base for empire. In the history of each the plain left its influence on the people, as Turner saw for America and Sir John Maynard for Russia. Each has shown an organizing capacity and a skill in amassing power. Most of all, both have shown the capacity (which stamps a strong civilization) to release locked-up energies.

The Russia which De Tocqueville saw was Czarist and not Communist, so that he could not have forseen the extent to which the Communist idea would become first a religious creed for the Russians and then a state church in which the religious fire had begun to burn out. His eye was, then, not on the dogma but on the land and the people. In them lay the capacity to give this or any other dogma its strength. In the American case, on the other hand, he noted the principle of freedom that has persisted to this day—a principle available for others as well as for Americans to develop. Thus what counted again was the land and the people, in whom lay the capacity to give the democratic idea its own brand of strength. What was latent in both cultures in 1835 has been realized in the mid-twentieth century. Every people has its high historical moments, when it feels a triumphant sense of national energy. What marks both the Russians and the Americans is that they moved beyond these short-lived spurts of intensity in a continuing arc of energy that they are still sustaining. This may be only a more complex way of putting what De Tocqueville calls "the will of Heaven" in explaining how each has come "to sway the destinies of half the globe."

The fact that America and Russia, who are today such determined rivals and whose social systems and principles are so at variance, should share certain common traits is a fact to infuriate as well as astonish the unthinking partisans of both. Yet reflection will show that there must be common elements which have led these two civilizations to steady growth and world power. These elements are not such as can be isolated by scientists and by their rigors of scientific method. Since they have to do with the intangibles of social energy and national character, they yield more readily to the intellectual imagination. I have mentioned the prophetic insight of De Tocqueville. Curiously, Walt Whitman, poet rather than political theorist, expressed a similar insight in his famous "Letter to Russia":

> You Russians and we Americans! Our countries so distant, so unlike at first glance—such a difference in social and political conditions, and our respective methods of moral and practical development . . . and yet in certain features, and vastest ones, so resembling each other. The variety of stock elements and tongues, to be resolutely fused in a common identity and union at all hazards—the idea . . . that they both have their historic and divine mission—the fervent element of manly friendship throughout the whole people, surpass'd by no other races—the grand expanse of territorial limits and boundaries—the unform'd and nebulous state of many things, not yet permanently settled, but agreed on all hands to be the preparations of an infinitely greater future—the fact that both Peoples have their independent and leading positions to hold, keep, and . . . fight for . . . the deathless aspirations at the inmost center of each great community . . . are certainly features you Russians and we Americans possess in common.

I do not cite these common traits to argue that there are no grounds for world struggle between Russia and America. The comparable historical elements in each system may be partly what has set them in opposition to each other. Neither in the life of nations nor of individuals do somewhat parallel personality structures insure the absence of conflict. The fact is that Russia and America are also strongly unlike each other, which implies not only a basis of conflict but means that each may at some future time manage to fit into a world culture which must feed on diversities.

The crucial difference does not lie in ideologies alone, important as they are: for the hold that Communism as an ideology has on the Russians and capitalist democracy on the Americans is something that itself needs explaining. The clues are in history and national character. Russia's long history of the oppression of peasants and the muzzling of intellectuals, along with psychological factors in the life history of the individual which await closer study, produced a strain of alternating violence and submission to authority. Children of an authoritarian church and a feudal social organization, the Russians never developed free institutions. They are burdened with the oppressive weight of dynastic history, and the experience of the Communist rulers did not abolish the dynastic pattern but left it intact. It is, moreover, a history marked by a succession of sharp breaks and catastrophes. The Kiev period was followed by a shift in trade routes, the weakening of Russian economic power, and by a Tartar rule which proved to be a long history of foreign enslavement. The Moscow period was one of domestic tryanny. Then came the rule of Peter and the awakening of Russian energies from their long Asiatic sleep—the fusion of Western and Eastern elements which evoked much of Russia's later strength. The witless misrule and corruption under the later Czars led to the double disaster of the defeat by Japan and the abortive 1905 revolution. Thus the 1917 break with the *ancien régime* was part of a continuing history of breaks and new starts which conditioned the Russian people to a long patience amidst a turbulent sequence of social disturbance and violent change.

One of the deepest differences between the two cultures lies in their divergent views of human nature and history. There is a messianic strain in the Russian tradition to which the American character is less conditioned, except for the influence of Biblical sin and salvation in the nineteenth-century Communist settlements and millennial movements. Students of Russian religion have noted that its core idea has been not the individual's responsibility to his conscience but the mystical sense of the congregation as a whole. To the Russian mind, therefore, both truth and salvation are likely to lie less in the individual soul than in the collective. The 1917 Revolution gave an explosive force to the Russian mystical and messianic strain, but it added also something the Russian thinkers from Belinski to Trotsky did not foresee—the will of a disciplined party seeking to transform the society according to a dogmatic scheme. Thus the Communist era imposed upon the *mystique* of the traditional Russia a rigid frame of planning based on a wholly rationalist view of human nature.

At first sight these may seem drastically opposed, leading to the conclusion that the Communist regime, with its optimist assurance that Russia and the world can be transformed according to a plan, could not thrive in a people with strong mystical and pessimistic strains. But this is to forget the common elements in past and present: the indifference toward individual values in the pursuit of some larger collective aim, whether it be the Holy Spirit-in-the-congregation, Socialism-in-one-country, or the triumph-of-the-world proletariat. Linked with the

Byzantine rather than the Western phase of European history, the Russians skipped both the Renaissance and the Reformation—which is to say that they skipped both humanism and the individual conscience. Toynbee has pointed out the inner link between what he calls "archaism" and "futurism." The former, as in the case of the Russian church, the peasant community, and the Slavophile movement, seeks to revive ancient forms for new situations; the latter, as in the case of Communism, seeks a short cut into the future. Both are examples of a mechanical Utopianism. Swinging from one to the other, the Russians have managed to stay within the same metaphysical frame.

Another difference lies in the pace of industrial growth. In a collectively willed process of industrialization the same act of planning which creates the economic structure creates also its political counterpart in the party and the state. Thus, the willed elements become central, and by a trial-and-error process of shifting party-line policies the effort is made to fit into the same pattern the strands of war and peace, industry and agriculture, education, family life, art, and philosophy. By comparison the process of industrialization in America and indeed the whole historic growth of the culture appear almost haphazard, a product of organic unfolding rather than of collective will. Where the whole growth has been so continuous, there is no need for drastic transformations by violence. Where individual career and conscience have counted for so much, there is a strong resistance to the short cuts which would by-pass both.

It is here that the strength of America's destiny lies. To be sure, a Communist system can drive ahead with a single-minded purpose and can make and consolidate gains with a swiftness denied to the more organic civilization like the American, which must feel out all the surrounding pressures in the very act of driving ahead. Yet the more tentative process of change has the merit of being more deeply rooted in the consent and energies of a people which feels itself part of what it has shaped freely out of its own process of growth.

Seeking to pierce the obscurity of the future, one may ask what will be the destiny of these two civilizations. There is one sense in which the two destinies are linked. It is impossible for each of them to establish its own pacifying and organizing force over the world which will parallel the *pax Romana*. On the other hand, if each pushes its claims and fears to their ultimate logic, the collision will be disastrous for both. An effort to divide the world between them seems futile, since such division could hold good only between two friendly powers, and even then any rigid formula imposed on the world would be bound to break before the strong currents of change.

If the struggle is fought out to the end, with nuclear weapons and germ warfare, the only prospect is a large measure of world suicide. If this is avoided, and the divergent social systems of the world manage to live side by side, the question arises whether there will be an inner collapse within one of the two great power structures, leading to a victory for the other without war. Here too America has the advantage. Since it uses the method of freedom and has established an unquestioned machinery for the succession of power, it does not run the risk Russia and China run of having the regime fall in the struggle over the succession. The old fears of internal collapse through economic breakdown have proved exaggerated, nor is there any institutional issue like slavery which might lead again to a bitter Civil War. Nor, despite the methods of Communist penetration, is there any great danger of an overthrow of the government from within. The greatest civil danger is that of the growth of an adventurist nationalist movement which would create a police state under the guise of saving the country from totalitarianism and would ally itself with the military elite. But if this were ever to happen it would be only as a consequence of a world atomic war or as prelude to it: America has shown the capacity to survive this kind of crisis short of a nuclear war.

The chances of civil struggle within the Communist systems and their satellites are greater. Once it loses the mastery of the coercive machinery of the state, a police regime must pay the price of inner strains and doubts. The suppression of competing opinion means that every leader or movement which might otherwise be a rival of the Administration becomes an enemy of the state itself. The method of Communism, as Albert Camus pointed out, divides the community into executioners and victims—and, one may add, the politically inert who are content to accept the rule of those on top. But while a one-party state and an iron party discipline are easy ways of eliminating inconvenient dissent and establishing party truth in science and human affairs, they cannot eliminate hunger as a spur to revolt, nor praetorian conflict, nor the survival of nationalist impulses in the satellite countries. The satellites are thus always ready to use the outbreak of war as an occasion for breaking away from the Communist imperium.

Along with the danger of suicidal destruction, this adds another argument against world war which may be persuasive to the Soviet mind. The alternative for both civilizations is not merely "coexistence" but corivalry in the struggle of ideas. One finds an interesting parallel in the era of European religious wars at the time of the Reformation and counter-Reformation. If both the Protestants and Catholics had been set on establishing a universal church, and if each had controlled a segment of state power, war would have been unceasing until one or the other had been wiped out. But there was a growth of secular authorities for whom peace and national unity were more urgent than the defense of the True Faith. The religious conflict was neither forgotten nor abolished, but it was transformed into a proselytizing rivalry within the frame of a secular authority—a rivalry that was only sporadically bloody but mainly peaceful. In this corivalry Americans have the advantage of presenting to the world a political and social system which will furnish a better and freer life for the large mass of people than its rival. Yet the struggle is bound to be a bitter one. It is not too hard, however, to conceive of an international secular authority which will similarly keep the struggle of the new political religions from engulfing the world in war and hold it within the frame of nonmilitary rivalry.

In such an event America's destiny in the calculable future will be to take a hand in creating this constitutional frame while it seeks to build friendly coalitions within it and help other peoples to reach in their own way their own institutions and method of freedom. This will mean a peaceful but exacting rivalry in which America will be one of a number of spokesmen for an open society, using with greater or lesser skill its statecraft and diplomacy, its technical and economic resources and its whole armory of ideas.

It is not easy to measure the relative equipment of each of the two groups of protagonists for this rivalry in the struggle for ideas. In the Communist case there is a political orthodoxy that has become a political religion and rouses dedicated energies among numberless men and women the world over. In the American case there is a stubborn belief in individual freedom—a belief so stubborn that it generated a revolution, survived a civil war and two world wars without being snuffed out, and has kept up a continuing struggle against the centralizing forces of both governmental and corporate power. This belief lacks the flamboyancy of a political religion, yet it sustains a formidable fighting faith.

Part of the fighting faith on both sides is the conviction that while material values count in life they are not the only values. Both America and Russia are materialist. They have a common activism, a masculine strength of purpose, a drive toward results, a genius for organization, a belief in progress, an obsession with production indexes and with magnitudes of all sorts, a conviction that their way of life will yield increasing satisfactions to their people. Each system can point to considerable accomplishment in raising living standards in a brief spell of time. But when one asks toward what ends these material gains are directed, the Communists answer that society sets the ends and that in the dialectic of history they are part of a process in which men transform themselves by transforming their environment. The answer of American democracy is that the free, creative personality forms both the method and the end of the social process.

The logical extension of an open society, as I have suggested earlier, is an open world. This does not call for either the dominance or anni- hilation of any culture but a respect for the characteristic traits of each, just as an open society must respect the characteristic traits of its members. There is also, of course, a Communist vision of an ultimate world society. It is the vision of a world federation of Soviet states, each retaining a measure of autonomy but each also surrendering to the central body the larger decisions about world policy and perhaps a veto over any basic changes in the system of internal power. The Federal structure of the Union of Socialist Soviet Republics is itself a probable model for what a Communist world society would be like. It would go beyond the *pax Romana* of the ancient world, since it would demand the kind of ideological conformity that one finds inside a Communist society.

To the differences in the vision of a world society one must add the differences in the kind of human being the two systems envisage. The Communists have made it clear that they base their view of human nature on the psychology of conditioned behavior: that men respond rationally to rational needs; there are no primal drives in men that cannot be exploited at will, or else expunged or deflected into other channels. For them the lesson of history is mainly that human nature is plastic and that the human mind, after adapting itself over millennia to every type of social organization, still presents an open slate on which new social experience can write new records. This is an instrumental view of man's essential nature, seeing man mainly as a bundle of poten- tials for manipulation by an elite of social engineers. The earlier Marxist thinkers, looking ahead, saw a "new society" in which the aliena- tion of men from one another would be ended, and new fulfillments of human values would be achieved by the release of individual and social energy. But unfortunately this humanist vision has not been translated into the current realities of Communist society.

The democrat also regards man as a bundle of potentials. But he is less brashly confident that he knows exactly what to do with those potentials. He has greater humility about his relation to the unknown forces of the Universe and more respect for the tenacity of the instinctual life of man. But he also has more belief in man's capacity to develop rich diversities of personality and find both emotional expressiveness and moral meanings in life within an open society.

Both views stress the material base of life, and both are activist: hence both may be said to have created their own types of economic man. Brooks Adams, writing about the English gentry in Cobden's day, who fought the repeal of the Corn Laws, saw them as "Nature's first attempts at creating an economic type" and noted that they were vanquished by the later and superior type of Manchester man. Writing today, one has to add that the economic man of Detroit and Stalingrad has replaced the Manchester man. What they have in common is their interest and skill in production and their use of an economic value scale for the whole range of values. But if one may draw the distinction that Peter Drucker has suggested between "economic" and "industrial" man—the latter using technology for the purposes of human life while the former cramps human life within the value scale of economics alone —then one may claim that the American vision (as vision, not as reality) is that of industrial man. In this sense it is where the material calculus ends that the conception of human personality begins. Whatever its shortcomings, the democratic vision is a humanist one. Like the Soviet view of man, it is oriented toward power and effectiveness. But where one tries to use the whole range of power and technology for the ends of the individual life, the other values the individual mainly as an instrument for the purposes of power and the state.

Another way of putting it is that one makes organization central while the other makes it instrumental. George Orwell's novel, *1984*, put into imaginative terms the logical end product of ideological or organizational man, who marks the triumph of the cerebral over the organic life processes and of automatism over personality and conscience. An American philosopher, Roderick Seidenberg, has projected this trend grimly into a future "post-historic man" who is reached when the processes of history have been wholly placed under cerebral and organizational control and when history in any meaningful sense has therefore ceased. Like his predecessors, Henry Adams and Spengler, Seidenberg interprets this trend as beyond the human will to resist.

If this tide should prove an historical reality, it may be that the differences our generation sees between the rival systems of society and views of life are only ripples on its surface. American thought has on the whole refused to accept such a determinism. On this issue the American thinkers diverge from Spengler, whose moral was that no change is possible and whose injunction to the ruling classes was to show iron resolution in repressing all challenges to their authority. There is a big gap between Spengler and Leninist thinking, but the despair over piecemeal change and the police-state methods of meeting every challenge to power are consequences of both.

The crucial question about America's destiny in the world frame brings us back to the tests of America's strength as a civilization. It is hard not to feel that while America is still on the rising arc of its world power it is on the descending arc of its inner social and moral vigor; that it has allowed itself to be switched off from the main path of its development into the futile dead ends of the fear of ideas and the tenacious cult of property. Toynbee has suggested how frequently a civilization has been weakened by its "pathological insistence upon pushing to extremes its master institution." That may be militarism or institutionalized holiness, imperial power or infallibility, but what always happens is its expansion far beyond its original meaning into a cult that becomes destructive of its utility. If the master institution of America is property, there is evidence of the beginnings of a "pathological insistence upon pushing [it] to extremes." Linked with it is a fear of subversive movements which may threaten or overthrow the institution—a fear that therefore induces a complacency about the idea-hunters and a loss of belief in the inherent efficacy of democracy. The result is a negativism of outlook which puts the stress upon the defense of the master institution rather than upon the affirmation of its linkage with democratic human values.

There is no question here of the imminent fall of America but of its long-range vitality. All that we can say for certain about the problem of the rise and fall of civilizations is that, under the conditions of modern economic and military power, a people needs the quality of creativeness for cultural survival over a long period. One may guess that America will lead the world in technology and power for at least several generations to come. But it is one thing to fill a power vacuum in the world with a transitional leadership, and quite another to offer to the world the qualities of leadership which it requires, attuned at once to the life of nature and the life of the spirit. Unfortunately American leadership in world affairs has not displayed this capacity: it has often been fumbling, hesitant, indecisive, without a clear picture of the direction in which it seeks to move or the kind of world it envisages, and with too much of a tendency to brandish its military strength and to use American wealth for purchasing things that simply cannot be bought.

America has not yet had to face many of the tests through which the other great civilizations have passed. Compared with the peoples of the European Continent, or of Russia or Asia, the history of America has been an epic continuity of almost unbroken success, with only the Civil

War as the kind of catastrophe that deepens consciousness by plowing up emotions. The French, for example, have been through a period of Roman rule, of imperial-barbarian battle, of feudal struggle, of bloody religious wars and equally bloody revolutionary upheavals; they have had the experience of invasion by the English, and of German armies sweeping three times across their country; at least twice they have had to eat the bitter bread of the conqueror's terms. Russia too has been crisscrossed many times by invading forces, steeped in a long night of Asiatic rule, torn by the bloody struggle of the Boyars, bled white by Czars and priests; it has been subjected to the battering of forces and ideas from both the East and the West, has had to meet attacks from Genghis Khan and the Tartars, from Napoleon and Hitler, has known a long history of serfdom, has been raked by revolutionary struggles and made a laboratory for the compulsive energies of a new regime.

The historic ordeals of America have been different. They have been the ordeals of endurance against a challenging frontier environment, and of having to weld a national unity out of widely divergent strains, even at the price of a terrible civil war. Its characteristic tests have, however, been technological, including the fashioning of new industrialism, and the swinging of the balance in the world wars in which it took part. Except for the Civil War, the inner crises have been those of the prosperity-depression business cycle. The typical crisis of character in an American novel is likely to turn on the endurance of economic hardship (note Norris's *McTeague,* Dreiser's *Sister Carrie,* Steinbeck's *Grapes of Wrath*), and the typical fall-from-grace situation is that of the well-to-do family which must endure a scaling down of its living standards.

As a civilization America has never had to meet the great test of apparently irretrievable failure. Except for the Civil War, its history has been without sharp breaks, and even the Civil War was (in the phrase of Allan Nevins) an "ordeal of union" rather than a break in history. Since the Revolutionary War, Americans have not as a nation had to meet the test of survival in the face of strong odds. They have never suffered decisive defeat in a war, nor the agony of internal revolutionary violence. Their history as a nation has never been cut in two by revolution, into an Old Regime followed by a New Regime. The closest they came was Franklin Roosevelt's New Deal, less a revolution than a successful attempt to forestall one.

Thus America as a civilization has been far removed from the great type-enactment of the Christian story, or the disasters of Jewish history or of the Asiatic empires: it has not suffered, died, been reborn. The weight it bears as it faces its destiny is the weight not of history but of institutions. Its great tests are still to come. One may guess that America will not meet them badly, but it would be tragic if it had to taste

.lisaster in order to learn the lessons of lost civilizations. One reason why the Christian metaphysic has never struck deep psychic roots among Americans lies in the gap between the moral experience underlying the Christian doctrine and the moral implications of the American life goals. Like all profound religious allegories, the Christian story presupposes the capacity to face suffering, failure, and death.

The American attitude toward death, which I have touched upon earlier,* is revealing on this score. The American today is preoccupied with death, but not in the way that the early Calvinists were or the later immigrants from Europe. He is interested in death in whodunit thrillers or the sudden death of auto and plane accidents: death is an illogical intrusion from without, or a curiosity to be taken apart like an intricate bit of machinery, but in either case irrelevant to life. Contrast this with the almost fatalist Russian acceptance of death, which has helped them bear the heavy burdens of a regime that regards human life as fodder for the Time Machine. Contrast it also with the ritualistic preoccupation with death that one finds, for example, in the literature of Mexico. For the Hispanic peoples death is not a cul-de-sac but a fruitful act, laying bare the values of life. For Americans it is an end to the possibilities of life, an obituary note in a newspaper signifying that a career is closed and blankness has set in.

Related to this is the span of the American time scale. Political observers have noted that in the calculations of foreign policy and statecraft both the Russians and Chinese operate on a longer time scale than do the Americans. This may be due to traditions stretching back into a dim past, plus the new Communist deification of history. The Americans are more concerned with the day-to-day and the here-and-now. Since life offers so much and death draws a blank, the habitual calculation does not stretch much beyond the lifetime scale. This does not mean that there is no sense of the future. But when Americans think of the future, it is again in terms of what is compassable—providing for the declining years of one's life and the education of one's children until they in turn can provide for their own future.

This belief in a compassable future is part of the organic optimism of American life. It is far removed from the mood of fatalism and renunciation which in most civilizations preceded the emergence of modern industrial man, as it also is far removed from the tragic pessimism which the great European thinkers from Nietzsche to Malraux have summoned in the twilight of the European experience. Because America has this sense of tragedy only in partial degree, its capacity to face national failure and disaster may well be questioned. It is limited by the unwillingness of the American as an individual to con-

* See Ch. VIII, Sec. 7, "The Middle and End of the Journey."

front the Medusa head of a life experience which includes penalties as well as gains, failure as well as success, tragedy as well as happiness.

But a nation can even surmount catastrophes and be deepened by them, provided its sources of creativeness have not dried up. The great enemy of any civilization is the enemy within. Its name is not subversion or revolution or decadence but rigidity. Just as every power group tends to limit its outlook as it hardens its position, so the temptation of a successful people is to make a cult of the artifacts of its success, rather than celebrate the daring and the large outlook that made the achievements possible. In the Russian case the original revolutionary Communism has become the hard ideological mask of a state church that aims to sustain its power elite and has forgotten that the revolutionary impulse came from a tradition of Socialist humanism. There are many who feel similarly that, whether through conformism, fanaticism or rigidity, American society will succumb to the final impersonality of the Age of the Insects. The long journey we have made through these pages should lead to a different conclusion. There is still in the American potential the plastic strength that has shaped a great civilization, and it shows itself in unexpected ways, at unpredictable moments, and in disguises that require some imaginative understanding to unveil. What Emerson said a century ago I would still hold to: "We think our civilization is near its meridian, but we are yet only at the cockcrowing and the morning star."

Acknowledgments

OVER THE SPAN during which this book was written I owe acknowledgments to my secretaries and assistants who labored faithfully along with me: to Frances Herridge, Carol Simon, Susan Steiner Satz, Gloria Howe, Alice Lide, and especially Ruth Korzenik, to whom fell much of the burden of helping prepare the book for press; to Donald McCormick for working with me during an entire summer at Southampton while a new draft came into being; to Jules Bernstein and Martin Peretz, my students at Brandeis University, who somehow survived a stormy and protracted siege during which we prepared the "Notes for Further Reading" together. I want to add my thanks to M. Lincoln Schuster, Henry W. Simon, Justin Kaplan, and Joseph Barnes of the staff of Simon and Schuster, who went far beyond their duty as publishers in order to help lick the book into shape.

Successive drafts of the book were mimeographed and used, year after year, as basic reading for my class in American Civilization at Brandeis University. I cannot overstate how much I owe to my colleagues and my students in that course, who put it to the test of using it as a tool for understanding the complex thing we call American Civilization, and gave it their best critical and creative efforts. I want to mention especially my colleagues in the course over a number of years—Henry Steele Commager, formerly at Columbia University and now at Amherst College, Merrill Peterson, now at Princeton University, Richard Akst, Bernard Rosenberg, Jerome Himelhoch, Arno J. Mayer, John Van Doren, and (most of all) Leonard Levy and Lawrence H. Fuchs. It is their book almost as much as it is mine. I want also to express my obligation to President A. L. Sachar of Brandeis University, who supported me enthusiastically in a drastically experimental venture in teaching American Civilization by cutting across all the established boundaries between the established disciplines.

Finally, and most of all, I want to thank my colleagues in the university world, and in the professions, business, labor, and the arts, who gave generously of their time and knowledge in a task which was obviously beyond my own powers. In a work of this scope no man's scholarship, even were he to spend a lifetime on it, could adequately cover every area treated in this book. Their generosity is all the greater because of the fact that, while many of them were friends of mine, others were willing to answer a stranger's call for help in the understanding of American Civilization. I do not dare to hope that together we have eliminated all errors, both of fact and interpretation. But I was determined, so far as humanly possible, to keep them to a minimum, and I was bold enough to ask some of the best people in every field to help me to that end. Each of them read a chapter or several chapters, or sometimes portions of a chapter, that were closest to his interests, and sent me both general criticisms and detailed—sometimes line by line—corrections and suggestions. In many cases I not only accepted their ideas but even adopted some of their phrasing because I could not hope to improve on it. To a great degree this book is thus

951

a collaborative work, and belongs not to me but to the collective of American scholarship. I hasten to add that some of my colleagues may fail to recognize or to be willing to acknowledge the book as in any way their product, and I want to make it clear that none of them is to be held responsible for my views or for my sins of omission and commission.

I want to thank especially Louis Hartz of Harvard University for reading and criticising the larger portion of the book, although I am certain that it still falls far short of his exacting standards. The others to whom I want to express my obligation and thanks are: Adam Abruzzi, Stevens Institute of Technology; Walter Adams, Michigan State University; Arthur Altmeyer, U.S. Department of Health, Education, and Welfare; Wayne Andrews, N.Y. Historical Society; Conrad Arensberg, Columbia University; Stephen Bailey, Woodrow Wilson School of Public and International Affairs, Princeton University; Read Bain, Miami University in Oxford, Ohio; Carlos Baker, Princeton University; Jacques Barzun, Columbia University; Catherine Worster Bauer, University of California in Berkeley; Daniel Bell, *Fortune;* Francis Bello, *Fortune;* Bernard Berelson, Ford Foundation; Adolf A. Berle, Jr., Columbia University; Herbert Bloch, Brooklyn College; Herbert Blumer, University of California in Berkeley; Daniel J. Boorstin, University of Chicago; Kenneth Boulding, University of Michigan; Carl Bridenbaugh, University of California in Berkeley; Robert R. R. Brooks, Williams College; Harrison Brown, California Institute of Technology; Stuart Gerry Brown, Syracuse University; Lyman Bryson, Columbia University; Gilbert Burck, *Fortune;* Roger Burlingame, New York City; and James MacGregor Burns, Williams College.

Also Richard Centers, University of California in Los Angeles; Eliot D. Chapple, E. D. Chapple Co.; Thomas I. Cook, Johns Hopkins University; Lewis Coser, Brandeis University; Avery Craven, University of Chicago; Maurice Davie, Yale University; Joseph S. Davis, Food Research Institute, Stanford University; J. Frederick Dewhurst, Twentieth Century Fund; Stanley Diamond, Brandeis University; John Dollard, Yale University; David Donald, Columbia University; Elisha P. Douglass, Princeton University; Peter F. Drucker, Montclair, N.J.; Joseph W. Eaton, Western Reserve University; Albert Ellis, New York City; Leonard W. Feather, *Down Beat;* Robert H. Ferguson, Cornell University; Donald Fleming, Brown University; Lawrence K. Frank, Belmont, Mass.; Charles Frankel, Columbia University; Lawrence Fuchs, Brandeis University; Lewis Galantiere, Free Europe Committee; Maxwell Geismar, *The Nation;* Siegfried Giedion, Harvard University; Nathan Glazer, University of California; Eric F. Goldman, Princeton University; William J. Goode, Columbia University; George W. Gray, Rockefeller Foundation; William Haber, University of Michigan; Oscar Handlin, Harvard University; Robert J. Havighurst, University of Chicago; Robert L. Heilbroner, New York City; Melville J. Herskovits, Northwestern University; Richard Hofstadter, Columbia University; Arthur N. Holcombe, Harvard University; Alfred J. Hotz, Western Reserve University; Irving Howe, Brandeis University; Cuthbert C. Hurd, International Business Machines; Stanley Hyman, Bennington College; and Howard Mumford Jones, Harvard University.

Also George Kennan, Princeton Institute for Advanced Studies; James Klee, Brandeis University; Otto Klineberg, Columbia University; Clyde Kluckhohn, Harvard University; Philip M. Klutznick, Park Forest, Illinois; Marshall Knappen, University of Michigan; Mirra Komarovsky, Barnard College; John A. Kouwenhoven, Barnard College; Oliver Larkin, Smith College; Eric Larrabee, *Harper's;* Harold D. Lasswell, Yale University; Leonard Levy, Brandeis University; Charles E. Lindblom, Yale University; Donald J. Lloyd, Wayne University; Nelson Lowry, University of Minnesota; Samuel Lubell, New York City; Robert D. Lynd, Columbia University; Fritz Machlup, Johns Hopkins University; Archibald MacLeish, Harvard University; Herbert F. Marcuse, Brandeis University; A. H. Maslow, Brandeis University; Alpheus T. Mason, Princeton University; Margaret Mead, American Museum of Natural History; Ida C. Merriam, U.S. Department of Health, Education, and Welfare; C. Wright Mills, Columbia University; B. F. Ashley Montagu, Rutgers University; Hans J. Morgenthau, University of Chicago; Samuel Eliot Morison, Harvard University; Lewis Mumford, Amenia, N.Y.; and Henry A. Murray, Harvard University.

Also Ernest Nagel, Columbia University; Theodore Newcomb, University of Michigan; James R. Newman, Washington, D.C.; Reinhold Niebuhr, Union Theological Seminary; Saul K. Padover, New School for Social Research; Talcott Parsons, Harvard University; Merrill Peterson, Princeton University; Gerard Piel, *Scientific American;* David M. Potter, Yale University; Phillip Rieff, Brandeis University; David Riesman, University of Chicago; John P. Roche, Brandeis University; Clinton Rossiter, Cornell University; George de Santillana, Massachusetts Institute of Technology; Edward N. Saveth, New York City; Meyer Schapiro, Columbia University; Arthur M. Schlesinger, Harvard University; Arthur M. Schlesinger, Jr., Harvard University; Frederick L. Schuman, Williams College; Gilbert Seldes, New York City; Jose-Luis Sert, Harvard University; Harold Shapero, Brandeis University; Edward A. Shils, University of Chicago; Edward W. Sinnott, Yale University; Henry Nash Smith, University of California in Berkeley; Herman Somers, Haverford College; Pitirim Sorokin, Harvard University; George Soule, Bennington College; Ralph Spielman, University of Kentucky; Mark Starr, International Ladies Garment Workers Union; Marshall Stearns, Institute of Jazz Studies; George Stewart, University of California in Berkeley; Cushing Strout, Yale University; Adolph Sturmthal, Roosevelt University; and G. E. Swanson, University of Michigan.

Also George Terborgh, Machinery and Allied Products Institute; Lionel Trilling, Columbia University; Christopher Tunnard, Yale University; Harry R. Warfel, University of Florida; W. Lloyd Warner, University of Chicago; Walter Prescott Webb, University of Texas; Rush Welter, Bennington College; William Wheaton, University of Pennsylvania; Leslie A. White, University of Michigan; William Foote Whyte, Cornell University; William H. Whyte, Jr., *Fortune;* Mitchell Wilson, New York City; Carl Wittke, Western Reserve University; C. Vann Woodward, Johns Hopkins University; and Dennis Wrong, University of Toronto.

Finally, I want to say how much I owe to my wife, Edna Albers Lerner, who retained her belief in what must have seemed at times a monstrously unreal venture and discussed with me every major phase of it and every draft.

June 1957   MAX LERNER
New York City

Notes for Further Reading

(These notes are arranged so as to accompany each chapter and section of the text. They give the books and articles from which I have drawn and are meant as a guide to the interested reader who may wish to pursue some particular theme further. To avoid cluttering footnotes I have also indicated here the sources of particular references in the text. The date and place of publication of each book or article referred to are given only with the first reference in the notes for each chapter. Later references give author and title only.)

Chapter VII: Class and Status in America

SEC. 1—*The Open-Class Society*, SEC. 7—*The Badges of Belonging*, and SEC. 8—*The Democratic Class Struggle:* For the larger picture of the class structure and social stratification, see the very useful book of readings, Reinhard Bendix and Seymour M. Lipset, *Class, Status, and Power* (Glencoe, 1953), and Bernard Barber, *Social Stratification* (New York, 1957), which also has a comprehensive bibliography. For a discussion of American status structure, see C. Wright Mills, *White Collar* (New York, 1951), Ch. 11. I have drawn heavily upon some of the classic works in American community studies: Warner *et al., Democracy in Jonesville* (New York, 1949), and Robert and Helen Lynd, *Middletown* (New York, 1929), along with their later study *Middletown in Transition* (New York, 1937). I have also been helped by W. Lloyd Warner and Paul S. Lunt, *The Social Life of a Modern Community* (New Haven, 1941); Robin Williams, Jr., *American Society: A Sociological Interpretation* (New York, 1951), and W. Lloyd Warner, Marcia Meeker and Kenneth Ellis, *Social Class in America* (Chicago, 1949). Also see Frederick L. Allen, *The Big Change* (New York, 1952), Ch. 15, "The All-American Standard," pp. 209-33; and Davis, Gardner, and Gardner, *Deep South* (Chicago, 1941), "Life in the Classes," pp. 253-62. See also August B. Hollingshead, *Elmtown's Youth* (New York, 1949), and an excellent recent community study by John R. Seeley, R. A. Sim, and E. W. Loosley, *Crestwood Heights* (New York, 1956). For an analysis of the class theory of the pioneer American sociologists, see Charles H. Page, *Class and American Sociology* (New York, 1940); see also Melvin Tumin, "Some Principles of Stratification," *American Sociological Review* (Aug. 1953). A comparative study of social mobility is Pitirim Sorokin, *Social Mobility* (New York, 1927). Also see Talcott Parsons, *The Structure of Social Action* (Glencoe, 1951); Robert K. Merton, *Social Theory and Social Structure* (Glencoe, 1949), and W. Lloyd Warner, *American Life: Dream and Reality* (Chicago, 1953). Selected readings on class are to be found in *Modern American Society*, eds., Kingsley Davis, Harry C. Bredemeier, and M. J. Levy (New York, 1949), Part 4. For a brief introductory study, along with a good bibliography, see Kurt B. Mayer, *Class and Society* (New York, 1955). See also my Notes for Further Reading on Ch. III, Sec. 8.

The reference to H. Dewey Anderson and Percy E. Davidson in the text is to their study of career patterns, geographical and vertical mobility, and occupational inheritance among men in San Jose, California, *Occupational Mobility in an American Community* (Stanford, 1937). The reference to F. W. Taussig and C. S. Joslyn is to their book, *American Business Leaders* (New York, 1932). The reference to W. Lloyd Warner and James Abegglen is to *Occupational Mobility in American Business and Industry* (Minneapolis, 1955). The reference to Veblen is to his *Theory of the Leisure Class* (New York, 1899). For Mayo and Roethlisberger citations, see Notes for Further Reading on Ch. IV, Sec. 4. The reference to John Dollard is to his work *Caste and Class in a Southern Town* (New Haven, 1937; with new introduction, New York, 1957). Also see Allison Davis, Burleigh B. Gardner, and Mary R. Gardner, *Deep South*, and Hortense Powdermaker, *After Freedom* (New York, 1939), which discuss the effect of class and caste on whites and Negroes in the South. For a discussion of Warner's "six-class system," see Walter R. Goldschmidt, "America's Six Social Classes," *Commentary* (Aug. 1950).

For an analysis of voting behavior and class, see Dewey Anderson and Percy E.

Davidson, *Ballots and the Democratic Class Struggle* (Stanford, 1943), especially Ch. 2, "Occupational Status and Political Behavior," and Ch. 4, "Class Consciousness and Political Behavior."

The quote from Irving Howe is from his *William Faulkner, A Critical Study* (New York, 1952). The reference to Karl Popper is to his book *The Open Society and Its Enemies* (Princeton, 1950). Richard Centers' work, *The Psychology of Social Classes* (Princeton, 1949), is an empirical cross-section study of subjective and objective class images. The quote from Russell Davenport is from his *The Dignity of Man* (New York, 1955).

SEC. 2—*The Seats of the Mighty:* On the American elites, I have drawn upon C. Wright Mills, *The Power Elite* (New York, 1956), a brilliantly conceived and written work which has left its impact on my thinking even where (as I have indicated in the text) I differ with it. In a vigorous article on Mills, Robert S. Lynd in "Power in the United States," *Nation* (May 12, 1956), argues that a dominant ruling class rather than a power elite exists in the American structure of power. For the background of much of the current discussion of American elites the reader can go back to Gaetano Mosca, *The Ruling Class* (New York, 1939), and Vilfredo Pareto, *The Mind and Society* (New York, 1939), and to my own essay, "Pareto's Republic," in *Ideas Are Weapons* (New York, 1939). José Ortega y Gasset, *The Revolt of the Masses* (new ed., New York, 1950) considers moral distinctions between mass and elite. I have also drawn upon David Riesman, *The Lonely Crowd* (rev. ed., New York, 1953), pp. 246-59, reprinted in Reinhard Bendix and Seymour Lipset, *Class, Status and Power*. In this same collection of readings, see Daniel Bell, "America's Un-Marxist Revolution"; E. Digby Baltzell, " 'Who's Who in America' and 'The Social Register': Elite and Upper Class Indexes in Metropolitan America"; Harold Kaufman, "Prestige Classes in a New Rural Community"; and Reinhard Bendix, "Social Stratification and Political Power." See also Floyd Hunter's survey, *Community Power Structure* (Chapel Hill, 1955). For a discussion of the elite tradition in America, see Gustavus Myers, *History of the Great American Fortunes* (New York, 1907; rev. ed., 1936), and Sidney Ratner, *New Lights on the History of Great American Fortunes* (New York, 1933).

SEC. 3—*The New Middle Classes:* On the middle classes, I have gained much from C. Wright Mills, *White Collar*, an outstanding book in this field. Russell Lynes, *A Surfeit of Honey* (New York, 1957) presents a fresh view of old class structures in dissolution and new ones in formation. The reference to Laski in the text is to *The American Democracy* (New York, 1948). See his *The Rise of European Liberalism* (London, 1936) for an earlier viewpoint in which middle class liberalism is interpreted as the bulwark of an emerging capitalism. In my discussion of middle class frustration I have taken Nietzsche's notion of "ressentiment" and carried it over from the proletariat (to whom Nietzsche applied it) to the middle classes. For a discussion of the same transition in the European context, see Svend Ranulf, *Moral Indignation and the Middle Class Psychology* (Copenhagen, 1938), and Max Scheler, "Das Ressentiment im Aufbau der Moralen" in *Vom Umsturz der Werte*, Vol. 1, (Leipzig, 1923; new ed., Berne, 1955). Also see Robert K. Merton, *Social Theory and Social Structure* (Glencoe, 1949). For commentary upon the relationship of wealth to social distinction in American history, see Dixon Wecter, *The Saga of American Society* (New York, 1937). For an analysis of business elites, see Robert A. Brady, *Business As a System of Power* (New York, 1943), and William Foote Whyte, ed., *Industry and Society* (New York, 1946).

SEC. 4—*Class Profile of the Worker:* On the working class as part of the American class system, see C. Wright Mills, *The New Men of Power* (New York, 1948); also Reinhard Bendix and S. N. Lipset, eds., *Class, Status, and Power*, especially Part 4, "Social Mobility in the U.S.," reprinting Katherine Archibald, "Status Orientations Among Shipyard Workers" and Herbert H. Hyman, "The Value Systems of Different Classes"; and S. M. Lipset and Joan Gordon, "Mobility and Trade Union Membership." See also Eli Chinoy, *Automobile Workers and the American Dream* (New York, 1955), and his "The Tradition of Opportunity and the Aspirations of Automobile Workers," *American Journal of Sociology* (March 1952).

SEC. 5—*The Minority Situation:* For the various minorities in American life, I have leaned upon G. E. Simpson and J. M. Yinzer, *Racial and Cultural Minorities* (New York, 1953), and Oscar Handlin, *Race and Nationality in American Life* (Boston, 1957).

On specific minorities: for the Jews see Oscar Handlin, *Adventure in Freedom* (New York, 1954) and Nathan Glazer, *American Judaism* (Chicago, 1957); on Puerto Ricans there is C. Wright Mills (in collaboration with Clarence Senior and Rose Kohn) *The Puerto Rican Journey: America's Newest Migrants* (New York, 1950); on Catholics, see John Tracy Ellis,

American Catholicism (Chicago, 1957); on Japanese-Americans there are both Carey McWilliams, *Prejudice: Japanese-Americans, Symbol of Racial Intolerance* (Boston, 1949), and Morton Grodzins, *Americans Betrayed* (Chicago, 1949). The history of anti-Semitism in the U.S. is discussed in Oscar and Mary Handlin, *Danger in Discord: Origins of Anti-Semitism in the U.S.* (Anti-Defamation League, New York, 1948). Also see Kurt Lewin, "Self-Hatred Among Jews" in Arnold Rose, ed., *Race Prejudice and Discrimination* (New York, 1951), pp. 321-32. The chapter on "America and its Minority Problems" in Laski, *The American Democracy*, pp. 452-86, has been helpful, as well as a number of articles in Swanson, Newcomb, and Hartley, *Readings in Social Psychology* (New York, 1952). Among these are Bruno Bettelheim and Morris Janowitz, "Ethnic Tolerance: A Function of Social and Political Control," pp. 593-602; Morton Deutsch and Mary Evans Collins, "The Effect of Public Policy in Housing Projects upon Interracial Attitudes," pp. 582-92, and August Campbell, "Factors Associated with Attitudes Towards Jews," pp. 603-11. Also see J. Himelhoch, "A Personality Type Associated with Prejudice," in Arnold Rose, ed., *Race Prejudice and Discrimination*, along with other essays in that volume. Also see Will Herberg, *Protestant, Catholic, Jew* (Garden City, 1955), and Stewart G. and Mildred Wiese Cole, *Minorities and the American Promise* (New York, 1954). The reference in the text is to Carey McWilliams, *A Mask of Privilege* (Boston, 1948). The T. W. Adorno *et al.* study which is cited is *The Authoritarian Personality* (New York, 1950). The Roper poll referred to in the text was conducted in September 1948 and was reported on in a radio broadcast of *Where the People Stand* over CBS on February 27, 1949.

SEC. 6—*The Negro in America:* On the situation of the Negro, I have drawn upon the wealth of material available including several works which concern themselves with the position of Negroes in America from an over-all perspective: Gunnar Myrdal, *An American Dilemma* (New York, 1944); Maurice R. Davie, *Negroes in American Society* (New York, 1949), and E. Franklin Frazier, *The Negro in the United States* (rev. ed., New York, 1957). On the question of school desegregation, see Robin M. Williams, Jr., and Margaret W. Ryan, *Schools in Transition* (Chapel Hill, 1954); Harry S. Ashmore, *The Negro and the Schools* (Chapel Hill, 1954), and Herbert H. Hyman and Paul B. Sheatsley, "Attitudes Toward Desegregation," *Scientific American* (Dec. 1956) On Negroes as a factor in American poli-

tics and labor, see Paul Lewinson, *Race, Class and Party* (New York, 1932); Henry Lee Moon, *Balance of Power: The Negro Vote* (New York, 1948); Horace R. Cayton and George S. Mitchell, *Black Workers and the New Unions* (Chapel Hill, 1944); Herbert R. Northrup, *Organized Labor and the Negro* (New York, 1944); Sterling D. Spero and Abram L. Harris, *The Black Worker* (New York, 1931). For an analysis of Negro social adaptations to their economic gains in American society, see E. Franklin Frazier, *Black Bourgeoisie* (Glencoe, 1957), which includes a discussion of the emerging Negro middle class. An intimate view of Negro life will be found in Arnold Rose, *The Negro Morale* (Minneapolis, 1949); see also E. Franklin Frazier, *The Negro Family in the United States* (rev. ed., New York, 1951), and St. Clair Drake and Horace R. Cayton, *Black Metropolis* (New York, 1945). On race, see Franz Boas, *Race, Language, and Culture* (New York, 1940), and W. Lloyd Warner, Buford H. Junker, and Walter A. Adams, *Color and Human Nature* (Washington, 1941); see also Melville J. Herskovits, *The Myth of the Negro Past* (New York, 1941).

Other sources which I have found useful are Otto Klineberg, ed., *Characteristics of the American Negro* (New York, 1944); C. Vann Woodward, *The Strange Career of Jim Crow* (New York, 1955); Roi Ottley, *Black Odyssey: The Story of the Negro in America* (New York, 1948), and Margaret Just Butcher, *The Negro in American Culture* (New York, 1956). Of the literature which has been written by Negroes in America the following novels are noteworthy: Countee Cullen, *One Way to Heaven* (New York, 1932); Richard Wright, *Native Son* (New York, 1940); Ralph Ellison, *Invisible Man* (New York, 1952), and James Baldwin, *Go Tell It on the Mountain* (New York, 1953), as well as his *Giovanni's Room* (New York, 1956), on a homosexual theme. For poetry, see Langston Hughes, *The Weary Blues* (New York, 1926) and *Montage of a Dream Deferred* (New York, 1951).

The reference in the text is to Oliver C. Cox, *Caste, Class, and Race* (New York, 1948). The reference to Franz Boas is to *Race, Language, and Culture*. The analysis by Kardiner and Ovesey will be found in *The Mark of Oppression* (New York, 1951). The study of interracial housing mentioned in the text is M. Deutsch and M. E. Collins, "The Effect of Public Policy in Housing Projects upon Interracial Attitudes" in Swanson, Newcomb, and Hartley, eds., *Readings in Social Psychology*. The reference to Henry Lee Moon is to *Balance of Power: The Negro Vote*. The reference in the text is to John Dollard, *Caste and Class in a*

Southern Town. The reference to Roi Ottley is to his *No Green Pastures* (New York, 1951).

Chapter VIII: Life Cycle of the American

SEC. 1—*The Personality in the Culture:* On the interplay of man and society, I have drawn upon several sources, among which are G. C. Homans, *The Human Group* (New York, 1950), Ch. 12, "The Individual and the Group"; Otto Klineberg, *Social Psychology* (rev. ed., New York, 1954), Chs. 12 and 13; J. J. Honigman, *Culture and Personality* (New York, 1954); James S. Plant, *The Envelope* (New York, 1950), and *Personality and the Culture Pattern* (New York, 1937), and John Dollard, *Criteria for the Life History* (New Haven, 1935). See also A. H. Maslow, *Motivation and Personality* (New York, 1954), and "Power Relationships and Patterns of Personal Development," included in Arthur Kornhauser, ed., *Patterns of Power in American Democracy* (Detroit, 1957); Ralph Linton, *The Cultural Background* (New York, 1949); David Riesman, *The Lonely Crowd* (rev. ed., New York, 1953); John Dewey, *Human Nature and Conduct* (New York, 1922); Ruth Benedict, *Patterns of Culture* (New York, 1934); Clyde Kluckhohn and Henry A. Murray, *Personality in Nature, Society, and Culture* (New York, 1948; rev. ed., 1953), and Prescott Lecky, *Self-Consistency: A Theory of Personality* (New York, 1945). An excellent discussion of the man on the periphery of his society is Bernard Rosenberg, *The Values of Veblen* (Washington, 1956), Ch. 1, "The Stranger." For something of the same problem, see Joseph Wood Krutch, *Henry David Thoreau* (New York, 1948). For a psychoanalytic discussion of the relation of society to man, see Sigmund Freud, *Civilization and Its Discontents* (New York, 1930), and Herbert Marcuse, *Eros and Civilization* (Boston, 1955).

The reference to Arnold Van Gennep is to *Les Rites des Passage* (Paris, 1909). The remark of James Klee is from correspondence with the author. The quote from John Dollard is from *Criteria for the Life History.* The reference to Ruth Benedict is to *Patterns of Culture.* Joseph Campbell's work is *The Hero with a Thousand Faces* (New York, 1949). The reference in the text to B. Malinowski is to his extensive work on the Trobriand Islands, particularly *The Sexual Life of Savages in North-West Melanesia* (New York, 1929) and *Sex and Repression in Savage Society* (new ed., New York, 1955). The reference to A. R. Radcliffe-Brown is to *The Andaman Islanders* (Cambridge, 1933). C. G. Homan's formulation will be found in *The Human Group.* The reference to Oscar Handlin is to *The Uprooted* (Boston, 1952).

SEC. 2—*The Family As Going Concern,* and SEC. 3—*Children and Parents:* On the structure and function of the family in American society and on the child-parent relationship in it, there are many good works available. On the family, see Ruth N. Anshen, ed., *The Family, Its Function and Destiny* (New York, 1949); Marvin Sussman, *Marriage and the Family* (Boston, 1955); Willard Waller, *The Family: A Dynamic Interpretation* (New York, 1938); Arthur W. Calhoun, *A Social History of the American Family* (New York, 1945); see also Meyer F. Nimkoff, *Marriage and the Family* (Cambridge, 1947); Talcott Parsons and Robert F. Bales, *Family Socialization and Interaction Processes* (Glencoe, 1955), and William Peterson, "The New American Family," *Commentary* (Jan. 1956), pp. 1-6. Further references are Howard Becker and Reuben Hill, eds., *Family, Marriage, and Parenthood* (Boston, 1948). Andrew G. Truxal and Francis E. Merrill, *The Family in American Society* (New York, 1947); Carl F. Zimmerman, *The Family of Tomorrow* (New York, 1949), and W. Allison Davis and Robert J. Havighurst, *Father of the Man* (Boston, 1947). For comparisons to the European family structure, see Max Horkheimer, ed., *Autoritaet Und Familie* (Paris, 1936), and Lewis Coser, "Some Aspects of Soviet Family Policy," *American Journal of Sociology* (March 1951). On the child-parent relationship, see Daniel R. Miller and Guy E. Swanson, *The American Parent in the Twentieth Century: A Study in the Detroit Area* (Ann Arbor, 1954); L. Joseph Stone and Joseph Church, *Childhood and Adolescence* (New York, 1957); Erik H. Erikson, *Childhood and Society* (New York, 1950) ; William E. Martin and Celia B. Stendler, *Child Development: The Process of Growing Up in Society* (New York, 1953), and Peter Blos, *The Adolescent Personality* (New York, 1941). See also J. H. S. Bossard, *The Sociology of Child Development* (New York, 1948); J. Piaget, *The Language and Thought of the Child* (New York, 1926), *The Child's Conception of the World* (New York, 1929), and *The Moral Judgment of the Child* (New York, 1932).

Of further interest will be Arnold W. Green, "The Middle Class Male Child and Neurosis," *American Sociological Review* (Feb. 1946), pp. 31-41, and Lawrence K. Frank, *Society As the Patient* (New Brunswick, 1948).

The reference in the text to Geoffrey Gorer is to *The American People* (New York, 1948). Philip Wylie's discussion of "Momism" is in his *Generation of Vipers* (New York, 1942). The reference to William J. Goode is to "Economic Factors and Marriage Stability," *American Sociological Review* (Dec. 1951). The reference to Lewis Mumford is to *The Conduct of Life* (New York, 1951). Arnold Green's discussion of "personality absorption" is in the article mentioned above.

sec. 4—*Growing Up in America:* On the maturing process, see Dixon Wecter, *Sam Clemens of Hannibal* (Boston, 1952). For other material on the growing-up years, see the Notes for Further Reading for Sec. 3 ("Children and Parents").

sec. 5—*Courtship, Love, and Marriage:* For the history of mating patterns, see Henri Birnbaum, *Love and Love's Philosophy* (New York, 1955), and E. S. Turner, *A History of Courting* (New York, 1955). On common problems of marriage, see Victor W. Eisenstein, ed., *Neurotic Interaction in Marriage* (New York, 1956). Also Philip Polatin and Ellen C. Phillips, *Marriage in the Modern World* (New York, 1956), and Abraham N. Franzblau, *The Road to Sexual Maturity* (New York, 1954). On divorce and its sequels, see William J. Goode, *After Divorce* (Glencoe, 1956). Other relevant material on this subject may be found in the notes for further reading for Sec. 2 of this chapter ("The Family As Going Concern"), and those on Ch. IX, Sec. 6 ("Morals in Revolution").

The reference in the text to Denis de Rougemont is to *Love in the Western World* (New York, 1939-40). The reference to Geoffrey Gorer is to *The American People* (New York, 1948). Margaret Mead's definition of a successful date will be found in *Male and Female* (New York, 1949). The reference to psychiatric views on marriage is from Victor W. Eisenstein, *Neurotic Interaction in Marriage.* The later reference in the text to Geoffrey Gorer is to *Exploring English Character* (London, 1955). William J. Goode's observations are in *After Divorce.* The reference in the text to Mirra Komarovsky is to *The Unemployed Man and His Family* (New York, 1940).

sec. 6—*The Ordeal of the American Woman:* On women in American society, I have drawn upon a large variety of works. On the role of women in American society, see Mirra Komarovsky, *Women in the Modern World* (Boston, 1953); Ferdinand Lundberg and Marynia F. Farnham, *Modern Woman, The Lost Sex* (New York, 1947); Eric John Dingwall, *The American Woman* (New York, 1956); Elizabeth Bragdon, ed., *Women Today* (New York, 1953). On female sexuality, see Alfred Kinsey *et al.*, *Sexual Behavior in the Human Female* (Philadelphia, 1953); Albert Ellis, ed., *Sex Life of the American Woman and the Kinsey Report* (New York, 1954); Marie Bonaparte, *Female Sexuality* (New York, 1953), and A. M. Krich, ed., *Women: The Variety and Meaning of the Sexual Experience* (New York, 1953). A background to the study of women in American society will be found in Viola Klein, *The Feminine Character: History of an Ideology* (New York, 1949). Also see B. F. Ashley Montagu, *The Natural Superiority of Women* (New York, 1953). For a foreign view of the position of women in society, see Simone de Beauvoir, *The Second Sex* (New York, 1953). The reference in the text to Simone de Beauvoir will be found here. The remarks of Stanley Diamond are from a correspondence with the author. Diamond's views are expanded in "Kibbutz and Shtetl," *Social Problems* (Oct. 1957). The reference to Margaret Mead is to *Male and Female.* The classic studies on female sexual dissatisfaction referred to in the text are G. V. Hamilton, *A Research in Marriage* (New York, 1929), and K. B. Davis, *Factors in the Sex Life of 2200 Women* (New York, 1929). The reference in the text to Mary Wollstonecraft is to *A Vindication of the Rights of Women* (London, 1792).

sec. 7—*The Middle and End of the Journey:* On growing old in America, I have gained much from David Riesman, "Some Clinical and Cultural Aspects of the Aging Process," in his *Individualism Reconsidered* (Glencoe, 1951), pp. 484-91, and Ruth S. Cavan, "Old Age in a City of 100,000," *Illinois Academy of Science Transactions* (1947). See also Martin Gumpert's articles: "Recharting Life for an Aging America," *New York Times Magazine* (Aug. 13, 1950); "Our 'Inca' Ideas About Retirement," *New York Times Magazine* (July 27, 1952), and "The Shock of Aging," *The American Scholar* (Jan. 1950). Research on aging and its effects has been in progress for a number of years under David Riesman and associates in Kansas City. The final results have not yet been published. However, see David Riesman, "A Career Drama in a Middle-Aged Farmer," *Bulletin of the Menninger Clinic* (Jan. 1954), pp. 1-8. See also reports of the National Conference on Aging, *Man and His Years* (Raleigh, 1951). On death, see Virginia Moore, *Ho For Heaven: Man's Changing Attitude Toward Death* (New York, 1946), and Margaret Mead and Nicholas Calas, *Primitive Heritage* (New York, 1953), Part 15, pp. 534-77. The reference in the text is to Margaret Mead, *Male and Female.* The reference to Havighurst and Albrecht is to their study, *Older People* (New York, 1953).

Chapter IX: Character and Society

sec. 1—*The Cement of a Society:* For the cohesive factors in American society, the best discussion is in De Tocqueville, *op. cit.*, Vol. I, Ch. 17; Vol. II, Book I, Chs. 1 and 2. The best brief contemporary analysis I have found is in Robin M. Williams, Jr., *American Society* (New York, 1951), Ch. 14, "The Integration of American Society"; see also Talcott Parsons, *The Social System* (Glencoe, 1951). Among those who discuss the need for some principle of cohesion, see R. Nisbet, *The Quest for Community* (New York, 1953), Erich Fromm, *The Sane Society* (New York, 1955), and Russell W. Davenport, *The Dignity of Man* (New York, 1955). My reference to Northrop in the text is to F.S.C. Northrop, *The Meeting of East and West* (New York, 1946), Ch. 3, "The Free Culture of the U.S.," discussing Locke's ideas, and Ch. 4, "Unique Elements in British Democracy," discussing Hooker's. The reference in the text to Polanyi is to Karl Polanyi, *The Great Transformation* (New York, 1944). The movie I mention in the text is *Crossfire*. The idea of "false personalization" will be found in Riesman's *The Lonely Crowd* (rev. ed., New York, 1953). The reference to Alistair Cooke is to his book of sprightly and perceptive essays, *One Man's America* (New York, 1952). The Ferdinand Tonnies book to which I refer is his *Gemeinschaft und Gesellschaft* (Berlin, 1920). The reference to Helen Mims is to an important but still unpublished manuscript on community and society in the modern Western world. See also Max Weber, *Wirtschaft und Gesellschaft* (Tubingen, 2nd enlarged ed., 1925), Part I, Ch. 3; Part III, Chs. 7, 8 and 10.

SEC. 2—*The Joiners:* On voluntary associations and "propensity to join," the classic passage in De Tocqueville on the "principle of association" is in Vol. I (Vintage ed.), Ch. 12, especially pp. 203-5. The best brief contemporary discussion is in W. Lloyd Warner, *American Life: Dream and Reality* (Chicago, 1953), Ch. 9, "Associations in America." For an interesting theoretical approach of the anthropologists, see Eliot D. Chapple and Carleton S. Coon, *Principles of Anthropology* (New York, 1942), Ch. 17, "Associations," pp. 416-42; see also several readings in Margaret Mead and Nicolas Calas, *Primitive Heritage* (New York, 1953), especially pp. 64-6 on "Blood Brotherhood," pp. 213-21, "The Mischievous Society of Boys," and pp. 22-30, "Graded Associations and Secret Societies." For the lesser participation of the lower-income groups in clubs and associations, see Genevieve Knupfer, "Portrait of the Underdog," *Public Opinion Quarterly*, Vol. II (1947), pp. 103-14, reprinted in Bendix and Lipset, *Class, Status, and Power* (Glencoe, 1953), pp. 255-63. On the "togetherness" compulsive in middle-class suburbia, see W. H. Whyte, Jr., *The Organization Man* (New York, 1956). For the crucial place of the church in Negro organizational life, see E. Franklin Frazier, *Black Bourgeoisie* (New York, 1957), pp. 87-90, and for other Negro associations, *ibid.*, pp. 90-5. See also C. W. Ferguson, *Fifty Million Brothers* (New York, 1937). For a recent little booklet intended as a guide to joiners, see *How to Be a Member* (New York, 1956). The reference in the text to Reuel Denney is to his article, "Hail Meeters: Greeters Farewell," *Commentary* (Oct. 1951).

SEC. 3—*Manners, Taste, and Fashion:* On manners and etiquette, the theme of American manners has held a continuing fascination for foreign travelers in America. De Tocqueville, *op. cit.*, devoted the whole of Vol. II, Book III to it, "Influence of Democracy on Manners, Properly So-Called," especially Chs. 1-4 and 14; Mrs. Frances Trollope also discussed it in *Domestic Manners of the Americans*, new edition by Donald Smalley (New York, 1949), and her son, Anthony Trollope, returned to the theme in his *North America*, new edition by Donald Smalley (New York, 1951); see also David Macrae, *The Americans at Home* (Edinburgh, 1871; new ed., New York, 1952), and Warren S. Tryon, *A Mirror for Americans*, 3 vols. (Chicago, 1952), which gathers together excerpts from American travelers between 1790 and 1870. On books of etiquette, see A. M. Schlesinger, *Learning How to Behave: A Historical Study of American Etiquette Books* (New York, 1947); of the books he considers, the most famous were Lillian Eichler, *Book of Etiquette* (1st ed., Oyster Bay, New York, 1922), and Emily Post, *Etiquette* (New York, 1955), which went through many successive printings; for a good essay on Emily Post, see Edmund Wilson, "Books of Etiquette and Emily Post," *The New Yorker* (July 19, 1947); see also *Amy Vanderbilt's Complete Book of Etiquette* (New York, 1952).

On taste I have relied heavily upon Russell Lynes, *The Tastemakers* (New York, 1954), and upon Oliver W. Larkin, *Art and Life in America* (New York, 1949). The widely quoted essay by Lynes, "Highbrow, Lowbrow, Middlebrow," first published in *Harpers* (Feb. 1949), is reprinted in *The Tastemakers* as Ch. 17. There is a brilliant analysis of "Pecuniary Canons of Taste" in Veblen's *Theory of the Leisure Class* (New York, 1899), Ch. 6, which is reprinted in *The Portable Veblen* (New York, 1948), pp. 151-96; see also Louis Kronenberger, *Company Manners* (Indianapolis, 1954). The quote in the text from Cooper will be found in Lynes, *op. cit.*, p. 7.

On dress and fashion, see A. L. Kroeber, "Order in Changes of Fashion" and "Three Centuries of Women's Dress," articles reprinted in his *The Nature of Culture* (Chicago, 1952). See also Veblen's *Theory of the Leisure Class*, Ch. 7, "Dress As an Expression of the Pecuniary Culture," reprinted in *The Portable Veblen*, pp. 197-214. For a commentary on Veblen's theory of dress and fashions, see Quentin Bell, *On Human Finery* (London, 1947). See also Douglas Gorsline, *What People Wore* (New York, 1952); Winthrop Sargeant, "Fifty Years of American Women," in *Life* (Jan. 2, 1950), p. 64; Edmund Bergler, *Fashion and the Unconscious* (New York, 1953), and Wilder Hobson, "Business Suit," on the American businessman's costume, *Fortune* (July 1948). The quote about obsolescence in the fashion industry is from *Time* (July 3, 1950), p. 72.

SEC. 4—*Varieties of American Character:* On the American personality in profile, I have found David Riesman's perceptive explorations into the minds of Americans, *The Lonely Crowd* (rev. ed., New York, 1953), and *Faces in the Crowd*, in collaboration with Nathan Glazer (New Haven, 1952) of considerable use. See also David Riesman, "Psychological Types and National Character," *American Quarterly* (Winter, 1953), pp. 325-43. Of further interest will be T. W. Adorno *et al.*, *The Authoritarian Personality* (New York, 1950); Daniel Bell, ed., *The New American Right* (New York, 1955); Robert Lindner, *Prescription for Rebellion* (New York, 1952) and *Must You Conform?* (New York, 1956); Peter Viereck, *The Unadjusted Man* (Boston, 1956), and Erich Fromm, *Man for Himself* (New York, 1947). For a specific personality orientation, see Karl Mannheim, *Ideology and Utopia* (New York, 1952), Ch. 9, "The Utopian Mentality." An excellent selection of readings will be found in Guy E. Swanson, Theodore M. Newcomb and Eugene L. Hartley, *Readings in Social Psychology* (rev. ed., New York, 1952). The reference in the text to Fromm's analysis of the "marketing orientation" is to *Man for Himself.* The reference to Peter Viereck is to *The Unadjusted Man.*

SEC. 5—*The Disorders of a Society:* In my discussion of social disorganization and pathology, I have drawn heavily upon Herbert A. Bloch, *Disorganization, Personal and Social* (New York, 1952). Other works which deal generally with criminology are E. H. Sutherland, *Principles of Criminology* (Philadelphia, rev. ed., 1955); Ruth S. Cavan, *Criminology* (New York, 1952); Walter Bromberg, *Crime and the Mind* (Philadelphia, 1948); Hans von Hentig, *Crime: Causes and Conditions* (New York, 1947), and

Gresham M. Sykes, *Crime and Society* (New York, 1956). On penology, see Robert M. Lindner, *Stone Walls and Men* (New York, 1946), and Donald Clemmer, *The Prison Community* (Boston, 1940). For an analysis of the life and mind of the criminal, see Hans von Hentig, *The Criminal and His Victim* (New Haven, 1946); Jean Evans, *Three Men* (New York, 1954); Sheldon Glueck and Eleanor Glueck, *500 Criminal Careers* (New York, 1930), and *The Professional Thief* by A Professional Thief (Chicago, 1937). Recent increases in the rate of juvenile delinquency in American cities have precipitated several studies. Among them are Albert K. Cohen, *Delinquent Boys: The Culture of Gangs* (Glencoe, 1955); William and Joan McCord, *Psychopathy and Delinquency* (New York, 1956), and Herbert A. Bloch and Frank T. Flynn, *Delinquency: The Juvenile Offender in America Today* (New York, 1956). See also Benjamin Fine, *1,000,000 Delinquents* (New York, 1955); Clifford Shaw and Henry D. McKay, *Juvenile Delinquency and Urban Areas* (Chicago, 1942); William F. Whyte, *Street Corner Society* (Chicago, 1943), and Frederick M. Thrasher, *The Gang* (Chicago, 1936). On alcoholism and narcotics addiction, see Ruth Fox and Peter Lyon, *Alcoholism: Its Scope, Cause and Treatment* (New York, 1955); Marie Nyswander, *The Drug Addict As a Patient* (New York, 1956); Isador Chein and Eva Rosenfeld, "Juvenile Heroin Users in New York City," *Law and Contemporary Problems* (Winter, 1957), and Isador Chein, "Narcotics Use Among Juveniles," *Social Work* (April 1956), pp. 50-60; also my *New York Post* columns on narcotics (June 4-8, 1956). On crime among the middle and upper classes, see Edwin H. Sutherland, *White Collar Crime* (New York, 1949), and Donald R. Cressey, *Other People's Money: The Social Psychology of Embezzlement* (Glencoe, 1953). A psychiatric approach to homicide will be found in Fredric Wertham, *The Show of Violence* (New York, 1949) and *The Circle of Guilt* (New York, 1956).

On social disorders, see also Robert M. Lindner, *Must You Conform?* and *Rebel Without a Cause* (New York, 1944); Franz Alexander and Hugo Staub, *The Criminal, The Judge, and The Public* (rev. ed., Glencoe, 1956); Glanville Williams, *The Sanctity of Life and the Criminal Law* (New York, 1957); W. C. Reckless, *The Crime Problem* (New York, 1950), and C. B. Vedder, Samuel Koenig, R. E. Clark, eds., *Criminology: A Book of Readings* (New York, 1953). For an insight into gambling, see Thorstein Veblen, *The Theory of the Leisure Class* "The Belief in Luck."

The reference in the text to statistics on juvenile delinquency is to Herbert A. Bloch and Frank T. Flynn, *Delinquency: The Juvenile Offender in America Today.*

SEC. 6—*Morals in Revolution*, and SEC. 7—*Society and Sexual Expression:* On the changes in American moral codes, I have found a number of works useful. See especially Alfred C. Kinsey and Associates, *Sexual Behavior in the Human Male* (Philadelphia, 1948) and *Sexual Behavior in the Human Female* (Philadelphia, 1953). For critical and interpretive material on the Kinsey studies, see Jerome Himelhoch and Sylvia Fleis Fava, eds., *Sexual Behavior in American Society: An Appraisal of the First Two Kinsey Reports* (New York, 1955); Edmund Bergler and William S. Kroger, *Kinsey's Myth of Female Sexuality* (New York, 1954); Seward Hiltner, *Sex Ethics and the Kinsey Reports* (New York, 1953), and Albert Ellis, ed., *Sex Life of the American Woman and the Kinsey Report* (New York, 1954). Other commentaries upon sexual expression in America include Abraham N. Franzblau, *The Road to Sexual Maturity* (New York, 1954); George W. Henry, *All the Sexes* (New York, 1955); Pitirim Sorokin, *The American Sex Revolution* (Boston, 1956), and Robert E. Fitch, *The Decline and Fall of Sex* (New York, 1957). See also Sydney Ditzion, *Marriage, Morals, and Sex in America* (New York, 1953); Albert Deutsch, ed., *Sex Habits of American Men* (New York, 1948), and Clennan S. Ford and Frank A. Beach, *Patterns of Sexual Behavior* (New York, 1951). For a description of the apotheosis of sex in America, see Winthrop Sargeant, "The Cult of the Love Goddess in America," *Life* (Nov. 10, 1947). On the standards of sexual normality, see Alfred Kinsey and Associates, "Concept of Normality and Abnormality in Sexual Behavior," *Psychosexual Development in Health and Disease* (New York, 1949). On homosexuality, see two books by Donald Webster Cory, *Homosexuality: A Cross-Cultural Approach* (New York, 1956), and *The Homosexual in America* (New York, 1951); also Edmund Bergler, *Homosexuality: Disease or Way of Life?* (New York, 1956); A. M. Krich, *The Homosexuals* (New York, 1954), and Gordon Westwood, *Society and the Homosexual* (New York, 1953). On the shifting moral basis of American life, see The American Roundtable Series on *The Moral and Religious Basis of American Society*, compiled by Lewis Galantiere and sponsored by the Advertising Council (April 14, 1952). Also see Frederick Lewis Allen, *Only Yesterday* (New York, 1931); Alexis de Tocqueville, *op. cit.*, Vol. II, Book III; Lloyd

Morris, *Postscript to Yesterday* (New York, 1947); L. T. Hobhouse, *Morals in Evolution* (rev. ed., New York, 1916), and Robin Williams, Jr., *American Society*, Ch. 10, in which the formulation by James Woodward mentioned in the text will be found.

The reference in the text to Lloyd Morris is to *Postscript to Yesterday;* Max Eastman's autobiography is *Enjoyment of Living* (New York, 1943). The reference to Albert Ellis is to *The Folklore of Sex* (New York, 1951). Sorokin's discussion of American sexual freedom will be found in *The American Sex Revolution*. The reference in the text to Arthur Hirsch is to *Sexual Misbehavior of the Upper Cultured* (New York, 1955). Herbert Blumer's remarks are from correspondence with the author.

SEC. 8—*Life Goals and the Pursuit of Happiness:* On the life hopes of Americans, I have drawn upon a number of pertinent and helpful works. I have found Howard Mumford Jones, *The Pursuit of Happiness* (Cambridge, 1953) most useful. See also Robin Williams, Jr., *American Society*, Ch. 11, "Value Orientations in American Society," pp. 372-442; Kenneth S. Lynn, *The Dream of Success* (Boston, 1955); David Riesman, *Individualism Reconsidered* (Glencoe, 1954), Ch. 2, "Individualism and Its Contents," pp. 15-120, and *The Lonely Crowd*. For a discussion of psychoanalysis and the psychoanalytic approach to happiness, see Karen Horney's works, including *New Ways in Psychoanalysis* (New York, 1939) and *The Neurotic Personality of Our Time* (New York, 1937); Clara Thompson, *Psychoanalysis: Evolution and Development* (New York, 1950), and Clarence P. Oberndorf, *A History of Psychoanalysis in America* (New York, 1953). See also Erich Fromm, *The Sane Society* (New York, 1955), *Man for Himself* and *Escape from Freedom* (New York, 1941); and Herbert Marcuse, *Eros and Civilization* (Boston, 1955).

The reference in the text to James Plant is to *The Envelope* (New York, 1950). The remarks of Lawrence K. Frank are from correspondence with the author. Lloyd Warner's stratification system is discussed in *Democracy in Jonesville* (New York, 1949). The reference in the text to Howard Mumford Jones is to *The Pursuit of Happiness*. The reference to Robert Lindner is to *Prescription for Rebellion*. Erik Erikson's observations will be found in *Childhood and Society* (New York, 1950). The reference in the text to Ernest Jones is to *The Life and Work of Sigmund Freud*, Vol. I (New York, 1953), Vol. II (New York, 1955), Vol. III (New York, 1957).

Chapter X: Belief and Opinion

SEC. 1—*God and the Churches:* The position and function of religion in American life were observed by Alexis de Tocqueville, *op. cit.,* Vol. II, Book I, Chs. 5-8, and Book II, Chs. 9 and 11. Ralph H. Gabriel, *The Course of American Democratic Thought* (rev. ed., New York, 1956) presents a profound understanding of the relationships between the development of Christianity and democracy in this country. See also Louis B. Wright, *Culture on the Moving Frontier* (Bloomington, 1955), for a competent discussion of English religious influences. Two European classics shed much light on the contributions of religion to the capitalist economic system: R. H. Tawney, *Religion and the Rise of Capitalism* (New York, 1926) and Max Weber, *The Protestant Ethic and the Spirit of Capitalism* (London, 1930). H. Richard Niebuhr, *Social Sources of American Democracy* (New York, 1929), and A. P. Stokes, *Church and State in the United States* (New York, 1950) contribute much toward an understanding of religion in America. The basic psychological and philosophic analysis is William James, *Varieties of Religious Experience* (New York, 1907). See also my "Christian Culture and American Democracy," *American Quarterly* (Summer, 1954). Robert Elliot Fitch, "American Presidents and Protestant Types," *Christianity and Crisis* (June 1952) is an interesting study of national policy in view of the faiths of its shapers. Also of value is the pamphlet of the American Roundtable, Lewis Galantiere, ed., *The Moral and Religious Basis of the American Society* (New York, April 14, 1952).

Charles Wright Ferguson, *Confusion of Tongues* (New York, 1928) was one of the first significant discussions of modernism. Will Herberg, *Protestant, Catholic, Jew* (New York, 1955) presents a fresh view of the subject. See also Herbert Schneider, *Religion in 20th Century America* (Cambridge, 1952). The symposium, "Religion and the Intellectuals," published by *Partisan Review* (New York, 1950), considers the conflict between secular attitudes and the growing return to religion in the English speaking countries. Other specialized volumes are Ludwig Lewisohn, *The American Jew* (New York, 1950); Elliot E. Cohen, ed., *Commentary on the American Scene: Portraits of Jewish Life in America* (New York, 1953), and *Catholicism in America* (New York, 1954), an anthology compiled by *Commonweal.* See also Simon Noveck, ed., *Judaism and Psychiatry* (New York, 1956), and Philip Rieff's critical analysis of this book and its subject in *Midstream* (Summer, 1956). The religious affiliations of the American Negro are considered in Wm. W. Sweet, *The American Churches* (New York, 1948) and Liston Pope, *Kingdom Beyond Caste* (New York, 1957).

The study by Ruby Jo Kennedy mentioned in the text is "Single or Triple Melting Pot? Intermarriage Trends in New Haven, 1870-1940," *American Journal of Sociology* (Jan. 1954). Edmund Wilson's article on Lincoln's faith is "Abraham Lincoln: The Union As Religious Mysticism," *The New Yorker* (March 14, 1953), pp. 116-36. Toynbee's view of Negro religious creativity is found in *A Study of History,* Vol. II (London, 1934), pp. 218-20.

Books on religious freedom and separation of church and state are mentioned in the Notes for Further Reading for Ch. VI, Sec. 10. Other material on religious minority groups is listed in the Notes for Ch. VII, Sec. 5. Additional references to studies of the religious roots of American thought are found in the Notes for the next section.

SEC. 2—*American Thought: The Angle of Vision:* On America's intellectual history, I have chosen for this bibliography comparatively few works from the mass of material available. The classic and indispensable work is Vernon L. Parrington, *Main Currents in American Thought,* 3 vols. (New York, 1927-30; new ed., New York, 1956), which laid the groundwork for later volumes of its kind; also Merle Curti, *The Growth of American Thought* (New York, 1943); H. S. Commager, *The American Mind* (New Haven, 1950); Louis Hartz, *The Liberal Tradition in America* (New York, 1955), and Ralph H. Gabriel, *The Course of American Democratic Thought.* See also for general surveys Charles and Mary Beard, *The American Spirit* (New York, 1942); Ralph Barton Perry, *Characteristically American* (New York, 1949); Daniel Boorstin, *The Genius of American Politics* (Chicago, 1953), and Richard Hofstadter, *The American Political Tradition* (New Nork, 1948). Hans Kohn's penetrating *American Nationalism* (New York, 1957), expanded from Ch. 6 of his *The Idea of Nationalism* (New York, 1944), discusses one of the basic ideological strains of American development. See also Harvey Wish, *Society and Thought in America* (New York, 1950-2).

The early period in American history is discussed in T. J. Wertenbaker, *The Puritan Oligarchy* (New York, 1947), and in several books by Perry Miller: *Errand into the Wilderness* (Cambridge, 1956); *Jonathan Edwards* (New York, 1949), and *The Puritans* (Boston, 1938), edited with Thomas Johnson. The transcendentalist period is studied in F. O. Matthiessen's remarkable *The American Renaissance* (New York, 1941), and in Lewis Mumford, *The Golden Day* (New York, 1926; new ed., New York, 1957), which includes a perceptive essay on "The Pragmatic Acquiescence"; see also Perry Miller, ed., *The Transcendentalists* (Cambridge, 1950). Van Wyck Brooks's monumental multi-volume *Makers and Finders: A History of the Writers in America, 1800-1915* (New York, 1936-42) is particularly outstanding in the middle period. It is, of course, impossible to understand that period without study of such basic sources as Ralph Waldo Emerson, *Complete Essays and Other Writings* (New York, Modern Library, 1940), and Henry David Thoreau, "On Civil Disobedience," from *Collected Works* (New York, 1906).

Richard Hofstadter, *Social Darwinism in American Thought* (Philadelphia, 1944) provided essential clarification of the post-Darwinian era. The spectrum of American reactions, in terms of their social import, to the appearance of Charles Darwin, *The Origin of Species* (London, 1859), is indicated by William Graham Sumner, *Essays*, 2 vols. (New Haven, 1934) and *Folkways* with introduction by W. L. Phelps (Boston, 1940); Lester Ward, *Dynamic Sociology*, 2 vols. (New York, 1883), and John Fiske, *American Political Ideas* (New York, 1885). The social protests emerging late in the nineteenth century as responses to the Darwinian status quo are expressed in Henry George, *Progress and Poverty* (New York, 1880); Edward Bellamy, *Looking Backward* (Boston, 1889), and Walter Rauschenbusch, *Christianizing the Social Order* (New York, 1912). *The Auto-Biography of Lincoln Steffens* (New York, 1931) sheds much light on the early 20th century reform movements. The pragmatic method first formulated during this period is discussed in Morton White's distinguished volume, *Social Thought in America: Revolt Against Formalism* (New York, 1949), and Morris R. Cohen, *American Thought* (Glencoe, 1954). See also Perry Miller, ed., *American Thought: Civil War to World War* (New York, 1954), especially the Introduction. The major primary sources are Chauncey Wright, *Philosophical Discussions* (New York, 1877); Charles Peirce (M. R. Cohen, ed.), *Chance, Love, and Logic* (New York, 1923); Oliver Wendell Holmes, Jr., *The Common Law* (New York, 1881); William James, *Pragmatism* (New York, 1907); John Dewey (Joseph Ratner, ed.), *Intelligence in the Modern World* (New York, 1939), and Thorstein Veblen (Max Lerner, ed.), *The Portable Veblen* (New York, 1948). The revolt among historians is best expressed in James Harvey Robinson, *The New History* (New York, 1912), and Charles A. Beard, *An Economic Interpretation of the Constitution* (New York, 1913). In the meantime, Josiah Royce, *A Philosophy of Loyalty* (New York, 1908) still held to the idealist tradition. Among the prognostic works of the period are Brooks Adams, *The Law of Civilization and Decay* (New York, 1896); Herbert Croly, *The Promise of American Life* (New York, 1909), and Henry Adams, *The Education of Henry Adams* (Boston, 1918). See also Louis D. Brandeis, *The Curse of Bigness* (New York, 1934). On William James, see Ralph Barton Perry, *The Thought and Character of William James*, 2 vols. (Boston, 1935); and on Veblen, See Joseph Dorfman, *Thorstein Veblen and His America* (New York, 1934); David Riesman, *Thorstein Veblen: A Critical Interpretation* (New York, 1953); Bernard Rosenberg, *The Values of Veblen* (Washington, 1956); my introduction to *The Portable Veblen* and my essay on Veblen in *Ideas Are Weapons* (New York, 1939). See also my article on Beard in the same volume, and my "The Political Theory of Charles A. Beard," *American Quarterly* (Winter, 1950).

Randolph Bourne, *Liberalism in America* (New York, 1919) and *A History of a Literary Radical and Other Essays* (New York, 1920), as well as Harold Stearns, ed., *Civilization in the United States* (New York, 1928), are volumes that confront critically the framework of American society. On Bourne, see my essay in *Ideas Are Weapons*, and Louis Filler, *Randolph Bourne* (Washington, 1943).

Daniel Aaron, *Men of Good Hope* (New York, 1951); Charles A. Madison, *Critics and Crusaders* (New York, 1947), and Harvey Goldberg, ed., *American Radicals* (New York, 1957), written from the position of the extreme Left, consider individuals within the tradition of protest. See also Louis Filler's valuable *Crusaders for American Liberalism* (New York, 1938). By far the best histories of the recent period are Eric Goldman, *Rendezvous with Destiny* (New York, 1952), and Richard Hofstadter, *The Age of Reform* (New York, 1955). For important literary trends, see Malcolm Cowley, ed., *After the Genteel Tradition: American Writers Since 1910* (New York, 1937), and Carl Van Doren, *Contemporary American Novelists, 1900-1920* (New York, 1949). Alfred Kazin, *On Native Grounds* (New York, 1942) is an outstanding discussion of contemporary American literature, with an awareness of its social context.

David A. Shannon, *The Socialist Party of America* (New York, 1955) is a relatively short but revealing history of American socialism. Donald Drew Egbert and Stow Parsons, *Socialism and American Life*, 2 vols. (Princeton, 1952) contains Daniel Bell's perceptive and lucidly written essay on "The Background and Development of Marxian Socialism in the United States," pp. 213-394. The second volume has the most complete bibliography available on the field. Theodore Draper, *The Roots of American Communism* (New York, 1957), a scholarly study of the formative years of the Communist party, is the first of a series of Fund for the Republic volumes under the general editorship of Clinton Rossiter. Others supervising volumes in the project are Daniel Aaron, Daniel Bell, William Goldsmith, Moshe Decter, Donald Egbert, Nathan Glazer, Robert Iversen, Earl Latham, John P. Roche, Ralph L. Roy, Draper, and David A. Shannon. Another forthcoming history of the American Communist party is by Irving Howe and Lewis Coser.

Walter Lippmann, *The Good Society* (Boston, 1937) is a classic statement of conservative thought. Significant also is the enthusiastic reception accorded by American conservatives to Frederich A. Hayek, *The Road to Serfdom* (Chicago, 1944), and Ludwig Von Mises, *Human Action* (London, 1949). See also Russell Kirk, *The Conservative Mind* (Chicago, 1953), written from the position of the radical Right, which contains an excellent bibliography of this position; Peter Viereck, *Conservatism Revisited* (New York, 1949), and Clinton Rossiter, *Conservatism in America* (New York, 1955). Daniel Bell, ed., *The New American Right* (New York, 1955) analyzes sources of the reactionary movements in contemporary America.

The disintegration of liberal militancy is chronicled in Edgar Kemler, *The Deflation of American Ideals* (Washington, 1941), of which the last sections are most relevant, and Arthur Ekirch, *The Decline of American Liberalism* (New York, 1955). Joseph Dorfman, *The Economic Mind in American Civilization*, 3 vols. (New York, 1946-49) is an exhaustive study of economic thought in the United States. Additional material on specific topics is cited in the Notes for Further Reading for the relevant sections.

SEC. 3—*The Higher and Lower Learning:* My discussion of education draws heavily on Thorstein Veblen, *The Higher Learning in America* (New York, 1918), and upon Merle Curti, *The Social Ideas of American Education* (New York, 1935). Also important here is W. Lloyd Warner and Robert J. Havighurst, *Who Shall Be Educated?* (London, 1946).

Among the most significant volumes of American educational philosophy are John Dewey, *Democracy and Education* (New York, 1916); Robert M. Hutchins, *Higher Learning in America* (New York, 1935), and *The Conflict of Education in a Democratic Society* (New York, 1953); Horace M. Kallen, *The Education of Free Men* (New York, 1949), and William H. Kilpatrick, *Philosophy of Education* (New York, 1951). See also two European works: Bertrand Russell, *Education and the Social Order* (London, 1932), and Karl Mannheim, *Freedom, Power, and Democratic Planning* (London, 1951), Ch. 10, "Education As Groundwork." Two helpful sources are the *Forty-first Yearbook* (Bloomington, Illinois, 1942), and the *Fifty-fourth Yearbook* (Bloomington, 1955) of the National Society for the Study of Education. Of relevance is Harold Rugg and Charles W. Withers, *Social Foundations of Education*, 2 vols. (New York, 1941). James Bryant Conant, *Education in a Divided World* (Cambridge, 1949) evaluates the goals of American education in the face of the Soviet challenge. David Riesman, *Constraint and Variety in American Education* (Lincoln, 1956) analyzes recent trends in the educational world. See also George Counts, *Education and American Civil Liberties* (New York, 1952).

The President's Committee on Education Beyond the High School, *Second Report to the President* (Washington, 1957) is an excellent appraisal of the current problems. See also Paul Woodring, *Let's Talk Sense About Our Schools* (New York, 1953). Arthur Bestor, *The Retreat from Learning in Our Public Schools* (Urbana, 1953) and *Restoration of Learning* (New York, 1955) are sharply critical of current educational procedures. A brief but sharp and documented attack on Hutchins, Woodring and Bestor is James C. Bay, "Our Public Schools: Are They Failing?" *Nation* (June 26, 1954). The Reconstructionist position is represented in Theodore Brameld, *Ends and Means in Education: A Mid-Century Appraisal* (New York, 1950); see also Marie Syrkin, *Your School, Your Children* (New York, 1944). See also "Education: Now and to Come," *Antioch Review* (Fall, 1955), as well as the chapter on education in Duncan Aikman, *The Turning Stream* (New York, 1948). John Walker Powell, *Learning Comes of Age* (New York, 1956) is a study of adult education. (See also C. Hartley Grattan, *In Quest of Knowledge* (New York, 1955). On teaching, see Jacques Barzun, *Teacher in America* (new ed., New York, 1956), and Gilbert Highet's work, *The Art of Teaching* (New York, 1950).

Problems of academic freedom are the subject of a Columbia University project which has produced two excellent volumes: Richard Hofstadter and Walter Metzger, *Development of Academic Freedom in the United States* (New York, 1955), and Robert MacIver, *Academic Freedom in Our Time* (New York, 1955). The Goslin case, to which there were many parallels, is the subject of David Hubbard, *This Happened in Pasadena* (New York, 1951). The "Textbook Problem" is discussed by Fred Hechinger and others in the *Saturday Review* (April 19, 1952). Other volumes on academic freedom are listed in the Notes for Further Reading for Ch. VI, Sec. 10.

SEC. 4—*Profile of the Press:* On the press, see Morris L. Ernst, *The First Freedom* (New York, 1946) for an affirmation of the principle of a free press and an attack on recent trends toward monopoly, and E. B. White, "The Vanishing Marketplace of Ideas," *The New Yorker* (March 16, 1946). The most significant discussion on press liberties and responsibility is *The Report of the Commission on a Free Press* (Chicago, 1947). I have dealt with this topic in "Freedom in the Opinion Industries," *Ideas Are Weapons*, and "Seven Deadly Press Sins," *Actions and Passions* (New York, 1949). For an excellent study of the daily press, see Alfred McClung Lee, *The Daily Newspaper in America* (New York, 1937), and Gordon W. Allport and J. Faden, "The Psychology of Newspapers," *Public Opinion Quarterly* (Dec. 1940). The role of the newspaper in American daily life is considered in Bernard Berelson, "What Missing the Newspaper Means," in Paul Lazarsfeld *et al.*, eds., *Communications Research: 1948-49* (New York, 1949), pp. 11-29.

Of interest also is Louis L. Snyder and Richard B. Morris, eds., *A Treasury of Great Reporting* (New York, 1949). I can only briefly cite the biographies of Barons of Opinion like Greeley, Bennett, Pulitzer, Hearst, and Scripps, as well as volumes on individual newspapers, but this listing would be incomplete if I did not mention Meyer Berger, *The Story of the New York Times* (New York, 1951).

The reference to Waldo Frank is from Ch. 10 of *Rediscovery of America* (New York, 1929). Marvin Craeger is quoted by Llewellyn White in "Milwaukee: A Good Paper Pays Off," *The Reporter* (Aug. 29, 1950). James Wechsler's statement comes from his discussion with August Heckscher on "Can Newspapers Survive Without Sex?" *The Saturday Review* (July 24, 1950). The Max Ascoli citation is his article in a special issue on the press of *The Reporter* (Feb. 14, 1950). Reuben Maury is discussed by John Bainbridge in "Editorial Writer," a Profile in *The New Yorker* (May 24, 31, June 7, 1947). The Irving Dilliard citation on press coverage of the 1952 campaign comes from the Louis D. Brandeis Memorial Lecture at Brandeis University in April 1953 and in 1957 from the Wm. A. White Foundation Lecture at the University of Kansas. Justice Holmes is quoted from his opinion in *Abrams vs. U.S.*, as cited in Max Lerner, ed., *The Mind and Faith of Justice Holmes* (Boston, 1943), p. 312.

SEC. 5—*Revolution in the Big Media:* On the transformation of public communication, I have found the following helpful: W. Lloyd Warner, *American Life: Dream and Reality* (Chicago, 1953), Ch. 10, "Mass Media"; Bernard Berelson and Morris Janowitz, eds., *Reader in Public Opinion and Mass Communication* (Glencoe, 1950), including especially David Riesman and Reuel Denney, "Do the Mass Media 'Escape' from Politics?"; and Daniel Katz *et al.*, eds., *Public Opinion and Propaganda: A Book of Readings* (New York, 1954). For further references to the Big Media, see the Notes for Further Reading for Ch. XI (The Arts and Popular Culture).

The reference in the text to W. Lloyd Warner is to *American Life; Dream and Reality*. The reference to Ernst Cassirer is to *An Essay on Man* (New Haven, 1944). Martha Wolfenstein and Nathan Leites' discussion of the "good-bad girl" will be found in *Movies: A Psychological Study* (Glencoe, 1950), pp. 25-46. W. Lloyd Warner's study of "Big Sister" is in W. Lloyd Warner and William E. Henry, "The Radio Daytime Serial: A Symbolic Analysis," *Genetic Psychology Monographs* (1948), Vol. XXXVII, pp. 7-13, 55-64. The reference in the text to Thurman Arnold is to *The Folklore of Capitalism* (New Haven, 1937).

Chapter XI: The Arts and Popular Culture

SEC. 1—*Popular Culture in America:* On the public arts in America, I have found useful Bernard Rosenberg and David M. White, eds., *Mass Culture: The Popular Arts in America* (Glencoe, 1957). In that volume, see especially Walt Whitman, "From 'Democratic Vistas,'" pp. 35-40; Leo Lowenthal, "Historical Perspectives of Popular Culture," pp. 46-58; which first appeared in the *American Journal of Sociology* (1950), Vol. LV, pp. 323-32; Dwight McDonald, "A Theory of Mass Culture," pp. 59-73, which first appeared in *Diogenes* (Summer, 1953), pp. 1-17; Clement Greenberg, "Avant-Garde and Kitch," pp. 98-107, which first appeared in *The Partisan Reader* (New York, 1946), pp. 378-89. The editors of this collection have expressed opposing views on the subject in Bernard Rosenberg, "Mass Culture in America," pp. 3-12, and David M. White, "Mass Culture in America: Another Point of View," pp. 13-23. See also Ernest Van Den Haag, "Of Happiness and Despair We Have No Measure," pp. 504-36; Leslie A. Fiedler, "The Middle Against Both Ends," pp. 537-47, which originally appeared in *Encounter* (1955), Vol. V, pp. 16-23, and Melvin Tumin, "Popular Culture and the Open Society," pp. 548-56. I have also found helpful the American roundtable series on *Cultural Aspects of the American Society* (Jan. 21, 1953; Feb. 25, 1953), sponsored by the Advertising Council and compiled by Lewis Galantiere. Further discussions of popular culture will be found in Gilbert Seldes, *The Public Arts* (New York, 1956); Louis Kronenberger, *Company Manners* (Indianapolis, 1954); Marshall Davidson, *Life in America* (Boston, 1951), Vol. II, pp. 1-98; Bernard Iddings Bell, *Crowd Culture* (New York, 1952); D. W. Brogan, "The Problem of High Culture and Mass Culture," *Diogenes* (1954), No. 5, pp. 1-13; Max Horkheimer, "Art and Mass Culture," *Studies in Philosophy and Social Science* (1941), Vol. IX. See also Leo Gurko, *Heroes, Highbrows, and the Popular Mind* (Indianapolis, 1953); Foster Rhea Dulles, *America Learns to Play* (New York, 1940); David Riesman, "Some Observations on Changes in Leisure Attitudes," in his *Individualism Reconsidered* (Glencoe, 1954), pp. 202-18; G. A. Lundberg, Mirra Komarovsky, and Mary A. McIlnerny, *Leisure: A Suburban Study* (New York, 1934), and David Riesman and Reuel Denney, "Leisure in Urbanized Society," in Paul K. Hatt and Albert J. Reiss, Jr., eds., *Reader in Urban Sociology* (Glencoe, 1951), pp. 469-80.

The reference in the text to Matthew Arnold is to *Culture and Anarchy* (London, 1869). The reference to Maxwell Geismar is to *Rebels and Ancestors* (Boston, 1953). Gilbert Seldes' changing view on popular culture may be traced from *The Seven Lively Arts* (New York, 1924) to *The Public Arts* (New York, 1956). The quote from Fernand Leger will be found in Katharine Kuh, *Leger* (Chicago, 1953). The references to W. H. Auden and Lewis Galantiere are from the American roundtable series on *Cultural Aspects of the American Society*, sponsored by the Advertising Council.

SEC. 2—*Writers and Readers:* On the development of fiction in America, the essential basic reference works are V. L. Parrington, *Main Currents in American Thought*, 3 vols. (New York, 1927-30; new ed., 1956); Van Wyck Brooks's series, *Makers and Finders* (New York, 1936-52), and Alfred Kazin, *On Native Grounds* (New York, 1942). A useful reference is Robert Spiller *et al.*, eds., *A Literary History of the United States*, 3 vols. (New York, 1948). See also F. O. Matthiessen's study, *American Renaissance* (New York, 1941). Of interest here is D. H. Lawrence, *Studies in Classic American Literature* (New York, 1923); see also Robert E. Spiller, *The Cycle of American Literature* (New York, 1955). Three volumes of Maxwell Geismar's projected multi-volume history of the American novel have al-

ready appeared: *Writers in Crisis* (New York, 1942), *Last of the Provincials* (New York, 1947), and *Rebels and Ancestors* which is the most mature. Essential also is the work of Edmund Wilson, the best of the contemporary critics: *The Shock of Recognition* (New York, 1943), which he edited; *Axel's Castle* (New York, 1931); *Classics and Commercials* (New York, 1950), and *Shores of Light* (New York, 1952).

A listing of the milestones in the growth of American fiction would be less useful here than several of the works of criticism on their authors: Newton Arvin, *Hawthorne* (Boston, 1929) and *Herman Melville* (New York, 1950); F. W. Dupee, *Henry James* (New York, 1951); see also Irving Howe's essays on "Henry James: The Political Vocation" and on Hawthorne, Henry Adams, and James, "Some American Novelists: The Politics of Isolation," in his penetrating book, *Politics and the Novel* (New York, 1957). An excellent work on Dreiser is F. O. Matthiessen, *Theodore Dreiser* (New York, 1951). On Ernest Hemingway, see Carlos Baker, *The Writer As Artist* (Princeton, 1952). Among the students of Faulkner, those who have most effectively dealt with his work are Malcolm Cowley in his introduction to *The Portable Faulkner* (New York, 1946), and Irving Howe in his *William Faulkner: A Critical Study* (New York, 1952).

Recent American writing is discussed by John Aldridge in *After the Lost Generation* (New York, 1951) and his article "America's Young Novelists: Uneasy Inheritors of a Revolution," *Saturday Review* (Feb. 12, 1949); also James T. Farrell, "The Fate of Writing in America," *New Directions 9* (New York, 1946). Of interest is Lionel Trilling's essay on "Contemporary American Literature and Its Relationship to Ideas," which first appeared in the *American Quarterly* (Fall, 1949) and was reprinted in his *The Liberal Imagination* (New York, 1950) as "The Meaning of a Literary Idea." See also my "Literature and Society" in *Ideas Are Weapons*. The reference to Harold Laski is to his *Faith, Reason, and Civilization* (New York, 1944), p. 171.

On the American literary audience, Alexis de Tocqueville wrote prophetically in *Democracy in America* of "Literary Characteristics of Democratic Times," in Vol. II, Book I, Ch. 12, pp. 58-64. Popular reading tastes in American history are studied in Frank Luther Mott, *Golden Multitudes: The Story of Best Sellers in the United States* (New York, 1947), and James D. Hart, *The Popular Book: A History of American Literary Taste* (New York, 1950). A curiously interesting work is Albert Johannsen, *The House of*

Beadle and Adams and Its Dime and Nickel Novels: The Story of a Vanished Literature, 2 vols. (Norman, Oklahoma, 1950).

Contemporary publishing trends are discussed in William Miller, The Book Industry (New York, 1949), and Freeman Lewis' pamphlet, Paperbound Books in America (New York, 1952). The nature and implications of current reading habits are considered in Douglas Waples, Bernard Berelson, and F. R. Bradshaw, What Reading Does to People (Chicago, 1940); Bernard Berelson, "Who Reads What Books and Why?" The Saturday Review (May 12, 1951), and Clifton Fadiman, "The Decline of Attention," ibid. (Aug. 6, 1949). See also Christopher La Farge, "Mickey Spillane and His Bloody Hammer," The Saturday Review (Nov. 6, 1954), and Edmund Wilson, "Why Do People Read Detective Stories?" in his Classics and Commercials (New York, 1950). Other valuable articles and bibliographical material are included in the sections on detective fiction, comic books and magazines in Bernard Rosenberg and David M. White, eds., Mass Culture: The Popular Arts in America.

SEC. 3—Heroes, Legends, and Speech: On folklore and language, source material on the nature of the contemporary American heroes will be found in the Notes for Further Reading for other sections of this chapter. The industrial capitalist heroes are discussed in the Notes for Ch. V, Sec. 2 ("The Rise and Decline of the Titan"). Constance Rourke, American Humor (New York, 1931) and The Roots of American Culture (New York, 1942) are valuable studies, and are discussed by Stanley Edgar Hyman, "Constance Rourke and Folk Criticism" in his The Armed Vision (New York, 1948).

Two excellent anthologies of American folk music are John A. Lomax and Alan Lomax, eds., Folk Song: U.S.A. (New York, 1948), and Margaret Bradford Boni, ed., Fireside Book of Folk Songs (New York, 1947). See also Clifton Fadiman, ed., The American Treasury: 1455-1955 (New York, 1955); Ben C. Clough, ed., The American Imagination at Work (New York, 1947); Ben Lucien Burman, Children of Noah (New York, 1951), and Mody C. Boatright, Folk Laughter on the American Frontier (New York, 1949). Wallace Stegner's article, "Joe Hill: The Wobblies' Troubadour," New Republic (Jan. 5, 1948) sheds much light on radical folklore during the early years of this century. Among useful regional studies are B. A. Botkin, ed., A Treasury of New England Folklore (New York, 1948) and his A Treasury of Southern Folklore (New York, 1949); Earl Clifton Beck, Lore of the Lumber Camps (Ann Arbor, 1949);

Vance Randolph, Ozark Superstitions (New York, 1947) and We Always Lie to Strangers (New York, 1951), and Harold Felton, ed., The Legends of Paul Bunyan (New York, 1947).

On language, see Margaret Schlauch, The Gift of Language (rev. ed., New York, 1955), and Bernard Wall, "Questions of Language," Partisan Review (Sept. 1948). The major study of American English is H. L. Mencken, The American Language, 3 vols., (New York, 1955). Other helpful volumes are Mitford M. Mathews, A Dictionary of Americanisms (Chicago, 1951); Donald Lloyd and Harry Warfel, American English in Its Cultural Setting (New York, 1956); Lester V. Berrey and Melvin Van Den Bark, The American Thesaurus of Slang (New York, 1947); Thomas Pules, Words and Ways of American English (New York, 1952); and Richard D. Mallery, Our American Language (New York, 1949). The reference to Leo Lowenthal is as quoted in C. Wright Mills, White Collar (New York, 1951), p. 236.

SEC. 4—Spectator and Amateur Sports: On American sports, there are regrettably few available sources. See Thorstein Veblen, The Theory of the Leisure Class (New York, 1899), Ch. 10, "Modern Survivals of Prowess," and Ch. 11, "The Belief in Luck"; David Riesman and Reuel Denney, "Football in America: A Study in Culture Diffusion," American Quarterly (Winter, 1951), pp. 309-25, and reprinted in Riesman's Individualism Reconsidered, pp. 242-57; S. K. Weinberg and H. Arond, "The Occupational Culture of the Boxer," American Journal of Sociology (March 1952), pp. 460-69. See also John R. Tunis, "Are We Sportsmen or What Are We?" New York Times Magazine (July 11, 1948), and the transcripts for the American Town Meeting, How Can We Clean Up College Sports? (March 13, 1951). An interesting discussion of baseball will be found in Jacques Barzun, God's Country and Mine (Boston, 1954), Ch. 8, "The Under-entertained."

SEC. 5—Dream and Myth in the Movies: On motion pictures in America, Hollywood and its inhabitants are discussed in Leo C. Rosten, Hollywood (New York, 1941) and Hortense Powdermaker, Hollywood, the Dream Factory (Boston, 1950). Bosley Crowther, The Lion's Share (New York, 1957) is a revealing study of an entertainment empire. For a content analysis of movies, see Martha Wolfenstein and Nathan Leites, Movies, A Psychological Study (Glencoe, 1950); also Siegfried Kracauer, "National Types As Hollywood Presents Them" in Rosenberg and White, Mass Culture, pp. 255-77, and "Hollywood's Terror Films," Commentary (1946), Vol. II, pp. 132-6. See also Frederick Elkin, "God, Radio, and the

Movies," Rosenberg and White, pp. 308-14; Herbert J. Gans, "The Creator-Audience Relationship in the Mass Media: An Analysis of Movie Making," *ibid.*, pp. 315-24, and Frederick Elkin, "The Psychological Appeal of the Hollywood Western," *Journal of Educational Sociology* (1956), Vol. XXIV, pp. 72-86. On the social function of movies, see David and Evelyn T. Riesman, "Movies and Audiences," *American Quarterly* (Fall, 1952), pp. 195-202, which has also been included in his *Individualism Reconsidered*, pp. 194-201. On censorship of the movies, see Ruth A. Inglis, *Freedom of the Movies* (Chicago, 1947). Further commentaries upon Hollywood and the movies will be found in Gilbert Seldes, *The Public Arts*, pp. 1-60; Parker Tyler, *Magic and Myth of the Movies* (New York, 1957); Eric Larabee and David Riesman, "Company-Town Pastoral: The Role of Business in *Executive Suite*," *Fortune* (1955), Vol. LI, pp. 108-9, reprinted in Rosenberg and White, *op. cit.*, pp. 325-37, and Arnold Hauser, "Can Movies Be Profound?" *Partisan Review* (1948), pp. 69-73. Also see Henry Popkin, "Hollywood Discovers the Bible," *Midstream* (Summer, 1956), pp. 48-57 and "It Was This Way . . . See?" *Midstream* (Winter, 1957), pp. 108-11; also James Agee, "Comedy's Greatest Era," *Life* (Sept. 5, 1949), pp. 70-88. Several novels dealing with Hollywood are of permanent value: Nathanael West, *The Day of the Locust* (New York, 1939); F. Scott Fitzgerald, *The Last Tycoon* (New York, 1941), and Budd Schulberg, *The Disenchanted* (New York, 1950).

The reference in the text to Gilbert Seldes is to *The Great Audience* (New York, 1950), which also includes a good discussion of the role of sex in the movies, "Sex," pp. 68-81. The reference to Simone de Beauvoir is to her *The Second Sex* (New York, 1953). On the Hollywood divorce rate, see Leo Rosten, *Hollywood* (New York, 1941). The reference in the text to Martha Wolfenstein and Nathan Leites, *Movies: A Psychological Study*. The reference to David Riesman is to his essay with Evelyn T. Riesman, "Movies and Audiences," *op. cit.*

SEC. 6—*Radio and TV: the World in the Home:* On radio and television, *Mass Culture, The Popular Arts in America*, edited by Bernard Rosenberg and David M. White, has been most helpful. In that volume, see especially Rolf B. Meyerson, "Social Research in Television," pp. 345-57; Gunther Anders, "The Phantom World of TV," pp. 358-67, which originally appeared in *Dissent* (1956), Vol. III, pp. 14-24; Murray Hausknecht, "The Mike in the Bosom," pp. 375-84; and T. W. Adorno, "Television and the Pat-

terns of Mass Culture," pp. 474-88. For an over-all analysis of radio and television in American society, see Gilbert Seldes, *The Public Arts* (New York, 1956), and Charles A. Siepmann, *Radio. Television, and Society* (New York, 1950). Leo Bogart, *Age of Television* (New York, 1956), is also useful. For several studies of the content and social implications of radio broadcasts, see Herta Herzog, "On Borrowed Experience: An Analysis of Listening to Daytime Sketches," *Studies in Philosophy and Social Science* (1941), Vol. IX, pp. 65-96; Harold Lasswell, "Radio as an Instrument of Reducing Personal Insecurity," *ibid.*, pp. 49-64; W. Lloyd Warner and William E. Henry, "The Radio Daytime Serial: A Symbolic Analysis," *Genetic Psychology Monographs* (1948), Vol. XXXVII, pp. 7-13, 55-64, which also appears in Bernard Berelson and Morris Janowitz, eds., *Reader in Public Opinion and Communication* (Glencoe, 1953), and Hadley Cantril, Hazel Gaudet and Herta Hertzog, *Invasion of Mars* (Princeton, 1940). See also Paul K. Lazarsfeld and Harry Field, *The People Look at Radio* (Chapel Hill, 1946); Robert Merton, *Mass Persuasion* (New York, 1946); John Crosby, *Out of the Blue* (New York, 1952), and Thomas Whiteside, *The Relaxed Sell* (New York, 1954). The reference to Whiteside is to that volume. The reference in the text to John Crosby is to "The Seven Deadly Sins of the Air," *Life* (Nov. 6, 1950). The 1950 study on TV viewing among children is cited in Robert Shayon, *Television and Our Children* (New York, 1951), pp. 26 ff.

SEC. 7—*Jazz As American Idiom:* On native American music, much of value has been written. For a general history of jazz see Rudi Blesh, *Shining Trumpets: A History of Jazz* (New York, 1946) and Barry Ulanov, *A History of Jazz in America* (New York, 1952); also see Marshall Stearns, *The Story of Jazz* (New York, 1956), which contains an exhaustive bibliography. For biographical and autobiographical material, see Alan Lomax, *Mister Jellyroll* (New York, 1950); Louis Armstrong, *Satchmo* (New York, 1954); Robert Goffin, *Horn of Plenty: The Story of Louis Armstrong* (New York, 1947); Barry Ulanov, *Duke Ellington* (New York, 1946), and Rudi Blesh and Harriet Janis, *They All Played Ragtime* (New York, 1950).

Jazz as a subject for novelists occurs in Dorothy Baker, *Young Man with a Horn* (New York, 1938), and Duke Osborne, *Side Man* (New York, 1956). For general background on American jazz, see Melville J. Herskovits, *The Myth of the Negro Past* (New York, 1941); John A. Lomax and Alan Lomax, *Folk Song:*

U.S.A., and Howard W. Odum and Guy B. Johnson, *Negro Workaday Songs* (Chapel Hill, 1926). Also see William L. Grossman and Jack W. Farrell, *The Heart of Jazz* (New York, 1956); Leonard Feather, *Encyclopedia of Jazz* (New York, 1955); Eddie Condon and Thomas Sugrue, *We Called It Music* (New York, 1957); Billie Holliday and Bill Dufty, *Lady Sings the Blues* (New York, 1956); Milton Mezzrow and Bernard Wolfe, *Really the Blues* (New York, 1956); Wilder Hobson, *American Jazz Music* (New York, 1939); Winthrop Sargeant, *Jazz: Hot and Hybrid* (New York, 1956); and André Hodier, *L'Homme et Problèmes du Jazz* (Paris, 1954). See also T. W. Adorno, "On Popular Music," *Studies in Philosophy and Social Science* (1941), Vol. IX, No. 1, pp. 17-64. In Bernard Rosenberg and David M. White, *Mass Culture: The Popular Arts in America*, see S. I. Hayakawa, "Popular Songs Versus the Facts of Life," pp. 393-403; Monroe Berger, "The New Popularity of Jazz," pp. 404-7, and David Riesman, "Listening to Popular Music," pp. 408-17.

The reference in the text to Alan Lomax is to *Mister Jellyroll*. The reference to Wilder Hobson is to *American Jazz Music*. The reference to Wilfrid Mellers is to *Society and Music* (London, 1950).

SEC. 8—*Building, Design, and the Arts:* For American architecture and design, De Tocqueville spoke of the nature of American artistic creativity when he discussed "In What Spirit the Americans Cultivate the Arts," *Democracy in America*, Vol. II, Book I, Ch. 11, pp. 50-56. Horace Kallen's theoretical work, *Art and Freedom*, 2 vols. (New York, 1942) is a classic discussion. Also see Russell Lynes, *The Tastemakers* (New York, 1954), Ch. 15 on "The Art World."

The American art histories of importance are Oliver Larkin, *Art and Life in America* (New York, 1949); John I. H. Baur, *American Painting in the Nineteenth Century: Main Trends and Movements* (New York, 1953); Virgil Barker, *A Critical Introduction to American Painting* (New York, 1931) and *American Painting: History and Interpretation;* and E. P. Richardson, *Painting in America* (New York, 1956). Particularly on the early period, see James Thomas Flexner, *First Flowers of Our Wilderness* (New York, 1947), and *The Light of Distant Skies* (New York, 1954). Of biographical interest are Larkin's *Samuel F. B. Morse and Democratic Art* (Boston, 1954), and Francis Steegmuller, *The Two Lives of James Jackson Jarvis* (New Haven, 1951). See also *Early American Painting: The Abby Aldrich Rockefeller Collection* (New York, 1957).

The later period is studied in John I. H. Baur, *Revolution and Tradition in Modern American Art* (Cambridge, 1951); Jerome Melquist, *The Emergence of an American Art* (New York, 1942); T. B. Hess, *Abstract Painting: Background and American Phase* (New York, 1951); Andrew C. Ritchie, *Abstract Painting and Sculpture in America* (New York, 1951); and Frederick S. Wight, *Milestones of American Painting in Our Century* (New York, 1949).

The work of Lewis Mumford has added much to my understanding of American architecture. See his *The Brown Decades* (New York, 1941); *The South in Architecture* (New York, 1941); *Roots of Contemporary American Architecture* (New York, 1952), and *From the Ground Up* (New York, 1956). Other notable works are Wayne Andrews, *Architecture, Ambition, and Americans* (New York, 1955); James Marston Fitch, *American Building* (Boston, 1948), and John A. Kouwenhoven, *Made in America* (New York, 1948). Particularly on the early period, see Hugh S. Morrison, *Early American Architecture* (New York, 1952), and Anthony N. B. Garvan, *Architecture and Town Planning in Colonial Connecticut* (New Haven, 1951). Of specific interest is Carl Bridenbaugh, *Peter Harrison: First American Architect* (Chapel Hill, 1949).

On recent developments, see Talbott Hamlin, *Forms and Functions of Twentieth Century Architecture* (New York, 1952); and Carl Condit, *The Rise of the* drews, "Looking at the Latest of Frank Lloyd Wright, see the Feb. 1948 issue of *Architectural Forum;* also Wayne Andrews, "Looking at the Latest of Frank Lloyd Wright," *Perspectives, U.S.A.* (Summer, 1953), and Wright's own *The Future of Architecture* (New York, 1953). Walter Gropius, *The Scope of Total Architecture* (New York, 1955) is very valuable. See also the symposium on "What Is Happening to Modern Architecture?" in *Museum of Modern Art Bulletin* (1948).

On the American theater, an excellent analytical history of recent times is Alan S. Downer, *Fifty Years of American Drama, 1900-1950* (Chicago, 1951); other significant books on the contemporary theater in the United States are Eric Bentley, *The Dramatic Event: An American Chronicle* (New York, 1954), and Mary McCarthy, *Sights and Spectacles* (New York, 1956). John Gassner, *The Theatre in Our Times* (New York, 1954) devotes much attention to American playwrights. See also the works of our most creative dramatists: Eugene O'Neill, the anthology *Nine Plays* (New York, 1941), *Ah, Wilderness* (New York, 1933), *The Iceman Cometh* (New York, 1946), and

Long Day's Journey into Night (New Haven, 1956); Tennessee Williams, *The Glass Menagerie* (New York, 1945), *A Streetcar Named Desire* (New York, 1947), and *Camino Real* (Norfolk, Conn., 1953); and *The Collected Plays of Arthur Miller* (New York, 1957), including *Death of a Salesman* and *A View from the Bridge.*

The reference in the text to André Malraux' "Museum Without Walls" is to his book of that title (New York, 1949), the first volume of his three-volume *The Psychology of Art* (New York, 1949-50). John Ruskin's "The Lamps of Power" is from his *Seven Lamps of Architecture* (New York, 1885).

SEC. 9—*Artist and Audience in a Democratic Culture:* On the relation of the creative artist to the public, several contributions have proved helpful. Among them are Gilbert Seldes, *The Great Audience;* Horace M. Kallen, *Art and Freedom,* 2 vols.; Kurt Lang, "Mass Appeal and Minority Taste," in Rosenberg and White, *Mass Culture,* pp. 379-84. See also the American Round Table series on *Cultural Aspects of the American Society.* Also of interest is William Phillips, ed., *Art and Psychoanalysis* (New York, 1957), which applies psychoanalytic theory to the creative process. See further André Maurois, "Art, Popular Art, and the Illusion of the Folk," *Partisan Review* (1951), Vol. XVIII, pp. 487-95; Max Horkheimer, "Art and Mass Culture," *Studies in Philosophy and Social Science* (1941), Vol. IX; and D. W. Brogan, "The Problem of High Culture and Mass Culture," *Diogenes* (1954), No. 5, pp. 1-13. On the man of letters in society, see Malcolm Cowley, *The Literary Situation* (New York, 1954); Allen Tate, *Man of Letters in the Modern World* (New York, 1955), and Edmund Wilson, *A Piece of My Mind* (New York, 1956), Ch. 10, "The Author at Sixty."

Chapter XII: America As a World Power

SEC. 1—*Among the Powers of the Earth,* SEC. 2—*The Shaping Currents,* and SEC. 3 —*National Interest and an Open World:* For the development of America in terms of her international role, among the most useful histories of American foreign policy are Samuel Flagg Bemis, *A Diplomatic History of the United States* (rev. ed., New York, 1942); S. F. Bemis and Grace Gardner Griffin, *Guide to the Diplomatic History of the United States, 1775-1921* (Washington, 1935); Thomas A. Bailey, *A Diplomatic History of the American People* (rev. ed., New York, 1950), and Julius W. Pratt, *History of U. S. Foreign Policy* (New York, 1955). An indispensable and monumental work is the 10-vol. Samuel Flagg Bemis, ed., *The*

American Secretaries of State and Their Diplomacy (New York, 1929). See also Ruhl J. Bartlett, ed., *The Record of American Diplomacy: Documents and Readings in the History of American Foreign Policy* (New York, 1947). An article that sheds much light on early American diplomacy is Felix Gilbert, "The English Background of American Isolationism in the Eighteenth Century," *William and Mary Quarterly* (April 1949).

A brief but highly significant study of the twentieth century is George F. Kennan, *American Diplomacy, 1900-1950* (Chicago, 1951); see also his *Russia Leaves the War* (Princeton, 1956), which is the first of his projected series on Russia. Trends in our relationship with Russia are studied in Thomas A. Bailey, *America Faces Russia: Russian-American Relations from Early Times to Our Day* (Ithaca, 1950). On relations with Asia, see A. Whitney Griswold, *The Far Eastern Policy of the United States* (New York, 1938), and Kenneth Scott Latourette, *The American Record in the Far East, 1945-1951* (New York, 1952). Daniel Aaron, ed., *America in Crisis* (New York, 1952) contains three excellent historical articles: Richard Hofstadter on "manifest destiny," Dexter Perkins on Woodrow Wilson, and Norman Holmes Pearson on the Nazi-Soviet pact.

The shaping of foreign policy in terms of national interest is discussed in Hans J. Morgenthau, *In Defense of the National Interest* (New York, 1951) and his *Scientific Man Versus Power Politics* (Chicago, 1947). For a comparable but not synonymous viewpoint, see George F. Kennan, *Realities of American Foreign Policy* (Princeton, 1954). For the work of Frederick L. Schuman, see *The Commonwealth of Man* (New York, 1952) and "International Ideas and the National Interest," in *Annals of the American Academy of Political and Social Science* (March 1952). Among other valuable contemporary analyses are Thomas K. Finletter, *Power and Policy* (New York, 1954); Thomas I. Cook and Malcolm Moos, *Power Through Purpose* (Baltimore, 1954); Charles B. Marshall, *The Limits of Foreign Policy* (New York, 1954), and Max Beloff, *Foreign Policy and the Democratic Process* (Baltimore, 1955). See also Richard C. Snyder and Edgar S. Furniss, *American Foreign Policy: Formulation, Principles and Programs* (New York, 1954), and Louis J. Halle, *Civilization and Foreign Policy* (New York, 1955). Brooks Adams, *America's Economic Supremacy* (new ed., New York, 1947) with commentary by Marquis Childs, contains some astute turn-of-the-century observations on America's role in the world.

On the role of the legislative branch in diplomacy, see Robert A. Dahl, *Congress and Foreign Policy* (New York, 1950), and Daniel S. Cheever and H. D. Haviland, *American Foreign Policy and the Separation of Powers* (Cambridge, 1952). On the impact of public opinion on foreign policy, Thomas A. Bailey, *The Man in the Street* (New York, 1948) is most useful. International affairs, atomic power, and limited war are discussed by Henry A. Kissinger, *Nuclear Weapons and Foreign Policy* (New York, 1957). A technical, specialized work is Richard C. Snyder, H. W. Bruck, and Burton Sapin, *Decision-Making As an Approach to the Study of International Politics* (Princeton, 1954). On the military influences, see the Snyder and Sapin pamphlet, "The Role of the Military in American Foreign Policy" (New York, 1954). For a discussion of General MacArthur's dismissal by President Truman and its meaning, see Arthur M. Schlesinger, Jr., and Richard M. Rovere, *The General and the President* (New York, 1951). On Henry L. Stimson, see Stimson and McGeorge Bundy, *On Active Service in Peace and War* (New York, 1947); on Dean Acheson, see Bundy, *The Pattern of Responsibility* (Boston, 1952), and on Arthur H. Vandenberg, see Arthur H. Vandenberg, Jr., ed., *The Private Papers of Senator Vandenberg* (Boston, 1952).

Sir John R. Seeley developed his views in *The Growth of British Policy* (Cambridge, England, 1895). The Josef Schumpeter citation is to his *Imperialism and the Social Classes* (New York, 1951). For the studies by Nicholas J. Spykman, see *American Strategy in World Politics* (New York, 1942) and *The Geography of Peace* (New York, 1944). The Herbert Croly reference is to *The Promise of American Life* (New York, 1909).

SEC. 4—*Landscape with Soldiers:* For the position of the military in America, Alexis de Tocqueville, in *Democracy in America*, discussed war and the military in Vol. II, Book III, Chs. 22-26, pp. 279-302. Thorstein Veblen gives particular attention to this area in *Imperial Germany and the Industrial Revolution* (New York, 1915) and *The Nature of Peace* (New York, 1917), both excerpted in Max Lerner, ed., *The Portable Veblen* (New York, 1948). On military conflict and the American experience, see Grayson Kirk and Richard Poate Stebbins, eds., *War and National Policy* (New York, 1942), and William F. Ogburn, *American Society in Warfare* (New York, 1944). See also Ernest W. Puttkammer, *War and the Law* (Chicago, 1944), and E. S. Corwin, *Total War and the Constitution* (New York, 1947). See also Samuel P. Huntington, *The Soldier and the State* (Cambridge, 1957).

Other works discussing the internal significance of military strength are Louis Smith, *American Democracy and Military Power* (Chicago, 1951); Hans Speier, *The Social Order and the Risks of War* (New York, 1952), and, especially, Walter Millis, *The Martial Spirit* (New York, 1931) and *Arms and Men* (New York, 1956). Particular discussions of the conflict between civilian and military power are Arthur Ekirch, *The Civilian and the Military* (New York, 1956) and Arthur M. Schlesinger, Jr., and Richard Rovere, *The General and the President* (New York, 1951), which considers the Truman-MacArthur controversy in terms of its institutional implications. On the soldier, see Samuel A. Stouffer's exhaustive study, *The American Soldier*, 2 vols. (Princeton, 1949), as well as Dixon Wecter's earlier *When Johnny Comes Marching Home* (Boston, 1944).

C. Wright Mills, *The Power Elite* (New York, 1956), in Chs. 8 and 9, considers the growth of the military elite and its relationship to other segments of the ruling group.

Vannevar Bush, *Modern Arms and Free Men* (New York, 1949), discusses the significance of "technical improvements" in modes of combat. An incisive discussion of government policies and public attitudes toward the atomic arms race is Rexford Tugwell, *A Chronicle of Jeopardy, 1945-1955* (Chicago, 1955). On the development of legislative policy on atomic energy, see Morgan Thomas, *Atomic Energy and Congress* (Ann Arbor, 1956). Of interest also is Richard A. Tybout, *Government Contracting in Atomic Energy* (Ann Arbor, 1956).

The Margaret Mead citation is to her *And Keep Your Powder Dry* (New York, 1942). The quotes from Holmes are found in Max Lerner, ed., *The Mind and Faith of Justice Holmes* (Boston, 1943), pp. 16, 23.

SEC. 5—*The American World Image*, and SEC. 6—*The World's Image of America:* On America in the community of nations, the notes for Secs. 1, 2, and 3 on American foreign policy, above, contain references to much material on America's own view of her position in the world. Several additional volumes, however, are important. Two books with great depth of understanding are Chester Bowles, *American Politics in a Revolutionary World* (Cambridge, 1956), and *Africa's Challenge to America* (Berkeley, 1956). Adlai E. Stevenson's perceptive 1954 Godkin Lectures at Harvard University, published as *A Call to Greatness* (New York, 1954), outline the pattern of American responsibility in the crisis world. Of interest also is Vera Micheles Dean, *The Nature of the Non-Western World* (New York, 1957). A three-part *Partisan Review* symposium on "Our

Country and Our Culture" (May-June, July-Aug., Sept.-Oct. 1952) reveals the feelings of intellectuals on the quality of American culture in comparison to the rest of the world.

American-Asian Tensions (New York, 1956) is the subject of a helpful work edited by Robert Strausz-Hupe, Alvin J. Cottrell, and James Dougherty. Reinhold Niebuhr, *The Irony of American History* (New York, 1952) places the national experience in a world perspective. Barbara Ward, *Interplay of East and West* (New York, 1957), discusses the relative position of America in the world. See the study by Max Beloff, "The Projection of America Abroad," *American Quarterly* (Spring, 1949). For broader discussions of this topic, see Holvdahn Koht, *The American Spirit in Europe* (Philadelphia, 1949), and Lewis Galantiere, ed., *America and the Mind of Europe* (New York, 1952).

Merle Curti, "The Reputation of America Overseas, 1776-1860" in *American Quarterly* (Spring, 1949) gives excellent background material on the foreign view of America. The most significant volumes of European observation of America are Alexis de Tocqueville, *Democracy in America;* Lord James Bryce, *The American Commonwealth* (New York, 1888; rev. ed., New York, 1891; new ed., New York, 1950), and Harold J. Laski, *The American Democracy* (New York, 1948). Two particularly useful anthologies are H. S. Commager, ed., *America in Perspective* (New York, 1948), and Allan Nevins, ed., *America Through British Eyes* (New York, 1948). See also André Visson, *As Others See Us* (New York, 1948). Among the writers of individual Englishmen, see D. W. Brogan, *The American Character* (New York, 1944), and *American Themes* (London, 1947); Geoffrey Gorer, *The American People* (New York, 1948), particularly Ch. 1, "Europe and the Rejected Father," and Ch. 3, "The All-American Child"; and Wyndham Lewis, *America and Cosmic Man* (London, 1948). See also Stephen Potter, *Potter on America* (New York, 1957), and Brogan's article on "America Through British Eyes" in *Saturday Review* (Oct. 13, 1951).

Other revealing estimates are Alfonso Reyes, *The Position of America and Other Essays* (New York, 1950); Luigi Barzini, *Americans Are Alone in the World* (New York, 1953); H. J. Duteil, *The Great American Parade* (New York, 1953); and on the Russian view, Frederick C. Barghoorn, *The Soviet Image*

of the United States (New York, 1950). An impressionistic but significant view is Jawaharlal Nehru, *Visit to America* (New York, 1950). See also Daniel J. Boorstin, "America and the Image of Europe," *Perspectives, U.S.A.* (Winter, 1956) and his "American Nationalism and the Image of Europe," *The Mississippi Valley Historical Association* (April 1954).

SEC. 7—*The Destiny of a Civilization:* In preparing the Notes for Further Reading for Sec. 7, I am aware that many volumes listed above—those that see America as an Orwellian nightmare, those that see it in idyllic terms, and those that imply a mature perspective between these extremes—should be included; most of them are referred to in the notes for preceding chapters and are too numerous to repeat here. Several books, however, are uniquely relevant to this section: Lewis Mumford, *The Transformations of Man* (New York, 1956); Roderick Seidenberg, *Post-Historic Man* (Chapel Hill, 1950), and Amaury de Riencourt, *The Coming Caesars* (New York, 1957). "The Human Situation Today" in *The American Scholar* (Winter, 1955-56) contains several relevant articles, including my own "The Flowering of Latter Day Man." An excellent analysis of the American linear time perspective is Kenneth Winetrout, "What Time Is It?" *Bulletin of Atomic Scientists* (March 1953). I have previously presented my concepts of our destiny in *It Is Later Than You Think* (New York, 1938; rev. ed., 1943); *Ideas Are Weapons* (New York, 1939); *Ideas for the Ice Age* (New York, 1941); "The Human Condition" and "We Move Toward Tomorrow" from *Public Journal* (New York, 1945); and "Toward a Tragic Humanism" from *Actions and Passions* (New York, 1949). Walt Whitman's "Letter to Russia" is noted on p. 161 and quoted on p. 251 in Joseph Clifton Furness, ed., *Walt Whitman's Workshop* (Cambridge, 1928). The quote from Alexis de Tocqueville is from the conclusion of "The Three Races in the United States," *Democracy in America*, Vol. II (Vintage ed.), p. 452. The Albert Camus reference comes from *Actuelles 2: Chronicles 1948-1953* (Paris, 1953). Peter Drucker's comment is from his *The End of Economic Man* (New York, 1939), and Arnold Toynbee's statement about pushing master institutions to extremes is developed in his chapter on "The Failure of Self-Determination" in his *Study of History* as abridged by D. C. Somervell (New York, 1947).

Index

Cain, James, 808

Calder, Alexander, 858

Calder, Ritchie, 107

Caldwell, Erskine, 798, 804

Calhoun, John C., 43, 198, 728; on the frontier, 6; as Sectionalist, 44, 192, 216; doctrine of, 406, 407, 718, 721; as seen by Hartz, 721

Calvinism, 706 ff., 905; on work, 240; on property, 298; on individualism, 298; on predestination, 703; revival of, 709

Campbell, Joseph, *The Hero with a Thousand Faces*, 547

Camus, Albert, 943

Caniff, Milton, 755

Cannon, Bishop, 671

Cannon, W. B., 211

Capek, Karel, *R.U.R.*, 259

capitalism, 39, 42, 267-352; opposition to, 31-33; and immigration, 88-89; and nature, 214; and personality, 253; comparative merits of, 270; in modern America, 267-274, 341; corporate, 292-293; and democracy, 366, 494-495; and middle class, 495; and religion, 708; and folklore, 801: as seen by Spencer, 30; by Veblen, 31; by Sumner, 31; by Laski, 31, 494, 305; by Mills, 31, 494; by Lynd, 31, 494; by Davenport, 33; by Berle, 33

Capp, Al, 785; *Li'l Abner*, 755, 804

Cardozo, Benjamin, *quoted*, 411, 466 ff., 513; judicial philosophy of, 428

Carey, Matthew, 365

Carlyle, Thomas, 27, 193

Carmody, John, 141

Carnegie, Andrew, 39, 45, 214, 239, 274, 275, 431; *quoted*, 572, 801

Carr, Robert, *quoted*, 522

Cash McCall (Hawley), 284

Cassirer, Ernst, 762

Caste and Class in a Southern Town (Dollard), 150, 197, 521-522

Cather, Willa, 606

Catholicism, 714, 790; in New England, 185, 186; politics of, 394, 513; opposition to, 512, 627; on birth control, 560; on steady dating, 588; on censorship, 668

Catlin, George, paintings of Indians, 14, 15

Catt, Carrie Chapman, 604

Celler, Emmanuel, committee on baseball under, 815,

censorship, 668; of movies, 829

Centers, Richard, 499, 538

Chadwick, George, 784

Chamberlain, Houston, 504

Chamberlain, John, 279

Chandler, Raymond, 808

Changes in Bodily Form of Descendants of Immigrants (Boas), 82-83

Channing, William Ellery, 27

Chaplin, Charles, 784, 785, 826, 827, 841, 870, 875, 876; *City Lights*, 830; *Monsieur Verdoux*, 830; *The Gold Rush*, 830

Chapple, Eliot D., 637

Chapters of Erie (Adams), 276

character, *see* National character

Charm Magazine, 601

Chekhov, Anton, 860

Chicago *Sun-Times*, 753

Chicago *Tribune*, 753, 924

Chicago, University of, 742, 745, 817

Child, Lydia, 604

Childe, V. Gordon, 215

children, 556, 560-570; growth of, 570-582; crime among, 658; television for, 839; *see also* Education

Chisholm, Brock, 564

Choate, Rufus, 45

Christian Science Monitor, 752

Christiana Securities Corporation, 291

Christianity, 705-712; and morality, 682-683; and capitalism, 708

About the Author

MAX LERNER, author, teacher, and columnist, received his B.A. at Yale in 1923, his M.A. at Washington University in 1925 and his Ph.D. at the Robert Brookings Graduate School of Economics and Government in 1927. He has been a member of the Social Science Faculties of Sarah Lawrence College, Harvard University, and Williams College. At present he is Professor of American Civilization at Brandeis University and a regular columnist for the New York *Post*. He has been Managing Editor of the Encyclopedia of the Social Sciences, editor of the *Nation*, contributing editor for *The New Republic*, on the editorial board of the *American Scholar*, and editorial director of the newspapers *PM* and the *Star*, and he is widely known as a lecturer and radio commentator. He is married, the father of six children, and he makes his home in New York City.

His previous books have included: *It Is Later Than You Think* (1938; rev. ed. 1943), *Ideas Are Weapons* (1939), *Ideas for the Ice Age* (1941), *The Mind and Faith of Justice Holmes* (1943), *Public Journal* (1945), *Actions and Passions* (1949), *The Unfinished Country* (1959), *Education and a Radical Humanism* (1962), and *The Age of Overkill* (1962). He has published editions of Machiavelli's *The Prince and the Discourses*, Adam Smith's *The Wealth of Nations*, the *Portable Veblen* and Jack London's *Iron Heel*.